American Literary Scholarship

1979

American Literary Scholarship

An Annual / 1979

Edited by James Woodress

Essays by Wendell Glick, David B. Kesterson, J. Albert Robbins, Hershel Parker, Willis J. Buckingham, Louis J. Budd, Robert L. Gale, George Bornstein and Stuart Y. McDougal, Panthea Reid Broughton, Scott Donaldson, William J. Scheick, Kermit Vanderbilt, David Stouck, Jack Salzman, Jerome Klinkowitz, Richard Crowder, Sandra M. Gilbert, Winifred Frazer, John M. Reilly, Jonathan Morse, F. Lyra, Maurice Couturier, Hans Galinsky, Rolano Anzilotti, Keiko Beppu, Rolf Lundén

Duke University Press, Durham North Carolina, 1981

© 1981, Duke University Press. Library of Congress Catalogue Card number 65–19450. I.S.B.N. 0–8223–04554. Printed in the United States of America by Heritage Printers, Inc.

Foreword

It is a pleasure to present to scholars in the field of American literature the 17th volume of *ALS*. There are no innovations in this year's annual, but we hope that the coverage is just as comprehensive and incisive as in the past. My co-editor, Professor J. Albert Robbins of Indiana University, and I continue the practice we began with *ALS 1978* of alternating the editorship. This is my year to edit the book, and Professor Robbins will put out the volume for 1980. We have to exert a considerable effort to keep the size of this work down to about 500 pages, and a number of the essays have had to be cut and trimmed to meet this objective. As in the past, *ALS* has not tried to cover all scholarship, and contributors have been instructed to be selective. We try to ignore minor or redundant scholarship, but the omission of an article or book does not mean that we regard it as not worth reviewing. It is an impossibility to catch everything of significance in our net, and again we urge writers of books and articles to see that our contributors receive copies.

There will be four new contributors to *ALS 1980*: G. R. Thompson (Purdue) on Poe, Jerome Loving (Texas A. & M.) on Whitman/Dickinson, Karl Zender (U.C., Davis) on Faulkner, Lee Bartlett (Univ. of New Mexico) on contemporary poetry. In addition the foreign contributors will change in France, Italy, and Japan; Marc Chénetier (Tour), Gaetano Prampolini (Pisa), Hiroko Sato (Tokyo), replacing Maurice Couturier, Rolando Anzilotti, and Keiko Beppu, to whom profound thanks are due. We are grateful also to our retiring contributors: Willis Buckingham, who has been doing Whitman/Dickinson, Panthea Broughton, who has been reviewing Faulkner scholarship, and Sandra Gilbert, who surveyed contemporary poetry for the present volume, for their valuable services. We also welcome several new contributors this year: David Kesterson (Hawthorne), Scott Donaldson (Hemingway/Fitzgerald), Kermit Vanderbilt (19th-century literature), Jerome Klinkowitz (recent fiction), John M. Reilly (black writers), and Jonathan Morse (themes, topics, criticism).

The apparatus of this book remains the same as in the past: The innovation begun last year continues of giving only an abbreviated name in the text for publishers and the full name and place of publication in the front matter. Thus instead of (Cambridge, Mass.: Harvard Univ. Press), we give only (Harvard) in the text. Festschriften and other collections of essays or books that deal with several authors and are dealt with by two or more contributors also are given shortened titles in the text and full data in the front matter.

We are grateful to Eileen M. Mackesy, managing editor of the *MLA International Bibliography*, for arranging to provide us with advance proof sheets of the American section of the bibliography. And thanks also to James L. Harner (Bowling Green State University), section head for festschriften, for providing us with appropriate entries from his files in advance of publication. This early information is essential to our tasks. We also wish to thank the Research Committee of the University of California, Davis, for a grant that supported the compilation and editing of this volume and Keith Kroll, who served as a research assistant.

James Woodress

University of California, Davis

Table of Contents

Key to Abbreviations

Festschriften, Essay Collections, and Books Discussed in More Than One Chapter

Allegories / Stephen A. Barney, *Allegories of History, Allegories of Love* (Archon)

American Autobiography / G. Thomas Couser, *American Autobiography: The Prophetic Mode* (Mass.)

American Character / J. A. Hague, ed., *American Character and Culture in a Changing World* (Greenwood)

American Imagination / Sonja Bahn, Arno Heller, Brigitte Scheer-Schäzler, and Sepp L. Tiefenthaler, eds., *Forms of the American Imagination: Beiträge zur neueren amerikanischen literatur*, Innsbrucker Beiträge zur Kulturwissenschaft, Special Issue 44 (Innsbruck: Institut für Sprachwissenschaft)

Articles on American Literature / Lewis Leary, ed., with John Auchard, *Articles on American Literature, 1968–1975* (Duke)

Black Literature / Eckhard Breitinger, ed., *Black Literature: Zur afrikanischen und afroamerikanischen literatur* (Munich:Fink)

Confidence Man / John G. Blair, *The Confidence Man in Modern Fiction* (Barnes and Noble)

Free Will and Determinism / Perry D. Westbrook, *Free Will and Determinism in American Literature* (Fairleigh Dickinson)

Gay Academic / Louie Crew, ed., *The Gay Academic* (Palm Springs: ETC Publications, 1978)

Handbook of Popular Culture / M. Thomas Inge, ed., *Handbook of American Popular Culture*, vol. 1 (1978); vol. 2 (Greenwood)

Harvard Guide / Daniel Hoffman, ed., *The Harvard Guide to Contemporary American Writing* (Harvard)

Home as Found / Eric J. Sundquist, *Home as Found: Authority and Genealogy in Nineteenth-Century American Literature* (Hopkins)

Homosexual Tradition / Robert K. Martin, *The Homosexual Tradition in American Poetry* (Texas)

Irish-American Fiction / Robert E. Rhodes and Daniel J. Casey, eds., *Irish-American Fiction: Essays in Criticism* (AMS)

Last Laugh / Ronald Wallace, *The Last Laugh: Form and Affirmation in the Contemporary American Novel* (Missouri)

Law of the Heart / Sam B. Girgus, *The Law of the Heart: Individualism and the Modern Self in American Literature* (Texas)

Literature Against Itself / Gerald Graff, *Literature Against Itself: Literary Ideas in Modern Society* (Chicago)

London Yankees / Stanley Weintraub, *The London Yankees: Portraits of American Writers and Artists in England* (Harcourt)

Madwoman in the Attic / Sandra M. Gilbert and Susan Gubar, *The Madwoman in the Attic: The Woman Writer and the Nineteenth-Century Literary Imagination* (Yale)

Mark and Knowledge / Marjorie Pryse, *The Mark and The Knowl-*

edge: Social Stigma in Classic American Fiction (Ohio State)

Mertner Festschrift / Herbert Mainusch and Diedrich Rolle, eds., *Studien zur Englischen Philologie: Edgar Mertner zum 70. Geburtstag* (Lang)

Mysterious Stranger / Roy R. Male, *Enter, Mysterious Stranger: American Cloistral Fiction* (Oklahoma)

Myth of the Picaro / Alexander Blackburn, *The Myth of the Picaro: Continuity and Transformation of the Picaresque Novel, 1554–1954* (N. Car.)

New Directions / John Hingham and Paul K. Conkin, eds., *New Directions in American Intellectual History* (Hopkins)

New World / Cecilia Tichi, *New World, New Earth: Environmental Reform in American Literature from the Puritans Through Whitman* (Yale)

No Castles on Main Street / Stephanie Kraft, *No Castles on Main Street: American Authors and Their Homes* (Rand McNally)

Northwest Perspectives / Edwin R. Bingham and Glen A. Love, eds., *Northwest Perspectives: Essays on the Culture of the Pacific Northwest* (Wash.)

Nye Festschrift / Joseph Waldmeier, ed., *Essays in Honor of Russel B. Nye* (Mich. State, 1978)

Only Kangaroo / Karl Keller, *The Only Kangaroo Among the Beauty: Emily Dickinson and America* (Hopkins)

Poznań Proceedings / Marta Sienicka, ed., *Proceedings of a Symposium on American Literature* (Poznań, Poland: Adam Mickiewicz Univ. Press)

Psychoanalysis and Text / Geoffrey H. Hartman, ed., *Psychoanalysis and the Question of the Text,* Selected Papers of the English Institute, 1976–77, n.s. 2 (Hopkins)

Puritan Influences / Emory Elliott, ed., *Puritan Influences in American Literature* (Illinois)

Shakespeare's Sisters / Sandra M. Gilbert and Susan Gubar, eds., *Shakespeare's Sisters: Feminist Essays on Women Poets* (Indiana)

Stoic Strain / Duane J. MacMillan, ed., *The Stoic Strain in American Literature: Essays in Honor of Marston La France* (Toronto)

Telling Lives / Marc Pachter, ed., *Telling Lives: The Biographer's Art* (New Rep.)

Universal Drum / Audrey T. Rogers, *The Universal Drum: Dance Imagery in the Poetry of Eliot, Crane, Roethke, and Williams* (Penn. State)

Where the West Begins / Arthur R. Huseboe and William Geyer, eds., *Where the West Begins: Essays on Middle Border and Siouxland Writing, in Honor of Herbert Krause* (Sioux Falls, S.D: Center for Western Studies, Augustana College, 1978).

Periodicals, Annuals, Series

ABBW / *AB Bookman's Weekly* (from Merger of *Antiquarian Bookman* and *Bookman's Weekly*)

ACRAA / *Annales du Centre de Recherches sur l'Amérique Anglophone*

AEB / *Analytical and Enumerative Bibliography*

AFs / *Alternative Futures: The Journal of Utopian Studies* (Univ. of Mich. and Rensselaer Polytech.)

AHumor / *American Humor: An Interdisciplinary Newsletter*

AI / *American Imago*

AL / *American Literature*

ALitASH / *Acta Littararia Academiae Scientarum Hungaricae*

ALR / *American Literary Realism*

ALS / *American Literary Scholarship*
America (National Catholic Weekly Review)
AmerS / *American Studies*
AmerSS / *American Studies in Scandinavia*
AmEx / *American Examiner*
Amst / *Amerikastudien*
AN&Q / *American Notes and Queries*
Anglia: *Zeitschrift für Englische Philologie*
APR / *American Poetry Review*
AQ / *American Quarterly*
AR / *Antioch Review*
ArQ / *Arizona Quarterly*
ASch / *American Scholar*
ATQ / *American Transcendental Quarterly*
AtM / *Atlantic Monthly*
ATR / *Anglican Theological Review*
BALF / *Black American Literature Forum*
BB / *Bulletin of Bibliography*
BBr / *Books at Brown*
BJRL / *Bulletin of the John Rylands Library of Manchester*
BMMLA / *Bulletin of the Mid-West Modern Language Association*
Boundary / *Boundary 2: A Journal of Post-modern Literature*
BRH / *Bulletin of Research in the Humanities* (formerly *Bulletin of the New York Public Library*)
BRMMLA / *Bulletin of the Rocky Mountain Modern Language Association*
BSch / *Black Scholar*
BSUF / *Ball State University Forum*
BuR / *Bucknell Review*
BYUS / *Brigham Young Univ. Studies*
Calamus: *Walt Whitman Quarterly International* (Tokyo)
C&L / *Christianity and Literature*
CanL / *Canadian Literature*
CE / *College English*
CEA / *C.E.A. Critic*
CEAA / Center for Editions of American Authors
CEA Forum
CentR / *The Centennial Review*
CH / *Church History*
ChildL / *Children's Literature*

ChiR / *Chicago Review*
CLAJ / *College Language Association Journal*
CLQ / *Colby Library Quarterly*
CLS / *Comparative Literature Studies*
CollL / *College Literature* (Westchester State College)
ComM / *Communication Monographs*
Comparatist (N. Car. State Univ., Raleigh)
Confrontation (Long Island Univ.)
ConL / *Contemporary Literature*
ConnQ / *Connecticut Quarterly*
CP / *Concerning Poetry*
CQ / *Cambridge Quarterly*
CR / *Critical Review* (Australia)
CRCL / *Canadian Review of Comparative Literature*
CRevAS / *Canadian Review of American Studies*
Crit / *Critique: Studies in Modern Fiction*
Crit I / *Critical Inquiry*
Criticism: *A Quarterly for Literature and the Arts* (Detroit)
CritQ / *Critical Quarterly*
DAI / *Dissertation Abstracts International*
Delta (Montpellier)
DicS / *Dickinson Studies* (formerly *Emily Dickinson Bulletin*)
Disposito: *Rivista Hispanica de Semiótica Literaria*
DLB / *Dictionary of Literary Biography* (Gale)
DN / *Dreiser Newsletter*
DQR / *Dutch Quarterly Review of American Letters*
EA / *Etudes Anglaises*
EAL / *Early American Literature*
EAS / *Essays in Arts and Sciences*
ECS / *Eighteenth Century Studies*
EEPSAPT / *Epistemonike Epeterida Philosophikes Scholes Aristoleleiou Panepistemiou Thessalonikes*
EIC / *Essays in Criticism*
EigoS / *Eigo Seinen: The Rising Generation* (Tokyo)
ELH / *English Literary History*
ELN / *English Language Notes*
ELWIU / *Essays in Literature* (Western Ill. Univ.)

Encounter (London, England)
ES / *English Studies*
ESC / *English Studies in Canada*
   (Toronto)
ESQ / *Emerson Society Quarterly*
ETJ / *Theatre Journal* (formerly *Edu-
   cational Theatre Journal*)
EuWN / *Eudora Welty Newsletter*
Expl / *Explicator*
FAR / *French-American Review*
FDP / *Four Decades of Poetry*
   (Toronto)
FemS / *Feminist Studies*
FForum / *Folklore Forum*
FHA / *Fitzgerald-Hemingway Annual*
FJS / *Fu Jen Studies: Literature &
   Linguistics* (Taipei)
FMLS / *Forum for Modern Language
   Studies* (St. Andrews, Scotland)
Freedomways
*Frontiers: A Journal of Women's
   Studies*
GaR / *Georgia Review*
GL&L / *German Life and Letters*
Glyph / Ed. Samuel Weber and Henry
   Sussman (Baltimore: Johns
   Hopkins Univ. Press)
GrLR / *Great Lakes Review: A Journal
   of Midwest Culture*
GRM / *Germanische Romanische
   Monatschrift, Neue Folge*
GyS / *Gypsy Scholar*
HC / *Hollins Critic*
HCN / *Hart Crane Newsletter*
HJ / *Higginson Journal* (formerly
   Higginson Journal of Poetry)
HJR / *Henry James Review*
HLB / *Harvard Library Bulletin*
Hn / *Hemingway Notes*
HSE / *Hungarian Studies in English*
HSN / *Hawthorne Society Newsletter*
HudR / *Hudson Review*
HUSL / *Hebrew University Studies
   in Literature* (Jerusalem)
IFR / *International Fiction Review*
IJAS / *Indian Journal of American
   Studies*
IllQ / *Illinois Quarterly*
IndL / *Indian Literature*
IowaR / *Iowa Review*
JAAR / *Journal of the American
   Academy of Religion*

JAE / *Journal of Aesthetic Education*
JAmS / *Journal of American Studies*
JEGP / *Journal of English &
   Germanic Philology*
JHI / *Journal of the History of Ideas*
JIL / *Journal of Irish Literature*
JLN / *Jack London Newsletter*
JLSt / *Journal of Literary Studies*
JMH / *Journal of Mississippi History*
JML / *Journal of Modern Literature*
JNT / *Journal of Narrative Technique*
JPC / *Journal of Popular Culture*
JWSL / *Journal of Women's Studies
   in Literature*
KAL / *Kyushu American Literature*
KN / *Kwartalnik Neofilologiczny*
KR / *Kenyon Review*
KS / *Kagoshima Studies in English
   Language and Literature*
LALR / *Latin American Literary
   Review*
L&P / *Literature and Psychology*
L&U / *The Lion and the Unicorn*
Lang&S / *Language and Style*
LC / *Library Chronicle* (Univ. of Pa.)
LFQ / *Literature/Film Quarterly*
LGJ / *Lost Generation Journal*
LitR / *Literary Review* (Fairleigh-
   Dickinson Univ.)
LJGG / *Literaturwissenschaftliches
   Jahrbuch in Auftrage der Görres-
   Gesellschaft*
LJHum / *Lamar Journal of the
   Humanities*
LRN / *Literary Research Newsletter*
LWU / *Literatur in Wissenschaft und
   Unterricht* (Kiel)
MarkhamR / *Markham Review*
MD / *Modern Drama*
MELUS / *Multi-Ethnic Literature of
   the United States*
MFS / *Modern Fiction Studies*
MichA / *Michigan Academician*
   (replaces *PMASAL*)
*MidAmerica: The Yearbook of the
   Society for the Study of Midwestern
   Literature*
MinnR / *Minnesota Review*
MissQ / *Mississippi Quarterly*
MLN / *Modern Language Notes*
MLQ / *Modern Language Quarterly*
MLR / *Modern Language Review*

MLS / *Modern Language Studies*
MMN / *Marianne Moore Newsletter*
Mosaic: A Journal for the Comparative Study of Literature and Ideas
MP / *Modern Philology*
MQ / *Midwest Quarterly*
MQR / *Michigan Quarterly Review*
MR / *Massachusetts Review*
MSE / *Massachusetts Studies in English*
MSEx / *Melville Society Extracts*
MSzA / *Mainzer Studies zur Amerikanistik*
MTJ / *Mark Twain Journal*
MTSB / *Mark Twain Society Bulletin*
MV / *Minority Voices: An Interdisciplinary Journal of Literature and the Arts*
N&Q / *Notes and Queries*
NAS / *Norwegian-American Studies*
NBR / *New Boston Review*
NCF / *Nineteenth-Century Fiction*
NConL / *Notes on Contemporary Literature*
NDQ / *North Dakota Quarterly*
NEQ / *New England Quarterly*
NER / *New England Review*
NewL / *New Letters*
NewRep / *New Republic*
NHSQ / *Nevada Historical Society Quarterly*
NLH / *New Literary History*
NMAL / *Notes on Modern American Literature*
NMW / *Notes on Mississippi Writers*
NOR / *New Orleans Review*
Novel: A Forum on Fiction
NYTBR / *New York Times Book Review*
NYTSM / *New York Times Sunday Magazine*
Obsidian: Black Literature in Review (Fredonia, N.Y.)
Odyssey: A Journal of the Humanities (Rochester, Mich.)
OhR / *Ohio Review*
OL / *Orbis Litterarum: International Review of Literary Studies*
ON / *Old Northwest* (Oxford, Ohio)
PAAS / *Papers of the American Antiquarian Society*

Paideuma: A Journal Devoted to Ezra Pound Scholarship
PAR / *Performing Arts Resources*
Parnassus: Poetry in Review
PBSA / *Papers of the Bibliographical Society of America*
PCL / *Perspectives on Contemporary Literature*
Phylon: The Atlanta Univ. Review of Race and Culture
PLL / *Papers on Language and Literature*
PMLA / *Publications of the Modern Language Association*
Poetics: International Review for the Theory of Literature
PMPA / *Publications of the Missouri Philological Association*
PoeS / *Poe Studies*
PPNCFL / *Proceeding of the Pacific Northwest Conference on Foreign Languages*
PQ / *Philological Quarterly*
PQM / *Pacific Quarterly (Moana): An International Review of Arts and Ideas* (Supersedes *New Quarterly Cave*)
PR / *Partisan Review*
Proof: Yearbook of American Bibliographical and Textual Studies
Prospects: An Annual of American Cultural Studies
PrS / *Prairie Schooner*
PSt / *Prose Studies* (Univ. of Leicester)
PsyculR / *Psychocultural Review*
PT / *Poetics Today*
PTL: *A Journal for Descriptive Poetics and Theory*
PULC / *Princeton Univ. Library Chronicle*
PVR / *Platte Valley Review*
QJLC / *Library of Congress Quarterly* (formerly *Quarterly Journal of the Library of Congress*)
RALS / *Resources for American Literary Study*
ReAl / *RE: Artes Liberales* (Nacogdoches, Tex.)
Renascence: Essays on Value in Literature

RES / *Review of English Studies*
RFEA / *Revue Française d'Etudes*
    Américaines (Paris)
RFN / *Robert Frost Newsletter*
RJN / *Robinson Jeffers Newsletter*
RLC / *Revue de Littérature Comparée*
RLMC / *Rivista di Letterature*
    Moderne e Comparate (Firenze)
RLT / *Russian Literature Triquarterly*
RS / *Research Studies* (Wash. State
    Univ.)
SAB / *South Atlantic Bulletin*
SAJL / *Studies in Jewish Literature*
SAF / *Studies in American Fiction*
SALIT / *Studies in American*
    Literature (Kyoto)
SAQ / *South Atlantic Quarterly*
SAR / *Studies in the American*
    Renaissance
SaSEL / *Salzburg Studies in*
    English Literature
SAVL / *Studien zur Allegemainen und*
    Vergleichenden Literaturwissen-
    schaft
SB / *Studies in Bibliography*
ScanR / *Scandinavian Review*
    (formerly *The American*
    Scandinavian Review)
SCR / *South Carolina Review*
SDR / *South Dakota Review*
SEA / *Studies in English and*
    American (Budapest)
SEEJ / *Slavic and Eastern*
    European Journal
SELit / *Studies in English*
    Literature (Japan)
SFQ / *Southern Folklore Quarterly*
SFS / *Science-Fiction Studies*
SHR / *Southern Humanities Review*
SIR / *Studies in Romanticism*
SJS / *San Jose Studies*
SLitI / *Studies in the Literary*
    Imagination
SLJ / *Southern Literary Journal*
SN / *Studio Neophilologica*
SNNTS / *Studies in the Novel*
    (North Tex. State Univ.)
SoQ / *The Southern Quarterly*
SoR / *Southern Review*
SoSt / *Southern Studies: An Inter-*
    disciplinary Journal of the
    South (formerly *LaS*)

Soundings: *A Journal of Inter-*
    disciplinary Studies
SovL / *Soviet Literature*
SR / *Sewanee Review*
SSF / *Studies in Short Fiction*
StAH / *Studies in American Humor*
StHum / *Studies in the Humanities*
StQ / *Steinbeck Quarterly*
Style (Fayetteville, Ark.)
SWR / *Southwest Review*
TCL / *Twentieth-Century Literature*
Thalia: *Studies in Literary Humor*
    (Ottawa)
ThQ / *Theatre Quarterly* (London)
ThR / *Theatre Research International*
TSB / *Thorean Society Bulletin*
TSE / *Tulane Studies in English*
TSLL / *Texas Studies in Literature*
    and Language
TUSAS / Twayne United States
    Authors Series
TWN / *Thomas Wolfe Newsletter*
    (Univ. of Akron, Ohio)
UDQ / *Denver Quarterly*
USP / *Under the Sign of Pisces*
UTQ / *Univ. of Toronto Quarterly*
VQR / *Virginia Quarterly Review*
WAL / *Western American Literature*
WascanaR : *Wascana Review*
WCPMN / *Willa Cather Pioneer*
    Memorial Newsletter
WCWN / *William Carlos Williams*
    Newsletter (Middletown, Pa.)
WHR / *Western Humanities Review*
WIRS / *Western Ill. Regional Studies*
WLT / *World Literature Today*
    (formerly *Books Abroad*)
WMQ / *William and Mary Quarterly*
WSIA / *Wiener Slawistischer*
    Almanach
WStJ / *Wallace Stevens Journal*
WWR / *Walt Whitman Review*
WWS / Western Writers Series (Boise,
    Idaho, State Univ.)
YER / *Yeats Eliot Review* (formerly
    T. S. Eliot Review)
YES / *Yearbook of English Studies*
YFS / *Yale French Studies*
YULG / *Yale University Library*
    Gazette

Publishers

A&W Publishers / Reading, Maine: Addison-Wesley Publishing Co.

AMS / New York: AMS Press

Appel / Mamaroneck, N.Y.: Paul P. Appel, Publisher

Archon / Hamden, Conn.: Archon Books

Atheneum / New York: Atheneum Publishers

Avon / New York: Avon Books

Barnes and Noble / New York: Barnes and Noble

Bobbs-Merrill / Indianapolis: Bobbs-Merrill

Basic / New York: Basic Books

Bowker / New York: R. R. Bowker Co.

Bowling Green / Bowling Green, Ohio: Popular Press, Bowling Green State Univ.

Brandeis / Waltham, Mass.: Brandeis Univ. Press

Brigham Young / Salt Lake City, Utah: Brigham Young Univ. Press

Bucknell / Lewisburg, Pa: Bucknell Univ. Press

Burt Franklin / New York: Burt Franklin and Co.

Calif. / Berkeley: Univ. of California Press

Cambridge / Cambridge, Eng.: Cambridge Univ. Press

Chicago / Chicago: Univ. of Chicago Press

Columbia / New York: Columbia Univ. Press

Cornell / Ithaca, N.Y.: Cornell Univ. Press

Crown / New York: Crown Publishers

Delacorte / New York: Delacorte Press

Dell / New York: Dell Publishing Co.

Doubleday / New York: Doubleday & Co.

Duke / Durham, N.C.: Duke Univ. Press

Eriksson / Middlebury, Vt.: P.S. Eriksson

Faber / London: Faber and Faber

Fairleigh Dickinson / Madison, N.J.: Fairleigh Dickinson Univ. Press

Farrar / New York: Farrar, Straus & Giroux

Feminist Press / Old Westbury, N.Y.: Feminist Press

Florida / Gainesville: Univ. Press of Florida

Free Press / New York: Free Press

Gale / Detroit: Gale Research Co.

Garland / New York: Garland Publishing Co.

Georgia / Athens: Univ. of Georgia Press

Greenwood / Westport, Conn.: Greenwood Press

Gregg / Boston: Gregg Press

Hall / Boston: G. K. Hall and Co.

Harcourt / New York: Harcourt Brace Jovanovich

Harper / New York: Harper & Row

Harvard / Cambridge, Mass.: Harvard Univ. Press

Hopkins / Baltimore: Johns Hopkins Univ. Press

Houghton Mifflin / Boston: Houghton Mifflin

Humanities Press / Atlantic Highlands, N.J.: Humanities Press

Huntington Library / San Marino, Calif.: Huntington Library Publications

Illinois / Urbana: Univ. of Illinois Press

Indiana /Bloomington: Indiana Univ. Press

Iowa State / Ames: Iowa State Univ. Press

Kansas / Lawrence: Regents Press of Kansas

Kennikat / Port Washington, N.Y.: Kennikat Press

Kent State / Kent, Ohio: Kent State Univ. Press

Kentucky / Lexington: Univ. Press of Kentucky

Lang / Frankfurt, Germany: Peter Lang

Little, Brown / Boston: Little, Brown

Longman / New York: Longman, Inc.

LSU / Baton Rouge: Louisiana
State Univ. Press
Mass. / Amherst: Univ. of
Massachusetts Press
McGraw-Hill / New York:
McGraw Hill Book Co.
Mich. State / East Lansing:
Michigan State Univ. Press
Miss. / Jackson: Univ. Press of
Mississippi
Missouri / Columbia: Univ. of
Missouri Press
MLA / New York: Modern Language
Association
Morrow / William Morrow and Co.
Nebraska / Lincoln: Univ. of
Nebraska Press
New Amer. Lib. / New York:
New American Library, Inc.
New Directions / New York: New
Directions Publishing Corp.
New Rep. / New York: New
Republic Books
N. Car. / Chapel Hill: Univ. of
North Carolina Press
No. Ill. / DeKalb: Northern
Illinois Univ. Press
Norton / New York: W. W.
Norton & Co.
Norwood / Norwood, Pa.: Norwood
Editions
NPF / Orono, Maine: National
Poetry Foundation
Ohio / Athens: Ohio Univ. Press
Ohio State / Columbus:
Ohio State Univ. Press
Oklahoma / Norman: Univ. of
Oklahoma Press
Oxford / New York: Oxford Univ.
Press
Pantheon / New York: Pantheon
Books
Penn. / Philadelphia: Univ. of
Pennsylvania Press
Penn. State / University Park:
Pennsylvania State Univ. Press
Pittsburgh / Pittsburgh: Univ. of
Pittsburgh Press
Prentice-Hall / Englewood Cliffs,
N.J.: Prentice-Hall
Princeton / Princeton, N.J.:
Princeton Univ. Press

Purdue / West Lafayette, Ind.:
Purdue Univ. Press
Putnam's / New York: G. P.
Putnam's Sons
Rand McNally / Chicago: Rand
McNally and Co.
Random House / New York:
Random House
Routledge / London: Routledge
and Kegan Paul
Rowman / Totowa N.J.: Rowman
and Littlefield
Rutgers / New Brunswick, N.J.:
Rutgers Univ. Press
St. Martin's / New York: St. Martin's
Scarecrow / Methuchen, N.J.:
Scarecrow Press
Scribner's / New York: Charles
Scribner's Sons
Seabury / New York: Seabury Press
Simon & Schuster /New York:
Simon and Schuster
S. Car. / Columbia: Univ. of South
Carolina Press
SMU / Dallas, Tex.: Southern
Methodist Univ. Press
So. Ill. / Carbondale: Southern
Illinois Univ. Press
SUNY / Albany: State Univ. of
New York Press
Taplinger / New York: Taplinger
Publishing Co.
Tenn. / Knoxville: Univ. of
Tennessee Press
Texas / Austin: Univ. of Texas Press
Thames and Hudson / London:
Thames and Hudson
Toronto / Toronto: Univ. of Toronto
Press
Twayne / Boston: Twayne Publishers
Ungar / New York: Frederick
Ungar Publishing Co.
Univ. Microfilms / Ann Arbor, Mich.:
University Microfilms Inter-
national
Univ. Press / Washington, D.C.:
Univ. Press of America
UPNE / Hanover, N.H.: Univ. Press
of New England
Utah State / Logan: Utah State
Univ. Press

Virginia / Charlottesville: Univ.
    Press of Virginia
Wash. / Seattle: Univ. of
    Washington Press
Wesleyan / Middletown, Conn.:
    Wesleyan Univ. Press
Whitson / Troy, N.Y.:
    Whitson Publishing Co.

Wiley / New York: John Wiley and
    Sons, Publishers
Wis. / Madison: Univ. of
    Wisconsin Press
Yale / New Haven Conn.:
    Yale Univ. Press

Part I

1. Emerson, Thoreau, and Transcendentalism

Wendell Glick

The most noteworthy trends in this year's published scholarship on the Transcendentalists were the attention paid to Thoreau's *Week* and the continued interest in Margaret Fuller. The finest single piece of scholarship, however, seems by consensus to be Joel Porte's study of Emerson.

Claims for the neglect of Fuller, not all of it benign neglect, have now become commonplace. This trend has been building for years, buoyed of course by the feminist movement. Some claims for Fuller as of now seem patently extravagant, but if the claims for her importance continue to build, the writer of this chapter may perforce in time be impelled to remove Fuller from the company of pedestrian minor Transcendentalists and accord her a niche of her own. That time, however, is not yet.

i. General Studies, Textual Studies, Bibliography

Taylor Stoehr's *Nay-Saying in Concord: Emerson, Alcott, and Thoreau* (Archon) raises once again the annual question of the rationale by which the Transcendentalists explained the distance they placed between themselves and the venality of their society. (For last year's study of the issue, see Richard Francis, *ALS 1978*, p. 4.) Students of Transcendentalism, and particularly social activists offended by the abstinence of these writers from an acceptable level of active involvement in the organized reform impulses of the time, have for years puzzled over the Transcendentalists' individual and collective responses to reform movements, associationism, communitism, solitary

Again this year I acknowledge the substantial aid of Professor Roger Lips in covering the year's Emerson scholarship.—W.G.

living, vegetarianism, manual labor, the family, and the rest, without coming up with an acceptable principle that would give these responses credibility. Stoehr suggests a principle that he terms "revolutionary abstinence" and advises us cogently that the record of the Transcendentalists' struggle to relate to the evils that they perceived likely to follow their own times provides, in both their saying and doing, guidance to us in the 20th century just as useful as that supplied by Hawthorne and Melville. Betty E. Chmaj in a long monograph in *Prospects* ([1978] 4: 1–58) develops the case for Charles Ives as "the musical historian of Transcendentalism and a Transcendentalist himself" (p. 12); and though her focus is on Ives, examines in detail Ives's interpretations of Emerson, Thoreau, and Alcott in both the *Concord Sonata* and *Essays Before a Sonata*. "America's Greatest Composer," Chmaj believes, was deeply influenced by all of them. Her findings as to Emerson's influence upon American music corroborate the common claim of historians for Emerson's deep influence upon 20th-century American culture. "Modernist Criticism and Transcendental Literature" by James Hoopes (*NEQ* 52:451–65) promises in its comprehensive title far more than it delivers: it is a narrow study of the erosion caused by I. A. Richards' "referential theory of language" upon the "transcendental effort" of James Agee in *Let Us Now Praise Famous Men*. To the mounting list of studies of the interest of the individual Transcendentalists in linguistic theory Philip F. Gura has now added a significant general monograph, "The Transcendentalists and Language" (*SAR*, pp. 1–16), pointing out that the prevailing philosophy of language in America in the first half of the 19th century has a "religious basis." Gura makes the point that the debate over language was a function of the conflict between the Unitarians, "who championed an empirical reading of scripture, and the Trinitarians, who attempted to defend a more orthodox reading of the Bible by adopting a 'symbolic' view of its language." A close connection existed, in other words, between Biblical exegesis and language theory.

A lull this year in the publication of authoritative texts presages a productive year for new texts in 1980. (As I write, a newly edited edition of *Woman in the Nineteenth Century* has been published, and Thoreau's *A Week* has appeared in the Princeton series.) O. M. Casale discovered and published "An Unpublished Thoreau Letter" (*NEQ* 51:98–100), particularly interesting for its late (1861) date when Thoreau correspondence is not abundant. The only other new texts of works of the Transcendentalists to see print in 1979 appeared in *SAR*. Joel Myerson's new text of Emerson's "Thoreau" (pp. 17–92) is accompanied by a historical introduction, editorial introduction, description of Emerson's printer's copy (Myerson's copy-text), tables of alterations, emendations, and textual notes, and a historical collation. Cruces are carefully documented. Myerson's study of Emerson's deletions and revisions suggests Emerson's design to soften the negative passages of the early draft. Francis B. Dedmond chose to record cancellations, editorial insertions, and authorial additions within the printed text of "Ellery Channing's 'Major Leviticus: His Three Days in Town'; An Unpublished Satire" (pp. 409–56), prefacing the text with an extended introduction and following it with copious notes. Had Alcott ("Speudo-Pistos") chanced to see the scornful ridicule of his eccentricities in Channing's satire he would have been deeply hurt. Thoreau ("Moses Bucolics"), who is accorded much less attention, might on the other hand have been amused. This short piece by Channing is a sequel to *Leviticus*, Channing's long, unpublished autobiographical novel, which I have been able to read through Professor Dedmond's courtesy. The earlier work contains Channing's finest satire, though personal hangups often reduce Channing's aesthetic distance to zero. I wish for Professor Dedmond success in getting a well-edited text of *Leviticus* into print. According to Frederick Wagner, 70 of the "Eighty-six Letters (1814–1882) of A. Bronson Alcott (Part One)" (pp. 239–308) seem not to have been published previously. In printing the first 41 of the letters, Wagner retains in the texts most of Alcott's scribal eccentricities and designates within the text by a system of editorial symbols all cancellations, insertions, editorial material, and questionable readings. Many of the letters are to members of Alcott's immediate family. One to Charles Lane and one to Thoreau are not included in the first published group. Interesting as many of these letters are, they add little that is new to our knowledge of Alcott or the other members of the Concord group.

Of use to scholars are two bibliographies published during the year. Joel Myerson's *Brook Farm: An Annotated Bibliography and Resources Guide* (Garland) is the result of a diligent search through major libraries and comprises about 600 items providing information about the farm, much of it primary material. Myerson's annotations are pithy, useful leads to the content of the entries, which are grouped topically in a format that increases their accessibility. A full index follows the listings. Gary L. Collison's "A Calendar of the Letters of Theodore Parker (Part One)" (*SAR*, pp. 159–230) is advertised by Collison as "both a research tool and a preliminary report on an edition of the letters of Theodore Parker" (p. 159); it lists chronologically all extant letters of Parker in the collections of 60 individuals and libraries. The 931 entries in part 1 of this "Calendar" are followed by a very useful "Index to Recipients." One notes that 33 of these letters are to Emerson, the largest number to any recipient except Convers Francis, Samuel May, and Charles Sumner.

Much useful primary material and several well-researched short articles appeared during the year in the *Concord Saunterer*, edited by the curator of the Thoreau Lyceum in Concord, and in the *Thoreau Society Bulletin*, edited by Walter Harding at Geneseo. The articles are too numerous for individual mention. The Winter issue of *The Saunterer* is noteworthy, however, for its studies of individual members of the Thoreau family: Thoreau's grandparents (by Dana McLean Greeley), Thoreau's father (Marcia Moss), mother (Anne McGrath), sister Helen (Linda Beaulieu), brother John (Malcolm M. Ferguson), and sister Sophia (Thomas Blanding). I know of no other single source of so much information on the Thoreau family. As always, students of Thoreau should keep in mind the up-to-date comprehensive bibliographies published in each issue of the *Thoreau Society Bulletin*, compiled by Walter Harding. The third of the "little" Thoreau journals, *The Thoreau Journal Quarterly*, after a brief lull in publication, will be edited in the Philosophy Department of the University of Minnesota.

ii. Emerson

a. **Life and Thought.**   After the burst of significant work on Emerson in 1978, it was perhaps predictable that 1979 would be fallow. The one notable exception is Joel Porte's *Representative Man: Ralph Waldo Emerson in His Time* (Oxford). Porte is a courageous and sensitive biographer who made the decision to direct his attention "not so much on Emerson the finished thinker as on Emerson in the act of thinking, working his way indefatigably to that land's end which was always just disappearing over the horizon of his thought"

(p. xiii). What distinguishes this book, therefore, is its imaginative use of facts to restore Emerson to us as a palpable, vibrant person; to the reader's consciousness comes a full man and a genius, living with his joys and sorrows, his highs and lows, his self-doubts and triumphs—"essaying to be" by "speaking in the service of self-culture," by "endeavoring to create himself in the very process, in the very act, of setting words on paper or uttering them aloud" (p. 153). Porte's fine sense of how to handle evidence with both sympathy and with cynicism leads him to speak candidly of Emerson's sexuality, his concern for money, his tragic sense of life, his feelings toward Thoreau and Margaret Fuller, toward reform movements and reformers; all of these elements are integrated into the pattern of Emerson's life, without the distortion of one at the expense of the others. This is biography so original, even when it deals with the old questions, that I am embarrassed to note the peccadillos I listed as I read it.

Richard Lebeaux, in "Emerson's Young Adulthood: From Patienthood to Patiencehood" (*ESQ* 25:203–10)—not a fortunate title—deals with the same period of youthful ambivalence and "identity formation" that Porte treats in broader perspective in his first chapter, "Rites of Spring." Using the psychology of Erik Erikson as a framework in which to place the physical and psychological events of Emerson's early life, as he did earlier in his biography of Thoreau, Lebeaux emerges with the thesis that Emerson consciously declared a moratorium on premature early commitments as a "constructive, even necessary, stage" in his development as a "genuinely healthy" individual. He does not force his point. Not so Louise Schleiner in her "Emerson's Orphic and Messianic Bard" (*ESQ* 25:191–202), which I find to be jargon-ridden. Assertions follow each other, moreover, with little supporting evidence. After citing a passage from Novalis, for example, Schleiner remarks that "whether or not Emerson knew this passage . . ." his thought "took exactly this direction." On such speculative slipperiness it is dangerous to erect anything. Schleiner builds on Yoder's book, *Emerson and the Orphic Poet in America* (see *ALS 1978*, pp. 9–10), itself, to my view, not the firmest of foundations. In "Literary Grieving: Emerson and the Death of Waldo" (*CR* 23:91–104), Bruce Ronda tests the proposition that Waldo's death "exposed the lack of a place for limitation and loss, decay and old age, in Emerson's thought, and forced him to account for death instead of continuing to focus on youth and creativity." "Threnody" becomes for Ronda the crucial definition of a precipitous shift in the Emersonian *weltanschauung*. Ronda's claim is in obvious conflict with that of scholars who view Emerson's thought throughout his life to have been in a constant state of change as a result of the act of thinking, and precipitousness therefore to have been uncharacteristic of him.

The year saw publication in Nebraska's Regents Critics Series of *Emerson's Literary Criticism*, edited by Eric W. Carlson, a selection and compilation of Emerson criticism from the essays, lectures, poetry, and journals. A 40-page introduction summarizing the scholarship on Emerson's critical theory precedes the selections, which are categorized under the headings "Art as Experience," "The Creative Process," "The Art of Rhetoric," and "Toward a Modern Critical Perspective," followed by a selection of criticism by Emerson of writers and books. A random check of Carlson's texts against the Centenary Edition reveals that the transcriptions are reliable, and there seem to be no omissions of major Emerson critical pieces. The short, introductory notes to the individual selections are particularly lucid and helpful, as are Carlson's many valuable notes supplementing those in the Centenary Edition. David Robinson's "Emerson and the Challenge of the Future: The Paradox of the Unachieved in 'Circles'" (*PQ* 57:243–53) is a carefully reasoned examination of "Circles" as the first sign of the waning of Emerson's early optimism as to human potential, "where Emerson begins to make clear that the assumption behind the possibility of self-culture, the recognition of the unachieved, itself has a tragic dimension." The plausibility of Robinson's case calls into question Ronda's thesis that Waldo's death was the precipitating factor in Emerson's change of mind. Luther Luedtke in "Ralph Waldo Emerson Envisions the 'Smelting Pot'" (*MELUS* 5:3–14) provides an excellent example of how to beat a metaphor to death in an attempt to extract every conceivable meaning from it. Carlos Baker's "Moralist and Hedonist: Emerson, Henry Adams, and the Dance" (*ESQ* 25:27–37), if it offers little new on Emerson, provides at least an intriguing illustration of Emerson's oft-repeated dictum that "all high beauty has a moral element in it": the sensuous dancing of Fanny Elssler, whom Longfellow's friend Sam Ward saw as "the ideal of a fascinating mistress," elicited from Emerson the comment that "she used the whole compass of her instrument"; and he went on to remark on the aesthetics of her grace and beauty. Baker credits Fraulein Elssler with dissipating Emerson's "early prejudice against the ballet." Stanley Cavell's "Thinking of Emerson" (*NLH* 11:167–76) is just that, a philosopher (who seemingly has not read widely in Emerson criticism) thinking about Emerson and linking him in a meaningful way with Thoreau, Kant, Heidegger, and Nietzsche. In his relating Emerson to the philosophers Cavell provides a broad perspective that most Emerson scholars are unlikely to have. Richard Lee Francis in "Completing the Sphere: Emerson's Revisions of the Mottoes of *Nature*" (*SAR*, pp. 231–36) uses the changes Emerson made in his mottoes in the second edition of *Nature* in 1849 to demonstrate the oft-remarked shift in Emerson away from his view of the centrality of man adumbrated in the 1836 edition. "The dynamism of the original essay is man-centered. The thrust of the new model is to suggest that man is the paradigm for vast activity within other sensate forms like the worm." Though in *ALS* we do not ordinarily comment upon reviews, I feel that Philip Gura's "essay review," "Emerson in Our Time" (*NEQ* 52:407–13) merits a remark or two. Gura reviews books by Scheick, Yoder, Porter (see *ALS 1978*, pp. 8–10), and Porte (above), and in so doing suggests the directions in current Emerson scholarship. The rash of new books on Emerson in the past few years should not blind us, however, to the value of such older studies as those by Holmes and Firkins in enabling us to capture the many sides of Emerson.

b. **Emerson and Other Writers.** Articles appeared during the year linking Emerson with Dickinson, Frost, Whitman, Pound, D. H. Lawrence, and Lucretius. Some are slight. Ina F. A. Bell in "Pound, Emerson and 'Subject-Rhyme' " (*Paideuma* 8:237–40) suggests "Emerson's version of Swedenborg as a context for Pound's notion of 'subject-rhyme' "; and claims that "Pound's echo of Emerson in 1927 sharpens our awareness of his [Pound's] debt to New England traditions." So broad a claim requires more evidence than Bell supplies. Gary Sloan ("An Emersonian Source for the Title *Sons and Lovers*" [*AN&Q* 160–61]) makes the tenuous suggestion that the optimism of the final paragraph of Lawrence's novel may be explained by Lawrence's having drawn his title from Emerson's "Experience." Jerome Loving's "Emerson's 'Constant Way of Looking at Whitman's Genius' " (*AL* 51:399–403) is, though brief, a substantial and well-researched piece of scholarship; Loving reopens the important issue of

Emerson's actual feelings toward Whitman and *Leaves of Grass* by examining the reactions to the note of Edward Emerson in *Emerson in Concord* (1889) to the effect that Whitman's later poetry was a great disappointment to his father. He cites a letter written by F. B. Sanborn to Traubel to show that Emerson, had he been living, would have demurred with Edward's appraisal of his feelings toward Whitman. The weakness in Loving's case for me is his willingness to accept Sanborn's appraisal of Emerson's feelings toward Whitman as "probably . . . an accurate assessment." Dr. S. A. Jones, who knew Sanborn (see Oehlschlaeger and Hendrick, p. 39, reviewed below), called Sanborn "a sham," a judgment that accords with my own studies for some years of Sanborn's handling of "facts" about Emerson, Thoreau, and Alcott. Loving's essay is a clear signal that the time has come for a new and thorough study of Emerson's estimate of Whitman and the nature of their personal relationship. Much new material, widely scattered, is now available to us.

Three of the comparative studies of Emerson with other writers are ambitious ones. The focus of Darrel Abel's "Two Philosophical Poets: Frost, Emerson, and Pragmatism" (*ESQ* 25:119–36) is less upon Emerson than upon Frost; though he announces as his essay's "central concern . . . to distinguish Frost's 'Aristotelian' pragmatism from Emerson's 'Platonic' pragmatism," he devotes none of the ten sections into which the essay is divided to an analysis of "Emerson's 'Platonic' pragmatism," nor does he allude to the copious research on Emerson as Platonist. Abel's central concern in this essay seems to me to be to find in Frost ("who had no consistent over-all philosophy") a "philosophizing tendency" somehow superior in its rejections to the affirmations of Emerson. The essay does not clarify Frost's assertion that "Emerson's name has gone as a poetic philosopher or a philosophical poet, my favorite kind of both." Nor does it make clear why Emerson was the only poet whom Frost conceded to have had a strong influence on his ideas. Roland Hagenbüchle sets out in "Sign and Process: The Concept of Language in Emerson and Dickinson" (*ESQ* 25:137–55) "to investigate further the differences between the two poets with particular reference to their underlying assumptions about the nature of language." The temptation to make forays into areas other than the nature of language is too much for Hagenbüchle, however; his essay diffuses into Whitman, Thoreau, Melville, Emerson's Puritan heritage, Wordsworth, Romantic aesthetics in general, the "Kierkegaardian malady of the infinite" and other Atlantean tangents; and though thoroughly researched, this essay becomes a welter of insights rather than a focused paper. Though I am unable to reduce the essay to a single statement, Hagenbüchle concludes that "while Emerson's poems—to overstate the point somewhat—are poems about process, Dickinson's are poems of process, are processes themselves." "Emerson and Lucretius on *Nature*: Questions of Method and Matter" by William H. Shurr (*ATQ* 38:153–67) has the potential for a worthwhile study. But that *De Rerum Natura* exerted so pervasive an influence upon the mind of Emerson at the time of the composition of *Nature* that it constituted "a force more fundamental, methodologically at least, than any other" I find impossible to accept, and Shurr's paper does not make the case. In this essay the studies by many fine scholars of the early, multiple influences upon Emerson's thought are ignored. I find little evidence of a deep knowledge of Emerson.

iii. Thoreau

a. **Life and Thought.** The only book-length work dealing with Thoreau in 1979 was *Toward the Making of Thoreau's Modern Reputation: Selected Correspondence of S. A. Jones, A. W. Hosmer, H. S. Salt, H. G. O. Blake, and D. Ricketson,* ed. Fritz Oehlschlaeger and George Hendrick (Illinois). The bulk of the letters here printed were between Jones, the Ann Arbor physician, whose interest in Thoreau postdated Thoreau's death by 30 years, and Hosmer, and were the consequences of Jones's intense interest in reclaiming for posterity every possible relic of Thoreau in order to get at the truth of the sort of person Thoreau had been. Little by little, as the letters show, Jones cleared the record of the misrepresentations of Sanborn and others, making possible preservation of Thoreau memorabilia that otherwise may well have been lost. The story the letters spell out will be an intriguing one to Thoreau scholars. I acknowledge to approaching this book with puzzlement as to why these posthumous documents about Thoreau merited publication; I confess after reading it to having found it interesting and informative. The long, distinguished, introductory essay developing Thoreau's 19th-century reputation and based in part on the letters here printed easily supersedes all other such studies that we have. Thoreau scholars will need this book; nonscholars will find in Dr. Jones a demonstration of what honest scholarship is all about. "Henry David Thoreau: Retreat and Pilgrimage" in G. Thomas Couser's *American Autobiography*, pp. 62–79, is a genre study whose purpose is to locate Thoreau, along with Franklin, Frederick Douglass, Henry Adams, Malcolm X, Mailer, Robert Pirsig, and others in what he labels the "prophetic mode," a subdivision of the genre of autobiography. The fit of these authors into Couser's "mode" is accomplished with some pressure: I am more struck in reading the book with the differences between Douglass, Mailer, Thoreau, and the rest than by Couser's "prophetic" linkage. "Henry Thoreau and the Wisdom of Words" by Philip F. Gura (*NEQ* 51:38–54) is an important addition to the study of Thoreau against contemporary philological theories, notably those of Charles Kraitsir, first investigated by Michael West. Gura shows that Thoreau's acceptance of the philological position of Kraitsir ("the highest form of mental activity, the study of language" is "the best way to worship the universal spirit") separated him from Emerson's notion of "a tripartite correspondence among words/things/spirit" and provides us with an essential interpretative tool to the understanding of such enigmas as the etymological section of the "thawing" passage in "Spring" of *Walden*. Richard H. Dillman in "Thoreau's Humane Economics: A Reflection of Jean-Baptiste Say's Economic Philosophy" (*ESQ* 25:20–25) calls attention to the parallels between the key principles of Say's economics and Thoreau's economic views. In reviewing once more the well-winnowed facts of Thoreau's relationship to John Brown, James Goodwin in "Thoreau and John Brown: Transcendental Politics" (*ESQ* 25:156–68) argues that an intensive explication of "A Plea for Captain John Brown" reveals no ideological tension between the Transcendental politics of "Resistance to Civil Government" and Thoreau's response to Brown—that Brown's violence and death in the service of the highest purposes were indeed consistent with Thoreau's earlier reform methodology. Goodwin's extended argument notwithstanding, it is difficult to view "Thoreau's response to Brown . . . not as a departure from or a moderation of transcendental individualism but as a further radicalization of its tenets and an escalation of its goals." No other Thoreau scholar so far as I am aware joins Goodwin in his position. Michael Meyer's "Discord in Concord on the Day of John Brown's Hanging" (*TSB* 146:1–3) prints interesting contemporary newspaper reports of the services for Brown on 2 December 1859, in which Thoreau participated. Wendell Glick in "The Jersey Tho-

reaus" (*TSB* 148:1–5), using genealogical documents from the Isle
of Jersey, traces the Thoreau (Thoreaux, Tiereau) line from the
Huguenot emigration from France in 1685 to the emigration of Tho-
reau's grandfather Jean from Jersey to America in 1773. In "Thoreau
and Frost: the Search for Reality" (*BSUF* 19,iv[1978]:67–72) Lyle
Domina offers several obvious parallels between the two writers.
Hugh Cook's discursive remarks in "Thoreau and the King James
Bible" (*Hearing and Doing: Philosophical Essays Dedicated to H.
Evan Runner*, ed. John Kraay and Anthony Tol [Toronto: Wedge
Pub. Co.], pp. 87–96) are far from the definitive analysis of this im-
portant issue.

b. **Studies of Individual Works.**   Four studies of *Walden* were published during the year. A somewhat more useful essay than that of
Cook is "The Bible and the Composition of *Walden*" by Larry R.
Long (*SAR* 309–53). Long's claim that "the essential qualities of
Thoreau's processes of composition become evident as one studies
his use of the Bible in *Walden*" seems extravagant; but his painstaking accounting of Thoreau's omissions and additions of Biblical material in the various stages of composition does provide leads to
Thoreau's intention in the book. Long's account of the significance of
his findings is perhaps less important than his listings of Thoreau's
Biblical sources. Richard H. Dillman in "The Psychological Rhetoric
of *Walden*" (*ESQ* 25:78–91) finds evidence that Thoreau in writing
Walden employed the principles of persuasion taught him by Edward Tyrell Channing at Harvard, using as texts Whately's *Elements*
and Campbell's *Philosophy*. George Monteiro's "*Walden* in *Albion*"
(*TSB* 149:6–7) publishes two newly found contemporary reviews
of *Walden*. Harold Hellenbrand in " 'A True Integrity Day by Day':
Thoreau's Organic Economy in *Walden*" (*ESQ* 25:71–78) construes
"economy" to include "managing household, body, mind, and spirit";
with few limits upon his scope, therefore, Hellenbrand can range
easily through Thoreau's "radically consubstantial" project at Walden in a comprehensive survey of fuel, housing, vegetarianism, hoe-
ing, masturbation, fecal disposal, etc. to Thoreau's final "metamorphosis" and successful fusion of all activities of human life. After
Hellenbrand's essay Mario L. D'Avanzo's uncluttered view of the
iron chest in "The Ponds" as a "deft trope" suggesting "the kind of
riches that Thoreau seeks . . . at Walden Pond" ("An Iron Chest in

Walden's Depths" [*NEQ* 52:397–401]) comes as something of a relief.

A Week drew more monographs than *Walden* in 1979. Michael Meyer in "A Case for Greeley's *Tribune* Review of *A Week*" (*ESQ* 25:92–94) cites substantial evidence that the 12 June 1849 review of *A Week* in the *New York Tribune,* usually attributed (following Sanborn) to George Ripley, was by Greeley himself. Ellen M. Raghavan and Barry Wood in "Thoreau's Hindu Quotations in *A Week*" (*NEQ* 51:94–98) provide the first comprehensive list of Thoreau's direct Hindu borrowings for his first book. Three long, interpretative monographs appeared, all of which derive from close textual study and analysis. Jamie Hutchinson in " 'The Lapse of the Current': Thoreau's Historical Vision in *A Week on the Concord and Merrimack Rivers*" (*ESQ* 25:211–23), building upon Sherman Paul, argues persuasively that Thoreau's journey "results in not only a confirmation of [his] belief in historical progress but also an awareness of his own essential, participatory role in bringing it about." *A Week,* Hutchinson concludes, "if one heeds its mythic design, demands to be read as an account of the growth of the individual's mind and what this signifies for a world fallen into decay and ruin." Eric J. Sundquist's findings to a degree coincide with Hutchinson's: his long monograph, "Plowing Homeward: Cultivation and Grafting in Thoreau and the *Week*," comprises chapter 2 (pp. 41–85) of *Home as Found* (Hopkins), a psychoanalytic study of Cooper, Thoreau, Hawthorne, and Melville. Sundquist analyzes Thoreau's tropes to show that what *A Week* records "is the unrelenting difficulty Thoreau has in finding Nature, that is, in uncovering something which is sufficiently far removed from his own defilement to qualify as that American garden at once primitive and Edenic." Thoreau discovers that "it is vain to dream of a wilderness distant from ourselves. There is none such." But of these three intensive readings of *A Week,* the most imaginative is John Carlos Rowe's " 'The Being of Language: the Language of Being' in *A Week on the Concord and Merrimack Rivers*" (*Boundary* 7:91–115). Taking his point of departure from Heidegger, Rowe sees Thoreau compelled by the corruption of the white colonists "to substitute a spiritual frontier for the vanishing physical wilderness": "*A Week* confronts directly man's alienation from nature by attempting to reflect on the essence of language." The voyage becomes "a metaphor for poetic composition." In short, "*A Week* is a way of

thinking the being of poetry as the poetry of being." With the publication of these three seminal essays, particularly that of Rowe, *A
Week* assumes a significance to the understanding of Thoreau's
thought hardly inferior to that of *Walden.*

Stephen Adams's "Thoreau Catching Cold: *A Yankee in Canada*"
(*ESQ* 25: 224–34) marshals the internal evidence from *A Yankee* to
show that this work was "Thoreau's account of a failure of vision and
his exploration of the social forces behind that failure." Thoreau's
cold was symbolic, this argument goes, representing "the petrifying
atmosphere created by Canada's feudal institutions." A commentary
on the symbolism of food in Thoreau's *Journal*, "Thoreau et La
Nourriture Dans Le *Journal*" (*EA* 32:303–11) by Colette Gerbaud
calls attention to Thoreau's supraphysical nourishment from his food:
"Sa fonction est biologique, psychologique et morale, et aussi spirit-
uelle."

iv. Minor Transcendentalists

Among this group Margaret Fuller is the center of interest this year,
to the exclusion of all others. One book or more a year on Fuller
is now standard. Belatedly, I call attention to Paula Blanchard's
Margaret Fuller: From Transcendentalism to Revolution (Delacorte,
1978), which I missed last year and which Dell published in paperback this year. The book is popular rather than scholarly, but it gives
a full sense of the frustrations faced by a woman of genius in the male-
dominated first half of the 19th century. This is the common note in
most of the books on Fuller, and the central emphasis also of Margaret Vanderhaar Allen's *The Achievement of Margaret Fuller* (Penn
State), with Emerson emerging as the villain who both "shaped and
stifled" (p. 25) Fuller's achievements. Allen's indictment of Emerson
is exceedingly harsh: beginning her research with "reverence" for
Emerson, she was led by her pursuit of the evidence, she observes, to
a hypocritical Emerson wholly trapped by his commitment to male
superiority. Allen's real eye-opener in this appraisal of Fuller, however, is her summary estimate (pp. 178–79): "She [Fuller] was easily
the equal of her contemporaries, Emerson and Thoreau . . . More civilized and more fundamentally social than either man, she achieved
greater balance as a thinker and human being." Nonetheless Robert
D. Richardson chose not to include his essay, "Margaret Fuller and

Myth" (*Prospects* 4[1978]:169–84), in his *Myth and Literature in the American Renaissance* (see *ALS 1978*, pp. 3–4). Fuller, according to Richardson, "found in myth a way to reverse the common tendency of idealistic thought," which moved from the actual into the ideal. Greek myth, in particular, helped her discover cultural paradigms that helped her to "formulate her concept of feminine individualism." I wish finally to mention an Alcott item overlooked in 1978, Joel Myerson's "William Harry Harland's 'Bronson Alcott's English Friends' " (*RALS* 8:24–60), a series of biographical vignettes discovered by Myerson at the Fruitlands Museum and published for the first time.

University of Minnesota, Duluth

2. Hawthorne

David B. Kesterson

If the output of Hawthorne scholarship for 1978 was "rather thin," as J. Donald Crowley reported in last year's *ALS*, 1979 certainly took up the slack. Three new books appeared which treat Hawthorne exclusively, another one focuses on Hawthorne and James, while a dozen or so others contain chapters on Hawthorne or else devote noteworthy space to some aspect of Hawthorne or his works. A concordance to the novels saw light at the end of the year, upwards of 40 articles appeared in learned journals, and well over a dozen doctoral dissertations prove that graduate students continue to find new clearings amidst the dense thicket of published Hawthorne lore. Though there were no new volumes of the Centenary Edition or *The Nathaniel Hawthorne Journal*, the *Hawthorne Society Newsletter*—containing bibliography, notes, queries, and other pertinent items—published spring and fall numbers.

The increased volume of scholarship brought its share of both the traditional and innovative, the valuable and the trivial. There were interesting trends toward comparative and multicultural approaches to the study of Hawthorne, directions evinced by the number of studies which treat Hawthorne and other authors and literatures (see section *v.*), works that focus on Hawthorne and the visual and performing arts, and even two travel-related books which depict Hawthorne places. Some examples, besides the studies detailed in section *v.*, are Rita K. Gollin's "Hawthorne on Film" (*HSN* 5,ii:6–7), John L. Idol, Jr.'s and Sterling K. Eisiminger's "A Preliminary List of Operas Based on Hawthorne's Fiction" (*HSN* 5,ii:5–6), Stephanie Kraft's descriptive "Hawthorne and the Old Manse" in *No Castles on Main St.*, and Marcella Thum's biographical-geographical sketch of Hawthorne and his environs in *Exploring Literary America* (Atheneum). The cross-cultural attention to Hawthorne was climaxed by the PBS television and radio productions of *The Scarlet Letter*, the media event that variously excited and disappointed Hawthorne devotees and prompted numerous reviews and articles on the adaptation and filming of Hawthorne's novel, one of the best being Peter Neill's "Challenge to BBC in Hester's Trials of our Puritan Era" (*Smithsonian* May :86–93).

i. Manuscripts, Texts, Bibliography

It was not a signal year for manuscripts or texts. There were no finds equivalent to the 1976 discovery of Hawthorne's early notebook. The scene is not totally bare, however. Mark F. Sweeney edited part 2 of "An Annotated Edition of Nathaniel Hawthorne's Official Dispatches to the State Department 1853–1857" (*SAR* 355–97). Covering the last two years of Hawthorne's official correspondence from Liverpool, 1856–57, this edition supplies text, annotation, and an informative introduction. Many of Hawthorne's dispatches are perfunctory, with little or no literary or biographical interest; others, however, treat substantive issues such as the need for merchant marine reforms and Hawthorne's chagrin over the lack of support granted his office by the State Department. In his introduction Sweeney earmarks letters of special interest. In all, this second and final installment of consulary letters is an important contribution to knowledge of Hawthorne's English public life.

Three other editions merit comment. The Ohio State Centenary text was used in Seymour Gross's and Rosalie Murphy's Norton Critical edition of *The Blithedale Romance* (Norton, 1978). Two special editions of *The Scarlet Letter* were prompted by the Public Broadcasting System's telecast. The more significant, edited by Joel Porte (Dell), has a timely introduction, "Viewing *The Scarlet Letter*," and the text is accompanied by eight pages of photographs from the production. The other (New Amer. Lib.) is billed as a television "tie-in" edition, but is merely an earlier edition with a new cover. Though of course not scholarly editions, both books attest to the popular and media attention given *The Scarlet Letter* during 1979.

The year saw into print several helpful secondary bibliographies. The main contribution is Buford Jones's "Current Hawthorne Bibliography" (*HSN* 5,i:11, and 5,ii:7–12), a checklist covering bibliographies, critical introductions, books, essays in books, articles, dissertations, and miscellaneous items such as a list of reviews on the PBS

Scarlet Letter. Jones's checklist is the most up-to-date guide to Hawthorne scholarship. The third volume of Lewis Leary's invaluable *Articles on American Literature* contains an impressive 21-page listing of essays on Hawthorne for the years 1968–75. Scholars will welcome this latest installment of Leary's comprehensive work. For more specialized findings two books compiled by Joel Myerson are helpful: *Margaret Fuller: An Annotated Secondary Bibliography* (Burt Franklin, 1977) and *Brook Farm: An Annotated Bibliography and Resources Guide* (Garland, 1978). Both checklists offer numerous items on Hawthorne in relation to Margaret Fuller, Brook Farm, Transcendentalism, and other literary personages and subjects. In sum, current Hawthorne bibliography is in the best shape it has enjoyed in years.

ii. General Studies

Two important books headline this section. Rita K. Gollin's *Nathaniel Hawthorne and The Truth of Dreams* (LSU) is the main interpretive study of the year. Taking a closer look at the long-recognized subject of dreams in Hawthorne's fiction, Gollin broadens the scope and focuses on Hawthorne's own propensity for dreaming (daydreams as well as actual dreams) plus the preponderance of dreams and dreamers in his fiction. She makes a good case for how crucial to life Hawthorne felt dreams to be. For all humans, dreams contain the various ingredients of idle fantasy, problem-solving, and self-exploration. To the writer, more particularly, composing is a form of dreaming in itself; repeatedly, Hawthorne's stories "are about the mind's uncertain struggles toward self-understanding; and their course is 'the real course of a dream.'" Gollin's innovative stance on the late fragments assumes that Hawthorne's failing artistry stemmed from a growing realization that dreams, formerly always fraught with meaning for him, might at bottom prove empty. And if there is no meaning to the "'disagreeable fantasms'" that one must confront and integrate with his own sense of the "realities of life," the implications for human life are "barely tolerable." Thus the protagonists of the fragments cannot find the keys to problem-solving or self-exploration in their dreams and remain confused, agonizing over "the insoluble secrets of mortality" just as Hawthorne himself in his last years must have groped for meaning in life's scheme. Gollin's convincing study is well-balanced, thorough, and scholarly. Its scope is the entire range of the Hawthorne canon, supplemented by a chapter on the historical and literary traditions from which Hawthorne drew and one chapter on the significance of dreams in his own life.

Of equal interest, though not so new in material, is Hyatt H. Waggoner's *The Presence of Hawthorne* (LSU). This collection of eight essays—all of which, except the final one, have been published earlier in some form during the author's 30 years of distinguished research and writing on Hawthorne—runs the gamut from Waggoner's self-proclaimed "neoorthodox" and "new critical" writing of the 1950s to current concerns with "questions of literary history and the creative process." Among the contents are studies of Hawthorne's artistic and religious beliefs, his tragic view in *The Scarlet Letter*, an appreciative introduction to *The House of Seven Gables*, and combinings of heretofore two separate statements on the recently discovered Hawthorne notebook as well as two pieces on Hawthorne and Melville. The initial selection, "An Allegorist of the Heart," is a slightly rebrushed version of Waggoner's 1962 University of Minnesota pamphlet on Hawthorne, still one of the best, brief general assessments of Hawthorne's life and art. Thus it is especially welcomed here. The title essay, written expressly for this volume, is based on the observation that Hawthorne has never suffered obscurity and that his "presence" has been continuously felt by readers and writers alike. Three chief American writers who were especially "inspired" by Hawthorne are James, Faulkner, and Robert Penn Warren (see section *v.*). Waggoner's collection is an interesting, insightful group of essays, threaded together loosely but effectively by the theme of Hawthorne's pertinence to readers and writers during and since his time. The only weak stitch is essay 6, "Hawthorne Explained," a review-essay of books on Hawthorne by Nina Baym, Edgar A. Dryden, and Kenneth Dauber. While it serves admirably as an apology for the new critical approach to Hawthorne which Waggoner represents, its topicality and narrower scope prevent its being coequal with the other selections.

Though not new, a third book-length study worth mentioning is the reprint of Elizabeth Lathrop Chandler's monograph, *A Study of the Sources of the Tales and Romances Written by Nathaniel Hawthorne Before 1853* (Darby, Pa.: The Arden Library, 1978). Though much has been learned about Hawthorne's sources since the original 1926 publication of this study, Chandler's brief work remains a classic which still offers the scholar and general reader much information about Hawthorne's life and authorship during the years before his residency abroad.

Among shorter general appraisals the best is Milton R. Stern's "Nathaniel Hawthorne: 'Conservative After Heaven's Own Fashion' " (*Nye Festschrift*, pp. 195–225). Stern presents Hawthorne as a "philosophical conservative" devoted to the "radical" calling of authorship. With obvious resulting tension Hawthorne's fiction becomes in part "a groping, political autobiographical exploration of his identity within his culture." Though Hawthorne was not a reactionary or "modal" conservative who shared the views of the marketplace, neither could he abide the radical championing of progress and change in 19th-century society. His compromise position was philosophical conservatism, characterized by a rational, chastened view of his times. Stern's argument is provocative, his presentation clear. Perhaps his promised longer treatment of the same subject will deal more specifically with individual tales and novels than does this otherwise solid contribution.

Tension in Hawthorne of another sort is suggested by Robert Glen Deamer in "Hawthorne's Dream in the Forest" (*WAL* 13:327–39). In *The Scarlet Letter*, "Young Goodman Brown," "The Maypole of Merry-Mount," and the portrait of "Mrs. Hutchinson," Deamer sees Hawthorne airing unresolved tension over the "dream of freedom and rebirth," represented by the American Western myth, and the Puritan idea that "evil is irremediable." To Hawthorne the East stands for the Puritan emphasis on social community and civil control, while the West represents freedom and control by individual conscience. The fact that Hester represents the spirit of the West and Dimmesdale the East creates "a tragic tension" in Hawthorne's best novel. Deamer's discussion is helpful in a sense, though the argument owes much to Leslie Fiedler's and Edwin Fussell's similar views on the subject. Deamer's point that Hawthorne's women represent the free, creative spirit of the West begs for qualification; Hawthorne's dark, free-spirited heroines, yes, but not the more conventional snow-maidens, surely. On a more specialized subject is Maria M. Tatar's chapter "Masters and Slaves: The Creative Process in Hawthorne's Fiction" in her book *Spellbound: Studies on Mesmerism and Literature* (Princeton, 1978), pp. 189–229. In this book designed to "trace the impact of mesmerist ideas on literature" Tatar discusses Hawthorne's propensity for adapting mesmerism to demonstrate "psychological domination and its inevitable concomitant, emotional bondage." Examining "Rappaccini's Daughter," "The Birthmark," "Ethan Brand," "The Prophetic Pictures," *The House of the Seven Gables,* and *The Blithedale Romance,* she shows how Hawthorne shifted his focus "from scientific experimenters [Rappaccini and Aylmer] to mesmerist wizards" and how he thereby added a "sexual and psychological component" to the relationship between "diabolical sorcerer and vulnerable maiden." Tatar offers cogent remarks on Hawthorne's reasons for using mesmerism. Her chapter is not as thorough or detailed on the background of mesmerism as Taylor Stoehr's discussion in *Hawthorne's Mad Scientists* (see *ALS 1978*), but she surpasses Stoehr in literary criticism. Not so clear in focus or fresh of insight in David Mayer's "Hawthorne's Theological-Psychological View of Sin and Forgiveness" (*KAL* 20:1–7). Mayer argues indisputably, if needlessly, that Hawthorne "treats sin seriously, aware of its theological roots," but that in the stories his interest "remains on the psychological, temporal level."

iii. Novels and Longer Works

If the PBS *Scarlet Letter* was the year's media event for Hawthorne as novelist, the major publishing venture was the weighty, two-volume *Concordance to the Five Novels of Nathaniel Hawthorne* (Garland), compiled by John R. Byers, Jr., and James J. Owen. The work is conveniently arranged and easy to use. For each entry the editors have elected to include the entire line (from the Centenary text) containing the concorded word, and they have arranged entries by novels in order of publication. Frequency counts are indicated with each entry. Despite some mistakes (errata are listed in an appendix), this is an excellent tool for scholars; and these volumes engender hopes of further concordances of notebooks, fragments, and miscellaneous pieces yet to appear in the Centenary Edition.

Two intriguing essays which treat the novels generically are Coleman W. Tharpe's "The Oral Storyteller in Hawthorne's Novels" (*SSF* 16:205–14) and Paula K. White's "The Melancholy of History: Hawthorne's Romances and the Futility of Escape" (*SDR* 17,i:20–38). By focusing on the "Alice Pyncheon" story in *The House of the Seven Gables,* "The Silvery Veil" legend of *The Blithedale Romance,* and the nymph of the fountain story in *The Marble Faun,* Tharpe contends that respective storytellers Holgrave, Zenobia, and Donatello are survivals of Hawthorne's earlier oral folk narrators (in "The Story-Teller" and *Grandfather's Chair.*) Though more complex characters than their predecessors, these three exhibit the folk narrator's talent of uniting "recollection and prophecy, history and the truth of the human spirit" in telling their distinctive legends. Since Hawthorne was not essentially a historian or interested in being one, Tharpe believes, he used folk tradition in his fiction because it is a nonhistorical yet viable method of arriving at the past and the "truth of the human spirit." Tharpe's approach is fresh, the handling interesting and judicious. Just as solid, if not so new, is White's argument that in Hawthorne's four major novels, knowledge of history brings gloom to the characters because of awareness of evil and a sense of inextricable involvement in the flow of history in which change is painfully gradual. Hester Prynne, of course, is a primary example and the one used most fully by White. What is most striking, though, is White's view that Hawthorne first introduced the concept of the "melancholy of history" in *Grandfather's Chair* and that its development there informed his use of it in the four novels. Furthermore, White posits that the endings of *The House of the Seven Gables* and *The Marble Faun* are flawed because in those two books, for various reasons, Hawthorne swerved from his belief in the sobering meaning of history, a stance firmly adhered to in *The Scarlet Letter* and *The Blithedale Romance.*

In treatments of individual novels *The Scarlet Letter* wins hands down as far as quantity is concerned. The seven essays range from general contextual views—historical, religious, cultural—to even further studies of the "Custom-House" introductory and individual characters. Quality, unsurprisingly, is uneven.

Sacvan Bercovitch in his remarkable book *The American Jeremiad* (Wis., 1978) allots brief but meaningful space to Hawthorne and *The Scarlet Letter* in his concluding chapter where he discusses the influence of the jeremiad on classic 19th-century American writers. Though Hawthorne, he feels, was not the Jeremiah that Melville, Thoreau, Emerson, and Whitman were, still he was affected by the myth of America and its strong rhetorical tradition. In *The Scarlet Letter* the influence is evident in Hester, who anticipates a "New World Eden to be" and seeks to "reconcile the conflicts between self and society," and in Dimmesdale, whose election sermon and its effect constitute "the most vivid rendering we have of the Puritan ritual of the jeremiad." Another view of the novel more strictly in religious context is that of Ronald J. Gervais in " 'A Papist Among the Puritans': Icon and Logos in *The Scarlet Letter*" (*ESQ* 25:11–16). Building on the thesis that the Puritans largely eliminated the icon and embraced logos to purge Catholic symbolism, Gervais holds that Hawthorne's novel shows neither position being complete without the other. Hester, in representing the icon, is a "picture looking for a text," while Arthur is "the word looking for instruction." Thus a resulting tension pervades the social and religious world of the novel. Only in the moment of the election sermon and revelation of the scarlet letter is there a "powerful and prophetic alliance" of icon and logos. Gervais's fruitful argument falters only with his conclusion that the book closes with the logos as it began with the icon; Gervais appears to overlook the irony of the heraldic emblem with which the novel ends. "Puritanism in *The Scarlet Letter*" (*KAL* 20:52–59) is Shinichiro Noriguchi's attempt to broaden the socioreligious picture of the novel, but Noriguchi offers nothing new in his examination of why Hawthorne chose Puritan times for his setting or how Puritanism is manifested in the novel.

Two views of the central characters of *The Scarlet Letter* in conflict with society are not wholly successful. Hugo McPherson in "How Hot Is the Scarlet Letter" (*Nye Festschrift*, pp. 141–50) contributes a piece of feminist criticism which concludes that in Puritan society there was no place for the complete woman such as Hester or the artistic temperament of a Dimmesdale and that these types were equally rejected in Hawthorne's own era. Woman has exerted her power in modern times, while men have generally lost the sway they enjoyed in Puritan New England. Unfortunately, McPherson's at times flamboyant style and flippant phrases (Hawthorne is a "sexy chap," Sophia a "tough" wife, Melville a "young buck," and Pearl a "little bastard") lessens the seriousness and effectiveness of his argument. Meanwhile Marjorie Pryse's "*The Scarlet Letter*: Social Stigma and Art," in her book *Mark and Knowledge*, pp. 15–48, argues the foregone conclusion that Hester, Dimmesdale, and Chillingworth are "marked" by the expectations of their society and that Hawthorne himself, as narrator-author, is "marked" or defined by the symbol he chooses to use. To survive, authors—like characters—must transcend the impositions and restraints of the "mark"; for the artist,

however, separation is inevitable. Pryse's undertaking is overly ambitious, and the uneven chapter at times lacks sharp focus and clear
conclusions.

Donald Darnell's illustrated "*The Scarlet Letter*: Hawthorne's
Emblem Book" (*SAF* 7:153–62) is a rewarding view of the novel's
connection with Renaissance emblem literature. "The Gentle Boy"
and other stories are also mentioned. The relating of prison house and
scaffold scenes to traditional emblems suggests a credible technical
pattern of development in Hawthorne's art. The article suffers only
in being too brief to allow sufficient detail and deeper probing into
the novel. Robert L. Berner and William Bysshe Stein establish new
positions on the character and significance of "The Custom-House"
and its relationship to the novel proper, though neither explains definitively (if such is possible) the nexus between novel and preface;
the dialogue will undoubtedly continue. Berner's "A Key to 'The Custom-House'" (*ATQ* 41:33–43) maintains that Hawthorne's essay is
so tightly and consciously structured that its four parts correspond
to the four stages in Hester's development, that the three inmates of
the Custom-House ironically correspond to Hester, Dimmesdale, and
Chillingworth (as does the Boston crowd to Hawthorne as narrator-
observer), and that these character types are repeated throughout
Hawthorne's other three major novels. While the essay is provocative
in discussing structure and themes, some of the projected parallels
are forced. In "The Rhetoric of 'P. P.' in *The Scarlet Letter*" (*ATQ*
39[1978]:281–99) Stein advances the view that both "The Custom-
House" and novel are examples of Hawthorne's rhetorical gamesman-
ship. Hawthorne's purpose in writing the preface was to offer "a
burlesque on the naive conception of the creative act," and in that
piece as well as the novel he constantly employs puns and other verbal tricks to undermine the gravity of his opening essay and the
seriousness of the tragic story itself. Often too cleverly written and
marred by sometimes questionable verbal discoveries, Stein's analysis fails to disclose major new meaning for either the preface or
novel. From customhouse to character, Nicholas Canaday takes "Another Look at Arthur Dimmesdale" (*CEA* 41,iii:13–16), concluding,
unsurprisingly, that far from being a coward Dimmesdale is "talented
and successful," a "great" man "whose very strengths have betrayed
him." But Canaday does well in discussing Dimmesdale's pride and
sexuality, offering an interesting interpretation of the midnight

scaffold scene where Dimmesdale's imagination constructs a titillating picture of the village maidens discovering him there at dawn.

The House of the Seven Gables attracted criticism ranging from Freudian to allegorical. Eric Sundquist's " 'The Home of the Dead': Representation and Speculation in Hawthorne and The House of the Seven Gables," Home as Found, pp. 86–142, offers a psychological view of Hawthorne's reaction to his personal and societal pasts. Holgrave and various protagonists from Hawthorne's stories are presented as author surrogates as they partake of what Freud termed the "sacramental totem meal"—an experience which simultaneously celebrates the seizure of authority and commemorates the dead or deposed. Both Holgrave and Hawthorne avenge and pay off historical family debts but also keep the past vibrantly alive, actions which create tension-filled dilemmas for each. Sundquist's thesis owes much to Freud as well as to Frederick Crews's Sins of the Fathers. Freudian readers of Hawthorne will find themselves comfortably at home here; others might grow weary of psychological jargon, intricate analyses, and frequent speculation. Hawthorne's novel derives from Renaissance allegorical tradition, according to Robert Emmet Whelan, Jr., in "The House of the Seven Gables: Allegory of the Heart" (Renascence 31:67–82). Featuring a battle between Flesh-Evil (Judge Pyncheon) and Spirit-Ascetics (Clifford) and involving Will (Hepzibah), Love (Phoebe), and Intellect-Conscience (Holgrave), the novel becomes an allegorical depiction "of the painful journey that an unregenerate soul takes from Paradise Lost to Paradise Regained" (Spirit wins, of course). Though Whelan is correct in emphasizing Hawthorne's concern with values, his approach stalls because of the complex interweaving of allegorical figures and meanings. He comes near rendering the novel as lifeless as Hawthorne feared his own insistance on moral import would.

Two articles with fresh insights into more specific aspects of Seven Gables are Jane Benardete's "Holgrave's Legend of Alice Pyncheon as a Godey's Story" (SAF 7:229–33) and Roger S. Platizky's "Hepzibah's Gingerbread Cakes in The House of the Seven Gables" (AN&Q 17:106–08). Benardete asserts that since Holgrave mentions having published in Godey's, the story of "Alice Pyncheon" is tailored to the Godey's formula. Hawthorne's purposes in writing a Godey's pastiche were to show his ability to produce the kind of story popular in the magazines and also to differentiate this "superficial manner" from the "complex, serious structure of his novel as a whole." Benardete's thesis is fresh and appropriately developed, though her reading of Hawthorne's inner story as superficial is questionable. The role of Ned Higgins and his ginger cakes is too easily dismissed by readers, claims Platizky. Rather, the little gourmand serves as a "unifying principle" for the whole novel; his timely appearances (beginning, middle, end) and even the kinds of cakes he chooses to eat symbolize central themes in the novel; for example, the "Jim Crow" represents a victim of greed and oppression, as do the Maules. Though not a major contribution and seemingly stretched in certain interpretations of the food Ned devours, the note certainly evokes new thoughts about little Ned's function in the novel.

A convincing statement on Hawthorne's view of history as expressed in both *The House of the Seven Gables* and *The Whole History of Grandfather's Chair* is made by John W. Crowley: "Hawthorne's New England Epochs" (*ESQ* 25:59–70). Relating the two works by means of a common chair (Grandfather's and the Pyncheon chair being based on the same model), Crowley demonstrates how they offer complementary views of historical epochs, *Seven Gables* picking up where *Grandfather's Chair* leaves off. Crowley's analysis of *Grandfather's Chair* is excellent, and the relating of the work to *Seven Gables* is generally sound, if somewhat speculative in projecting the complexion of the next "epoch" after Phoebe's and Holgrave's wedding. Commenting on another of Hawthorne's long framed narratives, James Duban in "The Triumph of Infidelity in Hawthorne's *The Story-Teller*" (*SAF* 7:49–60) argues that Hawthorne intended the frame structure of the first three tales, along with several of the later stories, to depict the theological decline "that marked American Protestantism in its Unitarian era." The storyteller himself, then, proves an infidel who rejects his Puritan heritage, adopts Arminian and Unitarian views, and indulges in "excessive mirth." The only trouble spots in this essay are Duban's tacit assumptions about which works were part of the original "Story-Teller," the contents of which are simply not wholly identifiable.

The Marble Faun was the subject of two essays, both on the timely subject of Hawthorne and art. Claudia D. Johnson's "Resolution in *The Marble Faun*: a Minority View" (*Puritan Influences*, pp. 128–42) presents Hawthorne as arriving at a solution to a problem he faced from his early years: how the artist can experience the necessary human cycle of fall and readaptation to society and not lose the sanctity of isolation needed for creativity. Whereas in the stories and earlier novels the artists often remain outside the "moral" realm, in *The Marble Faun* they experience the cycle of fall-regeneration as people and as artists; Kenyon and Hilda realize art has to be involved with the fluid forms of life. Thus art is regenerate and embraces morality. Johnson's careful and convincing analysis is weakened only by her last point proclaiming the reader is "co-creator" who assists Hawthorne in completing the creative process, an idea that is perhaps more overstressed than misstated. Also treating the subject of art— specifically sculpture—is Charles Thomas Walters' interesting "Hawthorne in Relation to Art: *The Marble Faun* and the Sculptural Aesthetic" (*IJAS* 8,i[1978]:36–45). Walters asserts convincingly that Hawthorne knew much more about American sculpture of the 19th century than charged by French critic Emile Montegut. In *The Marble Faun* he consistently shows fascination with two facets of the sculpting process (clay model and finished marble product) and deliberately focuses on sculptor William Wetmore Story rather than the sentimentalists to show that sculpture can exhibit dynamic conflict—in the case of Story's *Cleopatra*, "an acknowledgment of evil if not good."

iv. Short Works

Overshadowing all other work on the short fiction for the year is Lea Vozar Newman's much-needed, dissertation-based *Reader's Guide to the Short Stories of Nathaniel Hawthorne* (Hall). Devoting a separate chapter to each story, Newman considers its publication history, circumstances of composition, relationship of the story to other works of Hawthorne (especially helpful), and the significant scholarship on the story. Though the book covers only works defined by Newman as short stories (pieces with "an identifiable narrative pattern") and thus omits sketches and also the children's tales, the result is still an ambitious, useful amassing of pertinent information which will aid the scholar immensely.

As for essays on individual tales and sketches, the scales are slightly tipped toward Hawthorne's earlier works. James L. Williamson in "Vision and Revision in 'Alice Doane's Appeal'" (*ATQ* 40, [1978]:345–53) offers little new as he weighs the tones and effects

of the inner tale and frame of one of Hawthorne's earliest surviving
stories; but he is more original when emphasizing the autobiographical element in the frame. Just as the narrator is more successful with
his extemporaneous story of the witches' procession than with the
Alice Doane incident, so had Hawthorne grown in narrative skills
from his earliest attempts at story telling, Williamson theorizes. Roy
R. Male in his unique monograph *Mysterious Stranger*, pp. 16–17,
21–22, 47–49, affords "The Gray Champion" and "The Ambitious
Guest" brief treatment among stories which demonstrate the opposite
of the picaresque or narrator-seeker pattern, where rather a decision
is made "to stand firm and confront invasion" by a "mysterious
stranger." Male gives fuller and more effective treatment to "The
Gray Champion" than the White Mountain narrative. "The Gray
Champion" is also the subject of Takahiro Kamogawa's "History in
Hawthorne's 'The Gray Champion'" (*KS* 10:161–73). Kamogawa
treads a well-ploughed furrow in claiming that Hawthorne made romance out of a historical setting, but is closer to virgin territory when
emphasizing Hawthorne's use of the story to sound the theme of
American literary nationalism. What Hawthorne wanted to do in an
age that demanded a national literature using American materials
was to give readers "a significant sense of their being related to the
past." The article also contains good insights into Hawthorne's use
of the "Angel of Hadley" folk motif. In still another view "The Gray
Champion" is conjoined with other Revolutionary tales such as
"Howe's Masquerade," "My Kinsman, Major Molineux," and "The
Liberty Tree" in Celeste Loughman's "Hawthorne's Patriarchs and
the American Revolution" (*ATQ* 40[1978]:335–44). Loughman's
point is that Hawthorne uses patriarchs (or matriarchs) as central
symbolic figures in his stories on the American Revolution and that
"The Liberty Tree" is Hawthorne's most "accurate assessment" of
the American Revolution and past. Narrator Grandfather is neither
an "antique spirit or visionary" but rather a wise old man "who brings
to bear intelligence, experience, and objectivity on his judgments of
the Revolution." The remarks about "The Liberty Tree" are especially
cogent; one wishes Loughman had focused on this relatively un-
treated work more exclusively.

The unsurprising position that "The Wives of the Dead" is a
"psychological romance" and not a mere sentimental vignette is advanced by John L. Selzer in "Psychological Romance in Hawthorne's

'The Wives of the Dead' " (*SSF* 16:311–15). Selzer is more perceptive when demonstrating how Hawthorne uses "external devices" to dramatize "internal action" in depicting each woman's psychological reaction to her husband's prematurely announced death. Two examinations of "Young Goodman Brown" are less revealing and convincing. Holding the view that Hawthorne's story is a case study in paranoia is Edward Jayne in " 'Pray Tarry With Me Young Goodman Brown' " (*L&P* 29:100–13). Though somewhat fruitful in identifying a paranoiac narrative pattern in the story, the Freudian-Crewsian reading is reductive and at times overly clinical.

The later tales were not ignored. "Drowne's Wooden Image" is the main focus of Thomas Friedman's "Making Mysteries: Hawthorne's Use of the 'Hermeneutic Code' " (*HUSL* 7:298–322). Friedman's plausible conclusion, reached after a rather stilted examination of the story, is that Hawthorne's frequent "non-disclosure of secrets" in his stories, with resulting ambiguity, marks him as "distinctly modern." In "Aylmer's Alchemy in 'The Birthmark' " (*PQ* 57[1978]: 399–413), John Gatta, Jr., explores this Old Manse-era story from the standpoint of alchemy as guiding metaphor, supplying a new dimension to the reading and understanding of the story. Gatta holds that Hawthorne used the "neutral metaphor" of alchemy to "support the ironic structure" of the story and as symbol representing the "dangerous appeal" inherent in "any mode of false transcendence based on material suppositions." "Rappaccini's Daughter" is the subject of Stephen A. Barney's chapter "Blighting Words: Hawthorne's 'Rappaccini's Daughter' " in his *Allegories*, pp. 254–82. Though Barney carefully relates the story to various subtypes and stages of love allegory, his conclusions offer no real fresh interpretations of the story's meaning.

A popular culture-inspired study of a Hawthorne sketch is Roberta F. Weldon's "Hawthorne's 'Foot-prints on the Sea-Shore' and the Literature of Walking," a chapter in *America: Exploration and Travel*, ed. Steven E. Kagle (Bowling Green), pp. 127–35. Though her conclusions about the themes, structure, and inner discoveries of the narrator are not original, Weldon is successful in establishing this sketch in the history and development of walking literature in America, positioning it between Irving's classic excursions Eastward (to the past) and Thoreau's modern romantic treks Westward (to the future). The sketch that received an unusual amount of attention, however, is "The Haunted Mind." Rita Gollin's *Nathaniel Hawthorne and the Truth of Dreams* (see section *ii.*) analyzes it as a veritable paradigm of the dream experience (chapter 3). John E. Holsberry's "Hawthorne's 'The Haunted Mind,' the Psychology of Dreams, Coleridge, and Keats" (*TSLL* 21:307–31) proves to be more an analysis of the influence on Hawthorne by the philosophical and psychological associationists than it does a critical reading of the sketch itself. Holsberry's article in fact should be compared to Gollin's chapter 2, "Theories of the Mind," in its discussion of Hawthorne's knowledge of epistemology. Finally, in "Imagination and Point of View in 'The Haunted Mind'" (*ATQ* 39[1978]:263–67), Norman H. Hostetler reads the sketch as one of Hawthorne's best presentations "of the creative moral power of the imagination" and explores the implications of the rhetorical use of the second person singular pronoun throughout, an interesting point which, however, needs further references to the sketch and a closer following of its development to be wholly convincing.

v. Hawthorne and Others

Work on Hawthorne and other writers generally seems to be accelerating, there being nearly three times the number of comparative or influence studies this year as in 1978. Hawthorne's works are compared to a wide range of authors and times, from Spenser's Renaissance to John Updike's modern America and from Dickens to Nabokov.

Karen and Edward C. Jacobs offer a minor contribution to the corpus of Hawthorne-Spenser materials in "The Doves of Venus in Hawthorne and Spenser" (*AN&Q* 18:2–5). The Jacobs believe that Spenser's dove from Book IV of *The Faerie Queene* is borrowed for two appearances in *The Blithedale Romance* to show, conversely to Spenser's thematic handling, the absence of chaste love, a force which could have assuaged jealousy and united Coverdale with his friends. Their argument is tenuous, especially since the first bird to appear in *Blithedale* is not specifically identified by Hawthorne as a dove. An examination of similarities between Dickens and Hawthorne in their origins as writers (in periodical literature) and their divergent methods of societal delineation is the chief strength of Jonathan Arac's chapter "The House and the Railroad: *Dombey and Son* and

The House of the Seven Gables" in *Commissioned Spirits: The Shaping of Social Motion in Dickens, Carlyle, Melville, and Hawthorne* (Rutgers). For comment on an earlier version of this chapter see *ALS 1978*, p 28.

On the American front there is a surprising absence of new additions to the Hawthorne-Melville shelf. Of course, there is Hyatt Waggoner's chapter 7, "Hawthorne and Melville," in *The Presence of Hawthorne* (see section *ii.*), but this is essentially a reprinting of two earlier essays. Likewise Tyrus Hillway's revised *Herman Melville* (Twayne) offers essentially the same brief view of the Hawthorne-Melville relationship advanced in the original 1963 printing, disappointingly ignoring recent scholarly work on the subject.

Hawthorne and his Concord neighbors are the subject of several studies this year. Taylor Stoehr's *Nay-Saying in Concord: Emerson, Alcott, and Thoreau* (Archon) refers several times to how Hawthorne's views and practices (especially his Brook Farm experience) compared to those of the Transcendentalists. Hawthorne and Thoreau are the subject of Richard Predmore's "Thoreau's Influence in Hawthorne's 'The Artist of the Beautiful' " (*ATQ* 40:329–34), a not wholly convincing argument that Thoreau was a chief influence on Hawthorne's story since it was written during the time of his closest association with Hawthorne and bears several Thoreauvian markings in theme and symbol (especially the butterfly). A balanced, well-researched perspective of Hawthorne's relationship with Margaret Fuller is provided by Margaret V. Allen in *The Achievement of Margaret Fuller* (Penn State). Allen's brief but sensitive discussion of the two Concordians turns up nothing new about Fuller's being the model for Zenobia but is revealing on the subject of the two authors' feelings about each other—especially Hawthorne's "deeply ambivalent" attitude toward Margaret.

The year's major accomplishment on Hawthorne and related writers, however, is the book and three essays on Hawthorne and Henry James, a subject which has smoldered so long that this year's eruption seems a natural occurrence. The best and most comprehensive coverage is that by Robert Emmet Long in a remarkable influence study (see also chapter 7, section *ii.*), *The Great Succession: Henry James and the Legacy of Hawthorne* (Pittsburgh). In this only book ever to be devoted wholly to the literary relationship between the two, Long elects to demonstrate Hawthorne's influence on

James from the latter's apprentice years in short fiction, 1865–75, to his mid-career point with *The Bostonians* in 1886 (including, of course, James's seminal study *Hawthorne*). Long carefully delineates the specific influence of Hawthorne's tales and novels on James and suggests considerable indirect bearing as well. He is direct and sure-footed. He dutifully reviews existing scholarship on the Hawthorne-James question and is honest about other literary influences on James besides Hawthorne. The only disappointment is in Long's decision to end his book prior to James's major phase; we are left wanting more. Hyatt Waggoner also treats James in his final chapter and title essay, "The Presence of Hawthorne." He offers an incisive, objective analysis of James's three published assessments of Hawthorne, sees "kinship" as well as "influence," and concludes that Hawthorne "was immensely important to James, not as a model but as a felt presence." Richard Ruland explores how to read James's *Hawthorne* for what it reveals of his reaction to American culture and literary theory, in "Beyond Harsh Inquiry: The Hawthorne of Henry James" (*ESQ* 25:95–117). Though his Hawthorne-James discussion is not especially illuminating, Ruland presents a cogent reading of *Hawthorne* as it manifests James's mind and art as well as his cultural and artistic affinities with Hawthorne. Jesse Bier's "Henry James's 'The Jolly Corner': The Writer's Fable and the Deeper Matter" (*ArQ* 35:321–34) is a less successful attempt to prove that in "The Jolly Corner" James strove for "a delicate amalgam of his two predecessors" Hawthorne and Poe. Though provocative, Bier's argument is strained in its view that James seemed to be attempting such a conscious blending. He is on safer ground when drawing meaningful parallels between Hawthorne's and James's concepts and techniques.

Looking back across the Atlantic, two critics detect Hawthornean influence on Virginia Woolf and D. H. Lawrence. John B. Humma in " 'Time Passes' in *To the Lighthouse*; 'Governor Pyncheon' in *The House of the Seven Gables*" (*BSUF* 20,iii:54–59) takes the intriguing but unconvincing position that the "Governor Pyncheon" chapter of *Seven Gables* was possibly a major shaping force on Woolf's part 2, "Time Passes." Even Humma himself has to wonder, in concluding, whether the case is rather one of "art, all unconsciously, tend[ing] to imitate art." Sandra Whipple Spanier, in "Two Foursomes in *The Blithedale Romance* and *Women in Love*" (*CLS* 16:58–68) spots several remarkable parallels in setting, characterization, and theme between Hawthorne's and Lawrence's novels, concluding that if there is not direct Hawthornean influence, then at least "deep bonds" exist between the two works. Spanier writes convincingly until she assumes the same general motives behind the writing of each book.

The indebtedness of more recent American fiction to Hawthorne is the last point of comparison to be noted. Again, in "The Presence of Hawthorne," Hyatt Waggoner traces Hawthorne's influence on Faulkner and Warren, demonstrating that despite Faulkner's disclaimers to the contrary ("'Who's Hawthorne?'") he is obviously in the mold of Hawthorne and that Warren is the modern writer most conscious of Hawthorne's "presence." References to the Hawthorne-Faulkner-Warren relationship are also found elsewhere in Waggoner's book. In an article designed to prove that "contemporary writers create their precursors, justifying the older fiction by refining our critical handling of it," Chapel Louise Petty in "A Comparison of Hawthorne's 'Wakefield' and Nabokov's 'The Leonardo': Narrative Commentary and the Struggle of the Literary Artist" (*MFS* 25:499–507) skillfully demonstrates how in each story the narrators and their situations are closely intertwined with the characters and fates of their respective protagonists. She is less persuasive with her thesis that "Wakefield" essentially concerns "the theme of an artist's struggle with the materials of his story." Lastly, David B. Kesterson in "Updike and Hawthorne: Not so Strange Bedfellows" (*NMAL* 3:item 11) examines John Updike's indebtedness to Hawthorne, especially in *A Month of Sundays* where theme, structure, names, and characterization are analogous to those of *The Scarlet Letter*.

North Texas State University

3. Poe

J. Albert Robbins

Two years ago, 1977, there were half a hundred books, articles, and dissertations on Poe cited in the *MLA International Bibliography*. Last year, 1978, the total rose to nearly a hundred. This year it has subsided to 55. Of these we shall take notice of 33. The year 1979 is scant also by producing no texts or textual studies on Poe, no popular (commercial) books on Poe, only one brief bibliographical article, and nothing on *The Narrative of Arthur Gordon Pym* or *Eureka*. What we do have are three books: a general critical study, an edition of 19th-century correspondence about Poe biography, and a slender volume of three general essays; three articles on poems; and 22 articles on tales. Of the year's work in Poe studies the most substantial are David Ketterer's book, and essays by John Harmon McElroy, Stanley Kozikowski, and Taylor Stoehr.

i. Biography and General Studies

When Ingram, the British Poe enthusiast and biographer, died in 1916, he left the largest collection of Poe materials anywhere—a resource which five years later came to the University of Virginia. The late John Carl Miller spent a good part of his academic career cataloging, analyzing, and reprinting portions of these papers. In 1960 he published *John Henry Ingram's Poe Collection at the University of Virginia* (a catalog) and two years ago *Building Poe Biography* (see *ALS 1977*, pp. 37–38), a sampling of correspondence with Ingram's informants, with the exception of Sarah Helen Whitman. Now in *Poe's Helen Remembers* (Virginia), a well-edited and beautifully printed volume, he has joined the two halves of the remarkable Whitman-Ingram correspondence. In late 1873 Ingram approached Sarah Helen Whitman for help—the first of 71 letters from him and 94 from her. They document Ingram's obsessive exploration of Poe's tangled life and Mrs. Whitman's patient response to his questions until her death in 1878. Miller also includes 14 of Ingram's uncollected articles and reviews. His annotations to the letters are themselves a contribution to Poe scholarship and are retrievable through a detailed index. In *Poe Studies* (12:28–29) Miller corrects the record on several details about an Englishwoman who was a house guest in 1847, "Poe and Miss Anna Blackwell."

The year's most ambitious general study is David Ketterer's *The Rationale of Deception in Poe* (LSU). Of present-day critical approaches to Poe, Ketterer says, his is closest to *The Design of the Present*, in which John F. Lynen stresses Poe's lifelong search for unity (see *ALS 1969*, pp. 185–87); but Ketterer differs in seeing a developmental progression "from an immediately attainable supernal reality to a unified reality in the future"—from, to use the three topical headings by which the volume is organized, deception to fusion to intuition. He views the three topics (very loosely, I should emphasize) as evolutionary: "from a position where reason (viewed as productive of deception) is opposed to imagination, to a position where a species of reason allied with imagination is valued in an ambiguous concept of *intuition*." I am not convinced that such a sequential view of Poe is the most productive and prefer to read this book for new perspectives on old debates about Poe's writings.

As to proportion, one chapter treats biography; one, poetry; and seven chapters or parts of chapters discuss fiction. One (chapter 8) gathers up such odd pieces, analytic in one way or another, as "Maelzel's Chess-Player" and writings on cryptography, autography, phrenology, and literary criticism. Of the poems nine receive detailed attention and 11 get brief treatment. The poems, Ketterer suggests, form sequences around four key poems: "Tamerlane," "Al Aaraaf," "The Raven," and "Ulalume." It is the fiction which gets complete attention: every tale and sketch, plus *Pym* and "Julius Rodman," are noticed or discussed at length. Though analyses of individual tales are not always new and fresh, they are generally informative and occasionally stimulating.

In *Edgar Allan Poe, An American Imagination: Three Essays* (Kennikat) Elizabeth Phillips tries to persuade us that Poe was a complete—though not a typical—American artist. In essay 1 ("The Air of Democracy and the Imagination of Man") the strategy is to measure Poe's literary nature with America's literary prospects as described by Tocqueville in his *Democracy in America* (1835, 1840). Her thesis is that Poe *was* alert to the realities in Young America, but the proposition is not fully evident. And, as Phillips admits, there is no evidence that Poe ever heard of the Frenchman or was aware of his acute analysis of the American temperament and prospects. In essay 2 ("The Imagination of a Great Landscape") she argues that Poe drew significantly upon the American scene; but specific locales, and even allusions to place, are few in his creative work. She touches upon the collateral matter of awareness of American *spaces*, an intriguing aspect of the landscape topic, but inexplicably says nothing of "The Journal of Julius Rodman." Thus far I find little that persuades me of Poe's Americanness, but in essay 3 ("Mere Household Events: The Metaphysics of Mania") we encounter a new matter which is well researched and fascinating. After a routine summary of evidence on Poe's alcoholism, Phillips turns to contemporary medical opinion on alcoholism and on various forms of mania, hallucination, hostility, and murder—all elements in some of Poe's best tales. She proposes three works which a journalist such as Poe might at least have encountered at second hand—treatises by Dr. Benjamin Rush, 1812; by Dr. Charles Caldwell, 1832; and by Dr. Isaac Ray, 1838. Whether he knew the medical terminology and medical concepts or not, Poe utilized them again and again in his tales of mental aberration. Elements we regard as "Poe-esque" are straight out of the best medical opinion of that time. This portion of the third essay (pp. 112–37) is convincing and shows that it still can pay to explore the recorded thought of Poe's time.

Another essay is also on medical matters—the question of Poe's principal malady. It is impossible to diagnose a dead man's illnesses after a 130-year interval but the temptation is to speculate and B. Cowan Groves does ("The Death of Poe: The Case for Hypoglycemia," *ReAL* 5,ii:7–19). Hypoglycemia is "a condition in which there is insufficient glucose supply to the brain." Its manifestations resemble complaints Poe had: nervousness, weakness, apprehension, depression, anxiety, giddiness, and so on. Groves believes that Poe exhibited recurrent symptoms from West Point days to his death. Invariably his health worsened when he was away from home. Nutritional deficiency aggravates the disease and almost certainly Poe's meals and sleep patterns worsened when he was away from Maria Clemm's care.

A broad essay, more concerned with tales than with poems, is Samuel Coale's "The Primitive Poe: The Radical Awareness of his Gothic Art" (*EEPSAPT* 17 [1978]:35–51). Poe is "primitive" in his appeal to sensation and to the underside of the consciousness. The "radical awareness" in his art signifies a special and heightened sense of "a realm where fantasy and reality become interchangeable." This "awareness, rooted in the terrors of dissolution both of the world without and the world within, lies at the heart of Poe's art." Coale discusses four tales (including "The Fall of the House of Usher") and two poems. As to the latter, the persona in the poems resembles that of the tales, but the poetry is only "hollow replica or mere illusion." A good deal of this sounds familiar.

Thirty-six years ago Willard Thorpe discovered a malicious caricature of Poe in Thomas Dunn English's temperance novel *Walter Woolfe; or, The Doom of the Drinker* (1847). Others have addressed the bibliographical problem and now Dwight Thomas explores the full publishing history, including two serializations in 1843. In one brief scene an unnamed person's broad forehead identifies him as Poe—as do such details as "fine analytical powers" and "bitter and apparently candid style." English's animosity becomes visible in such phrases as "the very incarnation of treachery and falsehood" ("Poe, English, and *The Doom of the Drinker*: A Mystery Resolved," *PULC* 40:257–68).

ii. Poetry

The idea is not new, as Dwayne Thorpe fully knows: that "The City in the Sea" is Babylon and a primary source, the book of *Revelation* ("Poe's 'The City in the Sea': Source and Interpretation," *AL* 51:394–99); but Thorpe gives his reasons for preferring Babylon over Gomorrah, and he discusses correspondences with *Revelation* (so many that he concludes the poem "has so few original images that it may be seen as an embroidery on [St.] John's work"). But, unlike the city in *Revelation*, Poe's city is an emblem of "the power of death, and his vision is horrible because it is nihilistic."

The chief part of Katrina Bachinger's " 'A Fit Horror': Edgar Allan Poe's 'The Raven' " (*SaSEL* 87:48–60) is a reading which offers nothing new or fresh. The one new suggestion is bizarre: the Christian cross is a symbol of death and resurrection; the raven, if you will, is an anti-cross. The raven "negates the white bust of Pallas, i.e. negates the protecting presence of the household God, and the patroness of scholars, i.e. negates the poetic I or hope of the I."

Martin Roth's "Poe's Divine Spondee" (*PoeS* 12:14–18) is a summation of several arguments in Poe's "Rationale of Verse": the historical beginning of verse was the spondee (embodying simplicity and the beauty of a measure of equal duration); then came monotony and an engendering of new measures; the disappearance of the spondee accounts for degeneration in modern verse. Roth concludes that "as a critic [Poe's] mission was similarly paradoxical, pointing both to the rationale for increasing complexity in verse and to the lost spondaic basis of the ancient music."

iii. Tales

There is a wide range of interests and perspectives in articles on the short fiction—and, I might add, a wide range of quality. Seven essays and two notes are "general": studies of authorial deception, historical context, linguistic intent, ambiguity, role of the narrator, and such. Nine are psychocritical readings, and five treat influence and affinity.

a. **General Readings.**   Has everyone all these years been misreading "The Black Cat"? The thrust of John Harmon McElroy's article on the tale is to answer that question with a "Yes." The story "was designed as a skillfully wrought hoax requiring alertness to details to appreciate." The first clue comes in the fifth sentence, when the narrator says he will tell us "a series of mere household events." These "mere" commonplace events include compulsive drinking, fits of homicidal fury, carving a cat's eye out of its socket with a penknife, hanging the cat with a halter, cleaving his wife's skull open with an axe, concealing the evidence of his crime, perjury to escape justice, and almost certainly arson. (And, we should add, on the eve of his own hanging, composing this deceptive monologue full of hypocrisy, false remorse, insincere appeals for sympathy, and lies.) "Mere household events" indeed! The murderer's account of how the cat got thrown through the bedroom window to land and stick in fresh plaster and *with* the halter be impressed with the effect of bas relief (!) just above his bed on the day the house burned to the ground is, McElroy says, "the funniest thing in 'The Black Cat.'" With the exception of a Jungian reading five years ago (see *ALS 1974*, p. 38), this is the first article devoted to this tale in 20 years. "The Kindred Artist; or, The Case of the Black Cat" (*StAH* 3[1976; pub. 1979]:103–17) will accomplish what few essays do: permanently change the way we read a major Poe story.

The details of another major Poe tale have long been troublesome and in "A Reconsideration of Poe's 'The Cask of Amontillado'" (*ATQ* 39[1978]:269–80) Stanley J. Kozikowski proposes solutions to many of them. Kozikowski's chief arguments are these. The setting is not Italy but France, and not early 19th century but shortly after the French Revolution. Montresor is a French Catholic aristocrat, formerly wealthy but now financially reduced. Fortunato, an Italian, is an ambitious and injudicious alien in France and a follower of Napoleon, who had just taken rule of Italy. Montresor's family crypts, "modeled after the huge public catacombs of Paris . . . were probably visualized by Poe as being in or near Paris." Montresor and Fortunato are opposites in many ways: French/Italian; old money, declining/ new money, rising; fear of Freemasonry/"an ambitious Freemason"; a man disciplined by his hate/the clownish nouveau riche over-indulgent in the Mardi Gras festival. Moreover, it is likely that Poe knew that his audience would be familiar with the recent "William Morgan Excitement"—an exposé of Masonic secrets much publicized from 1826 to 1845. Some elements in this thesis are speculative, but Kozikowski makes good use of historical facts and argues his case persuasively.

There are two notes on this tale. In "Fortunato's Premature Demise in 'The Cask of Amontillado'" (*PoeS* 12:30–31) Jay Jacoby cites 11 articles and notes but he omits one (by Sam Moon, "The Cask of Amontillado," *N&Q* 199[1954]:448) which proposed the Fortunato premature-demise thesis 25 years ago. James W. Spisak's "Narration as Seduction, Seduction as Narration" (*CEA* 41,ii:26–29) is a summation of narrative and has nothing useful to say.

Taylor Stoehr's splendid essay, "'Unspeakable Horror' in Poe" (*SAQ* 78:317–22), undertakes a rationale of Poe's thought and art, a view of his ontology and linguistic/aesthetic theories. Again and again, in "Ligeia" for example, Poe claims that he cannot remember, cannot *name*—but "in the end the inexpressible always does seem somehow to get expressed." In concentrating upon three tales— "Ligeia," "Morella," and "The Fall of the House of Usher"—Stoehr makes cogent observations: "the essence of the tale lies in speaking of the 'unspeakable' "; a linguistic utterance is the medium by which the dead come to life. Indeed, "the essential task of Poe's art is to prepare the way, by various interlocking linguistic expectations and probabilities, for a culminating sentence that will somehow both say and be the desired apotheosis." Meaning and practice in these tales fit with precision into the larger frame of his general beliefs. The "power of words" is a potent creative force. The "theory of creation encompasses its end as well as its beginning." The fictive world is a thing apart, removed from everyday reality. There, on Poe's terms, the power is real, circumscribed, concentrated, brief (a tale to be read at one sitting), and fragile. "In his solipsistic world all reality will ultimately rest on words." The " 'unspeakable horror' is precisely that there is nothing there [after] the magic words are pronounced . . . [and] the story ends."

Ray Muzurek has interesting things to say about "Art, Ambiguity, and the Artist in Poe's 'The Man of the Crowd' " (*PoeS* 12:25–28)—specifying with clarity and brevity how much is suggested by "the mystery in [this] elaborate but 'unreadable' text." The effect comes from images of doubling and descent, from dramatic irony and parodic irony, from circularity and irresolution. Urban horror forms the surface meaning, beyond which we can find an unreliable narrator, a fascinating ambiguity, and commentary on Poe as artist. The tale, Mazurek affirms, points toward "a modernist aesthetic which conceives a literature as a concrete act of creation in language, and thus takes a critical stance toward its own practice."

Of the two essays on "Usher" the more substantial considers the inadequacies of the narrator ("Poe's House of the Seven Gothics: The Fall of the Narrator in 'The Fall of the House of Usher,' " *OL* 34: 331–51). Professor Frederick S. Frank reads the tale as an allegory on the powers (and weaknesses) of the imagination. The House (and for good reason he capitalizes the noun) is "the palace of art," "an abstraction" and "a dreamworld" imagined into existence. The fissure symbolizes "the taut harmony underlying the aesthetic composition of the House. Both the House and its lord dwell in tenuous balance." Sure that his end is near, Usher summons his friend to become his heir, but instead the narrator from the moment he looks upon House and tarn approaches with the inappropriate principles of materialism and reason. He is "a frustrated analyst who can see parts but never the whole"—the glorious unity of art. Not only is reason the wrong tool here, but the narrator "insists upon Gothicizing all that is potentially beautiful within the palace of art." It is "the narrator who is indeed the Gothic madman of the tale." At the end "rather than simply escaping from his Gothic predicament, the vain quester is literally disgorged or vomited forth by the submerging House as if he were some profane, foreign object." This reading pursues the unreliable narrator postulate with interesting results.

There are some noteworthy observations early in Katrina Bachinger's "The Poetic Distance of the House of Usher" (*SaSEL* 87:61–74). Poe establishes a poetic distance between the reader's commonplace reality and the tale's imaginary world of Gothic fancy; but then he chooses to compromise this distancing by addresses to the reader: conversational clichés such as "I have said" or "it will be remembered." He allies himself with the reader also by sharing his "worldly" wisdom (giving "mundane explanations for horrible improbabilities"). But then the article becomes lax and we encounter such undemonstrated assertions as "the House of Usher is fundamentally a logical house" and " 'The Fall of the House of Usher' is less a dream than a tale of ratiocination."

We are aware of Poe's use of two pseudosciences of the 1830s and 1840s—mesmerism and phrenology, but less aware of a third—physiognomy. Edward W. Pitcher discusses aspects of "The Physiognomical Meaning of Poe's 'The Tell-Tale Heart,' " (*SSF* 16:231–33). According to physiognomy, the moral nature is located in the breast and centrally in the heart, and intellectual nature in the head and centrally in the eye. Destroying the old man's eye and heart, the narrator believes, will demonstrate his own health of mind and moral sense. J. C. Lavater was a leading exponent of physiognomy and his works were widely translated into English. Poe referred to him once, but a close application of physiognomy to this tale strikes me as tenuous at best.

b. **Psychocritical Readings.** Poe lends himself to psychological, psychoanalytic, and psycholinguistic readings, and this year, with leftovers from 1978, there are nine which range from worthy to absurd and trivial. The best—because the clearest and most coherent—is "Poe and the Transcendent Self," a chapter in Sam B. Girgus' *Law of the Heart*, pp. 24–36. Calling Poe our early model American author of "the perverted self," he sees, through Poe, "the implications for the culture as a whole of the law of the heart." Girgus focuses upon several stories, principally "Usher" and "William Wilson," but there is space here only for a few generalizations. Many of "Poe's characters" develop a " 'schizoid way of being-in-the-world' as divided, disembodied, and false selves." Anxiety becomes his "regular mode of dealing with a world that threatens to destroy him." Schizophrenia can be a "means for a 'transcendental experience,' a 'journey of initiation.' The transcendent self . . . provides a vehicle for escape from an insane society that forces its citizens to accept mendacious standards of normality and that condones forms of insanity judged socially necessary. Madness need not be all breakdown. It may also be breakthrough." But, says Girgus, Poe seems minimally certain about the nature of reality beyond that breakthrough.

Joseph N. Riddel contributes an abstract and in-abstract-able exercise in deconstruction. There is word-play: decipherment/dicipherment and "ex-centric repetition" and the jest, "Poe died, as it were, in-text-ate." And liberal quotation from Derrida. He calls it "The 'Crypt' in Edgar Poe (*Boundary* 7,iii:117–44) and, of course, has a prefabricated, literal crypt in "Usher." In *Eureka* the crypt comes from verbal sleight-of-tongue. In the Dupin tales, the refuge-library is "indeed, a crypt." But this doesn't truly explain the essay. Best you read and judge it yourself.

Two seldom-discussed humorous tales—"The System of Dr. Tarr and Professor Fether" and "A Predicament"—were treated at some length last year by Barbara D. Winder in "Two Poe Stories: The Presentation of Taboo Themes Through Humorous Reversals" (*Thalia* 1,ii[1978]:29–33). The taboo element is that contemporary antebellum readers would easily have understood the tales as a veiled commentary on stereotyped behavior of blacks (childlike, unruly, naive, untrustworthy, etc.). Otherwise this essay is a psychoanalytic reading more informative about Freud than about Poe. There are two chief reversals, Winder claims (as parody, and of expected behavior of the fictional characters); the reader is aware of reversals on both unconscious and conscious levels. "Displacement" (defined as "replacement of an important but objectional element by one . . . that appears to be innocent to censorship") is "a significant technique" in these Poe stories. If you enjoy psychoanalytic criticism, you will appreciate this essay—and such truisms as this: "In 'The System' the techniques of humor are present in sufficient quantity . . . to assure us that the story will be taken as a joke on the narrator").

In 1966 Jacques Lacan published "Le séminaire sur 'La Lettre volée'" (*Ecrits*, Paris), and it has set up a chain reaction of sorts. Jacques Derrida (in *Poétique*, 1975) took issue in an essay called "Le facteur de la vérité." The former was partially translated in *YFS* 48[1972]:38–72 as "Seminar on 'The Purloined Letter'"; the latter in abridged form was translated in *YFS* 52[1975]:31–113 as "The Purveyor of Truth." The two pieces are extensively discussed by Barbara Johnson in "The Frame of Reference: Poe, Lacan, Derrida" (*YFS* 55–56[1977]:457–505) and in shorter form in *Psychoanalysis and the Text*, pp. 149–71. It is impossible to abstract the convoluted arguments of these pieces. As one would expect with Lacan and Derrida, the object is not to clarify "The Purloined Letter" but to use it as a laboratory specimen for their psycholinguistic discourse. This in turn becomes the topic of Johnson's summation and commentary.

Last year David R. Saliba published a Jungian reading of "Ligeia" ("The Nightmare in Miniature: 'Ligeia,'" *ATQ* 40[1978]:367–78). It goes like this. Both Ligeia and Rowena are anima figures and the narrator is unaware "that both female characters represent the same portion of his [unconscious] mind." Of the two Ligeia is the larger, more powerful force for she represents positive qualities (whereas Rowena stands for negative qualities). Ligeia is mystery and unknowability, a beneficent force, and a storehouse of knowledge and wisdom and of memories personal and collective. As the narrator seeks to increase his knowledge, his "strength is passing from the unconscious to the conscious side of the mind."

Before publishing pieces on literature, *American Imago* (which subtitles itself "A Psychoanalytic Journal for Culture, Science, and the Arts") should use a literary specialist as referee to caution against such weak essays as Robert N. Mollinger's "Edgar Allan Poe's *The Oval Portrait*: Fusion of Multiple Identities" (36:147–53). First error: Mollinger observes that the narrator is wounded, but he overlooks other highly relevant clues that tell us that the narrator is an unreliable witness: "delirium," "dreamy stupor," and in the deleted first paragraph of which the writer seems unaware, narcotic hallucination—all highly relevant in assessing the psychological state of the narrator. Second error: Mollinger uncritically accepts Marie Bonaparte's word that the oval portrait is of Poe's mother, Elizabeth, and reproduces the portrait (which indeed is oval). He quotes Poe's description in the tale, yet doesn't notice odd discrepancies: "it was a mere head and shoulders" [Elizabeth Poe's portrait extends *below* the waist] and this detail: "the ends of the radiant hair melted imperceptibly into the vague . . . shadows . . . [of] the background" [Elizabeth Poe wears a bonnet and almost none of her hair impinges on the background]. Mollinger's generalizations are no better. Sample: "Since the fusion makes all into a unity, the narrator is both murderer and murdered victim."

" 'The Purloined Letter': The Mystery of the Text" is a chapter in David I. Grossvogel's *Mystery and Its Fictions, From Oedipus to Agatha Christie* (Hopkins), pp. 93–107, and sounds promising. The mystery of the text turns out to be on "how to read *through* the surface of texts"—that is, what the text of this Poe tale may tell us of Poe's conscious and subconscious natures. This is largely a summarizing of Marie Bonaparte and Jacques Lacan's work. Disappointing.

Leonard W. Engel's "Edgar Allan Poe's Use of the Enclosure Device in 'A Descent into the Maelström' " (*EAS* 8:21–26)is unimpressive. A longer, more pretentious essay by William West ("Staying Alive: Poe's 'William Wilson,' " *Enclitic* 2,ii[1978]:34–49) ostensibly exists to challenge a passage in Daniel Hoffman's 1973 volume of Poe. It doesn't even do that effectively and soon lapses into pointless word-play, symbology, and Lacanean word-games.

c. Influence Studies. Five studies of Poe and his contemporaries propose the influence of Byron, E. T. A. Hoffmann, and Ludwig Tieck. George H. Soule, Jr., would extend the awareness of Byron and Byronism from *Tamerlane* and "The Assignation" to two other tales ("Byronism in Poe's 'Metzengerstein' and 'William Wilson,' " *ESQ* 24[1978]:152–62). After discussing the evidence the author concludes that "although neither Metzengerstein nor William Wilson is precisely Byron, they do reflect aspects of the Byronic character."

George B. von der Lippe has completed a doctoral study of the literary relationship of Poe and "the figure of E. T. A. Hoffmann," and two years ago he published an article on Hoffmann as a model for Roderick Usher (ses *ALS 1977*, pp. 42–43). Now there are two more. In one, "Beyond the House of Usher: The Figure of E. T. A. Hoffmann in the Works of Poe" (*MLS* 9:33–41), von der Lippe stakes a broad claim for the Hoffmann influence upon eight arabesque tales, from "The Assignation" in 1834 to "The Black Cat" in 1843. He places the beginning early: "At some point prior to 1835—perhaps as early as the 1826 appearance of [R. P.] Gillies' [English translation of] *German Stories*—Poe came under the spell of Hoffmann." In Poe, he asserts, there is "conscious implementation of the Hoffmann figure as a character model"—a claim, it seems to me, unprovable by internal evidence in the fiction. In the other essay, " 'La Vie d'artiste fantastique': The Metamorphosis of the Hoffmann-Poe Figure in France" (*CRCL* 6:46–63), von der Lippe admits that Poe never mentioned Hoffmann in his writing but, he contends, Poe could not have escaped the Hoffmann influence. About the time when the Hoffmann figure was fading from notice in France the Poe image revived it, thanks largely to the work of Baudelaire. Indeed, he concludes, the Hoffmann-Poe figure has become universal as "the archetypal image of Romanticism's creator and product—*l'artiste fantastique*."

Following a general discussion of the uses of Gothicism, Paul Lewis ("The Intellectual Functions of Gothic Fiction: Poe's 'Ligeia' and Tieck's 'Wake Not the Dead,'" *CLS* 16:207–21) suggests as a possible source the tale of Tieck translated into English at least a decade before Poe wrote his famous tale. The two stories deal "with almost identical material in radically different ways." Walter, the protagonist in the Tieck piece, marries a raven-haired woman, Brunhilda, who represents beauty, wisdom, sexual passion, and spiritual profundity. She dies and Walter mourns at her grave, though he has now married a blonde woman, Swanhilda—temperate, domestic, low on sexual ardour, and dull. And so on. Since Poe explored and developed two preparatory tales using this pattern—"Berenice" and "Morella"—I would say that he had no creative need of Tieck.

Many a painting by the 20th-century Belgian artist Magritte reflects a knowledge of Poe for visual details or mood or transcendent vision, William Goldhurst explains, with references to specific paintings ("Literary Images Adapted by the Artist: The Case of Edgar Allan Poe and René Magritte," *Comparatist* 3:3–14).

Indiana University

4. Melville

Hershel Parker

Again this year I am ignoring the most routine articles. Even the rest had the usual faults which I don't need to enumerate; as I said last year, the complaints in the opening paragraphs of *ALS 1972, 1973, 1975,* and *1977* still are valid. I do want to venture two observations. First, Henry Sussman was prophetic last year in the conclusion of his essay on *The Confidence-Man* (*Glyph* 4:32–56): we are in the long wake of deconstructionist criticism as it is co-opted, institutionalized, and formularized. After the recent trendy essays where "origin" and "absence" were merely critical catchphrases, we are seeing something much worse, vulgarizations in which a mix of structuralism, poststructuralist Freudianism, semiotics, speech act theory, deconstructionist criticism and what-not is relentlessly applied to one literary work after another, the way we used to get into print with a string of articles entitled "The Unity of . . . . " Second, the brightest of the new crowd will go on playing their wordgames only for themselves and their New Haven and Baltimore coteries as long as they ignore biographical and textual evidence (textual in the grubby CEAA sense of recovering words in manuscripts and editions, of identifying processes by which works reach their various forms). The best criticism of the 1980s, I'm convinced, will emerge from a combination of approaches, what I've been calling the New Scholarship. Surely this is not asking too much—for starters, Hayford-Sealts and Murray Krieger rolled into one.

i. Biography, Bibliography, Reputation, and Miscellaneous

Joyce Deveau Kennedy and Frederick J. Kennedy continued their important supplements to the *Log* with "Elizabeth Shaw Melville and Samuel Hay Savage, 1847–1853" (*MSEx* 39:1–7), letters the Kennedys found in the possession of descendants of Savage in South Carolina. Alice P. Kenney's "Relics of 'Grand Old Pierre'" (*MSEx* 40:1–2) contains illustrations of the camp bed tall General Gansevoort gave to another tall soldier, George Washington. The interest of the bed is that Gansevoort's grandson may have been describing a similar one in book 19 of *Pierre*; not a bed to encourage incest, one would think, but also not a bed to sit on for long. Of interest to Melvilleans and of profound interest to many others is a book I overlooked, G. J. Barker-Benfield's *The Horrors of the Half-Known Life: Male Attitudes Toward Women and Sexuality in Nineteenth-Century America* (Harper, 1976), in which five chapters deal with Dr. Augustus Kinsley Gardner, long-time friend of Melville's and the physician called in at Malcolm's suicide. In the light of these chapters it is spooky to think what sort of psycho-medico advice Gardner might have given the Melvilles. Nonspecialists needing a brief reliable survey of Melville's life and career may consult Hershel Parker's author introduction in *The Norton Anthology of American Literature*, volume 1 (Norton), pp. 2032–44, the first such survey to take the 1970s biographical discoveries into account.

Brian Higgins' *Herman Melville: An Annotated Bibliography, Volume I: 1846–1930* (Hall) is an important achievement. Following the Hall "Reference Guide" format, Higgins divides each year into two sections, one for books on Melville, one for shorter pieces, chronological within the year; since very few books on Melville appeared before 1930, the bibliography is all but chronological throughout. The result is a valuable reference tool which supersedes the Parker-Mailloux *Checklist of Melville Reviews* (except as a handy hunting-guide) and Hall's 1973 Ricks-Adams bibliography (for the years 1900–1930). Higgins' quotations and summaries are succinct, ranging from a line or two for routine reviews to almost two pages for John Freeman's 1926 book. The year 1849 gets 30 pages for 152 items (mainly reviews of *Mardi* and *Redburn*); 1909, during the eclipse of Melville's reputation, gets five items on one page. Aside from its scholarly value the compilation is a wonderful bedside book, a plum-pudding of quotations which will surprise and delight even the oldest Melville hands. Higgins also has a brief "Supplement" (*MSEx* 37:10–15). Lewis Leary's *Articles on American Literature*, pp. 354–72, supplies an alphabetical listing of critics and their criticism, ranging from "Anon." in *Extrapolation* to D. D. Zink in *Forum(H)*. I wondered in 1977 which parts of Marvin Fisher's book had appeared as articles; now it would be easy to find out by checking the nine items under his name. Despite such uses, I am skeptical of the value of a compilation arranged by critic instead of subject: is the purpose to show who has been getting into print? One who has (a dozen items, count 'em) is George Monteiro, whose latest is "Melville in the Chicago *Inter Ocean* and the London *Academy*" (*MSEx* 38:7–8). Catches from Monteiro's seining are diminishing: of the items in his "On the Author of the 'Greatest Sea-Book Known': Commentary on Herman Melville at the Turn of the Century" (*PBSA* 73:115–20) two were sampled in *Doubloon*. Nelson C. Smith supplies "Four New London Reviews" (*MSEx* 40:3–6), among them a rare English review of *Israel Potter*. Merton M. Sealts, Jr., takes account of new information in "A Second Supplementary Note to *Melville's Reading* (1966)" (*HLB* 27:330–35).

There were three curiously dissimilar contributions to the history of Melville scholarship and criticism. Egbert S. Oliver, author of the sixth dissertation on Melville, in *The Shaping of a Family* (Portland, Oreg.: HaPi Press) tells of a distant time at the University of Washington: "I now had a clear run for my dissertation, and I tackled it with enthusiasm. I had settled upon Herman Melville as a subject. I had read his sixteen volumes in the Constable edition twice and I had a theme which Harold Eby and the department approved." When's the last time a doctoral candidate read all of Melville twice before starting to write? Simultaneously, in a princelier setting, Charles Olson was meeting Melville descendants and working with Melville's own books and papers. In many of the recent studies of Olson there is mention of Melville; now Paul Christensen in *Charles Olson: Call Him Ishmael* (Texas) gives some details about Olson as a working Melvillean. The Melville passages in Lewis Mumford's *My Works and Days* (Harcourt) tell us almost more than we want to know, for after a fascinating account of his emerging interest in Melville and of the circumstances of the writing of his 1929 critical biography, Mumford reveals himself as spending more energy defending old positions than striving toward new insights. Still, his recollections and his quoted correspondence with Van Wyck Brooks and Henry A. Murray make a valuable addition to the history of Melville's general and academic reputation.

ii. General

Three books dealt with at least several of Melville's works: Edward H. Rosenberry's *Melville* (Routledge); Rowland A. Sherrill's *The Prophetic Melville: Experience, Transcendence, and Tragedy* (Georgia); and Carolyn L. Karcher's *Shadow over the Promised Land: Slavery, Race, and Violence in Melville's America* (LSU). Rosenberry surveys most of Melville's major writings and some minor works; Sherrill hopscotches, landing on six full-length prose works, missing the others, and missing all the short fiction and poetry; Karcher looks only at passages which relate to her topic or can be forced into relation to it. Although Rosenberry's biocritical study is designed to introduce Melville to the general reader, it is infused with the author's full knowledge of (and participation in) Melville scholarship and criticism. My copy will stand beside another gracefully written general account, John Freeman's *Herman Melville*. Sherrill's book gives fair warning: factual error in the first paragraph of the dust copy and the first paragraph of the introduction. Here is what Sherrill says he does: "In the interpretive effort of this study . . . the attempt has been to isolate and define the ways in which three of the early fictions—*Typee, Redburn,* and *White-Jacket*—each contributed to Melville's progress toward an idea of the transcendent, to assess the genesis, emergence, and shape of this idea in its most fully articulated form in *Moby-Dick,* and to discern in *Pierre* and *Billy Budd* how this idea became a controlling factor in Melville's mature vision of life." As Milton R. Stern says, all this was anticipated "decades ago" (*AL* 52:139–41). *Shadow* has the fault of the parts already reviewed here (e.g., *ALS 1975,* p. 66), misuse of evidence, for Karcher manhandles Melville into the role of persistent critic of social and racial prejudices: "Beginning with *Mardi,* in almost every piece of fiction Melville wrote, he addressed himself directly or indirectly, concertedly or in passing, to refuting the racist assumptions that justified slavery in the South and racial discrimination throughout the United States." The result is a series of readings which inflate mentions of racial topics or which inflate minor pieces such as "The 'Gees." In the best passage, an earnest attempt to "situate" Melville's supplement to *Battle-Pieces* historically, Karcher admits that Melville's consciousness was not raised to 1970-level. I say 1970 because this book is a belated product of the New Left: Karcher acknowledges

H. Bruce Franklin as "in a sense" its "spiritual father." The book has the weaknesses of its author's strong convictions.

The year's most influential general article is sure to be "Melville's Quarrel with Fiction" by Nina Baym (*PMLA* 94:909–23), both because of the circulation of the journal and the reputation of the author. Beginning with a reminder that the early books, being neither straight autobiography nor straight fiction, involved Melville in breaching "the genre contract with his readers," Baym argues that his career ended because "his revulsion from genre" was followed by "a revulsion from language itself, as it began to seem that every literary statement implied a literary world and that literature was no more than an elaborate game, a repertory of set forms whose rules foreclosed possibilities instead of opening them." Misdating Meville's close knowledge of Emerson's works, Baym brashly claims that "the contact with Emerson's thought was the single most significant influence on the shape of *Moby-Dick.*" She fails to distinguish Emerson's thought from pervasive Romantic and Transcendental thought available to Melville in Carlyle and others before he read Emerson; Jonathan Arac, below, provides a salutary reminder of Carlyle's importance to Melville. More basic is her failure to distinguish between fiction and imaginative literature: she dismisses *Clarel* as if Melville had not used "language" in writing it. Still more basic is Baym's failure to cite any of the abundant biographical evidence that Melville had urgent economic reasons for putting his literary career in abeyance. This vigorous foray into Melville's works and writing on him looks anachronistic—a survey for popular consumption such as Van Wyck Brooks might have written in the 1920s or 1930s—but it may be a wavelet in *PMLA*'s generalist-oriented future. (In fact, Baym's major point about Melville's uncertainty with genre was anticipated in the 1930s by a critic Baym does not mention, R. P. Blackmur; see the remarkable digression on Blackmur's reading of Melville in Susan R. Horton's *Interpreting Interpreting* [Hopkins], pp. 48–49.) Like the general essays of earlier decades, Baym's is error-ridden: the first paragraph gets Melville's death-year wrong; Baym charges Melville with ignoring "Feathertop" in his review of the 1846 *Mosses*— forgivable, since the story was not there; footnote 2 has two little errors in citations; other footnotes introduce "Werner" Berthoff and "G. Watson" Branch—strangers, in the extremest sense of the word. Often a skeptical view from outside the closed circle of specialists can be refreshing; here Baym's irritation at the way Melville writes (irritation needlessly obtrusive in her brilliant *Clarel* essay in 1974) seems to have led her into shortcuts with thinking and research in what ought to have been another landmark essay.

Jonathan Arac's *Commissioned Spirits: The Shaping of Social Motion in Dickens, Carlyle, Melville, and Hawthorne* (Rutgers) is awkward, from the choice of authors down to the arrangement of chapters and sections of chapters. It also limps into the long line of studies in which Dickens and Melville get discussed in the same breath without any memorable connection being established. When is someone going to improve on Leonard Woolf's impressionistic comments of 1923 (quoted in the Norton *Moby-Dick*, pp. 629–31)? But for Melvilleans the chapter on "Heroism and the Literary Career: Carlyle and Melville" is a treat, especially Arac's argument that the characterization of Ahab as manager and manipulator of his crew owes something to the section on Cromwell in "The Hero as King." Arac is convincing, and might even have strengthened his case by citing the paragraph on "great *silent* men" as an analogue to Melville's discussion of the "Divine Inert" (chapter 33 of *Moby-Dick*).

iii. Moby-Dick

An interesting piece in a dull year, Lawrence Buell's "Observer-Hero Narrative" (*TSLL* 21:93–111), puts *Moby-Dick* in the context of a fictional genre, or subgenre. I question only the assertion that Ishmael as observer seeks "to undercut the hero's pretensions—to reduce the hero, so to speak, to his own quotidian level." I would have thought that even a "poor old whale-hunter" passage (chapter 33) diffuses our skepticism about Ahab's heroism, exalting him even as it repudiates the aid of "outward majestical trappings and housings." A note by David Charles Leonard, "The Cartesian Vortex in *Moby-Dick*" (*AL* 51:105–09), cites entries from Melville's edition of Chambers' *Cyclopaedia* in arguing that "Melville's affinity with Cartesianism alienated him from the main-currents of nineteenth-century transcendental thought." Gustaaf Van Cromphout in "*Moby-Dick*: The Transformation of the Faustian Ethos" (*AL* 51:17–32), a phenomenological reading, argues at excessive length that the book, "a Faustian venture in its epic ambitiousness," represents Melville's endeavor "to understand some of the deepest spiritual tendencies shaping Western experience." Steven Mailloux's "Learning to Read: Interpretation and Reader-Response Criticism" (*SLitI* 12:93–108), in a fine special issue on "Critics at Work: Contemporary Literary Theory," attempts to describe the "assumptions and strategies" of reader-response criticism while maintaining "a metacritical perspective that uses reader-response criticism as an example of how approaches to literature generally function." Section 2 argues that Ishmael "disappears as narrator" because he has outlived his usefulness as a teacher: "The reader uses him up by learning his lesson—the lesson of how to read the novel." Familiar from a long section in the *College Literature* special issue on *Moby-Dick* (Fall 1975) is James William Nechas' *Synonomy, Repetition, and Restatement in the Vocabulary of Herman Melville's "Moby-Dick"* (Norwood, 1978). Nechas attempts "to prove that theme absolutely controls expression in a work of literary art" and that "the interpretation of any work of literary art must be primarily the interpretation of what its language is saying and how it is saying it." Marjorie Pryse in *Mark and Knowledge*, chapter 3, "*Moby-Dick*: Social Physics and Metaphysics," raises one good question: "Why include a study of *Moby-Dick* in a book about social stigma in American fiction?" Why, indeed? Pryse's justification is that "*Moby-Dick* becomes an implicit reflection on social stigma by focusing on the vision that results from Ishmael's social invisibility. His vision is not social, but his invisibility is. Thus Melville implies that wisdom for the American, symbolized in part by the omniscience Ishmael achieves as narrator, requires his social invisibility. This makes Melville akin to the Transcendentalists because, in going to sea, Ishmael escapes the landed concerns of his society, which include social hierarchy and social stigma."

iv. Pierre

Eric Sundquist's "Parody and Parricide in Melville's *Pierre*" (chapter 4 of *Home as Found*) is an examination of the book as "the record of Melville's exhaustion and burning out on the themes of authority and genealogy." *Pierre* may be "a more American book than *Moby-Dick*," Sundquist suggests, because if "*Moby-Dick* can be read as the longest dream in American writing of a crisis in paternal authority, of doing in the dismembering father, *Pierre* is in some sense the fulfillment of the dream. Pierre's father is gone before the book begins, and the sarcophagus passage announces that freedom—one so often sought by revolutionaries, frontiersmen, and other lunatic Americanists—in all its horrible splendor." Working from structuralist and poststructuralist rereadings of Freud, Sundquist comes up with a number of such suggestive comparisons between *Moby-Dick* and *Pierre*. Conspicuously weak on the facts of Melville's life, Sundquist has the bad luck to take over some legend and simple error from Edwin H. Miller. And in the overingenious wordplay which Hopkins delights to publish, mannerism degenerates into trashiness: I counted four uses of the voguish "early on." In "The Entangled Text: Melville's *Pierre* and the Problem of Reading" (*Boundary* 7:145–73) Edgar A. Dryden gets into *Pierre* through the *Mosses* essay, which, he says, "raises and then ignores the problems of derivation: authority and priority, tradition and the individual talent, literary fathers and sons." Sundquist found such themes in *Moby-Dick*, but Dryden thinks Melville postponed consideration of them until *Moby-Dick* was finished, then focused on them "with an almost desperate insistence" in *Pierre*. For Dryden, *Pierre* is "about reading and writing, about the consumption and production of literary texts—a double problem that fascinates Melville from the beginning to the end of his writing career." Where Sundquist is basically Freudian-cum-structuralist and Freudian-cum-deconstructionist, Dryden is phenomenologist, structuralist, poststructuralist, and specifically deconstructionist. Their vocabularies overlap, and both of them illustrate the tendency of critics to take any new literary approach and thematize it, argue that a writer is writing about the very themes the theory is most concerned with. The pitfall, which neither Sundquist nor Dryden avoids, is that the literary criticism will be more about literary criticism than about the work being criticized.

The hazards of applying postmodernist literary approaches are exemplified in an essay which reads like a travesty of Sundquist and Dryden: "The Writer's Procreative Urge in *Pierre*: Fictional Freedom or Convoluted Incest?" (*SNNTS* 11:416–30). Here Brook Thomas, grimly following Edward Said, sees "much narrative fiction in the nineteenth century" (including *Pierre*) as "linked intimately with an attempt to reproduce in language the mysteries of human procreation." Thomas makes a pat formula out of deconstructionist concern with origin and authority: "The uncertainty of a father's authority over his child is reflected in the uncertainty of an author's authority over his text. Just as after conception a child is totally cut off from his father, so after conception a text is cut off from an author." In this runamuck deconstructionism Thomas leaps over the major question of when intentionality is infused into a work of art—during the act of composition? at the moment of completion? during revision?

Ignoring all recent criticism (to look at the studies cited in the footnotes is to experience time-warp), Karl F. Knight in "The Implied Author in Melville's *Pierre*" (*SAF* 7:163–74) holds that the narrator ("a created figure distinct from Herman Melville") "is used precisely for the purpose of compounding the ambiguities of the book." For Knight "the central object of parody is the implied author; that is, the story represents the implied author's attempt to write a sentimental romance wherein he will anatomize the complexities of life in the vain expectation of clearing up the mysteries."

v. The Stories

In an important review-essay, "Melville's Short Fiction" (*ESQ* 25: 43–57), Merton M. Sealts, Jr., looks beyond Bickley (1975), Dillingham (1977), and Fisher (1977) to the likely consequences of the publication of the Northwestern-Newberry edition of the stories and miscellaneous prose: "Not only will the forthcoming volume provide a standard text; it will offer for the short fiction in particular that ' "hard-core" scholarship' so essential for really 'knowing' Melville, as Robert Milder has recently reminded us; the besetting sin of Melville studies is still the tendency to write interpretation and criticism before the facts are in—or, worse still, to ignore the facts even after they have been established and made readily available." M. Thomas Inge's long-promised *Bartleby the Inscrutable: A Collection of Commentary on Herman Melville's Tale "Bartleby the Scrivener"* (Archon) consists mainly of familiar essays. It also includes a reprinting of the known reviews of *The Piazza Tales*; Lewis Leary's pleasant overview of readings, "B Is for Bartleby"; three new (if already somewhat passé) critical essays by Hershel Parker ("The 'Sequel' in 'Bartleby' "), John Stark ("Melville, Lemuel Shaw, and 'Bartleby' "), and Stanley Brodwin ("To the Frontiers of Eternity"); as well as Bruce Bebb's "Bartleby'; An Annotated Checklist of Criticism" and (so long did the volume go unpublished) Elizabeth Williamson's brief supplement to Bebb.

Milton R. Stern's "Towards 'Bartleby the Scrivener'" (*Stoic Strain*, pp. 19–41), an analysis of the way critics have dealt with certain stumbling blocks in the story, is the year's best piece on Melville, packed with knowledge about Melville and Melville criticism and written in English prose. I think Stern goes awry only in finding "a meaningful change in the lawyer" halfway through the story; the change, as I argue in the Inge collection, is temporary, and the lawyer who tells the first half is, after all, the lawyer who has lived through the whole experience.

vi. The Confidence-Man

Despite huffing and puffing galore, no one said much of interest this year. The best is the briefest, Tom Quirk's "Two Sources in *The Confidence-Man*" (*MSEx* 39:12–13), a demonstration that chapter 14 owes something to a passage in Montaigne's *Essays* on inconsistency and that chapter 44 owes something to a discussion of originality in fiction which Melville read in *Putnam's*. The process of claiming real-life models for characters continues in "Three of Melville's Confidence Men: William Cullen Bryant, Theodore Parker, and Horace Greeley" (*TSLL* 21:368–95), a woeful misapplication of learning by Helen P. Trimpi, who leaves us with the threat to identify "all twenty-six of the major characters" with "their historical counterparts" in the future. William M. Ramsey's minor note in a major journal, "Melville's and Barnum's Man with a Weed" (*AL* 51:101–04), makes farfetched comparisons, then plays up the old news that the Drummond light passage is a recollection of Barnum (see the footnote in the Norton edition, p. 205). Another piece by Ramsey, "'Touching' Scenes in *The Confidence-Man*" (*ESQ* 25:37–42), belabors the obvious in showing how "the dialectics of plot are intimately tied to Melville's pervasive word play." Carolyn L. Karcher's "Spiritualism and Philanthropy in Brownson's *The Spirit-Rapper* and Melville's *The Confidence-Man*" (*ESQ* 25:26–36) is an incautious pursuit of Edwin Fussell's old suggestion that Melville's chapter titles might have been influenced by Brownson's. May not the similar chapter titles in the books in question derive from titles in *Amelia, Tom Jones,* or other 18th-century works?

Three pieces look good because they come in the guise of chapters rather than mere articles, but readers of this book should be wary of appearances. Stephen Barney's *Allegories*, chapter 5, fails to elaborate a potentially interesting view of *The Confidence-Man* as "a negative allegory, a Romantic allegory." Alexander Blackburn's *Myth of the Picaro*, chapter 4, "The Symbolic Confidence Man," never advances far beyond the initial banality ("But Melville was no common seaman."), never shows it matters that the book "is a picaresque novel in a nonautobiographical symbolic form." Chapter 2 of John G. Blair's *Confidence-Man* does not go much beyond 1960s interpretations, particularly Dryden's (1968).

vii. Clarel

Bryan C. Short's "Form as Vision in Herman Melville's *Clarel*" (*AL* 50:553–69) is ambitious but muddy. Interpreting the epilogue as "curiously buoyant," Short tries to make that brief passage bear far too much weight: "The lesson of Melville's changing art in *Clarel* is that truth-seeking, whether transcendental or objective, too easily produces a truth which is useless while ignoring opportunity after opportunity for beauty and satisfaction. The *Clarel* epilogue, in its marvelously complex self-consciousness, gives the best proof of Melville's faith in literature and playful delight in creative freedom since the early pages of *Moby-Dick*." In arriving at this idiosyncratic reading Short concerns himself mainly with the handful of lyrics sung or recited by a few characters; the bulk of the poem is all but ignored, and so major a figure as Rolfe is barely mentioned. Bernard Rosenthal handicaps himself by an ambiguous title, "Herman Melville's Wandering Jews" (*Puritan Influences*, pp. 167–92); he is concerned with all the characters in *Clarel*, Jewish or not, who agonizingly weigh the promise that Christ will return against the fear that he "had never come at all." Rosenthal is at some pains to defend Derwent against "the modern critic intent upon imposing a twentieth-century mythos upon a nineteenth-century writer," but I think Bezanson (in one of the appendices to his 1960 edition) puts the priest in correct perspective: "Derwent is part of a series of Melville characters who practise their law, medicine, or theology so professionally as to endanger their response to experience."

I have not seen Larry Edward Wegener's *A Concordance to Herman Melville's "Clarel: A Poem and Pilgrimage in the Holy Land"* (published for the Melville Society in the "Monograph Publishing" service of University Microfilms): you don't get review copies of books that cost $115.75. Word has it that this concordance is based on the right copy-text, the 1876 edition, that it lists each item by part, canto, and line for ready use with different editions, and that an appendix contains Melville's corrections in a set of proofs (changes not incorporated in the 1876 edition).

viii. Billy Budd, Sailor

Peter L. Hays and Richard Dilworth Rust carry forward suggestions by such earlier critics as Robert Penn Warren and Edwin S. Shneidman that Melville's relationships with his sons might be worked into his last fiction: see " 'Something Healing': Fathers and Sons in *Billy Budd*" (*NCF* 34:326–36). Barbara Johnson begins her modish post-Modernist wordplay in her title, "Melville's Fist: The Execution of *Billy Budd*" (*SIR* 18:567–99): the story is executed, not the title character. Veering from semiotics to speech act theory to structuralism to deconstructionism, Johnson makes heavy weather of her attempt to show that as "a political allegory" the story, "much more than a study of good and evil, justice and injustice," is "a dramatization of the twisted relations between knowing and doing, speaking and killing, reading and judging, which make political understanding and action so problematic." You would think a deconstructionist critic would be fascinated by the Hayford-Sealts Genetic Text, but Johnson scants it in her discussion of the "endings" of *Billy Budd*, a topic recently engaged by Parker and Binder (*NCF* 33:131–43). Johnson's is an extreme example of the mannered writing we've been getting from Yale and Johns Hopkins, a style with a supercilious and intimidating cast: look at her strewing of "curiously enough" and "precisely" and you'll see what I mean. And here's an illustration of the geometrical law that you write yourself into a corner when you write for a closed circle: "The very phrase 'the deadly space between' is, according to editors Hayford and Sealts, a quotation of unknown origin: the source of the expression used to designate what is not known is thus itself unknown." But as Stanton Garner has shown (*ELN* 14:289–90), Melville got the quotation from Thomas Campbell. It was Hayford and Sealts, mere benighted modern editors, who did not recognize the phrase.

Thomas J. Scorza's *In the Time before Steamships: "Billy Budd," the Limits of Politics, and Modernity* (N. Ill.) argues that Melville's last piece of fiction is "the timeless work of a poet of nature who took a complex stand against the otherworldly faith of Christianity, the secular confidence of modern radicalism, the mere conventionalism of modern conservatism, and the human hubris implied by either rationalism or protoexistentialism." Despite many lapses (such as talking about magnanimity without mentioning Bertoff's discussion) and idiosyncratic notions (the narrator is "presumably" an Englishman), much of the book can be enjoyed as old-fashioned quotation, paraphrase, and running commentary. The book concludes with a strange, outraged appendix in which Scorza fumes at Hayford and Sealts for stressing the book's unfinished nature: "the paramount critical need, once a usable text of *Billy Budd* was established, was to emphasize the artistic integrity and wholeness of the work." Here Scorza illustrates the way we are still entangled by the New Criticism: anything put between two covers, even a work left unfinished at the author's death, is by definition a unified work of art. For the theoretical problem raised here, see the Parker-Binder article mentioned in the previous paragraph; and for a fine review of Scorza's book, see Berthoff (*AL* 52:312–14).

University of Delaware

5. Whitman and Dickinson

Willis J. Buckingham

This has been a good year for Dickinson studies and at least a moderately good one for Whitman scholarship. Growing interest in the two poets' connections with other thinkers and writers continues with two books on Whitman's importance for later American poets and another in which Dickinson is nudged from the circumference closer to the center of American literary history. Dickinson is also the subject of a strongly original critical volume and a superb new bibliography. Of biographical contributions there is less to note, except to say that if overweening attention to Dickinson's affairs of the heart has sharply declined, a new occasion for tenuous speculation has emerged—the state of her physical health.

i. Whitman

a. **Bibliography, Editing.**   The first reprinting of Whitman's 1856 *Leaves of Grass* (Norwood Editions) does not reproduce its original binding, but is otherwise a facsimile and contains a useful introductory note on the importance of the second edition by Gay Wilson Allen. Two Whitman letters, both perfunctory, are published for the first time, a note of sympathy (William White, "Unknown Whitman Letter to Mrs. Colquitt," *WWR* 25:182) and an 1878 postcard to Sidney Lanier informing him that a copy of *Leaves of Grass* was in the mail (Artem Lozynsky, "Whitman to Lanier: A Rediscovered Letter," *WWR* 25:173–74). Also added to the record are two responses to the poet in his lifetime. Harold Aspiz has discovered quite a number of allusions to Whitman in Eliza W. Farnham's reform-minded women's treatise, *Woman and Her Era*, published in 1864

Preparation of this chapter was greatly facilitated by the research assistance of Norman J. Gerlein, Jr.—*W.J.B.*

("An Early Feminist Tribute to Whitman," *AL* 51:404–09). Though
it is not known whether Whitman was aware of this book, *Woman
and Her Era* has value in providing access to a matrix of liberal ideas
about women from which he may have drawn some of his views
concerning feminine perfectability, especially as they are enunciated
in his 1871 *Democratic Vistas*. The other recovered item is a humorous but apparently sympathetic review in verse of the 1860
Leaves of Grass (Scott Giantvalley, "A 'New' Whitman Parody,"
WWR 25:76–77).

Begun 23 years ago, William White's checklists of current Whitman publications continue to appear in quarterly issues of his *Walt
Whitman Review*. So well known among Whitman specialists that
they tend to be taken for granted in these pages, it is a pleasure to
mark their longevity and to note with esteem the indispensable record they furnish on Whitman's reception in our time. *The Mickle
Street Review*, published from the poet's Camden home by the Walt
Whitman House Association, issued its first annual number this year.
Its purpose, the editors say, is to publish "the best poems, stories, or
essays honoring Whitman or explicitly manifesting his influence on
American letters." Of the nearly 40 tributes in this issue—they are
mainly poems—most have not before been published, and a number
are by well-known writers.

b. **Biography.**   Recent interest in Whitman's relation to his disciples,
and of them with each other, continues this year in the expert account offered by Artem Lozynsky of the circumstances surrounding
publication of *Calamus*, a volume of the poet's letters to Peter Doyle
edited by Dr. Richard Maurice Bucke in 1897 ("What's in a Title?
Whitman's 'Calamus' and Bucke's *Calamus*," *SAR*, pp. 475–88). Lozynsky makes persuasive his belief that Bucke hastened these letters
into print, and titled them as he did, believing that their indications
of a merely Platonic relationship between the two men would scotch
the attempts of some, particularly a coterie of British homosexual
admirers of Whitman, to find a physical component of manly love
in the "Calamus" sequence. The tactless efforts in Whitman's behalf
by another disciple, Sadakichi Hartmann, are described in *The Whit-
man-Hartmann Controversy*, ed. George Knox and Harry Lawton
(Bern: Herbert Lang [1976]). Knox's introduction recounts Hartmann's visits to Camden in the 1880s, his abortive attempt to found

a Whitman society, and his public attribution to Whitman of some uncomplimentary remarks about contemporary literary figures. The latter two episodes (they do not quite add up to a "controversy") brought the young Hartmann into some disrepute, apparently more among other Whitmanians than with the poet himself. Hartmann's various recollections of Whitman, some published for the first time, complete the volume. They contain no surprises.

In "Whitman Among the New York Literary Bohemians: 1859–1862" (*WWR* 25:131–45) Gene Lalor capably reviews what little is known about this period in the poet's life. Lalor suggests that the ambiance at Pfaff's, and the views of some of its habitués, may have liberalized Whitman's beliefs about love and comradeship, but sensibly regards even these conclusions as speculative. The usefulness of Michael R. Dressman's description of Whitman's copious notes on language ("Walt Whitman's Plans for the Perfect Dictionary," *SAR*, pp. 457–74) is somewhat reduced by the appearance last year of most of that material in volume 3 of the *Daybooks and Notebooks* (see *ALS 1978*, pp. 59–60). Though evidence for his claim that Whitman had plans to himself compose a dictionary of American English is overestimated, Dressman rightly stresses that Whitman's "rapturous" interest in language was grounded in his conception of words as tangible links with the past. At work on a biography of Whitman, and taking him as his principal case, Justin Kaplan provides a leisured and stylish essay on difficulties in getting at certain plain facts about literary lives ("The Naked Self and Other Problems" in *Telling Lives*, pp. 37–55). Kaplan, who also considered some of these problems last year (see *ALS 1978*, p. 61), gives special prominence to Whitman's interest in animal magnetism, a topic taken up by O. K. Nambiar in "Is This a Then Touch . . . ? [*sic*] Walt Whitman's Paranormal Powers" (*Calamus* 18:3–20). Nambiar believes that hermetic wisdom regarding psychic energy transmission clarifies Whitman's passages on touch. This article consists of excerpts from a chapter in the author's *MahaYogi Walt Whitman: New Light on Yoga* (Bangalore, India: Jeevan Publications [1978]). As his title indicates, Nambiar uses Whitman primarily as an occasion for expounding yogic principles and symbols. In the annual "Walt Whitman Supplement" he edits for *The Long-Islander* [Huntington, N.Y.], William White rescues from near-obscurity 17 brief reminiscences by those who had met Whitman ("In the Eyes of His Contemporaries," 31 May, pp. 23–26). The recollecting authors range from Bram Stoker to Thomas Wentworth Higginson.

c. **Criticism: General.**   Although certain of Robert K. Martin's analyses of Whitman have already appeared (see *ALS 1975*, p. 87), his sense of the poet is given fuller expression in *Homosexual Tradition*, pp. 3–89. The merit of this study lies in its searching readings, particularly of those poems and parts of poems which are to a substantial extent erotic. Like Edwin H. Miller (see *ALS 1968*, pp. 52–53), Martin tends to identify quite specific acts of lovemaking in the poems, and there are those who, with some justice on their side, may prefer to grant the poet's lyrics a greater richness of ambiguity. Nevertheless, Whitman freely admitted to sexual indirection and his erotic lines manifestly invite imaginative completion by his readers. Martin's contribution in this area is performed with skill, spirit, and without the usual jowl-shaking over sexual and psychic regression. In regard to his argument about sexual politics, however, Martin's attempt to make Whitman a harbinger of current liberation movements sometimes lacks sufficient textual foundation. There is less to think about in Richard Lebeaux's "Walt Whitman and His Poems, 1856–1860: The Quest for Intimacy and Generativity" (*WWR* 25:146–63). Lebeaux draws more on the insights of Eric Erickson than others have to argue that the first three editions of *Leaves of Grass* reveal a poet experiencing personal loneliness and the hope of its mastery (or at least sublimation) through literary creation, but these conclusions are a staple of psychoanalytical study of the poet. The mischievousness of its title is carried through in Karl Keller's beguiling, if somewhat struck off, account of Whitman's humor as deliberate flamboyance ("Walt Whitman Camping," *Odyssey* 4:6–11). The poet's theatricality and verbal mannerism, Keller says, show him enjoying his ideas: "He is not making fun of the things he talks about but making fun out of them." For example, what Henry James laughingly referred to as Whitman's "too great familiarity with the foreign languages" Keller sees as Whitman's device for projecting his buoyant spirit through play and sportive extravagance.

Whitman's relation to a native tradition of millennial thought about the American landscape is explored in Cecelia Tichi's *New World*. Tichi is particularly helpful in providing literary and nonliterary sources for Whitman's geographical celebrations, mentioning such influential writers (to speak only of the 19th century) as William Gilpin, Frederick Law Olmsted, George Perkins Marsh, and Arnold Guyot. Since Whitman is still accused of merely echoing the journalistic boosterism of his age, this volume offers a corrective of fundamental importance in demonstrating how Whitman's symbolic understanding of the wilderness transcends polemic. Gay Wilson Allen's much briefer study of this topic, "How Emerson, Thoreau, and Whitman Viewed the 'Frontier,'" published in *Toward a New American Literary History*, ed. Louis J. Budd et al. (Duke), finds a profligate anticonservationist ideology in "Song of the Redwood-Tree," but Tichi rather suggests that in that poem and in "Song of the Broad-Axe" Whitman fuses frontier materials with millennial hopes to create an idealized geography of the heart which generates its own economics. The techniques of Whitman's landscape art, Charles Zarobila thinks, may owe something to the popularity of panoramas in Whitman's day, huge circular canvases depicting well-known historical or topographical scenes ("Walt Whitman and the Panorama," *WWR* 25:51–59). These paintings may have caused Whitman to compose some of his own images according to such panoramic principles as choice of a traditional subject (a river or a battle), and use of movement, variety, expansiveness, and a special vantage point. Robert E. Abrams pursues this subject in an observant phenomenological analysis, showing how Whitman uses language to evoke a sense of space as it is experienced from moment to moment by a central consciousness clearly positioned and embodied among the things of the world ("Space, Image, and Language in *Leaves of Grass*," *ATQ* 41:75–83).

To the increasing discussion these days of Whitman's place in American autobiography G. Thomas Couser provides a well-considered chapter in *American Autobiography*, pp. 80–100. Couser argues that whereas "Song of Myself" validates its prophetic vision within its literary performance, *Specimen Days* attempts to give more mundane autobiographical verification of the poet's calling and life. Reminiscent of Thoreau's shift from inward to outward self-portrayal, historicism thus replaces mystical experience "as the turning point and the analogue of the conversion experience in traditional spiritual autobiography." It is precisely in his more personally and historically grounded reflections on the Civil War, says Alfred Kazin, that Whitman makes his special contribution to American autobiography, one in which a certain extraordinary light or atmosphere is generated, showing "history itself as a character" ("Writing About Oneself," *Commentary* Apr.: 67–71). The literary importance of Whitman is also noted by Marvin Fisher, who demonstrates, by way of comparison with Longfellow, the pivotal effect of Whitman's more egalitarian, venacular style in shaping American writing ("The Centrality of Walt Whitman," *PVR* 7:32–47). But it is to the poet's thought rather than his artistry that Sam B. Girgus turns in *Law of the Heart*, pp. 52–65). Though the more recent theories of Norman O. Brown help explicate revolutionary components in Whitman's program for a sexually healthier national consciousness, Girgus believes it is Matthew Arnold who offers the most instructive parallel for the enormous humanizing importance Whitman gave to culture and education for nurturing the human spirit in the common man. Whitman's particularly American quality, "his attempt to find a structure for continual change," becomes apparent when he tries to synthesize the opposing forces of revolution and tradition.

d. **Criticism: Individual Works.**   A closely argued brief for the poet's philosophical integrity is presented by Diane Kepner in "From Spears to Leaves: Walt Whitman's Theory of Nature in 'Song of Myself' " (*AL* 51:179–204). Bringing welcome clarity to her subject, Kepner shows how Whitman's concept of energy inhering in atoms is crucial in his attempt to reconcile matter and spirit. This unified field theory of a continuous, cyclic interchange of particles within the universe seems plausibly derived from the poem, but as a readily teachable grand theory, one that can be as easily boxed into charts as it is in Kepner's essay, it does not fully accord with the playful and pedagogically evasive spirit of the poet's voice. In a related article Ward Welty identifies the speaker of the poem as neither body nor soul but transcending both, a "kosmos," a microcosm of the universe ("The Persona as Kosmos in 'Song of Myself,' " *WWR* 25:98–105). The speaker's unfolding relation to his reader occupied George Y. Trail, who sees the "I" and "you" of the poem becoming increasingly intimate and finally reversing active and passive roles (" 'Song of Myself': Events in the Microstructure," *WWR* 25:106–13).

   That Whitman tended to become less familiar with his reader over the span of his career is the impression reached by Dan Bogen after comparing first and last versions of a shorter poem (" 'I' and

'You' in 'Who Learns My Lesson Complete': Some Aspects of Whitman's Poetic Evolution," *WWR* 25:87–98). The evidence of textual change, however, though fairly presented here, seems overreached by the conclusion that the poet's words altogether lose their sense of spokenness and become merely abstract truths. In "Whitman's Lonely Orbit: 'Salut Au Monde,'" William L. Vance focuses on the meditative and dramatic qualities of another early poem (*WWR* 25:3–13). Vance believes that Whitman ends the poem reluctantly qualifying his egalitarian claims for mankind. In brief articles relating to the "Children of Adam" sequence Shirley Ann Chosy proposes that one of its poems answers Emerson's call for an imaginative literature that would discover the multiple meanings inherent in "every sensuous fact" ("Whitman's 'Spontaneous Me': Sex as Symbol," *WWR* 25:113–17), and Deborah J. Barrett points to special qualities of structure and imagery in one of the least studied poems in the cluster ("The Desire for Freedom: Whitman's 'One Hour to Madness and Joy,'" *WWR* 25:26–28).

As for the "Calamus" poems, Sowmu Francis offers a carefully worked-out analysis of the group, stressing ways in which water and grass imagery works to delineate subconscious processes of self-discovery ("Whitman's Use of the Pond Symbol in His 'Calamus' Poems," *WWR* 25:13–22). Francis regards the love of comrades as a means for illustrating how struggle between spiritual male friendship and a perverse, lacerating homoeroticism leads finally to mature self-understanding. The pond, which for Francis serves as the unifying setting for this drama, is interpreted quite differently as a refuge and love nest for healthy, same sex eroticism by Robert K. Martin ("Conversion and Identity: The 'Calamus' Poems," *WWR* 25:59–66; this article is incorporated, with additions, in Martin's *Homosexual Tradition*, noted above). For Martin the central conflict of these poems is between hiding and coming out. Whitman proclaims in "Calamus" his new identity as a homosexual. Others, like Russell A. Hunt (see *ALS 1975*, p. 91) take the view that "Calamus" is primarily about the making of poetry. According to Marilyn Davis De Eulis, Whitman revised one poem in the group to express his difficulty in writing verse free of refined and artificial literary devices ("A Short Analysis of Whitman's 'Roots and Leaves Themselves Alone,'" *WWR* 25:117–20). The repressive gentility of society at large is Whitman's theme in "The Dalliance of the Eagles," according to Gertrude M.

White ("The 'Dalliance' of Whitman's Eagles," *WWR* 25:73–76).
Chaviva M. Hosek offers an insightful survey of literary and linguistic strategies in the 1955 Preface ("The Rhetoric of Whitman's
1855 Preface to *Leaves of Grass*," *WWR* 25:163–73). In doing so she
only tangentially duplicates Ivan Marki's fuller treatment of this
subject (see *ALS 1976*, pp. 62–63).

e. **Sources, Affinities, Influences.** Whitman's concept of prudence,
enunciated in the 1855 Preface, as well as other of his most characteristic ideas about nature, immortality, and death, reveal something
of his interest in classical thought, according to Gay Wilson Allen's
"Walt Whitman and Stoicism" (in *Stoic Strain*, pp. 43–62). Allen
judiciously compares passages from Whitman and three works the
poet is known to have read with enthusiasm: Frances Wright's popu-
larization of Greek philosophy, *A Few Days in Athens*, the *Encheiri-
dion* of Epictetus, and Marcus Aurelius' *Meditations*. Arguments
made elsewhere for the poet's indebtedness to Lamarck's principles
of evolution are qualified, but not contradicted, in Harry Gersheno-
witz, "Whitman and Lamarck Revisited" (*WWR* 25:121–23; see also
ALS 1978, p. 65). The poet's lifelong reading of Emerson is con-
firmed by Michael R. Dressman, who shows that an article Whitman
wrote on American slang in the early 1880s contains a passage from
Nature virtually *verbatim* ("Another Whitman Debt to Emerson,"
N&Q 26:305–06). How Emerson viewed Whitman is the subject of
two essays by Jerome Loving, the first of which brings forward a
hitherto unpublished letter from F. B. Sanborn to Horace Traubel indicating that Emerson was not as negative toward his New York
admirer as Emerson's family portrayed him ("Emerson's 'Constant
Way of Looking at Whitman's Genius,' " *AL* 51:399–403). More speculative is Loving's argument in " 'A Well-Intended Halfness': Emerson's View of *Leaves of Grass*" (*StAH* 3[1976]:61–68) that Emerson
could only have liked the most abstract and spiritual passages in
Whitman. Of peripheral interest in this regard are amusing early reactions to Whitman by several of Emerson's correspondents published in full for the first time by Eleanor M. Tilton (*"Leaves of
Grass*: Four Letters to Emerson," *HLB* 27:336–41).

A number of studies this year treat of Whitman's relation to other
writers and artists, without attempting to trace influence. Among
those which compare and explicate parallel poems is Marilyn Davis

De Eulis' "Whitman's 'The First Dandelion' and Emily Dickinson's 'The Dandelion's Pallid Tube'" (*WWR* 25:29–32), the point of which seems to be that Whitman's flower is only a "natural artifact" betokening spring while Dickinson's is a "metaphorical vehicle" enacting resurrection. More substantial poems allow for instructive analysis in Barbara Schapiro's "Shelley's *Alastor* and Whitman's *Out of the Cradle*: The Ambivalent Mother" (*AI* 36:245–59). Schapiro finds that while both poems manifest a strong schizoid mother fixation, portraying her as at once comforting and annihilating, Shelley retreats into self-pity while Whitman reaches beyond contradictions to rapturous acceptance of the "one reality" of love and loss.

Several other studies consider the relation of Whitman's ideas to modern philosophy. The most difficult but rewarding of these is John T. Irwin's "Self-Evidence and Self-Reference: Nietzsche and Tragedy, Whitman and Opera" (*NLH* 21:177–92). Irwin draws on Schopenhauer and Hegel, as well as Neitzsche, to give depth and extension to the poet's sometimes baffling hints about the correspondence between his poetic language and his living, unmediated presence on the page. In a related essay Debra Harper discusses ways Whitman and Unamuno understand language as a vehicle for achieving continued personal existence in the world ("Whitman and Unamuno: Language for Immortality," *WWR* 25:66–72). Unfortunately, this comparison serves more to iterate than to illuminate well-known Whitmanian ideas, and the same is largely true of Stephen L. Tanner's "Religious Attitudes Toward Progress: Whitman and Berdyaev" (*Cithara* 17,i[1977]4–16), in which an over-simple account of Whitman's evolutionary cosmic optimism is set off against Berdyaev's nonprogressive eschatology. William Luther Moore's *Intuitional Vistas of Walt Whitman Paralleling Scientific Horizons of Pierre Teilhard de Chardin* (Tokyo: Taibundo Publishing Co. [1978]), apparently another philosophical study, was not available for examination.

A more literary perspective on Whitman's relation to Eastern mysticism than that offered by O. K. Nambiar (see section *b.*, above) is achieved in Ghulam M. Fayez's "Motion Imagery in Rumi and Whitman" (*WWR* 25:39–50). While Rumi was a 13th-century Persian, some of whose poems Whitman had read in translation, Fayez attributes similarities in flight and circle imagery not to Rumi's influence but to a "psycho-mystic temper" the two writers shared. Pictorial imagery of motion and fusing, and its linguistic equivalents in Whitman, is the subject of Barton L. St. Armand's thoughtful "Transcendence through Technique: Whitman's 'Crossing Brooklyn Ferry' and Impressionist Painting" (*BuR* 24 [1978]:56–74). St. Armand suggests that although the painterly "flashes and specks" of "Brooklyn Ferry," "its coloristic highlights, its sense of a special, timeless moment, its choice of a random, 'contentless' scene," all remind us of Impressionist canvases, the poem's use of these devices to accomplish a spiritual connection between poet and reader goes well beyond the self-contained surfaces of a Monet or Seurat.

Of Whitman's influence on others the principal work this year is James E. Miller, Jr.'s *The American Quest for a Supreme Fiction: Whitman's Legacy in the Personal Epic* (Chicago). It discusses Whitman as the originating and tutelary genius for a number of 20th-century American practitioners of the long poem, identifying as his direct heirs Pound, Eliot, Williams, Hart Crane, Olson, Berryman, and Ginsberg. While its central idea about Whitman's persistence in the 20th century is not new, and though its particular claims for the immediate descendance of each of these writers are not equally convincing, this volume brings consistently fresh, observant, and informed readings to the poems it considers. Robert Lowell's interesting and heretofore unpublished remarks as a teacher on Whitman are recorded by Helen Vendler in "Lowell in the Classroom" (*Harvard Advocate* Nov.: 22–26, 28–29). According to Vendler, "There was no poet he spoke of with more rueful affection." Whitman's populist aesthetics, adapted for fiction, are perceived by Nancy L. Bunge as informing the work of Sherwood Anderson, Sinclair Lewis, Ernest Hemingway, and Saul Bellow ("The Midwestern Novel: Walt Whitman Transplanted" (*ON* [1977]:275–87). Joseph Jones gives passing attention to Whitman's reception among Australian authors active in the 1890s in *Radical Cousins: Nineteenth Century American & Australian Writers* (St. Lucia: Univ. of Queensland [1976]), and Gari Laguardia carefully disentangles several strands of meaning in Lorca's "Oda a Walt Whitman" ("The Butterflies in Walt Whitman's Beard: Lorca's Naming of Whitman," *Neophil* 62[1978]:540–54). The American poet's importance for Eastern European literature is surveyed, though summarily and with only footnotes for a bibliography, by Thomas Eekman in "Walt Whitman's Role in Slavic Poetry (Late 19th–Early 20th Century)" (*American Contributions to the Eighth*

International Congress of Slavists, vol. 2, *Literature,* ed. Victor Terras [Columbus Ohio: Slavica Publishers, 1978], pp. 166–90). Ukrainian interest began a little later, according to John A. Barnstead, whose reception study, "Whitman in Ukraine" (*WWR* 25:22–26), notes that Whitman's translations in that language first appeared in the 1920s.

ii. Dickinson

a. **Bibliography, Editing.** Per Winther takes up most of the questions confronting the would-be editor of a popular or reader's edition of Dickinson's poems in "On Editing Emily Dickinson" (*AmerSS* 11:25–40). Such a volume, Winther feels, should include about 300 poems, be organized chronologically, sensitively choose among variants but not alter manuscript language or notational idiosyncrasies, only regularizing apostrophe placement in contractions. This essay is useful for its survey of editorial options, but the urgency of its recommendations is more than a little reduced by their already having been observed in Thomas H. Johnson's widely used selection from his variorum, *Final Harvest* (Little, Brown [1961]). The major difference between that volume and Winther's projected one has to do with the least principled issue Winther addresses, the question of how many poems to include (Johnson selected nearly 600). Pursuant to his preparation of a facsimile edition of the Dickinson fascicles for Harvard University Press, R. W. Franklin discusses how, based on pin effects and smudge links, he has been able to reattach the long separated first and last sheets of one of the poet's manuscript packets ("Emily Dickinson's Packet 27 (and 80, 14, and 6)," *HLB* 27:342–48). George Monteiro argues that a late worksheet attached to an earlier poem is not a redrafting but a newly conceived poem, and that it should be considered finished as it stands, in spite of its many variants ("In Question: The Status of Emily Dickinson's 1878 'Worksheet' for 'Two Butterflies went out at Noon,'" *ELWIU* 6:219–25). In "E[mily] D[ickinson] Forgeries," Anna Mary Wells wonders whether a series of love letters from Dickinson to Judge Lord may have been counterfeited by Mabel Loomis Todd, the poet's early editor (*DicS* 35:12–16). These letters and the verses they contain do not *sound* like Dickinson, she says. The problem is that the handwriting of these letters, to expert eyes, is not only identical with the poet's but changed in conformity with her own. Unfortunately Wells does not supply a reliable means for determining authenticity, only suggesting "close, analytical reading," nor does she offer a reason why Mrs. Todd might have felt a need to falsify the record so elaborately.

A most helpful new source for Dickinson studies is Joseph Duchac's *The Poems of Emily Dickinson: An Annotated Guide to Commentary Published in English, 1890–1977* (Hall). The fleeting and manifold quality of Dickinson's verse places her among those best served by a volume that will facilitate intensive study of individual works. Nevertheless, this compilation is not intended merely as an "explication index" based on New Critical assumptions about interpretative literary relevance, for textual discussions, material relating to sources and circumstances of composition, analyses of parts of poems, even study questions and paraphrases, all have been gathered in—over 6,000 items in all. Duchac is to be commended for designing a bibliography that is at all points accessible, exhaustive, and meticulous. It is an indispensable resource, one of the prizes among the growing list of G. K. Hall secondary bibliographies. A similarly organized guide to Japanese studies provided by Takao Furukawa gives welcome access to Dickinson's notable transpacific reception (*Interpretation Index to Emily Dickinson's Poems in Japan* [Tokyo: Kirihara-shoten]). This English-language volume analyzes over 500 books and articles on the poet published in Japan from 1927 to 1979.

Its sometimes obfuscating attention to detail notwithstanding, Roland Hagenbüchle's "New Developments in Dickinson Criticism" (*Anglia* 97:452–74) provides a useful review of major critical studies published during the last two decades. This essay, incidentally, exemplifies the traditional preoccupation of Germanic scholars with linguistic studies of Dickinson and their more recent interest in how her poems may be taken to exhibit *absence présente*, instantaneous reversals of being and nothingness. An update on recent scholarship and ana, and a list of overlooked items from the 1890s to the present are respectively furnished by Willis J. Buckingham ("Emily Dickinson: Annual Bibliography for 1977," *DicS* 36:50–57) and George Monteiro ("Still More on E[mily] D[ickinson]," *DicS* 35:52–54).

b. **Biography.**   Medical diagnosis undertaken 100 years after death, especially when the patient's records are as frugal of information as they are for Dickinson, is not easy. Nevertheless three studies this year seek to undermine theories of the poet's psychic stress by giving close attention to evidence of physical illness. All are guesswork, but the most plausible is Martin Wand's and Richard B. Sewall's " 'Eyes Be Blind, Heart Be Still': A New Perspective on Emily Dickinson's Eye Problem" (*NEQ* 52:400–406). The authors feel that extant images of the poet, her sister, and mother, reveal all three to have suffered from exotropia, a condition in which one eye turns out. But paintings and daguerreotypes are subject to distortion, and symptoms offered as corroborating evidence can as readliy be attributed to other disorders. Unfortunately Wand's and Sewall's article did not go unnoticed by the daily press, headline after headline proclaiming that the reason for Dickinson's seclusion had at last been solved, an inference they neither reached nor hinted at. Such an argument, however, is taken up by Jerry Ferris Reynolds, who believes that the letters and poems reveal signs of lupas erythematosus, a disease which could have appeared as early as 1848 and continued, with fluctuating severity, until it caused Dickinson's kidneys to fail (" 'Banishment from Native Eyes': The Reason for Emily Dickinson's Seclusion Reconsidered," *MarkhamR* 8:41–48). Disfiguring skin blotching from the disease primarily caused the poet's seclusion, the author says, but the evidence is tenuous. Reynolds argues that because Dickinson used an eight-ounce bottle of skin lotion as often as every 40 days, she must have been applying it to relieve an extensive rash caused by the disease. Maybe she just had dry skin. A spirit of play is helpful in reading Carla S. Sonntag's proposal that chronic brain dysfunction did not prevent Dickinson from carrying on an impassioned overseas epistolary romance with a famously dour "Master" ("Epilepsy and Thomas Carlyle," *DicS* 35:23–34).

One of the reasons Dickinson failed to publish, according to R. J. Wilson, was that she sought out Higginson's assistance on the basis of 18th-century patronage, rather than taking a more self-assertive approach demanded by the 19th-century literary marketplace ("Emily Dickinson and the Problem of Career," *MR* 20:451–61). But Robert A. Gross rightly replies that the early correspondence with Higginson shows her testing the water, not failing to swim ("A Response," *MR* 20:461–67). Whether Dickinson was capable of learning self-promotional techniques is beside the point when it cannot be said she predicated her business as a poet on achieving an audience. Though Dickinson herself is not given sustained attention in *Mary Lyon and Mount Holyoke: Opening the Gates* (UPNE), Elizabeth Alden Green provides useful background material on the poet's year in South Hadley. Of particular interest is Green's belief that religious pressure on Dickinson during college revivals has been exaggerated: "There is no evidence that she—or any of the other un-converted—was badgered or defiant."

c. **Criticism: General.** Rebecca Patterson's variously published es-says on Dickinson's symbolism are posthumously assembled in *Emily Dickinson's Imagery,* ed. Margaret H. Freeman (Mass.). Individual chapters discuss such metaphorical constellations as colors, gems, places, directions, and science. Patterson's discussions are clear and reasonably thorough, but there is a tendency to stress sexual implica-tions at the expense of other meanings and to be overspecific about an artist, one of whose signatures is the calculated imprecision of her imagery. A more thoughtful and elegant "life of the mind" approach to Dickinson is taken by Sharon Cameron in *Lyric Time: Dickinson and the Limits of Genre* (Hopkins). Though its argument is largely conducted through analysis of clusters of poems, the volume as a whole intends to produce a theory of the lyric, a genre Dickinson's verse is said to define by forcing the boundaries of its temporal struc-tures. A high order of critical intelligence is sustained in this volume. There have been excellent books on Dickinson, but at moments in this study one is almost ready to conclude that it is the first volume since Charles R. Anderson's 1960 *Emily Dickinson's Poetry* with the power single-handedly to raise the level of Dickinson criticism. Un-fortunately, so hermetic and cerebral are Cameron's delineations of the poems as acts of consciousness, they do not always leave the critic's workbench with the breath of life still in them. Presented as paradigms, dialectics, and intricate mental gestures, the poems begin to sound and look much alike and accuracy of reading is some-times undercut when they are drafted to serve an overarching speech-act theory of lyric discourse. Thus while fresh and perceptive things are said about "Because I could not stop for Death—," Cameron's sense that the poem's last lines express a "confession of disappoint-ment" better fits the larger design of Cameron's argument than the quickened pace and tone of accomplishment the last stanza conveys. In a "Letter to the Editor" of *PMLA,* in which a chapter from *Lyric Time* was published in part last year (see *ALS 1978,* pp. 71–72), Ro-land Hagenbüchle and Joseph T. Swann take issue with some of

Cameron's conclusions, to which Cameron replies in "Dickinson and the Dialectics of Rage" (*PMLA* 94:144–46).

Another limning of the poet's mental universe is attempted by David C. Estes in "'Out Upon Circumference': Emily Dickinson's Search for Location" (*ELWIU* 6:207–18). Dickinson commonly uses the language of spatial relationships as a strategy for controlling chaos, though without much success, Estes says, because her knowledge of being lost normally overwhelms her need for order. Indeed, not many readers nowadays see Dickinson as regularly finding stability and peace, though Daniel T. O'Hara charges that Allen Tate and the New Critics who followed his example mistakenly believe that her ironies achieve aesthetic integrations of experience ("'The Designated Light': Irony in Emily Dickinson," *Boundary* 7:175–98). Like Kierkegaard and other "negative theologians," O'Hara insists, Dickinson is passionately skeptical even when considering moments of epiphany and the sublime. This is a useful caveat, however often repeated, but uniformly applied, one wonders if it can take the full measure of a poet who would write to Higginson, evanescence notwithstanding, "Paradise is of the option." In a quite similar study, but without making sweeping claims, Carole Anne Taylor uses Kierkegaard as a model for showing how Dickinson's various tones of voice express different spiritual attitudes ("Kierkegaard and the Ironic Voices of Emily Dickinson," *JEPG* 77[1978]:569–81).

The most substantial treatment of Dickinson as a woman poet this year is a lengthy concluding chapter in Sandra M. Gilbert's and Susan Gubar's *Madwoman in the Attic*, pp. 581–650. The authors skillfully thread together various fictional lives impersonated in the poems, arguing that they enact quite a number of complicated relationships between the submissive female and the masterful male. Though many of their insights have at least been prefigured in recent feminist psychosocial discussions of Dickinson, Gilbert and Gubar are particularly helpful in catching the theatricality of the poems (especially their affinities with gothic romance) and in tracing the centrality of the "woman in white" motif as an index to the poet's meditations on the precarious situation of the woman artist. There is something wishful, however, in the way some of the poems are read to reinforce each other and proper self-restraint is not always exercised in plotting the poems. For example, though adult sexuality may well be at least partly at issue in "Before I got my eye put out," the speaker appears carried along by a feeling of exaltation and strategic mastery. To say, as the authors do, that the poem imagines an impassioned female apprehensively eyeing an intimidating, patriarchial male misses Dickinson's tone and makes up a story line that defeats the careful imprecision of the poet's text. The motif of abstinence, an "ethic" Dickinson shared with other women of her time, is well observed by Vivian R. Pollak in "Thirst and Starvation in Emily Dickinson's Poetry" (*AL* 51:33–49). Pollak believes that though Dickinson found some compensating resources in the life of the imagination, she never lost a sharp and bitter sense of the debilitating effects of her social losses on her ability to give as well as receive human sustenance. Nina Baym also considers poems of deprivation in "God, Father, and Lover in Emily Dickinson's Poetry," an essay in *Puritan Influences*, pp. 193–209. Baym argues that because Dickinson's *persona* undeifies God as an insensitive and punitive father, while deifying male lovers as divinely benevolent, and imagining her relation to both as that of a helpless little girl, the poet doubly expresses the dilemma of the woman subsumed within patriarchal structures.

d. **Criticism: Individual Works.** Dickinson's tumescence-prone "pink, lank worm" is summarily de-eroticized in Alice Hall Petry's "Two Views of Nature in Emily Dickinson's 'In Winter in My Room'" (*MLS* 9:16–22). The creature, she says, is merely an emblem for Nature—by turns friendly and threatening. Philip Cooper, on the other hand, finds an "inner metaphor" of erotic peril in "The Central Image of 'Because I could not stop for Death—'" (in *Studies in English and American Literature*, ed. John L. Cutler and Lawrence S. Thompson [Whitson, 1978], pp. 295–96). At the center of the third stanza's concentric circles, Cooper says, "bodies touch" and "In the genteel tradition, the enormity of death is as unacknowledged as the erotic facts of life." Linguistic problems in "Light is sufficient to itself—" are given structural analysis by Götz Weinold in "Some Aspects of Meaning in Literature" (*Dispositio* 3[1978]:127–35), but the poem's philosophical implications are left unaddressed. Giles Gunn offers a fine reading of an underestimated poem, "My period had come for Prayer—," paying attention to its use of the American landscape as a catalyst for ontological shock in his *The Interpretation of Otherness: Literature, Religion, and the American Imagination* (Oxford), pp. 192–95. In "Emily Dickinson's 'I know that He exists'" (*CEA Forum*

8, iii[1978]:11–12) Laurence Perrine hews close to the commonly accepted reading of the poem as a complaint about God's inaccessibility. The "hide and seek" dynamic of that poem (and others) is the primary aesthetic principle informing Dickinson's first five letters to her literary preceptor, according to John S. Mann's *Dickinson's Letters to Higginson: Motives for Metaphor* (*HJ* 22,ii:1–79). Mann's monograph explicates each letter line by line and concludes that their indirection is expressive of the poet's overall use of language as a way of making public, yet continuing to shield, her inner life.

e. **Sources, Affinities, Influences.** Though Dickinson's alliances with Puritanism and Transcendentalism have been looked at time and again, until the appearance of Karl Keller's provocative and most useful *The Only Kangaroo*, we have had no panoramic study of the poet's literary relations. Keller's initial preoccupation is with Dickinson as an inheritor of Puritan aesthetics, taking up, in separate chapters, that legacy as it was embodied in Bradstreet, Taylor, Edwards, and Harriet Beecher Stowe. Keller also seeks to estimate the poet's compatibilities with her own generation—Hawthorne, Emerson, her literary friends, her sister reformers, and Whitman. An illuminating final chapter considers ways later poets have made her their precursor, especially Stephen Crane, Amy Lowell, Hart Crane, and Robert Frost. In thus showing how Dickinson is like/unlike other American writers in reacting to Puritan thought, Keller wishes to give her a clearer place in literary history without eclipsing her singularity. Informed and refreshingly unlabored, Keller engages the issues well. His tendency to slight the poems, however, gives the intellectual history he constructs a largely presumptive character. More persuasively evidential is his essay on survivals of Puritan typology in Dickinson and others, "Alephs, Zahirs, and the Triumph of Ambiguity: Typology in Nineteenth-Century American Literature," published in *Literary Uses of Typology from the Late Middle Ages to the Present*, ed. Earl Miner (Princeton [1977]), pp. 274–314.

Dickinson's relation to the symbology of her forebears occupies other commentators as well, notably Roland Hagenbüchle in "Sign and Process: The Concept of Language in Emerson and Dickinson" (*ESQ* 25:137–55). Taking both Puritan and Emersonian poetics into account, Hagenbüchle regards Dickinson's version of the Romantic sublime as a dialectically applied faith in the sufficiency of the creative word. His amply documented and precise discriminations are missing in E. Miller Budick's "When the Soul Selects: Emily Dickinson's Attack on New England Symbolism" (*AL* 51:349–63). Budick believes, on the basis of singular readings of a few poems, that Dickinson wholly denied spiritualized New England ways of seeing. According to Brian Attebery, Emerson's techniques for making general terms more tangible, as demonstrated in his essay "Circles," are strategies also used by Dickinson ("Dickinson, Emerson and the Abstract Concrete." *DicS* 35:17–22).

Attending primarily to Dickinson's "concealment" imagery of armor, houses, and silence, Terence Diggory suggests that distinctively American male and female means of poetic expression may be traced to Whitman and Dickinson ("Armored Women, Naked Men: Dickinson, Whitman, and Their Successors" in *Shakespeare's Sisters*, pp. 135–50). The male tradition obeys an impulse toward openness and confession, the female toward withdrawal and protection. Dickinson's gifts as a correspondent are favorably compared with those of her most able American contemporaries in Daniel Aaron's eloquent if primarily descriptive report on the art of condolence writing, "The Etiquette of Grief: A Literary Generation's Response to Death" (*Prospects* 4:197–213). His essay a model of economy, William Mulder finds that Dickinson and Frost share a regional point of view: to see "New Englandly" for them is to see pictorially, morally, and, with some skepticism, symbolically ("Seeing 'New Englandly': Planes of Perception in Emily Dickinson and Robert Frost," *NEQ* 52:550–59). Though Dickinson's penchant for simulating epigrams, definitions, and sententiae is well known, her direct use of proverbs is not. In "Telling It Slant: Emily Dickinson and the Proverb" (*Genre* 12:219–41) Daniel R. Barnes shows how frequently Dickinson drew on proverbial wisdom and describes ways she charged it with new meanings or challenged its authority in her letters and poems.

Dickinson's marked interiority continues to lead to numerous studies linking her to various formal traditions of meditation. Rhoda Nathan feels Dickinson was familiar with the spiritual discipline of St. Augustine through his influence on Puritanism and the Metaphysical poets, and that, like *The Confessions*, Dickinson's religious poems are "a psycho-history of conversion" ("The Soul at White Heat: Emily Dickinson & Augustinian Meditation," *Studia Mystica* 2:39–54). Connections between Dickinson and Zen have been proposed by

Amy Horiuchi, whose essays on this and other Dickinson-related subjects are brought together in *Possible Zen Traits in Emily Dickinson's Perception* (Kawagoe, Japan: Toyo Univ. [1978]). The Zen material, by the way, takes up less than a third of this 500-page volume, the usefulness of which is hampered throughout by meandering thought and murky language. Martha Lindblom O'Keefe's privately published *The Farthest Thunder: A Comparison of Emily Dickinson and St. John of the Cross* (Chevy Chase, Maryland) reprints a complete translation of *The Dark Night of the Soul*, matching lines by Dickinson to St. John's text with only a minimum of analytical commentary.

Arizona State University

6. Mark Twain

Louis J. Budd

As the acknowledgments in many books and articles show over the years, scholarship suffered a great loss from the death of Frederick Anderson on 7 January 1979. Literary editor of the Mark Twain Estate since 1964, Anderson made a major contribution in several ways—through his patient helpfulness to all comers, his high standards that were all the more influential because expressed so directly yet unpretentiously, and his own publications. Perhaps most important of all for us survivors, he made the rooms holding the Mark Twain Papers an ideal place to do research because he believed in letting qualified persons forage almost at will, and tirelessly gathered copies of materials held elsewhere. Fortunately his successor, Robert H. Hirst, has the advantage of having worked for and with him.

Anybody examining the Papers cannot help noticing the stream of visitors who are often too interested to be called just sightseers. Whether or not Twainians like it, they have a large secondary public, starting with intellectuals in other fields. Typically, Alfred McLung Lee, in "Mark Twain: One of the Enduring Voices" (*Humanist* 39, iii:52–53), acclaims Twain as a "humanist critic," bestowing the adjective as a fairly precise term. The miracle of Twain's personality regularly inspires articles like "Mark Twain's Christmas" (*Historic Preservation* 31,v:18–21), a pleasant spread by Wynn Lee on Yuletide customs in the Clemens household when the three daughters were young; it makes good reading at the right season though I can't judge the recipe for sweet mince cake. General interest, presumably, also evoked "Mark Twain: Beneath the Laughter," an hour-long interpretation shown on nonprofit television. It rates notice here because five leading scholars served as active, paid consultants. Twainians will have to develop into drama critics. More is coming soon on television, and Hal Holbrook has several competitors, the most interesting of whom presents a Social Issues program.

i. Bibliography

We had better start adjusting to the decision of the second edition (1978) of *Anglo-American Cataloguing Rules* to enter items by and about Samuel L. Clemens under Twain. Though some libraries will no doubt resist, the desirable goal is uniformity, and the guiding principle adopts the commonly recognized name for authors who sometimes used pseudonyms. Almost a shibboleth for a few, the practice, first insisted upon by Albert Bigelow Paine, of treating the famous pen name as an inseparable unit (such as a trademark like Dr. Pepper) will now have to defy the American Library Association as well as popular usage. In conversation Frederick Anderson finessed any splits by invariably saying "Clemens."

But printouts programmed by *AACR2* will not lose any items relevant for us so long as we have Thomas A. Tenney deploying his net. With richer annotations than ever he has already produced "Mark Twain: A Reference Guide / Third Annual Supplement" (*ALR* 12:175–277), which still recovers obscure items for the 1870s and 1880s while coming as close to the present as printing schedules allow. Though the title of J. G. Riewald's long article, "The Translational Reception of American Literature in Europe, 1800–1900—A Review of Research" (*ES* 60:562–92), might indicate detailed commentary, it gives only a packed but knowledgeable summary. The three and a half pages on Twain are not complete either for the countries included or all the primary works; in fact the travels of Twain's short pieces along the newspaper network will always furnish surprises. But everyone getting into the subject will have to begin gratefully with Riewald. More interesting than a stark list might promise to be, "Southern Literary Culture: 1969–1975" (*MissQ* 32:33–42), compiled by William L. Andrews and Jack D. Wages, records about 150 theses and dissertations on Twain. However, any hope of new riches is dimmed by the repetition of titles and even more of themes, with some subjects so broad as to guarantee superficiality. Most often approached formalistically, the favored concepts are "Dreams," "Innocence," "Self," "Romance," and (still) "Pessimism." Nevertheless, experience predicts that within a few years some first-rate articles or a book will emerge from a gallimaufry that seems to profit only the typing agencies.

Though *Mark Twain's Early Tales & Sketches, Volume 1 (1851–*

1864) (Calif.) constitutes a big event critically, it first deserves mention as volume 15 of *The Works of Mark Twain* and therefore a sign that the Iowa/California Edition, which had wavered, is marching forward, with glossy yellow dust jackets as a flag of renewal. (The designation on the spine as volume 15 derives from the original overall plan: *Roughing It* [1972] is volume 2 and *What Is Man? And Other Philosophical Writings* [1973] is volume 19. By adding three new volumes in 1979, volume 15, volume 5 *[The Prince and the Pauper]*, and volume 9 *[A Connecticut Yankee in King Arthur's Court]* the Edition seems ready to capitalize on years of patient work.) In the "Textual Introduction" for this first part of a subset of perhaps four, Robert H. Hirst lays out the rationale for handling such problems as "radiating" texts for which the first printing is yet to be located. The questions behind preparing an authoritative text from journalistic work are complicated in the case of Twain, who compounded them by slapdash revision of his books, making painfully difficult the establishment of definitive texts. Critics more generally concerned with reading tastes and publishing standards during the 19th century will also find *Early Tales & Sketches* a major resource. Since textual editing breeds passion over points of detail, those who learn the most from its methodology will undoubtedly differ here and there, if only with its sterling conservatism in attributing pieces with unclear origins. Those wanting an easier first step into the current state of the art of editing might begin with John C. Gerber in "The Mark Twain Legacy for Present-Day Editors and Collectors" (*LRN* 4:59–66).

ii. Biography

Ulysses S. Smith, whose *Up a Tree with Mark Twain* (*ALS 1978*, pp. 81–82) claimed to uncover an illegitimate Clemens daughter in Hannibal, has mimeographed a three-page decoding of "anagrams" or cryptograms in *Pudd'nhead Wilson* that supports and elaborates his case. Until he adds other kinds of proof, however, the leading debate in this area of biography remains whether, as Hamlin Hill puts it in an important review (*ALR* 12:343–46), an "aging, flawed human being can write fascinating and interesting literature"; posterity should know that disagreements on this topic were stated eloquently by four panelists at the MLA meeting in San Francisco. The

clash of biographical and critical judgments will strike more fire in
the years ahead. Meanwhile outsiders who bear with William Baker,
in "Mark Twain in Cincinnati: A Mystery Most Compelling" (*ALR*
12:299–315), will smile at his title and my defense of it since his
minutiae produce nothing of consequence except the chance that the
dour McFarlane, whose philosophy impressed an itinerant typesetter,
may have existed after all. But by tenaciously digging for any Cincinnati evidence Baker demonstrates that we know almost nothing
about a rugged six-months stint in 1856–57 that should have left deep
impressions.

Justin Kaplan keeps returning to Clemens' subconscious. With
"The Naked Self and Other Problems" in *Telling Lives*, Kaplan
briefly probes the psychic effects of adopting a pen name, which put
a liberating distance between the artist-celebrity and private man
but also created the anxieties of becoming father to a new self. In
"Mark Twain's Punishing Profession" (*PMPA* 4:1–6) he speculates
questionably about the humorist's lack of "charity or respect" for
his difficult, risky trade as entertainer. Popularizing work already
published (*ALS 1978*, pp. 83–84), Robert R. Sears, in "Mark Twain's
Separation Anxiety" (*Psychology Today* 13,i:100–102), reintroduces
a restless "fear of losing love" into the psychological equation. Much
more substantive than the preceding items but angling too widely
for the space used, Judith Fetterley, in "Mark Twain and the Anxiety
of Entertainment" (*GaR* 33:382–91), expands on the common perception that Clemens felt ambivalent about amusing the public, that
after success eased the fears of failure he worried not only about staying on top but also about giving serious value for money paid. The
darkest side of this tension encouraged contempt for the gullible audience itself. Fetterley will convince most those who have the least
tolerance toward entertainment as a normal release and as a staple of
mass culture.

Among other biographical analysts the most interesting is Steve
Davis, in "Mark Twain, the War, and *Life on the Mississippi*" (*SoSt*
18:231–39), which infers from the book its author's divided and shifting attitude toward his inglorious service for the Confederacy. Davis
appears a bit divided himself, but he will make others think harder.
In "Mark Twain and Artemus Ward: A Bittersweet Friendship Is
Born in Nevada" (*NHSQ* 22:163–85) John J. Pullen's wit almost obscures the fact that nothing basically new is added, although the

subtly illogical ways in which Twain acted ungenerously toward Ward's memory until he no longer felt his mentor's competition is underlined. Still I wonder if Pullen appreciates how warmly Twain's lecture on Ward came across to reviewers. As extremist as the notorious faith in the Paige typesetter, Thomas Grant in "The Artist of the Beautiful: Mark Twain's Investment in the Machine Inventor" (*PMPA* 4:59–68) builds up to the notion of Twain as a writing mechanism himself. More tenably Grant argues that the fatal belief that the typesetter outshone mere humans evolved into the late view of man as a failed machine. Incidentally, before sharing the disdain over Clemens' delight in the latest indoor plumbing I would have to know how many times Grant has enjoyed a privy in the heat or snow.

On the ethereal plane Jeffrey R. Holland in "Soul-Butter and Hog Wash: Mark Twain and Frontier Religion" in *"Soul-Butter and Hog Wash" and Other Essays on the American West,* ed. Thomas G. Alexander (Brigham Young), pp. 5–32, unsuccessfully tried to say something original about Twain's well-known waverings of faith. Perhaps chapter 1, "Tedworth Square," in Stanley Weintraub's *London Yankees,* pp. 11–41, never meant to do more than reweave the familiar sources on Clemens' sojourns in London after 1896. All in all the major puzzles easily defied the year's hypotheses, while materials kept piling up; the next full-scale biography will have to be started by a youngish scholar under no pressure for results. He or she should take warning from "Katie Leary: 'She's Always There . . . ' " (*MTSB* 2,ii:1–2,5–6) by Robert E. Agan, a nephew of the Clemenses' housekeeper; it adjusts opinions now accepted through a book "dictated to a scribe who added her own strong coloring."

iii. General Essays and Books

One of the most impressive features of Twain's fame lies in his prestige with living authors, which two essays not intrinsically memorable support. In a short chapter in *Earthly Delights, Unearthly Adornments: American Writers as Image-Makers* (Harper, 1978) Wright Morris again traces respectfully the divergence between Twain's idealization of the past and gloom over the present; since Morris' scope of reading was evidently limited it would be interesting to know which critics guided him. In "The Necessary Miracle" (*Nation* 7 July:21–22), a loose-jointed speech, Kurt Vonnegut naturally salutes nonconformity but also comments trenchantly: "Only a genius [like Twain] could have misrepresented our speech and our wittiness and our common sense and our common decency so handsomely to ourselves and the outside world." Vonnegut reveals that he named his firstborn son after Mark Twain.

Among the longer interpretations, chapter 8 in *Dreams of Adventure, Deeds of Empire* (Basic) by Martin Green produces the most mixed results. While acquiring expertise too facilely from mainline scholarship, Green places *A Connecticut Yankee* within that Anglo-American zest for global adventuring which suited the needs of imperialism; a yet stronger point develops the significance of Clemens' reverence for Henry M. Stanley as explorer. Perry D. Westbrook in *Free Will and Determinism* very generally sets Clemens within a long running debate, a perspective too often blocked by dramatizing his private angst. Concrete as usual, Alan Gribben in " 'Stolen from Books, Tho' Credit Given': Mark Twain's Use of Literary Sources" (*Mosaic* 12,iv:149–55) examines his standards and practices in quoting from the work of others, especially for his travel books. Gribben's conclusion that literary sources cramped Twain's imagination might have considered that burlesque is ordinarily tarred by the faults it ridicules.

Though two critical books make a neat contrast from their style to their periods of emphasis, which virtually meet, each deserves separate discussion. David E. E. Sloane's *Mark Twain as a Literary Comedian* (LSU) builds an argument, much developed beyond a dissertation in 1970, that Twain's most valuable models lay not in southwestern humor with its socially elevated narrators and agrarian settings but in a northeastern school, exemplified by Artemus Ward, which held egalitarian attitudes and pitched its subjects much closer to a commercial society. To put the crux another way, Sloane faces the seldom-noticed questions of how Twain outgrew the frontier school and why he alone survives from the horde of literary comedians. Both answers lead into his combative rather than nostalgic thrusts against the "institutional complexity of the urban and industrial age" and his grasp of the new shapes of problems in "social ethics." Sloane writes with such compression that his 200 pages march relentlessly through the corpus of Twain's work up to a close analysis of *Huckleberry Finn* and even *Pudd'nhead Wilson*, whose flaws, he believes, reveal that the devices of the literary comedians did not allow scope enough for the emergent culture of the 1890s. So revisionist an interpretation will have its full impact only in time if at all. Most of us find it satisfying to overlook the bond with Ward as a youthful indiscretion.

William R. Macnaughton in *Mark Twain's Last Years as a Writer* (Missouri) bears the opposite handicap of lacking a striking thesis. Rejecting "despair" or "obsession" as keywords, Macnaughton contemplates the "complex states" of mind and feeling with which Twain tried to carry on his professional career after *Following the Equator*. Soberly he decides that some projects turned out better than others and many worked only in part. He suggests many unfashionable conclusions such as that the political essays between 1901 and 1903 marked a peak of effectiveness, that *What Is Man?* had the meliorative purpose of making human pride feel ridiculous, that Twain's autobiography (right now the hottest genre around) grew too self-indulgently to rate explication, that he could fall well short of *Huckleberry Finn* and still be worth reading, and that he had a right to abort some manuscripts without incurring accusations. Moving along with unpretentious grace, Macnaughton in effect achieves a civilized exchange with those willing to enjoy at least some of the 1897–1910 body of writing.

iv. On Individual Works

The importance of the first volume of *Early Tales and Sketches* (already discussed in section *i.*) requires further consideration as criticism here. Edgar M. Branch, who supplies a magisterial Introduction, has worked toward this project for 40 years or longer, not simply to recover all the apprentice writings, no more than a third of which were reprinted during Twain's lifetime, but to lay out the central materials for understanding his growth toward mastery. While the first volume gets in just 75 of the more than 365 items to come and ends with the Nevada years, it offers plenty to start with and much to learn from both literary editor Branch and textual editor Hirst. We can see the not-so-beginning writer floundering or achieving flights no longer than the first ones by the Wright brothers, and we can judge the few familiar sketches within a much larger context.

One of these familiar sketches is the subject of Lawrence R. Smith's "Mark Twain's 'Jumping Frog': Toward an American Heroic

Ideal" (*MTJ* 20,i:15–18), an essay dwarfed in the company of *Early Tales and Sketches*. Erecting an ambitious pattern of abstractions, Smith even elicits from the slender frame of the tale a condemnation by the narrator of insensitive and derivative ideals. Branch's and Hirst's next volume, which will include the famous sketch and related pieces, may help us judge better how much and what kind of meaning that frame was meant to bear.

In "Those Pirated Prints: Illustrating Mark Twain's *Roughing It* (*MTJ* 20,i:1–5) Beverly R. David has proved again that Elisha Bliss cheated Twain by borrowing illustrations from other books he had published and charging him for them as if they were originals. This article incidentally reenforces the idea now accepted that for many a 19th-century book the illustrations made part of its effect and in at least secondary ways reflected authorial intentions, especially in Twain's case. David already had helped to restore this viewpoint which the Iowa/California Edition now has adopted. Its volume 5, *The Prince and the Pauper*, ed. Victor Fischer and Lin Salamo (Calif.), reproduces all of the original 192 drawings. Indeed it holds to a generous scale throughout, including 30 pages of the author's working notes and 75 pages of his revisions in the manuscript. A patient mind can reconstruct the process of composition without visiting the Mark Twain Papers, though I suspect that the most dedicated researchers will still want to look for themselves.

Never again will I intimate that the chief approaches to *Adventures of Huckleberry Finn* have been covered or even that writing about it has slowed down. Scholarship and criticism spill over annual boundaries while our society has grown too quick at proclaiming trends. Wrecking any neat flow charts, a perhaps record number of capable essays had their say on Twain's masterpiece, and together they shake some apparently self-evident truths that have reigned for about 30 years.

The upsurge of writing about *Huckleberry Finn* can be sorted into three approaches, which still fail to accommodate Jeanie M. Wagner's prosaic theory (*MTJ* 20,i:5–10) that fascination with inventing a history game distracted Twain from winding up the novel at his best level. The first approach, roughly linguistic or stylistic, brings Walter Blair forward again with the catchy title "Was *Huckleberry Finn* Written?" (*MTJ* 19,iv:1–3) for an article which confronts the question of whether the text consistently tries to mimic a spoken account. After noting some anomalies in Huck's performance as scribe such as the stretches of good spelling, Blair disposes of them reasonably and concludes that the style was not "exactly that of talk. It was a talk *like* style, one modified to give the impression of talk—literary dialect." Lucille M. Schultz in "Parlor Talk in Mark Twain: The Grangerford Parlor and the House Beautiful" (*MTJ* 19,iv:14–19) compares kindred passages in *Life on the Mississippi* and *Huck Finn*, emerging with a preference for the latter's treatment, while I prefer to admire the versatility behind them both.

Taking too long, Louise K. Barnett in "Huck Finn: Picaro as Linguistic Outsider" (*CollL* 6:221–31) gives telling examples of Huck's resistance toward "official rhetoric that functions prescriptively to maintain group values and attitudes." Heightening our sense for the faintest echoes, Dale R. Billingsley in "'Standard Authors' in *Huckleberry Finn*" (*JNT* 9:126–31) stresses further the influence that borrowed "literary circumstances" exert on the characters' actions. If the American economy regains health, a bold grantsman will someday propose a variorum edition.

The major contribution was made by David Carkeet with "The Dialects in *Huckleberry Finn*" (*AL* 51:315–32). Evidently proficient in linguistics, Carkeet knows not only the relevant Twain scholarship but also the fiction of Twain's contemporaries who used dialect heavily. Mediating among fact, inference, and an author's workaday habits, he poses four questions about the "Explanatory" and answers them fully yet economically. Convincingly he decides that *Huckleberry Finn* records even more than the seven dialects promised, and he identifies those Twain had in mind. He rounds off with keen judgments on the moral and social implications of assigning a particular variety of speech to a character. We come away with higher respect for his craftsmanship even after agreeing that Twain did not bother to harmonize the dialect in the 1876 and 1883 stints on the manuscript.

The second approach, structural or formalistic, allows Gary A. Wiener in "From Huck to Holden to Bromden: The Nonconformist in 'One Flew Over the Cuckoo's Nest'" (*StHum* 7,ii:21–26) to compare three I-narrators neatly. In "The Huck Finn Swindle" (*WAL* 14:115–32) Barry A. Marks pushes very hard on his thesis that the tall tale formed the guiding technique and even the theme. Marks erects a definition cogent for the most appropriate episodes but then broadens it beyond oral performance to acted deception; still he does highlight the weaknesses of a plot about a pair whose motives for flight are "swindles" on the reader. In a ten-page section of *Myth of the Picaro*, pp. 178–87, Alexander Blackburn commits *Huckleberry Finn* fully to what he conceives as both a complex and enduring genre, resilient like its protagonist. Blackburn also thinks that Twain's "ideas of the novelist's art and function tended to be religious, even mystical," and holds that *Huckleberry Finn* is "certainly a very sad book" (p. 187). Those who can flow with such ideas or the notion that Pap embodies "civilization" will enjoy a multivalent analysis. By comparison Walter Shear in "Games People Play in *Huckleberry Finn*" (*MQ* 20:378–93) seems straightforward, though he interprets Eric Berne rather loosely. Lawrence B. Holland in " 'A Raft of Trouble': Word and Deed in *Huckleberry Finn*" (*Glyph* 5:69–87) almost defies classification for his ramble through all the central problems. Holland's most intriguing passage asks why Twain did not date Miss Watson's will a few weeks closer to the final action—a possibility that nobody else has elaborated on, to my knowledge.

From a thematic approach three essays justify or at least defend the Phelps farm episode on the very basis on which it supposedly fails, its intellectual coherence with the heart of the narrative. Richard and Rita Gollin in "*Huckleberry Finn* and the Time of the Evasion" (*MLS* 9,ii:5–15) chart the political currents of 1884–85 to argue that Twain wanted quicker results than most "white moderates" and therefore that the "often absurd efforts of Tom and Huck to liberate Jim" indict "polite society's continuing evasion," its turning the struggle for civil rights into a "satisfying game." If Alfred J. Levy is right in "The Dramatic Integrity of Huck Finn" (*BSUF* 20,ii:28–37), then a generation of undergraduates deserve a tuition refund. Without rancor Levy contends that Huck's innate decency never triumphs over the dominant code a boy is too weak to defy and that he acts firmly in character by sharing the racism in the final chapters. Albert J. von Frank in "Huck Finn and the Flight from Maturity" (*SAF* 7:1–15) defends the final chapters through a subtler, persuasive argument, here oversimplified as insisting on Huck's childishness (instead of untutored wisdom) which never rises into maturity because he is romantically rather than realistically conceived. However, intent on giving an original reading, Frank ignores the old fact that Huck was designed to function comically too.

If Levy and Frank gauge the sociomoral inflation of chapter 31 correctly, why has criticism taken so long to do so and will it ever achieve a stable currency? The most hopeful sign is a graceful synthesis by Harold H. Kolb, Jr. Kolb's "Mark Twain, Huck Finn, and Jacob Blivens: Gilt-Edged, Tree-Calf Morality in *The Adventures of Huckleberry Finn*" (*VQR* 55:653–69) first expands on the old idea that Huck's faults disguise an "angel in homespun," just another Good Bad Boy—which would mean that those who analyze Huck so ponderously have been ground in the very mill of the simplistic. Kolb's other major contribution is to spell out the three different systems of morality implicit in the action. From now on any unitary reading deserves rejection by editorial boards.

Only a gambler like Jim Smiley would bet that the sudden drought for the decade after *Huckleberry Finn* will continue. Volume 9 of the Iowa/California project, *A Connecticut Yankee in King Arthur's Court* (Calif.), should stimulate a flood of articles. Edited by Bernard L. Stein from a rich rather than just complicated manuscript and amplified by other primary materials along with the original illustrations, it also has a luminously factual introduction by Henry Nash Smith. All this makes a package that costs as much as a dinner for two with wine.

Aside from Sloane (see section *iii.*), *Pudd'nhead Wilson* elicited only Robert Gale's tracking of a key word (*Expl* 38,i:4–5), and aside from Macnaughton (see section *iv.*) the very latest writings went almost neglected too. In *Mysterious Stranger*, pp. 43–45, 55–56, Roy R. Male touches on "The Man that Corrupted Hadleyburg" and *The Mysterious Stranger* in a short book done with broad strokes. Holding on to the old Paine text, David Karnath in "*The Mysterious Stranger*: Its Mode of Thought" (*MTJ* 19,iv:4–8) proposes to convert flaws into deliberate virtue, reasoning that the regularity with which Christian and determinist sets of value are jumbled together amounts to a "comprehensive" questioning of philosophic categories. Karnath presents his case well, but Ruth Salvaggio in "Twain's Later Phase Reconsidered: Duality and the Mind" (*ALR* 12:322–29) sounds more convincing by not pressing her case so hard. Writing before Sholom Kahn's book (*ALS 1978*, p. 90) became available, Salvaggio identifies determinism and a freewheeling dreamself as the poles of a dialectic that the versions of "The Mysterious Stranger" struggled to resolve. She plausibly contends that the transplanted ending culminated in only one path of ideas. More broadly, she suggests that Twain's decline into solipsism was greatly exaggerated.

In summary I must confess worse luck than before in getting at newer periodicals, especially those published abroad. More are still being funded, giving urgency to Michael West's hope (*CE* 41:903–23) that the marketplace will do some winnowing. Still the turnabout in *Huckleberry Finn* criticism proves that standard positions need to be challenged. No doubt the revised Iowa/California Edition will enable further reversals and genuine amplifications. Also, scholars should work from its texts as soon as they become available. With *Early Tales & Sketches* they have no alternative if they want to understand Mark Twain's development as a professional writer.

Duke University

7. Henry James

Robert L. Gale

Is the James boom lessening at last, after about four decades of big publishing bangs? It is too early to say, but we should probably hope so. Only seven books (two of which are reference in nature and one of which is minor), about 75 essays, and a smaller than usual quota of dissertations appeared in 1979. As always, much is excellent. But new trends are notable. Relatively more work was done in 1979 concerning James and sources, parallels, and influence. Much material appeared on James and impressionism, and on James and silence. In my opinion the finest extended work in 1979 on James was by Nicola Bradbury, Robert Emmet Long, and H. Peter Stowell, while noteworthy essays were by Jean Frantz Blackall, Sara DeSaussure Davis, Ralf Norrman, Carl S. Smith, Adeline R. Tintner, and J. A. Ward. A partial shift is discernible as to works getting the most attention: in 1979 they were "The Turn of the Screw" (as always), *The Portrait of a Lady*, *The Bostonians*, *The Spoils of Poynton*, and *What Maisie Knew*. Of special importance to Jamesians was the establishment in 1979 of the *Henry James Review*, edited by Daniel Mark Fogel and published by the English Department of Louisiana State University.

i. Bibliography, Biography

Henry James 1917–1959: A Reference Guide (Hall) by Kristin Pruitt McColgan and *Henry James 1960–1974: A Reference Guide* (Hall) by Dorothy McInnis Scura comprise a two-volume descriptive bibliography of virtually all books, dissertations, and articles on James from 1917 through 1974 (well over 3,000 entries). Included are collections of criticism, citations of major reviews, foreign criticism, critical introductions to reprints of James's works, and allied material. Many aspects of this 900-page reference set are notable: the prefatory cautions, the thoroughness, the good sense of the descriptions, the helpful cross-referencing, the magnificent indexes, and the clean, readable format.

A fine biographical essay is Richard Hall's two-part "An Obscure Hurt: The Sexuality of Henry James" (*NewRep* 28 Apr.:25–28, 30–31; 5 May: 25–29), which concerns the "incestuous feelings of love" which Henry had toward his "handsome, vital and extroverted" brother William. Topics theorized on: Henry's "obscure hurt," William's early jealousy of Henry's steadiness and income, the brothers' escape from each other (Henry by expatriation, William by marriage), Henry's autobiographical "jilted and betrayed" heroines thereafter, his short-story plots in the 1890s as indicative of his jealousy of William's wife, Henry's later writing positively of physical love, and his post-1905 ascendancy over William.

ii. Sources, Parallels, Influences

A bewildering amount of work was done this year on James and his sources, on parallels to aspects of his work, and on his possible influence on later writers.

Adeline R. Tintner, source hunter extraordinaire, notes in "Hezekiah and *The Wings of the Dove*: The Origin of 'She Turned Her Face to the Wall' " (*NMAL* 3:Item 22) that when James describes Milly Theale's loss of hope and her acceptance of death as metaphorically turning her face to the wall, he is paraphrasing descriptions of Hezekiah literally doing the same thing (II Kings, 20.2, Isaiah, 38.2). Further, Milly resembles Hezekiah as to illness, reprieve, palatial hospitality and spoil-seeking friends. In "The Real-Life Holbein in James' Fiction" (*ABBW* 8 Jan.:278–87) Tintner details the fictional use James made of four of his views of Isabella Stewart Gardner: Mrs. Gardner the Boston hostess in the 1880s (Pauline Mesh in "A New England Winter"), gatherer of European art objects in the mid-'90s (Adela Gereth in *The Spoils of Poynton*), purchaser of the Holbein portrait of Lady Butts (Louisa Brash in "The Beldonald Holbein"), and Mrs. Jack "[t]he resident donor of a great museum, later to be bequeathed to . . . Boston" (Adam Verver in *The Golden Bowl*). The kernel of Tintner's overwrought "Two Innocents in Rome: Daisy Miller and Innocent the Tenth" (*ELWIU* 6:71–78) is simple and valuable. Late in *Daisy Miller* James analogically places his heroine on a seat before the Velazquez portrait of Pope Innocent X in the Palazzo Doria-Pamphili in Rome. Heroine and Pope seem to be a pair of innocents. But James's readers at once note that "contraries are set in motion": Innocent X is experienced, worldly, and cynical; Daisy, innocent, artless, virginal. Even more elaborate is "Velazquez and 'Daisy Miller'" (*SSF* 16:171–78) by Jeffrey Meyers, who says that we should visualize Velazquez's probing portrait of Innocent X as Winterbourne visualizes the meeting under it of Daisy and Giovanelli, that their tryst there relates "structurally and thematically" to others also "observed by the jealous but passive Winterbourne," and that ugly Innocent X contrasts with "angelically beautiful" Daisy.

In a pair of similar essays James is compared to groups of writers in general. Nancy K. Miller's "Novels of Innocence: Fictions of Loss" (*ECS* 11[1978]:325–39) mainly argues that "the sacrifice of innocence is a [sexualized] ritual of loss that tends to structure the fictional matrix of the eighteenth-century novel [particularly French]" but adds that such novels, being gynocentric, are scenically restricted, like many by James, in which "the themes of innocence and worldliness again become the province of an elite." In "From Reflective Narrators to James: The Coloring Medium of the Mind" (*MP* 76: 259–72) Darilyn W. Bock "redefines James's relationship to nineteenth-century fiction," moves from his criticism of Victorian novelists to his debt to them, and suggests ties between his fictive central consciousnesses and traditionally omniscient narrators. James disliked some Victorian fiction for its lack of structural innovation; yet he is part of the tradition of reflective narrators and reflector characters used by such writers as Nathaniel Hawthorne, George Eliot, and —after James—Joseph Conrad, Virginia Woolf, and F. Scott Fitzgerald.

Robert Emmet Long's *The Great Succession: Henry James and the Legacy of Hawthorne* (Pittsburgh) is the definitive, long-awaited discussion of the literary relationship between James and his most important American influence. Long shows how James transmutes Hawthorne's romantic forms and other aspects of his part in the American literary tradition into Jamesian psychological and social realism. In the process he considers Hawthorne's gardens, mesmerists, and fictive characters. Long treats Hawthorne's general influence on later American writers, then considers James's pro-Hawthorne apprenticeship, regards *Roderick Hudson* as implicit criticism of Hawthorne's provinciality, reads *The Europeans* and *Daisy Miller* as Hawthornean transfigurations, views James's *Hawthorne* as harsh, sees "Rappaccini's Daughter" and *The Marble Faun* as feeding into *Washington Square* and *The Portrait of a Lady*, and *The Blithedale Romance* as a major influence on *The Bostonians*. Related to Long's work is Richard Ruland's "Beyond Harsh Inquiry: The Hawthorne of Henry James" (*ESQ* 25:95–117), a slow, superbly articulated study which examines what James said about Hawthorne, largely in his 1879 book. Ruland theorizes that James's comments tell more about his opinions of "provincial" America and his literary theory than about Hawthorne. James saw Hawthorne as a moral romancer dramatizing his inherited Puritan conscience, not a Balzacian, Flaubertian realist of the sort that pro-European James intended to be and became.

Within a matrix of tangential material "Cruikshank's *Oliver* and 'The Turn of the Screw' " (*AL* 51:161–78) by Jean Frantz Blackall probes the thesis that James's celebrated tale gains force through his childhood poring over Charles Dickens' *Oliver Twist*, in the edition with George Cruikshank's illustrations. Many characters parallel each other, and tableau-like situations are similar. Blackall documents the appeal of Cruikshank's "dark vision" of a world which is "cramped, claustrophobic in its inwardness," all of which relates to "The Turn of the Screw," whose author visited the David Copperfield region of Suffolk just before he wrote his harmless *amusette*. In *George Eliot and the Visual Arts* (Yale) Hugh Witemeyer mentions James several times, noting that he criticized Eliot's sensitivity to plastic values as superficial but learned from the complex pictorial effects in her fiction. Witemeyer grants that Eliot's comments on pictures are "a bit wooden" compared to James's. Barbara Wilkie Tedford's "Of Libraries and Salmon-Colored Volumes: James's Reading of Turgenev through 1873" (*RALS* 9:39–49) is a meticulous record of the "approximate dates and specific translations" into French, German, English, and even what James called American of Ivan Turgenev's works with which James's essay on Turgenev for the *North American Review*, April 1874, "shows him to have been acquainted." James may have first encountered Turgenev in an English translation in London, winter, 1855–56, or, more likely, in French in Paris, summer, 1855 or 1856. The *Revue des Deux Mondes* soon featured many translations of Turgenev. James deepened his knowledge of the Russian by reading his works as they appeared in German.

There are two fine essays in *CLS* concerning influences on James.

D. Seed's "Henry James's Reading of Flaubert" (16:307–17) shows that the waning of Victorian moralism combined with praise of Gustave Flaubert by Paul Bourget and Emile Faguet caused James to modify his early dislike of Flaubert's fictive amorality, combined though it was with commendable technique. Then Sarah B. Daugherty's "James, Renan, and the Religion of Consciousness" (16:318–31) nominates Ernest Renan as a "vital influence" on James as he gradually substituted an "ideal of consciousness" for any "religious orthodoxy." James met Renan in Paris, 1876, and was awed by his intelligence and the "perfume" of his style, which expressed his consciousness. Later James found him too conservative politically but always shared his delight in nostalgia and "the moral occult."

"Henry James and Gustave Doré" (*MarkR* 8:21–25) by Adeline Tintner presents proof that Doré's illustrations, especially for Perrault's *Contes de fées*, La Fontaine's *Fables*, and Cervantes' *Don Quixote*, inspired James's pictorial imagery in many fictional and travel pieces. Further, on occasion James "invokes by name the classical fairy tales of Perrault to create literary analogues in his work."

In *The Educated Sensibility in Henry James and Walter Pater* (Tokyo: Shohakusha) wise and logical Keiko Beppu explains that James and Pater "shared basic affinities both in their attitude toward life and in their practice of art," and then "show[s] the confluence of their central concerns as translated or 'transcribed' into their fictional works." Her intention is neither to investigate influence nor to compare styles and critical tenets. What Beppu means by "educated sensibility" is the "harmony of the ideal and the sensuous elements in our consciousness." She explores "the relation between aesthetics and ethics" as it works well in Nick Dormer (*The Tragic Muse*), Florian Deleal (Pater's "The Child in the House"), James as a child (*A Small Boy and Others*), several characters in Pater's *Imaginary Portraits* (notably Antony Watteau and Duke Carl of Rosemold), the hero of Pater's *Marius the Epicurean*, Isabel Archer (*The Portrait of a Lady*), and Lambert Strether (*The Ambassadors*) and Maggie Verver (*The Golden Bowl*). Disharmony ruins the hero of *Roderick Hudson*, Gilbert Osmond and Madame Merle (*The Portrait of a Lady*), Chad Newsome (*The Ambassadors*), and Charlotte Stant (*The Golden Bowl*). Beppu is at her best when discussing Roderick Hudson, Strether, and Maggie and her enigmatic father. Beppu says little of fresh value concerning *The Portrait of a Lady* except to contrast

Ralph Touchett (generous, appreciative of moral beauty) and Osmond (restrictive, having taste without feeling). She unaccountably labels as "this whore of Babylon" poor Marie de Vionnet (*The Ambassadors*), whom she then compliments by comparing her with varied, dazzling Paris. Beppu suggests that *The Golden Bowl* is a kind of sequel to *The Portrait of a Lady*, since Prince Amerigo is redeemable whereas Osmond is not. Having constantly in mind Pater's belief that the cultivation of aesthetic sensibility elevates both moral and spiritual sensibility enhances our appreciation of James's best writings.

Stanley J. Kozikowski compares an 1899 James story and a 1903 Edith Wharton story in "Unreliable Narration in Henry James's 'The Two Faces' and Edith Wharton's 'The Dilettante' " (*ArQ* 35:357–72). In plot and handling of point of view the two are similar; but Wharton displays "a finer esthetic control," "an artistry that is more intact," and "a thematic integrity found lacking in James." Kozikowski interprets Lord Gwyther in "The Two Faces" as launching "an ingeniously calculated plan" to gain sympathy for himself and his bride regardless of jilted Mrs. Grantham's response to his request, Shirley Sutton as a not especially lucid reflector, and the narrator himself as puzzled; Kozikowski also contends that the careful reader understands Gwyther's strutting and fretting. Wharton more centrally places her reflector, who is Thursdale, the jilter revenged upon, whereas James's reflector, Sutton, watches but understands jilter Gwyther only imperfectly.

The most ambitious book of the year on James is H. Peter Stowell's handsomely printed *Literary Impressionism, James and Chekhov* (Georgia). It defines impressionism beautifully, relates impressionistic painting and literature, details the growth of impressionism in Anton Chekov and then James, and shows the impact of impressionism on modernism. Though brilliantly intelligent (if opinionated and phenomenologically wordy), Stowell cannot be definitive in a text of only 244 pages, which would have served Jamesians better if the theoretical introduction had been shortened, Chekhov (whom Stowell knows well) dropped, and more James texts considered than simply *The Portrait of a Lady* (three impressionistic scenes are well explicated), *What Maisie Knew* (the heroine perceives flux and impermanency), *The Sacred Fount* (the narrator "disrupts the balanced interface between subject and change, inner ego and outer world"), *The*

Ambassadors (with "impressionistic nuances of multiplicity and change" exploding "any certainty"), and *The Golden Bowl* ("*the* impressionist masterpiece" of alienation and immersion, passive perceptivity and heightened awareness, intratexturing silences, and spatial time). For me, Stowell's most helpful single sentence concerns *The Three Sisters* and *The Cherry Orchard* by Chekhov; the two plays "project the existential problems of being and becoming, phenomenologically perceived reality, ambiguity of speech and gesture, constant miscommunication, fragmentation of present surfaces, tension between metric and human time, multiple perspective, and change." (See also Suzanne Ferguson, in section *iii.* below.)

In "The Swiss Cottage's Owner: A Model for J. L. Westgate in James' *An International Episode*" (*AN&Q* 17[1978]:58–60) Curtis Dahl regards Colonel George T. M. Davis, New York "lawyer, businessman, railroad entrepreneur" in the 1870s, as a model for J. L. Westgate, and Davis' chalet, called the Swiss Cottage, overlooking Bailey's Beach in Newport, Rhode Island, as similar to the Westgates' Newport summer house.

Adeline Tintner's "Henry James and the Symbolist Movement in Art" (*JML* 7:397–415) is a major influence study, which shows that James appropriated "characteristic icons" of French, Belgian, and English painters, beginning with Gustave Moreau, in much of his later fiction. These icons include "[p]earls, masks, dying young women, chimaeras, sphinxes, doves, underwater images, decadent posters." Tintner relates Edward Burne-Jones's "The Mill" and "The Briar Rose Series" to James's "The Great Good Place" and "Flickerbridge," Fernand Khnopff's 'imagined world" to "The Altar of the Dead," billboard-poster females to the widow in "The Real Thing," interpretations of Pierrot by Aubrey Beardsley and James Ensor to the narrator of *The Sacred Fount*, Symbolist Byzantine princesses, poster people, and chimaeras to Milly Theale and Maud Lowder in *The Wings of the Dove* (as well as Maurice Maeterlinck's theatrical settings to Milly's crepuscular ambience), and Moreau's sphinx and lily-bearing femme fatale to May Bartram in "The Beast in the Jungle." Tintner concludes: "This analysis of the appearance of traditional Symbolist visual structures does not argue for a similarity of intention"; rather, James's diseroticising appropriation represents adverse but creative criticism of the highest order.

Four essays compare James and later literary figures. Kathy J.

Phillips, in "Conversion to Text, Initiation to Symbolism, in [Thomas] Mann's *Der Tod in Venedig* [*Death in Venice*] and James' *The Ambassadors*" (*CRCL* 4:376–88) sensibly chooses to compare two works of fiction with similar situations: aging men have regrets, move to exotic cities, guard young men, delude themselves, get initiated. But then what follows is a bewildering attempt to discuss narrative-voice shifts "between impersonality and opinion" and the "narrative technique of multiplying both foreshadowings and climaxes." Charlotte Cushman's "Henry James, D. H. Lawrence, and the Victimized Child" (*MLS* 10,i:43–51) observes that James's "The Author of Beltraffio" and Lawrence's "England, My England," and James's "The Pupil" and Lawrence's "The Rocking-Horse Winner" all concern the victimizing of children by family tensions caused mainly by mothers. Tenuous parallels lead Cushman to conclude that James may have influenced Lawrence. Charles W. Mayer in "The Triumph of Honor in James and Hemingway" (*ArQ* 35:373–91) offers a refreshing comparison of the Master and Papa in their devotion to literary art, their similarly "narrow vision and range," and the "moral force" resulting from it. Characters in both are treacherously defeated but "achieve . . . spiritual triumph over evil and death." The tone in the best fiction of each is marked by irony, which comes from awareness of the disparity between "wish and fulfillment, expectation and result." Victory can follow if one refuses to surrender, after knowledge of loss and exclusion, but instead honors "the rights and privileges of . . . expanding consciousness of reality." Success in life depends on "[c]ourage, endurance, magnanimity." Both James and Hemingway teach us how to live well: by dominating life and thus creating it, through unflagging intensity of perception. And they tell us how to die well: by accepting without illusion. Mayer establishes enough startling points of character paralleling in their respective fiction to outline a seminar in James and Hemingway. The ornament of the first issue of the new *Henry James Review* is J. A. Ward's "Henry James and Graham Greene" (*HJR* 1:10–23). Greene believes that the force behind James's writings was his sense of evil—betrayal, treachery, deceit, sometimes associated with sexual passion, with wrongdoers suffering so exquisitely as to merit pity. Ward compares James and Greene, especially as to *The Wings of the Dove* and *The Heart of the Matter*, which have central characters who similarly honor commitments, gain through moral refinement, but are will-paralyzingly scrupulous.

Greene distrusts goodness and creates weakly good characters, unlike James, whose good is thus "purer" and whose good people have "a supernal aura" and scatter grace this side of the grave.

Seven critical essays concern sources and parallels of a somewhat more specific nature. Adeline Tintner in her "James' Etonian: A Blend of Literature, Life and Art" (*ABBW* 19 Nov.:3419–38 *passim*) wittily overpleads her case that traits of Etonian Bob Bantling of *The Portrait of a Lady* derive from George John Whyte-Melville's *Digby Grand*, from personality elements in James's friend Arthur Christopher Benson, and from George Frederick Watts's painting "Sir Galahad." "Feminist Sources in *The Bostonians*" (*AL* 50:570–87) is a cogent, well-documented essay by Sara DeSaussure Davis, who discusses events of the feminist movement which occurred just before James wrote his controversial novel. The author points out parallels between real-life personages and fictional characters: Susan B. Anthony / Olive Chancellor, Whitelaw Reid / Basil Ransom, and Anna Dickinson / Verena Tarrant. Historical happenings are also "transmogrified." Davis splendidly suggests that in concluding his plot as he does James forecasts the actual "slow-down" of the feminist movement after 1884 (until 1897, she adds). (For related work, see Elizabeth McMahan in section *iv.* below.) Bernard Richards offers a pair of fine source studies. In "The Sources of Henry James's 'The Marriages'" (*RES* 30:316–22) Richards suggests that the plot of "The Marriages" derives from family circumstances of widowered Sir John Rose, James's distant British relative, who shocked his daughters by remarrying. His doing so prompted James to detail Adela Chart's neurotic campaign to stop her father's remarriage. (Richards prefers his source theory to that of Leon Edel, who mentions the remarriage of the third duke of Sutherland; but then he offers more evidence in support of Edel than Edel does.) He closes by relating Adela's hysteria to case studies in abnormal psychology by William James. More significant is Richards' "James and His Sources: *The Spoils of Poynton*" (*EIC* 29:302–22). In it Richards compares Mrs. Gereth's quarrel with her son Owen to the real-life dispute between Dame Rebecca Ross of Balnagown Castle and her son Sir Charles, who when he came of age in 1893 promptly married. Richards identifies Poynton with aspects of a Somerset house which James loved, and Waterbath with an ugly Victorian house in Surrey. Richards proposes other models for persons and places in *The Spoils of Poynton* with so much documen-

tation that James's "sheer inventiveness" seems to be played down.
But Richards' final paragraph is a spectacular defense of "this kind
of source study" as one means of asserting that realistic novels have
"palpability and specificity." May L. Ryburn in *"The Turn of the
Screw* and *Amelia*: A Source for Quint?" (*SSF* 16:235–37) notes that
Mr. Robinson of Henry Fielding's *Amelia*, which the governess reads
at Bly, is similar to Peter Quint as to facial features, height, and cloth-
ing. (See also Dennis Grunes in section *v.*, below.) In "An Illustra-
tor's Literary Interpretation" (*ABBW* 26 Mar.:2275–82 *passim*) Adeline Tintner ingeniously interprets the illustration by John La Farge,
James's friendly mentor, for the original 1898 *Collier's Weekly* publication of "The Turn of the Screw." The picture shows the governess and
Miles gazing at each other, an abstract rendition of Quint visible only
to the governess, and "inhuman horrors" framing the human pair.
Especially wild is the governess's having two right hands, which,
Tintner says, symbolize her maternal relations to the boy and also
the "repressed part of her nature." Jesse Bier in "Henry James's 'The
Jolly Corner': The Writer's Fable and the Deeper Matter" (*ArQ* 35:
321–34) suggests that Hawthorne was James's "conscious literary and
psychological model," and is to be equated with Spencer Brydon's
ego; further, that Edgar Allan Poe is James's "antimodel or alter ego,"
and relates to Brydon's alter ego too. James respected Hawthorne's
writings but "could not practice the Gothic mode, the ghost story in
particular, without having Poe in the back of . . . [his] mind."

Of tangential interest is "Filming James" by Nicola Bradbury
(*EIC* 29:239–301), in which the screenplay of *The Europeans* is
praised, as is the rich-toned work of the director. Bradbury opines
that the film lacks James's "discrimination" and thus "translat[es] a
peculiarly visual novel into a rather musical film." She praises the
movie scene in which Felix Young asks for Gertrude Wentworth's
hand, laments the inevitability that Lee Remick's Eugenia Münster
masks by beauty the pride and longing of James's heroine, and wishes
that her "darker and colder tones" were not absent from the film.

iii. Criticism: General

Little criticism of a general nature on James appeared this year.
Only that by Carl S. Smith and Nicola Bradbury appears likely to
prove influential. It is too early to say whether dissertation writers will

seek to publish their varied and important insights in years to come.

Carl Smith in "James's International Fiction: Sources and Evolution" (*CentR* 22:397–422) credibly develops a fascinating thesis. James's early contrast of Americans and their European friends and hosts was based on personal observation, including travel to out-of-the-way places, and also on nostalgia. Later, as hordes of tasteless tourists via better railroads cocknified and desecrated his old haunts, James found himself puzzled by modernity, grew harsh and intolerant, and stressed internationalism less. Finally, "Travel became for him . . . a figurative act which dramatized the 'foreignness' in all intercourse between the individual and the world," and so "he . . . examined the international situation . . . as a metaphorical device for dramatizing the mystery of each person to every other." Hence internationalism in the three big major-phase novels, though present, is secondary to the theme of the cryptic in personality and the mystery in all social relationships. (See also J. N. Sharma, *The International Fiction of Henry James* [New Delhi: Macmillan]).

B. D. Horwitz' protracted essay "The Sense of Desolation in Henry James" (*PsyculR* 1[1977]:466–92) discusses desolation in two types of Jamesian characters—self-exiled losers and victims of domineering mothers—and theorizes that James used the catharsis of art to avoid a breakdown in the face of a vapid father, a domineering mother, and a jaunty older brother.

Verily I believe that *Henry James: The Later Novels* by Nicola Bradbury (Oxford: Clarendon Press) is the most subtle book ever written on James. It concerns *The Portrait of a Lady* (mainly to discuss the unspeakable and the unsayable, distinguishable aspects of expressive silence), *What Maisie Knew* (in which the young heroine defines by negatives while learning to sense adult ineffables), *The Awkward Age* (full of inner silences, danger signals, and demands on the reader to fill with "potential meaning . . . the interstices of distorted form"), and *The Sacred Fount* (transitional, idiosyncratic, hence contrastive). Bradbury also theorizes that in the three major-phase masterpieces James unites author-narrator, reader, and protagonists in adventures of being and seeing, bafflement and recognition, "the process and the effect of representation." This Jamesian technique proceeds from *The Ambassadors* (in which James, reader, and Strether move to a central-perspective vanishing-point), through the elegiac, experimental *Wings of the Dove* (which has effective

double entendre, fine dialogue, a great Alpine scene, and a " 'double-
time' period in Venice"), to *The Golden Bowl* (in which Maggie
Verver is seen as both victim of immersion as in a bath and observer
as into a goldfish bowl). Bradbury needs more than 70 pages to posit
that *The Golden Bowl* strains and almost breaks the mold of the modern novel: "The question of loyalties and blame toward Prince or
Princess from the reader is evaded through a shift of terms between
the two halves of the novel: there is not merely a different centre of
consciousness, but a different kind." Bradbury treats James's post-
Bowl fiction badly, faulting *The Ivory Tower* harshly, saying little on
The Sense of the Past, and making too much of "A Round of Visits."
Her book is hypersubtle to the point of juicelessness, is merciless
with certain critics, but is thrilling on diction, imagery, James's demand for reader involvement, and Jamesian stillnesses.

Three essays concern various aspects of James's technique. Charles
W. Mayer in "Henry James's 'Discriminated Occasion': A Determi-
nant of Form" (*JNT* 9:133–46) theorizes on James's effacing the
author, encouraging the reader to share the narrator's limited point of
view, and dramatizing the scenic by shaping structural components
through selection. (Mayer's evidence comes mainly from *The Wings
of the Dove*.) The thesis of James W. Gargano's "The 'Look' as a
Major Event in James's Short Fiction" (*ArQ* 35:303–20) is that "in
story after story, James shows his fascination with glances that send
out waves of thought and express, in their special language, deeper
meanings than may often be found in stirring action." (Gargano analyzes such looks in "Madame de Mauves," "Four Meetings," "The
Liar," "The Real Thing," and "The Beast in the Jungle.") Suzanne
Ferguson in "The Face in the Mirror: Authorial Presence in the Multiple Vision of the Third-Person Impressionist Narrative" (*Criticism*
21:230–50) decries the critical misconception that the strategy of
fiction writers "most often seen as essential to impressionism" is "the
banishing of the author, so that all the fictional experience shall seem
to emanate from the consciousness of a character or characters in
the work." Ferguson notes that Flaubert and James, among other novelists, were mistaken in insisting that "they had eliminated their own
presence" from *Madame Bovary* and *The Ambassadors*, respectively.

"Henry James and the Demonic Vampire and Madonna" (*PsyculR*
3:203–24) by Elaine Zablotny is an interesting psychoanalytical essay
but is swollen by prolix plot summaries. In it Zablotny discusses two

types of women in seven usually neglected stories by James. The
women are virginal, comforting, Madonna-like, or vulture-like, vam-
piric, succubative; or, through credible ambiguity or change in the
course of time, a mixture of beneficent and demonic. The tales are
"A Landscape Painter," "De Grey: A Romance," "Poor Richard,"
"The Diary of a Man of Fifty," "The Story of a Masterpiece," "The
Great Condition," and "The Bench of Desolation."

Seven 1979 dissertations on James are listed in *DAI*. One concerns
the influence of James's family on his later fiction (L. D. Boren [40:
1465A]). Three relate James to other writers (J. L. Petrick, moral
concerns in Hawthorne and James [40:2123A]; G. E. Haggerty, James
in the tradition of Gothic fiction [40:4036A]; R. C. Funk, unity in
the past vs. chaos in James and others, especially Henry Adams [40:
2679A]). One concerns symbolism (E. V. B. Bowen, gardens in
James's fiction and Prefaces [40:7344A–45A]); two concern style
(G. O. Trotter, the evolution of James's process of selection [40:
5060A]; S. M. Grabler, symmetry in three James novels as it relates
to ideology [40:3299A]).

iv. Criticism: Individual Novels

Criticism this year on individual novels has been limited, with several old standbys ignored. *What Maisie Knew* wins the popularity
contest; following it are *The Portrait of a Lady*, *The Bostonians*, and
The Spoils of Poynton, all of which, as we have already seen, were
subjects of source studies.

In "Anglican Custom, American Consciousness" (*NEQ* 52:307–
25) Alan M. Kantrow takes evidence from the experience of Christopher Newman, hero of *The American*, in France and with Claire de
Cintré to support a sweeping theory that "Catholic Europe provided
the broad imaginative analogy by which the [too Puritan] American
mind covertly reclaimed its Anglican heritage." J. P. Telotte's "Language and Perspective in James's *The American*" (*SAB* 44:27–39)
relates Christopher Newman's changing world (from doing and buying in America to feeling, touring, observing, and inquiring in Europe)
to his—and the typical artist's—tragic task of learning a new language
to deal with "external reality" seen from altered perspectives.

Darshan Singh Maini's "*Washington Square*: A Centennial Essay" (*HJR* 1:81–101) is long and slow. In part 1, which surveys the

first century of criticism levied against *Washington Square*, Maini praises those few critics who like its modernity and its links to James's major phase, but taints most of his praise with dabs of superciliousness. Part 2 discusses "the nature of irony and evil" in *Washington Square*. The theme of the novel may well be "the *morality* of irony," with oedipally satanic Dr. Austin Sloper suffering the posthumous humiliation of having his verbal ironies, which "wither . . . into stylization," ironically defeated by his daughter Catherine, whose very sweetness and innocence preclude James's narrating the story from her point of view. High points in Maini's essay include subtle analysis of Sloper's Alpine iciness and the dialogue in the novel.

It's about time someone stood up again to praise recently maligned Isabel Archer. Harriet Blodgett, doing just that in "Verbal Clues in *The Portrait of a Lady*: A Note in Defense of Isabel Archer" (*SAF* 7:27–36), proves that "[t]he text of the first American edition . . . is laced with paired verbal clues to James's intentions which sustain . . . traditional assumptions of Isabel's worth." In revising the novel James retained the substance and often the wording of these clues. Evidence includes rosy light, Madonna and virgin imagery, comments in dialogue about the size of the world, and use of the words "turn" and "wait." Ergo, "Isabel is an admirable human being, without being a paragon." "Mrs. Touchett's Three Questions" (*AL* 51:641–44) by J. M. Treadwell is a perfect example of the useful explicative note. Treadwell proves that in chapter 54 of *The Portrait of a Lady* Lydia Touchett obtains her niece Isabel's permission to ask three personal questions but then asks only two. Why only two? Because James proofread the passage carelessly.

In an energetic but at times gratuitously antiphallic essay entitled "Sexual Desire and Illusion in *The Bostonians*" (*MFS* 25:241–51) Elizabeth McMahan deplores the fact that Verena Tarrant, like most of the other characters in *The Bostonians*, "confuses illusion with reality," also gives up her husbandlike (i.e., "possessive") partner Olive Chancellor, and—being too oft enchanted by stronger-willed people—succumbs to "nature's ploy," and falls for Basil Ransom. And all in spite of the sad fact that "her feelings [of love? sexual desire?] are illusory." Basil is defined here as stiff, rigid, provincial, conservative, possessed of "moral enervation," hypocritically unchivalric on occasion, simplistic—in short, "a narrow, authoritarian egotist" and "the classic male supremacist." McMahan makes me thoroughly ashamed of myself. Daniel H. Heaton begins his unconvincing essay "The Altered Characterization of Miss Birdseye in Henry James's *The Bostonians*" (*AL* 50:588–603) by reminding us that some critics have read Miss Birdseye as negatively portrayed, some as positively, while a few others "have sensed ambiguity in the portrayal, but have inaccurately found that ambiguity to be consistent throughout the novel." Heaton points out that in the first 14 chapters the old woman appears in a critical light, then drops from sight, then from chapter 20 on is praised as "a . . . noble and efficacious crusader who has . . . outlived her usefulness." Why this alteration? Not because William James complained that Miss Birdseye was being read as a caricature of Elizabeth Peabody or because the novelist tempered artistic with personal integrity, but because Miss Birdseye's change from "fool to saint" prepares the reader for psychosocially related Olive Chancellor's final-scene achievement of a parallel martyrdom. Could we say more simply that James was a bit inartistic?

Jule S. Kaufman's "*The Spoils of Poynton*: In Defense of Fleda Vetch" (*ArQ* 35:342–56) is a forthright vindication of an often-scorned Jamesian heroine. Kaufman praises Fleda Vetch for having genuine taste, being human (if a trifle perverse), loving Owen Gereth loyally (if partly for his negative qualities), striving to be honest and free, and having scruples and yet with them inconsistency and normal sexual feelings. Fleda loses, and this bleak novel "ends in . . . desolation." A notable virtue of this neat essay is its author's uncompromising treatment of previous critics. Charles Palliser in " 'A Conscious Prize': Moral and Aesthetic Value in *The Spoils of Poynton*" (*MLQ* 40:37–52) begins by citing a couple of critics only to allege their unreliability. Palliser believes that "James's attitude toward his heroine is a complex mixture of sympathy and irony." He explicates the main action, treating especially well the plot-swinging query Fleda makes about herself to Mrs. Brigstock to the effect that she might seem like a bad woman in a play, a remark Palliser calls "tasteless in both the aesthetic and the moral senses." He asserts that Fleda confuses idea and accident, is unaware of her ambivalent motives concerning both Owen and the spoils, is blind to Mrs. Gereth's unscrupulousness and Mona Brigstock's effective brutality, and seems to feel that the spoils are immutable. Palliser almost accuses poor, wretched Fleda of causing the climactic fire by naively thinking it could never happen.

In her "Moral Geography in *What Maisie Knew*" (*UTQ* 48:130–48) Jean Frantz Blackall maps the maturing of Maisie's perspectives and the increase of her knowledge and shows how "James sustains Maisie's point of view by objectifying rather than conceptualizing her alternatives," as in a morality play, especially in the crucial Boulogne scene. Blackall concentrates on how the gilt Virgin of the Boulogne church "symbolizes a new point of reference in Maisie's sensibility and thought." The shining figure replaces Ida Farange, among other "adult influences," and becomes a source of the girl's "intuitive understanding of brightness as an abstraction in certain modes of conduct." Blackall next interprets the *plage* as symbolizing qualities which Maisie enjoys with Sir Claude while the rampart serves to suggest Mr. Wix's sterner attributes. Taught to evaluate human elements epitomized by Virgin and beach, fearless Maisie freely chooses to "reject pleasure divorced from forms." Thomas L. Jeffers archly tells us in "Maisie's Moral Sense: Finding Out for Herself" (*NCF* 34:154–72) "what the prepubescent point of view actually achieves" for the heroine of *What Maisie Knew*. The young girl listens, looks, and enters "a symmetrical maze which she can talk through and finally out of." But she must learn to moralize on "morally neutral" maneuvers which are almost military, games of musical chairs, and adult couplings. Jeffers notes imagery of gardens and also of darkness yielding to light. The girl discovers the depths of *amour*, as Mrs. Wix certainly does not and as Sir Claude perhaps has not yet done, because it includes "reciprocity." Under Mrs. Wix's guidance, Maisie learns, though ultimately by herself, the moral sense through sympathizing with Sir Claude's frailty and then leaving the young man for unhoused isolation. Kenny Marotta notes in "*What Maisie Knew*: The Question of Our Speech" (*ELH* 46:495–508) that James's major-phase "style grew out of his characteristic theme: the redemptive power of innocence," but adds that in Maisie's story "language itself can become a weapon of the corruption James depicts" in opposition to such innocence. Readers and Maisie alike must resist the power of language to amuse and confuse; then "meaningful speech and . . . actions" are made possible. Maisie matures by learning to cut through the linguistic hypocrisy of adults. Marotta slickly relates Maisie's plea "for fidelity to language" to James's identical plea in "The Question of Our Speech," his 1905 lecture.

Alan W. Bellringer in " 'The Wings of the Dove': The Main Image" (*MLR* 74:12–25) praises James's much-debated novel by arguing that his main intention in it was to show, "not Milly's mind and character, but her illness in its ramifications, in its interrelating effects," that is, "to dramatize the pain and stimulus which Milly's grimness and silence cause to others." Bellringer explores Susan Shepherd Stringham, who causes "a kind of double blur" early in the narrative, Kate Croy, Sir Luke Strett, who "accommodate[s] her [Milly] to the negative," and Merton Densher, whom Milly uniquely detaches and redeems.

A delightfully different essay is Ralf Norrman's "Referential Ambiguity in Pronouns as a Literary Device in Henry James's *The Golden Bowl*" (*SN* 51:31–71), which begins by noting that the formula for determining the number of pairs in n number of people is $(n^2-n) \div 2$. Since *The Golden Bowl* "is a game of combinations" comprising a "*Vierpersonenkonstellation*" (Adam Verver, Maggie Verver, Prince Amerigo, Charlotte Stant), it yields six couplings. Complex enough; however, then Norrman not only demonstrates that James uses "he," "she," "you," and "we" so as to increase the ambiguity, but also "trace[s] the main pattern of the occurrence of actual *activated* ambiguity in the dialogues and their combination to the effect of intensity in the novel."

v. Criticism: Individual Tales

Fewer than a dozen of James's short stories were given separate essay treatment this year. Predictably, the unfathomable "Turn of the Screw" led the way, as it always does.

In "Culture and Rhetoric in Henry James's 'Poor Richard' and 'Eugene Pickering' " (*SAB* 44:61–72) Patricia Marks interprets both stories as "linguistic and cultural variants of the traditional fortunate fall." Each hero moves from linguistic immaturity through silence to control over expression. However, Richard falls from innocence by lying, whereas Eugene does so by learning to judge Mme. Blumenthal's unreal "aesthetic phraseology" and romantic pretentiousness.

William P. Safranek's "Longmore in 'Madame de Mauves': The Making of a Pragmatist" (*ArQ* 35: 293–302) is a tidy demonstration that Longmore moves "from an idealistic to a pragmatic way of thinking."

In a rambling essay entitled " 'An International Episode': A Cen-

tennial Review of a Centennial Story" (*HJR* 1:24–60) Adeline Tintner suggests that heroine Bessie Alden's rejection of Lord Lambeth,
about a century after the Battle of Lexington, symbolizes America's
tardy declaration of social independence from the British. Tintner
shows that James kept up with aspects of the Philadelphia Centennial while he was abroad. She relates history-minded Bessie to historians in general and Lambeth and his friend Percy Beaumont to
Alexis de Tocqueville and his friend Gustave de Beaumont. Tintner suggests a great deal of possible source material for James.

Now for "The Turn of the Screw." Brenda Murphy in "The
Problem of Validity in the Critical Controversy over *The Turn of the
Screw*" (*RS* 47:191–201) humorously summarizes the disparate interpretations of the controversial tale, disagrees with applicable comments in E. D. Hirsch's *Validity in Interpretation*, prefers elements
in D. W. Hamlyn's *The Theory of Knowledge*, and concludes that
James's conscious and unconscious aims, her interpretation (not
given), and our interpretations can never be reconciled. All the
same, other critics press on. Albert E. Stone's "Henry James and
Childhood: *The Turn of the Screw*," pp. 279–92 in *American Character*, builds on the author's extensive knowledge of American culture
and treatments of children therein. Stone relates the three childish
characters in "The Turn of the Screw" (that is, Miles, Flora, and
the governess) to the three main American stereotypes of children
(bad boy, precocious infant, virginal maiden). Then he relates James's
tale to his earlier indictments of careless parents. Next Stone shows
Bly "as microcosm of a [British] society lacking proper control and
moral responsibility," with Miles and Flora as "grandees," and below
them the immature governess, who as a vicar's daughter is both an
"ideal observer of social class" and a naive Christian ill-equipped
either to cope with evil or even to describe its complexities. "Another
Turn to James' *The Turn of the Screw*" (*CEA* 41,ii:9–17) by Marcella
M. Holloway provides a labored reading of "the Governess' story as
fiction, a kind of allegory sent from the borderland of death to a man
[Douglas] she loved." More convincingly, Holloway sees elements
of James in celibate, anguished Douglas. John J. Allen in "The Governess and the Ghosts in *The Turn of the Screw*" (*HJR* 1:73–80)
adduces evidence validating the authority of the governess and interprets the final scene of the story "as verification of the 'reality'
of the ghosts and hence of the governess's reliability." The main value

to me of Dennis Grunes's discursive essay "The Demonic Child in *The Turn of the Screw*" (*PsyculR* 2[1978]:221–39) lies in its comparing Miles and Flora to children in works by Charles Dickens, Mary Shelley, Herman Melville, Poe, Vladimir Nabokov, and Hawthorne. Less persuasive is Grunes's main concern: to show that James's tale is typical of those concerning possession "by the devil or the evil dead" through exploiting themes of "rebellion against authority, a lost redemptive capability, and incest." Grunes makes dangerous assumptions, for example, that Peter Quint is an image of the governess's incest-seeking father and that her childish charges are too intimate.

In "Mr. Mudge as Redemptive Fate: Juxtaposition in James's *In the Cage*" (*SNNTS* 11:63–76) Joel Salzberg suggests that "the telegraphist's relationship to Mudge is . . . distinguished by . . . substance and promise," whereas Captain Everard and Mrs. Jordan may, separately, be less fortunate. Compared to them and their shadowy partners, Mudge emerges as more noble "in character and action," and may even redeem his fiancée from her "solipsistic imagination" and "demeaning poverty."

J. Peter Dyson in "Death and Separation in 'Fordham Castle'" (*SSF* 16:41–47) traces the characterization of Abel Taker in "Fordham Castle" as "a consciousness which . . . survives as a spectator of its own tragedy resulting from 'defeat . . . failure . . . subjection'" back to more entries in James's *Notebooks* than were cited by the editors of those *Notebooks*.

Joan DelFattore in "The 'Other' Spencer Brydon" (*ArQ* 35:335–41) contends that the hero of "The Jolly Corner" is immature, self-centered, and ineffectual, and remains so even after seeing the specter, because he projects on the really "pusillanimous, ineffective, and passive" ghost those traits of courage, enterprise, and energy which he erroneously regards himself as possessing. Such a reading seems to downgrade the value of the hero's expatriation, misinterpret the seeming timidity of the alter ego, and trivialize the rebirth symbolism at the end.

vi. Criticism: Specific Nonfictional Works

James's nonfictional works were unaccountably slighted by critics in 1979. Only *Italian Hours*, the Prefaces, *The American Scene*, and a book James did not write were treated in separate essays.

"City as Self: Henry James's Travel Sketches of Venice" (*PSt* 2:73–87) by Frederick Kirchhoff suggests that James in his four essays on Venice in *Italian Hours* uses John Ruskin, who is didactic and pro-Gothic, by disavowing him, through being conversational and eclectic himself. Then Kirchhoff gets to his problematic thesis that as James writes of Venice he and the city "merge into a single identity": the city meets James's anticipations disturbingly, impressions unify writer and subject by actualizing both, one becomes essential to the meaning of the other, elements of Venice equate with elements of James's writings, and both are implicated in art and death.

William R. Goetz's "Criticism and Autobiography in James's Prefaces" (*AL* 51:333–48) is a convoluted argument that criticism of the Prefaces has generally failed. Critics too often have treated them either as critical aids to James's fiction or as a major statement of his theory of the novel. In reality each piece of fiction is "not so much a mimetic copy of an external reality as a palimpsest": beneath each fictive plot is "the history of the author and his imagination." A given Preface comments on both plot and history, is hence both "formalist analysis . . . and . . . autobiographical narrative," both "intrinsic . . . [and] extrinsic criticism." Goetz seems discontented with James and his Prefaces when we read that "the [prefatory] essays, instead of forming the single, continuous story of the author's growth, consist in alternating series of fragmentary, abortive narratives and discursive statements that attempt to redeem the failure of those narratives." But then Goetz adds that it would be wrong to conclude that the Prefaces are a failure. Instead, they succeed through trying to be simultaneously " 'structuralist' criticism . . . [and] an autobiography."

Related to Goetz's work is Gordon O. Taylor's beautifully written "Chapters of Experience: *The American Scene*" (*Genre* 12:93–116). Taylor sees James's book about his travels in America "as a kind of novel, in which an author protagonist re-enacts through interlocking and accumulating 'scenes' the journeys of interior discovery undertaken by his fictional protagonists, within an exterior context of a collision of cultures." Taylor says that James's theme here is "personal and literary discontinuity."

John L. Kimmey's "The 'London' Book" (*HJR* 1:61–72) is a neat demonstration that although James loved London, signed a contract with Macmillan in 1903 to write a book of 150,000 words on the city, planned to pattern his work on Francis Marion Crawford's *Ave Roma Immortalis*, and did a good deal of research, James was temperamentally unsuited to do the London book and therefore never did it. Kimmey shows that all was not lost, however, because James wrote evocatively about London in his autobiographical volumes, particularly in *The Middle Years*.

University of Pittsburgh

8. Pound and Eliot

George Bornstein and Stuart Y. McDougal

i. Pound

This was a busy year for Pound studies, with ten new books appearing. Continuing two of the three recent trends, significant work stressed either texts and biography (which for Pound often go together) or *The Cantos*, with relation to other writers receiving less emphasis than usual. Despite the flourishing activity, two problems arise. First, the heavy concentration of articles in *Paideuma* provides a handy gathering, but their scarcity elsewhere suggests that Pound scholars may be addressing an increasingly specialized audience of fellow initiates. Hence, the appearance of three books frankly aimed at neophyte readers is particularly welcome. Secondly, an earlier period when scholars, perhaps intimidated by the complexity of *The Cantos*, tended to focus on the earlier lyrics has reversed itself to the point where specific studies now neglect instead the poems up through *Mauberley*. One hopes that the spate of recent inquiries into Pound's epic—and several more book-length ones have been announced already—will lead to a consolidation enabling us to return to the great early poems with new eyes.

a. **Texts and Biography.** The most important contribution to texts and biography this year is also the most curious. H. D.'s *End to Torment: A Memoir of Ezra Pound*, ed. Norman Holmes Pearson and Michael King (New Directions), contains both H. D.'s 1958 journal-memoir of her contorted connection to Pound and the poems in his previously unpublished "Hilda's Book." A sort of sequel to her *Tribute to Freud* (1956), H. D.'s brief memoir illuminates a central

George Bornstein has contributed the section on Pound and Stuart Y. McDougal the section on Eliot.

relationship in Pound's life; it clarifies their early love, touches on the Imagist years, and proffers an interesting perspective on Pound's release from St. Elizabeths hospital. Intricately combining past and present, America and Europe, *End to Torment* both recreates the atmosphere of that early love and encapsulates such amusing anecdotes as the undergraduate Pound's being thrown into a lily-pond by incensed fellow students (they thereafter called him "Lily" Pound) or his later search for a London apartment in which to fence with Yeats. At a deeper level the nearly ideogrammic method of the account evokes both the impassioned stress of the early affair and a lifetime of brooding over its significance. Few readers may accept the Jungian framework of myth which H. D. evolves for the lovers' life stories, but nearly all will respond to the emotional depth of this portrait. A complementary text to the memoir, Pound's love poems in "Hilda's Book" reveal both his feeling for H. D. and his derivative literary output during 1905–07, the years of their composition. Of the 25 lyrics, 19 appear here for the first time (four of the others were printed with changes in Pound's early volumes and two more in the San Trovaso Notebook three years ago). Their mixture of medieval, Romantic, and late Victorian diction and conventions reminds us that Pound's later critiques of 19th-century poetry fit his own derivative early verse with even more force. The apparatus to both works is helpful but minimal; however, Guy Davenport has raised serious questions about the quality of the editing and transcription ("Poets' Romance," *NYTBR* 15 Jul.:12, 33–34). Although it is good to have both the memoir and the poems even in this form, it would be better if New Directions and the Ezra Pound Literary Property Trust would embark on a definitive edition of Pound's works rather than continue to dribble them out a book at a time.

Letters to Ibbotson: 1935–1952, ed. Vittoria I. Mondolfo and Margaret Hurley (NPF), both reproduces and transcribes 36 previously unpublished letters and cards from Pound to Joseph Darling Ibbotson, one of his teachers at Hamilton College and later librarian there. The first 25 date from the fascist years at Rapallo and the remainder from the postwar period at St. Elizabeths. Pound suggested books, surveyed the literary scene, boosted Vivaldi, blasted Usura, and hoped to influence American education. Occasional flashes of tart wit ("CONFOUND uncle Bill YEATS' paragraph on fug[u]e/ blighter never knew WHAT a fugue was anyhow," he fumed over Yeats's famous discussion of *The Cantos* in *A Vision*) relieve the antisemitic abuse and fascist orientation that pervade Pound's prose of the period. These letters contain no startling revelations, but they do usefully round out the record of these years and illuminate one of Pound's oldest friendships as well.

Of less interest but still worth having is S. Namjoshi's "Letters to John Buchan, 1934–1935" (*Paideuma* 8:461–83), which reprints seven letters together with Buchan's replies. More movingly, "The Poet Speaks" (*Paideuma* 8:243–47) offers the first English translation of Grazia Livi's 1963 *Epoca* interview in which an aged and remorseful Pound confesses to having "come too late to a condition of doubt." Natalie Harris' "New Pound Holdings at the Lilly Library" (*Paideuma* 8:141–46) announces the acquisition of letters pertaining to literary life in the '20s and to Pound's general preoccupations during the '50s.

Accounts of meetings with Pound threaten to turn into a minor industry whose products range from moderate utility to outright trivia. The best of the five reports in *Paideuma* this year is David Anderson's translation of "Rapallo, 1941" (8:431–42) by Romano Bilenchi, an Italian writer who met Pound almost daily for a month during the winter of 1941–42. Bilenchi is particularly good on Pound's isolation from the true nature of Italian fascism and on his "absurd" overestimate of Italian support for the war. At the other end of the scale B. L. Reid's "Four Winds" (*SR* 87:273–88) pointlessly records a 1964 interview during which Pound said only one word ("certainly").

Three other articles offer more biographical help. W. B. Clark's "'Ez Sez': Pound's 'Pithy Promulgations'" (*AR* 37:420–27) describes the circumstances of Pound's 17 sporadic columns for the Santa Fe *New Mexican* in the role of a folksy philosopher. Tim Redman's "The Repatriation of Pound, 1939–1942: A View from the Archives" (*Paideuma* 8:447–57) marshals good work on the records in the Beinecke Library and in the National Archives to establish the sequence of Pound's attempts to leave Italy and eventual decision to remain, but would be better without its assertions of Pound's purity then and later. Finally, Francis J. Bosha chronicles the gradual disappearance of support for Pound's release from St. Elizabeths within the Writers' Group of the People-to-People Program, in "Faulkner, Pound, and the P. P. P." (*Paideuma* 8:249–56).

b. **General Studies.** Michael Alexander describes his *The Poetic Achievement of Ezra Pound* (Calif.) as a chronological "introductory critical survey" aimed at the "uninitiated British reader." Replete with the ritualistic anti-academic gestures that infest this style of British academic writing, the book suffers in its early chapters from disproportion in design. Pound's translation of "The Seafarer" cannot justly claim 14 pages in a study which allots only six pages to *Mauberley,* four sentences to "The Return," and barely mentions Imagism. Simplistic views of 19th-century poetry ("After Shelley's directness of lyrical and emotional expression, Victorian poets had tried wearing their hearts off their sleeves") further weaken the section on lyrics by obscuring Pound's complex reaction to 19th-century traditions. The discussion of *The Cantos* is much better and may be recommended to both undergraduate and graduate students. There Alexander manages to combine an outline of the poem's main concerns and strategies with perceptive analysis of representative sections. He is especially good on the radical change that comes upon the work with *The Pisan Cantos:* "The fragmentariness and allusiveness and the simultaneous adoption of a subjective mode are inextricably associated, so that everything—even the hard history— in the hundreds of pages that remain, appears not as epic data but primarily as personal memory, perception, reflection, and reading—as contingent phenomena of the shocked and distractable mind of Ezra Pound." Alexander's gifts for formulation and for frankness will profit even the seasoned scholar.

The equally introductory *Ezra Pound* by James Knapp (Twayne) displays the obverse virtues to *The Poetic Achievement.* Detached and judicious where Alexander is often personal and polemical, Knapp provides a competent though uninspired account of Pound's career. Especially with the early work, Knapp weaves the prose and poetry together in a way that new readers will find helpful. He particularly illuminates Pound's progress from late Victorianism to modernism in terms of developing style and technique, while usefully recalling that Pound's favorite images and subjects recur throughout his various poetic periods. Knapp succeeds less well with *The Cantos,* where Alexander excelled. The decision to rely more on subject rhyme than on chronological progression might suit an advanced study but will likely confuse the neophyte audience at which this book aims. Knapp takes the poem very much on Pound's terms, in contrast to the sympathetic yet critical attitude which enlivens Alexander's remarks. The inadequate references to Pound's political involvement suffer particularly as a result. One can thus refer students to Knapp for the early poems and to Alexander for *The Cantos*, perhaps with a plug for Alexander's livelier style.

Peter Brooker's *A Student's Guide to the Selected Poems of Ezra Pound* (Faber) loses some of its value for American readers due to the lack of coordination between British and American editions of Pound's texts. The book itself offers glosses and notes in the manner of K. K. Ruthven's *A Guide to Ezra Pound's Personae* (1969), to which it is indebted. Because the two books overlap to a great extent, there is not enough new here to justify a second effort. And because it is keyed to the Faber rather than the New Directions *Selected Poems*, *A Student's Guide* does not annotate all the shorter poems in the American edition, still less of course those in the collected *Personae*. But Booker does treat all the selections from *The Cantos* in the American text, which prints four fewer than the British one. For that reason American teachers may well want to include *A Student's Guide* on reserve lists as a supplement to Ruthven.

A different sort of international enterprise, *Italian Images of Ezra Pound*, ed. and trans. Angela Jung and Guido Palandri (Taiwan: Mei Ya Publications), presents English versions of 12 essays on Pound previously published in Italian. Although some of the older pieces now seem dated, the volume does make available in one place and in English a range of essays by distinguished Italian contributors, of whom Mario Praz, Glauco Cambon, and Eugenio Montale are the best known in America.

New general articles this year cluster in the rival camps of political involvement and poetic technique. The best of the political articles, Robert A. Corrigan's "Literature and Politics: The Case of Ezra Pound Reconsidered," in *American Character*, pp. 81–98, may prove controversial as well. Drawing heavily on unpublished documents, Corrigan assigns much of the responsibility for Pound's long incarceration at St. Elizabeths to the "well-meaning, if misdirected efforts in his behalf" of his own family and friends. Along with charting personal and legal complications, he casts an interesting light on some of the more dubious attempts to refurbish Pound's reputation. Michael André Bernstein makes some worthwhile if at times fashionably obscure speculations on the wreck of fascism as irretrievably splitting the twin historical and mythic "codes" of *The Cantos* in "Mythos and Logos in Ezra Pound: The Splitting of the Realms" (*Paideuma* 8:543–48). Natalie Harris' "Aesthetics and/or Politics: Ezra Pound's Late Critical Prose" (*CentR* 23:1–19) surveys Pound's disastrous displacement of aesthetic values onto politics in *Jefferson and/or Mussolini, Guide to Kulchur*, and other prose of the 1930s. More superficially, W. G. Regier's "Ezra Pound, Adam Smith, Karl Marx" (*MinnR* 12:72–76) cites some of Pound's allusions before concluding with the pious regret that Pound did not read the two economists (nor Lenin) more thoroughly.

Turning not to politics but rather to poetic craft, two adjacent articles in *Paideuma* focus on Pound's versification. James A. Powell locates "The Light of Vers Libre" (8:3–34) in Pound's "adaptation of Greek prosodic techniques and rhythmic forms"; some of his analyses of passages from *The Cantos* are remarkable. In her briefer "Pound and the Modern Melic Tradition: Towards a Demystification of 'Absolute Rhythm'" (8:35–47) Sally M. Gall argues rather that "much of Pound's verse is metrical in the musical sense" and offers musical notation for six passages. Interested readers may compare her treatment of "The Return," "Dance Figure," and part of Canto 76 with Powell's remarks on the same texts. Approaching the sound of the poetry from a different direction, Max Nänny suggests in "The Oral Roots of Ezra Pound's Methods of Quotation and Abbreviation" (*Paideuma* 8:381–87) that Pound's practice parallels that of the ancient rabbis as discussed in Birger Gerhardsson's *Memory and Manuscript* (1961). The value of Jacob Korg's remarks on Pound in *Language in Modern Literature* (Barnes and Noble) lies in relating Pound to a broad modernist context rather than in probing him more deeply. Finally, Kevin Oderman's wandering "The Servants of Amor in Pound's Early Poems" (*Paideuma* 8:389–403) begins its discussion of the relation between sexual and visionary experience with an interesting gloss on Pound's allusion to Simon Magus and Helen of Tyre in the essay "Psychology and Troubadours." Researchers wanting comprehensive citations combined with brief descriptive notes on the sometimes bewildering array of past literature on Pound may find some guidance in *Paideuma*'s sporadic publication of annotated checklists. This year Hollis Sickles covers the years 1945–51 (8:97–140), Andrew Crosland 1961–65, part 1 (8:521–38), and George Rooks 1976 (8:303–16).

c. **Relation to Other Writers.** Most studies this year deal with Pound's relation either to his own immediate circle or to precursors in foreign languages. The most important work, Timothy Materer's *Vortex: Pound, Eliot, and Lewis* (Cornell), studies the "aesthetic, social, and philosophical principles [that] run through decades of collaboration and controversy to form the pattern Pound called the Vortex." Although not wholly convincing in its attack on the conventional view that the Vortex dissolved after 1919, Materer's argument does establish many fine congruities in the careers and concerns of the three writers. For students of Pound, the long chapter on Gaudier-Brzeska has most value, both in its lucid exposition of the sculptor's artistic development and in its presentation of the famous friendship through the hostile viewpoint of Sophie Brzeska's unpublished diary. Materer makes useful remarks on Pound's allegiance to nature, abhorrence of abstraction, and political predicaments before concluding with a chapter espousing the increasingly influential view that Pound, like Eliot, was "not a true anti-romantic." The book makes good use of some unpublished letters of Pound but occasionally slips up with published sources, for example in repeatedly identifying the author of *The Political Identities of Ezra Pound and T. S. Eliot* as Richard rather than William Chace. Readers bothered by Materer's neglect of Pound's impact on *The Waste Land* will find a sometimes brilliant but not always believable account of Pound pressing a classical rhetorical structure of five parts upon Eliot's initial preference for a Christian one of four exegetical senses in Marshall McLuhan's "Pound, Eliot, and the Rhetoric of *The Waste Land*" (*NLH* 10:557–80). Natan Zack's "Imagism and Vorticism" in *Modernism 1890–1930*, ed. Malcolm Bradbury and James McFarlane (Humanities Press), pp. 228–42, is a guidebook performance which specialists can skip.

Three studies revert to Dante and his circle. The first part of Stephen Paul Ellis' "Dante in Pound's Early Career" (*Paideuma* 8:549–61) traces the use of *De Vulgari Eloquentia* in *The Spirit of Romance* to minimize Virgil and to increase the importance of Dante's immediate predecessors; in reacting against the 19th-century emphasis on biography, Pound turned Dante into a pure craftsman. The weaker remainder of the essay downplays the importance of Cavalcanti and Dante to the development of Imagism. Gabrielle Barfoot's naive "The Theme of Usury in Dante and Pound" (*RLMC* 30[1977]:

254–83) laboriously rehearses parallel passages before reaching the dubious conclusion that usury provides the "moral core" for some of Pound's "finest and most appealing poetry." David Anderson's "The Techniques of Critical Translation: Ezra Pound's Guido Cavalcanti, 1912" (*Paideuma* 8:215–26) summarizes Pound's aims in translation well but is valuable chiefly for its quotations from manuscripts of Pound's earlier versions of many passages. Also concerned with Pound as translator, Nobuko Tsukui Keith's "*Aoi no Ue* and *Kinuta*: An Examination of Ezra Pound's Translations" (*Paideuma* 8:199–214) demonstrates differences between Pound's versions and the original Noh dramas, including a serious misunderstanding of the subject matter of *Aoi no Ue*. The other articles on Pound's interest in Oriental culture are disappointing, except for some items on *The Cantos* mentioned below.

The best of the numerous shorter notes, Ian F. A. Bell's "Pound, Emerson, and 'Subject Rhyme'" (*Paideuma* 8:237–39) posits Emerson's notion of "grand rhymes or returns in Nature" in the essay on Swedenborg from *Representative Men* as a source for Pound's concept and relates it to Pound's habit of seeking scientific analogies. Eva Hesse's "Mythopoiós" (*Paideuma* 8:293–95) provides the full context in Frobenius for the delightful anecdote in *A Visiting Card* about discovery of a bronze car with effigies of Dis and Persephone as ratifying a local folk tradition.

d. **Studies of Specific Works.**   Aside from E. A. B. Jenner's querying of the view of *Mauberley* recently taken by Jo Brantley Berryman and Donald Davie ("'Medallion': Some Questions," in *Paideuma* 8:151–57), attention focused again on *The Cantos*. Two books offer important insights of different kinds. Barbara Eastman's *Ezra Pound's Cantos: The Story of the Text, 1948–1975* (NPF) details the complicated bibliographic history of the poem in its postwar incarnations. Eastman understandably excludes from her already massive collation manuscript sources and prior printings of the poem in individual volumes and periodicals, though the omission of Mary de Rachewiltz's 1961 edition of Cantos 1–30 with its numerous emendations sanctioned by Pound himself is a loss. She does patiently track the divergences of the two chief collected texts—one published by Faber in England and the other by New Directions in America—both from each other and from their own successive printings and editions.

Surprisingly, textual problems persist even into the present. The now standard 1975 New Directions text, for example, eliminates the repetition of "A day when the historians left blanks in their writings,/ But that time seems to be passing" in the popular Canto 13, despite Pound's desire to retain the doubling, which itself originated in a printer's error. And not only those readers of Canto 97 who know a bawbee from a boodle (they are terms in old coinage) will worry over the reliability of a text that now substitutes the line "2 doits to a boodle, 13⅓ bawbees: 160 doits" for Pound's less accurate but more fluent "2 doigts to a boodle, one bawbee: one sixty doigts." Numerous questionable changes by printers, editors, and scholars still corrupt the text, sometimes against Pound's own instructions; in other places different readings sanctioned at different times exist. Eastman convincingly contends for a *Variorum Cantos* giving alternate possible readings. In the meantime, anyone writing on Pound's magnum opus had better consult the opening essays (including Hugh Kenner's capable introduction) and 100-page list of cruxes which this book provides.

Leon Surette's valuable but disjointed *A Light from Eleusis: A Study of Ezra Pound's Cantos* (Oxford) is really two books, as illustrated by two of its many statements contradictory in thrust if not in precise intellectual content. On the one hand, Surette properly and refreshingly calls for recognition that "the scholarly challenge presented by the poem [does] not lie in the search for some key which would render the cryptic, opaque, and heterogeneous text at once lucid and coherent, but rather in discovering why the poem is so intractable." That insight generates Surette's perceptive and helpful "biography of the poem" chronicling its diverse stages through its shifting relation to events in Pound's own life. On the other hand, Surette simultaneously believes that "the *Cantos* do contain within themselves a coherent and consistent metaphorical structure which thus far has gone almost entirely unrecognized." This key to all the poem's mythologies turns out to be Pound's revisionist rendering of the Odysseus myth in terms of the Eleusinian mysteries. In twisting it Surette unlocks some fascinating cabinets, though perhaps not as much of the entire structure as he contends. The strength of his study lies in its scholarly subjection of a beloved poem to a frank critical scrutiny, distinguishing successes from failures in a fashion standard for most poets but too often lacking in Pound studies. He particularly illuminates the poem's problematic relation to its sources. In short, not all the considerable light in Surette's book comes from Eleusis.

Three general articles by leading Poundians appeared this year. Guy Davenport's intricate "The House that Jack Built" (*Salmagundi* 43:140–55) begins with parallels between *The Cantos* and Ruskin's *Fors Clavigera* and then proceeds through a maze of literary and cultural correspondences to link the poem's "daedalian" art with that of Joyce and Zukofsky as characteristically modern. In seeking to become "daedalian" itself, the article ends up as yet another house that Jack built. Hugh Witemeyer takes Pound's recurrent phrase "ply over ply" to indicate the haiku and Imagist method of juxtaposition, in "Pound and the *Cantos* 'Ply over Ply' " (*Paideuma* 8:229–35). More briefly, John Espey's "Sidelights from the Italian and German *Cantos*" (*Paideuma* 8:297–99) suggests the usefulness of Mary de Rachewiltz's 1961 English/Italian edition of the first 30 cantos and Eva Hesse's 1964 English/German one for clarifying obscure passages, though Hesse's text needs more caution than Espey allows.

Fourteen items discussed individual cantos this year. I shall treat here only the three with broader implications. The others, all in *Paideuma*, concern Cantos 7, 42, 43, 56, 74 (four items), 97, and 110 (two items). (One may add in parentheses that as information accumulates over the years, Kay Davis' "An Index to Canto References in *Paideuma*," *Paideuma* 8:317–24, has some point.) "Pound's 'Ideogrammatic Method' as Illustrated in Canto XCIX" (*AL* 51:205–37) by Ben D. Kimpel and T. C. Duncan Eaves first summarizes Pound's ideogrammic method and then elaborately traces its workings in the adaptation of *The Sacred Edict* for Canto 99. The authors give a line-by-line gloss, often on the relation between Chinese characters and their English renderings, which sometimes loses the forest in the trees. At the other extreme, another pair of authors, P. H. Smith and A. E. Durant, offer pretentious theoretical assertions with little support in "Pound's Metonymy: Revisiting Canto 47" (*Paideuma* 8:327–33).

The most important article of the year is Barbara Eastman's "The Gap in *The Cantos*: 72 and 73" (*Paideuma* 8:415–27). Eastman circumspectly describes the two "lost cantos," which were in fact published first in the 15 January and 1 February issues of the Italian Navy newspaper *Marina Repubblicana* during 1945 and then in an obscure and virtually unknown 1973 edition (typewritten, photocopied, and paperbound) on behalf of the Estate of Ezra Pound, presumably to establish international copyright. Canto 72, entitled "Presenza," portrays Italy as an Inferno in which appear in order the Futurist Filippo Tommaso Marinetti, Pound's friend Manlio Torquato Dazzi, and the medieval figures Alberto Mussato and Ezzelino da Romano. Canto 73, entitled "Cavalcanti—Correspondenza Repub[b]licana," relates to Canadian troop movements (and an accompanying rape) in the invasion of Italy and apparently glorifies violence. Eastman states that "according to long-range plans of The Trustees of the Ezra Pound Literary Property Trust, the two Italian Cantos will make their next appearance in print in Mary de Rachewiltz's forthcoming Italian edition of *The Cantos* in which, presumably, they will be accompanied by Pound's incomplete English translation, never before published." However well-intentioned, the long and continued delay in making these two cantos readily available will likely result only in further damage to Pound's reputation by precluding responsible critical judgment. The Ezra Pound Literary Property Trust should reconsider its position, both on the lost cantos and on what one book cited in the present essay calls "the surprisingly heavy burden of permission fees for quotations from Pound's works."

ii. Eliot

The scholarship on Eliot this year is overshadowed by that on Pound, both in quantity and significance. Eliot's own critical pronouncements continue to shape the ways he is read and studied; very little criticism of Eliot's work reflects the theoretical turmoil of the last 15 years. It is clearly time for a reassessment of Eliot's career in terms other than his own.

a. **Texts and Biography.** Only two essayists ventured into the once forbidden area of biography, and both of them drew upon materials reviewed earlier in *ALS*. In "T. S. Eliot: Biography, Poetry and Anglo-Catholicism" (*ArQ* 35:249–69) William E. Meyer, Jr., extends the thesis advanced by James E. Miller, Jr., in *T. S. Eliot's Personal Waste Land* (see *ALS 1977*, p. 131) to "Ash Wednesday" and *Four Quartets*. Meyer asserts that in these two poems Eliot "moves progressively into history, but a history that is colored as much by his own life as it is by the events of his nation and generation or by the 'salvation history' of his Church," and he concludes by noting that "to some extent Eliot's

famous 'impersonal theory of poetry' and all that follows from it
may be a kind of defensive maneuver for the sake of screening his
own intensely personal poetry from the biographical or psychological
intrusions of insensitive critics." A less speculative approach to biography is taken by B. L. Reid in "Four Winds" (SR 87:273–88). Following the example of Donald Hall (Remembering Poets, reviewed
in ALS 1978, p. 120), Reid has recorded his own encounters with
Dylan Thomas, Robert Frost, Ezra Pound, and T. S. Eliot. But Reid's
impressions, unlike Hall's, add little to our sense of Eliot as man
or poet.

b. **General Studies.**   In *Thomas Stearns Eliot: Poet* (Cambridge),
A. D. Moody has written the best general study of Eliot this year as well
as the most comprehensive. Moody takes his method from Eliot's early
assertion that the critic "must simply elucidate: the reader will form
the correct judgment for himself." Although limited by this approach,
Moody's intelligent and gracefully written study forms a valuable
addition to Eliot scholarship. Moody illuminates "the author within
his poems," from the experimentation of the early poetry to the creation of a "poetic self" in "The Hollow Men" and "Ash Wednesday."
This "poetic self" becomes fully formed in *Four Quartets* where,
Moody suggests, the poet becomes "the protagonist of an ideal
English and European Culture." Through his exemplary readings of
individual works Moody greatly clarifies the contours of Eliot's
oeuvre. In addition, Moody reproduces the previously unpublished
syllabus of Eliot's "Course of Six Lectures on Modern French Literature" and includes three valuable appendixes, in which he considers
the texts of the poems, the drafts of *The Waste Land*, and "The Christian philosopher and politics."

Joyce Meeks Jones's booklet, *Jungian Psychology in Literary Analysis: A Demonstration Using T. S. Eliot's Poetry* (Univ. Press), is a
superficial treatment of a complex topic. Students will find the discussion of Jung's theories far too brief to be of use in applied literary
analysis. Jones's application of Jung's theories to Eliot's poetry is
reductive and misleading; moreover, Jones reveals an insufficient
knowledge of Eliot scholarship. Another simplification of Eliot's
work occurs in "Eliot's Quest for Man's Significance" (MQ 20:177–
86), where Sister Madeleine Kisner restates critical commonplaces
in a survey of Eliot's poetry from a Christian standpoint.

In *The Universal Drum* Audrey T. Rodgers examines the dance as image and symbol in the poetry of Eliot, Crane, Roethke, and Williams. Rodgers also discusses their interest in dance as an art form, and notes parallel developments between modern dance and modern poetry. She attributes Eliot's fascination with dance to his interests in music and primitive rites and rituals. On the basis of her analysis of Eliot's poetry she concludes that "the dance in Eliot's poetry turns on the duality of its fundamental references: as apotheosis and dance of death."

c. **Relation to Other Writers.** For the most part studies this year consider Eliot's relationships with his contemporaries and with well-acknowledged precursors. The most ambitious study is Timothy Materer's *Vortex: Pound, Eliot and Lewis* (Cornell) (see section *i.c.*), an examination of the literary and personal relationships of these three writers within a carefully documented cultural and historical context. Students of Eliot will find the chapter entitled "Abstract Entities" to be of great interest, especially for its succinct presentation of Eliot's relationship to F. H. Bradley's work. Materer contends that "Eliot's reading of Bradley made him critical of any philosophical pretentions to tell the facts of human existence, including even Bradley's very mild pretensions," and he compares Eliot's "skepticism concerning the scientific version of 'reality' " to the views Wyndham Lewis espouses in *Time and Western Man*. Materer's excellent book would have been strengthened, however, by a discussion of the close practical collaboration between Eliot and Pound, particularly in the period from 1918 to 1922 as revealed in reviews and annotations of each other's works.

Two other studies consider Eliot's indebtedness to Bradley. In *T. S. Eliot: The Critic as Philosopher* (Purdue) Lewis Freed argues at great length that "Eliot's critical prose is largely unintelligible apart from his philosophy" and then explicates Eliot's philosophy in terms of the work of Bradley. Although Eliot was surely indebted to Bradley, Freed exaggerates and simplifies the extent of this influence. Thus, "Eliot reads Flaubert," Freed remarks, "as he reads other writers, in the light of his Bradleyan philosophy." Freed weakens his argument by overstating his thesis and by focusing exclusively on Eliot's prose. Bradley's insights can also be used to illuminate the poetry, as Jewel Spears Brooker demonstrates in "The Structure of Eliot's 'Gerontion': An Interpretation Based on Bradley's Doctrine of the Systematic Nature of Truth" (*ELH* 46:314–40). Brooker bases her structural interpretation upon Bradley's notions of the "self transcendence of parts, the necessary and internal relations among objects, and the systematic nature of the whole." Her analysis of the fragmentary structure of "Gerontion" could easily be extended to other poems by Eliot. However, her analyses of specific images (such as her describing the "she" [1.38] as "a Brobdingnagian harlot bent on deceiving, seducing, and destroying her partners") are considerably less convincing.

The focus of Paul G. Stanwood's study, "Time and Liturgy in Donne, Crashaw, and T. S. Eliot" (*Mosaic* 2:95–105) is primarily the poetry of Donne and Crashaw. Stanwood assigns an aesthetic function to liturgy in order better to understand the ways in which "the form, the structure, and the rhetoric" of their poetry "presupposes ritual, ceremony, and liturgical action." For Stanwood the aesthetic function of liturgy is to "express the ordered movements of time in space," and he finds this tendency in Eliot as well. On this basis Stanwood makes substantive (but hardly surprising) connections between these poets. Aileen Shafer also considers Eliot's relationship to Donne in "Eliot Re-Donne: The Prufrockian Spheres" (*YER* 5,ii[1978]:39–43), but the echoes of "A Valediction: Forbidding Mourning" which she hears in "Prufrock" are too faint for most readers. In "Rilke, Eliot and Bonnefoy as Readers of Baudelaire" (*WLT* 53:456–61) John E. Jackson suggests that the "novelty of Baudelaire" for all three readers lies in his vision of death, which "however interior to the poet's eye . . . extends at the same time to the whole scene on which the Baudelairean ego prefers to situate its experience," an assertion which Jackson supports with examples from *The Waste Land*. A less convincing source for Eliot's work is cited by Jean MacIntyre in "A Source for the Rose-Fires in Eliot's *Four Quartets*" (*YER* 5,ii [1978]:36–38). MacIntyre traces these images to two of George MacDonald's fantasies for children, *The Princess and the Goblin* and *The Princess and Curdie*. There are certainly similarities here, but other sources appear far more likely.

Three very different studies consider the contributions of Pound and Aiken to *The Waste Land*. In "Pound, Eliot, and the Rhetoric of *The Waste Land*" (*NLH* 20:557–80) (see *i.c.*) Marshall McLuhan suggests that the first draft of *The Waste Land* anticipates "the four

divisions of *Four Quartets* in respect to the four seasons, four elements and four anagogical levels of exegesis." In revising the poem
Pound was guided by a "five division pattern of classical oratory."
McLuhan's incidental comments on the poetic strategies of both poets
are more illuminating than his thesis. A very different view of Pound's
relationship to *The Waste Land* is advanced by Lewis Turco in *"The
Waste Land* Reconsidered" (*SR* 87:289–95). After defining "musical
syntax" and "symphonic structure" as poetic terms Turco argues that
"it was Pound who recognized the indwelling musical structure of
Eliot's composition," a structure which he clarified and strengthened
through his editing. "Pound's editing was a singular act of genius.
Eliot's second act of composition was equally compelling." Fred D.
Crawford acknowledges "Conrad Aiken's Cancelled Debt to T. S.
Eliot" (*JML* 7:416–32) by citing numerous passages in Aiken's early
verse which *The Waste Land* seems to evoke. Crawford clearly demonstrates that "many of Eliot's more memorable scenes, images, and
lines owe much to Aiken," to which he adds, "the difference in Aiken's
expression and Eliot's expression of the same ideas demonstrates the
superior poetic genius of the latter."

Douglas Fowler examines Nabokov's extreme dislike of Eliot in
"Eliot, Nabokov, and the First Questions" (*YER* 5,ii[1978]:44–61).
Fowler attributes Nabokov's feelings to his perception of Eliot's anti-
semitism, although this assertion remains conjectural. Fowler then
contrasts the views of each artist on the nature of aesthetic experience.
In spite of their radically different positions, each created what Fowler terms "melodramatic art," the emotional content of which is
"negative, sadistic, masochistic, and vehemently antisocial." While
this is true of a small part of Eliot's work, it can hardly be said of his
later poetry.

d. **Studies of Specific Works.**   Apart from the works of Moody and
Freed, little attention was paid this year to Eliot's criticism or
drama. The most interesting work was devoted to drafts of poems
and suppressed poems.

In "Word Heard: Prufrock Asks his Question" (*YER* 5,ii[1978]:
33–35) J. Peter Dyson dares to ask of "the overwhelming question,"
"What is it?" He finds his answer in the allusion to Hamlet: "Which
should be read; No! I am not Prince Hamlet, nor was meant to be or
not to be, *that* is the question" (Dyson's italics). Carol Avins com-

pares "coincidences of imagery, tone and persona" in "Prufrock" and Oleša's short novel, *Envy*, in "Eliot and Oleša: Versions of the Anti-Hero" (*CRCL* 6:64–74) in order to demonstrate the "unconscious community" which exists "between the true artists of any time."

Vicki Mahaffey examines two interesting early poems in " 'The Death of Saint Narcissus' and 'Ode': Two Suppressed Poems by T. S. Eliot" (*AL* 50:604–12). After presenting very persuasive readings of these poems, Mahaffey suggests they "emphasize a more confessional aspect of Eliot's early poetic personality" and that his suppression of these two poems "shows that Eliot was attempting to emphasize in his collected poetry the rational aesthetic attitude that he so appreciated in Jonson, Gautier and Laforgue." Nancy R. Comley compares "The Death of St. Narcissus" with the revised lines from this poem in *The Waste Land* ("From Narcissus to Tiresias: T. S. Eliot's Use of Metamorphosis" [*MLR* 74:281–86]). Comley argues that "metamorphosis, or transformations of the self, are at the heart of T. S. Eliot's early poetry," and she suggests that the "hermaphroditism of Narcissus is absorbed into the more powerful figure of Tiresias."

The manuscript of *The Waste Land* continues to be the focus of critical attention. In "*The Waste Land* Manuscript: Picking up the Pieces—in Order" (*FMLS* 3:237–48) Peter Barry contributes a careful analysis of the composition of the sections of the manuscript. Barry suggests that the manuscript was composed in the following sequence: part 1 (Sheet [5]), London, 20 April to 9 May 1921; the remainder of part 1 and part 2, London, 12–18 November 1921; part 3, London, September-October 1921; parts 4 and 5, written in Lausanne, November-December 1921, and typed in Paris, January 1922.

Sister M. Christopher Pecheux offers an extended analysis of the lines deleted from the original "Death by Water" section of the manuscript of *The Waste Land* ("In Defense of 'Death by Water' " [*ConL* 20:339–53]). Pecheux observes that the deleted lines develop the "theme of redemption": "We do not have to wait for the voice of the thunder, so near to the end of the poem, to hear a note of hope." Although Pecheux overvalues the poetic strengths of these lines, she does show their thematic relationships with other sections of the poem and with the concluding lines of "Death by Water."

Vincent Daly has located a brief retelling of the Thunder Fable in English which would have been as available to Eliot as the German edition he cites in the notes to *The Waste Land* ("The Immediate

Source of The Thunder Fable: *The Waste Land* 396–423" [*YER* 5,ii (1978):31–32]). The source is a version which appeared in the opening paragraph of an essay by Eliot's Sanscrit Professor, Charles Lanman, published while Eliot was Lanman's student. Another essay which clarifies our reading of both *The Waste Land* and the notes which accompany it is Robert Currie's "Eliot and the Tarot" (*ELH* 46:722–33). Currie demonstrates that Eliot's knowledge of the Tarot exceeded his modest disclaimer. Eliot knew Arthur Edward Waite's book, *The Pictorial Key to the Tarot,* and also Waite's "poetic, metaphysical and mystical, Christian revision of the tarot cards" designed by Pamela Coleman Smith. Currie identifies four of the cards used by Eliot and suggests identifications for three others.

William V. Spanos attempts a radically new reading of *The Waste Land* in "Repetition in *The Waste Land*: A Phenomenological Destruction" (*Boundary* 7:225–85). Spanos' admirable if awkwardly stated goal is to "retrieve the body of great poetry that Eliot has left us heirs to from the oblivion to which the obsessively coersive panoptical perspective of Modernist hermeneutics has relegated it." In a display of overwrought earnestness, Spanos oscillates between simplification and obfuscation. The "'positive possibilities' concerning the being of the text" which Spanos hopes to uncover are unfortunately rendered less accessible by his analysis.

Perhaps the best single essay on Eliot this year is Eleanor Cook's "T. S. Eliot and the Carthaginian Peace" (*ELH* 46:341–55). Cook concentrates on "Eliot's vision of imperial apocalypse in *The Waste Land,* working from the hypothesis that a vision of Rome and the Roman Empire lies behind Eliot's vision of London and the British Empire." Cook identifies three maps within the poem, one of a city (London), one of an Empire (Roman), and one of a world (Dante's map of the inhabited world). She forcefully articulates the parallels between postwar London and this intricate web of allusions.

The complex modulations of voice in *Four Quartets* are identified and characterized by Andrew Kennedy in "The Speaking 'I' in *Four Quartets* (*ES* 60:166–75). By examining the different uses of this voice, Kennedy notes "the inner connection, in the poetry, between Eliot's early idea of impersonality and his later admiration for the expression of 'personality.'" Thus, Kennedy observes "a corresponding shift from *persona* towards 'confessional' poetry and from the dramatic/histrionic to the actual/empirical self." Recent criticism has revealed a greater personal element in the early poetry, and hence there is more continuity here than Kennedy recognizes. Still, Kennedy's distinctions provide us with a useful way of distinguishing the range of voices in the poem.

In *Time and Poetry in Eliot's "Four Quartets"* (Humanities Press) Rajendra Verma has written a guide to Eliot's poem which focuses more specifically on "Time Concepts and Philosophical Poetry" (the title of chapter 1). Verma's combination of summary and paraphrase makes little use of the considerable body of writings on this subject. Moreover, his observations are extremely impressionistic. For example, in discussing the fourth part of "Burnt Norton," Verma comments: "The rhythm is light and soft, evoking the sound pattern of a setting sun and the anguished query of the heart." Verma's best pages are on Eliot's reading of the *Bhagavad Gita* and his indebtedness to it in "The Dry Salvages." But this material would have been more effectively presented in an article.

University of Michigan

9. Faulkner

Panthea Reid Broughton

The past four years have been basically good ones for Faulkner studies. Fewer gross errors of logic, fact, and grammar mar the writings on Faulkner. Responsible bibliographical work has increased the amount of Faulkner materials available and enhanced our understandings of them. Biographical knowledge now locates our vision of the man and his work on solid ground. Concordances of the novels open entire new vistas for exploration. Subjects such as the allusions in and the forms of Faulkner's writings have received too-long-withheld attention. Excellent critical studies of works previously unknown, ignored, or dismissed as minor have appeared. The year 1979, for example, saw more attention paid to the stories than in any of the past several years.

These developments and others like them have made 1976–79 an especially exciting time to write the *ALS* Faulkner chapter. But if these years have seen much solid work, they also have seen much that is merely vapid and/or redundant. Given the emphasis upon publication in our profession, it is scandalous that so many publishing decisions are made so irresponsibly. If decisions were based upon information knowledgeable scholars and reviews such as this one provide, then less writing that "might just as well not have been" would get published.

i. Bibliography, Editions, and Manuscripts

The major bibliographical event of 1979 is the publication of Joseph Blotner's *Uncollected Stories of William Faulkner* (Random House). This volume makes accessible to scholars a number of stories previously available only in manuscript collections, obscure back issues, or limited editions so rare they are collectors' items. Also it includes some 20 stories (19 of them previously published) which were revised as parts of books.

The book itself is an enormous boon to the Faulknerian. Available at last are the famous "Afternoon of a Cow" and "Al Jackson" stories. Here is "A Portrait of Elmer"—the story Faulkner salvaged from his abortive 1925 novel *Elmer* but was never able to print. Here we find both "The Big Shot" and its later version "Dull Tale"; comparing them and the novels of the 1930s, we learn a great deal about Faulkner's use and reuse of motifs and situations. Here we can read "Evangeline," the first version of the Henry Sutpen/Charles Bon story. Here we find what were probably Faulkner's first short stories, "Adolescence" and "Moonlight." For the Faulknerian, these stories offer their own fascinating tale of the development of Faulkner's art. And the collection is followed by useful notes by Blotner which review the history of each story and suggest the ways Faulkner transformed these fledgling fictions in his later work.

Despite its value, however, this volume is often confusing. We might expect as much from a collection entitled *Uncollected Stories* which lists "Uncollected Stories" as one of its three subdivisions. There are problems with each of these divisions. The first—"Stories Revised for Later Books"—includes as subsections *The Unvanquished; The Hamlet; Go Down, Moses; Big Woods;* and *The Mansion*. But it does not include (or explain the omission of) "The Fire on the Hearth" (*Go Down, Moses*), "Notes on a Horsethief" (*A Fable*), "A Name for the City" (*Requiem for a Nun*), or "By the People" (*The Mansion*). Furthermore, these categories overlap, for a number of the stories in the other two subsections were also revised for inclusion in later books.

Blotner's statement about the other collections whose contents have not been reprinted is also confusing. Neither "The Hill" from *Early Prose and Poetry* nor any of the stories from *New Orleans Sketches* are included, but those volumes are not listed as excluded collections. Blotner explains that he has omitted "incomplete stories such as 'Love' and 'And Now What's To Do.'" Thus we have to assume that the unpublished stories "Christmas Tree" and "The Devil Beats His Wife," which Blotner refers to in the notes, were excluded because they fell into the category "incomplete stories." Such uncertainties could have been avoided simply by providing a detailed bibliographical note. Such a note could also have dealt with the nine apparently lost stories James B. Meriwether listed in *Proof I* (see *ALS 1971*, 105). Five of them have been found or identified since then and are printed in this volume. Presumably the other four remain lost, but information would have been helpful.

Apparently Random House wanted to make this volume a successful trade book. Thus the first category "Stories Revised for Later Books" includes those stories with mass appeal, as if to balance or disguise the fairly esoteric appeal of the rest of the collection. Perhaps in the gap between being a trade book and a scholarly edition certain bibliographical clarifications were lost. Nevertheless *Uncollected Stories of William Faulkner* is an enormously valuable publication, essential reading for any Faulknerian.

The special Faulkner edition of *MissQ*, ed. James B. Meriwether, includes several previously unpublished Faulkner pieces. "Pierrot and the Marble Faun: Another Fragment," ed. Judith L. Sensibar (32:473–76), is a poetic fragment Faulkner wrote on the blank end pages of his copy of Ralph Hodgson's poems. Sensibar offers fascinating speculations about Faulkner's inscriptions in that book and dates the poem from the spring or early summer of 1918. The poem opposes the sexual passion of the Pierrot figure to the resignation of the "Mute and impotent" faun. In *"Light in August*: A Manuscript Fragment"* (32:477–80) ed. Deborah Thompson presents some intriguing data. The fragment, a missing page 12 which corresponds roughly to pp. 332–34 of the first edition, tells us first of all how radical was Faulkner's process of revising and restructuring his discontinuous narratives. As editor of "An Unpublished Episode from 'A Mountain Victory'" (32:481–83) Meriwether explains the complicated textual history of this story. This episode has no relation to the Doctor Martino version of the tale, but is an episode Faulkner deleted, apparently at the request of the *Saturday Evening Post*, from the first printed version of the story. The fourth Faulkner text published in the 1979 *Miss Q* is the story "Don Giovanni," ed. Meriwether. (It also appeared in 1979 in the *Uncollected Stories*.) Written in 1925, the story relates a futile seduction attempt and shows Faulkner still reworking the basic subject of "Moonlight." George F. Hayhoe's "Faulkner in Hollywood: A Checklist of His Filmscripts at the University of Virginia: A Correction and Additions" (32: 467–72) follows the format of Hayhoe's original checklist (*ALS 1978*, p. 128) and offers a good example of responsible updating of bibliographical tools.

Carl Petersen's *On the Track of the Dixie Limited* (La Grange,

Ill.: The Colophon Book Shop) offers concise, authoritative, and at times entertaining annotations for its entries. Probably the most interesting items Petersen mentions are unpublished letters. His paraphrase of a 1919 letter, for example, suggests something of the double message Faulkner apparently was getting from his parents: both possessiveness and disapproval. Petersen makes a welcome plea for a new edition of Faulkner's letters: "It would ultimately be useful to have a freshly edited, usefully annotated, probably multi-volume edition published by one of the university presses having a special interest in Faulkner. If the compilation were done with a scholarly approach and a sensitive awareness for the concerns of the people who have these letters, both original recipients and present owners might be induced to release (with the permission of Mrs. Summers) texts that till now have been sequestered." Probably the possibilities for such an edition are less good than Petersen thinks, but he certainly has the right idea.

A second catalogue of a private collection—Robert W. Hamblin and Louis Daniel Brodsky's *Selections from The William Faulkner Collection of Louis Daniel Brodsky: A Descriptive Catalogue* (Virginia)—is a large, handsomely produced volume. Numerous photographs, variant versions of Faulkner poems, a list of books from the Stone collection, which augments our sense of what the young Faulkner probably read, a description of (with sample entries from) the Ripley Railroad Ledger, and the publication of previously unpublished poems, all make this an important bibliographical document. Its lists of such new materials provide interesting reading, but lists and descriptions of first editions (often autographed) comprise most of the catalogue. Therefore, though larger and much more lavishly produced than Petersen's, Brodsky's catalogue is less consistently entertaining to read. We Faulknerians are deeply in debt to collectors like Petersen and Brodsky. We look forward to the time when their collections (especially little-known materials) will be more available.

One portion of Brodsky's collection—the gift of 12 poems and one essay Faulkner made to Myrtle Ramey in 1924—is available now as a separate publication. Published as *Mississippi Poems by William Faulkner* (Oxford, Miss.: Yoknapatawpha Press), the volume reproduces the original sheaf of poems and the carbon typescript of "Verse, Old and Nascent: A Pilgrimage," and includes an introduction by Joseph Blotner and an afterword by L. D. Brodsky. Blotner's discussion offers a review of Faulkner's friendship with Myrtle Ramey. It considers the significance of the "Verse, Old and Nascent" essay and gives textual histories of the poems, most of which were published in radically altered form nine years later in *A Green Bough*. This is useful information, succinctly and clearly presented (though the history of one poem—the first—is difficult to follow). Brodsky's afterword sounds a note similar to Petersen's. He speaks of the collector "as a kind of curator and disseminator whose final responsibility is to the wider audience of the author he collects, rather than serving selfish motives of acquisitiveness or self-aggrandizement." As I have said before (*ALS 1976*, p. 123), protecting neither William Faulkner's reputation nor one's ego or investment seems sufficient reason to keep unpublished Faulkner materials from the public eye. The various collectors, presses, and editors who are now bringing such materials to light deserve our thanks.

Faulkner's various wills in the Brodsky collection are the source for the parallels Robert W. Hamblin suggests in his "Lucas Beauchamp, Ned Barnett, and William Faulkner's 1940 Will" (*SB* 32: 281–83).

ii. Biography

Judith Bryant Wittenberg's *Faulkner: The Transfiguration of Biography* (Nebraska) is the first comprehensive study of the fiction to make use of Blotner's biography. In many ways it is an extremely useful book. More compact than Blotner, it offers a readable summary of Faulkner's life. More analytical, it offers some real insights into the traumas Faulkner faced. More speculative, it suggests how the fiction reflects those stresses. Wittenberg consults only one source not available to Blotner: Dean Faulkner Wells's 1975 thesis on her father, Faulkner's youngest brother. Also, though she considers the sort of manuscript revision Faulkner did on *Sanctuary*, she apparently has not studied those revisions herself. Sometimes, therefore, the book seems like a third-hand summary of second-hand information. It articulates what one might infer from Blotner; it adds little further substantiation.

Nevertheless the book offers real understandings of the conflicts that wracked Faulkner's psyche. Wittenberg is good on the relation between Faulkner's personal anxieties and his early work. She writes,

"Perhaps Faulkner, like Yeats, was somehow paradoxically more fulfilled by frustration than by satisfaction." Her treatments of *The Sound and the Fury, Sanctuary, Light in August,* and *The Wild Palms* offer real insight into the ways in which Faulkner projected his own dilemmas into his writing and transformed them. Wittenberg helps us see how Faulkner's gradual (and belated) maturation was embodied in the fiction. She sees a "sort of moral and psychological advance" made by the Faulkner of *Absalom, Absalom!* and *The Unvanquished.* An issue raised, but not really addressed, is why relative psychic health produced great fiction in the former, not in the latter work. Wittenberg suggests that because Faulkner was in the 1940s "no longer driven by his private anxieties" he experienced writer's block for the first time and his fiction declined in power. She finds the later work less psychologically revealing, yet she provides rather laborious treatments of its connections with the biography anyway. Her summaries here, with the exception of a comparison between *The Reivers* and *The Sound and the Fury,* do not add to what we already understand. The final third of her book, then, is less good than the first two-thirds. Though this is an uneven book, it does offer intriguing suggestions about the terms of Faulkner's psyche and the ways they were translated into literature.

One special occurrence in 1979 was the privately printed publication of *The Making of William Faulkner's Books 1929–1937: An Interview with Evelyn Harter Glick* (Columbia, S.C.: Univ. of S.C. Southern Studies Program). Glick designed eight Faulkner books at Cape and Smith, Smith and Haas, and Random House. She tells a number of anecdotes about Faulkner and offers considerable information about publication circumstances during this period. The interview establishes with welcome clarity the personalities of Faulkner's various editors and the explanations for his shifts among publishers. Meriwether's foreword to this booklet promises the future publication of "a collection of several such taped and edited interviews with persons whose professional and personal relationships with William Faulkner were significant and have not before been adequately documented." If the other interviews are comparable to this one, such a publication will be of substantial benefit to Faulkner studies.

One full-length study which offers insight into the biography is Gary Lee Stonum's *Faulkner's Career: An Internal Literary History* (see section *iii. a.*). Among articles which offer (or promise) biographical information Jeffrey J. Folks's "Anderson's Satiric Portrait of William Faulkner in *Dark Laughter*" (*NMW* 12:23–29) is the most intriguing. Unfortunately, however, Folks raises more questions than he answers. His essay is based upon the hypothesis that Anderson added the satiric portrait of Faulkner to *Dark Laughter* between 5 March and 6 May 1925. Work with Anderson manuscripts would have made this scholarship more respectable. Nevertheless, Folks does manage to focus a blurred time frame. But he fails to draw the conclusions toward which his argument leads: that one possible reason for the Anderson/Faulkner breakup was Faulkner's relationship with Elizabeth Anderson. Whatever that relationship was (he did share her apartment for most of January and February of 1925 while Sherwood was on tour), Sherwood seemed to feel that a friendship had been betrayed. Francis J. Bosha's "Faulkner, Pound and the P.P.P." (*Paideuma* 8:249–56) is an interesting minor note. One gathers that the writers group of the People-to-People program disintegrated as much because of Faulkner's boredom with it as because of the dispute over freeing Pound from St. Elizabeths. In "On Faulkner's putting Wolfe First" (*SAQ* 78:172–810) Richard Walser reviews the circumstances of Faulkner's various statements about his contemporaries, adds information about Walser's own 1950 correspondence with Faulkner, and comments upon the Agrarian's hostility to both Faulkner and Wolfe.

iii. Criticism: General

a. Books.   One book published this year promises a significantly new emphasis. Gary Lee Stonum's *Faulkner's Career: An Internal Literary History* (Cornell) offers a definition of a literary career as neither an author's life nor work but instead as a composite of both having "its own distinctive properties and its own independent coherence." Stonum convinces us that Faulkner's consciousness of his development "gave rise to a long series of transformations, reappraisals, and altered understandings of what being a writer entailed." Because Faulkner's career had "its own direction and momentum" and was a perpetual "reconstitution of new designs out of old ones," Stonum believes that studying the career can illuminate aspects of Faulkner that neither exegesis nor poetics can. Stonum sees Faulkner's career as an on-going testing and revision of different aspects of the paradigm of arrested motion. Briefly, the stages he sees in Faulkner's career were: "art as a vision of the transcendence of life, art as a representation of life's motion, art as a problematics for arresting, and art as a meta-form for investigating the value of cultural forms." Stonum's discussion of the transition between Faulkner's poetry and his prose is particularly valuable. He illuminates the evolution of Faulkner's conception of art and shows how *The Sound and the Fury*'s four sections embody a gradual displacement of the visionary ideal.

Stonum points out that Addie and Darl seek "states similar to the absolute which is the goal of Faulkner's poetry." Also, he suggests the hypothesis that "Cash's last monologue is an embryonic version of the next phase of Faulkner's art. Unlike the other narrators, Cash consciously calls into question the ability to represent the world accurately." Faulkner, then, broached a problem at the close of *As I Lay Dying* which he worked through as the central issue in *Absalom, Absalom!*

Stonum offers a fascinating thesis which is especially helpful in explaining the remarkable transitions made during the 1920s. But his theory becomes a procrustean abstraction to which he shapes chronology and the canon, especially the final stage of Faulkner's career. I am not convinced that reworking the concept of arrested motion was as central in Faulkner's career as reworking, say, definitions of the novel or understandings of women and sex. Stonum's book is marred by two inexplicable errors (Hightower's first name is given as "Wayne" and Little Belle is called Horace's niece). But his study sensibly uses current fashions in criticism which afford a valuable way of seeing the interrelatedness of the Faulkner canon.

Of her earlier book on Faulkner, Elizabeth M. Kerr writes: "In *Yoknapatawpha: Faulkner's 'Little Postage Stamp of Native Soil'* [*ALS* 1969, pp. 110–11] I cover the mythic society and indicate factual parallels." In her new book, *William Faulkner's Gothic Domain* (Kennikat), Kerr covers the Gothic conventions and indicates how they are "played straight, ironically inverted, or parodied" throughout the Faulkner canon. Kerr does not see Gothicism as the only convention Faulkner adapted; she sees *As I Lay Dying*, for instance, as predominantly a quest-romance, albeit an inverted one. But she does see Gothicism as the dominant convention from which Faulkner worked. The only problem with this approach is that almost everything Faulkner wrote can become either Gothicism or truncated Gothicism. For instance, Kerr justifies including "Pantaloon in Black" in *Go Down, Moses* because of "Gothic elements in themes and patterns which serve as unifying devices."

Kerr includes numbers of useful correctives, such as her reminder that *Light in August* is a much more violent novel than *Sanctuary*. She is particularly good on the use of Christian allusions in *Light in August*. And Kerr makes valuable distinctions between Faulkner's Gothicism and that of his predecessors. One distinction is a matter of point of view; she explains that by "never telling a Gothic tale in the first person from the point of view of the hero or heroine at the time of the action or in retrospect, Faulkner dissociated himself from the multitude of run-of-the-mill writers of Gothic romance." Another distinction is a matter of psychological awareness. Kerr writes: "By great good fortune Faulkner had at his disposal what the original Gothic novelists, and even those of the generation before his, had lacked: the insight into the unconscious provided by Freud." Kerr's treatment of Gothicism is an informed approach which makes significant an aspect of the fiction that we have previously treated rather glibly. Nevertheless Gothicism still does not seem as central to Faulkner as Kerr would have it.

Another book on Faulkner (Donald Kartiganer's *The Fragile Thread: The Meaning of Form in Faulkner's Novels*) is reviewed in section *iv.b.* A final volume for 1979 is *Faulkner, Modernism, and Film: Faulkner and Yoknapatawpha, 1978*, ed. Evans Harrington and Ann J. Abadie (Miss.). This is the best of the volumes from the annual Faulkner conferences. The editors do a fine job in balancing and interrelating most speeches. And several of the speakers really said something new and/or suggested new and interesting approaches to Faulkner. Malcolm Cowley's "Magic in Faulkner" (pp. 3–19) is a moving reminder of Faulkner's ability to tap the unconscious wellspring of myth. In "Faulkner and Joyce" (pp. 20–33) Hugh Kenner shows how Faulkner might have been "dipping into" *Ulysses* without ever reading the copy Phil Stone gave him in 1924. Kenner does not believe that Faulkner learned from Joyce a mythological structuring device, but rather "a set of expressive devices effective on the plane on which sentences and paragraphs are constructed." Kenner's other essay, "Faulkner and the Avant-Garde" (pp. 182–96), insists that Faulkner had "none of the pedagogical fervor of the born avant-gardist." Without the interests, aims, or subjects of the avant-garde, Faulkner nevertheless learned from it, Kenner says, techniques which transformed normally local and folk materials. This essay is rather general, but it does open a topic for further, more detailed analysis. Ilse Dusoir Lind's "Faulkner's Uses of Poetic Drama" (pp. 66–81) provides useful historical background about Faulkner's interest in drama and makes a detailed and persuasive comparison of *All God's Chillun Got Wings* and *Light in August*. Lind argues convincingly that the distortions in *Light in August* are not failures in realism but rather are intentionally "adroit and most innovatively expressionistic" distortions. Lind's second talk was a discussion of the ways Faulkner after 1925 translated his "multiple creativity" in both visual and verbal arts into the verbal arts alone. Providing helpful examples of motifs and methods in painting which Faulkner adapted to fiction writing, Lind reminds us in "The Effect of Painting on Faulkner's Poetic Form" (pp. 127–48) that allusions may be visual as well as verbal.

In "The Montage Element in Faulkner's Fiction" (pp. 103–26) Bruce Kawin asserts that "repetition and montage are the two central linguistic and structural devices in Faulkner's fiction." Kawin makes a useful classification of montage forms and offers a distinction between dialectical and parallel montage devices. These comments upon Faulkner's methodology need to be further developed and applied. Kawin's "Faulkner's Film Career: The Years with Hawks" (pp. 163–81) offers a brief overview of its topic with introductory remarks about the films "Today We Live" and "The Road to Glory." The two other film speeches are interesting, though not very solid as printed essays. Horton Foote's "On First Dramatizing Faulkner" (pp. 49–65) is an autobiographical narrative telling as much about Foote as about Faulkner. Foote's "Tomorrow: The Genesis of a Screenplay" (pp. 149–62) fulfills its title's promise and provides an interesting discussion of the problems posed by converting one Faulkner tale into film, but we learn more about both "Tomorrows" from an essay by Carl E. Rollyson (see section *vii.*). Thomas Daniel Young's "Pioneering on Principle, or How a Traditional Society May Be Dissolved" (pp. 34–48) reviews the deterioration of Rosa Millard's character in the course of *The Unvanquished*. Young's thesis is that with Rosa, Drusilla, and John Sartoris we see a decline from what Ransom termed "Aesthetic" forms to mere "economic" forms. This terminology offers a fancy but not especially useful way to talk about moral decline. Young also spoke on that much rehearsed topic "Narration as Creative Art: The Role of Quentin Compson in *Absalom, Absalom!*" (pp. 82–102). Moving between *The Sound and the Fury* and *Absalom, Absalom!*, Young reconfirms Quentin's unreliability as a narrator and then asserts that Bon's black blood is merely a creation of "the disturbed imagination." But if so, what then was Sutpen's "trump"? and why did Sutpen's first wife not fit his design? Because he fails to consider such questions, Young's argument rings hollow.

b. **Articles.** As usual, articles under the heading "Criticism: General" tend to be too general to be useful. One partial exception is Michael Grimwood's "The Self-Parodic Context of Faulkner's Nobel Prize Speech" (*SoR* 15:366–75). Grimwood is really talking about a broader topic than the speech, but he makes it a useful point of departure. To him the speech represents one side of "an internal debate that preoccupied Faulkner throughout the 1940s and into the fifties." That debate is Faulkner's uneasiness about the value of art itself, an uneasiness I would date at least from the composition of the poems in *The Marble Faun*. Grimwood sees the image of man during an apocalyptic flood as a metaphor for Faulkner's sense of his own literary situation. Tracing recurrences of that image, Grimwood offers intriguing though sometimes procrustean interpretations. He writes a skillful but hardly exhaustive treatment of a central issue. Another essay, ostensibly on the same topic, John Rothfork's "The Concept of Time in Faulkner's Nobel Speech" (*NMW* 11:73–83) tries to do too much in too small a space. Several articles deal with large topics competently but hurriedly and offer no revelations. An article by Donald Palumbo deals with nothing less than "The Concept of God in Faulkner's *Light in August, The Sound and the Fury, As I Lay Dying,* and *Absalom, Absalom!*" (*So. Central Bul.* 34:142–46). A similar overview is Sybil Korff Vincent's "Sweet and Bitter Sweat: William Faulkner's Work Ethic" (*MarkhamR* 8:66–69). Another overview argues that "Yoknapatawpha County is not a geographical microcosm of the South but a place within the South." That argument is hardly news, but Charles S. Aiken's "Faulkner's Yoknapatawpha County: A Place in the American South" (*Geographical Rev.* 69:331–48) is at least partially new because Aiken argues as a geographer, presenting maps, photographs, and historical descriptions of real use to the Faulknerian. His map of downtown Memphis during the 1930s and 1940s, for example, tells us where Virgil and Fonzo might have gone to barber college and where the model for Miss Reba's establishment actually was. Robert V. Weston's "Faulkner and Lytle: Two Modes of Southern Fiction" (*SoR* 15:34–51) offers an appropriate warning against generalizing about southern writing, but the article is really more about Lytle than about Faulkner. The special Faulkner issue of *MissQ* includes a survey of research and criticism on Faulkner, with Thomas McHaney as general editor. That review differs somewhat in scope and emphasis from this one, but both are guided by an appreciation for sound scholarship and by a distaste for junk. Faulkner studies is enough of a major enterprise to warrant both reviews. Besides, each keeps the other honest.

iv. Criticism: Special Studies

a. **Ideas, Influences, Intellectual Background.**   Certainly the most unusual essay to appear this year is one on "Faulkner and Quantum Mechanics" (*WHR* 33:329–39). Steven T. Ryan's essay associates the techniques Faulkner first learned in *The Sound and the Fury* with scientific theories which were being formulated at about the same time. Ryan writes, "A common attitude toward Faulkner's approach is that he used a variety of perspectives to reveal a final, composite image. Actually, quantum mechanics offers a closer equivalent to Faulkner's approach. Each view is itself a composite of the observer and the observed, but together they contradict each other and can never reveal a composite image." In "William Faulkner and Some Designs of Naturalism" (*SAF* 7:75–82) Mick Gidley adds to his earlier work by suggesting affinities Faulkner had with the ideas of both Remy de Gourmont and Joseph Wood Krutch. Craig Werner takes on a large burden in writing "Beyond Realism and Romanticism: Joyce, Faulkner and the Tradition of the American Novel" (*CentR* 23:242–62). His thesis is that "Faulkner not only knew Joyce's works but adapted Joycean techniques to his own voice in a way which helped him . . . to rise at least momentarily above the conflict of the romantic and realistic traditions of the American novel." Some of these theories are by now familiar; nevertheless Werner offers reconceptualized, useful comparisons and specific instances of Joyce's influence upon Faulkner. Another note on Joyce and Faulkner is Thomas E. Connolly's "Joyce and Faulkner" (*James Joyce Quart.* 16:513–15). These essays should be read in conjunction with Hugh Kenner's (see section *iii.*).

"William Faulkner and Mario Vargas Llosa: The Election of Failure" (*CLS* 16:332–43) by Mary E. Davis offers testimony to Faulkner's continuing influence upon South American writers. Robert L. Johnson's "William Faulkner, Calvinism, and the Presbyterians" (*Jour. of Presbyterian Hist.* 57:66–81) testifies that Faulkner is being taken seriously in unexpected sectors. One would like to trust Johnson's theology and his information about Faulkner's Presbyterian connections. Since, however, he refers to William Faulkner's "great-grandfather, Murry Faulkner," one remains suspicious of his other information. This essay compares unfavorably with that of another nonspecialist, Charles Aiken (section *iii.b.*). Aiken writes like a geographer, not a literary critic; thus he tells us something. Johnson tries to write like a literary critic, not a theologian; thus he tells us very little.

b. **Style and Structure.**   I review Donald M. Kartiganer's *The Fragile Thread: The Meaning of Form in Faulkner's Novels* (Mass.) in this section because it purports to be a study of form and structure. Assuming that a "fragmentary structure is the core of Faulkner's novelistic vision," Kartiganer provides a first-rate summary of the ways in which Faulkner critics have skirted that issue. But then, though it is his avowed topic, Kartiganer partially skirts it too; for finally this book is more a study of themes than of structures. Kartiganer does provide insight into individual novels. He establishes how irrational is Jason Compson's mind, how toteming affects the Bundrens, how Joe Christmas really is like Christ, and how Quentin and Shreve establish that the "capacities of the imagination . . . are irrevocably rooted in our moral life." Kartiganer sees the novels of Faulkner's last 20 years (including *Go Down, Moses*) as minor works. He explains, "The reason for this comparative lack of success is, I believe, the fundamental inappropriateness of Faulkner's special fictional talents for the mythos form." Basically Kartiganer thinks that *The Hamlet* does not aspire to the mythos form, but that *Go Down, Moses* does and fails at the attempt. He argues that the late work lacks "serious moral concern in fiction," meaning that, though moral theories are present, there is little "evaluation of human conduct embedded in the nature and presentation of characters and action." That seems a meaningful distinction, and I find Kartiganer's readings sound. Even the highly questionable thesis about *Go Down, Moses* is plausibly articulated. The strength of the book is Kartiganer's welcome assertion that "all of Faulkner's major novels are studies in fragmentation, experiments in the nature and cause of disorder and in the possibility of working through it to some sense of coherence." My major regret is that *The Fragile Thread* is not a significantly different study; for Kartiganer does not travel much further than other critics have in showing how fragmented forms actually work in Faulkner's novels. In "Faulkner as Aphorist" (*RLC* 35:279–98) Calvin S. Brown provides a valuable review of the history of the aphorism as a literary form. Then he analyzes the kinds of aphorisms in Faulkner, discovers trends in Faulkner's usage, offers rough frequency counts, and generally helps us to see how a specific stylistic device becomes an element of tone, characterization, and even plot in Faulkner. This excellent essay is the only English language essay in the special Faulkner issue of *RLC*. In "The Influence of Poetry on the Narrative Technique of Faulkner's Early Fiction" (*JNT* 9:184–90) Jeffrey J. Folks makes a few valid generalizations, but he does not explore his topic in depth. Other articles dealing with style and/or structure are by Rabinowitz (see section *vii.*), Ryan (see section *iv.a.*), Ross (see section *vi.*), and Perry (see section *ix.*). Also see section *v.* for a book-length analysis of stylistics in *The Sound and the Fury*.

c. Race.   The only overt treatment of this topic, Heinrich Straumann's "Black and White in Faulkner's Fiction" (*ES* 60:462–70), is an unremarkable overview. In *Mark and Knowledge* Marjorie Pryse treats the topic more insightfully. Finding echoes of Hawthorne and Melville in "Dry September," "Red Leaves," and *Light in August,* Pryse theorizes persuasively about social stigmatizing (especially by race) as a perverse means of maintaining the American community. This work is a useful corrective for various idealizations of community. Pryse also suggests how Faulkner's fiction transcends its subject matter by itself refusing to stigmatize.

v. Individual Works to 1929

Faulkner's very early work received mostly bibliographical attention this year (see section *i.*). Also articles on "Mistral" and "Artist at

Home" may be found in section *ix.* Emily K. Dalgarno's "Faulkner and Gibbon: A Note on *Soldiers' Pay*" (*NMW* 12:36–39) offers some useful information about allusions to Gibbon in Faulkner's first novel, but the subject calls for further attention. Three minor articles on *Sartoris/Flags in the Dust* appeared in 1979. William Cosgrove's "The 'Soundless Moiling' of Bayard Sartoris" (*ArQ* 35:165–69) treats the significance of Bayard's inarticulateness. In "A Problem with the Internal Dating of *Flags in the Dust*" (*NConL* 9,iii:8–9) Jeffrey J. Folks deals with this topic very briefly. Katherine C. Hodgin's "Horace Benbow and Bayard Sartoris: Two Romantic Figures in Faulkner's *Flags in the Dust*" (*AL* 51:647–52) is a competent note on the Keatsian/Byronic associations characterizing these two men.

Irena Kaluza's *The Functioning of Sentence Structure in the Stream-of-Consciousness Technique of William Faulkner's "The Sound and the Fury": A Study in Linguistic Stylistics* (Norwood) is, to my knowledge, the first computerized study of Faulkner's technique. It is published in a limited edition of 150 copies and thus is not readily available. Though highly technical and even at times abtruse, the book shows how methodical stylistics can "describe the artistic structures of literary language in a systematic fashion." More specifically, Kaluza's analysis isolates the idiolects of each of the Compson brothers and establishes that each uses a syntactically unique structure. Examining every nonspoken sentence in the novel, Kaluza can categorize, for example, the components in Quentin's "syntax of fragmentation" and in Faulkner's rhetorical technique of organization. Her evidence suggests that "parallelism of structure" is "Faulkner's basic principle of organizing his material, not only in Quentin's idiolect but in the author's novels in general." Despite its tediousness I find this book a valuable reference work and model for future computer studies of Faulkner's style. The thesis of David Minter's "Faulkner, Childhood, and the Making of *The Sound and the Fury*" (*AL* 51:376–92) is that the principal impulses behind this novel were at once regressive and innovative—or back toward childhood and the interior and forward toward revolutionary narrative techniques. Minter argues, somewhat murkily, that these were corrolary impulses. He offers an interesting examination of the ways Faulkner's image of art as a vase is both aesthetic and erotic, but Minter fails to follow through with the psychobiographical implications of the materials he examines.

A study of two topics that have been exhaustively treated, Quentin Compson and southern Calvinism, Mary Dell Fletcher's "William Faulkner and Residual Calvinism" (*SoSt* 18:199–216) does at least offer a useful classification. Writing on a similar topic, Thomas Dukes in "Christianity as Curse and Salvation in *The Sound and the Fury*" (*ArQ* 35:170–82) works by assertion rather than by argument. Contrasting Dilsey with Mrs. Compson, the redeemed with the unredeemed, Dukes contends that Mrs. Compson is a believer in the "Wrathful God of the Old Testament"; here he ignores the difference between using a belief and actually believing it. The implication is that Mrs. Compson believes in the wrong God. I think that she believes in no God except herself.

vi. Individual Works, 1930–39

As I Lay Dying is the instance but not the subject for Stephen M. Ross's " 'Voice' in Narrative Texts: The Example of *As I Lay Dying*" (*PMLA* 94:300–310). Ross offers a distinction between mimetic voice and textual voice, saying that the two are in principle mutually exclusive. Separating them, Ross shows how mimetic voice in *As I Lay Dying* imitates "not how a character sounds but how one character sounds to another." Also he establishes how textual voice, or "the aspect of the printed text that generates signification without necessary reference to verbal signification" works. In other words, he talks about the function of the visual plane of the text itself. These terms are appropriate for *As I Lay Dying* and other nontraditional novels. The essay is one of the more interesting ones done this year. The Faulkner issue of *ArQ* included two articles on *As I Lay Dying*, neither of which could match Ross's essay for either insight or innovation. In "Vardaman's Journey in *As I Lay Dying*" (35:114–28) George Brooks reads the Vardaman sections closely to trace what he sees as Vardaman's psychological deterioration. In "A Wheel Within a Wheel: Fusion of Form and Content in Faulkner's *As I Lay Dying*" (35:101–13) Alice Shoemaker's wheel image is mostly a gimmick, thus her essay is not so much an examination of form as a rehashing of by-now familiar understandings. A similar gimmicky approach is Charlotte Goodman's "The Bundren Wagon: Narrative Strategy in Faulkner's *As I Lay Dying*" (*SAF* 7:234–42). LaRene Despain's "The Shape and Echo of Their Word: Narration and Character in *As I Lay Dying*" (*MSE* 6:49–59) is an often too schematic grouping of characters in the novel. *As I Lay Dying*, then, had a number of articles written about it, only one of which was of much value. *Sanctuary* did better with the percentages, having only one good article written about it. Arguing that Temple's problem is not an excess of will, but an absence of self, Donald A. Petesch in "Temple Drake: Faulkner's Mirror for the Social Order" (*SAF* 7:37–48) offers a sound reading of the novel. His attention to mirrors and other paralleling devices is specific and useful. The concordances to both *Light in August* and *Requiem for a Nun* appeared in 1979. The two-volume *Light in August: A Concordance to the Novel* (Univ. Microfilms) carries an excellent, seven-page introduction by Joseph Blotner. The lengthiest of these introductions, it is also the most useful. Blotner begins by showing what sort of support this concordance offers for the arguments of Richard Chase and Alfred Kazin in their classic studies of the novel. Blotner goes on to examine the attention Faulkner gives quantitatively to such subjects as Joe versus Lena, man versus female, white versus black, and "is" versus "was." He does so with appropriate cautions about the use of merely numerical tallies. But his introduction offers a variety of concrete examples of critical uses to which such tallies may be put. C. Hugh Holman's *Windows on the World: Essays on American Social Fiction* (Knoxville: Univ. of Tenn. Press) includes one chapter on *Light in August*. In "Faulkner's August Avatars" Holman makes two important points: (1) that *Light in August* is a Modernist, not a realistic novel; and (2) that Faulkner's characters are not so much realistic figures as avatars—"manifestations or embodiments of concepts, philosophies, or traditions." The chapter offers a broad understanding which should inspire other more specific readings of and approaches to this novel. An interesting article from 1978, Fredric V. Bogel's "Fables of Knowing: Melodrama and Related Forms" (*Genre* 11:83–108) includes a treatment of *Light in August* which Bogel sees as "an extended fable of knowing with a strongly melodramatic emphasis." Bogel offers the hypothesis that fables of knowing deal with the relation between two worlds—the seen and the unseen, but that in Faulkner the nature of those worlds is significantly altered. Other articles on *Light in August* fail to tell us anything we do not already know.

The year 1979 saw nine articles on *Absalom, Absalom!*, a few of which actually manage to add to our understanding of this much-discussed novel. The major exception to the pattern of essays, which are not so much wrong as redundant, is James H. Matlack's "The Voices of Time: Narrative Structure in *Absalom, Absalom!*" (*SoR* 15:333–54). Matlack's basic conception that *Absalom, Absalom!* is faithful to the oral tradition, as folklorists define it, is hardly new, but his terminology is. Matlack's outline of the novel's structure is useful, and his understanding of the connection between structure and theme is sound. Unfortunately, the essay was "shorn of most of its footnotes," but it remains of real value both to students and to Faulkner scholars. Three other competent essays approached *Absalom, Absalom!* from a variety of perspectives. Joseph W. Turner's "The Kinds of Historical Fiction" (*Genre* 12:333–55) mentions *Absalom, Absalom!* as part of a subgenre—the invented historical novel—which is "frequently structured to highlight the problems of historical interpretation." Turner offers a sensible reminder that even *Absalom, Absalom!* conforms to certain generic traditions. In his "Quentin Finally Sees Miss Rosa" (*Criticism* 21:331–46) J. Gary Williams explains that the "structuring principle of *Absalom, Absalom!* would seem to be Quentin's movement from the state of uncomprehending apathy in which he listens to Rosa in chapters 1 and 5 to the rigid, wide-awake 'Nevermore of peace' state of mind in which he finally 'sees' Rosa." Williams reads the text carefully, but his emphasis upon Rosa alone sometimes seems strained. Margaret Dickie Uroff's "The Fictions of *Absalom, Absalom!*" (*SNNTS* 11:431–45) offers a modestly altered perspective upon Shreve as the prototypical storyteller, but the author makes a questionable and undeveloped argument that Faulkner's ambivalence about fiction making here signaled the beginning of his decline as a fiction writer. Attention to Clytie is long overdue, but Thadious M. Davis' "The Yoking of 'Abstract Contradictions': Clytie's Meaning in *Absalom, Absalom!*" (*SAF* 7:209–20) is a series of assertions rather than an argument from the evidence. May Cameron Brown and Esta Seaton, in "William Faulkner's Unlikely Detective: Quentin Compson" (*EAS* 8:27–33) present a fairly obvious discussion of Faulkner's inversion of the detective genre. Thomas Daniel Young (see section *iii.a.*) offers an uninspired discussion of Quentin's unreliability. Like Young, Susan Resneck Parr in "The Fourteenth Image of the Blackbird: Another Look at Truth in *Absalom, Absalom!*" (*ArQ* 35: 153–64) argues that we do not know about Charles Bon's black blood. Both Young and Parr consider the value of conjecture and imagination

in *Absalom, Absalom!* Neither seriously entertains the possibility that
Quentin (as storyteller) might have withheld the information he got
from Henry Sutpen. Parr argues that for Quentin to have such knowledge would diminish the power and meaning of the novel and "the
subtleties of Faulkner's skill with multiple and unreliable narrators."
Here Parr insists unnecessarily upon either/or distinctions. The final
article on this novel, "The Narrative Frames in *Absalom, Absalom!*:
Faulkner's Involuted Commentary on Art" (*ArQ* 35:135–52) by Paul
Rosenzweig finds the source for the inability to love and the inability
to know truth as the "overbearing ego." Consequently, "the imaginative act of storytelling is equated with the act of love." This is so, but
hardly news for those of us who have been reading recent work on
Absalom, Absalom!

vii. Individual Works, 1940–49

The year 1979 was not a good one for *The Hamlet*. John McDermott's
"Mrs. Armstid: Faulkner's Moral 'Snag'" (*SSF* 16:179–82) is a
strained argument that endows Mrs. Armstid with more courage, rationality, and consciousness than I believe her creator intended. *Go
Down, Moses* received three treatments from three different perspectives. Wesley Morris' *Friday's Footprint: Structuralism and the Articulated Text* (Ohio State) uses *Go Down, Moses* as the principal
text for a deconstructionist analysis illustrating how history and myth
enter literary works. Morris' schematic treatment of the social taboos
which fragment and limit human possibility offers a fresh perspective
on *Go Down, Moses*. Morris' attention to the book's structure and design offers further evidence not only of the book's unity but of its
excellence. "Out of the Old Time: 'Was' and *Go Down, Moses*" (*JNT*
9:1–11) is a competent essay in which David Walker argues that "the
deliberate confusion of past and present, of distance and immediacy,
which the narrative technique of 'Was' achieves is an important introduction to the themes explored in the rest of the book." Walker's
notes are rather out-of-date and his thesis is hardly new, but his attention to the means for distancing us from Cass's perspective is useful. Charles Aiken's "A Geographical Approach to William Faulkner's
'The Bear'" (Memphis: Proceedings of the Southeastern Division,
Association of American Geographers) includes information about
the ways Faulkner altered actual landscapes in "The Bear" and even

tells Faulkner enthusiasts how they might find the prototype for Major DeSpain's hunting lodge still standing in a "snake infested soybean field." Aiken's geographical approach provides interesting footnotes for Faulkner studies. In "The Click of the Spring: The Detective Story as Parallel Structure in Dostoyevsky and Faulkner" (*MP* 76: 355–69) Peter J. Rabinowitz focuses upon *Intruder in the Dust*. Rabinowitz sees detective fiction as an aesthetic solution to problems posed by the discovery novel. His treatment of *Intruder in the Dust* effectively explains its composition as a successful execution of formal dilemmas posed by the discovery-novel genre. Carl E. Rollyson's "Faulkner into Film: 'Tomorrow' and 'Tomorrow'" (*MissQ* 32: 437–52) is a sensitive appraisal of the strengths of Horton Foote's 1971 film "Tomorrow." Rollyson argues that Foote's adaptation of Faulkner's "Tomorrow" works because Foote is faithful to the spirit, not the letter, of the story and because Foote does not transcribe the story but instead follows the dictates of the film medium. Foote's own comments upon the topic are reviewed above (section *iii. a.*).

viii. Individual Works, 1950–52

The year 1979 witnessed the publication of another in the series of the Faulkner concordances. *Requiem for a Nun: A Concordance to the Novel,* ed. with an introd. by Noel Polk (Univ. Microfilms). Because it applies to the text at hand, Polk's introduction is especially useful. Comparing the concordances of *Requiem for a Nun* and *Go Down, Moses,* Polk indicates how concordances can isolate differences between texts. Also he illustrates how this concordance establishes verbal linkage between the sections of *Requiem for a Nun*. The concordance raises at least one question it does not answer. It lists as variants "typed revisions to portions of Acts I and II pasted or stapled to the galley proofs"; but it does not explain why such obviously late revisions were not incorporated into the published text. A full discussion of the Faulkner Concordance Advisory Board's decisions in printing such matters as the variants would be most welcome. In the meantime the concordances themselves offer us invaluable research tools.

Stoic Strain contains one essay on Faulkner. In "His 'Magnum O': Stoic Humanism in Faulkner's *A Fable*" (pp. 135–54) Duane MacMillan argues, by philosophical rather than aesthetic criteria, that this novel is "Faulkner's masterpiece." More convincingly, MacMillan also contends that reading the book in the " 'Christ-reincarnated' tradition and mode" distorts the novel's focus; for MacMillan believes that the central wisdom of this novel follows stoic humanist rather than Christian traditions. Rosemary M. Magee's "*A Fable* and the Gospels: A Study in Contrasts" (*RS* 47:98–107) offers a useful tally of the differences between Christ's and the Corporal's stories. Magee also comments upon the significance of those differences. In "Faulkner's Noble Prince" (*ArQ* 35:129–34) Erik C. Nelson attempts a rather tenuous connection between Lucius Priest and Henry V.

ix. The Stories

Faulkner's stories have been misunderstood and/or neglected for so long that their sudden prominence makes 1979 seem a virtual *annus mirabilis*. The publication of Joseph Blotner's edition of *The Uncollected Stories of William Faulkner* (see section *i.*) has made numbers of previously unavailable stories accessible now. Also the principal emphasis of the Faulkner issue of *MissQ* was upon the stories. In "Faulkner, Anderson, and 'Artist at Home' " (32:393–412) Tony J. Owens provides an excellent account of this neglected story. Acknowledging "the presence of a biased, unreliable narrator," Owens avoids interpretive pitfalls. Placing the story in the contexts of the biography and of early work, he establishes the significance of this tale. In "A Forgotten Faulkner Story: 'Thrift' " (32:453–60) Hans H. Skei offers a competent treatment. Considering Faulkner's exclusion of "Thrift" from *These 13*, Skei also presents a persuasive thesis about Faulkner's sense of the unity of such collections. In another journal Skei further pursues that same topic. His "William Faulkner's Short Story Sending Schedule and His First Short Story Collection, *These 13*: Some Ideas" (*NMW* 11:64–72) is an excellent account which raises a number of questions about dating Faulkner's stories. Both Skei articles consider the unity of *These 13*. Kathryn Chittick's " 'Telling It Again and Again': Notes on a Horsethief" (32:423–35) argues that the story renders a prototypical transformation of the profane into the sacred, but Chittick does not carefully explain how that understanding deepens our appreciation of *A Fable*. Lisa Paddock's " 'Trifles with a Tragic Profundity': The Importance of 'Mistral' " (32:413–22) is a well-documented, insightful discussion of this early story. Paddock sees a number of parallels with later more important work and she also makes an intriguing suggestion about the psychic significance of this story. In "Faulkner's Priests and Fitzgerald's 'Absolution' " (32:461–65) Gail Moore Morrison points out allusions to "Absolution" in "The Priest" and "Mistral." Moore observes that allusions were direct and limited in the former, indirect and more generalized in the latter. In " 'Carcassone': Faulkner's Allegory of Art and the Artist" (SoR 15:355–65) Robert W. Hamblin discusses the ideas in this neglected but important story. There are ambiguities Hamblin neglects; for instance, he ignores the implied paradox between believing that art transcends this world and that it asserts "Kilroy was here." Nevertheless Hamblin offers sound, welcome coverage of "Carcassone" and of Faulkner's various statements about art. Hamblin also writes a competent but unremarkable essay on another story: "Before the Fall: The Theme of Innocence in Faulkner's 'That Evening Sun' " (NMW 11:86–94). And Jack F. Stewart's "The Infernal Climate of Faulkner's 'Dry September' " (RS 47:238–43) is good on images of hell, but it is by now hard to say anything new about either of these stories or about "A Rose for Emily." Menakem Perry almost manages to do the latter in "Literary Dynamics: How the Order of a Text Creates Its Meanings [with an Analysis of Faulkner's 'A Rose for Emily']" PT 1, i-ii:35–64, 311–54). Perry believes that "an entire body of criticism of this story ignores the functions of the text-continuum in a literary text and the reading process." Perry sets out to redress the balance, almost by the length of his essay alone. The essay would have profited from severe pruning, but it does provide a good example of the appropriateness of affective criticism for Faulkner studies. It discusses effectively the "traps" that the story sets up for its readers and persuasively argues that the device "archeseme" —the "hesitation between two possible conceptions" set up through "over-all opposition"—is a central device in Faulkner. (Section *iv.c.* also includes some reference to "Dry September" and "Red Leaves.") For the stories, then, 1979 was indeed a very good year.

Louisiana State University

10. Fitzgerald and Hemingway

Scott Donaldson

This report comments on eight books and more than 100 articles. Some of this work was first-rate, yet it stands as one measure of the year's output that the most significant publications resulted from gathering previously uncollected and somewhat peripheral writings of Fitzgerald and Hemingway themselves. These were the publication of the "last" 50 uncollected stories of Fitzgerald, and of the first authorized and unpirated edition of Hemingway's poetry. Both wells are running shallow now; with nearly all of the authors' creative corpus available in book form it is time to undertake critical editions. Meanwhile there remains plenty of room for critical commentary, bibliographical and textual study, and biographical examination that is both fresh and informed. One major conduit for such research has been at least temporarily dammed with the suspension of the *Fitzgerald/Hemingway Annual* following its 1979 number. Some compensation, however, will take place with the revival this year of *Hemingway notes* (*Hn*) after a hiatus of several years.

i. Bibliographical Work and Texts

With the publication of *The Price Was High: The Last Uncollected Stories of F. Scott Fitzgerald*, ed. Matthew J. Bruccoli (Harcourt) practically the entire Fitzgerald story canon is now available in book form. In considering the stories in *The Price Was High*, it will be well to bear in mind that Fitzgerald labeled many of them "stripped and permanently buried." As Bruccoli points out, "a writer deserves to be judged by his best work," and this is not Fitzgerald's best work. Yet —Bruccoli also maintains—"a writer's best work must be assessed in terms of his total work." The editor has supplied extremely helpful notes, giving time and place and circumstances of composition and adding key biographical detail.

In an excellent presentation of textual evidence James L. W. West III's and J. Barclay Inge's "F. Scott Fitzgerald's Revision of " 'The Rich Boy' " (*Proof* 5 [1977]:127–46) examines the alterations Fitzgerald made in this story between its original appearance in *Red Book* and its publication in *All the Sad Young Men*. Two of these changes obscure the identity of the model for Anson Hunter, but several other, more significant emendations present Hunter much less sympathetically. The shift in attitude is that of the narrator, not of Fitzgerald himself, the authors assert. West's "The Second Serials of *This Side of Paradise* and *The Beautiful and Damned*" (*PBSA* 73:63–74) traces the history (and usually the bowdlerization) of Fitzgerald's first two novels as they were serialized by newspapers in Chicago, Atlanta, Washington, and New York. Many readers—West estimates 50,000 for *Paradise*, 35,000 for *Damned*—gained their first or only impression of Fitzgerald from these "butchered or botched" texts, accompanied by advertisements touting him "as the chronicler of the flapper on the back page of the daily newspaper, right next to ads for corsets and corn plasters." This essay stands as a model of how bibliographical research accompanied by good writing can be brought to bear on questions of authorial reputation.

If they were someone else's poems, there would be little point in collecting them. But Hemingway's poetry, and particularly the early poems which make up the bulk of his verse, tell us something of the mind and values of the man who wrote the prose. Up to now the only editions of his poetry have been fragmentary and pirated, so that *Ernest Hemingway: 88 Poems*, ed. Nicholas Gerogiannis (Harcourt), represents a valuable contribution to Hemingway scholarship. Many previously unpublished poems are here, including the 1926 one savaging Dorothy Parker and another from the same period on Gertrude Stein. Besides unearthing these and other hard-to-locate poems Gerogiannis has supplied useful notes and a somewhat worshipful introduction which ends with Wallace Stevens' 1942 observation that Hemingway "obviously is a poet and I should say, offhand, the most significant of living poets, so far as the subject of EXTRAORDINARY ACTUALITY is concerned." A list of copy-texts used for this book and of changes made to correct errors in those copy-texts appears in Gerogiannis' "Editorial Apparatus for *88 Poems*" (*FHA* 383–88).

"The Unpublished Opening of *The Sun Also Rises*" (*Antaeus* 33: 7–14) prints Hemingway's aborted beginning for the first time and accompanies it with Fitzgerald's "Letter to Ernest Hemingway on *The Sun Also Rises*" (*Antaeus* 33:15–18) urging Hemingway to delete this beginning. Juxtaposed in this way, the documents testify to Fitzgerald's critical acumen in objecting to the rather snide, self-conscious way Jake Barnes introduces his cast of characters. Jake's narrative voice in this discarded section of two chapters and about 3,700 words resembles that of Hemingway in *A Moveable Feast*; indeed, the deleted portion concludes with the anecdote about Braddocks (Ford Madox Ford) "cutting" Hilaire Belloc that is reprinted, with slight alterations, in *Feast*. Hemingway's false start deserves close study with respect to telling vs. showing, point of view, and tone.

Through painstaking and intelligent study of the various texts and through reference to the Hemingway-Pound correspondence, E. R. Hagemann's "A Collation, with Commentary, of the Five Texts of the Chapters in Hemingway's *In Our Time*, 1923–38" (*PBSA* 73: 443–58) concludes that the Boni and Liveright printing of *In Our Time* represents the best text for the book's (inter)chapters. More work of this sort needs to be done.

Additions to the Hemingway and Fitzgerald bibliographies continue to turn up. George Monteiro's "Additions to Hanneman's Early Unrecorded Hemingway Items" (*PBSA* 72[1978]:245–46) cites several reviews in 1925 and 1926 that mention early Hemingway stories, particularly "The Undefeated" and "Soldier's Home." Ray Lewis White reports on previously unnoted reviews of Hemingway, Fitzgerald, and Zelda Fitzgerald in three separate articles. His "Hemingway's *Islands in the Stream*: A Collection of Additional Reviews" (*LC* 43[1978]:81–98) lists and briefly annotates 58 reviews unmentioned in Hanneman; "*The Pat Hobby Stories*: A File of Reviews" (*FHA* 177–80) adds 11 reviews to those in Jackson Bryer's *The Critical Reputation of F. Scott Fitzgerald*, and "Zelda Fitzgerald's *Save Me the Waltz*: A Collection of Reviews from 1932–33" (*FHA* 163–68) lists and presents excerpts from 13 previously ignored reviews, most of them favorable.

Finally, Jo August's "The Ernest Hemingway Collection" (*FHA* 237–45) uses photographs and illustrations from manuscripts of the year 1934 to indicate the wealth of the holdings in the Hemingway collection at the Kennedy library in Boston. This is a place to which all serious Hemingway scholars will want to repair. August is curator of the collection.

ii. Letters and Biography

Thomas J. Stavola's *Scott Fitzgerald: Crisis in an American Identity* (Barnes and Noble) advances the thesis that Erik Erikson's theory about the stages of growth applies both to Fitzgerald himself and to the protagonists in his four completed novels. Erikson's theory does shed some light on Fitzgerald, particularly on the question of identity, but is not of much help in interpreting his fiction. Stavola does not sufficiently differentiate between the author and his characters, and lacks the critical sophistication necessary to make his psychological reading stick.

A more modest biographical approach is offered in John J. Koblas' *F. Scott Fitzgerald: His Homes and Haunts* (St. Paul: Minn. Hist. Soc., 1978). This 50-page booklet uses standard sources in supplying an account of Fitzgerald's life in St. Paul, with attention to such matters as his parents, his girls, his frequent change of residence, and his partying. None of the written material is particularly fresh or revealing, but Koblas presents a fine photo gallery of the old homes (mostly still standing) where Fitzgerald grew up. Compared to Koblas' investigations, the brief remarks of Stephanie Kraft on Fitzgerald and St. Paul in *No Castles on Main St.*, pp. 203–06, seem pallid and uninformed. Oddly, Kraft's section on Hemingway and Key West, pp. 53–61, covers a great expanse of biographical territory in lively anecdotal fashion. Much the best production of this pictorial-biographical sort, however, is Robert E. Gajdusek's *Hemingway's Paris* (Scribner's, 1978). The times have changed the face of Paris, and the people and places are different now, but Gajdusek's pictures of the city of today still manage to suggest why Hemingway found it such a "well-organized" town to write in. After a brief introduction Gadjusek sensibly lapses into silence to let quotations from Hemingway (and occasionally from another commentator of the period) speak amid the handsome photographs of the streets and statues, cafes and hotels he once knew so well.

Four essays deal at greater or lesser length with aspects of Fitzgerald's life. Scott Donaldson's "F. Scott Fitzgerald, Princeton '17" (*PULC* 40:119–54) blends biographical information with Fitzgerald's published work to assess his attitude toward Princeton and Princeton's toward him. Fitzgerald is depicted as a socially ambitious middle-class young man who talked rather more about the question of class and becoming a big man on campus than was altogether to the taste of the university he attended and remained loyal to all his life. Roger Lewis' "Ruth Sturtevant and F. Scott Fitzgerald (1916–1921)" (*FHA* 3–21) fleshes out the record of Fitzgerald's correspondence with a young woman he met while in college. The ten letters printed here abundantly illustrate his charming epistolary manner. Lewis' introduction does not acknowledge what appears to be the case—that Fitzgerald regarded Ruth Sturtevant (Smith) more romantically than she was willing to be regarded—but contains some enlightening quotations from Mrs. Smith. Matthew J. Bruccoli's "Epilogue: A Woman, a Gift, and a Still Unanswered Question" (*Esquire* Jan.: 67) describes something of the relationship between Fitzgerald and another female friend, Mrs. Bertha Weinberg Goldstein, whom Fitzgerald met while returning to the United States to attend his father's funeral. In a more speculative manner William R. Anderson's "Fitzgerald after *Tender Is the Night*: A Literary Strategy for the 1930s" (*FHA* 39–63) postulates the existence of two Scott Fitzgeralds during the last half dozen years of the author's life, one of them "poor Scott Fitzgerald," the other the man who refused to be beaten, and who tried to create strong, self-sufficient heroes in his writing. Anderson sometimes confuses biography and literary intention, and parts of his article read like a turgid version of what Malcolm Cowley once said so eloquently about the third act of Fitzgerald's life, yet his conclusion that Stahr had the "capacity to continue functioning in the face of the breakdown of order, harmony, and established values that Fitzgerald most sought to instill in his post-*Tender* characters and in his own life" is, finally, convincing. Similarly persuasive is J. J. Fenstermaker's contention in "The Literary Reputation of F. Scott Fitzgerald, 1940–1941: Appraisal and Reappraisal" (*FHA* 79–90) that the author's reputation went through three distinct phases in the year after his death, from condescending comments about the Jazz-Age-chronicler through a period of reminiscence and appreciation by other established writers to the almost universally laudatory notices that greeted *The Last Tycoon*. Fenstermaker does a first-rate job of evaluating evidence in newspapers and magazines of the time.

In addition to the Sturtevant correspondence presented by Roger Lewis, Robert Hemenway's "Two New Fitzgerald Letters" (*FHA* 127–28) reprints two short letters written in 1921 and 1922 to John Franklin Carter, whom Fitzgerald apparently met in Rome during the spring of 1921. The reissuance of *Editor to Author: The Letters of Maxwell E. Perkins,* ed. John Hall Wheelock with new introd. by Marcia Davenport (Scribner's), serves to call attention to the usefulness of books of two-way correspondence, like *Dear Scott/Dear Max.* With Hemingway's letters now opening to public view, a *Dear Ernest/Dear Max* is in order.

Though no Hemingway letters were printed in 1979, two articles touch on biographical matters. Michael S. Reynolds' "The Agnes Tapes: A Farewell to Catherine Barkley" (*FHA* 251–77) consists of the edited transcript of Reynolds' six-hour taped interview with Mrs. Agnes (von Kurowsky) Stanfield in 1970. The interview reveals little that did not appear in *Hemingway's First War* except the vehemence of Agnes' insistence that Hemingway "would really have gotten to be a bum" if he'd remained in Europe after January 1919. Robert D. Crozier, S.J., in "'The Paris Church of Passy': A Note on Hemingway's Second Marriage" (*PLL* 15:84–86) resurrects the record of Hemingway's second marriage to Pauline Pfeiffer at St. Honoré d'Eylau Catholic Church in Paris. The marriage document gives Hemingway's birthdate as 21 July 1897, an error which Crozier construes as "an obvious ploy by Hemingway to make himself appear two years younger than his wife." Presumably the word "only" disappeared from Crozier's sentence.

iii. Criticism

The 1979 *Fitzgerald/Hemingway Annual,* edited by Bruccoli and Richard Layman, may have been the last. If so, its passing must be lamented, for although the material was sometimes uneven and the mixture of short and long pieces occasionally resulted in placing the trivial alongside the momentous, still the *Annual* could be depended upon to present much of the best scholarship on these two writers. Bruccoli decided that the journal should be suspended—and possibly closed entirely—when the level of articles *submitted* in the last two years (but not of those printed) showed a definite falling off in quality. In any event, the most recent *Annual* sounds an ominous valedictory note in printing a 46-page cumulative index to the entire 11-year series. In addition, Carol Johnston's "Fitzgerald Checklist" (*FHA* 453–61) and William White's 21-page "Hemingway Checklist" (*FHA* 463–83) range over a period of several years in citing publications.

Otherwise, the 1979 edition includes 32 items on Fitzgerald to 14 on Hemingway. The critical articles on Fitzgerald tend to be superior as well as more numerous, suggesting that Fitzgerald scholarship may suffer more from the apparent demise of the *Annual* than that on Hemingway.

a. **Full-Length Studies.** Robert Emmet Long's valuable *The Achieving of "The Great Gatsby": F. Scott Fitzgerald, 1920–1925* (Bucknell) attempts to follow the process of cultural assimilation that enabled Fitzgerald to write *Gatsby*. The section on literary forebears merely rehearses the Conrad influence Long pointed to in his 1966 essay. More useful is the emphasis on Fitzgerald's developing middle-class disillusionment with the rich and highly placed, and best of all Long's perceptively close reading of the novel's "structure of inter-woven detail and nuance."

Bernard Oldsey's *Hemingway's Hidden Craft: The Writing of "A Farewell to Arms"* (Penn. State) is the better of two critical books on Hemingway. Oldsey's unusually well-written study goes over the same manuscripts that Reynolds consulted for his 1976 book on the composition of *Farewell*, and by paying particular attention to titles, beginnings (Oldsey has located a second prospective beginning), and endings which Hemingway jotted down but decided not to use, un-covers some fresh approaches to the novel.

Raymond S. Nelson's *Hemingway: Expressionist Artist* (Iowa State) asserts that Hemingway's work belongs within the climate of opinion of artistic expressionism in philosophical attitude, subject matter, and technique. Nelson's argument grows weak where tech-nique is concerned, but his monograph supports and extends Emily Stipes Watts's 1971 finding that Hemingway's work was clearly in-fluenced by painting, particularly that of Cézanne. In this connection Meyly Chin Hagemann's "Hemingway's Secret: Visual to Verbal Art" (*JML* 7:87–112) establishes through careful research exactly which Cezanne canvases Hemingway saw at the Luxembourg mu-seum and at the Bernheim exhibit in the 1920s. Referring to these paintings, to Henri Bergson's aesthetic theories, and to three stories which Hemingway indicated had been particularly influenced by Cezanne, Hagemann concludes that "the secret" the writer acquired from the painter involved communicating temporal and spatial movement through the tension created by a "sequence of planes." This

interesting essay, together with a 1977 article by Alfred Kazin and
the books by Watts and Nelson, should help put to rest the persisting
notion of Hemingway as an artistic naif.

b. **General Essays.**   In addition to Hagemann's, a number of general essays on Hemingway's work appeared in 1979. Melvin Blackman's ambitious "Death and Birth in Hemingway" in *Stoic Strain*,
pp. 115–34, concentrates on the high incidence of "death comming-
ling disturbingly with birth" in Hemingway's work from the very
beginning on the quay at Smyrna and at the Indian camp. Ranging
across Hemingway's entire corpus, but with particular attention to
In Our Time and *For Whom the Bell Tolls*, Backman's essay sometimes invites objection as it becomes most reductively psychoanalytical—he finds wombs everywhere in Hemingway—yet a strong critical
intelligence operates throughout.

Nancy Comley's thoughtful if somewhat derivative "Hemingway:
The Economics of Survival" (*Novel* 12:244–53) maintains that Hemingway's "concern with money manifests itself in an economic structure of exchange values which the Hemingway hero learns to apply
to his life, most especially to his emotional relationships." His characters, Comley finds, try to achieve an economical emotional condition and to avoid investing in "complex human relationships." The
article's emphasis falls largely though not entirely on the most financially attuned of Hemingway's novels, *The Sun Also Rises*. Anders
Breidlid's "Courage and Self-Affirmation in Ernest Hemingway's
'Lost Generation' Fiction (*Edda* 5:279–99) builds on John Killinger's
book in discussing Hemingway's work through *Farewell* as illustrative of his existential posture. Characteristically, Breidlid points
out, Hemingway's protagonists confront instead of surrendering to
the "contingent forces" that threaten to make their existence meaningless.

One way of confrontation came through combat, and Peter Stine
argues in "Ernest Hemingway and the Great War" (*FHA* 327–54)
that though Hemingway's actual period of service in World War I
was rather brief, "remembering the war became for him a life work"
and much of his fiction can be read as an attempt to "witness or recreate the psychological coordinates of war." This coherent and highly
literate article effectively blends ideas from Philip Young, Paul Fussell, and others.

Anyone can think of the ways in which Hemingway's art differs from that of Henry James, but Charles W. Mayer's original "The Triumph of Honor in James and Hemingway" (*ArQ* 35:373–91) explores several significant similarities in their fiction, including a mutual emphasis on the dignity possible in defeat. Mayer categorizes both writers as belonging to an American tradition "that celebrates the individual." Edwin R. Booher draws a more predictable parallel in "The Image in the Prose: Ezra Pound's Influence on Hemingway" (*IllQ* 42,i:30–39). Booher presents examples in Hemingway's work of imagism, vorticism, and so forth, as demonstrative of Pound's influence on Hemingway, but his article does not much advance Harold Hurwitz' findings on the same subject.

In "De-coding the Hero in Hemingway's Fiction" (*Hn* 5,i:2–10) Charles Stetler and Gerald Locklin take issue with Young's concept of the code hero and with what they regard as his attempt to reduce Hemingway's work to a formula. Neither Young nor anyone else would be likely to disagree with their conclusion that both stories and novels of Hemingway should be read "as *separate* pieces of *fiction*." E. Nageswara Rao's "The Motif of Luck in Hemingway" (*JAmS* 13: 29-35) marshals a wealth of examples as evidence that luck, and usually bad luck, plays a disproportionate role in the chancy universe of Hemingway's fiction. That is undoubtedly true, but then to conclude that where "blind luck rules . . . human effort, idealism, and the will to do good are often frustrated by random combinations of circumstances" almost surely contradicts the theme of most major Hemingway fictions.

After accurately noting the proliferation of racial and ethnic epithets in Hemingway's stories, Paul Marx's "Hemingway and Ethnics" (*EAS* 8:35–44) goes on to maintain on the flimsiest of grounds that Hemingway respects Al and Max, the "probably Jewish" hit men in "The Killers," as professionals, and that counterman George exemplifies the small-town intolerance which has blocked the killers' entry "into the mainstream of American life." Equally nonsensical is Carol Gelderman's "Hemingway's Drinking Fixation" (*LGJ* 6,ii:12–14), which inveighs against the many references to drink in Hemingway's work (*"Across the River and into the Trees* is 300 pages long. Two hundred and seventy-five consist of cocktails, dinner, after dinner drinks, breakfast with wine and lunch") and decides on this basis that Hemingway, like his characters, was trying to dissolve "whatever

terror he was hiding from" in alcohol. Hemingway's propensities toward liquor have done him no harm in Russia, where, Elena Sabashnikova's "Word of Hemingway" (*SovL* 7:136–39) reports, "300,000
copies in the two-volume edition and 200,000 in the four-volume edition of his collected works" have been sold. On the basis of this readership and the evidence of two recent Russian television productions
based on *The Sun Also Rises* and *Islands in the Stream,* Sabashnikova
characterizes Hemingway as "one of those writers not subject to
fashion."

Robert N. Wilson, whose *The Writer as Social Seer* (N.Car.)
contains chapters on both Hemingway and Fitzgerald, also concludes
that Hemingway's work "does not risk going out of fashion." According to his "Ernest Hemingway: Competence and Character"
(pp. 42–55), gaps may exist between current views and Hemingway's
attitudes on male-female relationships, on the appropriate level of
commitment to one's vocation, and on warfare and violence, but
the author's emphasis on "solar joy" in living, on competence, and on
fidelity to oneself and others in human relations remains universal
enough that "one can scarcely envision a model of the good life that is
not instinct with Hemingway's virtues." Wilson's insightful chapter
on "F. Scott Fitzgerald: Personality and Culture" (17–41) depicts
both Fitzgerald and his fictional protagonists as examples of the "Ica-
rus complex" whose symptoms include "burning ambition and ex-
hibitionism, desire to ascend to great heights; desire to be the center
of all eyes; a precipitous fall; craving for immortality; depreciation
and enthrallment of women." This complex also reflects American
culture generally, and particularly its emphasis on the dream of the
future. Though one might wish for more reference to Fitzgerald's
texts, Wilson's fascinating essay opens a window from which to see
the writer and his work anew.

Two of the four remaining general essays on Fitzgerald start
from a consideration of his origins. Robert E. Rhodes's "F. Scott Fitzgerald: 'All My Fathers,'" in *Irish-American Fiction,* pp. 29–51, distinguishes between Fitzgerald's early fiction in which he tended to
dissociate his leading characters from the Irish, and the later work
in which he extended "the range of his Irish characters" and gave
them a more central position in his work. Though Rhodes sensitively
surveys these characters in the light of Fitzgerald's own Irish background, he has hardly exhausted the biographical implications there-

of. Barry Gross's "Fitzgerald's Midwest: 'Something Gorgeous Some-where'—Somewhere Else" (*MidAmerica* 6:111–26) proceeds from the caveat that Fitzgerald spent only about seven of his first 26 years in the Midwest and none thereafter to an assertion that there are really "two midwests" in his work: the secure and stable one of Nick Carra-way and Basil Duke Lee and the narrow and constricted one of Ru-dolph Miller and James Gatz. As Gross remarks, Fitzgerald knew them both well.

The remaining two essays deal with angles of vision. Dawn Trou-ard's "Fitzgerald's Missed Moments: Surrealistic Style in His Major Novels" (*FHA* 189–205) discovers surrealistic elements from the gong-announced appearance of Dick Humbird's ghost to the goddess Siva passing, Kathleen Moore aboard. Fitzgerald's surrealistic style is evident, Trouard states, in the "motif of missed moments" when the dream turns to nightmare, in the mingling of real and ideal through "fused contradictions and strident images," and in the ineffability of certain mysterious visions. Like Trouard, Robert A. Ferguson has hit upon an interesting subject in "The Grotesque in the Novels of F. Scott Fitzgerald" (*SAQ* 78:460–77). Ferguson's well-argued essay, again like Trouard's, locates elements of the grotesque in all of Fitz-gerald's novels, with its commonest expression coming through "our failure to orient ourselves to the physical world."

c. **Essays on Specific Works: Fitzgerald.**   As usual, articles and notes on *The Great Gatsby* (11) and *Tender Is the Night* (5) dominate Fitzgerald criticism. By contrast, there's but one essay and a note on *The Last Tycoon,* a note on *The Beautiful and Damned,* and nothing at all on *This Side of Paradise.* Two of the articles on *Gatsby* are devoted to visual imagery. Warren Bennett's "Prefigurations of Gats-by, Eckleburg, Owl Eyes and Klipspringer" (*FHA* 207–23) usefully looks back to Fitzgerald's earlier fiction for the genesis of the novel's obsession with eyes. Bennett proposes that the cobalt eyes of Rudolph Miller in "Absolution" may have inspired the famous dust jacket for *Gatsby.* Still better is Lawrence Jay Dessner's highly original "Pho-tography and The Great Gatsby" (*ELWIU* 6:79–90), a study which demonstrates once again the remarkable density of the novel. Fitz-gerald's characters, Dessner observes, "live in a world of photographic images, and have developed habits of mind, tacit philosophies, of ideal existence." Among other things, this point helps to account for the attention paid to the photographer McKee and his futile attempts to capture his all-too-actual wife in poses of ideality.

McKee also crops up in Keith Fraser's provocative "Another Reading of *The Great Gatsby*" (*ESC* 5:330–43), which takes Nick's drunkenly finding himself in the photographer's bedroom to be evidence of his "uncertain sexuality." In addition to this problematic scene, Fraser finds further evidence for his thesis in the novel's phallic imagery and in Nick's description of Tom Buchanan's physique. Fraser is oddly unaware of previous reservations about Nick's complete veracity as narrator and some of his conclusions seem farfetched, but Fitzgerald scholars will want to know of them. Murray L. Levith's note on "Fitzgerald's *The Great Gatsby*" (*Expl* 37,iii:7) also professes to uncover a wealth of sexual submeanings in *Gatsby*, including a "clearly masturbatory image" in the last sentence of the novel. A. B. Paulson's "The Great Gatsby: Oral Aggression and Splitting" (*AI* 35[1978]:311–30) offers a far more sophisticated psychological reading of that famous final passage which is at once deeply pessimistic and evocative of wonder and so displays typical Fitzgeraldian "duplicity." This suggests to Paulson the Freudian notion of splitting, which he then applies with excessive rigor to depictions of women as mother surrogates.

Irving S. Saposnik's "The Passion and the Life: Technology as Pattern in *The Great Gatsby*" (*FHA* 181–88) comments on the pervasive references to "those intricate machines"—automobiles, especially—whose use and misuse "reflect a severe imbalance between outward form and inner dislocation" in the novel. Saposnik's well-written article summarizes and integrates existing scholarship on the subject. Patricia Bizzell's "Pecuniary Emulation of the Mediator in *The Great Gatsby*" (*MLN* 94:774–83) combines concepts from that celebrator of technology, Thorstein Veblen, and from René Girard to account for Gatsby's pursuit of a transcendent ideal. These concepts, interesting in themselves, do not provide much by way of fresh insight into Fitzgerald's novel.

In shorter or less ambitious articles Peter L. Hays's "*Gatsby*, Myth, Fairy Tale, and Legend" (*SFQ* 41[1977]:213–23) calls for precision in applying terminology from folklore to *Gatsby*. According to this taxonomy, the novel can be regarded as part legend and part fairy tale, but not as part myth. The observation of Joseph B. Wagner's rambling "Gatsby and John Keats: Another Version" (*FHA* 91–98) that *The Great Gatsby* represents "an ironic version" of the Endymion myth continues the ongoing discussion of Keatsian influences on Fitzgerald's work. Gordon Bordewyck's fine note on "Gatsby: the Figure of the Host" (*AN&Q* 17:141–42) focuses on the paragraph in chapter 3 where "a wafer of a moon" shines on Gatsby's house and his riotous party while "the figure of the host" raises his hand, a secular priest presiding over "a pagan bacchanal," to bid distant farewell to Nick. David W. Cheatham's study of "Owen Davis's Dramatization of *The Great Gatsby*" (*FHA* 99–113) finds the play to be melodramatic in approach and shallow in characterization and theme.

The best of the articles on *Tender Is the Night* is Jeffrey Berman's "*Tender Is the Night*: Fitzgerald's *A Psychology for Psychiatrists*" (*L&P* 19:34–48), an interesting and long-overdue study of Fitzgerald's knowledgeability about psychiatry in general and the concept of "transference-love" in particular. Fitzgerald used the term "transference" rather vaguely to mean one person's absorption by another in a shifting love relationship, not in the specific analyst-patient sense which led Freud to assert that "an analysis without transference is an impossibility" and then to propose how its ill effects might be averted. Berman considers Diver generally unconvincing as a medical expert; certainly he does not sufficiently understand the "psychoanalytic dynamics of transference."

Two other essays aim to illuminate the character of Dr. Diver. Thomas Deegan's "Dick Diver's Childishness in *Tender Is the Night*" (*FHA* 129–33) lucidly and sensitively develops Piper's insight about the tension between Dick's charm and wit and his tendency toward waste and dissipation (H. D. Piper, *F. Scott Fitzgerald: A Critical Portrait* [1965]). As he descends into immaturity, Deegan states, Diver "progressively prefers the tender night of his romantic illusions to the daylight of reality." The article announces without qualification that Rosemary Hoyt had "sexual intercourse" during that train ride which haunts Diver's imagination, but how is anyone to be sure? Sam B. Girgus' enlightening "Beyond the Diver Complex: The Dynamics of Modern Individualism in F. Scott Fitzgerald" in his *Law of the Heart*, pp. 108–28, compares Diver's situation to that of Young Goodman Brown. Both fail because, having once thought too well of others, they are unable to reconcile themselves to their misbehavior. Thus Diver "is caught between feeling intense care and utter contempt" for other people and, eventually, for himself. Girgus

sometimes stretches Fitzgerald's text to find evidence for his assertions, as in the case of *his* misreading of the psychological effect on
Diver of the "Do you mind if I pull down the curtain?" phrase.

There are two notes on *Tender*. Peter Doughty in "The Seating
Arrangement in *Tender Is the Night*" (*FHA* 159–61) observes that
Rosemary leaves herself out in reciting who sat where at the Villa
Diana dinner party and attributes the error to a lapse in point of view.
Allen Shepherd's nicely crafted "Dick Diver in Nashville: A Note on
Robert Penn Warren's *A Place to Come To*" (*FHA* 173–75) detects
echoes of Diver and *Tender* in the portrait of J. Lawford Carrington
in Warren's 1977 novel.

In a beautifully written essay which smoothly blends criticism
with biography, Wendy Fairey's "*The Last Tycoon*: The Dilemna
of Maturity for F. Scott Fitzgerald" (*FHA* 65–78) asserts that the
Fitzgerald of 1940, despite the gloom of his letters to his daughter
back east, retained an "indomitable streak of optimism" and was
achieving real maturity. Thus *Tycoon* presents a hero who, like
Gatsby, was a romantic, but one whose romanticism is now sensibly
intermingled with pragmatism. And in the book's love story "we
move beyond Fitzgerald's earlier notion of men being destroyed by
their women to a more impartial and judicious sense of life simply
being very difficult." Even in this last fragmentary novel, however,
Fairey detects a note of immature self-pity in the emphasis on the exhaustion that breaks down Stahr, albeit from work rather than from
women or wine. T. Jeff Evans' note on "For Whom the Earth Moved:
A Fitzgerald Parody of Hemingway (*AN&Q* 17:127–28) detects a
dubious parallel between the earth-moving scene in *For Whom the
Bell Tolls* and Stahr's and Kathleen's sexual encounter at his skeleton
of a beach house. Wayne W. Westbrook's slight "Portrait of a Dan-
dy in *The Beautiful and Damned*" (FHA 147–49) points out an apparent link between Adam Ulysses Patch, Anthony's father, and Ward
McAllister, New York society arbiter of the late 19th century.

The best of the essays on Fitzgerald's stories is Alan Perlis' original and insightful "The Narrative Is All: A Study of F. Scott Fitzgerald's *May Day*" (*WHR* 33:65–72). Through meticulous attention
to the text Perlis provides an appreciation of Fitzgerald's skill in
handling point-of-view and structure. The initial compassion of the
novella's narrator gradually dissolves into indifference, Perlis ob-

serves, thus enabling Fitzgerald unobtrusively to "convey the sense of inevitability with which each character declines." In addition, the story is structured to counterpoint the personal violence of the major figures with the random violence of postwar New York.

Rochelle S. Elstein's "Fitzgerald's Josephine Stories: The End of the Romantic Illusion" (*AL* 51:69–83) correctly locates "a devastating and cataclysmic reversal" of Fitzgerald's treatment of love in "Emotional Bankruptcy," the last of his five Josephine stories. Elstein ranges broadly over such matters as Fitzgerald's preoccupation with youth and the sexual competitiveness of young girls, but her essay is awkwardly written and not particularly original.

The three remaining pieces on the stories are concerned with source-finding. Andrew Crosland's "Sources for Fitzgerald's 'The Curious Case of Benjamin Button'" (*FHA* 135–39) carefully shows where in Fitzgerald's reading he came across Mark Twain's notion that life might better begin with old age and go backwards. Significantly, Fitzgerald gave Twain's story idea—also set forth in Samuel Butler's *Note-Books*—a twist of his own. Tahita N. Fulkerson's "Ibsen in 'The Ice Palace'" (*FHA* 169–71) indicates the thematic weight which mention of Ibsen lent to Fitzgerald's story of contrast between North and South. Keith Cushman's concise "Scott Fitzgerald's Scrupulous Meanness: 'Absolution' and 'The Sisters'" (*FHA* 115–21) effectively maintains that "Absolution" owes a debt to Joyce's "The Sisters," the initial story in *Dubliners.*

Two separate articles argue for the artistic merit of Zelda Fitzgerald's *Save Me the Waltz.* Victoria Sullivan's "An American Dream Destroyed: Zelda Fitzgerald" (*CEA* 41,ii:33–39) asserts that *Save Me the Waltz* deserves critical attention on its own merits, not merely for the light it sheds on the Fitzgeralds. Sullivan blames Scribner's failure to promote the book on Scott Fitzgerald, but what chance would the novel have had for publication in the trough of the Depression had it not been written by the wife of one of Scribner's stars? Jacqueline Tavernier-Courbin's "Art as Woman's Response and Search: Zelda Fitzgerald's *Save Me the Waltz*" (*SLJ* 11,ii:22–42) argues along similar lines that though flawed, Zelda Fitzgerald's "moving and fascinating" novel remains "a searching portrayal of a woman's soul." Tavernier-Courbin relies upon the interpretations of Nancy Milford and Sara Mayfield in constructing a rationale for the worth of *Save Me the Waltz*, which presumably is more to be valued because Scott Fitzgerald appropriated his wife's thoughts and writings for his own professional use.

d. **Essays on Specific Works: Hemingway.**   Of 17 articles on Hemingway's novels, four are devoted to *The Sun Also Rises* and seven to *A Farewell to Arms*, but each of the novels except *Islands in the Stream* received some attention. The most stimulating essay on *Sun* uses the book as an example for Jane P. Tompkins' point in "Criticism and Feeling" (*CE* 39[1977]:169–78) that criticism should begin "where the literary experience begins, namely, with the critic's feelings." Tompkins' understanding of Hemingway's novel grew directly out of her "outrage" at the treatment of Robert Cohn: "First he says something good about Cohn, and then he says something mean." Tompkins wanted to identitfy with Cohn as an underdog, but was prevented from doing so by the awareness that he was a loser. Eventually this led her to judge *Sun* as an example of "repressive form" in which Hemingway seems intent, by making a virtue out of the inarticulate, on shutting out both thought and feeling. Where Tompkins attempts to mold a critical aesthetic out of emotional response, Robert B. Hellenga's "Macomber Redivivus" (*NMAL* 3:Item 10) allows subjectivity to reign entirely in asserting that Francis Macomber "proves to be in some ways an even more attractive figure than the hard-bitten white hunter" because he talks so openly of his feelings, of shame and of elation. Hellenga's celebration of Macomber on such grounds provides an almost classical case of reading into a work of art the prevailing values of one's own time—in this case the current preference for "openness" at the expense of rectitude and dignity.

David Goldknopf's witty "Tourism in *The Sun Also Rises*" (*CEA* 41,iii:2–8) proposes that Jake Barnes has a tourist's frame of mind—not the culture vulture type of tourist, but one who is determined not to be recognized as a tourist and so overcharged. Unfortunately, Goldknopf shows no indication of having read recent scholarship on *Sun*. Wayne Kvam's useful "*The Sun Also Rises*: The Chronologies" (*PLL* 15:199–203) holds that the confusion about dates within *Sun* can be cleared up by recognizing that Jake uses two different chronologies, "one to narrate the early chapters and another to narrate the trip to Pamplona." Though the two chronologies are not consistent with each other (and Kvam sensibly recognizes that Hemingway made a mistake, instead of arguing that the error is intentional and meant to reflect the chaotic world of his fiction), each one is accurate within itself. Cathy N. Davidson's brief "Death in the Morning: The Role of Vincente Girones in *The Sun Also Rises*" (*Hn* 5,i:11–13) demonstrates how the death of Girones during the running of the bulls underscores the theme of mutability in the novel. Less persuasive is Davidson's assertion that Hemingway's voice replaces Jake's in discussing this incident and what followed.

The two most important articles in a good group on *A Farewell to Arms* are Linda C. Parton's "Time: The Novelistic Cohesive in *A Farewell to Arms*" (*FHA* 355–62) and George Dekker's and Joseph Harris' "Supernaturalism and the Vernacular Style in *A Farewell to Arms*" (*PMLA* 94:311–18). Parton applies Eleanor N. Hutchens' concept of approaching fiction through time to Hemingway's novel, where time is found to be "the cement," "the catalyst which gives meaning to all else," "the illuminating perspective." In support of her claim, Parton adduces not only Marvell's chariot but the information that 33 of 42 chapters begin with a reference to time and Frederic Henry's observation after the ambulance bogged down during the retreat: "We walked along together all going fast against time." The artful essay of Dekker and Harris suggests that because Hemingway's fiction smacks of the vernacular, most readers have tended to ignore its wealth of literary allusion and its intimations of the supernatural. Thus the smooth vernacular surface obscures "the submerged folkloristic motifs of second sight and revenants" in *Farewell*, especially as exemplified in Catherine.

With his customary density and wit, John Seelye reveals in "Hyperion to a Satyr: *Farewell to Arms* and *Love Story*" (*CollL* 6:129–35) some of the ways—"description, characterization, dialogue, background, verisimilitude"—in which Hemingway's novel is superior to Segal's "exquisite piece of trash" and suggests that in our teaching we should not neglect such primary matters in favor of more fashionable approaches. In highly intelligent if somewhat ironically long-winded fashion Adam J. Sorkin's "From Papa to Yo-Yo: At War with All the Words in the World" (*SAB* 44,iv:48–65) contrasts Frederic Henry's repudiation of abstract patriotic language with Yossarian's word-play when censoring letters in *Catch-22*. The contrast takes us part of the way from Modernism to post-Modernism, since Hemingway seems to believe that (only) concrete language can accurately and morally reflect the world, while for Heller *all* language is "discredited, blacked out, annihilated" so that only a jocular approach remains.

Building carefully on recent criticism and adding his own insights, Edward Engelberg's useful and insightful "Hemingway's 'True Penelope': Flaubert's *L'Education Sentimentale* and *A Farewell to Arms*" (*CLS* 16:189–206) characterizes *Farewell* as a "mutation"—more violent, more telescoped in time, less obviously about "nothing"— of Flaubert's novel. In neither book does the protagonist learn anything that could be called wisdom, and the trouble with Frederic, according to Engelberg, is "what any good family doctor could diagnose as severe depression." What he has to be depressed about forms the subject of Terry Box's "Hemingway's *A Farewell to Arms*" (*Expl* 37,iv:7), which perceives *Farewell* as "a perfect reversal" of the Pygmalion-Galatea myth. Venus had been kind enough to let Galatea breathe, but Hemingway's gods convert Catherine to statuary.

Whether flesh or marble, Catherine Barkley is defended against her detractors in Roger Whitlow's "Mission or Love, Frederick Henry? You Can't Have It Both Ways" (*MarkhamR* 8:33–36). Far from being a vapid nonentity, Whitlow argues, Catherine is a sensitive and perceptive woman who fights back from the verge of insanity and escapes the demons of guilt and loss with the help of Frederick (*sic*) Henry. Two other articles by Whitlow attempt similar rescue missions on behalf of Hemingway heroines. "Adoptive Territoriality in *For Whom the Bell Tolls*" (*CEA* 41,ii:2–8) administers a healthy corrective to the stereotype of Hemingway's women as mindless creatures living solely to satisfy the wants of their men. Maria does indeed want to serve, and like Catherine to merge her identity with that of the man she loves, but such behavior is consistent with the psychological aftermath of the trauma she has undergone. Her "love ethic," according to Whitlow, provides the novel with its moral center, not the futile and murderous business of blowing the bridge. In "Critical Misinterpretation of Hemingway's Helen" (*Frontiers* 3,iii:52–54) Whitlow finds the character of Helen in "The Snows of Kilimanjaro" to have been unjustly maligned, partly because of the tendency to link this story with "The Short, Happy Life of Francis Macomber" and the bitchy Margot Macomber and partly because of a temptation to read "Snows" as a biographical portrait of Pauline Hemingway. Yet in the story itself, as Whitlow persuasively observes, Helen emerges as "strong, considerate, and deeply loving" and Harry as "weak, cowardly, dishonest, and cruel." Not all of Hemingway's female characters can be shoved into one pigeonhole or another.

John L. Cobbs's "Hemingway's *To Have and Have Not*: A Casualty of Didactic Revision" (*SAB* 44,iv:1–10) presents the doubtful proposition that the author "ruined what might have been the best proletarian novel of the thirties" by attaching extraneous material to the basic Harry Morgan story. This interpretation depends upon a view of Morgan as a common man of natural integrity and sensitivity. Cobbs and others who deal with Hemingway's texts should not do so without consulting the papers in the Kennedy library. John W. Crawford's blandly conventional "Robert Jordan: A Man for Our Times" (*CEA* 41,iii:17–22) celebrates a more likely hero than Morgan. According to Crawford, Jordan measures up to the standards of the "saintly" hero established by R. W. B. Lewis (*The American Adam* [1955]).

Two articles advocate the virtues of *Across the River and into the Trees*. Wirt Williams' "Tragic Patterns and Rhythms in *Across the River and into the Trees*" (*FHA* 389–405) asserts that Colonel Cantwell is a tragic hero who chooses "to rush toward death and dictate all the terms of the meeting" and that the novel itself, despite its faults, is "a composition of awesome plan and singular beauty." Roger Whitlow's "*Across the River and into the Trees*—Hemingway and Psychotherapy" (*IllQ* 40,iv:38–47) also attempts to rescue the novel from critical limbo. The tone may be "mawkish," the dialogue "contrived," and Cantwell "very nearly a caricature," yet the book deserves attention because it sets up "an intriguing moral dichotomy between a male sense of mission and a female sense of love." This article, like the three others by Whitlow mentioned above, have clearly been scissored from the same bolt. Gregory Green, in "The Old Superman and the Sea: Nietzsche, the Lions, and the 'Will to Power'" (*Hn* 5,i,14–19) does a nice bit of detective work in showing how Hemingway's book-borrowings in May 1926 led him to Nietzsche by way of James Huneker and then proceeds to argue, not entirely persuasively, that Santiago dreams of lions because they represent, for the German philosopher, a middle stage between man as beast and man as superman.

As usual, Hemingway's short fiction attracted considerable critical attention. In the course of advancing the twin theses that *in our time* possesses "a unity of form and argument" and constitutes "Hemingway's version" of "Hugh Selwyn Mauberley" and *The Waste Land,* Keith Carabine's "Hemingway's *In Our Time*: An Appreciation" (FHA 301–26) supplies sensitive readings of the "chapters" and ends with the extravagant claim that Hemingway "never surpassed the achievement" of that slim volume. Moving to the stories of *In Our Time,* upper case, Richard Fulkerson's "The Biographical Fallacy and 'The Doctor and the Doctor's Wife'" (*SSF* 16:61–65) intelligently points out that leaving biographical considerations aside, we would hardly be likely to conclude that Nick overheard either the Dr. Adams–Dick Boulton dispute or the Dr. Adams–Mrs. Adams exchange. Horace P. Jones, in "Hemingway's 'Soldier's Home'" (*Expl* 37,iv:17) observes that Krebs begins as an ex-Marine but is then transformed by Hemingway into a "soldier" who has served in the "army" and wonders why Hemingway describes him as returning to Kansas "years after the war was over" in the summer of 1919. This note, together with other recent scholarship, raises the issue of errata in Hemingway's work.

Three pieces concentrate in whole or part on "Big Two-Hearted River." According to Frank Kyle's unconvincing "Parallel and Complementary Themes in Hemingway's Big Two-Hearted River Stories and 'The Battler'" (*SSF* 16:295–300), Nick Adams begins his initiation into manhood with "The Battler" and completes it in "Big Two-Hearted River," tales which Kyle finds linked by parallel themes and imagery. Richard L. McCain's "Semantics and Style—With the Example of Quintessential Hemingway" (*Lang&S* 12:63–78) analyzes key passages from both parts of "Big Two-Hearted River" to illustrate how the syntactic strategy of sentences affects their meaning. Robert Gibb's "He Made Him Up: 'Big Two-Hearted River' as Doppelganger" (*Hn* 5,i:20–24) discusses the relationship between Hemingway's style and the content of Nick Adams' world in this story. This elegantly written article has, unfortunately, nothing particularly original to say. By way of contrast David R. Johnson breaks fresh ground in "'The Last Good Country': Again the End of Something" (*FHA* 363–70). Johnson maintains that this 60-page story formed the beginning of "the Michigan novel" Hemingway talked of and that he abandoned the project because there was no way to continue the idyllic sojourn of Nick and Littless with the threat of murder and even rape lying beyond Camp Number One.

Dennis Organ's "Hemingway's 'Hills Like White Elephants' " (*Expl* 37,iv:11) attempts to invest the curtain in this story with the metaphorical burden of representing—to the woman—her unborn child, and—to the man—the continuation of their present childless life. On similarly shaky evidence Myra Armistead's "Hemingway's 'An Alpine Idyll' " (*SSF* 14[1977]:255–58) concludes that the anecdote about the frozen wife is really a tall tale; the point, supposedly, is that the innkeeper in the story is prejudiced against peasants.

Two of the three essays on "A Clean, Well-Lighted Place" take up the familiar problem of attributing dialogue. Working from Hemingway's pencil manuscript, Warren Bennett in his persuasive "The Manuscript and the Dialogue of 'A Clean, Well-Lighted Place' " (*AL* 50:613–24) asserts that giving the speech "You said she cut him down" to the older waiter is Hemingway's mistake, one which he made in the process of fixing an earlier slip in dialogue. David Kerner's "The Foundation of the True Text of 'A Clean, Well-Lighted Place' " (*FHA* 279–300) sets out to refute Bennett by calling attention to numerous instances in which Hemingway gave two consecutive indented speeches to the same speaker. Kerner manages to cast some doubt on Bennett's proposed solution of this dilemma, which may resist solution. Steven K. Hoffman's "*Nada* and the Clean, Well-Lighted Place: The Unity of Hemingway's Short Fiction" (*ELWIU* 6:91–110) rather refreshingly avoids the attribution question in the course of differentiating among the three principal figures in the story.

John J. McKenna's note on "Macomber, the 'Nice Jerk' " (*AN&Q* 17:73–74) proposes that the four-letter word Robert Wilson was thinking of to describe Macomber was "jerk" and not "shit." Far more substantial is George Monteiro's lucid "Hemingway's *Samson Agonistes*" (*FHA* 411–16), which avers that more than any major writer of his time Hemingway evoked widely held cultural values and portrayed generally admired types in his fiction. Monteiro focuses on one such type, that of "the aging, disabled, or apostate professional" and particularly on Harry in "The Snows of Kilimanjaro," a man who achieves a measure of dignity by going to his death while "writing" once again. Finally, Kenneth G. Johnston's closely reasoned "Hemingway's 'The Denunciation': The Aloof American" (*FHA* 371–82) finds the narrator of this tale depicted as an "aloof American" who, along with his government, adopts a policy of strict neutrality toward the Spanish Civil War and so refuses "to assume the responsibilities which come with commitment."

e. **Dissertations.**   Four dissertations completed in 1979 deal with Hemingway alone, three with Hemingway and other writers, two with Fitzgerald alone, two with Fitzgerald and others, and one with Zelda Fitzgerald. Topics which sound promising in abstract form include "Hemingway's *In Our Time*: A Contextual Explication," "The Crafting of a Style: Hemingway and *The Sun Also Rises*," "The Image of the Artist in the Works of F. Scott Fitzgerald," and "F. Scott Fitzgerald and the South."

College of William and Mary

Part II

11. Literature to 1800

William J. Scheick

Considered collectively, studies of Colonial and early National American literature and culture lacked a distinctive heft this year. This admittedly impressionistic reaction emanates less from the proliferation of trivia per se than from the failure of this year's work to engage the scholarly community in a complex manner. Much of the critical output in Colonial studies is descriptive and enumerative reportage or documentation, a considerable amount of it editorial and bibliographic. Such endeavors are certainly legitimate, but when they dominate other modes of critical discourse, they tend to convey an impression of monolithic superficiality. Fortunately, however, as in 1978, Jonathan Edwards and Thomas Jefferson received notable attention. Now Benjamin Franklin joins them. Again like last year, Colonial American travel literature and Puritan interaction with Native Americans were treated in studies distinguished by a well-defined, sophisticated critical apparatus. More dubious than distinguished, two radically revisionist essays making the romances of Charles Brockden Brown more enigmatic than ever before also roiled the generally placid and lacklustre surface of colonial scholarship this year.

i. Puritan Poetry

Remarking a characteristic ambivalence behind the Puritan desire for and resistance to the depiction of the divine world, Lynn Haims initially synthesizes at great length much that is already well known, but her "The Face of God: Puritan Iconography in Early American Poetry, Sermons, and Tombstone Carving" (*EAL* 14:15–47) interestingly concludes that Puritan efforts to visualize the divine parent and to convert the image of a censuring father into one of a loving mother—a tendency to be treated in greater depth in a forthcoming book by David Leverenz—accord with patterns of childhood mental activity. For theory Haims relies principally on Ernst Kris, Jean Piaget, and Erik Erikson, appropriate sources which could have been usefully broadened by familiarity with Richard L. Bushman's application of Erikson's views to Edwards' life and with Bruno Bettelheim's investigation of mental patterns in children. Most problematic in Haim's essay is her approach to Edward Taylor's alleged need for poetic form and order, and the Taylorian parent-child drama she discusses is far more subtle aesthetically than she senses.

In "Edward Taylor's Metaphors of Promise" *(AL* 51:1–16) Michael North argues that Taylor's understanding of the Lord's Supper as a concrete assurance of grace encourages him to scan nature to discover, rather than create, metaphors which, as visible signs of divinity in the physical world, evince promises of salvation. Although North properly emphasizes the positive feature of Taylor's use of metaphor, he disappointingly devalues the integrity of imagistic arrangement in the poems, simplifies the relation between poetic narrator and his use of Biblical types, and overlooks any sense of play in the Taylorian persona of the lisping child. Structurally unifying imagery pertaining to the shape of two jaw bones and to Satan's use of rhetoric in a long poem by Taylor is the subject of William J. Scheick's "The Jawbones Schema of Edward Taylor's *Gods Determinations*" (*Puritan Influences*, pp. 38–54).

What boded to be a major assessment of Taylor's poetics greatly disappointed. Approaching Taylor in the context of John Donne, George Herbert, Henry Vaughan, and Thomas Traherne, Barbara Kiefer Lewalski attempts, with only partial success, to replace previous readings of these poets in terms of a rhetoric of silence and anti-aesthetic strategies with an understanding of their dedication to the establishment of a Protestant poetics based on Scripture. Lewalski's *Protestant Poetics and the Seventeenth-Century Religious Lyric* (Princeton) often belabors what is well known and frequently tends toward the descriptive, but it provides a wealth of valuable detail about Protestant views of the Bible as a work of art. Taylor is given prominent attention in the study and is instructively related to the Protestant tradition which considers life not as an orderly progress from penitence to contemplative ecstasy but as essentially an episodic sequence of trials; yet Taylor fails to get his just deserts. Aside from her minor mistake in having Taylor reside in Westfield, *Connecticut,*

Lewalski seems curiously unaware of the two modes of typology informing Taylor's Puritan culture and unable to detect any organizing principle in individual poems by him. In assessing Taylor's use of emblems, she concludes that his manner indicates an exhaustion of a literary mode; she is apparently unaware, for instance, that in "Meditation 2.3" Taylor ingeniously uses his own face as an emblem. Moreover, Lewalski seems perverse in asserting that Taylor's poems lack tension because the poet "does not actively grapple with his psyche or his art," that in his poems "the speaker is curiously serene: he writes as one sufficiently assured of election and regeneration." In Taylor's culture such assurance constitutes damning presumption, and in his poetic meditations an agonized psyche and a verbal tension comprise the very substance of his art. Lewalski may have put Taylor in good company, where indeed he deserves to be found, but she treats him as if he were a prickly pear among pomegranates.

Taylor's use of poetry as an expression of freedom and a source of meaning, as well as Edwards' emphasis on the process of spiritual awakening through epiphanic language and Anne Bradstreet's appreciation of the interior of the self as the locus of a grace-filled female identity, are treated in three chapters of Karl Keller's fascinating *Only Kangaroo*. If Keller's penchant for outre remarks and brusque generalizations at times evokes skepticism in the reader, his book, like his earlier one on Taylor, provides a pleasant encounter with intermittent flashes of illumination. Less self-assurance characterizes Anne Bradstreet in " 'The posy UNITY': Anne Bradstreet's Search for Order" (*Puritan Influences*, pp. 23–37), in which Emily Stipes Watts traces how the poet's earliest work reflects a failure to discover a comforting metaphorical unity in history, nature, or Biblical typology in spite of poetic assertions to the contrary.

The Latin and Greek poems of a contemporary of Bradstreet are printed and translated by Betty J. Parks in "The Latin and Greek Poetry of Charles Chauncey" (*EAL* 14:48–90). And a worthy, modest (in the best sense) biography of a contemporary of Taylor's appears in Donald P. Wharton's *Richard Steere: Colonial Merchant Poet* (Penn State). If it fudges occasionally and claims a mite too much for Steere's poetry, this monograph certainly contributes to our knowledge about Steere, whose magnitude has increased somewhat during the last decade.

ii. Puritan Prose

In their respective autobiographies Thomas Shepard, Increase Mather, Jonathan Edwards, and John Woolman function as exemplary
fathers and prophets, conflating personal and communal history as
well as urging their communities to fulfill a redemptive mission. This
is the generally convincing if not quite innovative thesis of G. Thomas
Couser's *American Autobiography*, pp. 10–50. Couser anachronisti-
cally designates the Great Awakening as the central influence on
Edwards' "Personal Narrative," disregards well-received previous
commentary when he asserts the absence of any urgent claims upon
the reader of this narrative, and makes a dubious distinction between
Puritan and Quaker revelation. Nevertheless, his book offers a sensible discussion of the conflict within Quaker views on idealism and
on consensus, of the tension between Mather's role as self-proclaimed
prophet and Calvinistic attitudes toward personal initiative, and of
the English and American sections of Shepard's account. Shepard,
as well as Taylor and Edwards, figures centrally in another tradition,
which Norman Grabo's "Colonial American Theology: Holiness and
the Lyric Impulse" (*Nye Festschrift*, pp. 74–93) defines as a search
for Godlike beauty in human forms, a search transcending the political and ethical concerns of American literature.

The man who had been instrumental in directing Shepard to his
first pulpit is the subject of Frank Shuffelton's lucid and informed
Thomas Hooker, 1586–1647 (Princeton, 1977). A fine concluding
chapter on the possible embodiment of a Hookerian heritage within
Edwardsian tradition notwithstanding, this book exhibits a conservative posture, which is certainly understandable but which also permits
certain questions of a more speculative nature to accumulate at the
fringe of the work to await probing by others. What others complete,
however, will not substantially modify Shuffelton's portrait, which
is as solid a contribution as is *Thomas Hooker's Writings in England
and Holland, 1626–1633* (Harvard, 1975)—a collection of ten Hooker
documents superbly edited by George H. Williams, Norman Pettit,
and Winfried Herget, with an essay on the Hooker canon and a bibliography of Hooker's writings by Sargent Bush, Jr.

A colleague of Hooker's in Rotterdam, with whom he co-authored
a book and who might well have been offered the presidency of

Harvard had he fulfilled his plan to emigrate to the New World, receives much needed attention in the first translation of William Ames's *Technometry* (Penn., 1978). Lee W. Gibbs provides an excellent translation, with commentary, as well as a lengthy, good introduction reviewing Ames's life, the sources of his work, and this work's influence on others. If after 1633 Hooker never saw Ames again, he saw too much of Roger Williams, with whom he debated anticlimactically in 1635. Williams' authorial perception of himself as vindicator and protector of the persecuted elect is contrasted with Milton's artistic role as persuader of erring humanity to prepare for grace in O. Glade Hunsaker's "Roger Williams and John Milton: The Calling of the Puritan Writer" (*Puritan Influences*, pp. 3–22). W. Clark Gilpin in *The Millenarian Piety of Roger Williams* (Chicago) excellently grounds Williams' notions in English contexts, while also limning various stages in Williams' thought, especially his conviction of divine appointment to perform eschatological tasks during what he thought were the latter days of the world. Such individualism is characteristic of sectarian enthusiasm, which diverges from the Presbyterian and Independent "middle way" emphasis upon the fulfillment of this millennial role through such official agencies as clergy and Parliament. However deficient in its grasp of typological traditions, Gilpin's work is on the whole satisfactorily clarifying. It convincingly discovers greater consistency than previously ascertained in Williams' behavior, particularly in his atttiude toward Native Americans, whom he did not seek to convert because he did not believe any true church yet existed to accommodate them.

An opportunity for an advancement in our appreciation of another little-understood but significant Colonial figure is missed in Ralph J. Coffman's *Solomon Stoddard* (*TUSAS* 295[1978]), which provides a few good thoughts and many textual and interpretive errors (see Thomas M. Davis' review-essay, *EAL* 14:110–17). The work of the son of Stoddard's chief antagonist is reviewed for undergraduates in Babette M. Levy's *Cotton Mather* (TUSAS 328). In the Introduction to *Ornaments for the Daughters of Zion* (Scholars' Facsimiles and Reprints, 1978) Pattie Cowell observes how Mather adhered to conventional ideas about women's responsibilities and at the same time emphasized, beyond what was average at the time, the value of their usual activities and the appropriateness of their exploration of new roles. All of Mather's writings for and about women, Cowell concludes, evince a contradictory attitude toward women's private equality and public subordination.

Mather at one time warned Joseph Dudley to beware the influence of John Leverett, to no avail and subsequent bad feelings. Leverett's transcription of Dudley's address given at the time of Leverett's installation as president of Harvard in 1708, the only extant example of Dudley's Latin, is reprinted in Leo M. Kaiser's " 'We Are All Filled with the Greatest Hope . . . ' An Installation Speech of Governor Joseph Dudley" (*HLB* 27:443–44). The private record of a man who tried to maintain a moderate response to Dudley's politics receives attention in Samuel Rogal's "A Survey of Published Works Identified in Samuel Sewall's Diary (1674–1729)" (*RALS* 9:50–69).

In "New England's Errand Reappraised" (*New Directions*, pp. 85–104) Sacvan Bercovitch uses a work by Samuel Danforth to reiterate conclusions made in the former's *The American Jeremiad*. The Latin text and an English translation of a 1722 lecture appears in "The Inaugural Address of Edward Wigglesworth as Hollis Professor of Divinity"(*HLB* 27:319–29) by Leo M. Kaiser, whose "On the Epitaph of Thomas Shepard II and a Corrigendum in Jantz" (*EAL* 14:316–17) suggests that Urian Oakes is the author of Shepard's prose epitaph. Finally, in a refreshing and thoughtful essay entitled "The World of Print and Collective Mentality in Seventeenth-Century New England" (*New Directions*, pp. 166–80) David D. Hall challenges recent views of a distinction between a ministerial elite and the popular mind, arguing for a continuity suggested by the fluid boundaries of the world of print and ministerial participation in the collective Puritan mentality; Hall speculates that the breakdown between the two might have occurred in Cotton Mather's time.

iii. The South

Students of Southern Colonial literature will appreciate the bibliography provided by Jack D. Wages and William L. Andrews in "Southern Literary Culture: 1969–1975" (*MissQ* 32:13–215). Wages also compiled *Seventy-four Writers of the Colonial South* (Hall), a well-done annotated bibliography of secondary works that is vague about its principles of inclusion but that nonetheless fills a genuine need. Noteworthy too is Richard Beale Davis' *A Colonial Southern Bookshelf: Reading in the Eighteenth Century* (Georgia), which re-iterates certain points made in his *Intellectual Life in the Colonial South* (1978) and which will be mentioned again when we turn our attention to Thomas Jefferson. Making good use of Davis' earlier study, Lewis P. Simpson's "The Act of Thought in Virginia" (*EAL* 14:253–68) nicely traces from John Smith, through Jefferson, to Poe a sense of history as something "shaped by an act of thought on the part of a novelist and rendered as a self-conscious exercise in achiev-ing the 'happiness of the living.'" A description of the contents and range of a Baltimore magazine appears in Janice Crabtree Wilson's "The *General Magazine, and Impartial Review*: A Southern Maga-zine in the Eighteenth Century" (*SLJ* 11,ii:66–77).

In "Upon the Attribution of 'Upon a Fart' to William Byrd of Westover" (*EAL* 14:143–48) Cameron C. Nickels and John H. O'Neill argue that the work under discussion was almost certainly written by an unidentified English author. Several other works attributed to Byrd, according to Gail Apperson Kilman's and John C. Kilman's "William Byrd II as Amateur Physician" (*LJHum* 5,i:46–65), give information about medical theory and treatment in the colonial South.

The crucial connection between medical practice, politics, and history in the formation of a national identity as it was assessed in the works of one of Byrd's neighbors in South Carolina is probed in "History, Politics, and Health in Early American Thought: The Case of David Ramsay" (*JAmS* 13:37–56) by Lawrence J. Friedman and Arthur H. Shaffer. Politics of a different sort a century earlier, specif-ically the transformation of the extreme individualism exhibited by soldiers, adventurers, and opportunists into regional values, inform T. H. Breen's "Looking Out for Number One: Conflicting Cultural Values in Early Seventeenth-Century Virginia" (*SAQ* 78:342–60).

iv. Edwards and the Great Awakening

In "The 'New Simple Idea' of Edwards' Personal Narrative" (*EAL* 14:193–204) R. C. DeProspo traces how Edwards harmonized Loc-kean psychology and Puritan piety, and suggests that the discon-nected paragraphs of the "Personal Narrative" deny the need for causal structure, thereby exhibiting Edwards' expansion of Locke's system. Not only does this approach contribute little to our present understanding of Edwards, but it is vexed by DeProspo's error concerning Locke's views of mental activity. In *An Essay Concerning Human Understanding* (book 2, chapter 21) Locke modified the Hobbesian view of causality by attributing a degree of freedom, or capacity for action, to the human mind so that in the mind the will "acts" originatively and the intellect "thinks" by combining simple ideas into complex concepts, which comprise real effects of real mental activity. In the Lockean system, in short, the mind evinces not only "passive power" but also an "active power," the capacity for asserting will and effecting change in itself.

At the heart of DeProspo's error is the chimera of our present sense of Edwards' genius for innovation, a notion which several recent studies have implicitly or explicitly exposed by indicating Edwards' extensive appropriation of sources. What is brilliant in Edwards will only surface when we close with what he borrowed or synthesized. Edwards' originality is certainly under attack in Michael J. Colacurcio's "The Example of Edwards: Idealist Imagination and the Metaphysics of Sovereignty" (*Puritan Influences*, pp. 55–106), a painstaking analysis, remarkable for its intelligence and lucidity, of the cohesion of Edwards' Calvinist theology of grace and his rational philosophy of idealism. Edwards' idealist imagination becomes most pronounced, Colacurcio observes, in the stunning metaphysical argument concluding *The Great Christian Doctrine of Original Sin Defended*. Edwards' idealism, as well as that of his grandson Timothy Dwight and of the Yale tutor Samuel Johnson, is mentioned in Edwin S. Gaustad's *George Berkeley in America* (Yale), an unpretentious, old-fashioned account of the Irish philosopher's activities and influence in America. The dependence of Edwards' idealism upon Puritan technometry, a heretofore undisclosed but significant factor, is discussed at length in Lee W. Gibbs's introduction to Ames's *Technometry*, noted above.

An unannotated list of "Doctoral Dissertations on Jonathan Edwards" (*EAL* 14:318–27) has been compiled by Richard S. Sliwoski. And in "The Pastorate of Jonathan Edwards" (*MR* 20:437–51) Patricia Tracy reviews a few details of Edwards' life to conclude that Edwards' real vocation was as pastor and communal leader rather than as intellectual.

"How is family government in a great measure vanished," lamented Edwards in the 1730s, when his work envisioned the renewal

of family hierarchy and harmony as a chief consequence of the Holy
Spirit during the revivals in Northampton. The importance of family
ties and of political power in a colonist's adoption of New Light
piety during the Great Awakening is studied by John W. Jeffries in
"The Separation in the Canterbury Congregational Church: Religion,
Family, and Politics in a Connecticut Town" (*NEQ* 52:522–49).

v. Franklin, Jefferson, and the Revolutionary Period

In "Franklin's Apprenticeship and the *Spectator*" (*NEQ* 52:377–96)
Albert Furtwangler remarks ministerial ambivalence toward the new
power of the emerging press and how nuances in the *New-England
Courant* disguise an editorial quarrel with the Mathers. The counter-
poise of Addison and Mather, Furtwangler reasonably concludes,
frames Franklin's apprenticeship as a writer. Stanley Brodwin seeks a
less sociological, more psychological basis for Franklin's literary
endeavors, especially his satire. In "Strategies of Humor: The Case
of Benjamin Franklin" (*Prospects* 4:121–67) Brodwin concludes:
"Through his comic sensibility Franklin played out dialectically the
contradictions and tensions of his own psyche couched in the terms
of formal Augustan categories and values. And because that sensibility contained within itself its own mode of opposites—Swiftian
irony, Rabelaisian exuberance, wit, invective, contemplative banter,
philosophical debate—it gave Franklin an epistemological tool by
which he could penetrate and understand the dynamics of his American life." Also concerned with how Franklin coped with contradiction and tension, Roger J. Porter's "Unspeakable Practices, Writable
Acts: Franklin's *Autobiography*" (*HudR* 32:229–38) points to Franklin's fear of fluidity as reflected in an accretive structure in his work.
This structure, Porter contends, embodies Franklin's effort to order
experience, minimize conflict, and repress individuality and self
through an artful construction (especially ironic undercutting) mimetic of how one should construct a life. Tension of a third kind
characterizes the *Autobiography*, in the first two parts of which the
personalities of father-figures emerge as complex and troubling. The
negative side of this conflict emerging from Franklin's response to his
father, Hugh J. Dawson explains in "Fathers and Sons: Franklin's
'Memoirs' as Myth and Metaphor" (*EAL* 14:269–92), was eventually
balanced by how much of the parent's example and personality be-

came incorporated into his son's life. Franklin's writings and national image receive attention in Brian M. Barbour's prudent selection of articles in *Benjamin Franklin: A Collection of Critical Essays* (Prentice-Hall).

A political colleague who described Franklin as "the greatest man and ornament of the age and country in which he lived" is treated unimaginatively in William K. Bottorff's *Thomas Jefferson* (TUSAS 327). The influence of a major figure of the Scottish Enlightenment upon Jefferson, as well as upon Edwards and Franklin, is assessed in Gilman M. Ostrander's "Lord Kames and American Revolutionary Culture" (*Nye Festschrift*, pp. 168–79).

Responding to other, larger questions concerning influences upon Jefferson's thought, Ronald Hamowy's vivisection of Garry Wills's argument that the Declaration of Independence was influenced by the moral philosophers of the Scottish Enlightenment is outstanding. In "Jefferson and the Scottish Enlightenment: A Critique of Garry Wills's *Inventing America: Jefferson's Declaration of Independence*" (*WMQ* 36:503–23) Hamowy exposes the differences between Jefferson's views and those of David Hume, Adam Smith, and Adam Ferguson, indicating how the former accord with the ideas of Locke, whose work significantly influenced Francis Hutcheson's writings. That Locke's Second Treatise was, contra Wills's assertion, well known in the colonies before 1750 is documented in Davis' *A Colonial Southern Bookshelf*, remarked above. Davis stumbles, however, in suggesting that praise (in a letter to Peter Carr, 10 August 1787) of the morality of Lawrence Sterne reflects Jefferson's devotion to *Tristram Shandy*. Extremely little evidence exists to support the notion that Jefferson ever read this work—a mere poem copied from the book in 1782 by Martha Wayles Jefferson and completed in her husband's hand. Rather, when he commented to Carr, Jefferson more likely had in mind Sterne's sermons, which as early as 3 August 1771 he recommended to Robert Shipworth as essential to a library, explicitly excluding all other works by Sterne.

Another implicit reply to Wills can be found in E. Brooks Holifield's *The Gentlemen Theologians: American Theology in Southern Culture, 1795–1860* (Duke, 1978), which indicates the influence of the French thinkers Destutt de Tracy and P. J. G. Cabinis upon Jefferson's thought. Holifield offers cogent and exemplary documentation of the thesis that educated southern clergymen (similar to their northern counterparts) were less concerned with spontaneous affectivity than with a reconciliation of reason with revelation, a revisionist thesis valuable in itself as well as for the light it casts on such matters as the southern response to Jonathan Edwards and Thomas Paine.

Reactions to Thomas Paine's writings are catalogued extensively in William S. Ward's *Literary Reviews in British Periodicals, 1789–1797: A Bibliography* (Garland), pp. 179–82, 253–56, 289–312. Whereas in "Black and White," a ballad printed in 1803, Paine was lampooned as a fiery-haired "ghost, with a message from hell," three of his contemporaries consciously sought to reduce such reactions to their political message. "Strategies of Candor in the *Federalist*" (*EAL* 14:91–109) by Albert Furtwangler cogently explores a rhetorical mannerism which closes the distance between author and reader as well as imparts an integrity to the essay series.

James Madison, one of the authors of the *Federalist*, apparently combined Locke's notions about contracts and Scottish ideas about reform, according to Roy Branson's "James Madison and the Scottish Enlightenment" (*JHI* 40:235–50). Madison once read in a letter from Jefferson that John Adams "is as disinterested as the being which made him: he is profound in his views: and accurate in his judgment except where knowledge of the world is necessary to form a judgment." Adams' vain effort to manage, as a means of assuring perpetual peace, an equilibrium among powers competing for the American marketplace is detailed by Gerald Clarfield in "John Adams, the Marketplace, and American Foreign Policy" (*NEQ* 52:345–57). Edith B. Gelles in "Abigail Adams: Domesticity and the American Revolution" (*NEQ* 52:500–21) reports that Adams' wife used letter writing as a form of therapy for the problems generated by her assumption of unfeminine roles during the absence of her husband in the Revolutionary years. Therapy in poetic form is noted in "Keeping the Faith: The Poetic Development of Jacob Bailey" (*EAL* 14:3–14), in which Thomas Brewer Vincent describes the work of an Anglican Tory who fled to Nova Scotia during the Revolutionary years.

The American Revolution, explains Emory Elliott, may in a sense be interpreted as a political Great Awakening. In "The Puritan Roots of American Whig Rhetoric" (*Puritan Influences*, pp. 107–27) Elliott convincingly describes how during this time the revival of 17th-century religious rhetoric combined with language pertaining to economic interests, thereby effectively focusing colonial discontent. Rhetoric of another sort characterizes contemporary responses to treason, and a readable and informed record of the image of Benedict Arnold in the late 18th-century can be found in Charles Royster's "'The Nature of Treason': Revolutionary Virtue and American Reactions to Benedict Arnold" (*WMQ* 36:163–93).

The mutation of the image of the frontiersman, in tandem with the change in the view of the frontier from a place of human degeneration to one of an opportunity for human progress, comprises the interest of J. A. Leo Lemay's "The Frontiersman from Lout to Hero: Notes on the Significance of the Comparative Method and Stage Theory in Early American Literature and Culture" (*PAAS* 88:187–223). Especially good is Lemay's review of how Crèvecoeur adapted notions of cultural evolution as applied to Native Americans to create a model for white civilization; especially mistaken is Lemay's reading of Washington Irving's response to Native American acculturation.

Concerning an acculturated figure of a very different kind Mukhtar Ali Isani has written three essays: "Phillis Wheatley in London: An Unpublished Letter to David Wooster" (*AL* 51:255–60), hinting at Wheatley's business sense; "'Gambia on My Soul': Africa and the African in the Writings of Phillis Wheatley" (*MELUS* 6:64–72), suggesting in Wheatley's work a secular note of protest against debauchery in Africa as well as against slavery in America; and "Early Versions of Some Works of Phillis Wheatley" (*EAL* 14:149–55), indicating that Wheatley did indeed revise her work sometimes.

vi. The Early National Period

A strong case can be made, explains William Hedges in "The Myth of the Republic and the Theory of American Literature" (*Prospects* 4:101–20), for an approach to the significant writings of the early National period that emphasizes the myth of the republic as the embodiment of the quasi-utopian faith typical of the age of Adams and Jefferson. Another major feature of the writings of this period is interestingly detailed in Robert A. Ferguson's "The Emulation of Sir William Jones in the Early Republic" (*NEQ* 52:3–26), which considers the nexus of law, literature, and public service as well as reviews Jones's influence on the neoclassicism of republican works. A third feature found in certain of the writings of this period is remarked in "Far from 'Gambia's Golden Shore': The Black in Late Eighteenth-Century American Imaginative Literature" (*WMQ* 36: 353–72), in which Mukhtar Ali Isani surveys literary attitudes preparatory to the antislavery literature of the 19th century; related matters are also remarked in "Theodore Dwight's 'African Distress'[:] An Early Anti-Slavery Poem" (*YULG* 54:26–36), in which Benjamin Franklin V comments on and prints the best poem by one of the Connecticut Wits.

The poet who hoped that the example of American freedom would eventually spread even to "Afric's burning sands" did not write 15 poems printed anonymously in his newspaper, according to Judith Hiltner Bair; the correct authors of said poems are now identified in Bair's "The Freneau Canon: Erroneous Newspaper Attributions" (*AL* 51:260–66). Equally dubious, according to Mary Weatherspoon Bowden's "In Search of Freneau's Prison Ships" (*EAL* 14:174–92), are the generally accepted biographical facts behind Freneau's *The British Prison-Ship.*

Faulty attributions and dubious assumptions are also exposed in "Fiction in *The Philadelphia Minerva* (1795–1798): A Contribution Toward the Establishment of the American Canon" (*RALS* 9:3–23), in which E. W. Pitcher identifies the sources of fiction printed in the *Minerva* to determine the nationality of respective authors. Pitcher identifies still another American author of periodical essays in "Nathaniel Cotton, the Elder: An Anonymous Contributor to Dodsley's *Museum* (1746–7) and William Dodd's *Visitor* (1760)" (*AN&Q* 17:124–25); and in "The Un-American Fiction of *The American Moral & Sentimental Magazine*, with a Comment on the 'Captivity Narrative'" (*EAL* 14:312–15) Pitcher proves that all ten stories in Thomas Kirk's short-lived magazine were reprinted from English sources and that one of them parodied the captivity narrative.

An early National work heavily indebted to English literature may also reflect the influence of the Common Sense School, according to Lucille M. Schultz's "Uncovering the Significance of the Animal Imagery in *Modern Chivalry*: An Application of Scottish Common Sense Realism" (*EAL* 14:306–11). Schultz's claim that in his satire Hugh Henry Brackenridge resorted to the dialectical manner of this school and considered the "swinish multitude" to be a mere minority

requires more substantial evidence of Brackenridge's interest in
Common Sense Realism and a more thorough probing of the dark
side of *Modern Chivalry*.

vii. Brown and Contemporaries

Jeremy Belknap's satirical and allegorical narrative, *The Foresters*,
received an unusual amount of attention this year. In "Jeremy Belknap's *The Foresters*: A Thrice-Told Tale" (*EAL* 14:126–62) Walter
H. Eitner observes Belknap's revisions; and in "The Names for the
American Colonies in Jeremy Belknap's *The Foresters*" (*BSUF* 20,
ii:22–27) Eitner annotates several allusions. An explication of a newspaper satire later incorporated into *The Foresters* appears in "Mother
Carey's Jacobin Chickens" (*EAL* 14:163–73) by Peter Kyle Mc-
Carter.

If Belknap's reputation as a literary artist is not likely to improve,
that of Charles Brockden Brown has appropriately enlarged ever
since the praise he received from such 19th-century writers as Percy
Bysshe Shelley, John Keats, William Godwin, John Neal, Edgar
Allan Poe, Nathaniel Hawthorne, and John Greenleaf Whittier. More
recent assessments have successfully plumbed the contexts and depths
of Brown's art. A contextual circumstance is revealed in "Yellow
Fever and Charles Brockden Brown: The Context of the Emerging
Novelist" (*EAL* 14:293–305) by Robert A. Ferguson, who remarks
how the yellow fever epidemic gave Brown an opportunity to emerge
as an artist and served in his works as a metaphor for his negative
attitudes toward American society. Concerning the depths of Brown's
artistry, many may well wonder at James R. Russo's two radical attempts to discover still more extensive authorial subterfuge in Brown's
works. In "The Chameleon of Convenient Vice: A Study of the Narrative of *Arthur Mervyn*" (*SNNTS* 11:318–405) Russo argues that the
narrator of *Mervyn* is a confidence man, a self-aware liar using pious
protestation, innocent looks, and the ambiguity of vice and virtue to
his advantage; and, moreover, that this narrator is not Mervyn but
Clavering posing as Mervyn and imputing his own criminal acts to
others. In "The Tangled Web of Deception and Imposture in Charles
Brockden Brown's *Ormond*" (*EAL* 14:205–27) Russo claims that
Ormond is a carefully plotted work of semiplausible lies, which explains why critics have failed to see, for instance, that Mr. Dudley

is the guilty party in the Craig affair, that Constantia is Craig's ac-complice and lover, that Helena Cleves is really Constantia, and that Ormond is no villain but merely a swindled man. That Brown's enig-matic romances can generate such readings is no surprise, but Russo's interpretations seem more wily than Brown's texts. *Caveat emptor.*

British reaction to Brown's work is recorded in William S. Ward's "American Authors and British Reviewers 1798–1826: A Bibliogra-phy" (*AL* 49[1977]:1–21), which also lists reviews of writings by Joel Barlow, William Dunlap, Timothy Dwight, John Penn, Susanna Rowson, and Royall Tyler. A useful overview of the career of the author of *The Algerine Captive* appears in *Royall Tyler* (*TUSAS* 344) by Ada Lou Carson and Herbert L. Carson. And in "*The Adula-teur* and How It Grew" (*LC* 43:103–33) and "The Quality of Mercy, or Mrs. Warren's Profession" (*GaR* 33:881–94) Gerald Weales con-cludes that Mercy Warren was in her time an exemplary professional woman author.

viii. Miscellaneous Studies

On the subject of Puritan attitudes toward Native Americans editors Richard Slotkin and James K. Folsom have created a superb anthology of works by Increase Mather, Benjamin Tompson, Thomas Wheeler, Samuel Nowell, Mary Rowlandson, and Benjamin Church. A few inaccuracies notwithstanding, the substantial introduction to *So Dreadfull a Judgment: Puritan Responses to King Philip's War, 1676–1677* (Wesleyan, 1978) is outstanding in its disclosure of the historic, mythic, and literary dimensions of the helpfully annotated works in-cluded in the volume. In "Conversion from Indian to Puritan" (*NEQ* 52:197–218) William S. Simmons studies the success of Thomas May-hew, Jr. in converting Native Americans of the Martha's Vineyard area and concludes that whenever the traditional culture was most intact the transference to dominant Christian culture was most com-plete.

A good essay on a heretofore somewhat mysterious troublemaker in 17th-century New England has been written by Philip F. Gura, "The Radical Ideology of Samuel Gorton: New Light on the Rela-tion of English and American Puritanism" (*WMQ* 36:78–100). And Hugh Barbour in "William Penn, Model of Protestant Liberalism" (*CH* 48:156–73) provides a first-rate discussion of Penn's effort to unite humanism and eschatology, to reconcile his recognition of truth as it appears in every individual with his response to the human need for social transformation.

Social transformation figures centrally in *New World*, in which Cecelia Tichi makes a strong case for an ideological relationship between environmental reform and the search for a spiritual utopia in the New World. Much that Tichi says about major American writers only reinforces current opinions, but her particular thematic context highlights these views in a special way and as a result intensifies our appreciation of them. Especially noteworthy are Tichi's chapters on Edward Johnson's *The Wonder-Working Providence* and Joel Barlow's *Columbiad*.

Concern with New World environment also informs Wayne Franklin's *Discoverers, Explorers, Settlers: The Diligent Writers of Early America* (Chicago), which delineates three modes of perception in the American travel documents of the 16th through the 18th centuries: the discovery mode recording the "simple timeless stare" or the "emotional stasis" of the ravished observer and generally evincing a series of descriptive set-pieces in lieu of true narrative action; the exploratory mode emphasizing physical and linguistic action (rather than stasis) in a New World void and evoking a vision of process in which the human will extends the moment of discovery into a future ideal colonization; and the settlement mode recognizing disagreeable facts in an ironic perception of the colonist as a pawn of forces quite opposed to those of idealized metamorphosis. Franklin's assignment of selected texts to these categories may strike some as arbitrary or as misrepresentational because whereas some texts yield passages which may be appropriated and inserted into categories, these passages do not necessarily prove that the entire texts from which they are drawn belong to the same categories. Moreover, context certainly qualifies whatever effect a given passage conveys, a problem particularly manifest in Franklin's discussion of Jefferson's *Notes on the State of Virginia*. Yet whatever its problems of this kind, Franklin's elegantly written, richly illustrated book emerges finally as a mature investigation of a neglected area of early American study, as an argument worthy in itself and of debate.

Reactions to landscape offer one means for critical assessments of colonial responses to the New World; the homes settlers built or envisioned in the landscape provide another. *The Palace or the*

Poorhouse: The American House as a Cultural Symbol (Mich. State) by Jan Cohn details colonial and early national attitudes about houses and reveals several significant contradictions, most notably the conflict between an ideal egalitarian society, symbolized by the cabin and cottage, and the pressure of economics, symbolized by the mansion and villa. A similar conflict, embodied in colonial responses to land, politics, and commerce, informs an American heritage combining an awareness of the persistence of corruption and the search for virtue: Milton M. Klein, "Corruption in Colonial America" (*SAQ* 78:57–72). Still another conflict involving early American economic concerns is remarked by Charles Constantin, who in "The Puritan Ethic and the Dignity of Labor: Hierarchy vs. Equality" (*JHI* 40: 543–61) explores the relation between the subordinate quality of all worldly activity and the belief in predestined vocations; he concludes that in principle at least no one calling was more or less superior to any other in Puritan society.

Finally, there is *American Prose to 1820: A Guide to Information Sources*, ed. Donald Yannella and John H. Roch (Gale), an annotated bibliography divided into sections on general reference, the Colonial period, the Revolutionary and early National periods, and principal authors. Such broad scope merits praise, but it has led to several problems which necessitate caution in the use of this work: lapses in citation of secondary sources (e.g., no entry for *The Will and the Word* under Taylor), factual errors (e.g., a mistaken date assigned to Edwards' *Distinguishing Marks*), a tendency toward vapidity in much-too-brief annotations, and an eccentricity in occasionally citing a critical judgment from a review of a work in lieu of presenting an abstract of that work.

If on the whole studies in New World Colonial and early National literature lack distinction this year, they nonetheless collectively contribute respectably to the ongoing pursuit of a deepening critical sensibility to American works written before 1800.

University of Texas, Austin

12. 19th-Century Literature

Kermit Vanderbilt

During a conversation not long before his death earlier this year Jay B. Hubbell recalled that when he arrived to teach at Duke in 1927, the library did not own a copy of *The Scarlet Letter*. Such frustration was common on campuses around the country where upstart American courses were being tolerated in the "English" department. The scholar-teacher of that time worked not only without adequate library or classroom copies of the longer American writings but also lacked ample bibliographies, checklists of manuscripts, and facsimiles of rare books. Fortunately Hubbell and other hardy prime movers of the study of American literature survived to witness the present-day abundance of all these resources and their effect on the scholarship that has flowed liberally through the 1970s. By all counts the great continuing event has been the appearance of the scores of volumes in the MLA-approved editions of 19th-century American authors (Edmund Wilson's grumble notwithstanding). In the year that closes out the decade Irving scholars have added three more titles to a burgeoning edition, the *Selected Letters* of Howells begins to arrive, and the first several of an expected 48 volumes in the definitive edition of Cooper are imminent. How fully all of this painstaking labor with manuscripts and earlier corrupted texts will stimulate revised criticism and biography in the next decade is beyond calculation or imagining.

i. General Studies

The most interesting thematic study published in 1979 is Sam B. Girgus' adventuresome *Law of the Heart*. Girgus ranges among judiciously selected works of the past century and a half to illustrate how an imperious individualism (after Hegel's "law of the heart") has resulted for America in a perversion of private liberty, severing of responsible social relationships, and estrangement of the anarchic "modern self." A second study of comparable insight, though considerably less sweeping than his subtitle suggests, is Eric Sundquist's *Home as Found*, which examines intersecting questions of alienation, family, home, democratic authority, and professional authorship largely in a single work of Cooper, Thoreau, Hawthorne, and Melville.

Robert K. Martin joins a further kind of alienation to a specific genre in *Homosexual Tradition*. Though Whitman and Hart Crane expectedly dominate whatever "tradition" of a shared homosexuality can be argued among American poets, Martin is very good on Fitz-Greene Halleck and especially Bayard Taylor. Because a homosexual in America is still the person who has just left the room, Martin's direct and open-minded approach may encourage a much-needed clearing of the air about a number of same-sex relationships among our authors and within their writings. Still another hopeful side of the year's general scholarship can be found in the high proportion of new dissertations by younger colleagues who have gone beyond the single-author subject to broad matters touching American culture and literary art—urban affairs, nature, the frontier, humor, naturalism, and the Romance.

ii. Irving, Cooper, and Their Contemporaries

After ten years of gradually accelerating activity, the CEAA-endorsed *Complete Works of Washington Irving* (Twayne) now boasts 14 volumes of an anticipated 27. The three books published this year include volume 2 of the four-volume *Letters* (1823–38). This generous collection of 868 letters in 942 pages (plus one page of errata) has been capably annotated, like its predecessor, by editors Ralph M. Aderman, Herbert L. Kleinfield, and Jenifer S. Banks (see *ALS 1978*, p. 201). Of the selections in *The Crayon Miscellany*, ed. Dahlia K. Terrell, the one currently most popular is *A Tour on the Prairies*, the subject of Terrell's textual dissertation (see *ALS 1967*, p. 136). Terrell's introduction, along with the editorial apparatus, is densely informative. It is also rather gracelessly written. The reader struggles through 150 footnotes, many in mid-sentence, in just 30 pages. In addition, Terrell presents little more than a half-hearted case for the need to republish these lesser works.

Even more self-defeating is editor Roberta Rosenberg's disparaging observation that *Wolfert's Roost* comprises "a grab-bag collection of Irving's unpublished manuscripts." The Introduction is marred, too, by carelessness—inept phrasing, wayward punctuation, misspellings, and erratic documentation. But this volume of short pieces, first published in 1855, tells us much that is important about Irving's irregular habits of writing and revising, thanks to Rosenberg's helpful scholarship.

A new biography of Irving, Philip McFarland's *Sojourners* (Atheneum), is a boldly imaginative effort to present Irving against the backdrop of contemporary history at home and abroad. The subordinate "sojourners" who appear within an otherwise unremarkable periodizing of Irving's life are his acquaintances Aaron Burr, Scott, Mary Shelley, and John Jacob Astor. Also, quite curiously, there is John Brown, whom Irving never met. McFarland apparently conceived the counterpoint of Brown's entries and exits to add continuity and dimension to Irving's international odyssey. And so "Don Washington Irving" muses over the legends of a Spanish past while Brown in the 1830s nurses an early humanitarian conscience; Irving associates with Astor during Brown's free-soil crusade in Kansas; and at the end, as in the opening pages, Irving in 1859 is dying at Sunnyside as Brown raids Harper's Ferry. Irving succumbs on 1 December, Brown is hanged the next day, "and as John Brown's body swung in space," McFarland concludes, "one age ended and another began." The Brown analogues do little for either structure or theme, but this book must be taken seriously. McFarland has faithfully attended to the required sources—criticism, biography, and the new texts of the "Complete Works."

A lighter moment for Irving enthusiasts is provided by the latest offering from the Sleepy Hollow Press, *The Wit and Whimsy of Washington Irving*, comp. and ed. by managing editor Bruce D. MacPhail. MacPhail has sprinkled this attractive little book with illustrations from Irving's special editions, and he serves up such frothy one-liners as "Whenever a man's friends begins to compliment him about looking young, he may be sure that they think he is growing old"—*Bracebridge Hall.*

There are three worthwhile articles on Irving this year. Earl N. Harbert, "The Manuscripts of *A Chronicle of the Conquest of Granada*: A Revised Census with Commentary" (*BRH* 82:124–29),

supplements H. L. Kleinfield's earlier census of Irving manuscripts
(see *ALS 1964*, p. 111). Harbert reviews the publishing history of
Granada and concludes that while these five manuscripts show Irving's inveterately sloppy writing mechanics, they also reveal his
"unwavering commitment through the years to historical accuracy
and improved narrative economy." Two stories receive psychological
scrutiny, the first in " 'Rip Van Winkle': Wheels within Wheels"
(*AI* 36:178–96) by David J. Kann, who regards "the mechanism of
the dream as the closest analogue to the process of Irving's tale."
While Rip's infantile wishes are ironically fulfilled in a regressive
death of the self, Irving ends on a satiric note that forces the reader
to withdraw from childish fantasy to mature analytic thought, though
not without hazardous ambiguity as to what point of view one can
truly assume. Kann's analysis is a worthy addendum to Philip Young's
pioneering essay two decades ago. Less ambitious but also provocative is James E. Devlin's "Irving's 'Adventure of the German Student' "
(*SAF* 7:92–95). As Devlin views it, Gottfried Wolfgang's escape from
his health-impairing fantasies of " 'female beauty' " in Goettingen is
a flight from the guilt of self-abuse; but in Paris he continues thus to
" 'lose himself.' " The guillotine and decapitated woman represent
castration punishment. When Gottfried is ushered off to a madhouse,
his insanity is, of course, an age-old penalty for masturbation. (Is
this a hidden dimension of Irving's wit and whimsy?) For anyone
whose library does not carry the journal cited, Devlin's reading can
also be found verbatim in *L&P* 29:120–22.

More than ten years have passed since James F. Beard completed
his invaluable six volumes of the Cooper *Letters and Journals* (Harvard). In 1979 the first two works in the new definitive-text edition
(SUNY) were scheduled but failed to appear. But some of the editors,
along with three dozen lovers of Cooper, gathered for a symposium
at SUNY College at Oneonta and Cooperstown, N.Y., in July 1978.
The seven papers have now been published by the conference in a
pamphlet, *James Fenimore Cooper and His Country, or Getting Under Way*, ed. George A. Test (Oneonta: SUNY College). Among the
editors who addressed the group Thomas L. Philbrick (*Wyandotté*)
traced Cooper's "best hopes and darkest apprehensions" in the four
Otsego novels; Donald A. Ringe (*Lionel Lincoln*) treated Cooper's
complex pictorial mode in three novels, especially *The Pioneers*;

Kay S. House (*The Pilot*) reminded participants that existing social and literary attitudes toward women influenced Cooper to portray angelic or mediating "females" in a man's world of adventure, and he was unusually skillful at this difficult task; and textual editor for the Cooper series, James P. Elliott, described the work on the first 14 volumes, including textual problems with *The Prairie*.

The fine opening chapter of Eric Sundquist's book, *Home as Found*, is the elaboration of a long article on Cooper previously summarized here (*ALS 1977*, pp. 212–13). Three new essays on the Leatherstocking fiction, all decently argued, contribute worthwhile grace notes, at least, to former criticism. Donald Darnell in "*The Deerslayer*: Cooper's Tragedy of Manners" (*SNNTS* 11:406–15) believes that Cooper in the 1840s viewed social striving not only as undesirable; it is also unnatural and can be ultimately tragic. In chapter 9 of *The Deerslayer* Natty points instructively to a leaping fish and advises Judith Hutter of nature's moral: one does not successfully strive upward out of one's element. Judith does not heed the lesson, and for her foolish social presumption Cooper goes beyond his practiced ridicule of climbers and levelers: he shows that "frustrated social aspiration can also be a source of tragedy and in the process creates his most memorable heroine in Judith Hutter." Despite Darnell's argument, some readers may have trouble discovering a particularly tragic note in Judith's frustrated "search for identity in the social world."

The other two essays supply a new wrinkle on well-worked themes in Cooper's most analyzed novel. Leland S. Person's "Cooper's *The Pioneers* and Leatherstocking's Historical Function" (*ESQ* 25: 1–10) stresses the older Natty's effort to merge his "wilderness values with those of the settlers" and to pass this vision on as an "active legacy" to the reborn Elizabeth and Oliver. Does the final sentence of the novel mean that Natty will duplicate his role for another society farther west? If so, Cooper later tempered his hope that such reconciling social leadership would ever appear in America. Natty as a reconciling voice does not, however, enter Peter Valenti's scheme in " 'The Ordering of God's Providence': Law and Landscape in *The Pioneers*" (*SAF* 7:191–207). Instead, Valenti devises the old battle line between civilization and nature, this time by invoking Gilpin's 18th-century "picturesque tour" to define the salient contrast between

Natty and Judge Temple. Natty corresponds to the picturesque traveler or artist who enjoys nature, her movement and grace and order, *as is.* Temple and his fellow civilizers, on the other hand, disrupt nature's order as they "improve" upon it. Natty fears that moving nature (the river) will soon become moving civilization (laden with the pioneers' boats). The contrast shapes the narrative movement, architecturally through forced versus intuitive aesthetics, scenically in rutted roads versus forest paths, and so on. One can be grateful for what illumination Valenti has brought to this familiar dialectic and at the same time plead, with regard to his subtitle, that a moratorium now be called on the trendy terms "landscape" and "law" in Cooper.

Cooper and Irving also receive summary sketches by Stephen Railton and Andrew Myers, respectively, in *Antebellum Writers in New York and the South* (see chapter 22), volume 3 of *DLB*. Among the 65 authors may be noted the entries for prominent contemporaries: Bryant (David Tomlinson), John P. Kennedy (J. V. Ridgely), and Simms (Keen Butterworth), the only significant space these three earned in 1979. Many of the lesser writers are amply treated: for example, Charles M. Lombard writes a crisp and sufficient sketch of Thomas Holley Chivers (pp. 57–61) and comments sensibly, "Today little attention is paid to his role as a poetic innovator apart from the limited notice taken of his connections with Poe." Despite this estimate, Lombard has then given us this year, as well, an 11-chapter monograph on Chivers (TUSAS 325).

A rare book that warrants its modest shelf space, however, is *Les Cenelles: A Collection of Poems by Creole Writers of the Early Nineteenth Century,* trans. with pref. by Régine Latortue and Gleason R. W. Adams (Hall). Because little is known about early literary attempts of "colored" Americans not influenced by British example—here the influence is from French romantic sources—these Creole poems, first published in 1845, are important to scholars. The editors acknowledge the poetry to be "superficial and imitative," lacking the poignancy and social protest of Haitian exile or abolitionist agitation (Creoles could own slaves). Still, the agony of a mixed-color identity is here. For readers who have assumed that Creoles possessed no written literature, no romance, no pressing anxieties beyond practical survival, these poems are welcome and necessary documents for an "American" literary history.

iii. Popular Writers of Mid-Century

Published last year as vol. 1 of the *DLB* (see *ALS 1978*, p. 491), *The American Renaissance in New England* is less satisfactory than the companion volume of New York and Southern writers just mentioned. Many of the 98 authors here are so minor as to merit only a paragraph of comment. Among the essays on the major figures Thomas Wortham's well-written, judicious assessment of Lowell can be recommended. Barry Menikoff is equally authoritative on Holmes. Wortham is also author of the extended essay on Holmes in *American Writers: A Collection of Literary Biographies,* ed. Leonard Unger (Scribner's), an enterprise that has incorporated the old University of Minnesota pamphlet series and continues it in this hard-cover format. Wortham touches all the bases with a critical awareness of which moments and works deserve close inspection. He offers no special pleading but instead a sane and civilized treatment of the sane and civilized Holmes. Vastly different in tone and approach is the only book on Holmes this year, *The Improper Bostonian: Dr. Oliver Wendell Holmes* (Morrow) by popular biographer Edwin P. Hoyt. Written in a journalistic, condescendingly chatty manner, with no critical analysis of Holmes's literary work (though Holmes's poetry is quoted at length), the book nevertheless benefits from Hoyt's usual careful research. His most original suggestion for Holmes's claim on our interest today is, oddly, not in literary history but gerontology. The keenness of this aging mind should attract the modern reader consumed by the fear of growing old in America.

Parallel to the crisis of aging today is a resurging, and less easily explained, interest in our past children's literature. Followers of this popular trend, on and off the campuses, will be happy to know about a compact overview of "The Captivity Narrative as Children's Literature" by James A. Levernier (*MarkhamR* 8:54–59). From 1820 to the Civil War the frontier experience of captivity was recast for the enjoyment and edification of WASP children as a struggle between the Satanic Indian and Providential Pioneering. Old-world children's stories were replaced by patriotic American adventure larded with the overt lessons of a McGuffey Reader. Courage, trust, friendship, and self-sacrifice were at the didactic center of these stories, though the young also learned, incidentally, about local folklore and geography. After the war, the popularity of these stories declined when the Indian gradually became absorbed into the American heritage, and a new sectionalism and urbanism shifted the national concern away from the moral precepts of prewar New England.

Adults of the same period also craved the adventure yarn, and one of the writers who served the demand for popular travel books was William Starbuck Mayo, the subject of Gerald C. Van Dusen's monograph (TUSAS 345). Mayo is remembered by Melville scholars for his *Kaloolah* (1849), a tale of captivity and escape in Africa, with the title character a version of Fayaway and her Yankee hero Jonathan Romer (along with his creator) a descendant of the Starbuck line to which Melville, supposedly in a literary tribute, would presently assign Ahab's chief mate. Van Dusen further argues convincingly Mayo's importance both as a pioneer of the urban novel of manners (*Never Again*, 1873) and a type of the struggling writer in the New York milieu of popular culture at mid-century.

Another popular writer of the period, Bayard Taylor, dazzled the young Howells but commands little readership these days. But Robert K. Martin may help to change Taylor's fortunes. His excellent "Bayard Taylor's Valley of Bliss: The Pastoral and the Search for Form" (*MarkhamR* 8:13–17) is also incorporated into the larger context of *Homosexual Tradition* (pp. 97–109), mentioned earlier. With the conventional subtitle of this article Martin springs a surprise on the unwary reader. Taylor used the pastoral in his aesthetic search for a form that could then allow the emotional release of a homosexual sensibility. He discovered this pastoral outlet in verses that treat Persian and Greek boys, the myth of Hylas, the Theocritean idyll, and other coded fare that was also welcomed by, in Martin's rather peremptory grouping, the Stedman-Stoddard "homosexual circle of genteel poets" (the Stoddard here being Richard Henry). Martin also resurrects Taylor's fourth novel, the quasi-pastoral *Joseph and His Friend* (1870), and calls Joseph's friend and mentor Philip Held "the first fictional spokesman for gay liberation in American literature."

Among the chief women authors at mid-century Margaret Fuller and Julia Ward Howe have new book-length studies and Harriet Beecher Stowe continues to attract a steady audience both in and out of her slavery fiction. Louisa May Alcott, in lesser degree, remains alive in at least one scholar's annual attention, and this year she is fortunate to have a perceptive new reading from Judith Fetterley,

"*Little Women*: Alcott's Civil War" (*FemS* 5:369–83). Fetterley notices a high degree of "anger and political perception" in the author of *Little Women*, and detects for once a stylistic tension in Alcott's literary art. The main cause of this advance beyond her "true style" is her discovery that the Civil War as a central fact of dominant male activity elsewhere can be translated into a "metaphor for internal conflict" among Jo and others in the world of little women. For them to conquer the self and live for others—the traditional morality of the little women's life in peace or war—is to Alcott "less a matter of virtue than necessity," Fetterley argues. Since men do the work of the world, the woman must please and honor them so that they will provide her with necessary love and an escape from the terrors of spinsterhood. This fear visits even Jo, the determined professional writer, and is "one of several unpleasant emotions simmering just below the sunny surface" of the novel. Fetterley challenges Elizabeth Janeway's calling Jo the one independent woman in 19th-century fiction, and reads a sharp ambivalence in Alcott's marrying Jo, the most resisting little woman, to Professor Papa Bhaer, the properly suppressive male "authority figure" whom she will, after all, come to serve.

Henry James found little to praise in the fiction of Alcott or, for that matter, the writings of Margaret Fuller. But Margaret V. Allen in *The Achievement of Margaret Fuller* (Penn State) judges her subject more favorably and has written a serious intellectual biography that ends up, however, with a rather strident assertion of Fuller's exalted significance (see also chapter 1). Allen gives full play to the vast influence of Goethe, who "humanized and liberated" Fuller from her stifling Puritanism and made her a creative citizen of the world. More than a legendary conversationalist, she was a gifted writer whose best work is still alive, as is her conviction, as critic and editor, that art must serve democracy. Allen helps us to realize why Julia Ward Howe should have thrown off the trammels of her own conservative upbringing after meeting Fuller at a "conversation" in Elizabeth Peabody's West Street Bookshop in Boston. Deborah P. Clifford in *Mine Eyes Have Seen the Glory: A Biography of Julia Ward Howe* (Little, Brown) recounts this decisive event and the turbulent inner life before and after for America's outwardly conventional lookalike of Queen Victoria. Clifford would have us remember the humanity of Mrs. Howe beyond the circumstances of the "Battle Hymn" (why are we then reminded of them in Clifford's title?)

Howe admirably battled for causes, firmly believed in human goodness and the power of reform, and not least, commemorated the most
admired woman of her life by writing, in later years, a characteristically modest biography of Margaret Fuller.

If perennial and seemingly inexhaustible scrutiny can be taken as
a measure of aesthetic excellence, *Uncle Tom's Cabin* assuredly is
near to the "great American novel" De Forest reckoned it might be.
This year Theodore R. Hovet adds the clinching evidence for Elizabeth Ammons' earlier essay on Uncle Tom's feminine characteristics
(see *ALS 1977*, p. 216) with the discovery of "Mrs. Thomas C. Up-
ham's 'Happy Phebe': A Feminine Source of Uncle Tom" (*AL 51*:
267–70). In her *Key to Uncle Tom's Cabin* Stowe wrote that Tom's
pious characteristics were derived from a "small religious tract" by "a
lady of Brunswick" who recounted the life of a "coloured woman,
named Phebe." Hovet found in Brunswick this eight-page source.
Like Tom, Phebe also marks her Bible, lives in a cottage, and prays
easily. Happy, humble, and patient, her feminine and domestic virtues also become Tom's. But at least since Richard Wright's *Uncle
Tom's Children* (1936), these have been odiously servile traits of the
black militant's "Uncle Tom," with Stowe castigated as an inad-
vertent racist. Moody E. Prior defends both author and character
in "Mrs. Stowe's Uncle Tom" (*CritI* 5:635–50). Prior views Tom as
a powerfully conceived Solzhenitsyn hero of mythic-Christian proportions who resists the oppressor as he struggles to maintain his
humanity.

The Stowe-Day Foundation has now brought all of Stowe back
into print with the publishing of *The Pearl of Orr's Island*, intro. by
E. Bruce Kirkham. Begun in 1852 after *Uncle Tom's Cabin*, the novel
was written by fits and starts during the next ten years. Kirkham first
acknowledges its flaws, but after remarking on echoes from *The
Tempest*, he grows inspired to deem it "worthy of a small niche in the
great hall of American classics." More likely it deserves to be repub-
lished as an instance of early local-color writing sufficiently effective
to have awakened 14-year-old Sarah Orne Jewett to the village world
of the Maine seacoast. The predictable love plot, too, appealed to the
sentimental magazine audience of the time, so that *The Pearl* enlarges the history of popular taste at mid-century.

Stowe also figures this year in two illuminating comparative studies. Karl Keller positions her as a "foil for talking about neglected sides of Emily Dickinson" in his *Only Kangaroo*, pp. 97–124. While Dickinson had Puritan affinities in her aesthetics, she did not, like Stowe, indulge in millennial reform hopes or the Puritan-historical analogies of typology. Stowe stood for public institutions and the ideal, Emily for private activity and actualities. Victor A. Kramer also adopts the example of Stowe to clarify the ideas and literary art of his figure in "Harriet Beecher Stowe's Imagination and Frederick Law Olmsted's Travels: The Literary Presentation of Fact," in *Olmsted South: Old South Critic / New South Planner*, ed. Kramer and Dana F. White (Greenwood), pp. 109–20. Stowe expressed her moral outrage and reformist sympathies in imaginatively powerful and seemingly accurate character and setting; Olmsted presented himself as an "agricultural economist" who sought objective truth and inquired into the practical shortcomings of slavery in a free-labor market. For a stylistic approach Olmsted took the subtle indirection of a "deliberately prosaic documentation" of detail and incident, but he meant, no less than Stowe, to expose the degrading effects of the plantation system on slave and master.

iv. Local Color and Literary Regionalism

An attempted redefinition of the local-color school and a new book on Bret Harte brighten an otherwise barren regional scene this year. "Universal and Particular: The Local-Color Phenomenon Reconsidered" (*ALR* 12:111–26) is Alice Petry's argument for the essentially universal in postwar local-color writing, and Petry examines the aesthetic methods that authors devised to expound these values. Faulkner in his Nobel Prize Speech made fashionable the view that the local is in fact universal, and the concept by now has grown a bit wearisome as a regional point of departure. Even so, Petry gives a helpful survey of writers who variously propounded Honor (Freeman), Heroism (Allen), Stoicism (Freeman), Adaptability (Harte, Austin), Human Responsibility (Cable, Garland, Harte, Hay, Murfree), Faith (Freeman), and Idealization (Allen). Five general aesthetic approaches appear in one author or another to universalize these matters. First is the device of the interloper, who is either a noncharacter (Harte) or a disruptive agent (Chopin) or a major character sympathetic to local ways (Westcott, Jewett, Harris, Page) or is merely felt through intrusive urban values (Dazey, Harris). Too, there is the yokel as a "reverse interloper" who takes his superior country notions to the city (Dazey, Westcott). Other universalizing techniques are the authors' uses of time (definite or indefinite past and assumed life after death), Biblical and classical parallels, generality of place and "home," and a direct, didactic narrative voice. Petry does not propose any author as the compleat practitioner. Do glaring exceptions in various works invalidate these formulae for the local-color mode? Petry's definitions make a useful target for future quibbles, qualifications, and addenda.

    Mark Twain, C. W. Stoddard, Ambrose Bierce, and others valued the critical opinion of Bret Harte, whose demand for realism when he edited the *Overland Monthly* (1868–71) put him just ahead of his time. These are reasons enough to welcome Patrick Morrow's modest *Bret Harte: Literary Critic* (Bowling Green). Harte's criticism is candidly presented here for what it is—practical expression and judgment of the work at hand, uninformed by a critical vocabulary or a definable stance beyond the requirement of believability (which Harte paradoxically flaunted in his own popular fiction). Morrow helpfully establishes the postwar climate of criticism in America and concludes that Harte should be especially known as a figure in transition between romance and realism who "maintained his allegiance to both." Harte's second career as a diplomat was aided by John Hay, his fellow balladeer of the West, when Hay helped to extract him from the German post to become U.S. Consul in 1880 at Glasgow. "The Unpublished Letters of Bret Harte to John Hay" (*ALR* 12:77–110) by Brenda Murphy and George Monteiro directs intimate light on Harte's restlessness and dissatisfaction in Glasgow. Harte was depressed almost at once by the smog, the people, and the cultural isolation. He wanted out. But he remained six years, then moved to London, and in 1888, wondered to Hay if there were a chance for another "post" in view of his efficiency in past appointments. This high estimate was not shared by officials in Washington, who, in James G. Blaine's words to Hay the next year, rated Harte "the worst consul thus far recorded."

    New England local-color fiction was represented this year by one essay on time (Jewett) and one note on space (Freeman). In the first

Mary C. Kraus, "Sarah Orne Jewett and Temporal Continuity" (*CLQ* 15:157–74), shows her author's consciousness to be that of Augustine rather than Yeats, Spengler, or Proust, with experience in Jewett felt as "the moving image of eternity" rather than disjunctive moments of time. "Her view of the interdependence and continuity between past and present," Kraus argues with ample evidence, "dictates the characterizations, themes, and techniques of her entire work." On the other hand, Freeman drew her characterization from psychic suggestions prompted by cramped physical space, at least on the occasion described in Marilyn De Eulis' appropriately restrictive note, " 'Her Box of a House': Spatial Restriction as Psychic Signpost in Mary Wilkins Freeman's 'The Revolt of Mother' " (*MarkhamR* 8: 51–52). De Eulis relies partly on Bachelard's *The Poetics of Space* to explain how the spaces of house and barn contain the psychic terms of Sarah Penn's revolt against the "system" her husband embodies.

A pair of articles study the indictment of southern character and society before and after the Civil War by two of the region's own. Though a New Yorker, Thomas Bangs Thorpe moved to Louisiana for his health in 1837, remained there 17 years, and wrote the sketches titled *The Hive of "The Bee-Hunter"* (1854), which Daniel F. Littlefield discusses in "Thomas Bangs Thorpe and the Passing of the Southern Wilderness" (*SLJ* 11,ii:56–65). Thorpe's accounts of the people and natural scenery in this lower Mississippi locale move into and then away from the realistic and humorous to become, at last, "an indictment of the wasteful destruction of natural resources." The "largeness and beauty of nature" seems not to have ennobled these inhabitants who, instead, despoiled the land, slaughtered the natural life, and routed the Indian. Robert O. Stephens shifts the historical scene to post-Reconstruction Louisiana as he brings together "Cable's *Madame Delphine* and the Compromise of 1877" (*SLJ* 11,i:79–91). In the final scene, when the heroine confesses her perjury regarding the mixed parentage of her daughter and Père Jerome exonerates her, Cable is venting his anger against the society that instituted the Black Codes which forbade interracial marriage, even with quadroons. More broadly, Stephens argues from biographical data, Cable indicts the entire nation for the Compromise of 1877 that left the fate of the black freedman to the southern states. Cable's rhetorical strategy is to entice his readers into the dramatic scene and then, through Père

Jerome's doctrine, awaken them to their complicity in the fierce contradiction his characters suffer between their "moral right and legal restriction."

v. Henry Adams and Late 19th-Century Nonfiction

The compound title of this section just barely applies, for Adams studies continue to be challenged by only the faintest competition. Richard F. Fleck continues to unfold the progress of John Muir's compassionate attitudes toward native cultures on this continent, now with an article on "John Muir and Eskimoan Cultures" (*RS* 47:48–53). Still another bibliography facilitates Muir scholarship: Ann T. Lynch's "Bibliography of Works by and about John Muir, 1869–1978" (*BB* 36:71–80, 84) provides a convenient and reliable listing, her only prominent omission being the work of Kevin Starr.

Barrett Wendell, Harvard's colorful professor and historian of American literature, is the central figure in Paul E. Cohen's pleasant chronicle, "Barrett Wendell and the Harvard Literary Revival" (*NEQ* 52:483–99). Stimulated by his creative students in freshman composition, Wendell helped to found the *Harvard Monthly* (1885–1917), and while those pages proclaimed the literary ideal of Oxford rather than Michigan or Nebraska, the journal inevitably flourished under the exacting standards of its famed advisor and the editorial and literary talents of brilliant young Harvard men like Baker, Berenson, Herrick, Santayana, Moody, Robinson, Stevens, and Dos Passos.

Henry and Marian ("Clover") Adams are each granted book-length appraisals this year, and some readers may learn more about Henry in Marian's book than in his own. Ferman Bishop's is the second monograph on Henry Adams from Twayne publications within five years (*TUSAS* 293). In his preface Bishop promises to correct earlier determinist misreadings of Adams caused by those who have missed the satire which affects his view of morality, human choice, and achieved optimism. Bishop underscores the role of choice in the Gallatin biography and *Esther*, relocates the "satiric norm" in *Democracy*, and distinguishes the multiple viewpoints in the *History* and *Education*. But no clearly defined satiric vision of Adams' ever unifies the variously truncated 13 chapters of this brief overview (118 pp.) of a highly complex and varied career. By contrast Otto Friedrich's volume is three times larger as he sifts far scantier data on Marian

Adams to produce this first biography of *Clover* (Simon and Schuster). Friedrich's analysis of Marian—a "Voltaire in petticoats" Henry James once tartly, though approvingly, called her—will intrigue students of Henry Adams for the same reason that Zelda's mental health seems necessary to appreciate parts of the Fitzgerald canon. Despite Friedrich's fascinating and at times protracted discussion of the various "evidence," literary scholars will continue to regard as open to diverse readings the presumably unflattering traits of Marian presumably embedded in the heroine of *Esther*, and the relation of all this to Marian's suicide.

Three substantial essays mark a real advance this year in exposing certain sides of Adams that are yet imperfectly understood. Several years after Marian's suicide, his *History* completed, Adams was recuperating emotionally in the South Seas and enjoying, with John La Farge, the sensual grace of native Samoan dancers. Carlos Baker imaginatively compares Adams' uninhibited response to this dancing with Emerson's more dignified aesthetic commentary in 1841 after accompanying Margaret Fuller to a Boston performance by Viennese ballerina Fanny Elssler. See "Moralist and Hedonist: Emerson, Henry Adams, and the Dance" (*NEQ* 52:27–37). Two more articles probe Adams' historical perception and mediating art. Lee C. Mitchell, " 'But This Was History': Henry Adams' 'Education' in London Diplomacy" (*NEQ* 52:358–76), poses chapters 8 to 11 of the *Education* over against Adams' confusion but lesser disillusionment in letters home during those Civil War years in London. Mitchell's conclusion is that "to dramatize his twin themes of chaos in the world and the failure of education," Adams in the later *Education* came back to the London period and "knowingly falsified motives and deliberately misinterpreted events to a degree previously unsuspected." David W. Marcell cuts a wider swath around the classic *Education* in "Henry Adams' Historical Paradigm: A Reexamination of the Major Phase," *American Character*, pp. 127–42. Applying Thomas Kuhn's structural model for scientific revolutions to the "peculiar unity of vision underlying Adams' diversity of style and subject in his later years," Marcell effectively places the *Education* as "keystone to the paradigmatic arch of the major phase," for it unites "the subjective, poetic evocation of order in *Mont-Saint-Michel and Chartres* with the objective, scientific description of impending chaos" found in the "Rule of Phase" and *A Letter to American Teachers of History*.

Finally, Charles Vandersee contributes a rudimentary offering to
the anticipated boom in Adams scholarship with "Henry Adams:
Archives and Microfilm" (*RALS* 9:70–79). Vandersee describes the
contents of the 36-reel microfilm edition of Adams' papers issued by
the Massachusetts Historical Society in 1979, as well as their relation
to the six-volume *Letters* being prepared by Ernest Samuels, J. C.
Levenson, Charles Vandersee, and Viola Winner (Harvard). In an
appendix he lists the books that Adams consulted.

vi. Realism and the Age of Howells

The current harvest in the Howells field proves more than ever that
Howells' life and work are among the most consistently fruitful for
study in our literature. On balance the impressive result this year is
found not in the criticism but in the materials assembled to provoke
criticism and reinterpretation in the years just ahead. To that end
John W. Crowley's two-part "Howells in the Seventies: A Review of
Criticism" (*ESQ* 25:169–89, 235–53) is not merely an orderly bibliography but also a lucid essay on Howells' critical fortunes over
the last ten years. Crowley organizes his review within the central
debate between, in his apt terms, the "revivalists" of the quiet, smil-
ing-aspects man and the "revisionists" of a "Howells Agonistes." He
ends by making some signposts for the critical territory ahead.

By far the signal event of the Howells year is the arrival of the first
two offspring of the six-volume *Selected Letters* (1852–72 and 1873–
81), edited, annotated, and delivered by a team of skilled textual
scholars: George Arms, Richard Ballinger, Christoph Lohmann,
John Reeves, Don Cook, David Nordloh, and Jerry Herron (Twayne).
Not only are the annotations as concise and helpful as those of the
Irving volumes, but the Howells editors conveniently group the letters according to pivotal moments in Howells' career and introduce
each section with brief, expert commentary. In the "General Introduction" they rightly boast that these letters are "forceful and sensitive communications and give us more explicit information about
the American literary scene than do the letters of any other figure of
the period." Indeed, Howells' correspondence reveals so much about
the man and his era that the editors have some weighty selections to
make as this edition opens the way to a forceful and sensitive new

interpretation of Howells. As one of Crowley's "revisionists," I look forward to a warts-and-all objectivity that daughter Mildred's two-volume edition understandably denied us for the later Howells. To remark briefly on one example for the volumes to come, Howells in the 1890s is a fascinating subject, wrestling in his own way with questions as disturbing as those raised by the later Henry Adams. The tormented novelist reveals his divided self in diverse outlets, the literary memoir, the Altrurian Romance, in renewed verse-writing, and here and there in his correspondence. At the Huntington Library where I am writing, there is a packet of letters Howells wrote in these later years to the homosexual bachelor Charles Warren Stoddard, longing for his company and addressing him with such uncharacteristic (for Howells) endearments as "Sweetest," "Dearest," "Sweetness and Light," and "My own!" The Houghton Library owns Stoddard's copy of *Literary Friends and Acquaintance* in which Howells takes the pains to compose a tender poem assuring Stoddard that he owns a sweet and sacred place in the author's heart. Should such troublesome evidence be whispered and then skittishly evaded and dismissed? (The best one gets even for Stoddard are the biographers' evasive euphemisms for his "bohemian," "hedonistic," or "Whitmanesque" propensities, so that we have only limited explanations of his fitful authorship, troubled life, and religious conversion.) Perhaps Robert Martin's frank new book will embolden the Howells editors and others to pull back the curtains of prudery and grant us a larger understanding of the private and creative ordeal of Howells and his friends.

The heavy pressures of Howells' busy life began as early as the *Atlantic* years, and Rayburn S. Moore illustrates the instance of Hayne's irritated and even wildly angered reactions to Howells' rejection of various poems that failed to meet the editor's presumptuous criteria ("'The Absurdest of Critics': Hayne on Howells," *SLJ* 12,i:70–78). Hayne, of course, was only one of many who resented Howells' increasing power in the eastern circles of literary influence. Maurice Thompson was another. Thompson's pique with Howells, though, was in fact not truly based on aesthetic disagreement, or so Gary Scharnhorst argues in "William Dean Howells and Maurice Thompson: At War Over Realism?" (*ON* 5:291–302). Just as Thompson squabbled with Hayne about regionalism, so Thompson resented that Howells did not celebrate the beneficent qualities of Indiana life—*vide* especially *A Modern Instance*—but dwelled on the tawdry aspects of Thompson's Midwest.

Thompson rightly feared the impact of *A Modern Instance*, Howells' most powerful novel, but village life in Tecumseh, Ind., is no more denigrated than the dead-end existence in Equity, Maine, as Jacqueline Tavernier-Courbin suggests in "The Village and After: Social Evolution through Character in *A Modern Instance*" (*ALR* 12:127–42). A spinoff and partial duplication of her essay on the city in *A Modern Instance* last year (*ALS 1978*, pp. 217–18), and largely indebted to earlier critical discussions, Tavernier-Courbin's article holds that Howells is even more devastating than Sinclair Lewis in his view of how "the city is what it is because it emerges from its roots in the village," a pregnant and complex idea that needs far more exploration. The other treatment of *A Modern Instance* this year also strains after some element of originality. In "Bartley Hubbard and Behavioral Art in William Dean Howells' *A Modern Instance*" (*SAF* 7:83–91) Geoffrey D. Smith elaborates the subtlety with which Howells gives the reader chiefly external indications from which to infer Bartley's inner responses, so that "the idea that observable behavior provides a valid criteria [*sic*] for psychological evaluation is basic to a modern interpretation of Howells." Quite so, but the principle has been illustrated, with different examples, in Howells criticism before.

"W. D. Howells: *The Rise of Silas Lapham* (1885)" is S. Foster's submission in *The Monster in the Mirror: Studies in Nineteenth-Century Realism*, ed. David A. Williams (Oxford, 1978). Foster cites nary a critical study for his presumably English audience and belabors them with such tame commonplaces as the contradictory presence of manipulated "romance" and morality in the work of this theoretical "Realist." Gregory L. Crider writes for an American readership with even less excusable ignoring of the criticism. In "William Dean Howells and the Gilded Age: Socialist in a Fur-lined Overcoat" (*Ohio Hist.* 88:408–18) Crider laboriously quotes well-known data in various manuscript holdings and writes conclusions after this fashion: "Yet even while publishing his most ascerbic [*sic*] novels, Howells' social commitment was an uneasy one." The only departure from familiar knowledge is a photograph caption of Howells and his wife, "Elizabeth."

Other work on Howells in the 1890s breaks new ground. James P. Elliott gives us a CEAA-inscribed new edition of *The Quality of Mercy* (Indiana) in which manuscript revisions are indicated where Howells had conceptual difficulties—a clear opportunity for interpretive studies to come.

Also in the decade of the 1890s came the socialism of Howells' Altrurian Romances which lead, in one fashion, on a direct line to the modern assumptions of Herbert Marcuse, as Sam Girgus views it in "Howells: The Rebel in the One-Dimensional Age," chapter 5 of *Law of the Heart*. Girgus here joins two studies on *A Modern Instance* and *Altruria* previously noticed in this chapter several years ago (*ALS 1972*, p. *197* and *1973*, p. *218*). Beginning with "rebel" Bartley Hubbard's corruption, Howells meditated on the impact of urban life upon personal freedom. By the time he wrote *A Traveler from Altruria* he had arrived at insights that sharply foresehadow Marcuse: a critique of materialism and inflated consumer wants at all levels of the citizenry and the resulting growth of socially conditioned, one-dimensional thought and false consciousness.

Howells' popular late story "Editha," his only fiction that conveniently fits into the classroom anthologies, attracted three new readings. Philip Furia, " 'Editha': The Feminist View" (*ALR* 12:278–82), shifts the focus from naive romanticism about war to the Howellsian "woman's struggle for sexual independence and domination." Both Editha and, less perversely, George's mother unconsciously work out their need for feminine mastery at George's expense. Michael O. Bellamy's "Eros and Thanatos in William Dean Howells' 'Editha' " (*ALR* 12:283–87) touches also on this same sexual politics but enlarges the issue, psychologically, to embrace George as well in a genneral eroticizing of death among the three characters. Only Editha's mother resists this morbid escape from actualities, though her inability to communicate why Editha is " 'wicked' " itself betrays the stigma of Victorian repression of sex. John B. Humma raises the story to the level of American myth in "Howells's 'Editha': An American Allegory" (*MarkhamR* 8:77–80). George represents a morally weakened Robin Molineux on the way to the degradation of American character in Jay Gatsby. His mother embodies earlier New England moral strength (Humma reads no irony in the portrait), Editha's mother signifies the decisive antiwar outlook of Shakerism, her father is the wartime profiteer, and Editha is Howells' sappy American woman gorged on melodramatic falsities. As he boldly casts these people into types, Humma overlooks some of the shadings that always complicate the individual portraits in Howells' fiction.

Two items on Howells in the miscellaneous category warrant brief notice. Bernard F. Engel considers Howells as a poet and groups all the verse under a heading, "The Genteel Poetry of William Dean Howells" (*MidAmerica* 6:44–61). But the risky premise of Howell's life-long "gentility"—moral, sentimental, or squeamish—binds Engel to a tyrannizing category and prevents him from gauging the full subtlety of revelation by and about Howells that may be extracted from his versifyings early and late. Lastly and somewhat peripherally to the literary interest in Howells is a biography of sister Annie, who married in 1877 a cultivated Canadian during her father's consulship in Quebec and enjoyed minor success in journalism and fiction. James Doyle's *Annie Howells and Achille Fréchette* (Toronto) will interest American readers who wish to know the woman who partly served as model for Kitty Ellison in *A Chance Acquaintance* and Parthenope Brook in *The Vacation of the Kelwyns*.

vii. Fin-de-Siècle America: Stephen Crane and the 1890s

By contrast to last year's far-ranging, orthodox scholarship on Crane, the work in 1979 may be termed somewhat diffuse and offbeat— and generally lively. First are contentious articles by Pizer, Binder, and Stallman. With "'*The Red Badge of Courage* Nobody Knows': A Brief Rejoinder" (*SNNTS* 11:77–81) Donald Pizer renews his quarrel with Crane's modern editors by refuting, this time, Henry Binder's rationale last year for a *Red Badge* text that eliminates later revisions supposedly forced on Crane by Appleton editor Ripley Hitchcock (see *ALS 1978*, pp. 220–21). Pizer contends that these revisions are typical of the ambiguous Crane at his best. But what is ambiguous and authorial to Pizer is incoherent and unauthoritative to Binder, and he replies to Pizer that Crane's "halfhearted . . . deletions were made in a cursory manner, producing a text that is incoherent in places and that cannot be taken to embody his intentions" ("Donald Pizer, Ripley Hitchcock, and *The Red Badge of Courage*," *SNNTS* 11:216–23). This altercation is of teapot proportions compared to "That Crane, That Albatross Around My Neck: A Self-Interview by R. W. Stallman" (*JML* 7:147–69). The Coleridge allusion in his punning title is apt, for Stallman assails with unrepentant acrimony and self-congratulation his critical adversaries of a lifetime. He regrets that others have stirred a witches' brew in the jungles of academe through the years. There are lighter moments, too, in this singular account of the Crane industry in our time.

A ramble of a different sort is William Wasserstrom's unorthodox but learned and rewarding "Hydraulics and Heroics: William James and Stephen Crane" (*Prospects* 4:215–35). Wasserstrom conducts us on a tour through Henry Adams, Walter Cannon, Freud, Santayana, and the James brothers to clarify "vital equilibrium" as a contemporary notion of energy and progress in human affairs. Through this principle he briefly illuminates the energy and tension of characterization, morality, and setting in *Red Badge*, wherein we experience the "dynamics of equipoise as prescribed by vitalist doctrine in Crane's time and nation." By coincidence Wasserstrom quotes a recent review of the dance for his analogy with "vital equilibrium" and an ultimate "faith in the certainty and sanctity of progress"; and Carlos Baker in his essay on Adams and the Samoan dancers (see section *v.*) quotes from the progressive Emerson's "Beauty": "The interruption of equilibrium stimulates the eye to desire the restoration of symmetry. . . . This is the theory of dancing, to recover continually in changes the lost equilibrium, not by abrupt and angular but by gradual and curving movements."

More direct readings of Crane's fiction have been remarkably sparse this season. The broadest is Joseph Kwiat's "Stephen Crane's 'The Effort Born of Pain'" (*Amst* 24:152–56). Kwiat's general criticism can be read with profit, especially in his crisp distinction between the immediacy of life and "precise but engaged observation" in Crane's art and the ideal of "'disinterested contemplation'" in Henry James. Because Crane was never burdened with conventional theories about fiction, Kwiat warns that we will continue to be frustrated by attempts to place Crane in any mode, school, or movement. In "The Nature and Significance of 'Experience' in 'The Open Boat'" (*JNT* 9:70–80) Bert Bender posits William James's view of knowing —beyond observation, inquiry, and information—to explain the essential "poetry of religious experience" in Crane's open boat. William K. Spofford, on the other hand, studies the same story against the earlier fiction to explain how Crane's previous images, occasions, and themes of private impotence and human solidarity in an indifferent universe converge in the treatment of "facts" in this later story ("Stephen Crane's 'The Open Boat': Fact or Fiction?" *ALR* 12:316–21). Necessarily absent in a condensed piece like this are the bewildering ironies that surround Spofford's earlier examples, let alone the context of their reappearance in "The Open Boat."

The Virginia Edition of Crane reaches a Signet paperback outlet in *The Western Writings of Stephen Crane,* ed. Frank Bergon (New Amer. Lib.), these being the letters, dispatches, and stories from Crane's trip west in 1895. And in the interest of biographical revision John Conway offers "The Stephen Crane—Amy Leslie Affair: A Reconsideration" (*JML* 7:3–14), a look at unpublished materials to show that Amy deserves better from Crane biographers. Not a whimpering female, Amy had valid reasons to sue the philandering Crane for nonpayment of a sizable loan and was not about to be, in Conway's words, "bamboozled by the likes of the itinerant Mr. Crane."

In England with the beleaguered Crane during those last years was the still underrated Harold Frederic. One useful article to report is by John O. Lyons, "Hebraism, Hellenism, and Harold Frederic's *Theron Ware,*" suitably fashioned for the *Arnoldian* (6,ii:7–15). Neither realism nor Hawthorne romance fully explains what is, at last, a philosophical novel, according to Lyons. Not two but three of Arnold's high-serious concepts trouble Theron Ware in the persons of Dr. Ledsmar (Hebraism), Celia (Hellenism), and Father Forbes (Racism). Only Sister Soulsby (American pragmatic common sense) supports Ware in his darkest hour of philosophical confusion, Lyons claims, and in the process he rather blithely sidesteps the strong case by Luther Luedtke that Soulsby is more likely an agent of moral blight (see *ALS 1975,* p. 261). Perhaps the too-exclusive fondness for Frederic's one best-seller will be distributed to his occasionally meticulous artistry elsewhere in the wake of Noel Polk's *The Literary Manuscripts of Harold Frederic: A Catalogue* (Garland), especially welcome for its data on the genesis of some of the writings, all the way from scraps to systematic outlines.

Frank Norris source materials appear in Joseph R. McElrath's "Frank Norris: Early Posthumous Responses" (*ALR* 12:1–76), the eulogies and memoirs from 1902 to 1914 alluded to in his essay last year on sources for a new biography (see *ALS 1978,* p. 224). The selection features both Norris' artistic development and his turn-of-the-century impact on other fiction. Those twin considerations are present also for Christian Messenger, who discusses two stories with athlete heroes in "Frank Norris and the College Sportsman" (*ALR* 12:288–94). "Travis Hallett's Half-back" (1894) contains some of the bestial aspects and machine metaphors of *Vandover*, while the hero of "This Animal of a Buldy Jones" (1897) inherits the tradition of the frontier roarers and looks ahead to the baseball world of Ring Lardner. In a second article McElrath compares Turner Ravis of *Vandover* and Condy Rivers' saving woman of *Blix* ("Allegory in Frank Norris's *Blix*: Its Relevance to *Vandover*," *MarkhamR* 8:25–27). Turner comes out second best. Readers should view her not as the ideal good woman but rather as the person so bound up in conventional proprieties that she fails to lessen the beast in poor Vandover.

Animal behavior in Norris also interests Edwin H. Miller, but not in its biological, naturalistic, or moral aspect. In "The Art of Frank Norris in *McTeague*" (*MarkhamR* 8:61–66) Miller studies the highly artful Freudian motifs and imagery, relating such symbols as the canary, the gold tooth, and the mine to the main characters' childish reversion to oral and anal, pregenital levels of unmet needs. Richard A. Davison's Norris is still artful as late as *The Pit* but also more instructively moral. "A Reading of Frank Norris's *The Pit*," in *Stoic Strain*, pp. 77–94, is an expectedly sober treatment of stoic virtues—duty, patience, courage, practical goodness, and Reason—that belong to those sturdy characters who either survive or die with dignity in Norris. These ameliorative ideals, implied or dramatized in *The Pit*, unify the business, culture, and love themes in a well-crafted novel.

Some perceptive and perhaps symptomatic criticism of Kate Chopin rounds out the current 19th-century scholarship. A wave of neoconservatism may be at hand, for no feminist interpretation of Chopin's heroines showed up among the largely women commentators. Moving through the fiction chronologically, we begin with Elmo Howell and the heroine of "Lilacs." Howell discovers in this earlier character, who annually retreats from her sensual life in Paris to embrace the moral boundaries of the convent, a parallel with the conflict of Edna Pontellier in *The Awakening*, another confused woman "pulled in two directions who cannot reconcile herself to the fact that she cannot go both ways" ("Kate Chopin and the Pull of Faith: A Note on 'Lilacs,'" *SoSt* 18:103–09). Howell sees no reason to believe Chopin was criticizing traditional marriage as an institution that suppressed Edna's individual development. Peggy Skaggs calls attention to "The Boy's Quest in Kate Chopin's 'A Vocation and a Voice'" (*AL* 51:270–76) as evidence that Chopin "was concerned far more with the identity problems of all human beings than with the peculiar difficulties society foists upon women. . . ." Nancy Walker in "Feminist or Naturalist: The Social Context of Kate Chopin's *The Awakening*" (*SoQ* 17,ii:95–103) agrees with Edmund Wilson that Chopin gave us not a problem novel about women's liberation but a portrait of an unthinking, sensuous woman. Walker notes that the Creoles, men and women, are not "rigidly moralistic" but in fact "openly sensuous people," and the married women in the novel are not unhappy. Edna flaunts her escape from earlier Kentucky Presbyterianism and goes out of control among the Creoles. Her suicide is not an existential act of choice but a sensual drift, for she is dominated "by her own emotion, not by men or society." In a virtual companion piece, "Kate Chopin's Awakening" (*SoSt* 18:261–90), Elizabeth Fox-Genovese also regards Edna's "personal immaturity" and suicide in terms of a "psychological regression," particularly a "repressed longing" for the mother who died early. In this light even the choice of Robert for a lover "cannot be reduced to Edna's revolt against patriarchal motifs. The longing that ultimately consumes her has its roots deep in her childhood." Charles W. Mayer likewise rejects the idea of a purposeful awakening for Edna. Mayer's "Isabel Archer, Edna Pontellier, and the Romantic Self" (*RS* 47:89–97) is a superior essay contrasting Edna, in her surrender to the "irresistible waves of temperament," to James's more responsible heroine. In a similarity, both are married to insensitive, possessive husbands, but "the fate of the wives is partly, perhaps mainly, attributable to other things—to their own egotism, willfulness, and perverseness."

The last two articles are also nonfeminist in orientation. Elizabeth B. House's "*The Awakening*: Chopin's 'Endlessly Rocking' Cycle" (*BSUF* 20,ii:53–58) plays some variations on previous analogies with Whitman's poem, this time in the birth-eros-death natural cycle that permeates both works and explains Edna's response at her death when "'she felt like some new-born creature.'" Patricia H. Lattin finally reminds us that Chopin is creator of "a believable fictional world with a dense social reality" that is cumulatively larger than the dramatic contours of her one impressive novel ("Kate Chopin's Repeating Characters," *MissQ* 33:19–37). Lattin's second premise, that the device of repeating them here and there "serves to make characters fuller, more complex human beings than they would be within the confines of one piece of fiction," is a dubious and arguable aesthetic proposition. But this attempt to see Chopin's characterization in the service of art and a many-sided social reality matches the spirit of the other essays and may indicate a decisive new turn in this area of literary scholarship as we enter the 1980s.

San Diego State University

13. Fiction: 1900 to the 1930s

David Stouck

The major writers of this period are given the critical distinction of being discussed at length in a book of essays by C. Hugh Holman titled *Windows on the World: Essays on American Social Fiction* (Tenn.). Holman's concern is to establish realism as a literary mode as important to American literature as romance. In essays on Sinclair Lewis, Glasgow, Marquand, and others Holman tries to show how individualism, materialism, and hard-headed practicality are as important to the imaginative assessment of America as romantic idealism. Several of the essays have appeared before, but the essay on realism as an American mode is new, as are pieces on Faulkner and Wolfe. The most interesting of the new pieces is an essay titled "The *Bildungsroman*, American Style" in which Holman distinguishes a particularly American form of the growing-up story where initiation for the hero results from witnessing action rather than participating in it. Cather's Jim Burden and Niel Herbert and Fitzgerald's Nick Carroway are examples of this type of initiate. This reflective form of initiation occurs in American literature, contends Holman, because its initiation stories are always violent and this allows the protagonist to survive and, in a realistic fashion, find a way to "make do."

There are also some articles of interest which treated the authors of this period collectively. Taking an interdisciplinary approach, Nelson Manfred Blake in "How to Learn History from Sinclair Lewis and Other Uncommon Sources" (*American Character*) illustrates how realistic fictions by writers like Dreiser, Cather, Wharton, and Lewis can be valuable sources of firsthand information for historians, while the latter at the same time must be wary of the novelist's romantic and satiric license. Also with some interest in history David D. Anderson in "The Midwestern Town in Midwestern Fiction (*MidAmerica* 6:27–43) discusses the environmental reality of the small midwestern town as a conservative agricultural community with high

moral standards, and then goes on to show how in the fiction of
Sherwood Anderson, Homer Croy, and Booth Tarkington the hero's
testing place is the small town, which supports him when he meets
its standards and also stirs in him an ambition to go out and meet
the challenge of the great world beyond. Also of interest to the cultural history of this period is "Second Countries: The Expatriate Tradition in American Writing" (*YES* 8[1978]:15–39) in which Malcolm
Bradbury gives a comprehensive account of the various occasions,
political, cultural, and personal for which American writers lived
and worked in Europe. Bradbury's belief is that the founding sensibility of the American arts was in a mode of exile, just as the national mythology has been one of movement and dissatisfaction
with provincial traditionalism.

i. John Dos Passos

Dos Passos garnered the lion's share of significant criticism in 1979.
The chief purpose of Linda W. Wagner's *Dos Passos: Artist as American* (Texas) is to relate all of Dos Passos' writings to his ever-growing
concern with the identity of America. Wagner divides his career into
three phases. His early books (*One Man's Initiation: 1917, Three
Soldiers,* and *Streets of Night*) she describes as being more self-
conscious than country-conscious as the protagonists search for a
sense of their identity against a background of World War I. *Manhattan Transfer,* she suggests, is a transitional work wherein Dos
Passos turns to the contemporary American scene and searches for an
objective method to record history. The result of that search is the
USA trilogy, the masterwork of Dos Passos' middle period, informed
by his leftist political and social views. The third phase is marked by
a shift in politics to the extreme right, which Wagner accounts for in
terms of a long-standing hatred for powerful organizations. As communism grew stronger as a political ideology and labor unions grew
more powerful and in some instances demonstrably corrupt, Dos
Passos retreated to a Jeffersonian ideal of democracy and individualism.

Wagner's book does not really constitute a new reading of Dos
Passos. The overall picture she presents of Dos Passos' career is
more or less a familiar one and the American theme has also been a
stock-in-trade of Dos Passos criticism. Also she avoids the use of

biographical materials which might have given greater depth to understanding Dos Passos' attitudes toward individualism and power. But the book does have its special virtues. Wagner has written probably the most comprehensive study of Dos Passos' work for she examines all his writings, poetry, plays, travel and political essays, as well as his fiction; and these readings are informed by her use of information from unpublished materials in the University of Virginia Library. Particularly good is her concern with Dos Passos' literary techniques. Wagner shows how the influence of such imagist poets as Blaise Cendrars and E. E. Cummings can be seen in Dos Passos' search for an objective style. Wagner does not slight any one portion of Dos Passos' work (there is a substantial discussion of the later, largely unread books) and the result is a sound critical study that is both thorough and balanced.

The best of the essays on Dos Passos is a structuralist piece titled "History, Fiction, and Satirical Form: The Example of Dos Passos' *1919*" (*Genre* 12:357–78) by Barbara Foley, who shows that the historical and the fictional elements of *1919* converge in the book's satirical mode which employs discrete units of history to make a critical statement about the state of human affairs. In a similar vein Charles Marz in "Dos Passos's Newsreels: The Noise of History" (*SNNTS* 11:194–220) points out that although the newsreels create a historical background for the trilogy, their significance lies in the grotesque ironies produced by the collision of various voices and events as the debris of history is heaped up. Garrett Epps in "Politics as Metaphor" (*VQR* 55:75–98) calls Dos Passos America's greatest political novelist and shows how he uses the workings of the political system in his *District of Columbia* trilogy to reflect the changes taking place in American civil society and to reflect the personal and moral dilemmas of individual Americans. There is a thoughtful overview of this writer's work in Harry Levin's "Revisiting Dos Passos' *U.S.A.*" (*MR* 20:401–15).

ii. Gertrude Stein

There are two valuable new books on Stein for the library shelves. Wendy Steiner's *Exact Resemblance to Exact Resemblance: The Literary Portraiture of Gertrude Stein* (Yale, 1978) is a sound and highly intelligent study of Stein in the tradition of Richard Bridgman's

Gertrude Stein in Pieces. Steiner makes clear in a preface that she is not concerned with Stein as a colorful personality but with Stein "as a writer with a training in psychology and philosophy that made her uniquely attentive to modernist problems." The question she poses at the outset is why should a radically experimental writer of the 20th century work out many of her most important critical ideas within such a conservative and secondary genre? Steiner believes the answer lies in the fact that the portrait from its earliest beginnings has always been both referential and self-reflexive and hence anticipates the central dilemma of modernist art. One of the best things about Steiner's book, so rich in observations on critical theory, is her historical study of the portrait as a specific genre in both painting and literature and her discussion of how Stein brings the two media together. For example, Steiner argues that the literary portrait did not really assume truly mimetic dimensions until biographers like Boswell began using direct speech, characterizing a subject through his own words. From there one moves to the Steinian monologue which renders directly the subject's habits of speech and thought. Steiner discusses how, under the influence of William James, Stein rejected the prevailing idea of the individual as a static configuration of physical and spiritual traits in favor of character as an ever-changing dynamic process, and how she developed a style of repetition with variation in order to render that process of being directly. Steiner relates this to Cubism in painting and explains how her experiments in portraiture broke down under the logic of a program which forced her toward complete self-reflexiveness. This is an excellent study in every way, and I highly recommend it to anyone seriously interested in one of the most intensely experimental periods in literary history.

With the rising tide of writings about Stein, Maureen R. Liston's *Gertrude Stein: An Annotated Critical Bibliography* (Kent State) is a welcome research tool for Stein scholars. This checklist is deliberately selective rather than complete so that it might serve as a practical and usable guide to the best and representative criticism of Stein. The annotations are at once succinct and informative. There are also some reviews of books about Stein which, in the light of Stein's controversial stature, is a significant inclusion.

The best of the recent essays on Stein is James E. Breslin's "Gertrude Stein and the Problems of Autobiography" (*GaR* 33:901–13), which asks how Stein could write autobiography when she did not believe in identity or the value of memory. She used "Toklas," says Breslin, to create the inside as seen from the outside, stylizing the gestures, rather as Picasso did the portrait, so that a mythical abstract figure emerges instead of a psychologically coherent personality. In "Gertrude Stein and the Translation of Experience" (*ELWIU* 3[1978]:105–18) James Rother discusses the part Stein played in freeing literary language from the exigencies of plot and meaning and redirecting its function to the objectifying of consciousness. Finally Laura Hoffeld's "Gertrude Stein's Unmentionables" (*L&U* 2,i [1978]:48–55) is a reading of the children's story, *The World Is Round*, as a narrative about a girl's quest for identity.

iii. Glasgow, Cabell

Although the essays published to mark Ellen Glasgow's centennial were not particularly distinguished, that event combined with the feminist interest in reexamining women writers has resulted in a substantial number of worthy essays on Glasgow being published in 1979. The majority of these are studies of *Barren Ground*. Three essays focus specifically on the significance of the landscape in the novel. In "Landscape of Revenge: Glasgow's *Barren Ground*" (*SHR* 13:63–77) Julius Rowan Raper shows how Glasgow makes the landscape in her novel a projection of the protagonist's psyche, dramatizing in Dorinda Oakley's control of the land her liberation from male abuse of her body and emotions. In a similar vein Linda W. Wagner in "*Barren Ground*'s Vein of Iron: Dorinda Oakley and Some Concepts of the Heroine in 1925" (*MissQ* 32:553–64) suggests that *Barren Ground* is "not so much an account of the way a woman learns to know the land, but . . . an account of the way a woman learns to know herself." The land and its development, says Wagner, is used to index the growth of the character. Wagner also views Dorinda in relation to other striving women in American fiction. Tonette L. Bond in an article titled "Pastoral Transformation in *Barren Ground*" (*MissQ* 32:565–76) suggests that Dorinda Oakley's search for a permanent design for her life is most completely fulfilled when she imaginatively "creates out of the barren chaos of Old Farm a pastoral garden which accords with her ancestral vision of potential order and harmony."

Two essays relate Glasgow to Thomas Hardy. In "Sexual Reversals in Thomas Hardy and Ellen Glasgow" (*SHR* 13:51–62) Velma
Bourgeois Richmond, with reference to *In This Our Life*, examines
the very different ways both authors cast a man in what is traditionally a woman's role. Hardy's Jude, writes Richmond, is passive and
lives by his instincts and is doomed to failure by the values of Victorian society; Glasgow's Asa Timberlake, on the other hand, not
only accepts feminine values as a way of living but also triumphs
through them. Glasgow's feminism is evident, says Richmond, in
this confident reevaluation and reapportioning of traditional sexual
roles. In "Hardy and Ellen Glasgow: *Barren Ground*" (*MissQ* 32:
577–90) James W. Tuttleton points to Schopenhauer's philosophy of
the Immanent Will as important to both Hardy and Glasgow and
shows how they were also both absorbed with the powerful role of
chance in determining one's fate. Tuttleton also points out that both
writers were fascinated with the relation of character to the land.

Barbro Ekman's published dissertation, *The End of a Legend:
Ellen Glasgow's History of Southern Women* (Uppsala: Almqvist &
Wiksell), is a very good study of Glasgow's women characters and
their historical credibility. She divides Glasgow's heroines into three
groups: the Southern Belle raised in the Genteel Tradition, the more
liberated woman appearing after the Civil War, and the "new
woman" who came after the feminist struggle and World War I.
Ekman argues that Glasgow is most successful in portraying the
Southern Belle in all her various manifestations largely because this
was her own background. Although she rebelled against it, she never
became a wholly liberated woman. Ekman refuses to label Glasgow
or her strong women as feminists, because when heroines like Dorinda succeed in a man's world, they do so in order to get revenge on a
man and not out of love for their endeavor. Ekman feels Glasgow's
significance to American literature is as a social historian who depicted truthfully the lives of southern women from 1850 to 1945.

Two remaining articles on *Barren Ground* deal with the question
of the novel's critical reputation and its universality. In "The Problematics of Regionalism and the Dilemma of Glasgow's *Barren
Ground*" (*SLJ* 11,ii:3–21) Wayne Lesser argues that it is not simply
Dorinda Oakley's quest for selfhood that gives the novel universal
reference, but the ironic narration and paradoxes of the text which
reconcile the particularity (even eccentricity) of the character to the

larger issues of conduct, value, and belief. Judith B. Wittenberg in
"The Critical Fortunes of *Barren Ground*" (*MissQ* 32:591–609) reports that the novel's popularity has been closely linked to that of its
author. During Glasgow's lifetime, Wittenberg tells us, *Barren Ground*
was frequently cited for its excellence and ranked much above the
works of Faulkner, but after the author's death the book went into
eclipse. Although interest in Glasgow's work has been growing, Wittenberg points out that *Barren Ground* curiously has not been the
subject of a feminist reading.

There were two articles of interest about Glasgow's Richmond
friend James Branch Cabell. In "From Virginia to Poictesme: The
Early Novels of James Branch Cabell" (*MissQ* 32:219–39) Joseph M.
Flora describes at length Cabell's first four novels in their first editions
before they were revised to become part of the "Biography of the
Life of Manuel." In these first Virginia fictions, observes Flora, it
was the life of the artist that most consistently engaged Cabell. In
"Cabell's Black Imagination" (*Kalki* 8:179–90) G. F. Morley-Mower
attributes the extreme morbidity and unhappiness in Cabell's novels
after *Figures of Earth* (1921) to the fact that about this time Cabell
learned that there was something wrong with his only son and that
the family name would not be carried on.

iv. Jack London

The ambitious program to give London the credentials of a front-
rank author has taken the form of making available fiction, essays,
and other pieces of London's writings that have long been out of
print and inaccessible. *Jack London: No Mentor But Myself*, ed.
Dale L. Walker (Kennikat), gathers together the pieces London
wrote about writing, including a number of selections never before
printed. This book allows us to see London in the role of critic
and reviewer of other writers' work, but more importantly, as Howard Lachtman points out in a foreword, it allows us to see London
discussing self-consciously the development of his own craft.

Jack London on the Road, ed. Richard W. Etulain (Utah State),
makes available a diary London kept at the age of 18 when he tramped
across the West with Charles Kelly's Industrial Army in the spring
of 1894. This volume also includes essays and stories London wrote
that were based on the tramp experience. In an excellent introductory

essay Richard Etulain describes the trip in full and evaluates the stories that resulted, conceding their limitations and asking why London never produced first-rate fiction on the basis of his experiences as a tramp. He put the best parts, notes Etulain, in *The Road* essays, but more significantly he was writing for a popular audience and the tramp was not acceptable to Americans as a fictional hero around the turn of the century. The experience was important in making London begin to question the American socioeconomic system and the writings, which combine the American escapist motif with the spectacle of social misery, are the first significant American writings about hoboes and migrant workers in a tradition that would later include writings by Dos Passos, Steinbeck, and Kerouac.

Jack London: Selected Science Fiction and Fantasy Stories, ed. Dick Wiederman (Lakemont, Ga.: Fictioneer Books [1978]), reprints five stories that London wrote in the fantasy vein, only one of which, "The Red One," is readily available elsewhere. The others are "The Strength of the Strong," "The Rejuvenation of Major Rathbone," "When the World Was Young," and "A Relic of the Pleiocene." Some of the best essays written on London in the past 20 years have been collected in *Jack London: Essays in Criticism*, ed. Ray Wilson Ownbey (Santa Barbara and Salt Lake City: Peregrine Smith [1978]). Finally, in this outfitting of a major author, there is Russ Kingman's *A Pictorial Life of Jack London* (Crown) to pay photographic homage to an important literary figure.

Most of the recent essays on London appeared in the *Jack London Newsletter*, which continues to provide a lively forum for views and information about this author. Probably the best of the articles is "The Unreliable Narrator in London's *The Sea Wolf*" (*JLN* 12:28–34) by Lee Lawrence Fischler, who argues interestingly that Van Weyden's profession of spiritual faith is not to be trusted, that at the end of the novel he has become a debased materialist like Wolf Larsen, that "his narration is frequently an exercise in self-deceit that betrays his spiritual confusion" rather than his spiritual growth. Another interesting piece is Susan Ward's "Toward a Simpler Style: Jack London's Stylistic Development" (*JLN* 11,ii[1978]:71–80), which considers London's transitional position in the shift toward a simpler, more vivid, vernacular style in American literature.

London continues to be a favorite subject for myth criticism.

There is another excerpt printed from James G. Cooper's study "The Womb of Time: Archetypal Patterns in the Novels of Jack London" (*JLN* 12:12–23). This sequence contains a somewhat mechanical application of male archetypes, including Primal Father, Father-Creator, the Wise Old Man, and the Hero, to the various characters in London's fiction. More interesting is Cooper's short piece "The Summit and the Abyss: Jack London's Moral Philosophy" (*JLN* 12: 24–27), in which Cooper describes London's consciously created myth as the search for enlightened moral freedom, which is to say a system of moral responsibilities based on the individual's conscious choosing. At the same time London's cosmogony is haunted, says Cooper, by a preconcious condition of moral freedom (the state of animals and Adam before the Fall) which comes close to being a pure archetype in itself. Jeanne Campbell's "Falling Stars: Myth in 'The Red One'" (*JLN* 11,ii[1978]:86–96) is a reading of the London story in terms of Jungian archetypes and psychic integration.

There also have been a couple of articles on humor in London's short fiction. In "Jack London's Yokohama Swim and His First Tall Tale" (*SAmH* 3,ii[1976]:84–95) Charles N. Watson, Jr., shows how the early London story, "A Night's Swim in Yeddo Bay," contains many elements of frontier humor including the deadpan narrator, the "whopper," the epic pratfall, and the sustained hyperbole of the barroom yarn. Similarly a short article by Denis E. Hensley titled "Jack London's South Seas Humor" (*BSUF* 20,ii:44–48) discusses London's incorporation of humorous folk legends and customs into his Hawaiian stories.

v. Sherwood Anderson

More of Anderson's writings are made available for study in *Sherwood Anderson: The Writer at His Craft*, ed. Jack Salzman, David D. Anderson, and Kichinosuke Ohashi (Appel). Some of the miscellaneous items gathered under the headings "Living in America" and "The Time and the Towns" are essays inspired by contemporary events in American life. More valuable to the study of Anderson as a creative writer are those pieces under the heading "Why I Write," especially the essay "Man and His Imagination."

The two most interesting articles on Anderson are studies of sexual ambivalence in his work by feminist critics. In "Sexual Metaphor and Social Criticism in Anderson's *The Man Who Became a Woman*" (*SAF* 7:17–26) Lonna M. Malmsheimer argues that Anderson's protagonist, Herman Dudley, does not experience homosexual longings in his fantasy of becoming a woman, but rather is unable to accept his role of maleness as socially defined. In all the role models available to Herman, says Malmsheimer, masculinity is a matter of aggressiveness, even brutality, which denies his humanity. Also fascinated by the androgynous element in some of Anderson's characters, Joyce R. Ladenson in "Gender Reconsideration in Three of Sherwood Anderson's Novels" (*MSE* 6:90–102) finds several rebels who defy sexual stereotyping but who are not fully developed characters. Anderson's view of marriage and the position of women, says Ladenson, advocates sexual liberation wherein women are recognized as self-determining persons by their own right; but at the same time she notes that Anderson's nostalgia for an irretrievable small-town past confines his ideal of woman to the civilized earth mother. Anderson's nostalgia for the past is also of interest to Philip Greasley, who in "Myth and the Midwestern Landscape: Sherwood Anderson's *Mid-American Chants*" (*MidAmerica* 6:79–87) argues that in Anderson's poetry there is a myth of song to revive agrarian values for 20th-century urban man.

There is only one short piece on Anderson's major work, *Winesburg, Ohio*. In "The 'New' Realism: A Study of the Structure of *Winesburg, Ohio*" (*CEA* 41,iii:9–12) Sylvia A. Holliday shows how Anderson employs an impressionistic montage of characters and events, linked only through association, to create a realistic picture of emotional unrelatedness between people. Two other Anderson articles are of biographical interest. David D. Anderson's " 'From East-Side to South-Side with Love': The Friendship of Sherwood Anderson and Paul Rosenfeld" (*Midwestern Miscellany* 7:41–55) is an account of the mutually supportive relationship between Anderson and Paul Rosenfeld, a New York fiction writer of minor acclaim and music critic for the Dial. Michael Fanning's "New Orleans and Sherwood Anderson" (*SoSt* 17[1978]:199–207) asks how the Louisiana city affected Anderson personally, philosophically, and artistically. Fanning believes that what Anderson responded to in New Orleans was its individuality ("in contrast to the 'standardization' of the rest of America") and its emphasis on the sensual life. New Orleans combined the primitivism and the laughter of the blacks and the *savoir-faire* and aesthetics of the French, values which were to inform his novel *Dark Laughter*.

vi. Willa Cather

Most of the articles on Cather are of secondary importance. Of most interest is Ann Moseley's "The Dual Nature of Art in *The Song of the Lark*" (*WAL* 14:19–32), which shows how the Dionysian-Apollonian polarities of passion and form are internalized in Thea Kronborg and how their balance is the secret of her greatness as an artist. This article is particularly good in its selection of illustrative detail, showing how the experiences of Thea's childhood were Dionysian in character and her recuperative stay in the Cliff Dwellings of Arizona was essentially Apollonian, or order giving.

Two articles examine possible influences on Cather's writing. In "The Sculptor of the Beautiful" (*CLQ* 14[1978]:28–35) Eben Bass argues that Hawthorne's "The Artist of the Beautiful" provided a theme and a number of images, including the butterfly as symbol of beauty, for Cather's "The Sculptor's Funeral." More strained is Patricia Lee Yongue's "Willa Cather's *The Professor's House* and Dutch Genre Painting" (*Renascence* 31:155–67), which relates scenes from Cather's novel to different types and periods of Dutch art. Two more articles compare Cather's work with the writings of two other women novelists. Pei-Tzu Hsu's "Love of Land in Buck and Cather" (*FJS* 12:71–82) compares the importance of landscape and the farm in Cather's work with its powerful portrayal in Pearl S. Buck's writing, while in "Two Visions of the Prairies: Willa Cather and Gabrielle Roy" (*The New Land: Studies in a Literary Theme*, Waterloo, Ont., Canada: Wilfred Laurier Univ. Press [1978]) Richard Chadbourne compares Cather to the Canadian novelist, whose imagination was also nourished by a prairie childhood. The comparison with Roy draws attention to Cather's agrarianism, her idealized and glorified conception of pioneer life, and her elegiac lament for its passing. The *Willa Cather Pioneer Memorial Newsletter* expanded its format a few years ago to include short articles and reviews. Two recent items again look at Cather in a comparative light. David Stouck's "Mary Austin and Willa Cather" (*WCPMN* 23,ii) compares briefly the two western writers on the basis of similar stories they wrote about

Chinese immigrants to California, while Michel Gervaud's "A Note on Willa Cather and Flaubert" (*WCPMN* 23,iii) connects Flaubert's belief that art should *faire rêver* with Cather's concern in art for the thing felt upon the page but not named there.

Two short articles look at opposing attitudes to farming expressed at different stages in Cather's writing career. In "Willa Cather's Early Short Stories: A Link to the Agrarian Realists" (*MarkhamR* 8:69–72) Virgil Albertini shows how very harsh the picture of pioneering is in the early stories and how this makes Cather closer to writers like Garland or Howe than she is usually considered to be. Meanwhile in "The Agrarian Mode in Cather's 'Neighbour Rosicky'" (*MarkhamR* 8:52–54) Edward J. Piacentino shows how the images of this story subtly and repeatedly connect Rosicky with the land he loves and affirm his choice of the simple, natural life in the country. Cather is also related to Garland in Randall L. Popken's "From Innocence to Experience in *My Ántonia* and *Boy Life on the Prairie*" (*NDQ* 46,ii[1978]:73–81). Popken is not so much interested in agrarian realism as he is in demonstrating that in the works of both authors the process of growing up is rendered fittingly in archetypal nature images: the garden of childhood, the snake's presence betokening evil in the world, the harsh conditions of farming and the burden of winter to define the nature of adult life. Finally, there is usually a feminist reading of Cather to report on. The most recent piece is Susan Rosowski's "Willa Cather's Pioneer Women: A Feminist Interpretation" (*Where the West Begins* [1978], pp. 135–42), which claims that Cather avoids sexist roles in presenting pioneer women, that a woman like Alexandra of *O Pioneers!* synthesizes the expansiveness attributed to the male pioneer with the stability of the female.

vii. Theodore Dreiser

The most important Dreiser essay is one which I failed to report on last year. This is Thomas P. Riggio's "American Gothic: Poe and *An American Tragedy*" (*AL* 49[1978]:515–32), which argues that "Poe stood out for Dreiser as the one American who had mastered the techniques of portraying criminal obsessions and mental disorders," and that when Dreiser describes at length Clyde Griffith's mental imbalance and evolution of a murder plan he turned to Poe for a model. Chapters 42–47 of *An American Tragedy*, says Riggio, "read like a Poe tale, complete with a nightmare landscape, the language of psychological analysis, and oriental and gothic trappings." Interestingly Del G. Khel in "*An American Tragedy* and Dreiser's Cousin, Mr. Poe" (*BRMMLA* 32[1978]:211–21) comes to the same conclusions when examining the imagery in Dreiser's most ambitious novel.

Library Chronicle contains a series of bibliographical notes and essays on *Sister Carrie*. There are pieces on the Heinemann edition of the novel, on the scrapbook Dreiser kept made up of letters concerning *Sister Carrie*, and on Arthur Henry's role in the publication of the novel. Again of most interest is a piece by Thomas P. Riggio titled "Notes on the Origins of *Sister Carrie*" (*LC* 44,i:7–26). Riggio writes first that the term sister is used in the title to suggest a working-class girl and also a kept woman. But the origin of the name "Carrie," says Riggio, probably goes back to Dreiser's school days, for in the manuscript version of *Dawn* Dreiser describes a Carrie Rutter who represents in his adolescent world both sensuality and a dreamy innocence. Her name was changed to "Cad" in the published version which is also Carrie Meeber's pet name in the novel. Tracking down the possible source of this name gives the reader an insight into the associative workings of Dreiser's imagination. There were two other articles on *Sister Carrie*. Examining the holograph manuscript of the novel, Stephen C. Brennan in "The Composition of *Sister Carrie*: A Reconsideration" (*DN* 9,ii[1978]:17–23) finds that many of the changes are really in the hand of Dreiser's first wife and that the sentimentalism and prudery that color the presentation of Carrie might very well be the result of Sarah White Dreiser's influence. In "Hurstwood Achieved: A Study of Dreiser's Reluctant Art" (*DN* 9,ii[1978]:1–16) Jacqueline Tavernier-Courbin tries to prove that Hurstwood is not a victim of chance circumstances but a weak, shallow character who lacks self-discipline.

There were two other articles on Dreiser, one on *Jennie Gerhardt* and one on the short stories. In "Loneliness, Death, and Fulfillment in *Jennie Gerhardt*" (*SAF* 7:61–73) Mordecai Marcus examines the relationships of the novel's central characters, demonstrating that Lester Kane's loneliness results from his deliberate choice not to love, whereas Jennie "gives herself up to loneliness as part of her expression of love." In "Dreiser's Short Stories and the Dream of Success" (*EA* 31[1978]:294–302) Joseph Griffin describes the majority of Dreiser's short fictions as "miniature 'American tragedies' in which

characters, given to believe . . . that the American dream is capable
of realization take the lure and suffer deception." Dreiser's stories,
says Griffin, though often rejected by publishers, were nonetheless
written in the context of magazine fiction, for they invariably deal
with the pursuit of romance and wealth.

viii. Edith Wharton

There are only five articles about Wharton to report on, but they are
happily of high quality. The richness of Wharton's fiction is reflected
in Elizabeth Ammons' latest article, "Edith Wharton's *Ethan Frome*
and the Question of Meaning" (*SAF* 7:127–40). Ammons reads *Ethan
Frome* as a frightening adult fairy tale, an inverted *Snow White*,
wherein the wicked witch, Ethan's wife Zeena, triumphs. Her triumph, says Ammons, is the result of the American economic system
which condemned women to servile and twisted existences. Ethan's
horror at Mattie, the fair maiden, also becoming a witch like Zeena,
expresses the male fear, says Ammons, that all women will eventually
turn into witches. Also exploring the mythic and sociological complexities of Wharton's fiction, Adeline R. Tintner in "Mothers, Daughters, and Incest in the Late Novels of Edith Wharton" (*The Lost
Tradition: Mothers and Daughters in Literature*, ed. Cathy N. Davidson and E. M. Broner [Ungar]) depicts *The Old Maid, The Mother's Recompense*, and *Twilight Sleep* as a Sophoclean trilogy wherein
the tragic dimension of human relationships stems from an element
of incest between fathers and daughters. But Wharton's novels, says
Tintner, are also concerned with the changing roles of women in
society and focus particularly on situations where mothers do not
raise their children although they remain central to their lives.

   Most of the articles written on Wharton continue to examine her
fiction for its views on marriage. In "Lily-Bartering on the New York
Social Exchange in *The House of Mirth*" (*BSUF* 20,ii:59–64) Wayne
W. Westbrook asserts that Wharton's novel belongs to a subgenre of
turn-of-the-century Wall Street novels and that Wharton describes
"a society which is a trading arena for those with something to sell
and those eager to buy, a social exchange where marriage deals are
negotiated and transacted." Cathy N. Davidson's "Kept Women in
The House of Mirth (*MarkhamR* 9:10–13) is another look at the way

women in Wharton's novels are trapped and exploited by their society's double standards. Finally, in a somewhat different vein, Allen F. Stein in "Wharton's *Blithedale*: A New Reading of *The Fruit of the Tree*" (*ALR* 12:330–37) writes that Wharton's third novel is not a reformist tract but a book about the limitations of human nature. Its central idea, says Stein, is that social betterment can never occur until human nature purges itself of meanness, folly, and egotism.

ix. Rølvaag and Other Western Writers

Since the Rølvaag Symposium in 1974 (See *ALS* 1975, pp. 292–93) a significant body of scholarship has continued to develop around this Norwegian-American author. There have been two good articles by Kristoffer F. Paulson. In "Berdahl Family History and Rølvaag's Immigrant Trilogy" (*NAS* 27[1977]:55–76) Paulson states that *Giants in the Earth* and its sequels do not constitute a literal history of the Berdahl family; but from reading diaries and autobiography in the Berdahl family and from interviews Paulson is able to show how "many of the actions and descriptions in the novel originated in the Berdahls' recounting of their personal experiences on the Dakota prairies." In "Ole Rølvaag, Herbert Krause, and the Frontier Thesis of Frederick Jackson Turner" (*Where the West Begins* [1978], pp. 24–33) Paulson outlines parallels in theme structure and characterization between Rølvaag's *Giants in the Earth* and Krause's *The Thresher*. Although Rølvaag's novel is more romantic, writes Paulson, both novels are about power struggles in the west and both novels reveal the tragic price, psychologically and spiritually, that the pursuit of power exacts. There is also a good article by Neil T. Eckstein, who in "*Giants in the Earth* as Saga" (*Where the West Begins* [1978], pp. 34–41) examines the affinities of Rølvaag's novel with the tradition of saga literature, finding similarities in the malevolence of nature, the nautical cast to Per Hansa's journey, and the brooding fatalism of his wife Beret. Rølvaag, says Eckstein, has "woven the many strands of a rich literary past into a coherent [new] whole."

There were three more articles on *Giants in the Earth*, all touching at some point on the cultural division in the immigrant and the immigrant author. In "Vision and Reality in *Giants in the Earth*" (*SDR* 17,i:85–100) Steve Hahn argues that there is a fundamental dichotomy in the novel between the physical world of the American plains and the psychological world of Norwegian religious and cultural structures. This essay is particularly effective in selecting details from the text to show how the two worlds penetrate each other without finally merging. In "Ole Edvart Rølvaag and *Giants in the Earth*: A Writer Between Two Countries" (*HSE* 12:77–87) Orm Øverland discusses the incongruities of language and the conflicting cultural themes in Rølvaag's best-known novel. Øverland points out that there are really two books and two audiences, Norwegian and English, but that they are both anomalies: the Norwegian book is written from a foreign point of view about a foreign experience; and while the English version is indisputably an American novel in content, it is nonetheless a translation from a foreign language. Finally, in a long article titled "Beret and the Prairie in *Giants in the Earth*" (*NAS* 28:217–44) Curtis D. Ruud shows how each of the settlers in Rølvaag's novel must come to terms with the prairie and how this process in turn is a key to understanding the characters and major themes of the novel. Ruud focuses on Beret's alienation and madness as a psychological struggle with the landscape.

There are two articles on Zane Grey and one on Wister worthy of mention here. The Grey articles focus on the author's attitudes to Mormonism. In "Zane Grey in Zion: An Examination of His Supposed Anti-Mormonism" (*BYUS* 18[1978]:483–90) Gary Topping argues on the basis of Grey's letters and articles that Grey was not prejudiced against the Mormons. He wrote in fact, Topping points out, pro-Mormon novels such as *The Heritage of the Desert*, and in all his fiction he has little sympathy for extremists of any order. Grey knew little about Mormon history, says Topping, but he recognized polygamy and authoritarian government as "good material for a raging Western story." This view is supported by Graham St. John Stott, who in "Zane Grey and James Simpson Emmett" (*BYUS* 18[1978]: 491–503) describes Grey's relationship to Emmett, whom Grey described as the man who influenced him most. Emmett was both physically and morally the archetypal hero for Grey and was also a Mormon. In "The Roosevelt-Wister Connection: Some Notes on the West and the Uses of History" (*WAL* 14:95–114) Forrest G. Robinson bases a comprehensive view of American culture on a comparison of Roosevelt's history, *The Rough Riders*, with Owen Wister's

The Virginian. In these parallel texts, argues Robinson, there is a vision of national unity based on ideals of manliness, self-reliance, and a strident Anglo-Saxonism. The conception of the American hero in those books as primitive, virile, at home in the great out-of-doors, whether as cowboy, adventurer, or soldier would dominate the national imagination, contends Robinson, until the Great War.

x. Women and Women Writers

Charlotte S. McClure has followed up her articles and Western Writers Series monograph on Gertrude Atherton with a book-length study. *Gertrude Atherton* (*TUSAS* 324) is a comprehensive examination of this California novelist whose place in American literary history, writes McClure, has not yet been determined. The abiding subject in Atherton's fiction, McClure tells us, is the woman searching not simply for happiness but for the goals that best express her internal nature and rhythms. Atherton wrote about "affinity" at the core of human relationships (especially the attraction between men and women), but that it had to be adjusted so that a woman might find her identity and purpose in life beyond the procreative function. On the largest scale Atherton's feminism, according to McClure, addressed the question of how to adjust a woman's aspirations and the exigencies of civilization. Although Atherton was a romantic novelist, she also saw herself, says McClure, as a social historian, recording the values and actions of her time, especially as observed in California. Her style was frequently faulted by critics but, writes McClure, it is distinctive with its unusual diction, its use of slang, its wit and lack of sentimentality. At its worst there are frequently turgid sentences in Atherton's prose and confusing arrangements of incidents. I knew little about Atherton before reading this book. I found it a fine introduction, which is what I assume the purpose of the Twayne series to be, and I recommend the book as such.

The active role frequently played by women writers in the early part of the century is reflected in *Literary America, 1903–1934: The Mary Austin Letters*, ed. Thomas Matthews Pearce (Greenwood). Most of the 115 letters selected from the Austin collection in the Huntington Library were written to Austin by a wide-ranging number of correspondents, including Jack London, Sinclair Lewis, Willa

Cather, Van Wyck Brooks, and Sherwood Anderson. The letters, grouped according to writer, are not chronologically arranged, but each letter is given an informative preface. Austin herself is the author of only seven letters, but most of the letters touch in some way on her work.

The search for feminist attitudes prevails even in the consideration of popular, relatively unsophisticated writers. Helen Lojek's "The Southern Lady Gets a Divorce: 'Saner Feminism' in the Novels of Amélie Rives" (*SLJ* 12,i:47–69) is a lengthy review of Rives's life and fiction. Lojek argues that in life the Virginia novelist never outgrew the traditional atttiudes inculcated in the southern belle, but that in her fiction she does demand greater freedom for women in the marriage relationship, that ideally "man and woman must be partners, friends." In "Woman on the Trail: Hough's *North of 36*" (*WAL* 14:217–20) Linda K. Downey describes Hough's originality in making "a proper lady the central character of a trail drive novel." Finally, C. G. and A. C. Hoffman in "Re-Echoes of the Jazz Age: Archetypal Women in the Novels of 1922" (*JML* 7:62–86) make the very interesting point that although male novelists of the 1920s generally portrayed women as love goddesses and female novelists portrayed women in terms of the mother imago, both were presenting women in terms of a psychological archetype rather than a realistic, social being. "Despite superficial and political changes in the status of women," these critics observe, "the novelist of 1922 envisioned the world of social and economic action as belonging to men and the world of moral and psychological sensibility as belonging to women." Among the American authors discussed are Wharton, Cather, and Fitzgerald.

xi. Proletarian Writers

Upton Sinclair's 1978 centenary was marked by a conference at California State University, Los Angeles, by a reissue of his novel *Boston,* and by the publication of the *Upton Beall Sinclair Centenary Journal.* I have not had the opportunity yet to read the new journal, so will wait to report on it next year. There is a good overview of this author and his work in Dennis Welland's "Upton Sinclair: The Centenary of an American Writer" (*BJRL* 61:474–94). One of the more interesting points that Welland makes is that Sinclair's openness to the experience of conversion was probably owing to his Methodist background. There is a long-winded article titled "Upton Sinclair's Escape from *The Jungle*: The Narrative Strategy and Suppressed Conclusion of America's First Proletarian Novel" (*Prospects* 4[1978]:237–66) in which Michael Brewster Folsom discusses the problems Sinclair had in writing a conclusion to *The Jungle* that would demonstrate the process whereby the masses of working men are converted to socialism. Folsom also compares the serial version of the story where at the end Jurgis is arrested and put in jail with the novel which ends with the socialist election victory speech. What Sinclair suppressed, says Folsom, is a realistic ending where socialism would be powerless to save the hero.

There is a good monograph, *Lincoln Steffens* (Ungar), by Robert Stinson, which examines the literary values of this muckraker's best work. Stinson shows that Steffens' most famous book, *The Shame of the Cities* (1904), with its vision of graft and bribery as central to American culture, is not without literary merit. To the melodramatic nature of muckraking, with its villainous robber barons, pathetic victims, and heroic reformers, Steffens brought a keen sense of how things looked, choosing exactly the right detail to bring the reality of the story home to the reader. According to Stinson, Steffens created a model for a new kind of journalism. Stinson also discusses the very successful *Autobiography of Lincoln Steffens* (1931), showing how it satisfies the various requirements of the genre. It is a conduct book, written to show his son the difference between political rhetoric and political reality. It is a confession of his inability to love fully the people close to him. It is above all an education wherein the innocent must unlearn the false education of his culture. Its literary success, says Stinson, derives from its heavy use of dialogue and its use of the self-contained story within the larger narrative. There is also a probing article titled "Muckraking Lincoln Steffens" (*VQR* 54[1978]:87–103) by Stephen J. Whitfield, who examines the inconsistencies in Steffens' thinking, the confusion in his attitudes (he shamed the cities but admired their feudal bosses), and the secretive nature of his private life.

The one article on Traven this year was of a bibliographical nature. In "Facts and Guesses: The Difference Between the First German and American Editions of B. Traven's *The Treasure of the Sierra*

Madre" (*PBSA* 73:315–31) Inge Kutt concludes from comparing the German and English texts that Traven was at home and wrote most effectively from a European point of view.

xii. Mencken, Lardner, and Others

George H. Douglas' *H. L. Mencken, Critic of American Life* (Archon, 1978) is a very good book about Mencken's ideas. This study is concerned chiefly with Mencken's writing of the middle and late 1920s, the period of the *American Mercury*, in which Mencken turned from literary criticism to criticism of American life. Fundamental to all of Mencken's writing, says Douglas, was a quarrel with the democratic belief that all men are equal. When this belief is practiced there is a leveling in the cultural life that results in the banal and mediocre being honored. It was Mencken's contention, writes Douglas, that the average man is not intelligent and reasonable but lives according to his emotions, especially fear, anger, and envy. Mencken felt the great malady of American life was living for its promises rather than its reality. However, says Douglas, he lauded the male principle of industry combined with imagination, regretting the prevalence of the female virtues—common sense, orderliness, and decorum. The latter, combined with the democratic ideal for education, produced an "anemic higher culture." Douglas makes some good observations on Mencken's style, the chief ingredients of which are wordplay, lampooning, but especially cataloguing. He also speculates on what Mencken's response would be to present-day American culture, convinced that he would see today's center stages (big government, the universities, and the technostructure of large corporations) as infected by Puritanism. He would surely see, says Douglas, the great pressure groups in modern society ("black power," "women's lib") as despotic, intolerant, and totalitarian in nature, as instances of democratic Puritanism where the "good" cause a man is caught up in is usually his own in disguise. This is a fine study of Mencken's thought—sound, compact, and very readable.

There are a couple of items on Lardner, who holds a minor but continuing critical interest. Both pieces are chiefly concerned with Lardner's vernacular style and his technique of story-telling. Donald Phelps in "Shut Up, He Explained" (*Shenandoah* 29,iv[1978]:84–100) argues that Lardner's writing was always concerned with the process of telling a story. He was particularly fascinated, says Phelps, by "the way in which even the most ignorant and fractured viewpoint could in effect create its own world." At the same time his laconic style, his refusal to use imagery or metaphor, kept the story to a literal reality. *Ring Lardner* (Ungar) by Elizabeth Evans is a brief but thorough introduction to this writer. Evans examines several of the stories in detail and argues that Lardner's concern with communication and American speech makes him still significant today.

Finally, two essays on writers from vastly different cultural backgrounds are both concerned with family values. In "David Levinsky: Modern Man as Orphan" (*TSE* 23[1978]:85–93) Bonnie Lyon asserts that Cahan's novel is a modern parable of man as a spiritual orphan in search of his parents, his home, "or any satisfactory center to give meaning to his life." This reading, says Lyon, gives focus and coherence to both David's business pursuits and his abortive love life. In "The Family in Booth Tarkington's *Growth* Trilogy" (*Mid-America* 6:88–99) Charlotte LeGates demonstrates that Tarkington's heroes are torn between the family and cultural traditions represented by the mother and the capitalistic, achievement-oriented life represented by the father. In all three novels, writes LeGates, the hero ultimately chooses the masculine world of industry and progress but retains something of the family's traditional values.

Simon Fraser University

14. Fiction: The 1930s to the 1950s

Jack Salzman

i. "Art for Humanity's Sake"—Proletarians and Others

The year 1979 saw the publication of several relatively brief but not insignificant works pertaining to the literature of the 1930s. In "Trouble on the Land: Southern Literature and the Great Depression" (*CRevAS* 10:153–74) Louis D. Rubin, Jr., begins by noting that the 1930s "were the high point, the culmination, of the South's literary history," then addresses himself to the problem of why such writers as Agee, Caldwell, and Wolfe, whatever the "considerable achievement" of the work they wrote about the Depression, "do not develop and sustain a believable and consistent artistic indictment of social injustice, whether of tenement or tenant shack, which was what they set out to do." A previously unpublished short story by Tess Slesinger, "A Hollywood Gallery" (*MQR* 18:439–54), is preceded by Janet Sharistanian's informative essay, "Tess Slesinger's Hollywood Sketches" (*MQR* 18:429–38). Joseph Cuomo's revealing "An Interview with Meridel LeSueur," the blacklisted midwestern writer, appears in *A Shout in the Street* (2:150–69), while *Quindaro* (3:29–37) includes "Edward Dahlberg: A Memorial," a transcript, slightly condensed, of a meeting in memory of Dahlberg held during the Midwest Conference on Alternative Journalism and Popular Culture in Kansas City on 3 June 1978. Meridel LeSueur was one of the participants in the memorial, as was Jack Conroy, many of whose stories, sketches, reminiscences, and essays have been collected for the first time in *The Jack Conroy Reader*, ed. Jack Salzman and David Ray (Burt Franklin). The last two sections of the *Reader*—"Reminiscences and Autobiography" and "Articles and Essays"—contain several pieces on the cultural and political fights which took place during the 1930s. A somewhat different view of the period is to be found in Malcolm Cowley's "1935: The Year of Congresses" (*SoR* 15:273–87)—a fre-

quently apologetic and distant account of the first American Writers'
Congress—which Cowley again refers to in the course of Diane U.
Eisenberg's "A Conversation with Malcolm Cowley" (*SoR* 15:288–
99).

A year after the first American Writers Congress was held the
Spanish Civil War broke out and became a matter of much concern
and debate to those on the Left. There is nothing in Ronald Fraser's
Blood of Spain: An Oral History of the Spanish Civil War (Pantheon)
which specifically deals with the writers covered in this essay, but
the book is indispensable for an understanding of an issue which was
central to the lives of many of these writers. (Fraser interviewed more
than 300 survivors of the war.)

A book of a very different kind but one which also provides some
sense of the political issues which dominated the attention of writers
of the Left during the 1930s and 1940s, and which had considerable
repercussion in the next two decades, is Norman Podhoretz's *Breaking
Ranks: A Political Memoir* (Harper). The book attempts to explain
how Podhoretz made his way from an essentially liberal to a "neo-
conservative" political position, and along the way there are sketches
of Dashiell Hammett and Lillian Hellman, of the Trillings, of William Phillips and Philip Rahv—of many others. It is all told in a cold,
self-congratulatory voice. Perhaps others take Podhoretz as seriously
as he takes himself, but I hope not.

a. **James Agee.**   Of the four essays to appear on Agee this year, two
are devoted to his only novel, *A Death in the Family*. In "Nobody . . .
Is Specially Privileged" (*Death Education* 2:369–80) Mildred L.
Culp suggests that the novel presents death on three levels: the physical death of Jay Follet, the stultifying death-in-life of Rufus' great-
great-grandmother, and the decline of a religious tradition. But these
forms of death are redemptive. In *A Death in the Family* Agee shows
us "the beauty of death, despite its irrevocable and irreversible qualities, in its ability to transform life-death on visible levels and death
viewed in light of faith." Gayle Whittier's focus in "Belief and Un-
belief in *A Death in the Family*" (*Renascence* 31:177–92) is somewhat different. According to Whittier, Agee's novel "reflects his adult
sensibility towards religion, while recasting his childhood impressions of formal faith." *A Death in the Family* "delineates the struggle
for and against faith, the goodness of human love reverently recog-

nized, and the possibility for an authentic, albeit limited, community within the family. . . ."

In "Agee's *Famous Men* and American Non-Fiction" (*CE* 40: 677–82) John O. Hussey addresses himself to the problem that, despite its reputation as a masterpiece, *Famous Men* is not regularly read or discussed in classrooms. The reason, Hussey suggests, has to do with the fact that Agee's book is nonfiction, and because we have not as yet established a single theoretical framework for our nonfiction much of it tends to go untaught. Yet *Famous Men* shares much in common with such nonfiction works as Edwards' *Personal Narrative*, Adams' *Education*, and Mailer's *Armies of the Night*: each "portrays a hero-narrator engaged in a solitary quest for spiritual and/or psychological renewal." And, significantly, these heroes achieve their ends. "They are not doomed, mad Ahabs or Gatsbys or Sutpens, and this fact makes for one of the strongest distinctions between these works and our great novels." James Hoopes also is concerned with *Famous Men*, but from a totally different point of view. In the most interesting piece to be published on Agee this year Hoopes considers the influence which I. A. Richards' referential theory of language had on Agee in general and *Famous Men* in particular. Hoopes argues that Agee mostly accepted Richards' theory of language "with unfortunate consequences for his study of tenant farmers." Because Agee came to believe that words could not embody his own perceptions of beauty, he failed to consider the possibility that they might do so for the tenants. Like the modernist critic considering his text, Agee was unable to consider "the place of the text in the lives of its artists, or even the possibility that they were artists."

b. **Jesse Stuart.** Much of the activity this year in Stuart studies has been provided by Stuart himself. Archer Editions Press has published a collection of 20 essays under the title, *Lost Sandstones and Lonely Skies and Other Essays*, while McGraw-Hill has issued *The Kingdom Within: A Spiritual Autobiography*. There is much about Stuart's life to be found in both volumes, though neither book is likely to tell the Stuart enthusiast anything new.

Stuart scholarship for the year has been entirely bibliographical. Hensley C. Woodbridge published the second edition of his *Jesse and Jane Stuart: A Bibliography* (Murray, Ky.: State Univ.), as well as two supplements to the bibliography: "Jesse and Jane Stuart: A

Bibliography (1979)—Supplement 1" (*JLN* 11[1978]:110–11) and "Jesse and Jane Stuart: A Bibliography (*JJS*³): Supplement 2" (*JLN* 12:93–94). In addition, H. Edward Richardson has provided "Addendum: The Jesse Stuart Bibliography of the L.M.U. Years: 1926–1929" (*JLN* 12:79–82), a listing of 42 titles published by Stuart during his years at Lincoln Memorial University and not included in Woodbridge's original bibliography. But the most substantial work of Stuart scholarship once again belongs to J. R. LeMaster, whose *Jesse Stuart: A Reference Guide* (Hall) is by far the most complete listing of works about Stuart. LeMaster covers the period from 1934— when *Man with a Bull-Tongue Plow* first appeared—to 1977; because Stuart has been out of fashion with academic critics, a vast majority of the items listed are from the popular press. In his introduction LeMaster tells us that "those who write about Stuart in the future will have to take seriously the fact that he is a modernist in his rejection of contemporary values, a humanist in his effort to create a habitable world, and a symbolist in his effort to abstract from a limited context the values which supposedly will make life meaningful for all of us." To this one can now add that those who write about Stuart in the future will have in LeMaster's annotated *Reference Guide* an invaluable tool to aid them.

c. John Steinbeck. The most valuable addition to Steinbeck studies this year is Thomas Fensch's *Steinbeck and Covici: The Story of a Friendship* (Eriksson). In actuality this is neither a story nor a study but a collection of letters between Steinbeck and his longtime editor and friend, Pascal Covici, with connecting comments by Fensch. The relationship between the two began in the mid-1930s and ended only with Covici's death in 1963. The volume is a fine supplement to *Steinbeck: A Life in Letters,* and is one of the few books we have which so fully discloses the relationship between a writer and editor.

Of almost no value whatever is Thomas Kiernan's *The Intricate Music: A Biography of John Steinbeck* (Little, Brown). This book purports to be the first full-scaled biography of Steinbeck. In fact it is a malicious and insensitive volume which has little to say about either Steinbeck or his work. Kiernan tells us that he found Steinbeck to be a disagreeable man—"politically pompous and literarily hostile, a person in whom vindictiveness and petty intolerance seemed to be the warp and woof of life." Yet he was an ardent admirer of Steinbeck's work and was curious about the disparity he perceived between Steinbeck the writer and Steinbeck the man. But Steinbeck was not very cooperative about a biography, and Elaine Steinbeck had agreed to cooperate with Jackson Benson, who wanted to do a biography of her husband and so was reluctant to cooperate with Kiernan, and then came *Steinbeck: A Life in Letters*. And so on: Kiernan obviously had a hard time of it. But that does not excuse the simplistic observations, the nastiness, the poor writing: Steinbeck, we are told, concluded early in his life that there was something perverted in the fact that society demanded the suppression of individuality and "the impulse to expose the perversion would become the engine of Steinbeck's forming literary vision"; the manuscript of *To a God Unknown* was rejected because "the nation, and its publishers, wanted not the sermons of muddled philosophers but the escapist adventures of sales-proven writers"; "probably the most illustrative of the boyhood-influenced works . . . was *The Red Pony*, a long short story or a brief novel, depending on one's interpretation of it." So it goes. This book is a disservice to Steinbeck and anyone who reads it; it should never have been published.

I'm not much more enthusiastic about Sunita Jain's *Steinbeck's Concept of Man* (New Delhi: New Statesman Publishing Co.; available from Humanities Press), which argues that from *Cup of Gold* through *The Winter of Our Discontent* Steinbeck shows man struggling "to attain dignity by imposing order on his dual existence as an individual and as a group animal." From his first novel through his last, "Steinbeck shows man caught up in the process of living, trying to rise above an individuality which prevents him from becoming a group animal, and trying, as a group animal, to retain his individuality." Twelve novels are discussed, all chosen to throw the maximum light on Steinbeck's concept of the individual, the social, and the ideal selves of man. It is all very repetitious and, I'm afraid, more than a little simplistic.

The fourth book to be published on Steinbeck this year is Tetsumaro Hayashi's *A Study Guide to Steinbeck* (Part II) [Scarecrow], a sequel to Hayashi's 1974 *A Study Guide to Steinbeck: A Handbook of His Major Works*. The volume begins with Hayashi's "A Guide to Steinbeck Studies: Questions and Answers" (pp. 7–18), and is followed by five essays by various hands covering ten of Steinbeck's works. The chapters include background material, plot synopsis, a critical explication, apparatus for research papers, suggested topics for research papers, and a selected bibliography. The volume, as Hayashi rightly notes, "is not for erudite or advanced scholars already conversant with the background of Steinbeck's literature"; it is geared, rather, "to non-English-majoring students who study Steinbeck's literature in humanities courses or in basic English composition courses."

Hayashi also is the editor of *Steinbeck's Women: Essays in Criticism*, Steinbeck Monograph Series 9 (Muncie, Ind.: Steinbeck Soc. of America), which consists of six essays about Steinbeck's female characters. Some of the essays were originally presented at the 1977 MLA Steinbeck meeting, and others appeared in the *Steinbeck Quarterly* and *Southwest Review*. The essays are uneven, but as Richard F. Peterson comments in his Introduction, collectively they reject the view that all Steinbeck's female characters before *The Grapes of Wrath* are pale precursors of Ma Joad, and "while still facing the issue of Steinbeck's sentimentality . . . [they] show that there is more to Steinbeck's women than have met other critical eyes."

The 1978 MLA Steinbeck Society Meeting Papers comprise a large part of *StQ* 12,iii and iv. (Although still a "quarterly," *StQ* now is issued only twice a year.) In "John Steinbeck: Selected Episodes" (pp. 78–86) Preston Beyer discusses some "episodes and thoughts in Steinbeck's life which lead his thinking, form his style, and portray the man or maybe are the man. . . ." In a slightly expanded version of his MLA talk Louis K. MacKendrick discusses "The Popular Art of Discontent: Steinbeck's Masterful *Winter*" (pp. 99–107), and most interesting of all, Robert DeMott in "The Interior Distance of John Steinbeck" (pp. 86–99) is concerned with "an analogous group of interior elements in Steinbeck's work which deserve more specific attention, and provide a means of placing Steinbeck in a shared intellectual and creative context." DeMott isolates four elements— symbolic landscape, images of enclosure, dreams, and creativity— which "spring from a linked generative point in the writer's unconscious, and rise to the surface of his work often enough to indicate a recognizable, and sometimes overlapping pattern." In the same number of *StQ* Tetsumaro Hayashi writes about "Steinbeck's *Winter* as Shakespearean Fiction" (pp. 107–15) and concludes that in *The Winter of Our Discontent* Steinbeck "tries to reverse the vision of

Shakespearean plays by placing an innocent hero (Ethan) against
a wicked world rather than a wicked villain (Macbeth or Richard)
against a good, but too innocuous world."

In *StQ*(12,i–ii) there is a section devoted to "Collecting Stein-
beckiana" (pp. 29–52), as well as articles by Laura F. Hodges on *The
Acts of King Arthur and His Noble Knights* (pp. 20–27), Steven J.
Federle's consideration of Steinbeck's unpublished novel, *Lifeboat*
(pp. 14–20), Ray Lewis White's discussion of a parallel occurrence
in Steinbeck's *The Grapes of Wrath* and Guy de Maupassant's
"L'Idylle" (pp. 27–29), and John Ditsky's "Steinbeck's *Bombs Away*:
The Group-man in the Wild Blue Yonder" (pp. 5–14), an interesting
article in which Ditsky argues that by the very slightness of the book,
Steinbeck betrays "the crucial point in his own intellectual development engendered by the collapse of the notion of the group-man with
which he had for so long been fascinated."

Ditsky also is the author of *"The Grapes of Wrath*: A Reconsideration" (*SHR* 13:215–20), in which he contends that *Grapes* "begs
recognition as the sort of book it really is: a classic of undiminished
power that is fundamentally a romantic epic of the U.S. highway."
The Grapes of Wrath is an episodic novel about a family's education,
a *bildungsroman* in the collective sense. It has attained the status of
a "classic," and what we are most in need of, Ditsky writes, "is a redefinition of why the book has attained that status." It would have
been far more valuable for Ditsky to have attempted such a redefinition, I think, than for him to tell us that a redefinition is needed.

Three more pieces need to be mentioned here, two of which are
really notes. In "Steinbeck's *East of Eden*" (*Expl* 38,i:11–12) Joyce
C. Brown suggests that Cathy Ames Trask not be seen as a serpentine
figure of evil but "as a figure of amorality," and in "The Cur in 'The
Chrysanthemums'" (*SSF* 16:215–17) Ernest W. Sullivan II argues
that the correspondences between people and dogs in "The Chrysanthemums" elucidate the social and sexual relationships of the three
humans in the story, "as well as foreshadow and explain Elisa's failure
at the end of the story to escape from her unproductive and sterile
lifestyle." More substantial is Louis Owens' "John Steinbeck's 'Mystical Outcrying': *To a God Unknown* and *The Log from The Sea of
Cortez*" (*SJS* 5,ii:20–32), which contends that most critics have mis-
read *To a God Unknown* as a teleologically causal act. Rather, Owens
suggests, Steinbeck developed a philosophy of man's oneness with all

things. He blurs the distinction between Christian and pagan because "he is interested in working toward an isolation of the crucial impulse within man which underlines formal religions by setting Joseph and all his religious gropings against a philosophical background of non-teleological thinking."

d. **Farrell, Dahlberg, Algren, Roth, and Fuchs.** The death of James T. Farrell on 22 August 1979 resulted in several memorial pieces in various newspapers and magazines, but nothing of any particular consequence was published during the year. Dennis Flynn discusses "James T. Farrell and His Catholics" (*America* 141:111–13), in which he notes that Farrell was the first writer "to contribute an image of the Catholic Church to American fiction"; what Farrell shows in his fiction is the Church's "practically impotent involvement with much of American society in a general failure of institutional structures to nourish or support human aspirations." Charles Fanning and Ellen Skerrett are concerned not only with Farrell's attitude toward the Church but also with the Street, the Park, and the Home, all of which are points of reference for Chicago's Washington Park, which, as they state in "James T. Farrell and Washington Park: The Novel as Social History" (*Chicago History* 8:80–91), "emerges in Farrell's fiction as a realized world, as whole and coherent as Joyce's Dublin and William Faulkner's northern Mississippi." Don Richard Cox in "A World He Never Made: The Decline of James T. Farrell" (*CLAJ* 23:32–48), a piece written well before Farrell's death, notes that Farrell's reputation "has decidedly suffered and has apparently been steadily declining since his first publications." But since only about half of Farrell's output has been seen as yet, his reputation may still rise on the literary market. James Finn would seem to agree. In "The Father of Studs" (*Commonweal* 106:622) Finn speaks of the achievement of the Studs Lonigan trilogy and the Danny O'Neill series: "Farrell captured a portion of Irish-American urban life at the beginning of the century. It is a life that is in the background of many American Irish; it is a part of their roots without some knowledge of which they cannot be fully understood or understand themselves."

Farrell's long-time nemesis, Edward Dahlberg, who died two years before Farrell, is the subject of a fine study by Earl Fendelman. In "Edward Dahlberg's Art of Memory (*JML* 7:113–26) Fendleman contends that the world Dahlberg writes about is "death-ridden," and Dahlberg's desire was "nothing less than to bring it back to life and to prove that it contains the means for his own survival." Dahlberg's subject—his hope for renewed life—became himself. For Dahlberg "the self, the world, and the relation between the two are all problematic categories, the subjects of an experiment which is endless before death." He explores the possibilities of memory in memory's agent, the autobiography—*Because I Was Flesh* and *The Confessions of Edward Dahlberg*—knowing all the while that memory "provides appropriate material for a monument only in a world where all else has failed."

Nelson Algren doesn't fare nearly as well as Dahlberg. John D. Raymer's "Nelson Algren and Simone de Beauvoir: The End of Their Affair at Miller, Indiana" (*ON* 5:401–07) informs us that the well-known affair "was an especially significant affair" because "it marked the first real post-war link between French and American intellectuals." Moreover, Raymer implies, Algren should not have been quite so disturbed by De Beauvoir's disclosures about the affair, since he has been "in the enviable position of having known one of the most important post-war European intellectuals and having introduced her to the American Midwest, a region she came to appreciate." Fortunately, the piece is not very long, so we don't have too much of this foolishness to endure.

Fuchs and Henry Roth have been much better served. In *Daniel Fuchs* (TUSAS 333) Gabriel Miller offers the first full-length study of a writer who has received relatively little critical attention. As Miller rightly notes, studies dealing with the 1930s and/or American Jewish literature tend to ignore Fuchs or mention him only in passing, when in fact "he should be singled out among the best artists in either classification." Miller concentrates upon Fuchs's first three novels—*Summer in Williamsburg, Homage to Blenholt*, and *Low Company*—which represent his "greatest achievement as a writer"—and also considers Fuchs's short stories, essays, and fourth novel, *West of the Rockies*; only his screen work is not discussed. The study does what its author set out to do: it begins to rectify the critical neglect which has befallen Fuchs, and it alerts "a wider audience to the richness and complexity of Fuchs's work." Henry Roth no longer suffers the critical neglect which only a few years ago he shared with Fuchs. The list of works about the author of *Call It Sleep* continues to mount, as do the number of interviews with its author. In "Henry

Roth in Jerusalem: An Interview" (*LitR* 23,i:5–23) William Freedman presents a transcript of a 1977 interview with Roth. Much of the
interview, as one might expect, is concerned with *Call It Sleep*, the
Depression, Roth's involvement with the Communist party, and his
literary silence. In "The Drama of Maturation: Henry Roth's *Call It
Sleep*" (*EA* 32:46–55) David Seed contends that of the various critical approaches to *Call It Sleep* those by Leslie Fiedler, Irving Howe,
and Walter Allen, which "stress the balance which Roth strikes between David's inner psychological experience and the outer world
of the streets," do fullest justice to the complexities of the novel, while
Daniel Walden in "Henry Roth's *Call It Sleep*: Ethnicity, 'The Sign,'
and the Power" (*MFS* 25:268–72), writes of the novel as a "book that
deals successfully and penetratingly with the traumas of dislocation,
the problems of the 'New Immigrants' as they were Americanized,
and the conditions (especially in the 1920s) of a country tied to industrialism, electricity, energy, power and disillusionment." Walden
also is the author of " 'Sleep' at the Switch: The NET Effect in *Call
It Sleep*," one of nine pieces published in a special issue of *SAJL*
(5,i) devoted to *Call It Sleep*. The issue has been guest edited by
Bonnie Lyons, who provides an "Interview with Henry Roth, March,
1977" (pp. 50–58). In addition to the interview and Walden's article
(pp. 18–21), the issue includes six other articles and Debra B. Young's
valuable "Henry Roth: A Bibliographical Survey" (pp. 62–71). None
of the pieces, I suspect, will change the way we see Roth and *Call It
Sleep*, but it is good nevertheless to have this tribute to Roth's extraordinary achievement.

ii. Social Iconoclasts—West and Salinger

As was the case last year, work on West and Salinger continues to
disappoint. Little has been written during the past two years which
adds much to our understanding of either writer. In "Nathanael West
and the Persistence of Hope" (*Renascence* 31:205–14), for example,
Martin Tropp argues not very convincingly that "in *Miss Lonely-
hearts* especially, and to a lesser extent in *The Day of the Locust* and
A Cool Million, there exist half-hidden indications of the potential, at
least, for an answer to the endless search of West's characters for a
way out of their nightmare labyrinth." Tropp would have us believe
that West "hints, at least, that there is a seemingly endless fund

of belief and love in the world which, merely by existing, helps purify the wasteland of his novel." Perhaps so, but to argue in terms of "hints" and "half-hidden indications" leaves one most dubious. More convincing is Deborah Wyrick's "Dadaist Collage Structure and Nathanael West's *Dream Life of Balso Snell*" (*SNNTS* 11:349–59), which contends that in *Balso Snell* West translates visual collage into literary collage. His "aesthetic sensibilities transform ugly material into a beautiful composition. He ends up with a Dadaist collage that, by its very artistry, celebrates that which it wishes to destroy."

Salinger in his criticism has been having an even more difficult time of it than West. Bernard Oldsey, for example, offers his "Salinger and Golding: Resurrection or Repose" (*CE* 6:136–44) as "penance" for having taken part in the Salinger and Golding industries "that have since gone bankrupt." Oldsey has little to say about Salinger save that he had "an almost perfect ear," and that his best works— *Catcher in the Rye* and *Nine Stories*—are "products of a passionate and highly perfected art." Even more disappointing, if only because it promises more, is James Lundquist's *J. D. Salinger* (Ungar). Lundquist discusses all the works—beginning with a chapter entitled "The American Brainscape and The Disappearing Man" and concluding with "Where He Has Been, Where He Has Gone: Patterns of a Career"—but almost all he has to say about the stories is marked by his conviction that Salinger is an autobiographical writer and a master of Zen; thus, he can conclude that Salinger has become "a stylist whose comic mastery of language approaches that of Mark Twain, and a writer of considerable religious vision whose books themselves remain in the mind as incarnations of spirit long after they are put down." I find very little of this to be a satisfying reading of Salinger. Lundquist speaks of Salinger's "essential optimism," but I think there is little of that in Salinger. There is, I suspect, far more irony in Salinger's work than Lundquist recognizes; it misses what is most basic to Salinger, it seems to me, to contend as Lundquist does that in Salinger's work "poignancy turns into hopefulness, and the objective is enlightenment, not despair." I wish Lundquist had paid less heed to the autobiographical and the mysticism and had taken a closer look at the texts. There is much more to Salinger than we get in this study. Indeed, despite its length it tells us far less about Salinger than does the brief but sensitive and insightful piece by John Romano, "Salinger Was Playing Our Song" (*NYTBR* 3 Jun.: 11,

48–49), who pointedly tells us that our inability to see that Salinger is one of the very best living writers has to do not with neglect but with our "careless, unrecast affection."

iii. Expatriates and Émigrés

a. **Henry Miller.** Although the number of works to appear about Miller this year is not large, the quality of the work is substantial. In "Caterwauling and Harmony: Music in *Tropic of Cancer*" (*Crit* 20,iii:40–49) Paul R. Jackson considers the way music "becomes an insistant metaphor both for Miller's own discordant lyricism and for the collapsing world that *Tropic of Cancer* exposes." Thematically, Jackson points out, music is used throughout the novel "as a sign of the flagging vitality Miller everywhere rejects." Lawrence J. Shifreen also is concerned with *Tropic of Cancer*, only his interest is with the roots of Miller's best-known work. In "Henry Miller's *Mezzotints*: The Undiscovered Roots of *Tropic of Cancer*" (*SSF* 16:11–17) Shifreen discusses the series of short fictions—what Miller called *Mezzotints*—with which Miller began his writing career in the early 1920s. Although only seven *Mezzotints* remain and are not available to most readers, Shifreen considers them to be the prototype for all of Miller's work. Although *Mezzotints* is an immature work, "the images and metaphors it contains form the basis for Miller's literary ideas"; the seven broadsides "form the basis for all of Henry Miller's major writings."

In addition to his essay on the *Mezzotints*, Shifreen has made one of the most important contributions to Miller studies with the publication of *Henry Miller: A Bibliography of Secondary Sources* (Scarecrow). This is the fifth Miller bibliography, and as Shifreen rightly states in his Introduction, it is the first fully annotated bibliography, and it is more inclusive than those which have preceded it. The volume is divided into five sections—Books About Henry Miller; Chapters, Prefaces & Introductions About Miller; Books With Significant References to Miller; Dissertations About Miller; Articles & Reviews on Miller—and the entries in each section are listed chronologically. There are two indexes. The annotations are somewhat uneven. Shifreen is most kind to those works which praise Miller, and some works are given no more than a line, but the annotations are helpful. The bibliography covers a period of 46 years—from 1931 (one item) to 1977—and is primarily aimed at the student and scholar rather than the bibliographer. It will in fact prove to be a valuable tool for anyone interested in the life and work of Henry Miller.

b. **Anaïs Nin.** The year 1979 saw the publication of Nin's *Little Birds: Erotica by Anaïs Nin* (Harcourt), as well as two substantial works of criticism. The more valuable of the two, I think, is Benjamin Franklin V's and Duane Schneider's *Anaïs Nin: An Introduction* (Ohio). The book is precisely what it claims to be: an "introduction to Nin's various works published during her lifetime." The authors make no attempt to place him in the context of contemporary literature or to "pursue her elusive biography." Rather, they present a sound and readable consideration of Nin's fiction, diary, criticism, and nonfiction. There is not much critical evaluation, but there is considerable elucidation. The volume argues convincingly what the authors state in their conclusion: Nin's "greatest value is as a legitimate cicerone through the feminine psyche, as an author who shows both women and men that the pursuit of one's completeness is a difficult task that must be undertaken, even though it is unpleasant to do so and even though it might not be successful in the end."

Also intended as an introduction to Nin, but a book of a very different kind, is Bettina L. Knapp's *Anaïs Nin* (Ungar). Knapp discusses fewer works than Franklin and Schneider, and her orientation is Jungian: Nin too, we are told, believed that the dream was a source of nourishment for the creative instinct; the dream, Knapp writes, enabled Nin "to interweave painting and music with the written word, and thus to convey feeling, incarnate an aesthetic, and dramatize a psychological credo." Throughout the study analogies are drawn between Nin's writing and music and the visual arts. The influence of Lawrence and Proust, of surrealism and alchemy are an essential part of the study. Knapp's reading of some of Nin's work—*House of Incest*, for example—is exceptionally fine. And yet the volume is less satisfying than it should be. Knapp's admiration for Nin becomes insufferable, and her prose becomes a part of that admiration. Thus Knapp concludes with the following: "The interplay of the powerful forces within Nin molded her into a woman of inner and outer beauty who danced, laughed, sighed, wept, breathed as she stilled the flowing, limited the infinite, personified the amorphous, and decanted her images in structured feelings and translucent arabesques. Love and joy, like nacre, lined her being." Unfortunately, such excess is not uncommon in what is otherwise a fine study.

Nin's mysticism is also discussed by Knapp in "'To Reach Out Mystically . . . ': Anaïs Nin" (*RS* 47:165–80), which is a distillation of much of her book. Here Knapp concludes that "Nin rendered the indeterminate palpable; she transformed by limiting. A visionary capable of traversing the frontiers that separate the material domain from the unmanifested and inner rhythms from a music of the spheres, she drew on unknown factors in her writing—a causal phenomena—to articulate her 'forgotten memory images.' " Nancy Scholar also is concerned with images but of a somewhat different kind than Knapp. In "Anaïs Nin's *House of Incest* and Ingmar Bergman's *Persona*: Two Variations on a Theme" (*LFQ* 7:47–59) Scholar notes that "Nin and Bergman alike wish to explore a realm of experience below or beyond rationality; they attempt to break down and through the comfortable masks and surfaces by which most of us live." Scholar does in fact demonstrate that there are similarities between *House of Incest* and *Persona*. What she fails to make clear, however, is what difference it makes that the similarities do exist.

Two interviews with Nin were published during the year. In "Link in the Chain of Feeling: An Interview with Anaïs Nin" (*NOR* 5:113–18) Jeffrey Bailey offers excerpts from a conversation between Nin and himself, and *USP* (10,iii) offers "Anaïs Nin: An Unpublished Interview" by Maryanne Raphael, which was conducted during the Spring of 1974. Neither interview adds much to our knowledge of Nin, but the interview in *USP* clearly is the more interesting and substantial of the two.

In addition to the Nin interview, this year's issues of *USP* includes several other pieces on Nin. The articles continue to be a little too informal, but *USP* itself remains an essential source for anyone interested in Nin.

c. **Vladimir Nabokov.** Certainly the most important addition to Nabokov studies this year is *The Nabokov-Wilson Letters: Correspondence Between Vladimir Nabokov and Edmund Wilson, 1940–1971*, ed. Simon Karlinsky (Harper). There are a total of 264 letters in the collection, including the extant correspondence between the two from the summer of 1940 to the spring of 1958; there are also a few letters which were written between 1958 and 1971. Most of the letters in this volume, then, were exchanged before Wilson's celebrated attack on Nabokov's edition of *Eugene Onegin*. As Simon Karlinsky notes in his Introduction, these letters show the "close personal and intellectual contact" between Nabokov and Wilson; they also make clear that Nabokov's second literary career—as an American author writing in English—"can hardly be imagined without Wilson's help, advice and literary contacts." Yet at the same time, as Karlinsky points out, "For all of Edmund Wilson's awesome scope as a literary critic, the one major writer whose reputation he did not help to establish or assert was, paradoxically, his close friend and correspondent Vladimir Nabokov." We do not learn why Wilson liked *Lolita* "less than anything you wrote," or why he attacked the *Onegin* edition as he did. But despite what we do not learn, the volume is of great value for what it does tell us about Volodya and Bunny.

Two other volumes published during the year, though without the same intrinsic excitement of the *Letters*, also make a valuable contribution to our understanding of Nabokov's art. In *Vladimir Nabokov: A Reference Guide* (Hall) Samuel Schuman offers a bibliography of secondary sources which "aims at a completeness that stops just this side of pedantry." Schuman includes not only articles and books about Nabokov in English, as well as critical articles and books which deal in substantial part with Nabokov, a wide selection of works in foreign languages and foreign publications, a "generous sample" of reviews and news stories, and Ph.D. dissertations; he also includes reviews of the movie versions of *Lolita* and *Laughter in the Dark*, as well as a checklist of Russian émigré criticism. Schuman also provides a brief but informative introduction in which he discusses both the basic outlines of Nabokov's life and literary output and the general direction and evolution of writings about Nabokov. All in all, a fine volume.

So is the Nabokov number of *MFS* (25,iii), for which Schuman provides "A Selected Checklist" of criticism of Nabokov (pp. 527–54). The special issue, guest co-edited by Charles S. Ross, includes David I. Sheidlower's insightful discussion of the chess motif in *Bend Sinister*, "Reading Between the Lines and the Squares" (pp. 413–25), and among three essays which focus on *Lolita* is Robert

Merrill's "Nabokov and Fictional Artifice" (pp. 439–62), which also focuses on *Pale Fire* in an attempt "to clarify the nature of Nabokov's fiction, early and late." *Ada* is the subject of Ellen Pifer's "Dark Paradise: Shades of Heaven and Hell in *Ada*," which argues that *Ada*'s "carefully arranged aesthetic effects offer us fresh perceptions of our own psychic world and the way it is structured." The issue concludes with two notes devoted to Nabokov's shorter works, in one of which, "*Bend Sinister* and 'Tyrants Destroyed': Short Story into Novel" (pp. 508–13), Dan E. Burns compares the two works by Nabokov and concludes that the primary difference between the two "is merely *the degree to which the 'world' of the work is particularized*."

One of the contributors to the *MFS* issue, D. Barton Johnson, had two other pieces on Nabokov to appear during the year. In "The Index of Refraction in Nabokov's *Pale Fire*" (*RLT* 16:33–49) Johnson wonders why Nabokov compiled and included a seemingly useless index in *Pale Fire* and concludes that far from being ornamental, "Nabokov has made a bogus index the key to the novel." Johnson also offers "A Guide to Nabokov's 'A Guide to Berlin'" (*SEEJ* 23: 353–61), the story in Nabokov's early collection, *The Return of Chorb: Stories and Poems*, which he feels "stands out in that it presages the later works in their *tour de force* integration of style, plot, and theme."

The remaining works to be discussed cover a wide range of material, although three essays are devoted to Nabokov's most popular novel, *Lolita*. Brenda Megerle is concerned with "The Tantalization of *Lolita*" (*SNNTS* 11:338–48), for she believes the novel is about tantalization, "specifically the tantalization which Nabokov finds in the aesthetic experience." Language, Megerle writes, "is Nabokov's Lolita, the tantalizing source and repository of the great promised, the never-to-be-had—the perfect novel." Ronald Wallace, in "No Harm in Smiling: Vladimir Nabokov's *Lolita*," a chapter in *Last Laugh*, sees Humbert's claims of artistry and love as being comically balanced by Nabokov's exposure of perversion and lust. It is impossible to choose one view over the other, Wallace writes. "Revising and expanding our comically balanced notions of morality and art, Nabokov's parody forced the reader to hold all the contradictory impulses in mind at the same time." And Nomi Tamir-Ghez writes an article about "The Art of Persuasion in Nabokov's *Lolita*" (*PT* 1:i–ii:65–83). Tamir-Ghez describes the major rhetorical devices which are used by Nabokov while practicing his art of persuasion in *Lolita,* and notes that "the same arguments that are used by Humbert to justify himself, are often used (indirectly) by Nabokov to expose the narrator's guilt. In short, the narrator is but a pawn in the author's general scheme."

In addition to the three pieces on *Lolita,* this year's work on Nabokov includes W. W. Rowe's "A Note on Nabokov's Erotic Necks" (*RLT* 16:50–57), which first considers instances of the male's attraction to the female neck and then concludes, "Just as he is so sensitive to the edges of human sanity, perhaps Nabokov also perceives, and uses female necks partially to suggest, the somewhat predatory edge of a man's intense physical desire for the body of a woman whom he more soberly, and less savagely, sees as possessing not only a neck but a heart and even a brain."

In addition, Dick Penner looks at "*Invitation to a Beheading*: Nabokov's Absurdist Initiation" (*Crit* 20,iii:27–39), and after examining various critical approaches to the novel suggests that we see Cincinnatus as the "uninitiated man-child" in what is "a classic work of absurdist literature." E. Warwick Slinn is concerned with "Problems of Consciousness in Nabokov's English Novels" (*WascanaR* 13,ii[1978]:3–18), and finds that "Nabokov requires his readers to be conscious of consciousness, in works where the texture of verbal patterning provides a qualitative guide to the texture of human consciousness." A. M. Pjatigorsky offers "A Word About the Philosophy of Vladimir Nabokov" (*WSlA* 4:5–17) but the word—or words—add up to a somewhat confused and bewildering consideration of Nabokov's "inner philosophizing." And, finally, a work that is not at all confusing and is perhaps a fitting conclusion to this section, Dmitri Nabokov's touching memoir "On Revisiting Father's Room" (*Encounter* 53:77–82). It is a lovely piece: simple, clear, and affectionate.

iv. The Southerners

a. **Allen Tate, Robert Penn Warren, and Andrew Lytel.** The death of Tate on 9 February 1979 brought forth a number of tributes, including those by William Meredith, Malcolm Cowley, Cleanth

Brooks, Louis Coxe, Eudora Welty, and William Jay Smith in *QJLC*
("For Allen Tate," 36:349–55), as well as Louis D. Rubin, Jr.'s "Allen
Tate, 1899–1979" (*SR* 87:267–73) and Robert Buffington's "Young
Hawk Circling" (*SR* 87:541–56).

Also published in *QJLC* is Thornton H. Parsons' "The Education
of Lacy Buchan" (36:365–76), a study of *The Fathers*, which Parsons sees as "a concentrated version of the enigmas of human life."
It would be a mistake, Parsons argues, to read the novel simply as an
account of the great disruption caused by the Civil War. The personality of George Posey and its influence upon Lacy Buchan are
the center, "and the war provides the context for Lacy's discovery that
irrationality governs in human life and that the necessity to act in a
condition of imperfect knowledge or even of ignorance is unrelenting." This essay, as well as "*The Fathers*: A Pictorial Introduction"
(*QJLC* 36:357–64), which precedes and accompanies it, are meant
as an invitation to read Tate's novel: "There could be no better way
to honor his memory."

Of the five pieces to appear on Robert Penn Warren this year
two are devoted to *All the King's Men*. William E. McCarron notes
in "Tennyson, Donne, and *All the King's Men*" (*AN&Q* 17:140–41)
that at two junctures in the novel Warren alludes to Tennyson's
"Flower in the Crannied Wall" and Donne's "A Valediction: Forbidding Mourning" to illuminate Jack Burden's cynical view of
mankind. Earl J. Wilcox, in a somewhat more substantial piece, " 'A
Cause for Laughter, A Thing For Tears': Humor in *All the King's
Men*" (*SLJ* 12,i:27–35), contends that despite the critical attention
accorded *All the King's Men*, little attention has been given to the
numerous witty and clever remarks made by Jack Burden, whose
humor "is his scheme for rationalizing what he sees. . . ." At the end,
ambivalent about his future but clearer and wiser about his choices,
"Jack Burden is a man whose 'cause for laughter' has turned to a
'thing for tears.' "

Two of the three essays yet to be discussed were written by Allen
G. Shepherd. In "Dick Diver in Nashville: A Note on Robert Penn
Warren's *A Place to Come To*" (*FHA* 173–75) Shepherd notes that
Warren's J. Lawford Carrington seems to be influenced by "a num-
ber of pages" from Fitzgerald's *Tender Is the Night*, while in "Pro-
totype, Byblow and Reconception: Notes on the Relation of War-

ren's *The Circus in the Attic* to His Novels and Poetry" (*MissQ* 33: 3–17) he discusses Warren's short fiction—which generally is acknowledged to be his least satisfying artistic form. Shepherd concentrates on four stories—"Prime Leaf," "The Circus in the Attic," "When the Light Gets Green," and "Goodwood Comes Back"—and concludes that despite the merit of much of his short fiction, "the form itself seems to have inhibited Warren's natural talents and inclinations."

Andrew Lytle never has received much critical attention, nor have his books been widely read. Yet in "Faulkner and Lytle: Two Modes of Southern Fiction" (*SoR* 15:34–51) Robert V. Weston argues that three of Lytle's characters—Nuno Tovar in *At the Moon's Inn*, Henry Brent in *A Name for Evil*, and Jack Cropleigh in *The Velvet Horn*—not only "rival anything in Faulkner for complexity, fullness of rendition, and imaginative vitality," but "are among the most complete characters in modern Southern fiction." Weston's claims on behalf of Lytle do seem somewhat exaggerated, but better the exaggeration than the usual silence.

b. **Carson McCullers.** McCullers continues to fare less well than one might expect. This year there are only two pieces to report, and neither adds very substantially to the literature about McCullers. In " 'A Voice in a Fugue': Characters and Musical Structure in *The Heart Is a Lonely Hunter*" (*MFS* 25:258–63) Michael C. Smith argues that the novel does not center on John Singer; five voices, not one, make up the novel. McCullers was strongly influenced by her early training in music, and the fugue pattern—to which she refers in her outline for *Hunter*—provides a key to understanding the form of her first novel and perhaps her later fiction as well. Patterns of a different sort are explored by Charlene Clark in "Male-Female Pairs in Carson McCullers' *The Ballad of the Sad Cafe* and *The Member of the Wedding*" (*NConL* 9,i:11–12). Clark notes that there are "remarkable parallels" between Miss Amelia and Cousin Lyman in *Sad Cafe* and Frankie Adams and John Henry West in *Wedding*. In each case the males are effeminate and the females masculine. What is clear from an examination of the two novels, Clark writes, is that Carson McCullers was "so totally absorbed with the idea of presenting an aggressive female–passive male pair that she styled the characters of both novels according to exactly the same pattern but succeeded in producing exactly the opposite effect." In *Wedding* the children behave like adults, while the adults in *Sad Cafe* behave like children.

c. **Katherine Anne Porter.**   Porter criticism continues to be somewhat fuller than that of McCullers. This year, to begin with, we have a volume in the Twentieth Century Views series, *Katherine Anne Porter: A Collection of Essays*, ed. Robert Penn Warren (Prentice Hall). As is usual with the volumes in this series, the essays have been published previously, as has Hank Lopez's interview with Porter, "A Country and Some People I Love" (pp. 20–35). It is, however, good to have these essays—by Glenway Wescott, Eudora Welty, V. S. Pritchett, Cleanth Brooks, and Mark Schorer, among others—in one volume; and it is very good to have Robert Penn Warren's Introduction, which contends in part that the most powerful tension in Porter's work "is between the emotional involvements and the detachment, the will to shape and assess relations in experience."

Thomas F. Walsh is responsible for identifying and reprinting a 1921 sketch published annonymously in the *Christian Science Monitor* ("Identifying a Sketch by Katherine Anne Porter," *JML* 7:555–61). It is, according to Walsh, "the earliest known published work based on Miss Porter's personal experience, and gives further proof that her creative energies were soon released upon her arrival in Mexico." In *CollL* (6:57–63) Walsh also discusses "Miranda's Ghost in 'Old Mortality,'" in which he notes the "deep similarities between Miranda and her dead aunt Amy in 'Old Mortality,'" and argues that the similarities between the two emphasize the barriers to understanding between one generation and another. Miranda's optimistic philosophy "is a romantic heirloom which experience will force her to discard; in Miss Porter's world, living is not a progress but a downward path. Miranda is hopeful only because she is ignorant."

Charlotte Goodman also deals with similarities, only her concern is with "Despair in Dying Women: Katherine Anne Porter's 'The Jilting of Granny Weatherall' and Tillie Olsen's 'Tell Me a Riddle'" (*ConnQ* 1:47–63). Goodman sees the two stories as celebrations of the "self-abnegating dedication of the two mothers, Granny Weatherall and Eva, as well as "probing explorations of personal anguish."

Two essays devoted to Porter's nonfiction need to be mentioned here, since both reflect upon her fiction. Joan Givner writes about

"Katherine Anne Porter, Journalist" (*SWR* 64:309–22), in which she considers how Porter's journalism gave shape to her lifelong philosophy that "evildoers are not the most reprehensible people in the world because they at least have the courage of their convictions . . . The people who really need to be watched are the so-called innocents who stand by and allow others to perpetrate evil." And in "Katherine Anne Porter's Feminist Criticism: Book Reviews from the 1920's" (*Frontiers* 4,ii:44–48) Jane Flanders notes that although Porter is seldom recognized as a feminist and is little known as a literary critic, she was in fact both: a study of her early reviews "show the emergence of her feminist views in print and her preparation for the splendid portraits of women which fill her works."

d. **Eudora Welty.** Last year I began this section by noting that the criticism and scholarship devoted to Welty showed no sign of abating. That continues to be true. If anything, this year's work is even more rewarding than last year's. To begin with, we have been given two important collections devoted to Welty. *Eudora Welty: A Form of Thanks*, ed. Louis Dollarhide and Ann J. Abadie (Miss.) contains the papers presented at the University of Mississippi in 1977 honoring Welty. The collection includes Cleanth Brooks's "Eudora Welty and the Southern Idiom" (pp. 3–24), Michael Kreyling's "Clement and the Indians: Pastoral and History in *The Robber Bridegroom*" (pp. 25–45), Peggy W. Prenshaw's insightful essay on the women in Welty's fiction, "Woman's World, Man's Place: The Fiction of Eudora Welty" (pp. 46–77), and Noel Polk's "Water, Wanderers, and Weddings: Love in Eudora Welty" (pp. 95–122). Even more valuable, I think, is *Eudora Welty: Critical Essays*, ed. Peggy Prenshaw (Miss.). This really is an extraordinary collection: 27 essays, all previously unpublished, divided into four sections: General Studies, Early Fiction, Later Fiction, and Photography and Criticism. Some of the contributors are well-established scholars, others are just beginning their careers. The general level is very high indeed. My own preferences are Chester E. Eisinger's "Traditionalism and Modernism in Eudora Welty" (pp. 3–25), John Alexander Allen's "The Other Way to Live: Demigods in Eudora Welty's Fiction" (pp. 26–55), Albert J. Devlin's "Eudora Welty's Mississippi" (pp. 157–78), Seymour Gross's "A Long Day's Living: The Angelic Ingenuities of *Losing Battles*" (pp. 325–40), and Ruth M. Vande Kieft's

"Looking with Eudora Welty" (pp. 423–44). In her Introduction
Prenshaw states that the purpose of this collection is "quite simply to
increase the reader's enjoyment and understanding of Welty's fiction." It cannot help but do so; this volume should be essential reading for Welty enthusiasts for years to come.

I should mention here that *EuWN* (3,ii) includes a review (pp.
11–15) by Michael Kreyling of both *A Form of Thanks* and *Critical
Essays*. In addition, *EuWN* continues to print its valuable "Checklist
of Welty Scholarship" as well as information of all kinds about Welty
scholarship and criticism. A supplementary issue of *EuWN* (3,i–B),
issued on the occasion of Welty's birthday, contains an unpublished
1956 prose sketch by Welty—"Chodorov and Fields in Mississippi"—
as well as contributions by three of her close friends: Elizabeth Spencer, Reynolds Price, and Charlotte Capers. Welty and her readers
continue to be well served by *EuWN*.

Of other essays about Welty perhaps the most interesting are
those by Welty herself and her close friend, Charlotte Casper. In
"Looking Back at the First Story" (*GaR* 33:751–55) Welty tells the
story of how "Death of a Traveling Salesman" came to be written
and published. It is a piece which tells us much about Welty's art,
about how she never doubted, "then or now, that imagining yourself
into other people's lives is exactly what writing fiction is." Charlotte
Capers tells about the "chancy life" of another Welty story in "The
Narrow Escape of 'The Petrified Man': Early Eudora Welty Stories"
(*JMH* 41:25–32). Here we learn that Welty originally threw the
manuscript of "The Petrified Man" in the stove, burned it, and then
"wrote it over" when *Southern Review* wanted to take another look
at it.

Elmo Howell's "Eudora Welty and the City of Man" (*GaR* 33:
770–82) is, in essence, an appreciation of Welty's art. Welty, Howell
tells us, is a very private person with a bent for writing about private
experience; like the poet, "she explores the inarticulate region of the
mind and heart." St. George Tucker Arnold, Jr., in "The Raincloud
and the Garden: Psychic Regression as Tragedy in Welty's 'A Curtain
of Green'" (*SAB* 44,i:53–60), notes that critics have commented on
the way "A Curtain of Green" epitomizes Welty's philosophical focus,
which is "pessimistic and existential." But this theme, Arnold writes,
is interwoven with the thread of the less discussed but equally important psychological emphasis upon "the growth or retardation of

individual consciousness on its progress toward an imagined ideal awareness." And Ann Romines in "The Powers of the Lamp: Domestic Retual [*sic*] in Two Stories by Eudora Welty" (*NMW* 12:1–16) addresses the matter of domestic ritual in "Death of a Traveling Salesman" and "The Demonstrators," and observes that in the two stories as well as in much of the fiction between them "we find the same ritual-ringed center: the house, the lamp, and the eager, uncertain heart. Their relation is always mysterious, volatile and unavoidable, and the deepest mystery—so deep that it is only broached in these two stories—is the relation of the women to domestic rite, to house and lamp."

e. **Thomas Wolfe.** The year 1978 was not a particularly productive year for Wolfe scholarship, and 1979 was even less so. Scribner's reissued *Editor to Author: The Letters of Maxwell Perkins*, ed. John Hall Wheelock, but with the exception of Marcia Davenport's Introduction, there is nothing new here. Nor is there very much new information to be found in Carole Klein's *Aline* (Harper), the first biography of Aline Bernstein. Klein obviously admires Bernstein, and she writes sympathetically and intelligently about the Bernstein-Wolfe affair; indeed, *Aline* offers what is certainly the fullest picture we yet have had of the relationship. But, finally, *Aline* is about Aline Bernstein, not Thomas Wolfe.

Croissant & Company once again has put Wolfe scholars in its debt with the publication, in an edition limited to 250 copies, of Clayton and Kathleen Hoagland's *Thomas Wolfe Our Friend: 1933–1938*, ed. Aldo P. Magi and Richard Walser. This is a loosely written "journal" of the Hoaglands' relationship with Wolfe, which was compiled by them from pocket and desk diaries, noting the times when Wolfe visited them in Rutherford, New Jersey—beginning in August 1933—or when they were with him in the city.

In addition to co-editing the Hoagland "journal," Richard Walser has given us an account of "On Faulkner's Putting Wolfe First" (*SAQ* 78:172–81), in which he tells about the time Faulkner rated Wolfe ahead of Dos Passos, Hemingway, Caldwell, and himself, and the distortions that then ensued. Faulkner, Walser points out, did not contend that Wolfe was the greatest American writer of modern times, but that he "had made the best failure because he had tried hardest to say the most." In *TWN* (3,ii:19–25) Walser also writes about "The Angel in North Carolina," an account of the reaction to the appearance of *Look Homeward, Angel* in North Carolina. Walser's piece appears in a special issue of *TWN* devoted to *Look Homeward, Angel* to commemorate the 50th anniversary of the novel's publication. The essays here and in *TWN* 3,i tend to be too brief, but *TWN* continues to serve its readers by offering an attractive newsletter which contains important sections on bibliography and news and notes. If Wolfe scholarship continues to disappoint, the fault certainly is not with *TWN*.

v. Popular Fiction

a. **Best-Sellers.**   Critical attention to popular writers continues to grow. The outstanding work this year certainly must be Millicent Bell's *Marquand: An American Life* (Little, Brown). Bell tells us that she wanted "to tell the storywriter's own story, visible not only in the autobiography of his fiction but in the full factuality of an exceptionally available record." Marquand's personal history was of such a prototypical nature, "so representative in its essentials as to constitute a kind of metonymy for all our lives, a work of the personal will and imagination collaborating with fate to produce an artistic fable of the general experience." Bell has told her story well. Her biography will not make much of Marquand's work less tedious, but she has made him considerably more fascinating.

Linda Simon's biography *Thornton Wilder: His World* (Doubleday) is not in the same class as Bell's biography of Marquand, but it is a respectable book nonetheless. What is missing here is Bell's ability to put Marquand into a larger cultural context. Still the publication of Simon's biography, together with a collection of Wilder's essays, *American Characteristics and Other Essays*, ed. Donald Gallup (Harper), as well as the publication of Gerry R. Wright's "Thornton Wilder: A Bibliography of Secondary Sources, 1963–1978" (*BB* 36:185–93), Peter Gontrum's brief piece on "The Influence of Thornton Wilder on Max Frisch" (*PPNCFL* 29,i[1978]:14–17), the writer's brother Amos N. Wilder's " 'He Didn't Go to Paris': Thornton Wilder, Middle America and the Critics" (*LJGG* 20:183–207), and even Ka Naa Subramanyam's negligible "The Novels of Thornton Wilder" (*IndL* 22,iv:167–81), make this an outstanding year for Wilder studies.

Although none of the other writers to be discussed here has fared quite as well as either Marquand or Wilder, some have been the recipient of exceptionally fine work. Matthew J. Bruccoli has continued his efforts on behalf of James Gould Cozzens by putting together a collection of ten essays and seven tributes by such critics as James William Ward, Robert Scholes, Bernard DeVoto, and Malcolm Cowley (*James Gould Cozzens: New Acquist of True Experiences* [So. Ill.]). Bruccoli sees the collection as part of the "long process of reappraissal" of Cozzens' career, which has just commenced. When it is accomplished, Bruccoli believes, "the novels of James Gould Cozzens will be secure among the enduring achievements of American literature." Perhaps, but if it is not, Bruccoli certainly will not be at fault. Nor will Morris H. Wolff, who in "The Legal Background of Cozzens' *The Just and the Unjust*" (*JML* 7:505–18), adds to the reappraisal by examining "Cozzens' innovative techniques in transforming the notes of testimony in the Wiley-Farrell trial into an exciting and realistic courtroom trial." John O'Hara, too, continues to have his adherents. Although there is nothing this year on O'Hara from Bruccoli, Vincent Balita continues his excellent work with the *John O'Hara Journal*, which this year includes a long essay by Charles W. Basset on "John O'Hara—Irishman and American" (1,ii:1–81), a consideration of "The Reception of John O'Hara in Germany" (2,i: 1–12) by Thekla Zachrau, and John L. Cobbs's "Caste and Class War: The Society of John O'Hara's *A Rage to Live*" (2,i:24–34). At the same time one must note the attack on O'Hara by Joseph Browne in "John O'Hara and Tom McHale: How Green Is Their Valley?" (*Irish-American Fiction*, pp. 127–38). Browne contends that O'Hara wanted to make every "Irish character in his writings pay for being an outsider," and "never seemed to get beyond a contemptuous sniggering at his Irish characters."

Erskine Caldwell is the subject of two essays this year, as are Ross Lockridge, James M. Cain, and Walter Van Tilburg Clark. Ronald Hoag addresses himself to "Irony in the Final Chapter of *Tobacco Road*" (*NConL* 9,v:8–10), while Guy Owen in "*The Sacrilege of Alan Kent* and the Apprenticeship of Erskine Caldwell" (*SLJ* 12,i:36–46) looks at Caldwell's "strangest and, in some ways, most original book." A close study of *The Sacrilege of Alan Kent*, Owens insists, will help to illuminate much of Caldwell's important fiction of the 1930s. Donald J. Greiner discusses "Ross Lockridge and the Tragedy of *Raintree County*" (*Crit* 20,iii:51–63), which he considers to be one of the ten best American novels published since World War II, and Fred Erisman, in "Raintree County and the Power of Place" (MarkhamR 8:36–40), argues that Raintree County "is an ecological novel written before its time." In "James M. Cain Papers" (QJLC 36:419–23) we learn of the Cain papers housed in the Library of Congress, and in David M. Fine's "James M. Cain and the Los Angeles Novel" (AmerS 20,i:25–34) we are told that "Cain gave us the chief metaphors for the literary identity of Los Angeles," as well as a sense "of what it was like to live, work and dream in Los Angeles in the thirties." Joseph M. Flora in " 'Woman with Parrot' in The Ox-Bow Incident" (AN&Q 17:74–76) points out that the painting hanging in Canby's saloon is one of the most obvious signals of Walter Van Tilburg Clark's "intention to transcend the genre of the popular western," while John Alt offers an interesting study of Clark's "The City of Trembling Leaves: Humanity and Eternity" (SDR 17,iv:8–18).

Four items remain to be discussed, none of which is without some importance. Lucille S. Zinn has compiled "The Works of Pearl S. Buck: A Bibliography" (BB 36:194–208), which consists of both primary and secondary sources. Robert H. Barshay has given us the first full-length work devoted to Philip Wylie: The Man and His Work (Univ. Press). The study, as Barshay writes, "is devoted to an account of Wylie's life, his contributions to popular fiction, and his controversial and interesting social criticism." It is all done rather superficially, and the photo-offset is unpleasant to read, but at least it has been done. Esther Forbes's Johnny Tremain also has received scant critical attention, as John B. Rosenmon points out in "The Rising Eye in Johnny Tremain" (Claflin College Review 3,ii:44–48). The reason for the neglect, Rosenmon writes, no doubt is due to the book's strong appeal to adolescents. Yet even a moderately close reading of the novel reveals that Forbes has not only "an exciting tale of adventure about a young boy growing up in Boston just before the Revolutionary War, but also a national epic of symbolic and thematic complexity." Finally, to conclude this section, there is Barbara Meldrum's fine essay in Northwest Perspectives, "Vardis Fisher's Antelope People: Pursuing an Elusive Dream" (pp. 153–66). Meldrum examines Fisher's Toilers of the Hills, Dark Bridwell, and April: A Fable of Love and concludes that for Fisher "the West became much more than the meeting point between savagery and civilization; it became a state of mind, a paradise that must be found within, and that blossoms only through the dynamics of love."

b. Detective Fiction. Although the number of pieces devoted to detective fiction this year is not as great as it was last year, what has been published is of considerable value. The University of Pittsburgh Press has issued two new volumes in its Pittsburgh Series in Bibliography, one on Dashiell Hammett by Richard Layman and one on Raymond Chandler by Matthew J. Bruccoli. Both volumes— *Dashiell Hammett: A Descriptive Bibliography* and *Raymond Chandler: A Descriptive Bibliography*—are models of their kind. Facsimiles of title pages, copyright pages, and dust jackets are provided, and in accordance with the series plan, full treatment is given to the American and English editions. Both volumes are well edited and handsomely produced. It is a pleasure to see such care given to the work of these two popular writers.

Another volume of considerable interest is *The World of Raymond Chandler*, ed. Miriam Gross (A & W Publishers, 1978). The contributors include Julian Symons, John Houseman, Michael Mason, Natasha Spender, and Jacques Barzun; there also is an interview with Billy Wilder. Many of the pieces in the collection are rather informal, yet the 15 essays do provide the reader with a clear sense of Chandler's intriguing personality as well as considerable insight into his work. The volume also includes 24 pages of illustrations and a bibliography, which lists Chandler's books, stories, and articles.

Chandler also receives considerable attention, as do Hammett and Ross MacDonald, in Bernard A. Schopen's "From Puzzles to People: The Development of the American Detective Novel" (*SAF* 7:175–88). Chandler, Hammett, and MacDonald, Schopen contends, "make up the 'Great Tradition' of the American detective novel." The inner apprehension of good and evil which constitutes the codes of Marlowe, Spade, and Archer forces them to sever all meaningful ties with their fellow men. They are "avatars of the central character in the American novel, the tragic victim of the dark and violent conflict between the individual and society."

Finally, mention should be made of the reprint of Cornell Woolrich's *Rendezvous in Black* (Gregg), with a new introduction by Francis M. Nevins, Jr. This is one of a number of books which have been appearing in The Gregg Press Mystery Fiction Series, under

the general editorship of Otto Penzler. Some of the volumes are reprinted with new introductions, some have no introduction. *All* the
books are well produced and are worth having. This little publicized
series is of great value and deserves far wider attention than it has
received.

c. Science Fiction. In addition to *Opus 200* (Houghton Mifflin)—a
selection from his second 100 books—and *A Choice of Catastrophes:
The Disasters that Threaten Our World* (Simon and Schuster), Isaac
Asimov also published *In Memory Yet Green: The Autobiography of
Isaac Asimov 1920–1954* (Doubleday). I really don't have a good
word to say about the 732-page volume, which I find to be incredibly
dull. Much less so is Ina Rae Hark's study of "Unity in the Composite Novel: Triadic Patterning in Asimov's *The Gods Themselves*"
(*SFS* 6:281–86), which finally notes that to demonstrate the symbolic
connection between the triad of "The Gods Themselves" and the
overall construction of *The Gods Themselves* "does not in any way
absolve Asimov of his grave miscalculation in writing the conclusion
of the novel." Less interesting but still better than Asimov's *In Memory Yet Green* is Darko Suvin's comments about Asimov's *I, Robot* in
"Three World Paradigms for SF: Asimov, Yefremov, Lem" (*PQM*
4:271–83), which is seen as an example of a science fiction "characterized by a failed search for solutions outside of human creativity."

For several important works devoted to Ursula K. Le Guin this
year, see chapter 15, section *xviii.*

Two interesting additions have been made to Lovecraft scholarship. Dirk W. Mosig's "Lovecraft: The Dissonance Factor in Imaginative Literature," which appeared twice during the year—*PVR* 7:
129–44 and *Gothic* 1:20–26—argues that Lovecraft reveals unusual
insight when his remarks are viewed within a dissonance-theory
framework. Barton Levy St. Armand and John H. Stanley offer with
commentary "H. P. Lovecraft's *Waste Paper:* A Facsimile and Transcript of the Original Work" (*BBr* 26[1978]:31–52), a work which they
feel is in danger of being undervalued by its own author.

Briefly, let me mention W. Dale Hearell's "Longevity and Superman: Robert A. Heinlein's Debt to George Bernard Shaw" (*ReAL*
6,i:21–25) and Richard Lupoff's poorly written "The Realities of
Philip K. Dick" (*Starship* 35:29–33), which originally appeared in
slightly different form as the Introduction to the Gregg Press edition

of Dick's *A Handful of Darkness.* It should be noted, finally, that under the general editorship of David G. Hartwell, Gregg Press is issuing The Gregg Press Science Fiction Series, which, if anything, is even more impressive than the Mystery Fiction Series.

Hofstra University

15. Fiction: The 1950s to the Present

Jerome Klinkowitz

A wide range of scholarship on a now-larger-than-life novelist, Saul Bellow, dominated 1979's scholarly activity. Eleven of the 52 doctoral dissertations filed this year concentrated on his work; a full shelf of Bellow essays filled special issues of journals and two hardcover collections; and one of the first substantial books on his writing has been updated in a revised edition. Saul Bellow, it seems, is one current author critics can deal with conclusively.

Bellow indisputably shares the stature which merits such consideration, but who else—especially among writers whose major work was accomplished in the 1950s—deserves dozens of articles each year? Flannery O'Connor? Norman Mailer? The thin nature of recent publication on these and other familiar figures belies the fact that they are no equal to Melville or Shakespeare for inspiring an endless flow of good scholarship. Yet younger and more innovative writers continue to be ignored while eminently safe opinions are ventured forth on writers already buried in their own secondary bibliographies. A quick test of the worth of this year's criticism: the author of this chapter planned to photocopy any essay which seemed worth keeping; sad to report, he left the library most days with his roll of nickels intact.

i. General Studies

A happy exception to the blandness of the year's scholarship is Manfred Pütz's booklength study, *The Story of Identity: American Fiction of the Sixties* (Stuttgart: Metzler). Pütz's common theme—the struggle to define oneself in a world which makes self-definition increasingly impossible—is prefaced by several chapters on aesthetic and social theory. Complementing the work on *récit* theory, folklore, and the *"sujet text"* with considerations of social theory developed by

Erving Goffman, Ralph Linton, and David Riesman, Pütz shows how
Barth, Brautigan, Sukenick, and Company have faced a different
world picture than the dead-end fictionists described in Ihab Hassan's *Radical Innocence* and Marcus Klein's *After Alienation*. In these
younger contemporaries' hands defining the self leads step-by-step
to the text's assumption (with the reader's cooperation) of this role.
Contexts to be so energized by self-definition are epoch and country
(John Barth), society (Richard Brautigan), culture and history (Pynchon), personal being (Luke Rhinehart), and finally literary genres
and conventions themselves (Ronald Sukenick and Vladimir Nabokov). Barth tests the imagination's creative powers in a variety of
philosophical contexts before turning to subgenre itself; Pynchon
creates a "fiction of history"; Brautigan revives the pastoral; Rhinehart experiments with psychology as self-definition; while Sukenick
and Nabokov make the leap from *histoire* to *discours* as a strategy to
make the true identity-quest the job of the reader, rather than of
author or protagonist.

Pütz's study of 1960s fiction, by virtue of its comprehensive opening chapters, summarizes the full development of American literary
history and analyzes the status of fiction since World War II; the
1960s themselves are simply a paradigm for post-Modern experience.
For three other general studies, however, the 1960s seem never to
have happened. Josephine Hendin's chapter, "Experimental Fiction,"
for the *Harvard Guide* is not about experimental fiction at all. Not a
word is said about Ronald Sukenick, Clarence Major, Steve Katz,
Walter Abish, or any of the other formal innovationists who over-
threw earlier standards of mimesis; indeed, Hendin ignores even
Joseph Heller's *Catch-22* in favor of a paragraph on the thematics of
Something Happened, which enhance her rather unliterary thesis,
that "innovative in neither style nor form, postwar experimental fiction uses modernist or standard literary devices to conduct its own
experiments with human subjects." Psychology, and not literary art,
is Hendin's topic; the fiction itself is regarded as traces of a pathology
("fragmentation of personality") which must be cured before fiction
is conventionally readable again. "Power and vulnerability" are all
that need to be examined, and experimental techniques are merely a
"variety of adaptive devices used to minimize feelings of violence,
humiliation, and vulnerability." If this sounds like Hendin's 1978
study, *Vulnerable People: A View of American Fiction Since 1945*

(Oxford), one should not be surprised: fully two-thirds of the paragraphs in this *Harvard Guide* chapter are lifted intact from the earlier study, with the term "experimental" careted in. Far more helpful is Nathan Scott's chapter on black literature in the same volume; here are careful notes on the truly experimental work of Ishmael Reed, Clarence Major, Charles Wright, William Demby, and their colleagues (in addition to excellent treatments of mainstream black writers such as James Baldwin, Ralph Ellison, Alice Walker, and others).

Warner Berthoff's *A Literature Without Qualities: American Writing Since 1945* (Calif.) admits that the postwar years encompass two aesthetically (and politically) distinct eras: the balance of the 1940s and 1950s, and then the much more innovative decades of the 1960s and 1970s. But Berthoff comes to grips with only the first. Even then, his interest is in what he considers the period's pathology: "a lapse of interest in good *writing* in the traditional sense," an "epidemic yearning, against all privation and disappointment, for restitution and some palpable consequence of our own. . . . It is as if human sensation itself had lost coherence." Berthoff's own difficulty at understanding contemporary fiction becomes the basis of his judgment that it is indefensibly bad. Very few contemporaries are discussed in individual terms; half of the book (on "Writing Since 1945," as its subtitle proclaims) is devoted to the traditionalist sides of Henry Miller and Wallace Stevens.

In *Last Laugh* Ronald Wallace singles out five novels for chapter-length analysis: Barth's *The Floating Opera*, John Hawkes's *Second Skin*, Nabokov's *Lolita*, Ken Kesey's *One Flew Over the Cuckoo's Nest*, and Robert Coover's *The Universal Baseball Association*. The most recent novel comes from 1968; the others now average 25 years old. Wallace's method is more positively inclined than Berthoff's; rather than pathological pessimism, contemporary fiction speaks in tones of "comic affirmation: detachment, irony, and wit; love, humor, and compassion; expulsion, parody, and balance; laughter, satire, and escape through artistic creation." The distinguishing mode of this recent work is that it is a hybrid of two traditional roles in comedy. In the novels discussed the protagonist becomes at once the *eiron* (witty self-deprecator) and the *alazon* (boastful antagonist, impostor or fool); this internal conflict structures the plot. Here is where Wallace's originality ends, for his essays on the novels simply explicate this theory with plot summaries and basic character analysis. None of his readings adds anything of note to the most basic previous essays on Barth, Hawkes, Nabokov, Kesey, or Coover.

Unhappiness with the state of contemporary fiction and its respondant criticism has been prominent enough to make the cover of the *New York Times Sunday Magazine* ("The Sound and Fury Over Fiction," to be discussed with John Gardner), to occupy prominent sections in weeklies and quarterlies, and to pervade Gerald Graff's *Literature Against Itself.* "Both literature and our ways of talking about it have been conditioned by social pressures and how they have in turn influenced social life," Graff argues, concluding that "literary thinking is inseparable from moral and social thinking." He therefore rejects contemporary fiction, which abandons mimesis, and its supportive criticism (deconstructionism), which challenges the sanctity of critical meaning (for Graff they go hand in hand). That his critical stance contradicts the very essence of American fiction and aesthetics in general since the 1940s (including Abstract Expressionism in art and nonpredictability in music) does not dissuade Graff from making such judgments as "literature does make truth claims, and makes them in the same way non-literary statements do" (*BMMLA* 13[1980]:11–13).

Personal crankiness and sarcasm toward new and only vaguely understood innovations—a sure sign of a conservative establishment's resistance to its own overthrow—pervade the symposium "Who Reads Novels?" conducted by the editors of *ASch* 48:165–90. John Updike and Saul Bellow are those cited among the "younger" writers being read (Bellow, of course, is 65); the only commentator to discuss newer fiction is Gerald Graff, who complains that novels no longer supply "news about the way people live" (which he professes as the sole reason to read them) and that writers after Joyce "did not know how social life works in the sense in which Dreiser did know it," thus rejecting Modernism as his *Literature Against Itself* dismissed the post-Modern aesthetic. A more open-minded section on "The State of American Fiction" (*Commonweal* 106:265–69) reviews not only the mainstream writers but reports Thomas LeClair's monumental symposium held at the University of Cincinnati, which hosted John Barth, John Gardner, John Hawkes, and William H. Gass in a colloquy on both fiction and new styles of criticism. Gardner defended his thesis from *On Moral Fiction* (1978) that contemporary fiction should be representational, while his colleagues argued (in varying degrees) that a novel was foremost an artifact added to the world, representing only itself. Janet Groth's "Fiction Vs. Anti-fiction Revisited" (*Commonweal* 106:269–71) suggests that John Hawkes's risk-taking in the definition of nothingness is in fact a higher moralism on the order of Paul Tillich. Suspension of disbelief in the case of such postrepresentational moralism is then a hindrance, and the 19th-century standards of Gerald Graff become inapplicable. (Sections of LeClair's transcript appear in *NYTBR* 1 Apr.: 7, 31–33; *NewRep* 10 Mar.: 25–33; 10 Nov.: 26–29.)

Two similarly constructive analyses of the moral fiction/innovative fiction debate are Thomas LeClair's "Moral Criticism" (*ConL* 20:508–12) and Walter Cummins' "Inventing Memories: Apocalyptics and Domestics" (*LitR* 23:127–33). LeClair describes the retreat from formal experimentation in the later works of Gass, Coover, Donald Barthelme, Thomas Pynchon, and William Gaddis; Cummins characterizes the new realists (John Irving, Larry Woiwode, and John Gardner) as "Domestics," whose invention of personal memories replaces the invented cosmologies of the "Apocalyptics," who include the earlier Pynchon, Coover, Barth, and Kurt Vonnegut. In "Eight Digressions on the Politics of Language" (*NLH* 10:467–77) novelist Ronald Sukenick outlines the conservative pressures in publishing and academics which have repressed innovative impulses.

Major studies on outright innovation continue to appear. Robert Scholes's *Fabulation and Metafiction* (Illinois) reprints Scholes's pioneering *The Fabulators* (1967) with major essays and new commentary prepared in the intervening years. Scholes's discussions of the Americans in the first edition—Kurt Vonnegut, Terry Southern, John Hawkes, and John Barth—are in all but Southern's case updated through the 1970s, and are in turn complemented with theoretical chapters on fabulation (storytelling which self-consciously emphasizes its own joy in the act of telling) and metafiction (fiction which explores its own fictionality as theme), in which Robert Coover, Donald Barthelme, and William H. Gass are added to the fold. The basis for metafication is traced back to Charles Saunders Peirce, who taught that "the products of the imagination are real in the sense that we really imagine them." In fiction this means that reality may be absolute (à la Gardner and Graff) but that human attemps to signify it are relative—in other words, fictional. Reality is too subtle for realism to catch it—but by invention, by fabulation, we may open a way

toward reality that will come as close as human ingenuity may venture. Reality in fiction, therefore, is created; and that creation is ordered by the religion of structuralism (as Scholes sees it). Because
of this latter influence Scholes has come to distrust the imagination
purely on its own and to yearn for a fiction which will reflect a greater
harmony with the operations of the cosmos. For Scholes science fiction
is the answer, though others—notably Ronald Sukenick—have dis-
avowed it as being the final gasp of realism.

A more formally positive study is June Schlueter's *Metafictional
Characters in Modern Drama* (Columbia), which mentions fictionists
Raymond Federman and John Barth. A fiction which posits itself as
free of creator, narrator, voice, and storyteller becomes free to establish its own rules of order and chaos—to create genuinely new meanings, the end point argued by Sukenick and Gass. Instead of being
passive vehicles for the recording of reality, metafictions strive for an
independent reality of their own, akin to music or abstract art. In
"The Critic as Riot Police" (*ChiR* 31,i:30–42) Mas'ud Zavarzadeh
characterizes the resultant texts as "readerly . . . nontotalizing . . .
receivable," in the sense that their product is "continually outside of
any likelihood"—the paradigm of art espoused by such triumphant
American artists as Jackson Pollock and John Cage, but still resisted
by conservative critics. That social and political conditions in the
recent decade did in fact help create such a fiction is borne out by
two analyses of Vietnam War fiction: Philip D. Beidler's "Truth
Telling and Literary Values in the Vietnam Novel" (*SAQ* 78:141–56)
and the introduction by Jerome Klinkowitz and John Somer to their
Writing Under Fire: Stories of the Vietnam War (Dell, 1978).

The shortsightedness of critics such as Hendin and Berthoff, the
contentiousness of those like Graff, and the uncertainty of such earlier
mentors as Scholes and LeClair emphasize how rare the reliable
critics of truly contemporary fiction are. Several book-length publications in 1979 indicate that Richard Kostelanetz is one of the few
to be trusted. His comprehensive *Twenties in the Sixties* (Greenwood) integrates several of his pioneering essays on the avant-garde
(dating from 1959) with many unpublished pieces to form both a
personal and aesthetic coming of age. Genuinely synthetic pieces
worthy of attention are Kostelanetz's "The American Absurd Novel,"
"Dada and the Future of Fiction," " 'New American Fiction' Reconsidered," and numerous essays on the state of criticism. His *A*

Critical Assembling (Brooklyn: Assembling Press) gives several score critics (from Hugh Kenner to Zbigniew Lewicki) *carte blanche* in order to come to terms with fictionists as diverse as Susan Quist and Crad Kilodney, the genuinely "young" writers more established media have never touched. That an entirely new form of fiction is being written is apparent from Kostelanetz' collection of original essays, *Visual Literature Criticism* (So. Ill.), which in addition to general pieces features essays on Raymond Federman, Maurice Roche, and John McClurg. Kostelanetz' ongoing battle with the conservative forces in publishing is summarized in his *"The End"/Appendix, "The End"/Essentials* (Scarecrow).

ii. Saul Bellow

Scholarship on Saul Bellow overpowers contributions on other writers; only the very best of the several score essays published during the year can be mentioned here. An essential contribution is Chirantan Kulshrestha's book-length study, *Saul Bellow: The Problem of Affirmation* (New Delhi: Arnold-Heinemann, 1978), which is based on a year's study of Bellow's papers at the University of Chicago and lengthy conversations with the novelist. Bellow first establishes the power of art and the compatibility between art and life (as opposed to Modernist stances of alienation and hostility), but then struggles through the fraudulent styles of affirmation (mankind's essential unity, the ego's command of experience, abstractions of reality) to his own hierarchy of victims, adventurers, and survivors (the three progressive segments of his novelistic career). "Bellow's protagonists show a consistent attempt to outgrow their feelings that life is without pattern and move over to a position where they can exercise choices discriminately."

Mr. Sammler's Planet, Humboldt's Gift, and *To Jerusalem and Back* are the later works added to the second edition of John J. Clayton's *Saul Bellow: In Defense of Man* (Indiana). Clayton interprets the first novel as an expression of the Jewish literary tradition through the myth of Oedipus in a peculiarly exclusive way: Oedipus as son is replaced by Oedipus as father. *Humboldt's Gift* is more successful because it retains a structuring dichotomy: the "experience of distraction" versus the poet's "experience of inner light," or the natural against the supernatural. *To Jerusalem and Back* supplements Sammler's character with Bellow's own persona; each argues the rhetoric of annihilation/survival, with an emphasis on traditional values.

Four book-length collections of essays on Saul Bellow contain several important essays. Stanley Trachtenberg has edited *Critical Essays on Saul Bellow* (Hall), including Philip Stevick's "The Rhetoric of Bellow's Short Fiction" (the rhetoric of a voice attempting to persuade), Eusebio Rodrigues' "Reichianism in *Seize the Day*," and Daniel Fuchs's "*Herzog*: The Making of a Novel" (based on the careful unity of tone established in careful redraftings by Bellow). The proceedings of a 1977 conference at the Free University of Brussels have been edited by Edmond Schraepen and published as *Saul Bellow and His Work* (Brussels: Centrum voor taal en literatuurwetenschap, 1978); in India a special number of *JLSt* (1,ii:1–132) contains studies which are mostly derivative of established interpretations. Similarly derivative (in many cases by the very critics who first proposed these theses) are the essays in the Bellow number of *MFS* (25:1–171), though worth reading are James M. Mellard's "Consciousness Fills the Void: Herzog, History, and the Hero in the Modern World" and Bruce J. Borrus' "Bellow's Critique of the Intellect," the latter of which suggests that after rejecting the intellectual's role in America Bellow may be turning toward a subtle mysticism to fill this position.

The consensus of most critics is that Saul Bellow is now America's premier literary spokesman for conservative moral values. Sam B. Girgus uses the figure of Artur Sammler to protest radical individualism (absolute equality not just in opportunity but in economic, political, and cultural spheres) "as an indulgence that opposes the dying humanistic and liberal tradition which he embodies as a remnant" (*Law of the Heart*, pp. 140–50). Daniel Fuchs goes even further, declaring Bellow to be our own equivalent of a grand Russian novelist, making the "essentialist affirmation, desperate though it may be, of irreducible moral truths defining a sort of rhythm of the ethical sphere" ("Saul Bellow and the Example of Dostoevsky," in *Stoic Strain*). In "Saul Bellow and the Moral Imagination" (*NER* 1:475–88) Irving Halperin aligns Sammler's dictum of "choice to be ourselves" with Bellow's own pronouncements in his essay, "The Writer as Moralist"; the question each asks is, "In what form shall life be justified?" The struggle to be human—as a heroic task—is discussed by Michelle Loris in "*Mr. Sammler's Planet*: The Terms of the Covenant," *Renascence* 30[1978]:217–23, in which moral spokesmanship elevates itself to the status of religion. Two final essays from other journals are worthy additions to scholarship: Helge Normann Nilsen's "Anti-Semitism and Persecution Complex: A Comment on Saul Bellow's *The Victim*" (*ES* 60:183–91), which studies the environment of antisemitism as a way of expressing shared democratic responses to America, and Allan Chavkin's "Bellow's Alternative to the Wasteland: Romantic Theme and Form in *Herzog*" (*SNNTS* 11:326–37), which cites Wordsworth as a model for Bellow's imaginative transcendence over alienation as a way of reconciling oneself to the world.

iii. Singer, Malamud, Roth, and other Jewish Americans

As for Saul Bellow, several studies of other Jewish-American writers emphasized their relationship with the traditions of Jewish literature. In *The Resonance of Dust: Essays on Holocaust Literature and Jewish Fate* (Ohio State) Edward Alexander describes the challenge to the imagination posed by the Nazi atrocities. Realizing that thematic comprehension is impossible, that any response on this level is bound to be inadequate, holocaust writers have adopted modes of uncertainty and despair as a means of expressing their subject; the Jewish religion itself is a frequent touchstone. Full chapters are devoted to Isaac Bashevis Singer and to Saul Bellow.

Lothar Kahn departs from this recent trend by claiming that Singer's true talent is found outside of the Yiddish literary tradition. Kahn's essay, "The Talent of I. B. Singer, 1978 Nobel Laureate for Literature' (*WLT* 53:197–201) argues that Singer's fiction is informed by an atypical political skepticism, which moreover questions God's will. Ruth R. Wisse extends this same ambivalence into Singer's novelistic structure, which she sees as informed by a tension between containment and license; Singer's literary progress is effected by counterposing legend and reality, and especially past with present ("Singer's Paradoxical Progress," *Commentary*, 67,ii:33–38). Two interesting interviews, each of which emphasizes literary as well as purely biographical matters, are Lance Morrow's "The Spirited World of I. B. Singer" (*AtM* 243,i:39–43) and Clive Sinclair's "A Conversation with Isaac Bashevis Singer" (*Encounter* 37,ii:21–28).

A most remarkable and fresh approach to Bernard Malamud's fiction forms part of Evelyn Gross Avery's thesis in *Rebels and Vic-*

tims: The Fiction of Richard Wright and Bernard Malamud (Kennikat). Avery's justification for comparing black literature with Jewish
American fiction is that each is ethnic, standing somewhat apart from
mainstream writing, and celebratory of the hero as outsider. This
alienation, however, is handled in two quite different ways, with
Malamud preaching Job-like acceptance while Wright's heroes pursue a course of violent action. Yet each shares a posture of rejecting
conformity with the present, as Morris Bober assumes responsibility
for the past while Bigger Thomas seeks to eradicate it with his vio-
lently self-assertive action. Similar questions apply to each, and
deepen our appreciation of their roles in fiction: "How should individuals respond to a cruel or indifferent environment? How can the
poor and powerless survive with dignity in modern society?"

The single major essay on Philip Roth also takes a novel approach
to that author's most scandalously popular work, *Portnoy's Complaint.*
In Steven David Lavine's "The Degradations of Erotic Life: *Portnoy's
Complaint* Reconsidered" (*MichA* 11:357–63) psychoanalytic theory
is used to establish a Freudian conflict, in which sex (the pleasure
principle) triumphs over simple ethics. The hero, however, opts for
"independent moral action" as a way of transcending this impasse.

Other Jewish-American writers—Bruce Jay Friedman, Elie Wiesel,
and Edward Lewis Wallant—were subjects of studies less original
but helpful nonetheless for understanding their novels. David R.
Mesher's "Three Men on the Moon: Friedman, Updike, Bellow, and
Apollo Eleven" (*RS* 47:67–75) is an interesting comparison of ethnic
and mainstream writers on a self-evidently Transcendental topic:
their reactions prove to be less stylistically typical and more media-
ized, granted the nature of their topic. Elie Wiesel is elevated to the
stature of a religious writer (if not prophet) in Michael Berenbaum's
*The Vision of the Void: Theological Reflections on the Works of Elie
Wiesel* (Wesleyan); Wiesel's vision is apocalyptical even without
the enabling subject matter of the holocaust. David Galloway tries
to build Edward Lewis Wallant into a major novelist (TUSAS 319)
sharing the status of those studied in his *The Absurd Hero* (Updike,
Bellow, Styron, and Salinger), but establishes only that Wallant
was an excellent craftsman in his role as a second echelon writer.
A comic vision of a nightmare world seems too reminiscent of Nathanael West, though Wallant turned his own talents to a celebration

of joy (as opposed to West's bitter irony). His written work is eclipsed by Sidney Lumet's film of *The Pawnbroker*, a fact Galloway cannot escape in his own study (which returns to this event several times).

iv. Norman Mailer

The autobiographical figure of Norman Mailer—by virtue of his self-considering works since *Armies of the Night*—seems to have replaced the Mailer canon as the most popular subject among scholars. In *American Autobiography* G. Thomas Couser links Mailer's on-going autobiography with those of John Woolman, Benjamin Franklin, Frederick Douglass, and others (Thoreau, Whitman, Adams, and—with less success—Robert Pirsig) as a prophet of the American dream. Mailer's imagination mediates between self and history, seeks analogies between personal experience and that of the community, and struggles toward a new vision to present to his audience. Couser presents Mailer's work of the 1960s—*Armies of the Night, Miami and the Seige of Chicago, Of a Fire on a Moon*, and *A Prisoner of Sex*—as cut from one cloth, whereas other Mailer critics have seen the true story to be in Mailer's struggles toward wholeness of persona.

Five pieces in *NOR* (3:211–342) extend the biographical treatment of this literary artist who has made his own sensibility his foremost subject and—as these essays show—his technique. An interview conducted by Matthew Grace and Steve Roday is supplemented by Robert B. Cochran's stimulating "St. Norman of New York: The Historian as Servant to the Lord," George H. Douglas' "Norman Mailer and the Battle of the Sexes," George Held's "Men on the Moon: American Novelists Explore Lunar Space" (which also treats Bellow and Updike), and the thesis-piece which unifies this collection of commentary on Mailer's personal "critifiction," Jeffrey Gillenkirk's "Mailer is the Message." In Martha S. Banta's *Failure and Success in America* (Princeton) Mailer appears as the male imagination seeking power, trying to control the "inner space of femininity"; love and death within the context of history is the battle field, as Mailer describes it. Barry A. Marks in "Civil Disobedience in Retrospect: Henry Thoreau and Norman Mailer," *Soundings* 62:144–65 takes exception to Mailer's method as morally arrogant, distorting of history, and dangerous to society and self; Marks sees *Armies of the Night* as an extraliterary effort perverted by Mailer's ego. The ins and outs of that ego are the proper subject of Andrew Gordon's insightful study, *An American Dreamer: A Psychoanalytic Study of the Fiction of Norman Mailer* (Fairleigh Dickinson), which argues for these same para-journalistic structures within Mailer's supposedly conventional fiction. Finally, Paul N. Siegel presents a surprisingly successful Marxist reading of *The Naked and the Dead* in *Revolution and the 20th-Century Novel* (New York: Monad Press), in which the Army is a concentrated version of America ready for counterrevolution.

v. Jack Kerouac, Ken Kesey, and Joseph Heller

The act of publishing a brief critical biography of Massachusetts-born Jack Kerouac in a "Western Writers Series" is itself part of the thesis of Harry Russell Huebel's *Jack Kerouac* (WWS). Huebel's point is that the American West was Kerouac's sustaining image—doomed to failure, of course—and that both his writing and his personal life declined after 1960 when Kerouac abandoned both the West and the nomadic life-style he had fashioned as its epitome.

Studies of Ken Kesey continue to center on *One Flew Over the Cuckoo's Nest* and its protagonist, Randall Patrick McMurphy (even though Ronald Wallace's *Last Laugh*, described in section *i.* above, insists Chief Broom is the center of the novel and its true hero). Gary A. Wiener agrees that the Chief is thematically central ("From Huck to Holden to Bromden: The Noncomformist in *One Flew Over the Cuckoo's Nest*," *StHum* 7,ii:21–26), while Michael M. Boardman advances a political argument for McMurphy's transformative power in "One Flew Over the Cuckoo's Nest: Rhetoric and Vision" (*JNT* 9:171–83). Madelon F. Heatherington scores an important point in an essay whose title describes its thesis: "Romance Without Women: The Sterile Fiction of the American West" (*GaR* 33:643–56), a study (including works by Thomas Berger and Owen Wister) which effectively undercuts the universality of McMurphy's revolt. An interesting parallel between Kesey's major novel and a work no less than *Moby-Dick* is drawn by Edward Stone in his airtight case, "*Cuckoo's Nest* and *Moby-Dick*" (*MSEx* 38:11–12), in which Ahab is compared to McMurphy, the Whale to the Nurse, and Ahab's madness to Mac's shrewdness as an implement of self-destiny.

Joseph Heller's *Catch-22* still attracts attention. Leon Seltzer argues in "Milo's 'Culpable Innocence': Absurdity as Moral Insanity in *Catch-22*" (*PLL* 15:290–310) that the novel's satire is in fact a highly moral attack on capitalism; Thomas L. Hartshorne makes a similar point about Heller's almost quaint, "straight" moralism by contrasting a notable later effort in "From *Catch-22* to *Slaughter-house-Five*: The Decline of the Political Mode" (*SAQ* 78:17–33), arguing that Yossarian's social effectiveness yields to Billy Pilgrim's passivity in Vonnegut's novel. That Heller himself has changed in the intervening decade is borne out by Susan Strehle Klemtner in her study of his second novel, " 'A Permanent Game of Excuses': Determinism in Heller's *Something Happened*" (*MFS* 24:550–56), which argues that Slocum is an unpleasant protagonist because of his willing submission to forces of determinism.

vi. Flannery O'Connor and Walker Percy

Future O'Connor scholarship will be aided by the publication of *The Habit of Being: Letters*, ed. Sally Fitzgerald (Farrar), but even the best of this year's essays on Flannery O'Connor repeat familiar themes (very little is given to technique) of the grotesque, the personal, and the visionary within the sphere of her Catholicism and southern womanhood. Charles W. Mayer discusses O'Connor's revisions toward comic effect in "The Comic Spirit in 'A Stroke of Good Fortune' " (*SSF* 16:70–74), while Cheryl Z. Oreovicz makes a cogent point in "Seduced by Language: The Case of Joy-Hulga Hopewell" (*SAF* 7:221–28), that in "Good Country People" theme and technique are fused in O'Connor's consideration of "how people use and are used by language." A sacramental view of authorship, the product of region and religion, is Suzanne Allen's topic in "Memoirs of a Southern Catholic Girlhood: Flannery O'Connor's 'A Temple of the Holy Ghost' " (*Renascence* 31:83–92). Steven T. Ryan argues against the emphasis on climax and visionary denouement in "Greenleaf," claiming the story's key is found in the three realms of its setting which correspond to Heaven, Hell, and Earth ("The Three Realms of O'Connor's 'Greenleaf,' " *C&L* 29,i:39–51). A biographical study intended to correct improperly autobiographical readings, Barbara McKenzie's "Flannery O'Connor and 'The Business of the Purified Mind' " (*GaR* 33:817–26) discusses "transformations" as the key.

A uniformly strong collection of essays on Walker Percy, *The Art*

of Walker Percy: Strategems for Being, ed. Panthea Reid Broughton
(LSU), contains studies which cover all facets of this novelist's work.
Broughton's introduction discusses Percy's most prominent feature:
that his fiction presents more complication than the reader sometimes
bargains for, although the resolution of love and faith over disruption
and discovery repay one's investment in patience. *The Moviegoer* is
treated by Max Webb, Martin Luscheli, and Janet Hobbs in the first
three essays. Webb uses Binx Bolling as the symbol of "the permanent
human tensions involving life and death" with an emphasis on the
"continuing necessity of new beginnings"; Luscheli explores the limits
of film technique in showing "nonbeing"; Hobbs traces Binx's progress through the Kierkegaardian stages toward faith. Richard Pindell,
Simone Vauthier, and Panthea Reid Broughton apply their talents
to *The Last Gentleman,* discussing (respectively) entropy versus
news of salvation, narrative triangulation reinforced by the triadic nature of language (which Percy adopted from Charles Saunders
Peirce), and the "bisected reality" of mind and body against which
Percy's fiction protests. *Love in the Ruins* is treated by J. Gerald
Kennedy ("what went wrong" in America, summarized by a need
to transcend the Cartesian dualism of mind versus body) and William Leigh Godshalk (the unreliable narrator as a prophet of this
same transcendence). In "Walker Percy's Devil" Thomas LeClair
finds an "unfulfilled promise" in Percy's existential counterposing of
Faust and Don Juan. Turning to Percy's scholarly work on language,
Weldon Thornton reports the author's fear of a depletion of experience by overreliance on specialists; the power of language reaches
beyond physical signs, for the symbol is "nucleus and prototype
of human knowledge." William H. Poteat adds that Percy is equally
concerned with a Cartesian sundering of roots, by which the more
complex sensibilities in communication drop out. Lewis A. Lawson
and William J. Dowie contribute essays on *Lancelot,* the former
showing how the subjective/objective split of the early novels is here
resolved by virtue of a human bonding, a communion of full consciousness, the latter admiring the past for its decisive deeds (and
even sins) as opposed to the eventlessness of the present day. Two
general pieces conclude the volume: Cleanth Brooks's "Walker Percy
and Modern Gnosticism," which argues that modern man is impover-
ished by his view of reality (à la Eric Voegelin's *Order and History*)

and Ted R. Spivey's "Walker Percy and the Archetypes," which claims Percy's fiction speaks with a philosophical tone lacking in Hemingway and Fitzgerald, and deficient even in Bellow, O'Connor, and J. F. Powers; for Percy, Kierkegaard supplies the frame for a basically Jungian meaning.

Of the five other significant essays on Percy noted this year, three are philosophically inclined. Similar to Cleanth Brooks's reflections on Voegelin's theory of history is Lewis A. Lawson's well-written "The Gnostic Vision in *Lancelot*" (*Renascence* 32:52–64), while J. P. Telotte objects to the existential pigeonhole a narrowly linguistic (Peircean) reading creates for Percy's fiction ("Walker Percy: A Pragmatic Approach," *SoSt* 18:217–30). A major essay by Lewis J. Taylor, Jr., "Walker Percy's Knights of the Hidden Inwardness" (*ATR* 56[1974]:125–51), uses Kierkegaard to trace an influence throughout Percy's essays and novels; responding to one's situation in life in order to become a self is the imperative, which Taylor finds atypical for southern writers, even Faulkner. Rounding out the year's work is a concise reading by Jack Hicks, "The Lesions of the Dead: Walker Percy's *The Last Gentleman*" (*EA* 32:162–70), which —for once—treats Percy less as a southerner than as a truly universal contemporary, plus a third useful essay by Lewis A. Lawson: "*The Moviegoer* and the Stoic Heritage" (in *Stoic Strain*). Percy's stoicism is seen as a northern mode in contrast to the prevailing southern ecclesiastical structure, making Binx a rare protagonist in his region's literature.

vii. John Updike, John Cheever, and Joyce Carol Oates

John Updike's remarkable productivity—a book each year for the past quarter century—has helped scholarship on his work to remain fresh and unpredictable. This year's essays range widely over his novels and short stories, rarely repeating previous criticism.

Two original essays by the editors are included in the Twentieth Century Views collection, *John Updike: A Collection of Critical Essays*, ed. David Thorburn and Howard Eiland (Prentice-Hall). Thorburn's introductory comments remind us of Updike's conservatism, a writing style based on a "radical empiricism"—yet Updike's "anxiety of influence" remains the lyrical sexuality preached by

James Joyce. Eiland's "Play in *Couples*" shows how a subtle self-consciousness (akin to Nabokov) structures this novel. In *American Imagination* Jerome Klinkowitz's "John Updike Since *Midpoint*" argues that as the innovative styles of the 1970s evolved, Updike kept pace with his culture by exhibiting a more self-conscious sense of authorship and an ability to make language a subject of his story. Joseph Waldmeir's editing of the *Nye Festschrift* includes his own "Rabbit Redux Reduced: Rededicated? Redeemed?" which shows how the first novel's idealism is replaced by a more mundane pragmatism echoing the alternatives of *The Centaur* versus *Of the Farm*. A corrective to earlier readings of *The Centaur* itself is supplied by Ronald Wesley Hoag in "A Second Controlling Myth in John Updike's *The Centaur*" (*SNNTS* 11:446–53), indicating Peter as a factor in the Sisyphus myth of Albert Camus; James M. Mellard calls upon Jung to document the elegaic feelings Peter expresses for his father ("The Novel as Lyric Elegy: The Mode of Updike's *The Centaur*," *TSLL* 21:112–27). A *Month of Sundays* is shown to reflect the structural motif of *The Scarlet Letter* in David B. Kesterson's "Updike and Hawthorne: Not So Strange Bedfellows" (*NMAL* 3:Item 11), focusing on Marshfield's four sermons; Robert Detweiler's "Updike's *A Month of Sundays* and the Language of the Conscious" (*JAAR* 47:609–25) argues for more subtlety in Updike's use of the minister and a stronger emphasis on the structuralist play of his meditative language. A theologically expressed presence of God accounts for the union of thought and style —and also for resistance to entropy—in this same novel, argues Terrence A. Doody in "Updike's Idea of Reification" (*ConL* 20:204–20).

Updike's short fiction is the subject of George W. Hunt, S.J.'s "Reality, Imagination, and Art: The Significance of Updike's 'Best' Story" (*SSF* 16:219–30). Between 1964 and 1966, Hunt says, Updike's craft underwent a transition toward artistic self-consciousness; the stories collected from this period in *The Music School* are distinguished by their recreation of the past and of memory itself; each acts as an analogy for art itself. A little noted story from *Museums and Women* is Diana Colbertson's subject in "Updike's 'The Day of the Dying Rabbit' " (*SAF* 7:95–99), in which Colbertson sees the story as told through "a series of underexposures" which emphasize "the difficulty of seeing beyond the space-time pictures" assumed to be reality. "Getting the picture" becomes Karl Barth's "moment of vision"—a gratuituous act which man cannot merit (moral struggle may precede it, but no personal triumph merits it). Finally, James Atlas provides an excellent biographical study of Updike's remarriage in "John Updike Breaks Out of Suburbia" (*NYTSM* 10 Dec. [1978]: 60–61 ff.).

John Cheever (*TUSAS* 335) by Lynn Waldeland emphasizes Cheever's treatment of family relationships—especially between the sexes—within his self-proclaimed affirmative posture regarding American life and its freshness of promise. George Hunt extends one of Waldeland's important points by insisting that there is fine art and great depth of imagination behind Cheever's apparent sociology ("A Style Both Lyrical and Idiosyncratic: Beyond the Cheeveresque," *Commonweal* 106:20–22), while Robert Pawlowski finds even deeper structural dimensions in "Myth as Metaphor: Cheever's 'Torch Song' " (*RS* 47:118–21).

Joyce Carol Oates is feted with two book-length studies and a partially original collection of essays, in addition to numerous critical articles. In *Dreaming America: Obsession and Transcendence in the Fiction of Joyce Carol Oates* (LSU) G. F. Waller decides Oates's short fiction is superior to her novels, for it better expresses the Lawrencian mode he finds in her work; like D. H. Lawrence, Oates is a prophet whose obsessive vision (often expressed in violent forms) sees past human tensions and passions into the transcending ego (or "psyche" as it is called here). Realism becomes something more than transcription: as the language of her characters' feelings, it is in fact a creative function. Complementary studies are Sanford Pinsker's "Joyce Carol Oates and the New Naturalism" (*SoR* 15:52–63), which shows Oates's development toward the Gothic and away from genteel respectability, and Steven Barza's "Joyce Carol Oates: Naturalism and the Aberrant Response" (*SAF* 7:141–51), which claims that Oates departs from the classic form by making her deterministic forces unknowable, and hence more interesting to contemporary readers bored with simple Naturalism.

Jeanne V. Creighton's *Joyce Carol Oates* (*TUSAS* 321) relies more heavily on earlier interpretations—stories of violent liberation through love, and a search for wholeness among the fragments of personal existence. Many of these same ideas run through *Critical Essays on Joyce Carol Oates*, ed. Linda Wagner (Hall), although

Ellen Friedman makes a good comparison (on the basis of style, theme, and structure) between *Wonderland* and Lewis Carroll's fable, and Eileen T. Bender charts in *Childwold* a convincing development from earlier pessimism to emerging success over despair. Wagner's Introduction, "Oates: The Changing Shapes of Her Realities," reprinted from *GrLR* 5:15–23), outlines Oates's "variations" against realism and her eschewing of the "controlling artist" (in favor of the "artist-as-recorder").

Two separately published essays each make their own specific point. James R. Giles in "Oates' *The Poisoned Kiss*" (*CanL* 80:138–47) discusses the unreality of landscape as a new phase—mystic and visionary—in Oates's fiction, in which literature functions "as a process of sanctification." In "The Process of Fictionalization in Joyce Carol Oates' *them*" (*IFR* 6:121–28) Anthony Decurtis describes how Oates's characters feel compelled to "deny the substantiality of their shattering experiences and perceive their lives as fiction." The future is a threat, "contentment and hope are taunting invitations to disaster," and maturity "consists of realizing and accepting that there is no design or permanence in one's surroundings."

viii. John Barth, Donald Barthelme, Raymond Federman, and Jerzy Kosinski

As a writer John Barth is fascinated by myth, and his critics have been caught up by that interest: every study on him published this year uses myth as part of its topic. In "Myths and Fiction in the Contemporary American Novel: The Case of John Barth" (*HSE* 12: 89–106) John B. Vickery shows that myth interests a contemporary such as Barth because it is "a fiction of a particular order" and therefore pertinent to a generation whose primary interest is in the mechanics of storytelling. Thom Seymour makes a similar point in "One Small Joke and a Packed Paragraph in John Barth's 'Lost in the Funhouse'" (*SSF* 16:189–94), paralleling the retelling of myth with the author's role in creating the story at hand. Joseph A. Cosenza draws another myth-based parallel in "*Giles Goat-Boy* and Zeno's Paradox" (*NMAL* 3, Item 13), which demonstrates "man's inability to arrange life's endless contradictions into a coherent, communicable, universal truth." The idea of a labyrinth provides a comparative study for

Wendy B. Faris in "Butor and Barth in the Labyrinth" (*FAR* 3:23–39), while Susan Stewart finds Barth a master of the nonsensical use of infinity (*Nonsense* [Hopkins]), reinforcing the notion of play. Barth's own commentary on his work shares the stage with John Hawkes in part of the transcript from Thomas LeClair's conference in "Hawkes and Barth Talk About Fiction" (*NYTBR* 1 Apr: 7, 31–33).

For Steven Jones the Perseus Legend is a test of the mythologist's methodology ("The Legend of Perseus and John Barth's *Chimera*," *FForum* 11 [1978]:140–51), but Joe and Sher Weixlmann have used it for a comparative judgment in "Barth and Barthelme Recycle the Perseus Myth: A Study in Literary Ecology" (*MFS* 25:191–207). "Whereas Barthelme uses the myth to add a dimension to a contemporary character," the Weixlmanns say, "much as Joyce does in *Ulysses* or Updike in *The Centaur*, Barth confronts the myth directly, much as Perseus confronts his past"; Barthelme transforms while Barth reinterprets.

A common complaint of past criticism about Donald Barthelme has been his fragmentary structure and opacity of meaning. In the most singly helpful essay on Barthelme yet written, "Meaning and Non-Meaning in Barthelme's Fictions" (*JAE* 13,i:69–79), Larry McCaffery uses these problems to approach the reading and teaching of Barthelme's work. A "Theory of Meanings" approach establishes correlations between content and form, but more successful is the "Theory of Non-Meaning or Art as Object" method previously used for abstract expressionist art, in which the act of writing is its own point of reference. James Hiner's "I Will Tell The Meaning of Barthelme" (*UDQ* 13:61–76), though marred by outright errors in primary bibliography, makes a useful catalogue of Barthelme's more apparent techniques (tremulous allusions, bland literalism, gratuitous enumeration, shocking juxtaposition, etc.) which combine to form an absurdity of method (which Hiner calls "an absurd but real structure").

Paul R. Lilly, Jr.'s "Comic Strategies in the Fiction of Barthelme and Kosinski" (*PMPA* 4:25–32) actually enhances Jerzy Kosinski's work, which is usually described as tragic (or perhaps morbid). Studies of individual works are Betty Catherine Dobson's "Mythological, Biblical, and Literary Allusions in Donald Barthelme's *The Dead Father*" (*IFR* 6:40–48), which catalogues these references with perhaps more seriousness than Barthelme might intend, Carl Malmgren's "Barthes' S/Z and Barthelme's 'The Zombies': A Cacographic Interruption of a Text" (*PTL* 3[1978]:209–21), and Frank W. Shelton's brief comments on what is perhaps Barthelme's funniest story, "Barthelme's Western Tall Tale: 'Porcupines at the University'" (*NConL* 9,i:2–3). The best study of an individual work—in terms of widening our understanding of Barthelme in general—is Maurice Couturier's "Barthelme's Uppity Bubble: 'The Balloon'" (*RFEA* 8:183–201), which argues for the distinction between subject and object (between the balloon and "the balloon" as it exists as a factor in people's texts). Citing Roland Barthes and Jacques Lacan, Couturier establishes how Barthelme's balloon "is constituted by each individual subject who uses it as a pre-text in his struggle to found or reinvent his own problematical unity."

Raymond Federman—already the subject of several dissertations and a Beckett scholar in his own right—is given center-stage attention in the anthology *Visual Literature Criticism*, ed. Richard Kostelanetz (So. Ill.). In "Raymond Federman's Visual Fiction" Jerome Klinkowitz describes the unspeakable atrocity suffered at the center of Federman's autobiographical work, which makes his use of the visual (as opposed to the spoken) necessary, and how the otherwise speakable incidents fail to make a story on those terms. In "Principles of Concrete Structuralism" John Jacob shows how Federman structures his first novel, *Double or Nothing*, according to the integrity of each single page, and how the evolving narrative is framed within the more obvious story of the book's own composition. Federman's own "Why Maurice Roche" considers how texts cancel themselves by placing contradictory voices within voices.

After years of shocking critics with its abrasive thematics, Jerzy Kosinski's fiction has begun to merit attention for its technique. Cinematic montage can be seen as the principle behind the fragmented narrative in *Steps*, reports Byron Petrakis ("Jerzy Kosinski's *Steps* and the Cinematic Novel," *Comparatist*, 3[1978]:16–22), tying Kosinski's mastery of this form to his experience in photography and cinema school; but Kosinski's true genius is that narrative depth is not sacrificed (in the manner of the French New Novel), since by exploiting "language's connotative and metaphorical function" Kosinski creates striking visual descriptions without sacrificing the power of his narrative. An essay further emphasizing Kosinski's creative use of the written word is J. Bakker's "Language as Failed Therapy: Kosinski's *The Painted Bird* and *Blind Date*" (*DQR* 9:203–17). A more familiar study of theme made worthy by its considerations of myth is Patricia Meszaros' "Hero with a Thousand Faces, Child with No Name: Kosinski's *The Painted Bird*" (*CollL* 6:232–44).

ix. Robert Coover, John Hawkes, William H. Gass, and John Gardner

Fictions exist in constructs of language—so argues Brenda Wineapple in "Robert Coover's Playing Fields" (*IowaR* 10,iii:66–74). Hence reality is not a matter of direct reference, but rather of authorial construction reenacted by the reader; there is no existence beyond meaningless ritual, as the imbedded structure of *The Universal Baseball Association* shows. Such metafiction, Susan Kissel adds, makes especial demands of readers ("The Contemporary Artist and His Audience in the Short Stories of Robert Coover," *SSF* 16:49–54), and of character as well (according to Kathryn Hume in "Robert Coover's Fiction: The Naked and the Mythic," *Novel* 12:127–48); by removing meaning, Coover strips his characters to their most vivid components, leaving them only the protection of myth. The master of this narrative technique is, of course, Jorge Luis Borges, to whom Ronald Christ makes the now-familiar comparison ("Forking Narratives," *LALR* 14:52–61).

Scholarship on John Hawkes has in recent years adopted the tone of treating a major novelist, though always with disclaimers that he is too little read. A good essay to unravel Hawkes's complexities of theme and manner is C. J. Allen's "Desire, Design, and Debris: The Submerged Narrative of John Hawkes' Recent Trilogy" (*MFS* 25: 579–92). There is "a submerged narrative in which the power of the conscious mind to create idyllic visions is gradually undermined by unconscious needs and fears." What is implicit in *The Blood Oranges* is parodied in *Travesty* "as a result of the threatening portrayal of the unconscious in the middle volume, *Death, Sleep & the Traveler*"; what begins as sexual multiplicity ends with "cataclysmic destruction." In his own interview with Hawkes, Thomas LeClair draws out penetrating comments on the author's use of "the language of vision" and "the essential beauty of the ugly." "I see writing as an act of eroticizing the landscape," Hawkes reveals (*New Rep* 10 Nov.: 26–29).

As a seemingly inevitable reaction to John Gardner's attack on his style of fiction last year in *On Moral Fiction* William H. Gass found himself pitted against Gardner in two pieces of 1979 scholarship, both of them debates—one actual, the other mock. Larry McCaffery supplies the very telling parody in "The Gass-Gardner Debate: Showdown on Main Street" (*LitR* 23:134–44). Gardner is made to repeat his theses from *On Moral Fiction* and to condemn most of contemporary culture, while Gass articulates his aesthetics from the "Medium of Fiction" essay in his 1970 collection, *Fiction and the Figures of Life.* "To provide new, wonderful objects to the world" is Gass's answer to Gardner's claim that literary art preach moral truths. In his own commentary McCaffery surmises that Gardner is operating from optimistic, humanistic premises "that many modern writers, scientists, and philosophers have decided to abandon"; Gass, on the other hand, writes in a world which has abandoned "the old epistemological assurances" (Gass studied under Wittgenstein at Cornell while Gardner was studying Chaucer at Iowa). What interests Gass most is not the content of narrative but rather the "ontological shifts" which happen when words are taken out of life and placed in a literary context. Tom LeClair's transcript of an actual debate (at the University of Cincinnati, 24 October 1978 and printed in *NewRep* 10 Mar.:25, 28–33) corresponds almost perfectly to McCaffery's fantasy. Gass countered Gardner's call for moral relevance by suggesting that a fiction writer cannot be as certain as a social scientist, that the writer's job is to make beautiful objects (hence backing up beyond Gardner's Tolstoy to John Keats). Beyond this attempt to out-traditionalize each other, Gass and Gardner each deepen their positions and clarify the consequences of moral preachment versus objecthood.

John Gardner himself was treated as a politically hot figure. "The Sound and Fury Over Fiction" was the headline splashed across the front page of the *NYTSM* on 6 July, and Stephen Singular's feature article (pp. 12–15, 34, 36–39) played up the contentiousness which Gardner's critical stances had created for his own fiction. "A near-Messianic complex about the purpose of art, and of fiction in particular" is what Singular sensed in Gardner's work; quotes from other novelists, including John Updike and Saul Bellow, read as attempts to distance themselves as far as possible from Gardner's ideals. Gardner's own posturing in the subsequent discussion makes one suspect that *On Moral Fiction* may have been more publicity stunt than reasoned criticism, since little of its thesis holds up in the face of challenges which emerge from these debates.

Gardner fares better in the critiques of specific works. In "John Gardner and the Defense of Fiction" (*MQ* 20:405–15) W. P. Fitzpatrick finds that the interior novel within *October Light* establishes that art is weaker than life as a substitute for fiction—Gardner's claim in the aesthetic debates. Moreover, the stories of *The King's Indian* challenge John Barth's "Literature of Exhaustion" thesis by creating fresh fictions within familiar modes.

x. Kurt Vonnegut

Petty insults of Vonnegut's talent still abound, but defenses of his art are being made as well; ten years after the adolescent furor of his pop-culture fame has died down, neither would seem to be necessary. Yet both sides of the Vonnegut question yield interesting points about his fiction. In *Confidence Man* John G. Blair dismisses Vonnegut—"In fifty years or less he will be read as a minor figure representing a certain stage in the cultural decay of the West"—yet finds the novelist's work in *Cat's Cradle* essential to his thesis: "Vonnegut's novel depicts an absurd and hopeless world in which the only coherence is supplied artificially by a confidence man." Less appreciative is David Bosworth, whose "The Literature of Awe" (*AR* 37: 4–26) complains that "a fiction that loses faith in man must eventually lose faith in itself: a literature of defeat must eventually become self-defeating and deny its own validity." Bosworth mistakes Vonnegut's discarding of the suspension of disbelief (in fact a claim for art to believe only in itself, and not in some sham representation) for "an entire body of literature whose basic perspective is one of despair," "too abstracted to capture that whole, 'felt' truth that the best fiction has always rediscovered for us."

Intelligent rejoinders to such neo-Tolstoyan, "good-old-days" criticism may be found in John M. McInerney's "Children for Vonnegut" (*NMAL* 3: Item 4), which argues that the author's "deliberately primitive prose fits in with the general trend toward the devaluation of language," which in turn is necessary so that "his childlike perspective . . . becomes the means for restoring the reader's imaginative consciousness" otherwise dulled by the smooth manipulations of society. A most eloquent defense of Vonnegut's work comes from his former student and successful novelist, John Irving ("Kurt Vonnegut and His Critics," *NewRep* 22 Sept.:41–49), who praises Vonnegut for making the reader's job easy (which for a writer is difficult work). Vonnegut survives his own pessimism by virtue of "sunny little dreams," which, when taken away, create the true pathos of his work. His moral harshness in such sunderings is equal to that of Conrad and Dickens ("Dickens, by the way, was also an entertainer"). The supposed pessimism of Vonnegut's endings is explained by his refusal to insult our intelligence: "He won't make a grander claim." His characters' own pledge to personal kindness is Vonnegut's own optimistic message.

Some measure of Vonnegut's spreading international fame may be gauged from Jerzy Kutnik's survey, "Vonnegut in Poland" (*AmEx* 6,iii:33–44). In Poland, as in the Soviet Union, Vonnegut is not only the most popular and best-selling American contemporary, but has been the subject of much recent criticism (which, as in the United States, was for a time retarded by the author's disarming simplicity).

xi. Thomas Pynchon and John Irving

Thomas Pynchon, whose three novels have proved to be conservative critics' favorite examples of innovative fiction, will be the subject of even more scholarship now that *Pynchon Notes* (Wesleyan Univ.) is underway. With a running bibliography by John M. Krafft and news notes by Khachig Tololyan, this typewritten newsletter plans to expand into a journal, and its 1980 numbers have already begun publishing full-length critical essays. Tololyan also shows how Pynchon overwhelms critics ("Prodigious Pynchon and His Progeny," *SNNTS* 11:224–34) and creates a Post-Modern crisis in values ("Criticism as Symptom: Thomas Pynchon and the Crisis of the Humanities," *NOR* 5:314–18). Sara M. Solberg underscores this distance from conventional Modernism in "On Comparing Apples and Oranges: James Joyce and Thomas Pynchon" (*CLS* 16:33–40).

Benny Profane and Herbert Stencil continue to occupy critics as the two poles of Pynchon's first novel, *V.* Melvyn New sees them as two approaches to understanding (as in the deciphering of texts) in "Profaned and Stenciled Texts: In Search of Pynchon's *V.*" (*GaR* 33:395–412); each seeks a new, imaginative system of order within a romance structure (albeit lacking "amelioration"). Steven Weisenburger reminds readers that for the mass of historical information which distinguishes both *V.* and *Gravity's Rainbow* Pynchon is in fact using unexperienced source material; close detail is his own way of bearing witness to the individual versus the system. A closer identification with Benny Profane, however, is Michael H. Begnal's argument in "Thomas Pynchon's *V.*: In Defense of Benny *Profane*" (*JNT* 9:61–69). Common mistakes in reading Pynchon are diagnosed by Brian McHale ("Modernist Reading, Post-Modern Text: The Case of *Gravity's Rainbow*," *PT* 1,i–ii:85–110) and Antonio Marquez ("The Cinematic Imagination in Thomas Pynchon's *Gravity's Rainbow*," *BRMMLA* 33:166–79). Two source studies whose titles say all are David Cowart's "Pynchon's Use of the Tannhaüser Legend in *Gravity's Rainbow*" (*NConL* 9,iii.1–3) and "*V.* in Florence: Botticelli's *Birth of Venus* and the Metamorphosis of Victoria Wren" (*SHR* 13:345–53). Robert L. Nadeau posits Alfred North Whitehead as a God-figure in "Readings from the New Book of Nature: Physics and Pynchon's *Gravity's Rainbow*" (*SNNTS* 11:454–71), while Raymond J. Wilson settles for a more mundane catalog of corresponding characters and themes in "Cozzen's *Guard of Honor* and Pynchon's *Gravity's Rainbow*" (*NConL* 9,v:6–8). A masterpiece in miniature—a lesson to all Pynchon critics that much can be said in a very few words— is Khachig Tololyan's "The Fishy Poisson: Allusions to Statistics in *Gravity's Rainbow*" (*NMAL* 4: Item 5). Tololyan finds the sources for Pynchon's statistics, describes how they are used, and outlines their importance. As structuring devices in the novel, they establish figures of menace as both metaphor and symbol within the languages of science.

John Irving would seem to have entered the ranks of important novelists only with the publication of his fourth work, *The World According to Garp* (1978), but this year's scholarship has already yielded two dissertations. In a penetrating interview with Michael Priestly ("An Interview with John Irving," *NER* 1:489–504) Irving discusses the influences of his writing of *Garp*, particularly those from autobiography. With the Random House republication of his first

three novels in one volume (1980) Irving should become the subject
of further studies soon; a television documentary on his fifth novel
(in progress) has already been aired.

xii. The New Journalists: Tom Wolfe and Hunter S. Thompson

The New Journalism—once the province of racy feature writers who
used fictional techniques to dramatize their news narratives—has split
into two factions along lines similar to the Gardner-Gass debate.
Tom Wolfe continues to use the techniques of traditional novels—
character, image, development by dialogue—to throw light upon contemporary experience. Richard A. Kallan shows how this works in his
essay, "Style and the New Journalism: A Rhetorical Analysis of Tom
Wolfe" (*ComM* 46:52–62), while Thomas Powers makes specific
application to Wolfe's *The Right Stuff* in "Wolfe in Orbit: Our
Mercurial Interests" (*Commonweal* 106:551–52). But in Hunter S.
Thompson's hands the New Journalism becomes more like the New
Fiction, in which the adoption of innovative techniques allows the
writer to report on his own sense of involvement with the story—with
his own writing of the story, in fact, much as the narratives of Ronald
Sukenick, Clarence Major, and Steve Katz present themselves. John
Hellmann describes the process in "Corporate Fiction, Private Fable,
and Hunter S. Thompson's *Fear and Loathing: On the Campaign Trail
'72* (*Crit* 21,i:16–30). "The page and deadline . . . becomes the life
and death of his narrative," Hellmann reports; composition is its own
act, and the true story of Thompson's narrative. "Distancing and symbolic forms of parody" are available to Thompson by virtue of his
flair for consciousness-altering drugs (another part of his writer's
pose). Digressive freedom, irresponsibility, and disarming candor
are by-products of Thompson's stance. "He has had to replace the
detective-role of the conventional reporter—based on the assumption
of a rational, cause-and-effect world—with the artist-role of the new
journalist—based on a realization that the evidence of the macrocosm
has already been artificially distorted and invented." This is precisely
the issue of the John Gardner–William H. Gass debate, and the point
of contention in Gerald Graff's attack on contemporary innovative
fiction. That the journalists are thrashing it out as well suggests that
the new approach has indeed penetrated the full popular culture.

Thompson's own collected work of the past two decades has been published as *The Great Shark Hunt* (Simon & Schuster), which contains an exhaustive primary and secondary bibliography of the good doctor of gonzo journalism.

xiii. Other Innovators

William Burroughs' debt to Mikhail Bakhtin's theory of polyphonic structure in *Naked Lunch* is computed by Roger Fowler in "Anti-Language in Fiction" (*Style* 13:259–78). "*Death Kit*: Susan Sontag's Dream Narrative" (*ConL* 20:484–99) is Larry McCaffery's account of how Susan Sontag rejects the blatantly self-conscious techniques of Barth and Barthelme in favor of the "dream tale of Kafka or Borges, or the nightmarish works of Djuna Barnes, John Hawkes, and Anaïs Nin." Yet Sontag's fiction is far from being representational, for its landscape and logic have their own peculiar structure which is best approached as a formal problem.

E. L. Doctorow fascinates critics with his use of history (in both *The Book of Daniel* and *Ragtime*), and has thus encouraged a series of source studies. Daniel L. Zins considers historian William Appleman Williams as "Daniel's 'Teacher' in Doctorow's *The Book of Daniel*" (*NMAL* 3:Item 16), and Josie P. Campbell brings to modern production-line technology in "Coalhouse Walker and the Model T. Ford: Legerdemain in *Ragtime*" (*JPC* 13:302–09). A more ambitious study—one of the most revealing, in fact—is Constance Pierce's "The Syncopated Voices of Doctorow's *Ragtime*" (*NMAL* 3: Item 26), which shows how a singular narrative voice emerges in the book's closing pages—that of the little boy, who has been an astute observer all along. Does this influence the book's meaning? Indeed, it forms the meaning: "When the little boy and the narrator merge, so do pieces of time," changing a somewhat realistic work into a triumph of impressionism. This same technique is studied by Daniel L. Zins in "E. L. Doctorow: The Novelist as Historian" (*HC* 16,v:1–14), where we are told that when facts are viewed as illusion we can judge the historian as a creative writer.

xiv. Women Writers

Though few women fictionists describe themselves by gender, scholarship (in most cases by women) chooses to treat them as a group, even though there are vast formal differences between the works of, say, Erica Jong and Grace Paley. One deliberately political study which justifies its subgenre claim is Anne Z. Mickelson's *Reaching Out: Sensitivity and Order in Recent American Fiction by Women* (Scarecrow). "Is there a new woman emerging in literature" on the heels of recent feminist declarations and activities? "Lois Gould's women, in her first three books, seem to view themselves as ugly and unattractive. They emerge as living proof of the influence of the Judaic-Christian code which formed the basis of the concept of woman's body as mysterious and unclean." Gail Godwin's heroines, on the other hand, revolt against this posture; the tension in woman's position leads to fear and violence in the works of Joyce Carol Oates. Yet the damage caused by men in Oates's work is answered by "a kind of symbolic ritual baptism in the celebration of the female body" in the novels of Erica Jong. "The meaninglessness of existence," not always an effect of being female, is Joan Didion's response. Yet there is a literature of survival and strength: of black women writers such as Sarah E. Wright, Toni Morrison, and Alice Walker. The true future of writing by women is explored in an aptly titled chapter, "Piecemeal Liberation: Marge Piercy, Sara Davidson, Marilyn French, Grace Paley." Paley in particular, through her celebration of style (humor, irony) in the lives of common city people, offers "an air of reconciliation, a soothing perspective, a breakthrough to something better."

As for towering reputations, Joan Didion has replaced Erica Jong among women writers, at least in terms of attracting bitter attacks and spirited defenses. What some critics describe as Didion's depressive thematics seems a culturally appropriate 1970's reaction to the sexual exuberance and flamboyant personality (born in the 1960s) of Jong's fiction. On the personal level of character, these maniac-depressive rhythms can be productive, claims Sybil Korff Vincent ("In the Crucible: The Forging of an Identity as Demonstrated in Didion's *Play It As It Lays*," PCL 3,ii[1977]:58–64); but in terms of larger meaning the message is one of loss, as H. Jennifer Brady argues in "Points West, Then and Now: The Fiction of Joan Didion" (*ConL* 20:452–70). "The closing of the frontier, the termination of America's original dream of new beginnings in that unknown country of the setting sun" has yielded for Didion a "sense of obsolescence" which creates a climate of cultural loss, overpowering her characters and their hopes. Barbara Grizzuti Harrison is more personal in her attack. "Joan Didion: The Courage of Her Afflictions" (*Nation* 229:277–86) claims that "Didion's 'style' is a bag of tricks" pointed more toward surface effect than meaning, and that her characterizations are similarly superficial, in which "exquisite desperation" is superior to being "tacky." Didion "romanticizes insanity" and expresses "her revulsion against the struggle for meaning." Writing "paens to the futility of human endeavor" and elevating "pain to a sacrament," Didion's fiction and essays are more the expression of a personal insufficiency and shallowness than admirable works of art.

Harriet Arnow's work, on the other hand, is seen to enhance the position of women in art, even though women's roles are often held to be in tension with the demands of aesthetic freedom, says Glenda Hobbs in "A Portrait of the Artist as Mother: Harriet Arnow and *The Dollmaker*" (*GaR* 23:851–66). A special issue of *Shenandoah* (30,iii) on Jean Stafford is largely given over to memorials and biographical statements (by Peter Taylor, Howard Moss, Nancy Flagg, and Dorothea Straus); Joyce Carol Oates, however, contributes a critical essay, "The Interior Castle: The Art of Jean Stafford's Short Fiction" (pp. 61–64), which emphasizes the meditative, "the patient accumulation of sharply-observed impressions."

xv. New Realists: James Dickey, Stanley Elkin, and Others

Stanley Elkin represents a new style of American fictionist who returns to realistic forms of narrative in full knowledge of the antimimetic innovations wrought by William H. Gass (Elkin's colleague at Washington University in St. Louis). In "The American Salesman as Pitchman and Poet in the Fiction of Stanley Elkin" (*Crit* 21,iii: 52–58) Robert Edward Colbert stresses how attention to a character's voice and language carries Elkin's fiction beyond the "Black Humor" label affixed to it at its inception. Larry McCaffery's analysis of *The Franchiser* ("Stanley Elkin's Recovery of the Ordinary," *Crit* 21,ii: 39–51) shows just how Elkin's magical language transforms the ordinary. Peter Matthiessen's more lyrical transformative works, *At Play in the Fields of the Lord* and *Far Tortuga*, are the subjects of respective studies by Richard F. Patterson and James P. Grove in this same issue (*Crit* 21,ii:5–38), which concludes with a checklist of Matthiessen studies.

Another fictionist of the city landscape is Richard Price, whose novels are examined by Frank W. Shelton in "Family, Community, and Masculinity in the Urban Novels of Richard Price" (*Crit* 21,i: 5–15). To the expectable realism Price adds a touch of surrealism "to heighten his portrayal of urban decay and violence." Family life is important for its absence; the gang becomes an alternate form of community life, even though the gangs perpetuate ideals of parental and cultural value their members had supposedly rejected. The one unique feature of Price's gangs is their rejection of women in favor of male companionship.

James Dickey continues to be regarded as a master of the underside of human nature. The release of the bestial, a familiar theme in criticism of his novel, is reexplored by Edward Doughtie in "Art and Nature in *Deliverance*" (*SWR* 64:167–80), with this difference: art is the mediating force between the natural and civilized life. A title which tells all we might suspect about Frederick Exley's work is Donald R. Johnson's "The Hero in Sports Literature and Exley's *A Fan's Notes*" (*SHR* 13:233–44). An introductory study of a new, young writer is David Boxer's and Cassandra Phillips' "*Will You Please Be Quiet, Please?* Voyeurism, Dissociation, and the Art of Raymond Carver" (*IowaR* 10,iii:75–90).

xvi. Older Realists: J. P. Donleavy, William Styron, and Others

Early in his career J. P. Donleavy expatriated himself from America and took on the personality of an Irish country gentleman; Johann A. Norstedt examines the problems presented between a romanticized Ireland and the real thing in "Irishmen and Irish-Americans in the Fiction of J. P. Donleavy" (*Irish-American Fiction*). "Ancestral reconciliation" of this sort is central to *The Ginger Man*, but its protagonist "is the prototype of a series of Donleavy heroes," and so the theme remains central throughout Donleavy's canon. Out of disgust for America Donleavy himself seems to have created a myth for himself of Romantic Ireland. This same collection features similar nationally inclined studies of Elizabeth Cullinan (by Maureen Murphy), Edwin O'Connor ("Priests and Politicians" by David Dillon), J. F. Powers (as a comic satirist, by James P. Degnan), and "Women's Perspectives in Irish-American Fiction from Betty Smith to Mary McCarthy" (by Bonnie Kime Scott). "An Interview with J. P. Donleavy" conducted by Kurt Jacobson presents Donleavy's own views on his adopted Ireland (*JIL* 8,i:39–48).

Sophie's Choice, especially as related to his earlier novels, occupies most of Valarie Meliotes Arms's "An Interview with William Styron" (*ConL* 20:1–12). Denise T. Askin makes a valid point in "The Half-Loaf of Learning: A Theme in Styron's *The Confessions of Nat Turner*" (*NMAL* 3: Item 6), that his fragmentary and shallow education "is made whole by the revelation of the merciful nature of the Christian God" evident in Margaret's sacrifice.

In "Ross Lockridge and the Tragedy of *Raintree County*" (*Crit* 20,iii:57–63) Donald J. Greiner reexamines the fact (first established by John Leggett) that the young novelist's confidence was challenged by doubt. Truman Capote's transformation of journalistic material is reviewed by Jack DeBellis in "Visions and Revisions: Truman Capote's *In Cold Blood*" (*JML* 7:519–36). William Goldman's career is surveyed in chronicle-like fashion by Richard Andersen (*TUSAS* 326), and two contemporaries of the period are given checklist treatment: *Adam and His Work: A Bibliography of Sources by and About Paul Goodman*, comp. Tom Nicely (Scarecrow), and *Gore Vidal: A Primary and Secondary Bibliography*, comp. Robert J. Stanton (Hall).

xvii. Native American and Western Writers

"The Quest for Mythic Vision in Contemporary Native American and Chicano Fiction" (*AL* 50:625–40) is Vernon Lattin's investigation of the quest for harmony between man and nature in a culture which has "betrayed neither the land nor the dream." Rejecting the conqueror's Christianity, heroes in this literature return to a vision of the sanctity of all life in a transcending unity. Edith Blicksilver describes the crisis between these two cultures of belief in "Traditionalism versus Modernity: Leslie Silko on American Indian Women" (*SWR* 64:149–60), describing Silko's attempt to preserve the literary treasures of her Native American heritage. Reaching back from even more "civilized sources" is the quest described by Thekla Zachrau in "M.

Scott Momaday: Towards an Indian Identity" (*American Indian Culture and Research Journal* 3,i:39–56).
Frederick Manfred (*TUSAS* 329) by Robert C. Wright treats the novels and stories of this Western writer from his first novel, *The Golden Bowl* (1944) through his recent fictionalized reminiscence, *Green Earth* (1977). The five Buckskin Man Tales which include *Lord Grizzly* (1954) are at the center of Wright's analysis. A great deal of Wright's information is derived from Manfred's previously published "Conversation"; new interview topics might have been pursued, and the myth criticism of other scholars on Manfred's work might have been better consulted.

Larry McMurtry's novels are given exhaustive treatment in Dorey Schmidt's collection of original essays, *Larry McMurtry: Unredeemed Dreams* (Edinburg, Tex.: Pan American Univ.), to which Schmidt has contributed an interview. The volume's most insightful essay is Izora Skinner's "Description: The Lyrics of Strange Music," in which McMurtry's apparently realistic description of Texas landscapes and people proves to be a lyrical stylization of the artist's own sensibility. Wright Morris is the subject of a special issue of *PrS* (53,ii), which includes a perceptive essay by Randall K. Albers covering new ground in *Field of Vision* and *Ceremony at Lone Tree* ("The Female Transformation: The Role of Women in Two Novels by Wright Morris"). A nicely synthetic piece which sums up Wright's importance as a regionalist is Raymond L. Neinstein's "Wright Morris: The Metaphysics of Home." The Starkweather case is researched for its influence by Ginny Nachann in "*Ceremony at Lone Tree* and *Badlands*: The Starkweather Case and the Nebraska Plains."

Jack Schaefer, best known as the author of *Shane*, is studied as a more deeply brooding author by Michael Cleary in "Jack Schaefer: The Evolution of Pessimism" (*WAL* 14:33–47). Demographics and Schaefer's thematization of the expanding American civilization are treated by James C. Work in "Settlement Waves and Coordinate Forces in *Shane*" (*WAL* 14:191–200), while Gerald Haslam searches out a more mystical trend in "Sacred Sources in *The Canyon*" (*WAL* 14:49–55). A westerner whose influence has spread by virtue of his teaching is Wallace Stegner, according to Bill Henkin's "Time Is Not Just Chronology: An Interview with Wallace Stegner" (*MR* 20:127–39), where in addition to discussing his own work Stegner comments candidly on his experience with Ken Kesey and Larry McMurtry as students.

xviii. Science Fiction

The science fiction boom continues, and this year has centered on Ursula Le Guin as its premier practitioner. Le Guin's versatility as a stylist (as opposed to more traditional SF writers who limit themselves to novels of ideas) helps account for the wealth of scholarship on her, including two book-length collections. Of the two Joseph D. Olander's and Martin Harry Greenberg's *Ursula K. Le Guin* (Taplinger) is clearly the superior volume, largely because of its attention to how Le Guin writes (as opposed to what she writes about, which are matters of greater concern to the social scientists who figure prominently in the other book). The essay which tells nonspecialists the most about Le Guin's fiction is Thomas J. Remington's "The Other Side of Suffering: Touch as Theme and Metaphor in Le Guin's Science Fiction Novels," which characterizes Le Guin as a writer whose characters reach out in sympathy past the Hobbesian bleakness of life. Essays focusing on Le Guin's structure and technique are N. B. Hayles's "Androgyny, Ambivalence, and Assimilation in *The Left Hand of Darkness*" and John H. Crow's and Richard D. Erlich's "Words of Binding: Patterns of Integration in the Earthsea Trilogy." The remaining pieces are sound explications of individual works and more personal characterizations of Le Guin as a thinker. Joe DeBolt is the editor of *Ursula K. Le Guin: Voyager to Inner Lands and to Outer Space* (Kennikat), which features DeBolt's own biography of the author plus a number of strongly sociological interpretations of her work. Indicative of this style is Karen Sinclair's "Solitary Being: The Hero as Anthropologist." Le Guin's protagonists are more than critical of the action as it unfolds; they become participant-observers whose judgments separate them from the worlds in which they find themselves, and are thus characterized as detached, objective anthropologists (and the author's primary vehicle for the expression of meaning). Le Guin criticism (a story in itself) is surveyed by James W. Bittner, Le Guin's authorized bibliographer and foremost student of her work, in a dissertation completed this year (*DAI* 40:3286A).

Separate essays on Le Guin's fiction are addressed to specific interests. Patricia Dooley's "Magic and Art in Ursula Le Guin's Earthsea Trilogy" appears in *ChildL* 8:103–10; John Fekete writes a structuralist critique in *"The Dispossessed* and *Triton*: Act and System
in Utopian Science Fiction" (*SFS* 6:129–43); Virginia L. White covers
familiar ground in "Bright the Hawk's Flight: The Journey of the
Hero in Ursula Le Guin's Earthsea Trilogy" (*BSUF* 20,iv:34–45);
and in the most helpful of these separate essays Susan Wood shows
how Le Guin maps out imaginary worlds as "a framework for an
exploration of the varieties of physical life, social organizations, and
personal development open to human beings" ("Discovering Worlds:
The Fiction of Ursula K. Le Guin," in *Voices for the Future: Essays
on Modern Science Fiction Writers,* vol. 2, ed. Thomas Clareson
[Bowling Green]). Clareson's collection is also distinguished by cogent essays on such major talents as Robert Silverberg (by Clareson
himself), Phillip José Farmer (Thomas L. Wymer), John Brunner
(Joe DeBolt), and Roger Zelazny (Joe Sanders). A comprehensive
collection of original essays of an introductory nature is gathered by
Patrick Parrinder in *Science Fiction: A Critical Guide* (Longman),
which features (in addition to the usual historical pieces on the subgenre) country-by-country surveys on the state of SF today.

That science fiction writers use language itself as the substance
of their fictions, as opposed to the more traditional staging of ideas,
is discussed in three essays. Patrick Parrinder handles Samuel Delany
in "Delany Inspects the Word Beast" (*SFS* 6:337–41). L. T. Biddson
reviews another classic figure in "Ray Bradbury's Song of Experience"
(*NOR* 5:226–29), and Eric S. Rabkin explores the different uses of
language in "Metalinguistics and Science Fiction' (*CritI* 6:79–98).

xix. Mysteries and Crime Thrillers

Several distinguished works, critical and bibliographical, on this long-
maligned subgenre suggest that it may succeed science fiction as the
latest cottage industry within the literary establishment. David I.
Grossvogel's *Mystery and Its Fictions* (Hopkins) traces crime literature back to Sophocles to establish a tradition of "descriptive, meditative mysteries." Ending up with the self-conscious texts of Robbe-
Grillet and Borges, Grossvogel suggests that texuality may be the

incitement behind mystery writing all along. A more popularly based study is Jerry Palmer's *Thrillers: Genesis and Structure of a Popular Genre* (St. Martin's). Agreeing that the reader's consciousness of and delight in the textuality of formula is the genre's unifying principle, Palmer insists that social attitudes toward crime and punishment are the reasons for its continued popularity, growing from an interest in competitive (even radical) individualism.

Ross MacDonald is praised for expanding the genre (his Lew Archer is compared to Fitzgerald's Nick Carraway) in Bernard A. Schopen's "From Puzzle to People: The Development of the American Detective Novel" (*SAF* 7:175–89). The "fusion of character with the pattern of investigation" is MacDonald's triumphant achievement. Rites of passage, magic, and sacrifice are seen as the key in "Stephen King's *Carrie*—A Universal Fairytale" by Alex E. Alexander (*JPC* 13:282–88). Finally, two giants of the 1940s are the subjects of descriptive bibliographies published by the University of Pittsburgh Press: *Dashiell Hammet* (Richard Layman) and *Raymond Chandler* (Matthew J. Bruccoli).

xx. Afterword: Secondary Bibliography

For nearly two decades this chapter has been the longest (and not necessarily the most detailed) in *American Literary Scholarship*. That so much work on emerging (and hence critically unestablished) figures exists creates a double irony—it is too much to read, yet it must be read. Therefore the most significant event of the year is the publication of a tool to help contemporary critics with this very problem. John Somer and Barbara Eck Cooper are the authors of the massive *American and British Literature, 1945–1975: An Annotated Bibliography of Contemporary Scholarship* (Kansas). Far more than a comprehensive checklist (which by itself would be immensely helpful), this volume abstracts books and cross-indexes both books and critical essays according to the authors and material covered (in fairly close detail). With its help, scholarship should become far less redundant; individual scholars may now approach an author with the responsibility formerly reserved for the more traditional areas of research.

University of Northern Iowa

16. Poetry: 1900 to the 1940s

Richard Crowder

i. General

More dissertations about our poets are listed in *DAI* this year than in any year since I began writing this chapter (*ALS 1969*). Thirty-nine tyro scholars give consideration to 15 poets. In some cases a poet relevant to this chapter shares attention with others, but most of the writers focus on individuals. MacLeish, Wylie, Davidson, Tate, Cummings, Williams, and H. D. are treated in one dissertation each. Appearing in two studies are Aiken, Robinson, Ransom, Jeffers, and Moore. Crane is a subject four times, Stevens eight, and Frost ten. This is a large increase for Frost, who has been the subject of only four dissertations a year for the most part in the last decade, whereas Stevens has been the subject of ten or more annually in recent reports.

The Poet's Work, ed. Reginald Gibbons (Houghton Mifflin), is subtitled 29 *Masters of 20th Century Poetry on the Origins and Practice of Their Art*. It includes, in relation to this chapter, prose comments by Stevens, Crane, Williams, Bogan, and Moore. In his preface Gibbons observes that our century has produced comparatively more accounts than formerly by poets about their work—its sources and motives and the writer's practice. Modern poets, he thinks, may be moved to prose comment and explanation because readers find their work obscure. Also included in this book are excerpts from Pound, Eliot, younger Americans, and several British and European poets.

In their Introduction to *The "Poetry" Anthology: 1912–1977* (Houghton Mifflin) (pp. xxv–xlvii) Daryl Hine and Joseph Parisi, narrating the events of the founding of the monthly magazine, contribute vignettes of such early contributors as William Carlos Williams. Hine and Parisi sketch Harriet Monroe's effective role as editor, both in selection of poems and in suggestions for revisions. Their opinion is that her "greatest achievement" was probably the discovery and encouragement of Wallace Stevens. They frankly admit, however, that, along with the amazing amount of work of the highest level, there appeared much that was mediocre, especially from 1919 to 1932.

Jacob Korg uses quotations from both Stevens and Williams, among others, to show how modern poets, by experiment as opposed to experience, have often called into question the relationship between observer and observed, proposing new forms, idioms, and modes of imaginative perception. Such an operation breaks up the conventional principles of cognition and delivers the reader over not only to confusion but to outrage. One method transforms ritual into experiment, as in Williams' "Burning the Christmas Greens," which inverts the sacred values of the Biblical nativity scene. Korg cites Stevens' "Sunday Morning" as another example of this daring to experiment with ritual attitudes. His essay is entitled "Ritual and Experiment in Modern Poetry" (*JML* 7:127-46).

Language and the Poet: Verbal Artistry in Frost, Stevens, and Moore (Chicago) is the title of Marie Boroff's study relating language (and statistics) to poetry (subject matter and theme). The first chapter looks at brief passages from the three poets to demonstrate Boroff's "method." The second chapter focuses on Frost, paying special attention to "Mending Wall" (early) and "Directive" (late). The subtitle, "The Uses of Simplicity," points at once to the author's approach to Frost's language. Turning to Stevens, Boroff devotes two chapters to his "World of Words." She concludes the first ("The Uses of Diction") with an interesting diagram titled "The Spectrum of Diction in English" as it has developed in her consideration of Stevens. In the other Stevens chapter, "An Always Incipient Cosmos," she quotes from the late "St. Armorer's Church from the Outside," among others, to illustrate the nature of the poet's language, "abstract, changing, pleasure giving, and human."

The two chapters on Moore are based on Boroff's bold statement that the poet's work is significantly indebted to advertisements and feature articles in newspapers and magazines, "promotional prose." The subtitles are "The Uses of Syntax" and "A Poet's Guise at Last." Boroff introduces a travel advertisement from the *Illustrated London News* of 1930 to support her argument.

Audrey T. Rodgers in *Universal Drum* has chosen to study the relationship of the dance to the work of four American poets, two of whom are relevant to this chapter. The material on Crane was published last year in *FDP* 2 (see *ALS 1978*, pp. 328–29). As for Williams, Rodgers starts with the poet's tribute to Isadora Duncan in 1909 and then traces the importance throughout Williams' work of physical movement and especially the function of dance in expressing the otherwise inexpressible, as "the rhythmic pattern . . . that encloses the past and present into a permanent, enduring reality." The poets here treated were at their best, the author maintains, when holding the dance image "in perfect tension" with "scaffold, language, and rhythm." Each chapter is thoroughly documented.

Prose works by our poets will be briefly mentioned here. Thomas M. Linehan's "Style and Individuality in E. E. Cummings' *The Enormous Room* (*Style* 13:45–59) notes what we all are well aware of, "the wide diversity of style and tone"—from "derisive imitation of official language and mentality" to the unemotional tone akin to documentary. Linehan quotes passages in Cummings' many "stylistic voices." Harry Marten in "'The Stranger Becomes Oneself': Visual Surfaces and Patterns in Conrad Aiken's *King Coffin*" (*JNT* 933–40) looks at the structure of Aiken's third novel. Marten says, "A contrast of mental motion and visual stasis is established" at the very beginning of the book. Allen Tate's *The Fathers* is given consideration in *QJLC* 36. "*The Fathers*: A Pictorial Introduction" (pp. 357–64) presents a group of Civil War pictures connected with the novel. Thornton H. Parsons in "The Education of Lacy Buchan" (pp. 365–76) discusses the growth of the central figure in *The Fathers*, supplemented by interesting photographs. Reevaluating "Tate's venture into Confederate biography," Steve Davis' "Turning to the Immoderate Past: Allen Tate's *Stonewall Jackson*" (*MissQ* 32:241–53) sees the theme of the book as "the meaning of the hero as symbolized by General Jackson." Devoutly religious, Jackson was at the same time an aggressive warrior, courageous even when doomed, belonging to "a timeless heroic tradition."

ii. Women Poets

Edward Butscher's *Adelaide Crapsey* (TUSAS 337) follows the pattern and simplicities of the other books in the series. It is 40-50 pages shorter than the books about our other poets (94 pages of text as contrasted, for example, with 150 for Frost and 147 for Millay). This brevity is explained by the subject's relatively short life (36 years) and the small quantity of her work. More descriptive than analytical, the book details Crapsey's undergraduate poetry and prose at Vassar and delineates her obsession with English prosody, beginning about 1902. Her early verse is admittedly weak, but in 1911 Crapsey invented the cinquain, her most important achievement, and continued to write with vigor and compression in this five-line form until her death. Her book of poems (1915) was published only after her death.

In "H. D.: A Symbolist Perspective" (*CLS* 16:48–57) Heather Rossario Sievert says that H. D.'s attempt to reveal an object's "interiority" without naming it relates her to the Symbolists, though the poems in her earliest volume, *Sea Garden* (1916), differ from other Symbolist literature in enjoying "the force and fervor of fresh wind blowing throughout." Another essay on H. D. is Susan Gubar's "The Echoing Spell of H. D.'s Trilogy," in *Shakespeare's Sisters*, pp. 200–218. It was first published in *ConL* 19 (reviewed in *ALS 1978*, p. 324).

Russell Anne Swafford and Paul Ramsey have collaborated on "The Influence of Sara Teasdale on Louise Bogan" (*CEA* 41,iv:7–12). Bogan, they find, thought of herself as "more permissively modern" than the older poet. Though Teasdale and Bogan differed in tone and texture, they both gave "classic form and depth to romantic perceiving." In writing *Sara Teasdale: Woman and Poet* (Harper), William Drake interviewed and corresponded with everyone available who knew the poet and examined papers of friends no longer living. The result is a biography closely aligning the events and situations of Teasdale's life with the contents, tone, and implications of her work. Drake clearly shows how the poet worked to break away from her 19th-century genteel upbringing to enjoy the new freedoms women were finding in the 20th century. He places Teasdale in the feminine tradition alongside Christina Rossetti, Elizabeth Barrett, Emily Brontë, and Emily Dickinson. Her frail health and her inbred reticence hindered efforts at confronting the world. Drake recounts "with respect and sympathy" the story of her travels, her interest in Vachel Lindsay and John Hall Wheelock, her marriage to Ernst Filsinger, her craftsmanship, and at last her suicide. The author writes lucidly and indeed vividly, with insight fed, of course, by his fresh materials. This is an important book about a sensitive poet who ought to be more widely considered.

Drake mentions Teasdale's long-time intimate, Harriet Gardner

Curtis, only very briefly in two places 50 pages apart. In an essay entitled "Sara Teasdale's Friendships" (*NewL* 46,i:101–07) Ruth Perry and Maurice Sagoff draw data from "a small packet of hitherto unrecorded letters and cards" from Teasdale to Curtis and from the "diary record" of Curtis' "relationship to the poet." The authors discuss briefly Teasdale's friendships with Margaret Conklin (whom Drake often relies on as Teasdale's literary executor) and Marion Cummings Stanley, then turn at greater length to the Curtis connection. These documents, they discover, "make it clear how much more significant were her relations with other women [than with any man], how central they were to her emotional and artistic life."

Also in *Shakespeare's Sisters* (see H. D., above) is an essay by Jane Stanbrough on "Edna St. Vincent Millay and the Language of Vulnerability" (pp. 183–99), which asserts that the poet's public image of self-assurance and braggadocio masked underlying suffering and anguish. Millay revealed her concept of reality through assaulting, bombarding words. Her language shows her to have been "a misfit and a failure," oppressed and victimized. She felt restricted because she was a woman—dreams denied, body attacked, mind and spirit extinguished. This is a strong feminist statement. Similarly, Patricia A. Klemans considers the sonnets of *Fatal Interview* (1931) a "unique contribution" to the cause of feminism, "the first female counterpart to Donne's sophisticated lover." " 'Being Born a Woman': A New Look at Edna St. Vincent Millay" (*CLQ* 15:7–18) says the sonnets bring order out of a chaotic love affair, demonstrating Millay's honesty and intelligibility. Klemans points out how contemporary the poet is: skillful in her craft, she underscores the agelessness of the "message of feminine individuality." Also feminist in its approach is Jeannine Dobbs's "Edna St. Vincent Millay and the Tradition of Domestic Poetry" (*JWSL* 1:89–106), which shows how Millay coped with the tone, attitude, and materials often formerly adopted by women writers. Annie S. Woodbridge's "Millay in Spanish" (*JLN* 11 [1978]:105–06) evaluates Salomón de la Selva's translations.

iii. Reznikoff, Crane, Williams

Paul Auster ("The Decisive Moment," *Parnassus* 7:105–18) has made a critical survey of the prolific, though obscure writer Charles Reznikoff, whose poetry is "a transcription of the visible into the brute,

unciphered code of being." As Reznikoff wrote, he discovered the
real, became Adam, seeing things "as if for the first time." "The world
comes into being only in the act of moving towards it." The poet is
always trying to perceive. Reznikoff learned from imagism the power
of the unadorned image itself; he put down what he saw (an "objectivist"), without comment, without metaphor, trying to remain himself invisible.

Gregory R. Zeck does some psychological probing in "Hart
Crane's 'The Wine Menagerie': The Logic of Metaphor" (*AI* 36:
197–214). Zeck suggests that the poem in question dramatizes Crane's
obsessive search for identity, a result of unsatisfactory communication
in his family. After a complex explication he concludes that the poet
"has to be self-mothering, self-othering," for he fears castration.
Crane sees himself, then, as a literary hermaphrodite. The article
explains puns and Freudian references of many kinds to be found in
the poem.

Marc Simon's *Samuel Greenberg, Hart Crane, and the Lost Manuscripts* (Humanities Press, 1978) is in two parts: a biography of
Greenberg (1893–1917) and the story of his papers (including their
influence on Crane) ending with their final resting place in 1964 at
New York University. The appendix consists of the 41 poems from
the Greenberg manuscripts (not to be confused with those in Crane's
collection, now at Yale). The documentation is full; a select bibliography lists the sources consulted; and the index is good. Dennis
M. Read's "Hart Crane's Letters to *The Little Review*" (*BRH* 82:
249–61) discusses the poet's communications with Margaret Anderson's stimulating journal. The six letters, now in the Special Collections of the University of Wisconsin at Milwaukee, were written between 1923 and 1929 from Cleveland; Brooklyn; Patterson, N.Y.;
New York City; the Isle of Pines; and Paris, this last after Crane's
release from prison following a drunken brawl. Parts of two books
discuss Crane as homosexual. *Gay Academic* devotes seven pages to
the topic (pp. 193–99); and Robert K. Martin in *Homosexual Tradition*, pp. 115–63, discusses the situation at greater length.

We welcome William Carlos Williams to this group. Up to now
he has been included (for some esoteric reason) with the younger
poets of the next chapter. A postwar German poet published 58 Williams poems in a bilingual volume in 1962 as well as a strong essay on
the American. In "Hans Magnus Enzenberger and William Carlos

Williams: Economy, Detail and Suspicion of Doctrine" (*GL&L* 32: 153–65) W. S. Sewell shows how the German has followed Williams in seeking greater control through reduction to essentials not only in word choice but also in subject matter, though, unlike Williams, Enzenberger rarely finds altogether satisfying the "contemplation of the local and particular." Thomas H. Jackson claims that Williams as "Modernist" excelled Pound, Eliot, and Stevens in realizing the goals of Mallarmé and Yeats, that he resolved better than any other poet in English the problems presented by the limits of reason in the Positive sense. Jackson's article, "Positivism and Modern Poetics: Yeats, Mallarmé, and William Carlos Williams" (*ELH* 46:509–40), points out how the American poet's lyrics transform, with tensions, "a visible scene into a verbal structure," as, for example, in "Spring Strains" of 1916, and how Williams carried through the theories of both his predecessors with even more power and elegance, using "words and words alone" to make fresh the experience of the senses, the meaning of a word at the same time being "what the word has become to language-users through use."

In an article entitled "The Four Elements of Poetic Consciousness in William Carlos Williams' *Paterson*" (*SDR* 17,i:101–11) Helen H. Roulston emphasizes that the poet uses the four Heraclitean elements throughout the books of his major poem (with the exception of book 1, which stresses chaos) in a theme-and-variations form: earth as "raw poetic materials," air as "imagination," fire as creative energy, and water as "human community and communication." Roulston carefully traces the use of the elements in all five books. This is a helpful addition to the understanding of Williams' craft in knitting Paterson together.

Andrew Hudgins turns to the insights of Freud's *Civilization and Its Discontents* (e.g., how the mind carries both the present and the past at the same time) in a reading of *Paterson*. In "*Paterson* and Its Discontents" (*ArQ* 35:25–41) Hudgins calls this long work a "triple-piled homologue": the city, the doctor, and the poem—all named Paterson. Through the five books id and ego "are brought into harmony." Steven Weiland's "Where Shall We Unearth the Word? William Carlos Williams and the Aztecs" (*ArQ* 35:41–48) points to pre-Columbian cultures as a rich and vital force for the poet. Weiland compares the tone of Williams' Aztec translations with the attitudes of Octavio Paz and finds that his *In the American Grain* (essays) suggests Stephen Berg's *Nothing in the Word* (translations of Aztec poems). The uneasy Aztec alliance between "worldliness and abnegation," on the one hand, and the "unadorned poetic style," on the other, struck a sympathetic chord in Williams.

William B. Ober, M.D., has published an off-beat volume, *Boswell's Clap and Other Essays: Medical Analyses of Literary Men's Afflictions* (So. Ill.). Chapter 7, "William Carlos Williams, M.D.: Physician as Poet" (pp. 206–32), previously published in a medical journal, notes: "Williams was more concerned with the poetic process than the finished product," whereas "the common reader is a consumer and is likely to form his judgment on the finished product: the container and the thing contained."

"Voyage to Ithaca: William Carlos Williams in Paris" (*PULC* 40: 193–214) by Noel Riley Fitch describes the poet's experiences on his various visits to Paris, especially in 1924 and 1927, when Williams met and mingled with the literati who found a welcome at Sylvia Beach's Shakespeare and Company. Williams developed a hostility toward America which was later subdued, even replaced by a renewal of love. He finally insisted that Americans must write about America in the American idiom.

iv. Santayana, Robinson, Aiken, Cummings

William G. Holzberger has edited the *Complete Poems of George Santayana* (Bucknell). His introduction is in effect a 60-page biography of the poet-philosopher covering the early life in Spain, the schooling in America, the undergraduate years at Harvard, the graduate studies in Europe, the years as instructor back at Harvard, the 14 years as professor, the years (1913–40) as independent writer, and the last 12 years, spent in the care of the Blue Sisters in Rome. The emphasis throughout, naturally, is on Santayana's activity as poet. The appendix supplies elaborate notes on the poems (pp. 561–695) and on textual problems (pp. 696–712). This work appears to be exhaustive and definitive.

Nathan A. Scott, Jr., does not discuss Santayana's poetry in his article "Santayana's Poetics of Belief" (*Boundary* 7:199–224) but rather his philosophy, which he called "materialism," not in the scientific sense, but as "an absolutely recalcitrant kind of otherness which can in no way be thought to be called into being by any creative act of the human spirit itself." Rather, Santayana's inalterable belief was that man is "the creator of forms." Here he differed from the New Critics, who would divorce the poem from the writer and, indeed, "from the existential world." Santayana is at the opposite pole, also, from the current proponents of symbolic forms, destructiveness, and phenomenology. A reconsideration of the tenets of his philosophy, says Scott, might well "bring us to the threshold of a new *decision*, as to whether or not we shall give our suffrage to a poetic that does, at bottom, contend for the essential worthlessness of literary art." Santayana's homosexuality is the subject of a passage (pp. 109–14) in Martin's *Homosexual Tradition* (see Crane, above).

There is at least a temporary decline of interest in Robinson. Only two articles have come to my attention this year. William H. Pritchard's "Edwin Arlington Robinson: The Prince of Heartachers" (*ASch* 48:89–100) uses "The Book of Annandale," "Luke Havergal," "For a Dead Lady," "Eros Turannos," "The Sheaves," and other poems to develop the thesis that the lyrical poems of 1910 and 1916 are Robinson at his best—a verbal poet rather than moral or psychological, a reveler "in the felicities of language," as Frost said. Pritchard presents a fair-minded reappraisal of Robinson's work.

Jeffrey L. Spear addresses the often-mentioned comparison between Robinson and Thomas Hardy, finding similarities (with caution) between the two poets. In "Robinson, Hardy, and a Literary Source of 'Eros Turannos'" (*CLQ* 15:58–64) Spear links the Robinson poem with Hardy's "Wives in the Sere" (published a dozen years before "Eros Turannos"). Eight-line stanzas and alternation of masculine and feminine rhymes characterize the structure of both poems. Robinson focuses on one wife rather than "a class of wives" and achieves a "rhetorical masterpiece" by extending Hardy's two-stanza structure to six stanzas, "infinitely more complex." They are similar in another way, however: Robinson's lady, like the women in Hardy's poems, is a victim of time, decay, and death.

Conrad Aiken, a very strong poet, has never received his due. Arthur Waterman finds parallel themes in the short stories and the poetry: consciousness, horror, chaos, death, love, nightmares, and so on. In "The Short Stories of Conrad Aiken" (*SSF* 16:19–31) Waterman resorts to quoting from the last Prelude in *Time in the Rock* because he must acknowledge Aiken's greater gift as writer of poetry than of short stories, which as a whole fail to "develop toward a di-

vine pilgrimage as does the poetry" and are hence "secular" in tone
and interest. As in his poems, but to a less heightened degree (and
frequently less skillful) in the stories, Aiken shapes "two worlds—
things as they are and our imaginative version of them." William W.
Hoffa in "Conrad Aiken: Music and the Poetics of the Prelude" (*FDP*
2:127–44) concentrates on the considerable influence of music (syn-
esthesia and imagery, in part) on the poems many critical readers
consider the product of the peak of Aiken's genius (the 1930s).

Rushworth M. Kidder's *E. E. Cummings: An Introduction to the
Poetry* (Columbia) is another in a good series under the general
editorship of John Unterecker that includes introductions to Marianne
Moore and Wallace Stevens (see *ALS 1969*, pp. 284–85, and *ALS
1977*, p. 363). In a substantial Foreword Unterecker defends Cummings' constancy of style and subject matter. He has selected 96
poems (from all periods) as the poet's best. Kidder's work itself
is comprehensive, interesting, and worthy of attention. His opening
pages straighten out some usually distorted details of the poet's life,
both fact and gossip, as we should expect from his essays on Cummings as artist (see *ALS 1975*, p. 372, and *ALS 1976*, p. 330). True
to his profession as teacher, Kidder provides initially seven "general
rules for paraphrasing." The rest of the book examines each volume
in chronological order from *Tulips and Chimneys* to *73 Poems*. The
author explains the publishing situation of each collection, points out
the meaning of the arrangement of the poems, and explicates many
of them with relation to each other.

JML 7:173–393 provides an "E. E. Cummings Special Number,"
ed. Richard S. Kennedy, author of an upcoming biography. This is
an important issue, containing a dedicatory poem by Nancy Cummings de Forêt, seven solid articles, 24 Cummings poems (20 never
before published and four early versions), documents concerning the
poet's World War I experience in France, and Artem Lozynsky's "Annotated Bibliography of Works on Cummings." This last describes
eight already existing bibliographies, 13 books on the poet, nearly
150 articles (of varying quality), and reviews and comments on
his books, from *The Enormous Room* (1922) through *95 Poems*
(1958). There is also a list of explications of 60 poems.

Cummings is an attractive subject for linguists. Richard D. Cure-
ton has published "E. E. Cummings: A Study of the Poetic Use of
Deviant Morphology" (*PT* 1:213–44), in which, after presenting a

theory of morphological deviation, suggesting "exactly how a reader uses his grammatical competence to arrive at an acceptable reading of the deviant word," the author surveys the morphological processes Cummings departs from, discussing coinages and compiling tables, using quotations from the poems as well as word lists. The longest section of the article is devoted to the prefix "un-."

Guy L. Rotella's *E. E. Cummings: A Reference Guide* (Hall) joins Nancy Carol Joyner's *Edwin Arlington Robinson* and Craig Abbott's *Marianne Moore* in a convenient and practicable series (see *ALS 1978*, pp. 325 and 328). Rotella's book follows the pattern of the others in being devoted to chronological listing and summarizing of "Writings about E. E. Cummings, 1922–1977." The prefatory material includes, besides a selected list of the poet's work, an analytical introduction, which traces by decades the history of Cummings criticism and reviews—an intelligent and helpful account for the reader. "The index interfiles author, title, and subject entries." Rotella has a blanket entry—"Reviews"—to accommodate all such items, including those without indication of title or author. Using Rotella's book as a base, Richard Crowder in "'he's free into the beauty of the truth': A Review Essay" (*AEB* 3:268–83) follows the history of Cummings bibliographical studies from 1940 to 1979, paying particular attention to the notable work of Paul Lauter, George J. Firmage, and Lewis Leary. The essay compares and contrasts Rotella's volume with others in the Hall series and with such works as Bruce Morton's *John Gould Fletcher* (see below) and *Robert Frost* by Frank and Melissa Christensen Lentricchia (*ALS 1976*, pp. 319–20).

v. West, South, Midwest

In "John G. Neihardt and the American Epic (*WAL* 13:309–25) Lucile P. Aly says that *A Cycle of the West* deserves to be called an epic for several reasons: "a rousing story of heroes and heroic action"; "spaciousness" of setting; expansiveness of theme ("the relation of man to the cosmos and to other men"); "movement through archetypal images [and] themes"; and the work's appeal to "the wide audience of ordinary people." Whether or not, as Aly suggests, *A Cycle of the West* will become *the* American epic, her argument for such eventual judgment carries firmer conviction than the earlier statement of Kenneth S. Rothwell (*ALS 1971*, pp. 295–96).

On the occasion of the republication of certain Jeffers books and the appearance of William H. Nolte's *Rock and Hawk* (*ALS 1978*, p. 331) and some heretofore "suppressed poems," Robert Ian Scott reminds us that critics "calling themselves Christians, classicists and humanists" attacked Jeffers and his work quite viciously. In "The Ends of Tragedy: Robinson Jeffers' Satires on Human Self-Importance" (*CRevAS* 10:231–41) Scott comments that such critics probably could not see beyond their emotions, could not "see the world on which our lives depend" in order to escape the miseries their "emotional reactions" were bringing on. Christians probably resented the poet's presenting the death and resurrection of Jesus as a traditional seasonal metaphor of tragedy and were angered by the suggestion that Jesus himself was paranoid and gave us "not salvation . . . but twenty centuries of needless misery." Readers failed to understand (did not want to?) that Jeffers, through satiric contrasts between man's self-importance and the immensity of the universes, was working at ending "the lies men live by."

Douglas L. Peterson maintains that Yvor Winters' poetry, though traditional, modifies the conventions to assist in expressing his profound concern with public and philosophical issues, in flexible verse, skillful and sophisticated. "Yvor Winters' 'By the Road to the Air-Base'" (*SoR* 15:567–74) demonstrates the poet's complexity, compression, power, and intellectual concern in his maturity. Peterson contrasts Winters' "post-Symbolist" method with that of Stevens, a method difficult for Winters to master—the use of "brilliantly descriptive details" to make clear "the conceptual structures of which they are a part."

Bruce Morton's *John Gould Fletcher: A Bibliography* (Kent State) undertakes to make a record of the poet's entire career. The annotations are as noncritical as Morton can make them, providing, rather, an account of "trends of prolificacy, the stature of periodicals in which work was published, geographical trends in output and reception, trends in critical attention and critical reception." The book is divided into the conventional three large parts—works by Fletcher, works about Fletcher, and indices. The section on Fletcher's monographs details 30 items. The listing of book reviews ranges in number from one on *The Crisis of the Film* to 11 each on *Irradiations: Sands and Spray* and *The Burning Mountain*—all told, a comparatively modest amount of reviewing interest. The book as a whole indicates

Fletcher's involvement in two of the most important cultural movements of the first part of our century—Imagism and Southern
Agrarianism.

The poems Donald Davidson was writing in the summer of 1922
were experiments in modern techniques, as Martha E. Cook discloses
in "Dryads and Flappers: Donald Davidson's Early Poetry" (*SLJ*
12,i:18–26). Allen Tate told Davidson "Corynba" was "the finest
you've written." In this so-called "Pan" series Davidson was contrasting the aridity of modern life ("flappers") with the hidden vitality of
life which the protagonist alone, apparently, was aware of ("dryads").

Tate himself was memorialized in several essays. Roy Fuller
("Allen Tate: A Note in Memory," *SoR* 15:521–23) recalls various
meetings with Tate in England. Fuller's judgment: "In Allen's case
the current fashion for poetic disorder seems to have affected somewhat the reputation of his disciplined, intellectual, but turbulent and
sonorous verse. This can only be evanescent folly." Louis D. Rubin,
Jr., testifies that Tate was "the bravest man I ever knew." In "Allen
Tate 1899–1979" (*SR* 87:267–73) Rubin sums up the subject's life and
influence and explains his limited publication as stemming from the
autobiographical nature of his material controlled by his "impeccable
taste." He concedes that his opinion is open to disagreement that
"Allen's conversion to Roman Catholicism was desperate, wholly
sincere, and intense." William Meredith and other friends of the poet's
contribute an anthology of praise, "For Allen Tate" (*QJLC* 36:349–
55). Besides Meredith the eulogists include Malcolm Cowley, Cleanth
Brooks, Louis Coxe, Eudora Welty, and William J. Smith.

Periods in Tate's life are the subject of some biographical essays.
Robert Buffington in "Young Hawk Circling" (*SR* 87:541–56) writes
of the poet's leaving the South in the 1920s and experiencing New
York, England, and France. Tate's marriage to Caroline Gordon
came at this time, and the poet made stimulating contacts with Malcolm Cowley, Hart Crane, Kenneth Burke, the Fugitives (continued),
and other figures of that exciting decade. By 1931 Tate had completed
a circle: the South, New York, Europe, and the South again, always
with deepening perspective. He also enjoyed two sojourns at Princeton in 1939–42 and again in 1949–52. Willard Thorp reports on "Allen
Tate at Princeton" (*PULC* 41:1–21), using as his source the 57 boxes
of Tate papers in the Princeton library. Thorp discusses the poet's
Program in Creative Writing, the various lectures he gave, his rela-

tions with the English Department, his involvement in the Ezra
Pound fracas over the Bollingen Prize, and his conversion to Catholicism with its intellectual problems. The article is packed with biographical detail lighted by Thorp's insights and extended with interesting photographs. Robert Kent in "Allen Tate in Minneapolis" (*NBR*
Apr.–May:3–5) recalls some informal evenings he enjoyed as a student with Allen Tate during the 1960s at the University of Minnesota. Through Tate Kent met interesting and well-known people. On
more public occasions he had a chance to observe Tate's manner of
introducing visiting lecturers. Though throughout his account Kent
emphasizes Tate's gentlemanliness, he shows the man to have been
capable of "backyard wit," albeit tempered by "discretion, even prudence." The picture here drawn of Tate as professor is both vivid and
analytical.

Evelyn Schroth's "Image of Womanhood in the *Spoon River* Portraits" (*MidAmerica* 6:62–71) divides Edgar Lee Masters' female
characters into four categories: the fulfilled ("heroines"), the com-
promisers (they "sublimate"), the beaten ("stifled by oppression"),
and the revolters ("enlightened spirits"). Schroth's classifications are
supported by many quotations. The author concludes, rather obviously, that Masters appeared to favor the first and fourth groups. Herb
Russell continues his analysis of Masters' career with "Imitations of
Spoon River: An Overview" (*WIRS* 2:173–82). Russell sites satiric
imitations from the columns of Franklin P. Adams and lists several
book-length derivatives, from the pens of Henry Savage, August
Derleth, and George Jessel, whose *Elegy in Manhattan* (1961) provides cemetery verses about such celebrities as Fanny Brice, Al Jol-
son, and Babe Ruth. Russell finds "most novel" J. C. Squire's satire in
Reedy's Mirror (1918), "If Gray Had Had to Write His Elegy in the
Cemetery of Spoon River Instead of in That of Stoke Poges." He
thinks these imitations testify to the lasting international appeal of
Masters' most famous work.

William A. Sutton has edited *Carl Sandburg Remembered* (Scarecrow), a collection of reminiscences. Sutton's own meeting with the
poet is recorded on pages 256–62. Part 1, "The Perry Friendship,"
consists of excerpts from a manuscript by Lilly Perry of Los Angeles.
The second part, "A Host of Encounters" (pp. 75–281), presents 76
accounts varying in length and importance of contacts with Sandburg. The contributors range widely: Harry S. Truman, Harry Gold-

en, Cyril Clemens, William O. Douglas, Lesley Frost Ballantine, and Fanny Butcher, to name a few. The book is an enchiridion of impressions and opinions, a few of them unfavorable. (E.g., E. Merrill Root found Sandburg to be "a poseur masquerading as a poet . . . a tedious, artificial mediocrity" [p. 234].) An elaborate division of the index is devoted to Sandburg himself: activities, artistic characteristics, attitudes, events in his life, interests, personal appearance, personal traits, publications, and unpublished materials. With the help of the index, the book should aid would-be biographers and analytical scholars considerably.

Bernard Duffey says that, unlike Masters and Lindsay, Sandburg "located a poetically constructive imagination of" America. This is his conclusion in "Carl Sandburg and the Undetermined Land" (*CentR* 23:295–303). Though, like the other two, Sandburg was to a degree tentative and open, he nevertheless developed "a close and living sense of the native." His total poetic output discloses "a wholeness of perception." With a few overblown exceptions the poems add up to specifics of "the land's own spatial and temporal indeterminateness." As craftsman Sandburg was more concerned with actual practice than with elaborate theory. (Contrast Pound, Eliot, Crane, Stevens, Williams.) Duffy sees the poetry as holding "back from willed ideality." The world is just the commonly presented spectacle, "a sort of proto-naturalistic poetic vision."

What Duffey has done is to contribute to the reevaluation of Sandburg which Paul Ferlazzo says is due in "The Popular Writer, Professors, and the Making of a Reputation: The Case of Carl Sandburg" (*MidAmerica* 6:72–78). Such a new look should be based on honest judgment of his "poetic merits and failures" to free us from "the burden of opinion we have inherited." Sandburg's poetry, says Ferlazzo, is taught mostly in high schools, is hardly mentioned in the colleges, though his prose has fared somewhat better. The problem as Ferlazzo sees it is that the professors and literary critics have not conceded greatness to him. What has worked against Sandburg has been his popularity, his social philosophy, and "the long reign . . . of the New Critics."

Owen Hawley's "Lindsay's 1908 Walking Trip" (*WIRS* 2:156–72) describes the second of Vachel Lindsay's three walking tours, this one from New York City to Hiram, Ohio. (The first was in 1906; the third, in 1912). Details come largely from the last 94 pages of *A Handy*

Guide for Beggars (1916), which has received little critical attention. Hawley also uses two Lindsay holographs, a letter and a three-page manuscript, published here for the first time. He illustrates his article with photographs of people Lindsay met while tramping through Pennsylvania. The trip lasted from 28 April to 16 May, during which time the poet developed many ideas to be used in writing and illustrating in the years to come.

Dennis Camp in "Vachel Lindsay and the Chicago *Herald*" (*WIRS* 2:70–88) extends the rather casual comment of Eleanor Ruggles that Lindsay was an occasional contributor to the *Herald* in 1914. This article gives a chronological account of his contributions during 1914 and 1915—33 poems, 12 of which were never printed elsewhere, and a number of prose pieces. These items back up Lindsay's "continuing interest in moon poems and chants," in film, women's rights, travel, and "the wretchedness of the world at war" and his resulting ambivalence. Incidentally, the first item in the "Notes and Documents" section of this issue of *WIRS* (pp. 89–90) is a detailing of the contents of Lindsay's Springfield house, of interest to biographers and other scholars. Dr. Camp and his wife are the curators.

Marc Chénetier has edited the *Letters of Vachel Lindsay* (Burt Franklin), with a Foreword by Nicholas Cave Lindsay, the poet's son. The editor has carefully selected 199 letters to show Lindsay in his various roles—as family man, teacher, higher vaudevillian, troubled celebrity, and poet. Many letters are excluded because of careless composition, shallow comments, and publication elsewhere; so there are some biographical gaps in the collection. The portrait comes through, however, of a "rich and many-colored personality" reduced to paranoia and mere entertainment while at the same time (the 1920s) continuing to write a number of memorably beautiful pieces. Recipients of the letters include many prominent literary figures. Chénetier has given us a warm, vigorous, exciting collection, to be highly recommended to scholars devoted to midwestern poetry, but also to other readers interested in biography, in vivid style, and in the world of American life and letters in general.

vi. Wallace Stevens

"Manuscripts of Wallace Stevens" by Louis L. Martz (*YULG* 54:51–67) describes in detail the 1974 gift of the Rev. John Curry Gay to the

Beinecke Library at Yale: pencil autographs of four poems; seven typescripts or carbon copies; "an early version of the first four sections of 'The Comedian as the Letter C'" under its first title, "From the Journal of Crispin"; two letters (one from Gilbert Seldes); a wallet; and a snapshot of the poet's daughter Holly.

In preparing a doctoral dissertation Glen MacLeod has discovered "some important, uncatalogued material" in the Princeton library. In "A New Version of Wallace Stevens" (*PULC* 41:22–28) MacLeod discusses the poet's correspondence with Whit Burnett, editor of *Story Magazine* and of the anthology *This Is My Best* (1942). He lists the poems Stevens selected to be included in the anthology and analyzes them to arrive at the thinking behind the choice. Stevens apparently wanted to say that the poet must always be receptive ("ignorant") in order to be always surprised and to find richness in his observations.

On the problem of ultimate belief Lawrence S. Cunningham's "The Poet as Theologian of Secularity" (*Commonweal* 106:619–22) indicates that Stevens apparently read little theology but felt that the duty of the poet is to show the imagination as the "primal source" of satisfaction. Stevens himself was always noodling over the interplay of imagination and reality. Cunningham quotes Bruce Kauffman as saying that Stevens found it impossible to "trust in the beneficence of life." The author also cites Allen Tate's comment that Stevens, disliking the commonplace, wanted to touch "the essential and the eternal," though he could not "accept the sacramentality of the world." Differing from Roethke, who saw a "possibility of transcendent experience," Stevens, says Cunningham, worked unsuccessfully all his life to bridge the "chasm between self and world." On the same subject Andrew J. Angyal's "Wallace Stevens' 'Sunday Morning' as Secular Belief" (*C&L* 29,i:30–38), in a careful exegesis of the famous poem, sees in it "a stoical strength" derived from "the rhythms of change in nature." Angyal quotes "The Emperor of Ice Cream" to show, however, that Stevens was not merely resigned to the fact of death but could present it as tawdry and vulgar, in other words, far from transcendent. He also cites "Of Heaven Considered as a Tomb" and "A High-Toned Old Christian Woman." In the first the self looks to "itself for strength and courage." The second replaces orthodoxy with the triumphant imagination.

Again, pursuing a related theme, Michael Hattersley builds his study, "Wallace Stevens' Poetry of Perspective: 'The Auroras of Autumn'" (*MSE* 6:60–76), on the previous brilliant work of Helen Vendler and Harold Bloom. Hattersley sees "Auroras" as interpreting "the existence of a world external to text or self." The poem has exorcised from the auroras any "divine figuration." The new-found human innocence looks at the earth's innocence. "The Auroras of Autumn" refines a method; it does not attempt to possess the world. This essay strikes me as a fresh and supportive statement of the poet's point of view.

The Stevens poems in relation to the other arts engage the interest of some writers. Judith Rinde Sheridan develops the influence of Picasso on Stevens. "The Picasso Connection: Wallace Stevens' 'The Man with the Blue Guitar'" (*ArQ* 35:77–89) elaborates on the long-acknowledged relation between the poem and the blue-period *The Old Guitarist*. Then Sheridan points out that both artists worked at illumination rather than distortion. For them both, however, a work of art was not a reality, but actually "an ingenious contrivance designed to delight the imagination." For Stevens a poem was "word play." For him "Things as they are, are things as they seem." Music was another art that Stevens was interested in. To *The Arts and Their Interrelations* (*BuR* 24,ii[1978]), ed. Harry R. Garvin, John N. Serio contributes "The Ultimate Music Is Abstract: Charles Ives and Wallace Stevens" (pp. 120–31). Working from opposite sides, Stevens and Ives make many connections between poetry and music. For example, Stevens often thinks of "the imagination as an instrument, usually a guitar, and the poet as musician." Both he and Ives try to attain "an abstract sense of the music of poetry and the poetry of music." They both consider music "feeling . . . not sound." They differ in that Ives affirms an idealism derived from Emerson, whereas Stevens cannot "admit a transcendental reality." Rather Stevens finds satisfying the act of pursuit, "a state of mind,/Nothing more," which can renew through transformed reality. For both Ives and Stevens, however, the "ultimate poetry . . . may be known, but never reached."

Relating the work of Stevens to that of other poets seems to be inevitable. Robert Greer Cohn in "Stevens and Mallarmé" (*CLS* 16: 344–53) compares "The Snow Man" with "Le vierge, le vivace." "Notes toward a Supreme Fiction," says Cohn, is a kind of "summing-up in the later Mallarmé manner." Stevens' themes and images often resemble Mallarmé's. Cohn piles up details in proof. He thinks of the "marvellous shimmer" of Mallarmé's *Poesies* when he reads of Stevens' various ways of looking at sea-clouds or a blackbird. Stevens, however, adds an American freshness and an "extended daring." Patricia A. Parker has elaborated on her dissertation (under Geoffrey Hartman, Yale) in *Inescapable Romance: Studies in the Poetics of a Mode* (Princeton). After discussing Ariosto, Spenser, Milton, and Keats as romantic poets (i.e., both searching for and always avoiding any conclusion), in an Epilogue Parker comes to Mallarmé, Valéry, and at last Stevens. On pages 236–43 she opines that the American's poetry looks back "on the meaning of romance for English poetry since Spenser." Stevens appears to write in anti-Romantic style, clearing out the "rotted names." He nevertheless senses that such reduction will not be enough, for romance is inescapable: it is impossible not to see the sun as "gold flourisher"; romance must remain "open-ended."

Excerpted from Peter A. Brazeau's forthcoming biography of Stevens (Seabury), "'My Dear Old Boy': The Wallace Stevens-Arthur Powell Friendship" (*Antaeus* 36:148–65) outlines the 30-year friendship of the poet and the Georgia-born jurist. This southern connection is frequently reflected in the Stevens poetry. Powell encouraged his friends to read Stevens. The fact that the poet went south often to enjoy jaunts with his "dear old boy," Judge Powell, should dissipate the frequent impression that he was quite reclusive. One poem reflecting the southern experience is central to Celeste Turner Wright's "Stevens and the Black Emperor of Key West" (*ArQ* 35:65–76). Wright believes Stevens had black people in mind when writing "The Emperor of Ice-Cream." She draws elaborately on biographical evidence (especially the poet's visits to Key West) to explain the provenance of the poem.

In "Folk Etymology in Sigmund Freud, Christian Morgenstern, and Wallace Stevens" (*CritI* 6:65–78) Samuel Jay Keyser and Alan Prince use examples from the past of how people are persuaded that language itself can create a world. (The second chapter of Genesis is a case in point.) Quotations from both Freud and the German poet Morgenstern support the thesis. Stevens, Keyser and Prince find, provides the "final, subtler example" in "Infanta Marina." The assumption is that words are "saturated with meaning" to be found "through a kind of inspired analysis"; that is, Stevens creates, not religion (see Genesis), but poetry, through the application of the principles of folk etymology. For example, the two lines "In the roamings of her fan,/Partaking of the sea . . ." illustrate their point; for one thing, they combine "fan" and "sea" into "fancy" and take off from there.

Robert DeMaria, Jr., sees Stevens' image of his reader as closer to Coleridge's view than to Samuel Johnson's. His essay, " 'The Thinker as Reader': The Figure of the Reader in the Writing of Wallace Stevens" (*Genre* 12:243–68), recalls the poet's dictum that to the "right reader" his poetry presents no problems. For the most elevated kind of reader "the object and its image become inseparable." Just as "Stevens's voice is solitary," so "his reader" is "solitary, individual." In other words, nothing comes between the reader and the text. (Here he differs from Coleridge, whose reader is one with the author of the text.) For Stevens the poem is a written, not an oral, phenomenon and hence requires, not a listener or a viewer, but a reader.

For Stevens aficianados *SoR* 15:769–984 will prove a treasure trove. "The Wallace Stevens Centennial Essays" begin with two notes on the origin of "The Emperor of Ice-Cream." Holly Stevens and Donald E. Stanford scotch the rumor that the poem was written for Holly. For one thing, Holly was not even born at the time of its composition. The ten substantial essays that follow are frankly too rich to be treated in any detail here. Roy Harvey Pearce uses "Chocorua to Its Neighbor" as his text (pp. 777–91). Grosvenor E. Powell works out from Crispin toward "central poetry" (pp. 792–810). Milton J. Bates studies the Nietzsche-Stevens parallel (pp. 811–39). Herbert J. Stern considers the Coleridge-Stevens axis (pp. 840–50). William H. Pritchard underscores the delights of what friendly critics list as the best Stevens poems (pp. 851–76). George S. Lensing analyzes the contents of a Stevens notebook (pp. 877–920). Samuel French Morse focuses on the concrete illustrations by which the poet illuminates his ideas (pp. 921–32). Price Caldwell startles us with the title of his essay—" 'Sunday Morning': Stevens' Makeshift Romantic Lyric" (pp. 933–52). Betty Buchsbaum draws on ideas from a forthcoming book to study the poems of Stevens' old age (pp. 953–67). Lynette Carpenter argues that Stevens was inclined to give meaning to groups of poems, as in "The Man on the Dump," "On the Road Home," and "The Latest Freed Man" from *Parts of a World* (pp. 968–84). This stimulating series of studies is a worthy successor to a similar collection in *SoR* 7 (*ALS 1971*, pp. 308–10).

Finally, Craig Raine makes an assessment of Stevens' entire work in "Wallace Stevens, 1879–1955: A Centenary Essay" (*Encounter* Nov.: 59–60 ff). Raine's judgment is that the early poems ("full of life") and the last (informed with an awareness of approaching death) are much better than those of the middle period, when the poet's rhetoric was needless and even emptily resounding. Raine's theory is that Stevens, disappointed at having virtually no readership for the early work, underrated the importance of being understood: sometimes "the syntax simply melts." In his final period, however, the work returned to lucidity, to poems "beautiful and intelligible." "He was at ease with his audience at last."

vii. Robert Frost

"Robert Frost and Edward Thomas: Two Soldier Poets" (*NEQ* 52: 147–76) by Paul M. Cubeta is a biographical account of the brief friendship between the two poets: their early insecurity, moodiness, and melancholy, their feeling that they had failed. Cubeta follows Frost's and Thomas' translation of their companionship into poetry and illustrates their appreciation for each other's verse as well as their concern about the public reception of their work. Echoes of Thomas appear in Frost's work as late as 1958. For the short time that they were privileged to know each other they "enjoyed the creative and sustaining power of poetry, of love, of nature, of a moment shared." Laurence Perrine in "Frost's 'Iris by Night'" (*CP* 12:35–43) defends this poem (about Frost and Thomas) against superficial and outright mistaken readings of other critics. It is a metaphorical affirmation of "the true miracle" of the friendship between these two men—American and British.

Kathryn Gibbs Harris examines the works of Lawrence Thompson and Robert S. Newdick in "Two Difficult Biographies of Robert Frost" (*L&P* 29:19–24). Gibbs decides that, though Thompson introduces more data and "dramatization," Newdick is important because he adds to, reinforces, and contrasts with Thompson. She discusses at length the influence of William James on Frost. She disagrees with William A. Sutton, editor of the Newdick material (*ALS 1976*, p. 320): the evidence, for her, indicates that Frost's father's personality disintegrated because of excessive drinking and physical illness. She concludes that the two biographies prove that the poet was "an imperfect man like any other man." Frost's attempted suicide in Virginia's Dismal Swamp in November 1894 has been mentioned but not explained by biographers. Rosemary F. Franklin thinks the young man, depressed by what he thought was failure in his suit for the hand of Elinor White, was possibly following the route of the youth in Thomas Moore's "A Ballad: The Lake of the Dismal Swamp" (1803). In telling of the episode in later years with a mixture of teasing amusement and disdain for his youthful self-pity, Frost was perhaps undertaking to "exorcise . . . the demons still with him." Franklin makes this conjecture in "Literary Model for Frost's Suicide Attempt in the Dismal Swamp" (*AL* 50:645–46). She also studies the influence of Francis T. Palgrave's *Golden Treasury*, second series (1896), on the poet. Her article, "Frost's 'Worn Book of Golden Song' " (*ELN* 16:315–21), names several Victorian poems as sources for Frost, both echoes and departures, "absorption and transmutation."

The poet's familiar comment about the importance of hazards (meter, rhyme, stanzaic structure, etc.) in the game of composing verse is the subject of Wayne Tefs's "Measures as Countermeasures: The Function of Form in Frost's Poetry" (*GyS* 6:3–17). Victor E. Vogt in "Narrative and Drama in the Lyric: Robert Frost's Strategic Withdrawal" (*CritI* 5:529–51) argues that narrative and dramatic modes have made strong contribution to the survival of Frost's lyric poetry, though he agrees with Radcliffe Squires that Frost actually cared little about narrative in his poems. Vogt calls "Mending Wall" lyrical in that its chief value is "the speaker's revealed state of mind." He maintains that most of Frost's dialogue poems strategically withdraw from emphasized interest in story to create "new potentials for the lyric genre."

Turning to another form, Noam Flinker discusses "Robert Frost's Masques: The Genre and the Poems" (*PLL* 15:59–72). Flinker presents a case for the masques as modifications of the Renaissance genre. He faces up to possible objections to his comparison of Frost with Renaissance poets by examining closely the history and form of the genre and arriving at an interpretation of Frost masques as "generically relevant to the titles," there being, for example, more words than action as well as recognizable "machinery and devices."

Daniel Pearlman's ingenious reading of "Neither Out Far Nor In Deep" is the basis of "Robert Frost: A Political Satire Unveiled" (*Agenda* 17,ii:41–63). Pearlman finds that this poem, in a guarded manner, is attacking leftist intellectuals as "potential traitors to

America." He draws particular attention to the third line: "They turn their back on the land." He refers to "Build Soil," a letter to Louis Untermeyer, and an interview in *Rural America* as sources for the poem. In the light of Frost's conservative view, this is quite a convincing interpretation.

Frost's geographical consciousness is the concern of two items. William Mulder's "Seeing 'New Englandly': Planes of Perception in Emily Dickinson and Robert Frost" (*NEQ* 52:550–59) presents both poets as drawing the provincial picture, finding the moral in nature, and getting at the psychic meaning ("to search the landscape for signs of grace"). For Dickinson "the vision is both beatific and agonized," whereas for Frost it "is pastoral and stoic, courageously humanistic." Mulder thinks of both poets as "profoundly religious."

John C. Kemp's *Robert Frost and New England: The Poet as Regionalist* (Princeton) aims to correct what Kemp feels to be critical misconceptions about Frost's relation to New England. In lengthy dissections of "Mending Wall" and "Christmas Trees," Kemp points up the poet's inconsistency and even fallibility in the use of New England scene and character, then delineates Frost's actual struggle with the fact of New England and how in his "greatest poems" he passes beyond an adopted regionalism (local color) in attaining a a kind of religious attitude, reverential and sacred. In its task of revising glib and stereotyped views of Frost's Yankee stance, the book presents full and complex rereadings of many familiar poems. A 25-page appendix provides a list of commentaries on Frost's regionalism, many of the entries being annotated.

Another kind of withdrawal than that described by Vogt (above) is the topic of Lyle Domina's "Thoreau and Frost: The Search for Reality" (*BSUF* 19,iv[1978]:67–72). Domina reminds us that both Thoreau and Frost withdrew from "reality," not to escape, but to find its meaning. Frost had less confidence than Thoreau "in man's capacity to discover the nature of reality." Though they both wanted to know exactly what life is, Domina says Frost went at the quest calmly, whereas Thoreau's search was urgent and colored by excitement. Neither wanted to be separated from the earth, but rather to participate in both the spiritual and the physical, not an impossibility if each level of consciousness were granted both "respect and integrity."

Darrel Abel has added two more fruitful essays on Frost to the two he published last year (see *ALS 1978*, pp. 340–41). In discussing "Two Philosophical Poets: Frost, Emerson, and Pragmatism" (*ESQ* 25:119–36), Abel says that Emerson was the strongest influence on Frost among the poets and that William James's pragmatism was a congenial view. Frost found reality "a process of becoming," the product of imagination, will, and "a vital principle" in nature and insisted he was no Platonist but "more of an Aristotelian." Imagination and energy are accompanied by "awareness of the immense mystery of the physical world." For Frost the self is elemental, even existential. The reader can reconcile the Frost dichotomy of the static quality of philosophy and his unwillingness to hold to a creed. What matters is sincerity, not content, of belief. As Frost grew older, he became more and more "philosophical" and moved away from the concrete toward generalizations.

"Robert Frost's 'Flirting with the Entelechies' " (*Renascence* 32: 33–49) again places the poet on the side of William James in defining "the fear of God" as a fear of being unworthy in the sight "of someone who knows us at least as well as we know ourselves." In this essay Abel thinks that Frost felt one must devote time to enriching oneself in order to make a contribution of any value to society. He concludes that communication does not always require "contiguity and language." As for entelechies, if some men find it impossible to appreciate and believe in values above them, those with belief in the transcendent are at fault if they "trample down and despise" those others, for men must tolerate one another and work together while at the same time recognize, even if not understanding, the rights and values of others.

The industrious Kathryn Gibbs Harris has edited, written an introduction for, and contributed an article to *Robert Frost: Studies of the Poetry* (Hall), a collection of 15 essays, which are separated into four sections. The first, "Form," consists of two articles, one looking at Frost's efforts at "old ways to be new," the other using both textual and linguistic methods to produce a fresh reading of "Nothing Gold Can Stay." The second pair of essays, "Attitude," present (1) Frost's view of the world and (2) the tension between commitment and irony. The section "Problems" (four essays) points up the paradox of necessity as against freedom and the practical difficulties confronting biographer and bibliographer. The final group, "Background," includes discussion of Frost's knowledge of Latin and Greek, his acquaintance with Wordsworth's Lucy poems, his reliance on his own life and on a kind of psychology as source material, his lyric impulse, his employment of Biblical material, and the feasibility of psychoanalytical techniques for making meanings clearer to the general reader. Of the 15 contributors I will name only a few: in addition to Harris, essays have been written by Donald J. Greiner, Philip L. Gerber, Nancy C. Joyner, and Mordecai Marcus. This collection, full of solid scholarship (always, of course, open to difference of opinion) is both reliable and stimulating. It should have wide appeal, not only to Frost researchers but to lay readers as well.

Purdue University

17. Poetry: The 1940s to the Present

Sandra M. Gilbert

Commenting on contemporary literature is in a way like sketching your own image as you move in front of a mirror or recording the stream of your own consciousness. Because you are both observer and observed, you are so deeply ensnared in your subject that your own motion necessarily skews the lines with which you try to record that motion. Besides, the mirror's right hand is reality's left hand, so you are deceived by your own participation. At the same time, however, just because you are in some sense inseparable from your subject, you obviously have a privileged knowledge of many of its inmost details. If you look away from the mirror of your own mind, you see that for miles around, in every direction, there are familiar trees, solid as newspapers or magazines of verse. No future critic will ever confront them so clearly and closely as you do. But, lost in such a maze of dailiness, how can you hope to determine the shape of the forest?

The enormous mass of material I confronted in preparing this review suggests that platoons of ambitious critics have, in fact, nourished a hope of drawing the figure in the mirror, or at least describing the shape of the literary forest. Like my predecessor, James E. Breslin, I found much of their work dull or trivial; like him, too, I thought some of it was disfigured by angry partisanship or critical pretentiousness. Nevertheless, of the more than 25 books and 85 articles that I surveyed, a respectable number were worth serious consideration, with particularly admirable contributions coming from Charles Molesworth, Warner Berthoff, Jonathan Holden, Barbara Gelpi, and Robert K. Martin (on various aspects of the contemporary "scene"), from Helen Vendler (on Robert Lowell), from Jay Parini and Audrey Rodgers (on Theodore Roethke), from Gary Lane, Sister

This chapter could not have been written without the invaluable research assistance of Roger Gilbert.

Bernetta Quinn, Margaret Dickie Uroff, J. D. McClatchy, and Jon
Rosenblatt (on Sylvia Plath), and from Harold Bloom (on John Ashbery and John Hollander).

i. General Studies

In one way or another all the writers who published criticism of contemporary poetry in 1979 grappled with the obvious yet often overwhelming problems of the participant/observer, even while they
reaped the rewards of contemporaneity. But in attempting to provide
overviews of the field the most ambitious general works on the subject necessarily encountered the deepest difficulties. As encyclopedic
surveys of recent poetry, Daniel Hoffman's three chapters on postwar
poetry in the *Harvard Guide*, together with Elizabeth Janeway's essay
on "Women's Literature" and Nathan Scott's discussion of "Black
Literature," dramatically illustrate the contemporary critic's interlocking advantages and disadvantages.

Himself a poet of stature, with six collections of verse to his credit,
Hoffman has an intimate knowledge of the current poetry scene that
few future historians will ever duplicate. In addition, because he is a
notably responsible critic, he is able to set neat summaries of the
careers of major contemporary figures into the context of an accurate
and impartial history of American poetry from about 1945 to about
1970. Thus, although he has no special theory about the period—
indeed, one feels keenly at times the lack of a serious intellectual
context—he is a good guide to its major features, with his chapters on
"Poetry: After Modernism" and "Poetry: Schools of Dissidents" offering useful overviews of post-Modernist phenomena that are past or
passing or to come. His account of the stylistic experimentation that
so many poets undertook in the early 1960s as the "academic" style
of the 1950s slowly disintegrated is particularly lucid, as is his
analysis of the different schools ("confessional," Beat, Black Mountain, New York, Surrealist) that marked the emergence of a self-
consciously post- (or anti-) Modernist poetry. In addition, new readers of such important figures as Lowell, Berryman, Bishop, Olson, and
Ashbery will undoubtedly find that Hoffman's concise introductions to
these poets provide valuable guidance as they enter what may sometimes seem bewilderingly various *oeuvres*. Finally, Hoffman's surveys of recent poetry are helpfully supplemented by Scott's discus-

sions of a few major black poets (Brooks, Hayden) together with Janeway's accounts of the works of women like Rich, Rukeyser, Levertov, and Kumin.

Unfortunately, however, the third chapter illustrates some of the major difficulties with which the critic of contemporary writing must grapple. Not too felicitously entitled "Dissidents from Schools" (mainly, one supposes, to balance the earlier "Schools of Dissidents"), it finally seems as empty of real ideas as its title's artifice suggests. Discussing such diverse figures as Ammons, Wagoner, Hecht, Kinnell, and Levine—poets whose work has not been primarily associated with any particular school or style—Hoffman produces what is merely a list, with no special point or shape: the forest has been obscured by the trees. Again, in noting the contributions of even more recent writers like Gerald Stern, Norman Dubie, and Marilyn Hacker, he offers merely a sketchy compendium, for which he himself apologizes ("this is not intended as a definitive list"). His failure here argues that the critic who is unable to theorize about the literary forest he himself inhabits may ultimately be unable to offer guidance through its lesser-known dells and thickets. But of course—to continue the metaphor—how *can* a critic, contemplating careers very much in process, predict the shapes of trees to come? Hoffman's weakness in grasping the nature of the poetry that this time and this place are producing raises a serious question about the value of a project which defines itself, the way this book does, as a *guide* to contemporary literature. Will chapters on recent fiction and poetry be updated annually, or at least every decade? If not, the work will obviously soon be a guide not to the present but to the past; at the very least, it will have to be retitled.

The organization of the *Harvard Guide*, with its partial separation of black and women poets from "mainstream" poets, raises yet another general question. While it is, of course, important to help readers understand the ways in which blacks and women participate in special literary subcultures, such separation-for-analysis can turn into unhealthy ghettoization unless the critic-historian is careful to note the reciprocal dynamics that govern relationships between such literary subcultures and "mainstream" poetry. Both as editor of the *Guide* and as author of the work's three chapters on contemporary verse, Hoffman seems to have been insufficiently aware of this problem. No doubt because he supposed Scott and Janeway would deal definitively with black poetry and women's poetry, he omitted discussion of all black poets and of many women poets from his three chapters. In fact, however, because they had such large fields to cover, both Scott and Janeway were far more perfunctory in their accounts of black and female poetic movements than Hoffman was in his accounts of white male poetic movements. Yet the new black poetry produced by writers like Baraka, Evans, Sanchez, Harper, and Lorde has been a contemporary literary phenomenon at least as vital and influential as the Beat poetry of the late 1950s and early 1960s. Similarly, the self-consciously female and sometimes consciously feminist poetry of women like Wakoski, di Prima, Griffin, Grahn, and alta has been as notable a phenomenon as the playful Surrealism of the New York school. Intentionally or not, then, the effect of the Scott and Janeway chapters, both important and commendable efforts in themselves, has been to distort literary history by filtering out the achievements of blacks and women. Indeed, Hoffman's three chapters leave the impression that most truly significant contemporary poetry has been written by white men, with the Scott and Janeway essays offering supplementary notes on what appear to be subordinate kinds of poetry written by blacks and women.[1]

Charles Molesworth's *The Fierce Embrace* (Missouri) is less ambitiously encyclopedic than the *Harvard Guide* and thus encounters fewer major problems than Hoffman's chapters. At the same time, however, because Molesworth makes a more serious effort than Hoffman does to formulate a general *theory* of contemporary poetics, his book sometimes seems partial or incomplete, precisely because he bases his ideas primarily on the works of just ten supposedly representative writers (Roethke, Lowell, Ginsberg, O'Hara, Kinnell, Bly, Levine, Ashbery, Plath, Sexton). Finally, then, his is a lively, sometimes quirky collection of not entirely integrated essays, many of which have already been individually reviewed in earlier volumes of *ALS*. What is especially notable about his work as a whole is its engagement with the problem of audience, a problem that in Molesworth's view ranks with the struggle for publication and the "anxiety of influence" as a difficulty which particularly shapes the plight of contemporary poets. A "fretful struggle *just to be heard* dominates

1. The distortion described here also has been a problem for *ALS*. We have compromised by reviewing all scholarship on black writers in a separate chapter, but women writers are treated wherever they belong by period or genre—Ed.

much of contemporary poetry, and thereby shapes its idiom," this critic argues. Nevertheless, as his fairly diverse, if limited, pantheon of poets suggests, a number of poets *are* heard, and he provides them with a line of descent, proposing that Roethke is a poetic father of us all who begot not only confessional poetry but also such phenomena as "deep imagery, neosurrealism, and the return to a kind of pastoral ecstasy, as well as the use of mythical parable."

In a similarly useful and imaginative chapter Molesworth juxtaposes Lowell and Ginsberg to suggest wittily that "their fullest voices were achieved through their ability to make the public events they often deplored into something like private musings." Though he is good on its lineage and some of its practitioners, however, his discussion of "confessional poetry" itself is disappointing, with an especially cursory dismissal of Plath and Sexton. Yet he partly compensates for this failing by a fine chapter on Bly as well as a lively discussion of the contemporary role of "magazines and magazine verse," in which he advances the somewhat chilling idea that for poets, reduced to anonymity by an indifferent or even hostile society, the literary magazine is "often just an elaborate form of correspondence, a sort of postal salon."

Warner Berthoff's *A Literature Without Qualities* (Calif.) offers even more sweeping theses, based on sketchier evidence, than *The Fierce Embrace*; nevertheless Berthoff is probably more interesting than either Hoffman or Molesworth. Since 1945, Berthoff suggests, American writers, novelists and poets alike, have been in the grip of a mass paranoia, in which a sense of the overwhelming power of modern society's "control systems"—reflected in plots like those of Burroughs, Pynchon, and Heller, where "nothing . . . is contingent or accidental"—is coupled with a corollary consciousness of the individual writer's helplessness and invisibility, even inaudibility. For poets in particular, says Berthoff, such a sense of anonymity (close to some of the literary phenomena Molesworth describes) means that nothing matters as much as "the writer's overmastering concern with staying alive as writer," and consequently even "the myth of power and creative efficacy implicit in the very words *poetry* and *poem* begins to seem a hollow joke."

Ultimately, Berthoff argues, poets carry on the fight against such anonymity in the verse-journal (e.g., *Notebook*, *Sphere*, etc.), "our reigning formal solution" which is also possibly "our chief instrument of performative self-deception," for in this fragmentary and tentative record of daily experience dehumanized, exhausted artists prove to themselves that they are still alive. Ambitious and sometimes excessive, this critic's vision of recent poetry is worth attention, especially because it proposes a continuity between the concerns of the contemporary poet and those of the contemporary novelist, but this theory would have appeared more notable and less extravagant if it had been more carefully grounded in serious readings of major poems that he mentions only in passing.

Berthoff's theorizing would have profited, too, from a more serious reading of the many self-defining aesthetic testaments now becoming available from poets themselves. Ironically, this critic did prepare his hypothesis about contemporary poetry by marshalling a good deal of empirical evidence. Little of it, however, was drawn directly from poets; rather, as Berthoff takes pains to explain, he studied essays and reviews that appeared in the first two-years' run of the critical journal *Parnassus*. Reading *A Field Guide to Contemporary Poetry and Poetics*, ed. Stuart Friebert and David Young (Longman) —a book which may well be this year's most significant collection of prose-about-verse—one cannot help wondering why so perspicacious a writer as Berthoff based his ideas on what are essentially secondary sources when poetry magazines like *Field*, the *American Poetry Review*, and the *New York Quarterly* (as well as many others) regularly print strikingly helpful primary sources. That criticism of contemporary poetry has become criticism of criticism is particularly disheartening when one considers the easy availability of such direct evidence. For if the disadvantage of critics of contemporary literature is an inherent blindness to the shape of the forest, surely it is to their advantage that as they wander, unseeing, along winding paths, they may suddenly hear the trees begin to speak.

Reprinting five sets of essays that have appeared over the years in *Field*, Friebert and Young have put together a particularly useful compendium of tree-speech. Their anthology is, of course, uneven, as any such collection must inevitably be. But it includes Denise Levertov's revealing "Work and Inspiration: Inviting the Muse," Donald Hall's wonderful "Goatfoot, Milktongue, Twinbird: The Psychic Origins of Poetic Form"—a work that is a particularly apt illustration of one post-Modern aesthetic, Robert Bly's "Reflections on the Origins of Poetic Form," Galway Kinnell's "Poetry, Personality, and Death," and Adrienne Rich's "Poetry, Personality, and Wholeness: A Response to Galway Kinnell," as well as an energetic symposium on "the poetic line" and a group of meditations on the prose poem highlighted by a crotchety, half-allegorical, half-confessional piece by Russell Edson. Altogether, the scholar seeking real evidence of the state of the art of poetry this year could not find a richer collection of documents. Ranging from quiet analyses to bitter polemics, these essays illustrate, as few critical exegeses could, the special assumptions and reservations that mark the thinking of at least one major group of post-Modernist poets.

Six volumes published by the University of Michigan Press as part of a series called "Poets on Poetry" attempt the same task of documentation that *A Field Guide* does so well. In fact, a number of the pieces reprinted in the Michigan series may have originally been stimulated by queries from Friebert and Young, who increasingly appear as the twin Diogeneses of contemporary verse, seeking, lanterns in hand, some Ultimate Truth about mid-20th-century poetics. Notably the Michigan volumes reproduce a few of the most striking *Field Guide* essays (e.g., "Goatfoot, Milktongue, Twinbird"). Nevertheless, as primary sources these collections nicely supplement the Friebert/Young anthology. The series includes Galway Kinnell's *Walking Down the Stairs: Selections from Interviews* (1978), William Stafford's *Writing the Australian Crawl: Views on the Writer's Vocation* (1978), Donald Hall's *Goatfoot, Milktongue, Twinbird: Interviews, Essays, and Notes on Poetry, 1970–76* (1978), Donald Davie's *Trying to Explain*, Diane Wakoski's *Toward a New Poetry* (1980), and Maxine Kumin's *To Make a Prairie: Essays on Poets, Poetry, and Country Living*, with Hall's perhaps the single strongest volume but all offering evidence that will surely be useful to the student of recent verse.

Besides the *Field Guide* and the Michigan series, 1979 saw the publication of three other lively anthologies of writings by poets on poetry. Robert Peters' *The Great American Poetry Bake-off* (Scarecrow) is a witty collection of essays and reviews by a poet who is also an accomplished critic-teacher. The title essay, a scathing-but-funny putdown of W. S. Merwin, may be the best example of this writer's comic-polemic mode, but the book also includes scathing-but-revealing pieces about major Po Biz journals like *APR* and *Poetry*, pieces which illustrate the plight of the eager poet in a ferocious market-place far more tellingly than, say, Charles Molesworth's graver medi-tations. Similarly, Richard Eberhart's *Of Poetry and Poets* (Illinois) assembles a poet's particularly vivid reminiscences of recent writers from Pound and Frost to Lowell and Roethke. Eberhart's "West Coast Rhythms" offers a glimpse of the so-called Beat movement in its innocent youth, and his dazzling "Literary Death" is a bravura essay in tragicomedy: "When Eliot died he had laid down so many words that it seemed a natural transition to further words and con-siderations. The death of Hart Crane was so far back that it seems a fable, but it seemed a fable then." This book will interest students of both Modernist and post-Modernist poetry. Finally, many students of recent verse will also want to read *Earth Poetry: Selected Essays & Interviews of William Everson, 1950–1977*, ed. Lee Bartlett (Berke-ley: Oyez), an anthology of aesthetic and mystical statements that spans this poet's lively career, from his days as "Brother Antoninus" to his more recent incarnation as plain "William Everson."

Yet another kind of primary source that the student of recent verse should not ignore is, of course, the literary interview. Along with *Candid Camera*, home movies, oral history, and polaroid snapshots this uniquely contemporary genre is a product of our strikingly self-conscious and electronically adept age of tapes and films. As every writer knows, and every critic should know, anyone who has pub-lished a few books gets interviewed incessantly, so that many of the intellectual playlets regularly offered in periodicals and anthologies will be trivial or repetitious. Still, some are worth reading, especially for their occasionally unguarded revelations about the aesthetic as-sumptions upon which contemporary writers operate. A number of the Michigan volumes mentioned earlier include such useful con-versations with authors. Other interviews published during 1979 include dialogues with William Dickey (*NER* 2:127–44), with David Ignatow (*Paris Review* 76:54–59), with Galway Kinnell (*ConL* 20: 423–33), with Maxine Kumin (*WHR* 33:1–15), with Josephine Miles (*SJS* 5,iii:80–89), with Howard Nemerov (*SoR* 15:605–16), and with Diane Wakoski (*GyS* 6:61–73).

Not all this year's discussions of poetic *praxis* were confined to formal or informal statements made by writers themselves, however, for a number of the year's essays and articles on "general" subjects were concerned with questions of prosody. Such a concern is not really surprising, since both poets and critics have been involved for the last few years in a massive reevaluation of the prosodic theories that gained widespread acceptance in the 1960s. Now, more than a decade after preoccupations with breath and speech swept away the formalism of the 1950s, many writers seem obsessed by an overwhelming question about the freedom of so-called "free" verse. This year the most notable essays that ask (or answer) such a question are by Alan Helms, Roy Fuller, Denise Levertov, and Jonathan Holden. In "Intricate Song's Lost Measure" (*SR* 87:249–66) Helms berates contemporary poets from Ammons to Wakoski for prosodic sloppiness. Verse rhythm, he argues, should either be "regular" in its commitment to a "rhythmic contract" or it should somehow reflect the thoughts the poem expresses; recent writers, Helms insists, tend to waver between a regularity they do not understand and a freedom that is meaningless. Helms's essay is cogent in its criticism of the flaccid verses produced by some inexpert post-Modernists but occasionally disturbing in its suggestion that a Wintersesque backlash against prosodic innovation may now be gathering strength. Certainly Roy Fuller's "The Fetish of Speech Rhythms in Modern Poetry" (*SoR* 15:1–15) reinforces my worry that such a backlash might take strange forms. Declaring that Gerard Manley Hopkins' prosodic theories have been a pernicious influence on 20th-century versification, Fuller fulminates against the lifeless *vers libre* and end-stopped prose he feels he finds even in the work of such major artists as Williams, Lowell, and Ashbery. In its own structure, however, Fuller's essay is far more shapeless than any of the poetry he decries, while his concluding citation of songwriter Stephen Sondheim's remark that "Rhyme gives point to a word" is simply silly.

Where Helms and Fuller are conservative, even "reactionary" in their commitment to metrical orthodoxy (with Fuller hinting that he prefers Bridges' traditionalism to Hopkins' innovations), Denise Levertov remains, of course, a spokesperson of Black Mountain poetics. Her brief meditation on "The Function of the Line" (*ChiR* 30,iii:30–36) is firm in its praise of the possibilities implicit in "open forms," which she thinks "more apt to express the sensibility of our age," and she argues that the best poems in such modes employ linebreaks to establish "*pitch patterns*" as well as rhythmic patterns. Like most such primary statements by poets, Levertov's essay will be especially useful to critics interested in her own aesthetic assumptions even while it is vulnerable to attacks from Derridean poststructuralists who insist upon the primacy of written rather than spoken words. Interestingly, however, her antitraditionalist essay begins with an assertion that supports the complaints of Helms and Fuller: "Not only hapless adolescents, but many gifted and justly esteemed poets writing in contemporary non-metrical forms, have only the vaguest concept and the most haphazard use, of the line." The recent concern for reevaluation of craft is pervasive indeed.

In two fine essays that elaborate upon this concern Jonathan Holden manages to steer a skillful course between Fuller's fulminations and Levertov's affirmations. His "The 'Found' in Contemporary Poetry" (*GaR* 33:329–41) begins by considering a limited definition of the "found" poem as a "rearranged" passage of prose, then broadens the "found" rubric to include all poems that deliberately exploit the "verse format" to frame what might otherwise seem to be ordinary prose. Finally, Holden argues convincingly that most contemporary verse emphasizes "closure"—that is, the sense of the poem as self-contained artifact—rather than "measure and tempo": thus "the 'feeling' in a poem, which has traditionally been borne by the 'music' of verse as song, is now, more often than not, borne by metaphor." Holden's " 'Affected Naturalness' and the Poetry of Sensibility" (*CE* 41:398–408) usefully illustrates this last point by demonstrating how a hypothetical verse-writing workshop might rewrite Conrad Aiken's highly stylized and musical "Annihilation" to transform an intricately wrought early 20th-century poem into an apparently casual and antimetrical contemporary work. At the same time, however, Holden observes that the surface relaxation of a good post-Modernist poem is essentially illusory, for he insists through an analysis of Mark Strand's "Lines for Winter" that "the sensibility of the contemporary 'pro' poet bears the same relation to the craft of composition that the body of a professional athlete bears to its conditioning and training." Clearly, though he would reject Levertov's emphasis on "melody," Holden would agree with her that the skill of the writer in "open forms" is not inferior to, but simply different from, the art of the Elizabethan sonneteer.

Several other important general essays that were published in 1979 focused on major contemporary poetic schools, and were therefore at least peripherally concerned with questions of craft. Charles Altieri's "The Objectivist Tradition" (*ChiR* 30,iii:5–22) offers a densely written exposition of Objectivism that is finally more subjective manifesto than objective critical analysis. As if to counteract Holden's use of a Strand poem to exemplify contemporary skill, Altieri cites another Strand piece as an instance of what might be called "workshop-ese"—the phrase is mine, not his—and ends like a latterday T. E. Hulme with a paean to the hard, the tough, the "sincere" (a word he uses in strange ways). In general what his fiercely partisan essay gains in power, it loses in credibility, for, as Holden and others demonstrate, the Pound/Olson/Zukofsky tradition is not the "onlie begetter" of impressive contemporary verse. In "Lowell, Berryman, Roethke, and Ginsberg: The Communal Function of Confessional Poetry" (*LitR* 22:329–41), for instance, Steven K. Hoffman speaks up for the so-called "confessional" writers of mid-century America. Far from being solipsistic and private, he declares, these poets worked in a tradition of public-spirited self-exposure that goes back to Wordsworth and St. Augustine; in fact, insists Hoffman, the apparently ill-assorted quartet of Lowell, Berryman, Roethke, and Ginsberg were all "self-appointed exorcists of contemporary psychological, sociological, and even political demons . . ." Like Altieri, Hoffman is plainly a partisan of the poets he discusses, but while he is less crotchety and even (to this reader) less irritating than Altieri, he is also rather less original in his formulations.

As if to propose that there *is* something else to think about beyond all this fiddle, five major essays this year join discussions of craft with analyses of contemporary poetic schools to explore recent ideas about the visibility and viability of a "feminist poetic." As its title suggests, Mary Carruthers' "Imagining Women: Notes Toward a Feminist Poetic" (*MR* 20:281–307) is perhaps the most ambitious in its scope and the most sweeping in its generalizations, yet it is finally the most disappointing. Arguing that there is a significant difference between women poets who began to write before the feminist revival of the late 1960s and those who began after that revival, Carruthers tends both to distinguish and to praise writers who are politically "correct" —that is, writers who act as, and write about, what are now called

"positive role models"—rather than those who struggle against or
are defeated by the constraints of their times. Ultimately, in making
such an argument, she loses touch with aesthetic concerns and transforms most of the texts she cites into historical documents rather than
literary ones. Nowhere, moreover, does she attempt a serious reading
of any of the poems she quotes, so that her engagement with "poetics"
is quite minimal. A better subtitle for her essay might be "Notes on
the Politics of a Feminist Poetics."

Interestingly, where Carruthers is self-consciously committed to a
poetry that is both polemical and political, Marjorie Perloff is suspicious of such verse, and, in "Beyond the *Bell Jar*: Women Poets in
Transition" (*SCR* 11,ii:4–16), Perloff clearly dissociates herself even
from the label "feminist," defining herself simply as "female." In a
curious way, however, she makes a more convincing case than does
Carruthers for the existence of a distinctively female or feminist poetic, if only because she attends more closely to the literary qualities
of literary texts. Yet her basic thesis is oddly extravagant: contemporary women poets, Perloff argues, have continued "to favor the metaphoric mode as if Williams had never written *Spring and All*," and
she goes on to show considerable contempt for such a "mode," at least
as it appears in the writings of women from Millay to Atwood. In her
conclusion she cites a rather incoherent prose ramble by Bernadette
Mayer as a positive, metaphor-free example of "the kind of poetry
women will be writing in the decade to come"—that is, if women poets
are lucky enough to forget the sins of their literary foremothers. One
can only wonder what Perloff would make of Holden's theory that
almost *all* contemporary verse is in some sense structured through
metaphor rather than music.

Holden's work is apropos here in another way, for just as Holden
steers a sensible course through the difficult shoals of prosodic argument by substituting description for prescription, Linda Wagner
manages to mediate between Carruthers' overemphasis on politics
and Perloff's overreaction against "metaphor" by taking a calm and
relatively disengaged look at the shapes of two women's careers in
her brief "Levertov and Rich: The Later Poems" (*SCR* 11,ii:18–27).
As if restating Hoffman's low-keyed defense of the confessional poets,
Wagner observes that "the best poems of feminism become poems of
'community.' " Though her argument that Levertov's recent poems
restate past concerns while Rich's go beyond such concerns isn't strik-

ingly original, her essay is refreshing in its fairness, its commitment to analysis rather than advocacy.

Two selections in *Shakespeare's Sisters* also explore the general question of a feminist poetic, basing their arguments in whole or in part on readings of a wide range of contemporary poets. Barbara Charlesworth Gelpi in "A Common Language: The American Woman Poet" (pp. 269–79) surveys the art of poets from Marianne Moore to Lucille Clifton in order to construct a theory of female literary history that is considerably more complex and convincing than the hypotheses proposed by Carruthers and Perloff. Basing her historical analysis on models of victimization and its effects drawn from Margaret Atwood, Arnold Rampersad, and Frantz Fanon, Barbara Gelpi eschews literary (as opposed to political) advocacy to argue that American women poets have moved through four stages in their reactions to social oppression. If they are talented, she observes, they have written good poetry of many kinds at *each* stage, but through their "shared experience of victimization and of the shared attitudes which that creates [they] have found common themes" and what Adrienne Rich calls "a common language." In "The Critique of Consciousness and Myth in Levertov, Rich, and Rukeyser" (pp. 280–300) Rachel Blau DuPlessis focuses on an even smaller group of writers to demonstrate that "in poems about women, politics and war, and myth [these three] poets construct critiques of culture and ideology from a radical and often feminist point of view." DuPlessis' readings of key texts by these writers are notably sensitive and her definitions of sociohistorical contexts are equally attentive.

In the same way that critics like Carruthers, Gelpi, and DuPlessis have attempted to describe a feminist (or at least female) poetics by examining the intersections of gender and genre, sexuality and creativity, Robert K. Martin in *Homosexual Tradition* tries to identify the characteristics of a male homosexual literary tradition that extends from Walt Whitman through Hart Crane to such recent poets as James Merrill and Alfred Corn. Martin's exploration of recent verse in this mode is organized into separate sections on Allen Ginsberg, Robert Duncan, Thom Gunn, Edward Field, Richard Howard, James Merrill, and Alfred Corn, each of which offers illuminating analyses of its subject's individual achievement as well as discussions of his literary relationship to his gay peers and precursors. Taken together, however, these essays also provide a persuasive argument for the

existence of a homosexual tradition in American poetry, a tradition
that "has operated through a series of more or less coded references"
to create a distinctive "literature of indirection." Like the histories
and analyses of lesbian poetry that many feminist critics have lately
begun to produce, this book is valuable for its examination of a subject
whose name critics have for too long refused to speak.

A last volume that should be mentioned here is *A Book of Rereadings in Recent American Poetry*, ed. Greg Kuzma (Crete, Neb.: The
Best Cellar Press). This wide-ranging anthology contains 30 essays
on contemporary poets, including pieces on Berryman, Bishop, Bly,
Lowell, Plath, Roethke, Snyder, Stafford, and Wagoner. I will mention the most important of these in discussions of works about individual writers, but though these "rereadings" vary greatly in quality
—some are naive or perfunctory while others are sophisticated and
imaginative—in the aggregate they offer an invigorating vision of
contemporary verse in all its complexity. Such a vision should help
students of this genre resist the twin temptations of hasty partisanship and gloomy generalization.

ii. Blackmur, Eberhart, Jarrell, Miles, Rukeyser, Schwartz

A scattering of articles dealt with these writers in 1979, and though
no individual piece seems of major significance, a few should be taken
into account. Two essays on R. P. Blackmur, for instance, use the occasion of the publication of a definitive collection by this poet to
meditate on the shape and significance of his career. John Peck reminds us in "R. P. Blackmur, Romanticism, and Poetic Language"
(*Poetry* 133:290–301) that Blackmur belonged to what Yvor Winters
(not pejoratively) called "the Reactionary generation," and he offers
an appreciation of the Princeton poet-critic's "struggle for a poetic
language, line by line if necessary, which recently it has become unfashionable to wage." Similarly, Russell Fraser surveys Blackmur's
verse in "The Poetry of R. P. Blackmur" (*SoR* 15:86–100) to argue
that this admittedly "minor" writer made "six permanent poems"—
no mean achievement, at least by Randall Jarrell's lightning-rod
standard. Examining Blackmur's debts to Yeats, Eliot, Hopkins, and
others, Fraser explores also his "mock aesthetic" that weds despair
and reason. In the same vein Richard K. Cross's "Richard Eberhart:

Reading God's Fingerprints" (*CP* 12,i:13–20) examines the contradictory impulses that inform Eberhart's verse: on the one hand, the spiritual desire to confront God directly, and on the other, the pragmatic realization that we must live in an ordinary reality where the transcendent rarely emerges. To maintain a balance between the spiritual and the pragmatic, Cross suggests, Eberhart seeks fleeting traces of divinity in the clutter of this world, an enterprise central in his *oeuvre*.

Two essays on poems by Randall Jarrell were slighter than the pieces on Eberhart and Blackmur but will nevertheless be of interest to some readers. Charlotte H. Beck's "Unicorn to Eland: The Rilkean Spirit in the Poetry of Randall Jarrell" (*SLJ* 12,i:3–17) considers similarities in theme and image between Rilke and the poet's American admirer, predictably enough noting in both writers "the poet's need for distance from his creation," the use of children to represent essential human innocence, the employment of death as a perspective from which to criticize life, and the "theme of the imprisoned spirit." Less predictable is Linda Bradley Funkhauser's "Acoustic Rhythm in Randall Jarrell's 'The Death of the Ball Turret Gunner'" (*Poetics* 8: 381–403), a daunting attempt to apply laboratory techniques to aesthetic analysis. Comparing 21 readings aloud of Jarrell's famous short poem—one by the poet himself, ten by English professors, and ten by a "control group" of "non-literary persons"—Funkhauser uses elaborate graphs and charts of each reading's "acoustic levels" to prove (perhaps surprisingly) that in its placement of pauses and stresses Jarrell's own reading implicitly presented a subtler interpretation of the work than the readings of the professors. (As for the "non-literary persons," the less said the better.)

In another somewhat surprising development Josephine Miles was the subject of an interesting appreciation by Lawrence R. Smith. In his "Josephine Miles: Metaphysician of the Irrational" (*Book of Rereadings*, pp. 22–35) Smith develops the oddly telling notion that the verse of the University of California's apparently rational and sensible poet-critic is really a surrealist art which "partake[s] of the world of dreams and the irrational."

Finally, Elizabeth Sewell's "Reflection in a Dark Mirror" on Muriel Rukeyser (*Parnassus* 7,ii:51–65) and David Lehman's "Delmore, Delmore: A Mournful Cheer," on Delmore Schwartz (*Parnassus* 7,ii:

215–30) are both particularly serious and substantial review-essays, which usefully illuminate the careers of two poets who should be read and reread like this more often.

iii. Berryman, Bishop, Lowell, Roethke, Shapiro

As might be expected, a number of important articles and books were devoted to these poets this year, with Lowell and Roethke receiving— as might also be expected—the most attention, and Berryman coming in third. Diane Ackerman's "Near the Top a Bad Turn Dared" (*Parnassus* 7, 141–50) focuses on *Homage to Mistress Bradstreet* and *Delusions, Etc.* Densely written yet cheerfully relaxed, this essay is more meditative than argumentative, more impressionistic than analytical, but nevertheless rich with insights that seem to arise, associatively, from the Berryman texts themselves. John Haffenden's "John Berryman: The American Poet at Cambridge" (*CQ*, 8:129–50) is similarly relaxed and almost as interesting. Excerpted from a forthcoming biography, the article includes a number of revealing anecdotes about the poet's "mad escapades" and restless intellect. More sharply focused, Paul Mariani's impassioned " 'Lost Souls in Ill-Attended Wards': Berryman's 'Eleven Addresses to the Lord' " (*Book of Rereadings*, pp. 8–21) is a lively and illuminating meditation on the crucial concluding section of *Love & Fame*, one of the best essays in Kuzma's anthology. Less lively and more tentative but also concerned with Berryman's theological struggles, Kenneth MacLean's "Berryman's 'Delusions'—On Poetry and Religious Pain" (*Book of Rereadings*, pp. 156–70) complements and supplements Mariani's piece. Finally, four short pieces by Kathe Davis Finney, Jack V. Barbera, Joseph Mancini, Jr., and Carol Ames, all published in "A John Berryman Miscellany" that appeared in *NMAL* (4: Items 1–4) deal briefly with Berryman's language, two of his *Dream Songs*, and the connections between his poetry and his unfinished novel, *Recovery*.

Of three essays on Elizabeth Bishop's work Jane Shore's "Elizabeth Bishop: The Art of Changing Your Mind" (*Ploughshares* 5: 178–91) is the fullest and most useful. Through a wide-ranging study of Bishop's use of metaphor, Shore emphasizes the uncertainty of much of this writer's imagery, the constant self-questionings and "changes of mind" that contribute to the "dazzling dialectic of her vision." Unlike Shore's piece, David Shapiro's "On a Villanelle by

Elizabeth Bishop" (*IowaR* 10,i:77–81) is both brief and ponderous, for the most part substituting a kind of intellectual name-dropping—by actual count 52 names are invoked from Nietzsche to Deleuze to Mallarmé to Kierkegaard—for real critical insight. Similarly disappointing is Anne R. Newman's "Elizabeth Bishop's Roosters'" (*Book of Rereadings*, pp. 171–83), a needlessly long and somewhat mechanical explication of a poem worth more imaginative analysis.

Among the many elegies and eulogies, essays, and reminiscences published about or for Robert Lowell in 1979 Richard J. Fein's expansion and revision of his 1970 *Robert Lowell* (*TUSAS* 176) is perhaps the most engaging, if not necessarily the most useful. To "extend the range" of his study and bring it up to date, Fein has added new chapters and rewritten old ones from the first edition so as to present "evaluations and conclusions under the sad recognition that the poet's work is no longer in process." His final assessment of Lowell's career is intelligent and sensible, while his newly composed "Prologue: Memories of Brooklyn and Robert Lowell" and "Epilogue: Looking for Robert Lowell in Boston" are particularly lively and readable essays in what we might call confessional criticism, pieces Fein has written to show himself and his audience that "my investment in [Lowell's] poetry . . . was not simply an academic one, but was a reflection of my own development."

Two memorial collections of appreciations and reminiscences also explore the vein of confessional criticism in which Fein works, as if only Lowellesque "imitations" could adequately honor and interpret the memory of the author of *Life Studies*. The first, *Robert Lowell: A Tribute* (reviewed in chap. 21, section *iv.*), brings together a wide range of essays by important Italian and American critics, while the second, the *Harvard Advocate's* commemorative Lowell issue (Nov.: 1–2), contains for the most part briefer and more personal pieces, but quite a few of them will also be useful to serious students of Lowell's career. The most interesting of these include the contributions by Blair Clark, Christopher Ricks, Robert Fitzgerald, and Helen Vendler. Ricks on Lowell's sense of himself as a *Lowell*, together with Vendler on Lowell's teaching of poetry, provides especially illuminating insights into the poet's own sense of his literary ancestry.

A number of separate essays were also published on Lowell in 1979, with a surprising majority concentrating on the writer's earlier

work, and most devoted to the analysis of single poems. J. Barton
Rollins' "Young Robert Lowell's Poetics of Revision" (*JML* 7:488–
504) is a careful study of three successive versions of Lowell's "Death
from Cancer." Rollins makes sound though not startling points about
the ways in which Lowell transforms his imagery and symbolism from
the mythological to the Christian while particularizing abstractions,
but this essay would have been more useful if he had printed the
drafts themselves along with his analysis of them. In a much briefer
study of "An Early Version of Lowell's 'The Drunken Fisherman'"
(*NMAL* 3: Item 19) Rollins examines yet another of the poet's draft
manuscripts, while in a longer piece on "Robert Lowell's Apprenticeship and Early Poems" (*AL* 52:67–83) he brings these scholarly explorations together with studies of other manuscripts and biographical reminiscences to theorize about Lowell's already quite famous
student years, arguing that the first tones of "the Lowell voice" that
break through in the writer's apprentice manuscripts owe a good
deal to the influence "not only of William Carlos Williams, but also
of Richard Eberhart, who so strongly supported Lowell's personal
lyricism in his first poems." Finally, other analyses of individual Lowell poems include Carolyn Allen's brief but helpful "Lowell's 'After
the Surprising Conversions': Another Look at the Source" (*NMAL*
3: Item 17), Steven K. Hoffman's "Private Poet, Public Role: Lowell's
'For the Union Dead'" (*NMAL* 3: Item 18), which formulates some
of the same points Hoffman makes in his essay on the confessional
poets (discussed earlier), and my own "Mephistophilis in Maine: Rereading Lowell's 'Skunk Hour'" (*Book of Rereadings*, pp. 254–64),
which attempts to combine confessional criticism in the mode of Fein
and Vendler with archetypal analysis to explore the revisionary impulses that inform "Skunk Hour."

Though Lowell inspired such a flood of regret and reminiscence,
it was his slightly older contemporary, Theodore Roethke, who received the most serious attention this year. Jay Parini's *Theodore
Roethke: An American Romantic* (Mass.) is an intelligent though
sometimes predictable study which skillfully places Roethke among
his poetic precursors—Blake, Wordsworth, Yeats, Emerson, and Whitman—while also examining his relationship to such crucial older
peers as Stevens and Eliot. Parini particularly emphasizes "the American quality" of Roethke's Romanticism, but notes that this poet
whose central symbol became the greenhouse where nature and cul-

ture intersect was "a poetic ventriloquist of sorts, able to speak through masks of those whom he called 'the great dead' " yet at the same time he had "a voice at his core which is unmistakably his own." In exploring the contexts that shaped Roethke's texts, Parini makes good use of the writer's unpublished notebooks and correspondence; his discussions of the ways in which mentors like Humphries, Bogan, and Kunitz nurtured the apprentice poet's art will be especially useful to students of Roethke's development. Finally, though his conclusion that *The Last Son* is "this poet's most durable achievement and the key to his work" is hardly startling, Parini does a notable job in providing that volume (and others) with a sensible literary history.

A related though slightly different literary history of Roethke is traced by Audrey T. Rodgers in a chapter of *Universal Drum.* Arguing that this poet who had once struck Stanley Kunitz as "a blond, smooth shambling giant . . . with a cold pudding of a face" was, to use Roethke's own phrase, "Dancing-Mad," Rodgers sees his Bennington colleague Martha Graham as both emblem and precursor for the author of "My Papa's Waltz," "The Dance," and "I Knew a Woman." "Like other American poets before him," she declares, "Roethke would be a modern Siva: visionary like Whitman, shaman like Hart Crane, dancing bear and waltzing prophet, creating in poetry the patterned movements of rite and ceremony as an affirmation of the spirit." Rodgers' study of his dancing measures and metaphors is extraordinarily articulate as well as exceptionally illuminating. And yet a third historical/biographical context for Roethke's poetry is provided in Kermit Vanderbilt's "Theodore Roethke as a Northwest Poet," a piece collected in *Northwest Perspectives*, pp. 187–216. Though Vanderbilt concedes that Roethke was not a regional writer in the ordinary sense, he argues convincingly (if unsurprisingly) for the significance to his later poetry both of his life as "a frustrated citizen in Seattle" and his love for "his adopted Northwest landscape."

Other essays that dealt with Roethke in 1979 had narrower ambitions, tending to concentrate on individual poems and sequences rather than on their biographical or literary-historical backgrounds. John Carpenter's somewhat unfocused "Theodore Roethke—The Shapes of Fire" (*Book of Rereadings*, pp. 127–55) begins by trying to refute Kenneth Burke's assertion that "Ted's gong struck . . . when he hit the greenhouse line." Roethke "had other voices, other 'gongs,' " Carpenter insists. Despite his best intentions, however, Carpenter devotes most of his meditation on Roethke's achievement to a discussion of the greenhouse sequence; only at the end of his essay does he consider the problem of the poet's later, pseudo-Yeatsian formalism and his ultimate transcendence of that compulsive borrowing, which Auden called "a rhythmic tic." Similarly concerned with "the greenhouse line" is Sandra Whipple Spanier's "The Unity of the Greenhouse Sequence: Roethke's Portrait of the Artist" (*CP* 12,i:53–60), an interesting if somewhat rigid reading which sees this famous series not as "an album of snapshots" but as a unified, chronologically organized "portrait" of the process of poetic creation, beginning with the "preconscious beginnings" of "Cuttings" and concluding with the "perfection and timelessness" of "Carnations."

Rather more general analyses of Roethke's achievement are offered in Sanford Pinsker's "An Urge to Wrestle/A Need to Dance: The Poetry of Theodore Roethke" (*CEA* 41,iv:12–17) and T. R. Hummer's "Roethke and Merwin: Two Voices and the Technique of Nonsense" *WHR* 33:273–80). As their titles suggest, the first of these essays is a somewhat cursory and unfocused appreciation of the Whitmanesque way in which Roethke's poetry contains and reconciles contradictions, while the second is a more innovative piece in which Hummer elaborates on Stanley Plumley's distinction between the "hero-voice" and the "guide-voice" in modern poetry, suggesting that Roethke is a paradigmatic "hero" and Merwin a paradigmatic "guide," and showing how, as a result of such different self-definitions, the two poets make different uses of "nonsense": as a "hero" Roethke enacts and experiences the "irrational" directly, whereas Merwin merely *points* "beyond the rational." Though his intricate apparatus is tedious at times, Hummer does produce some good individual readings, especially of Merwin. His vision of Roethke, moreover—like the visions of Parini, Rodgers, Vanderbilt, and others—cannot help reminding us once again that Molesworth was absolutely right to consider Seattle's "American Romantic" a crucial poetic father of us all.

Finally, the kind of work needed to begin the study of a writer appeared this year in Lee Bartlett's *Karl Shapiro: A Descriptive Bibliography, 1933–1977* (Garland), an accurate, detailed compilation that is enhanced in interest and value by transcriptions of taped interviews with Shapiro. There also is a checklist of reviews and criticism compiled by David Huwiler.

iv. Creeley, Duncan, Everson, Ginsberg, Olson, Snyder, Zukofsky

There was no full-length study devoted to any of these poets in 1979, but a number of book-length essay collections appeared, along with a few pamphlets and articles as well as a small but interesting section of a more general critical study. The last of these, on Robert Creeley, is "The Cry of Its Occasion," which constitutes the final chapter of John Vernon's commendably brief and lucid *Poetry and the Body* (Illinois). Exploring Creeley's notion that a poem exists "as primarily the fact of its own activity," Vernon uses Sartre's meditations on Giacometti's attenuated sculptures to illuminate the American poet's apparently minimalist struggles with language.

A far more substantial and significant publication is *Robert Duncan: Scales of the Marvelous*, ed. Robert J. Bertholf and Ian W. Reid (New Directions) for the series entitled "Insights: Working Papers in Contemporary Criticism." This serious and wide-ranging anthology is a volume that no student of Duncan's poetry—or, indeed, of "San Francisco poetry" more generally—should be without. Contributions emphasizing biography include engaging and illuminating personal reminiscences by Hamilton and Mary Tyler, Joanna and Michael Mc-Clure (in a conversation with Robert J. Bertholf) and Denise Lever-tov, while more straightforward literary contexts are explored in Don Byrd's "The Question of Wisdom as Such" (on Duncan and Olson), Mark Johnson and Robert DeMott's " 'An Inheritance of Spirit': Robert Duncan and Walt Whitman," Jayne L. Walker's "Exercises in Disorder: Duncan's Imitations of Gertrude Stein," and Eric Mottram's "Heroic Survival Through Ecstatic Form: Robert Duncan's *Roots and Branches*," as well as in essays by Ian W. Reid, Nathaniel Mackey, Gerrit Lansing, Séan Golden, and others. A fine discussion of "Homosexuality in Robert Duncan's Poetry" by Thom Gunn brings together biographical and literary considerations to place the San Francisco poet in the important tradition that Robert K. Martin's book has also (as noted earlier) begun to define. In addition, a "Selected Checklist" of Duncan's works offers useful bibliographical information, including an up-to-date listing of the journals where portions of this writer's now almost mythic "H. D. Book" have appeared. There are only two faults to be found with this excellent collection:

first—and this is a major problem—because of the growing significance and size of the "H. D. Book," many readers will keenly regret the omission of any essay on Duncan's important relationship with that crucial Modernist, H. D.; second—and this is minor but nevertheless irritating—because the book has been offset from reduced typewritten pages instead of being typeset (no doubt to save money), many hapless Duncan admirers will find it almost blindingly difficult to read—and surely even people who pay "only" $4.95 for a paperback book deserve legibility!

Scholars of Brother Antoninus/William Everson may find *Benchmark & Blaze: The Emergence of William Everson*, ed. Lee Bartlett (Scarecrow), almost as useful in their researches as Duncan students will find *Scales of the Marvelous* in theirs. Unlike the former anthology, whose contributions are all new, *Benchmark* contains very few previously unpublished essays; rather, it delineates Everson's poetic evolution by reprinting a montage of reviews and critical appreciations that mark the different stages of his career. Many of the pieces date back to the poet's "Antoninus" days, including a brief but sensible piece by Jerome Mazzaro and a comical review from *Time* magazine, almost self-parodically entitled "The Beat Friar." More recent essays include Albert Gelpi's fine "Everson/Antoninus: Contending with the Shadow" and Bill Hotchkiss's rather baroquely Jungian "The Roots of Recovery: Ten Meditations." Finally, a good but short selected bibliography rounds out this collection, whose editor, Lee Bartlett, compiled the definitive bibliography of Everson's work from 1934 to 1976 (Scarecrow, 1977) and also this year edited Everson's *Earth Poetry* (mentioned in section *i.*).

The treatments of Ginsberg, Olson, and Snyder came in articles and pamphlets this year. Mark Shechner's "The Survival of Allen Ginsberg" (*PR* 46:105–12) is a review-essay that uses the publication of three new volumes by Ginsberg to speculate briefly on the shape of the poet's career, in particular on his "standard brew of homosexuality, metaphysics, pacifism, political outrage, muddled prophecy, and homemade Buddhism that is as familiar now as the morning coffee, and about as alarming." Both more focused and more feverishly enthusiastic, Paul Christensen's "In Cold Hell, In Thicket" (*Book of Rereadings*, pp. 54–78) is a rambling introduction to an early Olson collection, which, says Christensen, "delivers the whole man in the tumult of his first years." By the end of this piece, the critic has worked himself into such a frenzy of admiration that he begins flinging his copy of the book around. By comparison Joseph N. Riddel's "Decentering the Image: The 'Project' of American Poetics" is blessedly restrained. In *Textual Strategies: Perspectives in Post-Structuralist Criticism*, ed. Josué V. Harari (Cornell), pp. 322–58, this essay offers a decidedly poststructuralist overview of the more radical innovations of modern American poetry, linking Olson's key notion of the poem as a field of interacting forces with Derrida's concept of the "free play" of the text.

In a very different mode from either Christensen or Riddel, Bert Almon's pamphlet on *Gary Snyder* (WWS) presents an overview of Snyder's career that has little critical vision at all, whether prestructuralist or poststructuralist. Though his summaries of the poet's achievements are accurate enough, Almon's style is both naive and patronizing. Sadly, Del Ivan Janik's "Gary Snyder, The Public Function of Poetry, and *Turtle Island*" (*NMAL* 3:item 24) is no sharper in focus though it is, fortunately, shorter. Whatever readers may think of Snyder's new (or old) work, surely most will agree that he deserves more serious attention than he gets from either of these critics.

Yet another 1979 entry in the anthology sweepstakes is the excellent *Louis Zukofsky: Man and Poet*, ed. Carroll F. Terrell (NPF). This fat commemorative volume does in a definitive way for Zukofsky what *Scales of the Marvelous* and *Benchmark & Blaze* begin to do for Duncan and Everson. Carefully organized into sections on "The Man," "The Poet," "The Thinker," "The Translator," and "The Testament," it includes, in the first section, Carroll F. Terrell's fascinating "Louis Zukofsky: An Eccentric Profile," a biographical memoir based on a long, relaxed series of interviews with the poet's wife, Celia; in the second, reprints of essays on Zukofsky's art by Hugh Kenner, Peter Quartermain, and M. L. Rosenthal among others, together with a brilliant and witty piece on the poet's Jewish literary contexts by Harold Schimmel; in the third section, a reprint of L. S. Dembo's valuable "Louis Zukofsky: Objectivist Poetics and the Quest for Form"; and in the fourth and fifth sections, a good essay on "Zukofsky as Translator" by Burton Hatlen, along with useful biographical pieces by Celia Zukofsky, Marcella Booth, and Carroll F. Terrell. Throughout, there are many other strong contributions. A number of the essays date back to last year's special issue of *Paideuma*, but the volume brings together so much else, and is so well organized, that it will no doubt be helpful to Zukofsky researchers for a long time.

v. Plath, Rich, Sexton, Wakoski

It does not seem insignificant that of all the poets treated in this section of *ALS* Sylvia Plath got the most critical attention in 1979. Reevaluations and *re*reevaluations of this charismatic poet continue, and even accelerate in pace, as readers go on trying to come to terms with the persistent charisma of Plath's art. As revealed by the essays collected in a superb anthology, *Sylvia Plath: New Views on the Poetry*, ed. Gary Lane (Hopkins), Plath's work is still controversial. Yet even those who dislike it find it absorbing, even mesmerizing, as if this 31-year-old woman who died in 1963 were in some troubling sense what Keats might call a "figure of allegory."

It is, in fact, a troublesome inability to distinguish biography from allegory, life from art, that invariably undermines the weakest essays about Plath in Lane's book, whose authors often feel obliged to take a moral position on this artist's career, especially on the suicide that ended it, apparently in the belief that by dying the poet of *Ariel* somehow wrote an enormous and vulgarly flashy advertisement for death. (It is curious that many fewer critics take this position about the suicides that ended the poetic careers of Crane and Berryman, or about the equally "allegorical" deaths of Thomas, Roethke, and Lowell.) Ironically, critics of this sort melodramatize the dénouement of Plath's "story" in much the same way that they accuse the poet herself of having done. Worse, in their preoccupation with a theatrical plot that they themselves project into the poetry, such critics almost always fail to read the poems *as* poems. Rather, Plath's texts become merely the occasions for extratextual sermons and partisan polemics.

The two most problematic essays in Gary Lane's anthology constitute such sermons. In his "Sincerity Kills" Hugh Kenner fulminates against "the obligatory note of the theatrical" in the poet's life/work but then goes on (as his title indicates) to perform a set of not very original variations on that note: Plath's early career was marked by "sheer calculation," Kenner asserts, conjuring up a vision of the poet-as-Duessa and concluding that "Poems like 'A Birthday Present' . . . have a Guignol fascination," a notion which in its turn dredges up the old clichés about Plath's poetry-as-Russian roulette. Similarly (as its title also indicates) David Shapiro's "Sylvia Plath: Drama and Melodrama," undertakes "the unpleasant task of demystifying [Plath's] critics in their constant enchantments"—a project whose very formulation suggests a vision of the poetess/sorceress not unlike Kenner's and even more melodramatic than anything to be found in *Ariel* or Plath's other volumes. However, where Kenner's assertion that Plath was "calculating" at least implies a backhanded compliment—this artist *could* be artful!—Shapiro refuses to admit that Plath was ever anything but "student and imitator." Finally, his essay deteriorates into an incoherent attack upon all the writers and thinkers with whom he associates Plath. Not only such an obvious relative as Hughes but also Laing, Brown, Lowell, Berryman, Bly, Ginsberg, Thomas, Williams, D. H. Lawrence, and James Wright are ritually cursed and dismissed in three astonishing pages, which feature sentences like "she was twisted upon the poles of a hyperbolic melodramatic masquerading as a realism" and "[she lost] the whole delicious sense of the nondiscursive in poetry," and which petulantly complain that Plath was not as good as Georg Trakl, Frank O'Hara, and Gertrude Stein. I devote so much space to this essay because in its contrivance of an aesthetic based almost entirely on ill will it seems to me to be a model of poor criticism—badly written, self-indulgent, arrogant, and inattentive. This is, alas, an example of the fever of partisanship into which observers of the contemporary scene may fall as they wander through the groves of poetry, confusing trees with forest and—worse—encountering the white face of hate that Plath, too, saw in "its strangle of branches."

Exemplary criticism of an entirely different kind is offered in Sister Bernetta Quinn's "Medusan Imagery in Sylvia Plath," an essay on Plath's difficult "Medusa," which begins as a brilliant explication of the text but broadens into a marvelously illuminating exploration of the poem's many contexts. Both sophisticated and learned, Quinn's contribution reminds us that the best way to deal with an important poet is still through serious reading rather than angry sermonizing, for finally, in its conservatism and apparent modesty, Quinn's elegant analysis makes a general statement about the Plath canon and about "Plath's logic even in the constructions of Freudian dream-work" that is far more convincing than the generalizations produced even by critics who are more convincing and responsible than Shapiro. Another fine essay in the Lane book that shares Quinn's commitment to literary analysis is J. D. McClatchy's "Short Circuits and Folding Mirrors," a particularly serious and scrupulous account of Plath's stylistic development, which concedes "that it is difficult not to read her life—with its gestures of defiance, compulsion, and despair—rather than her work, in which those gestures are reflected or reimagined" but which draws strength from a clear understanding of the ways in which all written language both masks and shapes the self.

Other notable essays in Gary Lane's volume include Richard Allan Blessing's "The Shape of the Psyche: Vision and Technique in the Late Poems of Sylvia Plath," still another piece which concentrates intelligently on the poems *as* poems; Lane's own "Influence and Originality in Plath's poems," a good essay whose author is, fortunately, not too anxious about Plath to explore her influences; and J. D. O'Hara's "Plath's Comedy," a sophisticated piece which argues convincingly for the notion that late poems like the obviously lunatic "Daddy" and even the more stately "Berck-Plage" are informed by what Samuel Beckett has called "the mirthless laugh . . . the laugh laughing at the laugh . . . in a word the laugh that laughs—silence please—at that which is unhappy." Other essays in the anthology are by Calvin Bedient, Barnett Guttenberg, Marjorie Perloff, Murray M. Schwartz and Christopher Bollas, Carole Ferrier, and Jerome Mazzaro. A few of these flog the old biographical horse (e.g., Schwartz and Bollas, and to a lesser extent Bedient), while others attempt feminist or pseudo-feminist analyses that are not altogether successful (e.g., Perloff and Ferrier), but all will be of interest to students of Plath's development and reputation, as well as, more generally, to critics of contemporary verse.

Two other substantial works dealt with Plath in 1979, neither quite as engaging or potentially controversial as the Lane anthology but both of major interest to critics of this persistently interesting artist. As its title suggests, Margaret Dickie Uroff's *Sylvia Plath and Ted Hughes* (Illinois) offers complementary analyses of the poetry that these two mutually dependent writers produced as they evolved through a loving/hating "working relationship" to the twin milestones of *Ariel* and *Crow*. That each poet influenced, energized, and perhaps occasionally inhibited the other has always seemed undeniable, but Uroff is the first critic to attempt a serious study of this sometimes uneasy marriage of true minds which had such far-reaching implications for contemporary verse. Her readings are sound and her identifications of influence equally competent, though overall her juxtapositions of works by the two poets too often tend to be more mechanical than imaginative.

Similar competent analyses of Plath's life/work are offered in Jon Rosenblatt's brief, lucid, and illuminating *Sylvia Plath: The Poetry of Initiation* (N. Car.), a book which begins with a refreshing insistence on separating this writer's poetry from her biography and which, when it does digress into biography, sensibly observes that Plath "was brought to suicide by pressures and forces that would ultimately be satisfied neither by art nor by any other human activity." Arguing that all Plath's work was structured around a metaphoric "drama of initiation" in which the speaker of the poems moves through the three phases of "entry into darkness, ritual death, and rebirth," Rosenblatt borrows an explanatory vocabulary from the theologian Mircea Eliade to account for Plath's "search for identity." Rosenblatt's work is sometimes reductionist, sometimes naively hostile toward what he takes to be a "feminist stance," and sometimes, despite his criticism of Judith Kroll, reminiscent of Kroll's *Chapters in a Mythology*, but the students of Plath's art whom Kenner contemptuously calls "Plath fans" will have to take his argument seriously if only because he takes Plath's poetry seriously.

Three briefer essays on Plath published last year confront some of the same problems that Lane's contributors, Uroff and Rosenblatt, also face. Eileen Aird's " 'Poem for a birthday' to 'Three women': development in the poetry of Sylvia Plath" (*CritQ* 21,iv:63–72) is a somewhat unfocused study of the poet's stylistic evolution that tries but fails to do what McClatchy's essay succeeds at doing so well. Ellin Sarot's "To Be 'God's Lioness' and Live: On Sylvia Plath" (*CentR* 23:105–28) is too short for its own ambitions: drawing on readings of *The Bell Jar* as well as many of the later poems, Sarot compares Plath with Lowell, studies the evolution of what might be called *Ariel's* "Jewish theme," and considers the significance of the poet's gender in relation to all this. Many of her individual points are strong ones but Sarot needs more space in which to sustain the generalizations she wants to make. It is interesting, though, that a number of her best passages—like those in Sister Bernetta Quinn's far more successful essay—emphasize the allusiveness and wit concealed within or behind Plath's flights of staccato metaphor, phenomena that are also emphasized in Deborah Gilbert's "Transformations in 'Nick and the Candlestick'" (*CP* 12,i:29–32), a sometimes strained and unconvincing reading of one of the more difficult *Ariel* poems which at least has the virtue of being a *reading*. Criticism of this kind should remind writers who feel tempted to throw away the text and moralize that, no matter how casual Plath's motions of the mind may seem, they were as intricately patterned as those of any other artist. More important, this kind of criticism should remind scornful readers that, after all, such waltzing is not easy, either for the poet or the critic.

A volume overlooked two years ago should be noted here: *Sylvia Plath: The Woman and the Work*, ed. Edward Butscher (New York: Dodd, Mead, 1977), which is a useful collection that includes eight reprinted essays, an introductory piece by the editor, and five original memoirs of Plath.

The intellectual and aesthetic strategies of Rich, Sexton, and Wakoski all received some useful analysis in 1979, though nothing like the attention given Plath. Perhaps the most notable piece on Rich was Alicia Ostriker's "Her Cargo: Adrienne Rich and the Common Language" (*APR* 8,iv:6–10), which uses the publication of *The Dream of a Common Language* to argue with passion and lucidity that "Adrienne Rich is a poet of ideas" who refuses to allow her reader to think, "Oh, it is only *poetry*." Exploring the evolution of those ideas, Ostriker vigorously engages Rich's thought, simultaneously debating, refuting, and appreciating—no easy task. Her piece is as much a review-essay as it is a critical article, but it is worth attention from readers with a special interest in Rich, as is Carol Muske's "Backward into the Future," another review-essay on *The Dream* (*Parnassus* 7,ii:77–90) which also traces the shape of this changed and changing poet's career so far. Finally, Joyce Greenberg's candid, even confessional "By Woman Taught" (*Parnassus* 7,ii:91–103) offers an account of the Rich classroom which interestingly complements and supplements Ostriker's and Muske's readings of the Rich canon.

Entirely different in tone and quality from most of the work done on Plath and Rich were this year's publications on Anne Sexton, most of which had a biographical cast, though, unlike the nastier essays on Plath's life, these tended to be chummy memoirs. "Two Perspectives on Anne Sexton," for instance (*SWR* 64:209–17), consists of Nancy Yanes Hoffman's "A Special Language," a piece that is little more than a friend's rather indulgent eulogy, in tandem with Jeffrey L. Lant's "Another Entry in *The Death Notebooks*," an essay that serves up a slightly more impersonal mixture of biography and reminiscence. Two items in *NMAL*'s special Robert Lowell and Anne Sexton number (3:3) are no more substantial. Brian Gallagher's "The Expanded Use of Simile in Anne Sexton's *Transformations*" (Item 20) studies imagery in the poems of "Dame Sexton's" fairytale volume to conclude, unsurprisingly, that "one of the more remarkable aspects" of these works is "how much they sound like 'Anne Sexton,'" while Kathleen L. Nichols' "The Hungry Beast Rowing Toward God: Anne Sexton's Later Religious Poetry" (Item 21) puts together a few mechanical Jungian observations about "archetypal amniotic fluid" and so forth. (Like Snyder, Sexton deserves better, despite all her faults.) Finally, two consciously feminist essays on Sexton and Wakoski respectively are both more political and, paradoxically, more literary. Suzanne Juhasz's "Seeking the Exit or the Home: Poetry and Salvation in the Career of Anne Sexton" (*Shakespeare's Sisters*, pp. 261–68) is a forceful meditation on the aesthetic implications of Sexton's situation as a woman/poet, while Catherine Gannon and Clayton Lein's "Diane Wakoski and the Language of Self" (*SJS* 5,ii:85–98) is an uneven but ambitious analysis of the imagery through which Wakoski defines her femaleness in *The Motorcycle Betrayal Poems*.

vi. Ammons, Ashbery, Bly, J. Dickey, O'Hara, Merwin

Of these poets Ashbery and O'Hara continued, predictably enough, to receive the most attention this year. Nevertheless some notable work was also done on Ammons, Bly, James Dickey, and Merwin. In "The Poetry of A. R. Ammons" (*SCR* 12,i:2–9), for instance, Alfred S. Reid attempts to define the nature of the post-Modernist aesthetic that shapes works like *Tape for the Turn of the Year* and *Sphere*. Reid's generalizations are sometimes naive or easy—Ammons "has challenged the formalist theories and practices of modernism," etc.— but admirers of *Tape* and *Sphere* will doubtless want to read this essay, as well as Hugh Luke's "Gestures of Shape, Motions of Form: On Some Poems by A. R. Ammons (*Book of Rereadings*, pp. 79–107), a longer, less focused and sometimes embarrassingly breathless appreciation which offers several interesting paragraphs about Ammons' relationship to his literary friend and advocate, Harold Bloom.

David Shapiro's *John Ashbery: An Introduction to the Poetry* (Columbia) is part of the useful series of introductions to contemporary poetry that Columbia has recently started to publish, under the general editorship of John Unterecker, who has contributed a lively foreword to this volume. In one respect, however, Unterecker is misleading, for in warning us that Shapiro "approaches Ashbery neither as New Critic nor as historian, but as fellow poet" Unterecker fails to prepare us for the relentless barrage of aesthetic jargon and intellectual jingoism with which this critic assails us. As in his essays on Elizabeth Bishop and Sylvia Plath, Shapiro loads every rift of this book with names, which he seems to consider weightier than any other ore, and some of his pages radiate a kind of graduate school ecstasy, a rapturous devotion to "the meditative dialectic of a Paul de Man and the equally inspiring tones of Meyer Schapiro," to "the passion of Shkovsky, Yakubinski and Mukarovsky" as well as to "Wittgenstein's 'ladder of propositions,'" "the humor of polysemy," and "that poem of which Benjamin Lee Whorf spoke." Since Ashbery is surely a poetic nephew of Wallace Stevens, who shares the older poet's belief that "the gaiety of language is our seigneur," one assumes that such pollyanalytics must drive him right in one side of his convex mirror and right out the other. Still, this book does have *a* redeeming feature: when Shapiro forgets for a moment or two his hectic conviction that "the best poetry of our day is . . . a form of literary criticism, both in drab and golden tones" he has a few interesting points to make about a few individual poems by John Ashbery.

Both more moving and more illuminating is Harold Bloom's paradoxically more modest "The Breaking of Form," a chapter in a volume on *Deconstruction and Criticism* that Bloom jointly authored with not *a* but *the* Paul de Man, Jacques Derrida, Geoffrey Hartman, and Hillis Miller. Taking as a "proof-text" Ashbery's *Self Portrait in a Convex Mirror*, Bloom reads through this difficult poem with characteristic eloquence in an attempt to review and restate his own controversial theories of influence. What is finest about this surprisingly traditional *explication de texte* is that though it seems to begin as an attempt at deconstruction of *a* poem it ends up as a reconstruction of *this* poem: after reading Bloom's reading, one really does understand the work better—that is, to be Derridean, one finds oneself stepping under Ashbery's text and assuming for a moment the burden of its beliefs and unbeliefs.

Two other essays on John Ashbery appeared in connection with the publication of part 2 of *Litany* as a special supplement in *APR* (8,iv). In "Syntax and the Poetry of John Ashbery" (pp. 37–40) Jonathan Holden argues interestingly that Ashbery's poetic achievement is founded on his "abstract-expressionist" use of syntactical structures as principles of composition, while in "A Movement out of the Dream: Poetry of John Ashbery" (pp. 33–36) Cynthia Evans undertakes a wider survey of the poet's career, emphasizing his phenomenological awareness of "the moment in which he exists as he perceives it" and "the passage of that moment into the past."

Considering their sometimes controversial positions on the contemporary scene, Robert Bly and James Dickey were relatively neglected in 1979. Some of the secondary materials that appeared, though, will be useful to many readers. Philip Dacey's brief but charming "The Reverend Robert E. Bly, Pastor, Church of the Blessed Unity: A Look at 'A Man Writes to a Part of Himself'" (*Book of Rereadings*, pp. 1–7) defines Bly both as "a heterodox Lutheran minister successfully disguised as a poet" and as a religious Romantic obsessed with the problem of the divided self. Two other essays in the *Book of Rereadings* deal with Dickey's work: Stephen Dunn's "A Rereading of a Sort, James Dickey's 'The Sheep Child'" (pp. 109–11) and Peter F. Dusenbery's "The Three Dimensional Parlor of James Dickey's 'The Shark's Parlor'" (pp. 327–35). Both are appreciative though somewhat unfocused explications of individual poems. Finally, Jim Elledge's *James Dickey: A Bibliography, 1947–1974* (Scarecrow) is a lightly annotated but carefully organized volume that is bound to be essential for serious students of this poet's career.

Several essays on W. S. Merwin and a book-length study of Frank O'Hara also appeared this year. In "W. S. Merwin: Rational and Irrational Poetry" (*LitR* 22:309–20), Victor Contoski argues that Merwin's poetry is neither irrational nor obscure but instead structured by a "faith-ful" quest for a "meaningful life." Similarly, in "Order and Energy in Merwin's *The Drunk in the Furnace*," Linda Trengen and Gary Storhoff offer a rather naive discussion of Merwin's work in terms of well-worn existentialist concepts. T. R. Hummer's readings of Merwin in his essay on Roethke and Merwin, discussed earlier, are probably more useful than either of these pieces. Finally, Alan Feldman's *Frank O'Hara* (TUSAS 347) is a useful if somewhat diffuse introduction to the life/work of this contemporary writer, whose achievement can now be seriously evaluated in light of Donald Allen's posthumous editions of his poetry and other recently published volumes. Feldman's style is clear and unpretentious; his readings are both illuminating and evaluative without being excessively enthusiastic or hastily censorious; and he pays particular attention to biographical pressures that helped shape O'Hara's aesthetic—his work at the Museum of Modern Art, his homosexuality, his friendships with Koch and Ashbery, and so forth. The most sophisticated students of O'Hara may consider Feldman's analyses somewhat elementary or at least preliminary, but many readers of contemporary verse will probably find his book helpful, if only because of its strong grasp of the period and place in which the so-called New York school took shape.

vii. W. Dickey, Hollander, Howard, Meredith, Merrill, Oates, Ortiz, Weiss

Neither equally "major" nor equally well known, the poets in this last group don't by any means represent a definitive rounding out of the list of recent poets whose work critics studied this year. On the contrary, I'm deliberately devoting this final section of my review to an extraordinarily various but vigorous selection of writers, meant to suggest, once again, the complexity of the "scene" we confront when we try to describe and analyze contemporary verse. Not only in their styles, but also in the "traditions" they represent, the genres they employ, and the systems of reference they draw upon, these artists confront readers and scholars with a striking range of literary problems. Dickey, Howard, and Merrill, for instance, are now being studied as, among other things, writers who participate significantly in the homosexual tradition that Robert K. Martin and others have begun to define. Ortiz has been placed—and places himself—in a separate but equally important tradition of poetry that explores and exploits Native-American roots. Oates must be understood not only as a poet but also, of course, as a major novelist who is a poet, while

Hollander can be read as a critic/scholar who is also a poet. And clearly these writers represent only a random literary gathering, a particular collection of poets who have surfaced simultaneously in 1979 through some coincidence of criticism or publishing.

William Dickey's *The Rainbow Grocery*, for instance, was the subject of a particularly fine review-essay by Frances Mayes (*NER* 2: 145–48), a piece that traces Dickey's growth from the early, tightly controlled verse in *Of the Festivity* to a wilder, more comically Surrealistic poetry that explores new erotic and aesthetic possibilities. Similarly, the title poem of John Hollander's 1978 volume, *Spectral Emanations: New and Selected Poems*, evoked an elegant meditative explication by Harold Bloom, whose "The White Light of Trope" (*KR* 1 [n.s.]:95–113) relates Hollander's brilliant but difficult work to Hawthorne's *The Marble Faun* as well as to a variety of Hebraic sources. And although Richard Howard's poetic career was treated in two essays that were more general in focus, these too, like the pieces on Dickey and Hollander, seemed to be important preliminary gestures in a process that is just gathering force. Michael Lynch's "The Life Below the Life," collected in *The Gay Academic*, offers an overview of Howard's career as a homosexual poet, while Greg Kuzma's "Howard's Flowers" (*Book of Rereadings*, pp. 452–88) is a similar survey that emphasizes *Untitled Subjects*, especially the Wilde-Whitman fantasy recorded in "Wildflowers."

Helpful mid- or early-career appraisals of poetry by Meredith, Merrill, Oates, Ortiz, and Weiss also appeared this year. Henry Taylor's "In Charge of Morale in a Morbid Time: The Poetry of William Meredith" (*HC* 16,i:1–15) is an overview of the poet's career which pays special attention to Meredith's debt to Berryman. Illumination of James Merrill's *The Book of Ephraim* is provided in J. D. McClatchy's lively "*DJ*: A Conversation with David Jackson" (*Shenandoah* 31,ii:23–44), while Peter Stevens' "The Poetry of Joyce Carol Oates," in *Critical Essays on Joyce Carol Oates*, ed. Linda W. Wagner (Hall) is, again, a generalized introduction to a body of verse deserving of more attention than it has yet received. Finally, Willard Gingerich's "The Old Voices of Acoma: Simon Ortiz's Mythic Indigenism" (*SWR* 64:18–30) is an expanded review of a work by a fairly recent poet—Ortiz's *Going for the Rain*—which considers this writer's use of places and patterns associated with his Native-American heritage, while Robert Stock's "A Passion Equal to all Hope:

Theodore Weiss" (*HC* 16,ii:1–12) is a sophisticated survey of a more established writer's achievement, which analyzes the poet's rhetoric as well as his influences in an attempt to account for his impassioned optimism.

There is much important recent verse that has *not* been adequately treated this year—I think particularly of the new feminist poetry I mentioned earlier, work by writers like Lorde, Griffin, and Grahn—but nevertheless, many of the essays in this last group, though they're uneven in quality and though they vary in sophistication and scope, are commendable attempts to trace the figures of contemporary poetry that we all see, as we see ourselves, in a mirror that distorts our vision even as it seems to promise honesty. Or, to return to my alternative metaphor, the best of these essays, like some of the others I've been discussing, are serious efforts to name the forest while standing in the shadow of the trees.

University of California, Davis

18. Drama

Winifred Frazer

i. From the Beginning

At the end of the decade historical studies of American drama take a back seat to those of contemporary playwrights and movements. There are, however, several articles concerning 18th-century theatre performances and influences of early drama on that to come. In "The Province of Speech: American Drama in the Eighteenth Century" (*EAL* 13:24–33) Jay Martin shows that early American drama, in an analysis of manners, portrayed a superior social class as based on superior consciousness or on great service to the community, or finally, on the creation of a new American character as produced by a new society in a new land. As such it was influential between 1740 and 1800 in laying the groundwork for assumptions on which 19th-century Americans based their literature and their beliefs. In a companion piece, "Royall Tyler's 'Bold Example': *The Contrast* and the English Comedy of Manners" (*EAL* 13:3–11), Donald T. Siebert, Jr., illustrates that Tyler encouraged in Americans an independent spirit by his literary independence in combining licentious, Restoration-like comedy and didactic 18th-century sentimentality. If the world is a stage, Americans obviously must prefer, Tyler implies, those who are themselves, to those who are putting on an act.

In "Plays and Amusements Offered for and by the American Military During the Revolutionary War" (*ThR* 4[1978]:12–24) Jared A. Brown documents that, in spite of restrictions by the Continental Congress in 1774, performances allowed by commanders of various military units served to raise morale and to keep a theatrical tradition alive until after the war, when it flourished. Philadelphia; Portsmouth, N.H.; and Reading, Pa., as well as Valley Forge, were the scenes of productions of such plays as *Cato, Coriolanus, The Lying Varlet,* and *Revenge.* A drama presented not for edification or amusement but to reconcile two divergent religious factions failed to

achieve its aim, according to George B. Bryan and Mary Bashaw-
Horton in "Drama as Social Corrective: A Performance at Windsor,
Vermont, in 1791" (*NEQ* 51:99–105). *The French Revolution*, originally performed at Dartmouth College, brought only continued strife
between the opposing parties.

Two studies concerned with the 18th century to the present are
Abe Laufe's *The Wicked Stage: A History of Theater Censorship
and Harassment in the United States* (Ungar, 1978) and Richard
Palmer's "The Aristocratic Motif in the Drama of Russia and the
American South" (*SoQ* 17,i[1978]:65–88). In the first Laufe, beginning with Puritan and political censorship before 1800, recounts numerous instances of closings of plays and musicals on the American
stage through the 1970s. Although the 19th century comes in for only
brief mention, each decade of the 20th gets extended treatment. The
style is chatty rather than legalistic and deals with harassment as
well as official censorship in New York and regional theatres illustrated by some 35 photographs of offending performances. In the
second Palmer considers numerous Russian and American plays portraying aristocrats, from Robert Mumford's *The Candidates* (1770)
and Denis Ivanovich Fonvizin's *The Minor* (1782) up to the plays of
Tennessee Williams and Anton Chekhov. Both Russian and southern
American aristocrats feel a superiority in their class, which is reinforced by the caste system and ritualized customs.

Adding a footnote to 19th-century American theatre history, Barbara Barker in "Maria Bonfanti and *The Black Crook*, New Orleans,
1872" (*ETJ* 31:88–97) details the 20-year career in America of ballerina Bonfanti, including incredibly taxing tours in which Bonfanti
would arrive one day and dance with a local chorus to a local orches-
tra that night.

ii. 20th Century

Henrik Ibsen figures in four items on late 19th- and early 20th-century
drama. In *James A. Herne: The American Ibsen* (Chicago: Nelson
Hall, 1978) John Perry documents the life and work of the author of
Shore Acres, Margaret Fleming, and *Sag Harbor*, which, representing a break with 19th-century sentimentality and melodrama, showed
the way, as did Ibsen, for later 20th-century realists. As a popular
actor, as well, Herne played the lead in many of his own dramas op-

posite his wife, Katharine Corcoran, never, however, losing his concern for the rural, the poor, and economic inequalities, for which he advocated Henry George's single tax. Frederick Marker and Lise-Lone Marker in "Early Ibsen Performances in America" (*ScanR* 66, iv[1978]:20–34) point out that *The Pillars of Society* appeared in Milwaukee in 1879, a year before any Ibsen play was performed in London. Between then and Alla Nazimova's two-month run of *The Master Builder* in 1907 in New York, Ibsen's plays were so frequently produced that Walter Prichard Eaton called him "one of the most popular playwrights in America today." Robert Brustein in "The Fate of Ibsenism" (*ScanR* 66,iv[1978]:7–19) discusses modern productions of the playwright, along with an appeal to moderns to recognize the value of his example of standing alone in a critical world. In "The Culture of the Provincetown Players" (*JAmS* 12: 291–310) Arnold Golman makes clear that political and social radicals helped found the group to produce plays, which, like Ibsen's, declared a new social freedom and equality for men and women. Hutchins Hapgood's liberalism was replaced by John Reed's left-wing socialism, but both had encouraged aesthetic and social freedom through the Players.

Orville K. Larson's "Robert Edmond Jones, Gordon Craig and Mabel Dodge" (*ThR* 3[1978]:125–33) provides an interesting sidelight on the imaginative stage designer for the Provincetown Players and his frustrating attempt to study in Florence under the great innovator Craig. Craig's refusal to see Jones was apparently because of the letter of introduction which the young man brought from that patron of arts and artists, Mabel Dodge, with whom Craig was at outs. As the Provincetown went professional, new radical theatre groups arose, as documented in *People's Theatre* (Rowman, 1978) by David Bradby and John McCormick. Building on the thesis that the most significant development in the theatre during this century is the broadening of its social basis, the authors describe the rise of democratic and radical theatres in Britain and on the Continent. In the United States agit-prop grew in the late 1920s and 1930s with such groups as the Workers' Theatre League, the New Playwright's Theatre, the Theatre Union, Clurman's Group Theatre, and the Federal Theatre.

In an extremely useful reprint Hugo Rorrison has translated with helpful additional notes Erwin Piscator's *Das Politische Theater*

(1929). *The Political Theatre* (Avon, 1978) consists of Piscator's account of his years in Germany preceeding and following World War I, along wtih some 100 photographs illustrating the many plays and films Piscator directed during the time for the Volksbühne and Piscator-Bühne and other Berlin theatres. The account does not extend to Piscator's post–World War II years in New York with the Dramatic Workshop and the Group Theatre, but his modern staging in Germany of such plays as Upton Sinclair's *Singing Jailbirds* and *What Price Glory?* and others had great effect on traditional American stage design and direction during the early decades of the century.

iii. Ruth Draper, Rachel Crothers, Clifford Odets, William Saroyan, Lillian Hellman

Again this year (see *ALS 1978*, pp. 368–69) Ruth Draper's unique work is noted. With high praise for her creation of innumerable characters in her one-person dialogues Neville Rogers in "The Art of Ruth Draper" (*OhR* 19,i:6–23) speculates that Draper (who was admired by Ellen Terry, Sarah Bernhardt, Eleanora Duse, Henry Adams, Henry James, and Bernard Shaw) may have been the greatest actress of all times. Surely she was America's best ambassador of good will abroad up until her death in 1956. Another woman prominent in the theatre during the first half of the century is the subject of Lois C. Gottlieb's *Rachel Crothers* (TUSAS 322). As playwright, producer, director, and actor Crothers held her place in a male-dominated theatre world, illustrating in her own career the difficulties of some of her women characters. Although *Susan and God* was her most important commercial success, today's audiences prefer plays like *He and She*, in which a talented sculptor is torn between her career and her family.

Harold Cantor's thesis in *Clifford Odets: Playwright-Poet* (Scarecrow, 1978) is that, far from being only the leftist social realist of the 1930s, Odets achieved great success with three post–World War II dramas, the best of which is *The Flowering Peach*. As a portrayer of Jewish family life, Odets broke ground for Jewish writers of two decades later, and as a writer of resonant dialogue he portrays an imaginative, poetic world beyond the mundane. Richard J. Dozier in "Recovering Odets' *Paradise Lost*" (*ELWIU* 5:209–21) is also full of high praise. Odets' vision of the wasteland is set in a crumbling house, inhabited by a troubled family and homeless outsiders, but is so rich as to "spill out of its frame." If it is "a litany for the dead," it speaks dramatically to the modern era, which no longer judges a play in terms of theatrical realism. It is true that although Odets' reputation rests partly on his leftist drama (and a revival of *Waiting for Lefty* in Washington, D.C.'s The Studio Theatre this year testifies to its timeliness), he may be remembered most as a portrayer of family life in mythical terms and semipoetic language.

William Saroyan figures in two collections of essays: Nona Balakian's *Critical Encounters: Literary Views and Reviews, 1957–1977* (Bobbs-Merrill, 1978) and *The Old Century and the New: Essays in Honor of Charles Angoff*, ed. Rosa Alfred (Fairleigh Dickinson, 1978). In "The World of William Saroyan" Balakian reviews the work of the still prolific writer, stressing that the same optimism of *The Time of Your Life* appears in Saroyan's most recent fiction and drama, which, whether it is all printed or not, is therapeutic for the creator of it. In "Michael Arlen and William Saroyan: Armenian Ethnicity and the Writer," from the second collection, Harry Keyishian contrasts the response to social ostracism on the part of the smart British novelist of the 1920s and the homely American fiction and drama writer of the 1930s. Arlen's response was to sharply satirize the artificiality of sophisticated British society, Saroyan's to create simple, good-hearted Californians. Both pieces testify to Saroyan's contented acceptance of a world he made.

Steven H. Bills in *An Annotated Bibliography of the Life and Works of Lillian Hellman* (Garland) includes, with at least brief annotation of all, everything from biographical material to reviews of her major plays as well as scholarly works on each play, and reviews of her screenplays and of her three autobiographical works of recent years. The division of the material into eight sections and many subsections, as well as careful indexing, makes it easy for the scholar to locate items on any aspect of Hellman's life and works. Although she is the author of eight important American plays and in late years three enlightening autobiographical volumes, Hellman only now has made it into the Twayne series. In *Lillian Hellman* (TUSAS 338) Katherine Lederer's main thesis is that Hellman's enduring artistry lies in her ironic vision rather than in her political leftism or her well-made play structures, as commonly thought. From *The Children's Hour* through *The Little Foxes* and on to *Toys in the Attic*, Hellman's interest

is essentially moral, rather than political or dramaturgical, climactic-
ally exemplified in her stand during the McCarthy era as recounted
in *Scoundrel Time.*

iv. Eugene O'Neill

Leading off the studies on O'Neill this year is a collection of essays—
Eugene O'Neill: A World View, ed. Virginia Floyd (Ungar)— on the
playwright's reputation in England, Europe, and Scandinavia. In informative essays Clifford Leech writes on the production of O'Neill's
plays in England; Josef Jarab, in Czechoslovakia; Timo Tiusanen, in
Europe and Scandinavia; Peter Egri, in Hungary; Marta Sienicka, in
Poland; and Tom Olsson, in Stockholm. Critical essays on various
plays by Finnish, Danish, and Russian cities, along with some ten by
American critics and actors, supplemented by Floyd's extensive introduction, fill out this useful volume, which testifies in particular to
O'Neill's popularity abroad, even during the decades of the 1940s and
1950s when it was at a low ebb in his own country. Those wanting a
competent summary of the playwright's life and works will find Frederic I. Carpenter's revised *Eugene O'Neill* (TUSAS 66), with its
new concluding chapter and updated bibliography, useful. Louis
Sheaffer, well-known biographer of O'Neill, in response to questions
on his methods—"O'Neill's Way" (*Confrontation* 17:167–70)—replies
that he invented no conversations, considered O'Neill's plays to be
fictionalized biography, and took an attitude of skepticism toward the
playwright's own claims about himself.

Three essays which, from different viewpoints, stress O'Neill's
recognition of America's failure to live up to its dream are: John Gatta
Jr.'s "The American Subject: Moral History as Tragedy in the Plays of
Eugene O'Neill" (*ELWIU* 6:227–39), Thomas F. Van Laan's "Singing
in the Wilderness: The Dark Vision of Eugene O'Neill's Only Mature
Comedy" (*MD* 22:9–18), and Winifred L. Frazer's "'Revolution' in
The Iceman Cometh" (*MD* 22:1–8). In the first, claiming that O'Neill
saw as tragic the failure of America to live up to Emersonian ideals,
Gatta describes the struggle in many of O'Neill's characters between
admirable self-reliance and acquisitive greed. Such plays as *Desire*
and the *Mourning* trilogy illustrate the tragedy of the failure of the
New England conscience to bring the American Eden to fruition. In
the second Van Laan points out that *Ah, Wilderness!* has undertones

of criticism of the family life it seems to extol, besides satirizing the sentimental, stereotyped characters and their chauvinistic responses to the Fourth of July. Recognition that the playwright's view is different from that of the characters makes the play much richer than an average family comedy. In the third Frazer shows that a poem called "Revolution" by a 19th-century German revolutionary and lyric poet, Ferdinand Freiligrath, is the source of two important thematic lines in *Iceman*. "The days grow hot, O Babylon!/ 'Tis cool beneath thy willow trees!" is repeated with variations some dozen times by anarchist Hugo Kalmar (Karl Marx), a character based on a friend whom O'Neill knew in the Hell-Hole bar. Besides fortifying the love-death, bridegroom-iceman connotations of the play, the lines illustrate that revolution is one of the foolish illusions by which men try to improve society.

Two essays on *Long Day's Journey* throw light on O'Neill's psyche. The first, Judith E. Barlow's "*Long Day's Journey into Night*: From Early Notes to Finished Play" (*MD* 22:14–28) is a very illuminating commentary on the changes O'Neill made from first draft to last in his autobiographical play. The very harsh portraits of the Tyrones in early versions are modified finally to tone down the cruelty and anger and to present complex individuals caught between love and resentment. For example, such a description of Mary as "possessed by an alien demon of revenge" is omitted in the final script in which the earlier portrait of a viciously spiteful woman is modified. James and Jamie too become worthy of compassion as O'Neill worked out his own frustrations in later drafts. In "Ghosts of the Past: O'Neill and Hamlet" (*MR* 20,ii:312–23) Normand Berlin begins with Jamie's remark about Mary—"The Mad Scene. Enter Ophelia"—at the end of *Journey*, and enumerates many similarities between it and the scene in *Hamlet*. From there Berlin cites Jamie's association of his mother with a whore, as does Hamlet, and his similar wish for death, which in *Moon* Josie prays may come for him soon. Without belaboring minor points Berlin makes an interesting case for the psychic pressures on O'Neill, exerted by his extensive knowledge of *Hamlet*, and for Jamie as the portrayal of O'Neill himself.

In a third very perceptive essay on the play—"The Phenomenology of the Glance in *Long Day's Journey into Night*" (*ETJ* 31:343–56)—David McDonald makes his case that "watchers-being watched" is of the essence in *Journey*. The three men watch Mary, who watches them watching her until she absents herself from their glances through drugs. Taking Sartre's view that "the look" results through four steps in absence of the self, McDonald proposes a sequence of four comparable phases in *Journey*. McDonald thoroughly demonstrates the extent of the visual interplay and the dramatic effect of seeing and being seen on the identity and the outcome of each character in *Journey*.

Two items on techniques which O'Neill uses in several plays are James A. Robinson's "O'Neill's Symbolic Sounds" (*MLS* 9,ii:36–45) and Carol Billman's "Language as Theme in Eugene O'Neill's *Hughie*" (*NMAL* 3:Item 25). Enumerating the extensive sound effects in *The Emperor Jones, The Hairy Ape, Lazarus Laughed,* and *Dyamo,* Robinson points out how they symbolize, as O'Neill himself claimed of these early plays, "the inscrutable forces behind life." In a more original piece about a more sophisticated drama Billman contends that O'Neill's sense of dialogue and use of dialect in *Hughie* dramatize his theme that human beings can get through to one another by means of the link of language, the failure of which is the cause of violence in other one-acts like Edward Albee's *Zoo Story* and Amiri Baraka's *Dutchman*.

The Eugene O'Neill Newsletter, ed. Frederick Wilkins, has carried more essays of substance in each year of its existence, along with continued coverage of staged productions, conferences, books, articles, and dissertations about O'Neill. Essays in the first issue of 1979 (2,iii) include three on possible influences on the playwright. In "Crane's *Maggie*: A Source for *The Hairy Ape*" (pp. 8–10) Robert McIlvaine tellingly cites similarities of language and action between Maggie's brother and her lover and O'Neill's seaman Yank. In "Another Biblical Parallel in *Desire Under the Elms*" (pp. 10–12) Patrick Bowles equates Abishag, a fair damsel sent to warm the blood of old King David, with Abby, who tries to warm Ephraim, as well as equating Adonijah, who is executed for loving Abishag, with Eben, who comes to the same end. In " 'Splendid Twaddle' ": O'Neill and Richard Middleton" (pp. 13–16) Michael Hinden, having unearthed a volume of this mediocre poet, whose poems, according to O'Neill's wife Agnes, O'Neill often quoted, finds that Middleton, a suicide at age 29, and his moody, love-sick verse affected the young O'Neill, possibly supplying the name of Richard to the like young man in *Ah, Wilderness!*

In the Spring issue (3,i) two essays concern O'Neill's attitude toward life in early plays. Patrick Bowles in *"The Hairy Ape* as Existential Allegory" (pp. 2–3) sees Yank as a symbol of the Self, caught like Rodin's *The Thinker,* whose pose he imitates, between ape and essence crying out in despair, "Where do I fit in?" Frank R. Cunningham in *"The Ancient Mariner* and the Genesis of O'Neill's Romanticism" (pp. 6–9) points out that O'Neill's early adaptation of Coleridge's poem, dramatizing the reconciliation of man with nature, showed an interest which the playwright never lost in what he called "an unquenchable flame in man which makes him triumph over his miseries." A final bibliographical item by Winifred Frazer, "A Lost Poem by Eugene O'Neill" (pp. 4–6) provides external and internal evidence that an anonymous poem in Emma Goldman's *Mother Earth* of May 1911 is the earliest work of the playwright to appear in print. A satirical, political takeoff on a section of "The Rubaiyat," it illustrates the young man's knowledge of the poem as well as his radical proclivities at that time.

The most notable item in the third issue of the year (3,ii) is "John Howard Lawson on Eugene O'Neill, Man and Playwright" (pp. 12–14), in which LeRoy Robinson summarizes previously unpublished comments by Lawson on O'Neill and *Dynamo,* which has close resemblance to Lawson's earlier play, *Nirvana.*

v. Arthur Miller, Tennessee Williams, Edward Albee

A volume—*Critical Essays on Arthur Miller,* ed. James J. Martine (Hall)—consists of a collection of reviews and essays written by various critics during the past 35 years and an introduction in which Martine selectively reviews the scholarship on Miller. Martine also includes an interview with Miller, completed specifically for this volume, in which the playwright elucidates his views of critics, plays, academics, television, his own playwriting, and his future work. In a brief answer to the question as to the most important event of the century Miller replies to the editors of *Confrontation* (No. 15[1978]: 152–53) that the Holocaust caused at least a subconscious recognition by everybody that "vileness is possible" at any time.

In *After the Fall,* however, Miller places the evil in the individual. Clinton S. Burhans, Jr., in "Eden and the Idiot Child: Arthur Miller's *After the Fall (BSUF* 20,ii:3–16) believes that in what he considers Miller's best drama Quentin's evil is a *felix culpa,* whereby Quentin recognizes his former arrogance through growth of consciousness and accepts with joy the tragic vision of what it means to be human. He rejects the illusionary lie of Eden to embrace the idiot child of life from Holga's dream. In a review of a recent autobiographical piece—the Hallmark television play, *Fame*—Enoch Brater ("The State of Things," *MichA* 11:217–18) praises the medium which can be a vehicle of quality drama, and the play, in which Miller's hero, Meyer Shine, finds that being a celebrated playwright and an individual in our American culture are not easily reconciled.

Miller's ever-challenging *The Crucible* elicits two worthwhile essays this year: John Ditsky's "Stone, Fire and Light: Approaches to *The Crucible*" (*NDQ* 46,ii:65–72) and William T. Liston's "John Proctor's Playing in *The Crucible*" (*MQ* 20:394–403). Praising the structure, the settings in home and court, and the Shakespeare-like language, Ditsky finds that the images of fire and light in stony New England convey the crises of personal and social conscience which make *The Crucible* Miller's most produced play. Liston, on the other hand, holds that Proctor, a character who speaks in metaphor, has a playful imagination which makes him, like Plato's poet, a revolutionary and a threat to the community.

In a sociological essay, "Sports and the Competitive Ethic: *Death of a Salesman* and *That Championship Season*" (*BSUF* 20,ii:17–21) Frank W. Shelton compares the themes and the different eras of the two plays. They are alike in that an older man—father or coach—has been the advisor to younger men who have failed in life because of the false ideals of their mentors. Separated by a generation, the plays illustrate a growing disintegration in America through the competitive ethic. In Arthur Miller's play Biff's game is football with its implication of at least some green spaces surviving. In Jason Miller's play the urban game of basketball has guided the men to even more fruitless and brutal lives than those of Willy's sons.

In Karl Harshbarger's Freudian interpretation of *Death*, it turns out that Linda is at fault in keeping her three men childishly dependent on her and that Willy's problem is his homosexual love for Biff, whom he longs to admire and identify with, at the same time hating his need of a male figure which his missing father never supplied. In reality, less deconstructionist than a summary makes it seem, *The Burning Jungle: An Analysis of Arthur Miller's Death of A Salesman*

(Univ. Press), although a slight volume, does offer some close readings of crucial lines which call for new interpretations.

Tennessee Williams usually rates two or more volumes a year. This year, in a *Life*-sized book and with a *Life* format of several pictures for almost every one of its 160 pages, the outline at least of his life and career is made visual in *The World of Tennessee Williams*, ed. Richard R. Leavitt (Putnam's, 1978). Ever since *The Glass Menagerie* changed the course of American drama, Williams has, will it or not, been in the limelight of the American theatrical scene. Leavitt's is therefore a valuable collection of memorabilia and pictures of productions. Much of the material for the book is housed in the Williams collection in the Humanities Archives at the University of Texas, where much more remains. Although Foster Hirsch in *A Portrait of the Artist: The Plays of Tennessee Williams* (Kennikat) purports to show new relationships between the life and plays of Williams, he covers a subject already vastly explored in a slight volume containing such an error as that Sebastian is cannibalized on "a South American mountaintop."

It's an unusual year as well that doesn't produce at least one extensive interview with Williams in a scholarly periodical. In Cecil Brown's "Interview with Tennessee Williams" (*PR* 45[1978]:276–305) the two discuss a variety of subjects at the playwright's home in Key West. In such interviews Williams obligingly reveals his plans. hopes, reactions, and other matters of interest to his public. In this one, for example, he explains his intention in 1937 of writing a long play about D. H. Lawrence and of his traveling to Taos to confer with Frieda and all who knew Lorenzo there. Inspired, he wrote *Phoenix*, planned to be the end of a much longer play, until his agent told him, "Nobody is interested in Lawrence," at which point he dropped what he now believes could have been a great play.

Making a case for the reading of Williams' plays, Nancy Anne Cluck in "Narrators in the Drama of Tennessee Williams" (*AL* 51: 84–93) notes that Williams' only narrator on stage is Tom in *Glass*, who takes license with dramatic convention to narrate the play. In *Cat on a Hot Tin Roof* the narrator takes the reader into his confidence in the stage directions. In *Streetcar* the reader picks up biographical data about Stanley.

The Tennessee Williams Newsletter, ed. Stephen S. Stanton, began

its first year of publication with very respectable Spring and Fall
issues, each containing book reviews, notes on productions, abstracts
of articles and books, forthcoming publications and productions, and
reviews of productions of Williams' plays. Several short articles as
well are of interest. Carol F. Reppert in "Suddenly Last Summer":
A Re-Evaluation of Catharine Holly in Light of Melville's 'Chola
Widow'" (1,ii:8–11) makes the case that Catharine may be emotionally unstable and hence as ambivalent a character as Sebastian, by
her comparison of Catharine to the disoriented woman in Melville's
sketch "Norfolk Isle and the Chola Widow." Lee Quimby traces a
theme in "Tennessee Williams' Hermaphroditic Symbolism in The
Rose Tattoo, Orpheus Descending, The Night of the Iguana, and
Kingdom of Earth" (1,ii:12–14) and finds that Williams in early
works represents the hermaphrodite as psychically whole, but the
ideal perishes as the playwright's creative powers have faded, until
Lot in Kingdom sounds its death knell.

In a well-titled article, "Surviving with Grace: Tennessee Williams
Today" (SoR 15:753–62), Kenneth W. Holditch reviews four recent
volumes on the playwright, acknowledging his aesthetic failures in
the last years and hoping that he will still "surprise us with magic."
In spite of difficulties the playwright holds an honored place in the
literature and the theatre of America.

Edward Albee is the only American dramatist to receive treatment in June Schlueter's Metafictional Characters in Modern Drama
(Columbia), which examines artistic self-consciousness in such foreign playwrights as Pirandello, Beckett, Genet, and Stoppard. Opposing the view that a fiction can be real, the metafictional view is
that admitted artifice is closer to the truth of reality in declaring itself to be what it is. In Who's Afraid of Virginia Woolf? George and
Martha put on an act of pretending to be parents, a role they throw
off at the end under the direction of artist-director George.

Two notes, each entitled "Albee's Who's Afraid of Virginia Woolf?"
by J. Albert Robbins (Expl 37,iv:17–18) and by Vernon Hall (Expl
37,ii:32), make the point that George's line "ice for the lamps of
China" derives from Albee's satire of Alice Tisdale Hobart's mediocre novel of 1933, Oil for the Lamps of China, thus doubly demolish-
ing Kai-Ho-Mah's case for the line's referring to a turning Chinese
lamp which gives the illusion of running horses (Expl 35,iv:10–11).

A rather lengthy summary of the action causes Porter M. Gilbert in

"Toby's Last Stand: The Evanescence of Commitment in *A Delicate Balance*" (*ETJ* 31:398–408) to conclude that the Nothing or Terror that causes Harry and Edna to leave their home corresponds to what Tobias comes to realize as the Emptiness or existential Nothingness of all their lives. The circularity of the play leads back to the beginning with Tobias in the center, no more able than at the start to commit himself to others or to action of his own. Thomas P. Adler takes a more hopeful view in "Albee's *Seascape*: Humanity at the Second Threshold" (*Renascence* 31:107–17). Claiming that the last line of *Balance*—"Come now; we can begin the day"—like that of *Seascape*—"Begin"—foretells a new start for mankind after a night or an eon of despair or failure, Adler sees these plays as a contrast to the play whose title and last line is *All Over*.

About this last play James Neil Harris in "Edward Albee and Maurice Maeterlinck: *All Over* as Symbolism" (*ThR* 3[1978]:200–208) claims that Albee is familiar with Maeterlinck's life and works and the dictates of static theater and symbolist drama. *All Over* is not naturalistic but symbolistic as from a tomb, the title of which may come from Maeterlinck's last words in the throes of a heart attack. Albee may be saying that for 19th-century patriarchal society it is all over. As in other years Albee's plays create some differing opinions, none of which this year seems of great note.

In *The Language of Modern Drama* (Rowman, 1977) Gareth Lloyd Evans pays tribute to O'Neill, Miller, Williams, and Albee, for although these "American cousins" fail when they try to achieve an English classicism, they succeed in creating a "strange, indigenous hard poetry" when they remember their own language. Even in the naturalistic mode, American playwrights have an oratorical tradition which emboldens them to use a largesse of expression beyond the ability of their British contemporaries.

vi. Contemporary

In the "Drama" section (pp. 396–438) of the *Harvard Guide* Gerald Weales traces the work of the major playwrights, cites trends and landmark productions, summarizes the accomplishments of minor playwrights, points out the increasing use of Off-Broadway plays on Broadway through the 1950s, describes the history of black drama during the period, comments on the genres of farce and musical

comedy in America, and emphasizes the growing importance of regional theatres today. Not feeling sure that his summary will prove to
have been accurate in years to come, Weales concludes: "Everything
about the period [sinceWorld War II] seems tentative to me."

One thing that doesn't seem tentative is the number of books on or
by theatre people that pour from the presses. George S. Kaufman is
good for two this year: Malcolm Goldstein's *George S. Kaufman: His
Life, His Theater* (Oxford) and *By George: The Collected Kaufman*,
ed. Donald Oliver (St. Martin's). The first is a thorough recording of
the creation and production of all of Kaufman's dramas as well as a
presentation of his personal life. The book includes details of his
collaborations with some 25 other writers and musicians and their
part in productions ranging from *The Time of Your Life* (1930)
through hits like *The Solid Gold Cadillac* (1953). The second is a
slighter work with an introduction by Dick Cavett, full of praise for
this volume of Kaufman's articles, playscripts, and an entire year of
silly calendar dates.

Anyone as successful as Neil Simon deserves a book summarizing
his work, which Edythe M. McGovern efficiently does in *Neil Simon:
A Critical Study* (Ungar). Considering each of 13 nonmusical plays
in chronological order from *Come Blow Your Horn* (1961) through
Chapter Two (1977), McGovern includes a picture and synopsis of
each, along with brief biographical and critical comments. In "Notes
from the Playwright" Simon says that although he never rereads his
old plays, the book was "enormously revealing to me"—adding a second reason for its existence besides its use as a reference summary of
America's most popular writer of comedy. A popularized biography
about a playwright of stature is Linda Simon's *Thornton Wilder: His
World* (Doubleday). Numerous photographs add to a lively account
of the life and works of Wilder, who won two Pulitzer Prizes for
Our Town and *The Skin of Our Teeth* and experienced great success
with the play *The Merchant of Yonkers*, which became *The Match-
maker*, which became *Hello, Dolly!* Simon makes clear that in spite
of a small dramatic output Wilder holds a firm place in mid-20th-
century American drama.

John Houseman's *Front and Center* (Simon and Schuster) is a
well-written second volume of his autobiography. Writing in order
that the theatre and film history in which he participated will not be
lost, Houseman describes his directing work with the Theatre Guild,

the Mercury Theatre, the Negro Theatre Project of the WPA, the Voice of America during the war, and in succeeding years his work on both coasts in directing and producing such plays as *Galileo, The House of Bernarda Alba, King Lear,* and *Lute Song.*

In another autobiographical account Ralph Bellamy in *When the Smoke Hits the Fan* (Doubleday) recalls incidents from his 57 years on the American stage and in moving pictures. Since his career included some 200 to 300 plays in stock and rep, several Broadway hits, almost 100 films, and innumerable television shows, Bellamy has much to choose from.

Three lesser volumes are Marian Seldes's *The Bright Lights: A Theatre Life* (Houghton Mifflin, 1978), *Actress: Postcards from the Road* (New York: M. Evans, 1978) by Elizabeth Ashley with Ross Firestone, and *170 Years of Show Business* (Random, 1977) by Kate Mostel and Madeline Gilford with Jack Gilford and Zero Mostel. In the first Seldes, who teaches drama at the Julliard School, describes the parts she has had in such plays as *The Milk Train Doesn't Stop Here Anymore, Tiny Alice, A Delicate Balance, The Chalk Garden,* and *Equus* on and off Broadway during the past 30 years. In the second, Ashley, at age 38, recounts the story of her 20 years of ups and downs in and out of the theatre and cinema. In the third the Gilfords and Mostels relate their adventures during a total of 170 years in musicals and plays, closing with Zero's death in 1977. Taken together, all these biographies do enliven theatre statistics with personal memories and photographs not available elsewhere.

Several essays concern productions and movements of recent decades while many more cover the last few years.

Two which appear in collections are Ruby Cohn's "Camp, Cruelty, Colloquialism" in *Comic Relief: Humor in Contemporary American Literature,* ed. Sarah Blacher Cohen (Illinois, 1978) and Ronald Hayman's "Albee and Shepard" in his *Theatre and Anti-Theatre: New Movements Since Beckett* (Oxford). In the first Cohn illustrates the three C's of types of humor in many modern American playwrights—including Camp in Martha's imitating Bette Davis, Cruelty in Megan Terry's *Viet Rock,* and Colloquialism in John Guare's contemporary slang in *House of Blue Leaves* (pp. 281–303). In the second Hayman writes on "Albee and Shepard" (pp. 147–77) and their eclecticism. Although Albee borrows speech rhythms and ideas from other modern playwrights and from *Faust* in *Tiny Alice,* Shepard goes him one better in borrowing more imaginatively from contemporary playwrights, adding rock music, film, cartoon strips, and disc jockey chatter. Fascinated with language itself and "pulled toward images that shine in the middle of junk" Shepard has had 27 plays (listed in the appendix) performed at various small theatres throughout the country between 1964 and 1977.

Several essays are concerned with movements and types of American drama popular in post–World War II years. Joan Holden in "Satire and Politics in America; or, Why Is That President Still Smiling?" (*Theater* 10,ii:104–07) says it is because there is no good political satire in American drama which draws blood. Playwrights like Gelber and Baraka, and troupes like The Living Theatre, the Bread and Puppet Theatre, and Modern Times Theatre are not encouraged. As a footnote Barbara Garson, answering the question by the editors of *Confrontation* (No. 15[1978]:157–58), says that the "Non-Event of the Half-Century" is the lack of such an audience for satire as she had in the 1960s for her antiwar teach-in production of *MacBird*. Further evidence of the same view is found in Barnett Kellman's interview "The American Playwright in the Seventies: Some Problems and Perspectives" (*ThQ* 8,xxix[1978]:45–58), in which he finds that writers like Jack Gelber, Lanford Wilson, and Michael Weller are more interested in the *how* than in the *why* of drama, unlike British playwrights, who are interested in the political effect of the theatre.

In the main, Americans seem to go for right-wing morality. Richard Powers in "One G-Man's Family: Popular Entertainment Formulas and J. Edgar Hoover's F.B.I." (*AQ* 30[1978]:471–92) points out that in spite of the popularity on TV and screen of the G-Man show, some sponsored by the F.B.I., it lost audiences in the 1960s, as evidence appeared of the heroic figure's overstepping the bill of rights. Richard M. Palmer has gathered interesting evidence, which he presents in "Moral Re-Armament Drama: Right Wing Theatre in America" (*ETJ* 31:172–85), of the widespread production of MRA plays between 1940 and 1964. Extremely propagandistic, the plays stressed communism as the major enemy and spiritual conversion of the individual as the solution to life's ills.

Allen E. Hye throws a somewhat similar light on a play usually considered to portray the triumph of reason over that old-time religion. In "A Tennessee Morality Play: Notes on *Inherit the Wind*"

(*MarkhamR* 9:17–20) Hye sees in this drama by Jerome Lawrence and Robert E. Lee the archetypal morality play with its didacticism, its contrast of good and evil, its issue of whether mankind is to be saved or damned, even its reporter devil Hornbeck—all of which with the added local color of this rural state in 1925 make it a Tennessee morality play.

Critics attempt to place Ferlinghetti, Foreman, and Rabe aesthetically and culturally. Michael Skau in "Toward a Third Stream Theatre: Lawrence Ferlinghetti's Plays" (*MD* 22:29–38) proposes that between the well-made play and spontaneous improvisation runs a third stream of theatre characterized by the subversion of language, the intermixing of audience and actors, and the inaction of characters who look on rather than engage in life. Ferlinghetti's plays—*Unfair Arguments with Existence* and *Routines*—in the third stream, replace conventional theatre with experimentation which contributes to liberation and hence to the evolution of new audiences. Kate Davy contributes "Richard Foreman's Ontological-Hysteric Theatre: The Influence of Gertrude Stein" (*TCL* 24:108–26). Foreman uses multiple beginnings to get the effect of momentarily intense images, as Stein says she experienced drama as a child. Foreman also puts pressure on the mind to work at perceiving the event, like Stein, who forces the reader to notice himself trying to comprehend the whole. David Rabe, according to Robert Asahina in "The Basic Training of American Playwrights: Theater and Vietnam War" (*Theater* 9,ii[1978]:30–37), is the only dramatist to make successful use of the war. Rabe's trilogy, though faulty, provides cultural critics with an interesting example of the art of drama on the contemporary subject of the most unpopular war in America's history. Thomas P. Adler elevates the first of Rabe's trilogy by his comparison of it to Shakespeare in " 'The Blind Leading the Blind': Rabe's *Sticks and Bones* and Shakespeare's *King Lear*" (*PLL* 15:203–06). Rabe's allusions to *Lear* include the pattern of reason in madness and sight in blindness as Vietnam-blinded David tries to make Ozzie and Harriet *see*. David's poetic imagination creates sense of nonsense, like Lear's fool. Ozzie sets up a court scene like Lear's in which Rabe puts American ideals on trial and urges the audience to "see better."

Besides playwrights as well known as the three above, new theatre groups and playwrights emerge from year to year. Laurence Shyer in "Journey to *New Jerusalem*" (*Theater* 11,i:65–72) describes

the production of Len Jenkins' play by the New York Shakespeare
Festival Workshop at the Public Theater. Set on an island for international criminals, all objects are charged with changing lights, and
noises assault the senses, until the end when to the accompaniment of
vast organ music, all vanishes. Stage fever affects the West Coast
as well: Jules Aaron describes "The Playworks Festival at the Mark
Taper Forum" (*Theater* 11,i:73–79) where twelve plays at three
theatres were presented by playwrights from all over the country. In
"Directing the Holocaust Play" (*ETJ* 31:526–40) Robert Skloot describes the difficulties of directing *Throne of Straw* by Harold and
Edith Lieberman at the University of Wisconsin in July 1973, a play
concerned with the possible collaboration of the Jewish leader of the
ghetto of Lodz, Poland.

In "Notes from the Avant-Garde" (*ETJ* 31:5–24) Xerxes Mehta
provides an extremely useful description of the differences in theory
and practice of four experienced American groups who performed
at The New Theatre Festival in June 1978 in the Mount Vernon
Square area of downtown Baltimore: The Performance Group (New
York), Kraken (Baltimore), American Contemporary Theatre (Buf-
falo), and the Mabou Mines Group (New York). Mehta analyzes
the "creation that emerges from collectives" among those who during
the past decade have achieved the security to be able to "shed
worn-out skins."

Among professional critics evaluating the New York theatre scene,
Sam Shepard requires the most, perhaps somewhat grudging, at-
tention. Gerald Weales in "American Theater Watch, 1978–79" (*GaR*
33:569–81) comments at length on the Pulitzer-Prize-Winning *Buried
Child*, during which year Shepard also starred in the film *Days of
Heaven* and had three other plays on the boards: *Seduced, Getting
Well*, and *Jacaranda*. This "unhousebroken" playwright is thus the
most produced of the season in spite of his playing "a dirge for the
end of the American dream." Along with Bernard Pomerance's *The
Elephant Man*, Ernest Thompson's *On Golden Pond*, Michael Weller's
Loose Ends and a Sondheim musical *Sweeney Todd*, Shepard's con-
tribution makes Weales conclude, somewhat querulously, that crea-
tivity is not dead in New York. John Simon in *"The Elephant Man"*
(*HudR* 32:403–10) pans this play. In "Theater Chronicle: Kopit,
Norman, and Shepard" (*HudR* 32:77–88), however, Simon has kind

words for three nontraditional playwrights on the boards. Arthur Kopit's *Wings* is his best play to date. Marsha Norman's *Getting Out* is "an astonishing first play." And Shepard's *Buried Child* is full of symbols that "play absorbingly, disturbingly, and finally overpoweringly on stage."

Stanley Kauffman makes the case in "New York: the City and the Theatre" (*ThQ* 8,xxxii:34–40) that despite vast activity in many cities, New York is still the theatre capital of the United States. Broadway may have lost theatres and glamor, but Off-Broadway and Off-off-Broadway continue to grow with thriving companies which receive large proportions of national and state grants. Shepard comes in for note by Kauffman, as he does in Carol Rosen's "Sam Shepard's *Angel City*: A Movie for the Stage" (*MD* 22:39–46). Green film-slime engulfs the characters of the city of angels, signifying perhaps the fate of film-addicted America. If Shepard is our new O'Neill, he foretells an even greater revolution in American drama than that of the 1920s.

vii. Reference Works

A very useful bibliographical essay by Jackson R. Bryer and Ruth M. Alvarez is "American Drama, 1918–1940: A Survey of Research and Criticism" (*AQ* 30:298–330). Divided into sections on Reference Works, Anthologies, Histories, General and Specialized Criticism, and some two dozen individual playwrights, the volume cites works published mainly from the 1930s through the 1970s, which are described as to their content and purpose. Another is C. W. E. Bigsby's "Drama as Cultural Sign: American Dramatic Criticism, 1945–1978" (*AQ* 30:331–57). Bigsby sees criticism of American drama as poorer than criticism of the novel and relatively ignored by serious critics. Although principal periodicals dealing with drama arose only in the last two decades, Bigsby reviews a large number of books and articles on American theatre and playwrights since World War II.

A volume useful in conjunction with the two essays above stresses production more than drama as literature: Don B. Wilmeth's *The American Stage to World War I: A Guide to Information Sources* (Gale, 1978). Two large sections of the volume are "State and Local Histories" by states and "Individuals in the American Theatre." There are helpful lists of current and past periodicals in the field as well as listings of theatrical collections in various libraries—a means used more and more by researchers in specialized fields. Wilmeth also has two bibliographical essays in *Handbook of Popular Culture*, vols. 1 and 2, in which he discusses the major sources of history and criticism for such popular kinds of stage entertainment in America as the minstrel show, vaudeville, burlesque, musical revue, dime museum, melodrama, circuses, and other outdoor entertainment (see also chap. 22).

Import of British productions to America is not all one-sided, as is testified to by William T. Stanley's *Broadway in the West End: An Index of Reviews of American Theatre in London, 1950–1975* (Greenwood, 1978). Including 3,000 reviews of 339 productions, the volume lists playwrights alphabetically with their plays, the date, theatre, and length of run, and often 10 to 15 newspaper and periodical citations where reviews appeared, under each writer. To find information on deceased or no longer active American and British stage personalities, Gale Research Company has composed from 15 volumes of *Who's Who in the Theatre* a four-volume *Who Was Who in the Theatre, 1912–1976: A Bibliographical Dictionary of Actors, Actresses, Playwrights, and Producers of the English-Speaking Theatre* (1978). The annual bibliography of "Modern Drama Studies," comp. Charles A. Carpenter, includes a section on American drama (*MD* 22:142–50) divided according to general works and individual playwrights for the year 1978.

Among specialized bibliographies are L. Terry Oggel's "A Guide to the Edwin Booth Literary Materials at the New York Public Library" (*BHR* 82:90–104). Mainly housed in the Theatre Collection of Lincoln Center, the Booth material includes 515 letters to his daughter Edwina, stage plans of stage machinist Benson Sherwood, and numerous promptbooks, scrapbooks, ledgers, and manuscripts. Other Booth material is listed in Oggel's earlier "A Short Title Guide to the Edwin Booth Literary Materials at the Players" (*PAR* 3[1976]: 98–142). George B. Bryan's "Vermont Drama: A Bibliography" (*Vermont History* 46:175–93) is an extensive alphabetical listing of plays set in Vermont or by Vermonters and an alphabetical list of playwrights, with the names and dates of the plays they wrote. *The Encyclopedia of Southern History* (LSU) includes a summary of the history of the theatre in the South by James M. Dorman with high-lights from theatrical firsts in the coastal cities to present trends in the Southeast today. If no landmark works of scholarship emerged in 1979, at least great interest in the theory and practice of the contemporary American stage is evinced by serious scholars and critics.

University of Florida

19. Black Literature

John M. Reilly

The vigor of Afro-American literary studies has never been greater. The quantity of scholarship published in 1979 is as high as it has ever been. Articles on black literature are more frequently to be found in general journals, indicating editorial recognition of the broadened interest among all academics in a literature that provides the specialized journals its able contributors and loyal audiences. And the completion of 16 dissertations in the field at North American universities during the past two years marks the arrival of a new cohort of scholars prepared to build upon the work of the last decade.

Along with the quantity of production has come also growing diversity and exciting suggestions of new theoretical development. The recent scholarship still refers to the classic texts identified by previous critical study. Increasingly, though, there is awareness of precedent, coterminous, and succeeding texts that togther constitute Afro-American literary tradition. Once hypothesized by critical practice, the idea of a unique tradition creates fascinating problems. To be sure, essays are still being written on the premise of simple reflection theory in which literature is presumed to be notable for its burden of documentary social fact. Since it is so attractive for classroom use such writing will always have its place; yet, more and more, scholars are seeking to answer such questions as: What are the specific structures of black narratives? What inherent patterns are there in the writing of black female artists? Precisely how does folklore or dialect work in written literature? And how does Afro-American writing relate to the other literatures of America?

Instances of the energy with which the new tasks are being undertaken can be found in three anthologies and four special issues of journals. *Sturdy Black Bridges: Visions of Black Women in Literature*, ed. Roseann P. Bell, Bettye J. Parker, and Beverly Guy-Sheftall (Doubleday) presents 15 critical essays strongly emphasizing con-

Black Literature

temporary American women writers. *Afro-American Literature: The Reconstruction of Instruction*, ed. Dexter Fisher and Robert B. Stepto (MLA) develops the results of a two-week seminar on "Afro-American Literature from Critical Approach to Course Design." In a foreword to *Chant of Saints: A Gathering of Afro-American Literature, Art, and Scholarship*, ed. Michael S. Harper and Robert B. Stepto (Illinois) John Hope Franklin suggests this new anthology might serve "as a yardstick by which to measure the evolution of Afro-American literature and culture, and as a commentary on what has happened in these areas since the appearance of *The New Negro* in 1925." The analogy with Alain Locke's compilation has merit, for *Chant of Saints* attempts to represent Afro-American arts so that their abundance and their varied, yet associated, colorings will portray the tradition that has succeeded the Harlem Rennaissance.

The special journal issues devoted to black literature include the fourth quarter *Freedomways* on Lorraine Hansberry, the summer issue of *Black American Literature Forum* on Clarence Major, the July/ August issue of *Black Scholar* on theatre, and the December *Colby Library Quarterly* given over to general black studies topics. Significant articles from these journals will be discussed in their appropriate place.

i. Bibliography

Edward Margolies and David Bakish have prepared *Afro-American Fiction, 1853–1976* (Gale). Their alphabetical checklist identifies 728 novels, 83 short-story collections, and 16 anthologies. All entries provide publication data for first printing. An appendix giving works chronologically makes the book doubly useful. The editors have also made a choice of 15 major authors for whom they provide a selected and well-annotated listing of bibliographies and critical studies. If one is tempted to question exclusions from that list, the book's other features, including a listing of 50 general bibliographies and 73 general studies of black fiction, will reduce criticism to quibble.

William P. French, Michel J. Fabre, and Amritjit Singh offer a companion guide, *Afro-American Poetry, 1760–1975*, bound in the same volume with Geneviève Fabre's *Afro-American Drama, 1850–1975* (Gale). The two-thirds of the volume given to poetry opens with a listing of standard reference works, presentation of general studies, and a checklist of anthologies. Individual authors appear in three chronological groups. The strength of the poetry guide is comprehensiveness. On the other hand, Geneviève Fabre's drama guide finds its strength in a substantial overview of dramatic development of black theatre in the introduction. Fabre's essay traces the emergence of black theatre as an institution and provides a convenient typology for the work of recent playwrights. This listing of general studies includes references to library resources, bibliographies, collections, and critical studies. The main body of the guide also arranges authors chronologically. Published and unpublished plays are included, with selective indication of secondary studies. There is overlap between Fabre's work and James V. Hatch's and Omanii Abdullah's *Black Playwrights, 1823–1977* (Bowker, 1977); for a review of the two see *BALF* (14 [1980]:44–46).

Charles D. Peavy's *Afro-American Literature and Culture Since World War II: A Guide to Information Sources* (Gale) appears intended for a readership that finds such earlier bibliographies as *Blacks in America*, ed. James M. McPherson et al. (Doubleday, 1971), *The Negro in America*, ed. Elizabeth W. Miller (Harvard, 1970), and *The Negro in the United States*, ed. Dorothy B. Porter (Library of Congress, 1970) insufficient for coverage of literary topics. Yet Peavy's book is marred by unanswered questions about its own selectivity. The 56 individual writers given entries are justifiable enough, though the principle for selecting secondary sources is unclear. In a section on "Subjects" Peavy covers 28 topics that "reflected the Zeitgeist of this period." The Black Aesthetic is included, but not the work of Stephen Henderson. Black Power appears, but not Black English.

Perhaps because of tighter focus, but certainly because of greater assiduity, three reference guides recently published by Hall are consistently more dependable. Curtis W. Ellison and E. W. Metcalf, Jr., illustrate the model in their volume *William Wells Brown and Martin R. Delany: A Reference Guide* (1978). Brief introductions outline critical responses to Brown, 1844–1975, and Delany, 1838–1975, while the body of the book presents listings of books and shorter items alphabetized year by year. R. Baxter Miller's *Langston Hughes and Gwendolyn Brooks: A Reference Guide* (1978) uses the introduction to relate the poets' work to scholarship and reviews. Works on Hughes proceed from 1924 to 1977, on Brooks from 1944 to 1977. As in other Hall guides secondary sources are preceded by listings of primary works. The test of the model G. K. Hall employs comes this year with a volume on a writer about whom commentary is vast. *James Baldwin: A Reference Guide* by Fred L. Standley and Nancy V. Standley includes in the notation of primary works reviews Baldwin wrote for *The New Leader* in the 1940s, dialogues, interviews, essays, short stories, excerpts from stories, plays, and, of course, the novels. Secondary materials are heavily annotated, reprinted studies cross-referenced.

Jessamine S. Kallenbach's *Index to Black American Literary Anthologies* (Hall) offers references to 142 collections ranging from *The New Negro* through books issued by Associated Publishers during the 1930s and up to compilations from the mid-1970s. Arranged alphabetically by author, works are keyed to anthologies by page number, and a separate index by title refers to the author in the master list. Another guide directed to students is Robert L. Southgate's *Black Plots & Black Characters: A Handbook for Afro-American Literature* (Syracuse: Gaylord). Southgate explains that he has determined the shape and content of his book on the basis of practical teaching experience. The result is a melange of aids. There are 95 plot summaries: Toomer's *Balo* is included, but not *Cane*; John A. Williams' *Captain Blackman*, but not *The Man Who Cried I Am!*. Omitted also are *Up From Slavery* and *Souls of Black Folk*. A second section of the book provides a short companion to literature with explanatory notes on various subjects. A section of author bibliographies lists primary works and such secondary sources as *Contemporary Authors* and the *New York Times*. One may well have doubts about a book of plot summaries, but in this case the fault lies in the absence of any clear indication of editorial principles.

Dee Beich Cameron's "A Maya Angelou Bibliography" (*BB* 36: 50–52) provides a record of the many editions and reviews of the major works, short annotations for minor works, and a section of biographical articles and interviews. "A Checklist of the Creative Writings of W. E. B. DuBois" by Paul G. Partington (*BALF* 13: 110–11) explains that the unpublished creative work has been at the University of Massachusetts since 1973. Sooner or later all will appear in print, but meanwhile the short creative pieces have to be found in *The Horizon*, which DuBois edited from 1907 to 1910, but not in *The Crisis* where he published the creative efforts of others. There are some pieces in *Moon Illustrated Weekly*, but only 10 percent of the file exists. As a result of the paucity of published material Partington can only list the five novels, *Selected Poems* published in Ghana in 1963, books with short stories in them, 21 poems from magazines, eight other stories, and two very short dramas. Robert Fikes, Jr., gives a full listing of works by James Alan McPherson under the title "The Works of an 'American' Writer" (*CLAJ* 22:415–23). Fikes is also responsible for "Echoes from Small Town Ohio: A Toni Morrison Bibliography" (*Obsidian* 5:142–48) arranged in the same way as the McPherson bibliography. The special issue of *Black American Literature Forum* on Clarence Major contains "Toward a Preliminary Bibliography of Clarence Major compiled by Joe Weixlmann and Major" (*BALF* 13:70–72). "User-oriented" rather than all-inclusive, it attempts to locate all works by Major in each of the genres he adopts. Adding further to the project, Weixlmann reprints along with the "Preliminary Bibliography" previously unpublished reviews by Ron Fair and Ishmael Reed of *All-Night Visitors* and Kofi Awoonor's unreleased introduction to *The Syncopated Cakewalk* (*BALF* 13: 73–74). For the Lorraine Hansberry issue of *Freedomways* Ernest Kaiser has collaborated with Robert Nemiroff, the playwright's former husband, on a comprehensive "Lorraine Hansberry Bibliography" (19: 285–304).

Kaiser also serves as the most dependable recorder of new books in his regular column "Recent Books" in *Freedomways* (19:54–64, 118–28, 174–77) where he lists new books with annotations referring to related or similar works in all fields concerning blacks in the United States. Vèvè A. Clark performs a similar service for dramatic works and theatrical production in "Enough of the Blues: The Year's Work in Black Theatre, 1978: A Biblioreview (*BSch* 11,i:69–80).

The anthology *Sturdy Black Bridges* must also be noted for its inclusion of selected bibliographies of primary and secondary sources on 24 writers discussed or represented in the volume, as well as listings of writings by male authors on female characters, African women writers' works, and criticism or creative writing by Caribbean women.

ii. Fiction

a. Griggs, Chesnutt, DuBois, J. W. Johnson. Over 30 years ago Hugh M. Gloster noted that Sutton E. Griggs was one of the most

popular authors among the black working class at the end of the
19th century. Nevertheless, it has been Griggs's fate to be practically
dismissed by critics. With his essay "Literary Garveyism: The Novels
of Reverend Sutton E. Griggs" (*Phylon* 40: 203–16) Wilson J. Moses
hopes to begin a proper appreciation of the author who believed
popular literature should serve the political purpose of fostering
racial patriotism. Although the essay rambles, Moses describes Grigg's
style as "splendidly primitive, clear, forceful, and colorful," many of
his characters as embodiments of "twoness," and the structure of his
novels as determined by folklore motifs.

This year's essays on Charles W. Chesnutt, who is in no danger
of neglect, show varying degrees of success. Trudier Harris in "Chesnutt's Frank Fowler: A Failure of Purpose?" (*CLAJ* 22:215–28) concentrates on character portrayal in *House Behind the Cedars*. Despite his virtues the dark-skinned Fowler is described in ways that
recall the Plantation Tradition, including a personal acceptance of
inferior status. Since Chesnutt's similarly virtuous mulatto characters
are always represented as worthy of entry into the white world, Harris
concludes that Fowler's portrayal reflects Chesnutt's own caste prejudice. The argument almost persuades until one recalls the satiric treatment of mulattoes in Chesnutt's short stories and the heroic black
figure of Josh Green in *The Marrow of Tradition*. Recognition of the
complexity of Chesnutt's beliefs during the nadir of American race
relations informs Susan L. Blake's "A Better Mousetrap: Washington's
Program and *The Colonel's Dream*" (*CLAJ* 23:49–59). Ordinarily
Chesnutt's story of a privately sponsored plan of reconstruction is read
as a frustrated utopia. Blake cogently argues, though, that Colonel
French's industrial dream is founded on the idea popularized by
Booker T. Washington that whites would accept blacks if they showed
themselves willing to sacrifice and offered economic advantage to
cooperative whites. Chesnutt rebutted Washington's belief in an
essay of 1903, "The Disfranchisement of the Negro," and in 1905
rendered his refutation in the novel.

Both 1979 essays on Chesnutt's short fiction are clever, but each
is strained in fundamental conception. In "The Mask as Theme and
Structure: Charles W. Chesnutt's 'The Sheriff's Children' and 'The
Passing of Grandison'" (*AL* 50:364–75) P. Jay Delmar expands the
significance of mask beyond the familiar reference to shuckin' and
jivin' to include the structural principles of reversed expectations and

absence of foreshadowing plus the metaphor of perception obscured by racism. Relating the Afro-American cultural practice of masking to fiction is ingenious, but it does not add essentially to an explanation of the texts. Karen Magee Myers writes on "Mythic Patterns in Charles Waddell Chesnutt's *The Conjure Woman* and Ovid's *Metamorphoses*" (*BALF* 13:13–17) in demonstration of similarities in the use of four historical ages, transformations, and a frame story the author says represent universal mythic patterns. The theoretical premise of archetypes is simply taken for granted by perfunctory reference to J. G. Frazer's *Golden Bough*, so one is left with questions unanswered about Myers' view of the relationship between Afro-American and other cultures.

Arnold Rampersad, who published *The Art and Imagination of W. E. B. DuBois* (see *ALS 1976*, p. 374), uses "W. E. B. DuBois as a Man of Literature" (*AL* 50:50–68) to survey the numerous ways DuBois anticipated later developments in Afro-American creative writing. DuBois was the first to break with rhyme and blank verse ("A Litany of Atlanta"), first to celebrate human blackness ("Song of the Smoke"), first to write a *Bildungsroman* and promulgate the doctrine of the Third World (*Dark Princess*). Rampersad is wonderfully successful, because while he relates DuBois' creative ferment to the political and intellectual turmoil within himself he also sustains an engaging analysis of DuBois' search for suitable genres.

Until recent criticism characterized him as a morally obtuse figure, the narrator of James Weldon Johnson's *The Autobiography of an Ex-Colored Man* had been treated as ambiguous. It is the purpose of Maurice J. O'Sullivan, Jr., to return to the earlier interpretation in "Of Souls and Pottage: James Weldon Johnson's *The Autobiography of an Ex-Colored Man*" (*CLAJ* 23:60–70). The measured prose of the novel, says O'Sullivan, along with the narrowed responsiveness of the narrator provides both a sense of ambivalence felt by readers and the means to suggest that the protagonist of the novel is irresolute about his choices. "Themes and Cadences: James Weldon Johnson's Novel" (*SLJ* 11,ii:43–55) by Ladell Payne summarizes the action of the novel in order to remark similarities to the work of other southern authors.

b. **Fisher, Fauset, Toomer, Hurston.** Leonard J. Deutsch gives a memorable introduction to a neglected writer of the Harlem Renaissance in " 'The Streets of Harlem': The Short Stories of Rudolph Fisher" (*Phylon* 40:159–71). The chronological survey of Fisher's career shows him creating a world and an imaginative language that constitute a principal history for the Renaissance. Technically Fisher depends greatly on realistic depiction of topography and the problems of urban adjustment faced by migrants, but his eye for tragedy and his ironic mode transform the history into literature.

Joseph J. Feeney, S.J., aims to redeem the reputation of Jessie Fauset's fiction from classification as conventional and middle-class. His title tells it all: "A Sardonic, Unconventional Jessie Fauset: The Double Structure and Double Vision of Her Novels" (*CLAJ* 22: 365–82). Three out of Fauset's four novels, Feeney says, have a counterstructure darkening the love story, and each posits an underworld where blacks recall past suffering even while they strive hopefully within the realm of bourgeois sentiments.

Publication on Jean Toomer has slackened for the time being, but fascination with *Cane* will never be quelled. Richard Eldridge in "The Unifying Images in Part One of Jean Toomer's *Cane*" (*CLAJ* 22:187–214) joins the band of critics who seek integrating principles for the experimental book. Expanding upon earlier criticism, Eldridge traces images of man and nature, dusk and song, pagan and Christian elements, beauty and ugliness running throughout the tales and verse. In "Frustrated Redemption: Jean Toomer's Women in *Cane*, Part One" (*CLAJ* 22:319–34) Michael J. Clark sees the male characters seeking to possess the instinctive, elusive women in order to impose pattern on life's chaos, but their quest is frustrated because chaos is inner, a condition illustrated by the careers of the female characters who retreat before carnality and materiality. Clark's essay, like Eldridge's, continues a discussion critics have been conducting for at least ten years about redemptive themes in *Cane*. Synthesis provides another way to describe redemption for Elizabeth A. Schultz in "Jean Toomer's 'Box Seat': The Possibility for 'Constructive Crises' " (*BALF* 13:7–12). In the *Earth-Being* manuscripts Toomer repeatedly sets up conditions for dialectical resolution of crisis. Schultz applies the schemes to Dan Moore, the character who fluctuates between creative love resulting from his capacity to translate material reality into spirituality and the brutality he expresses in frustration with mechanistic life. His epiphany and the tale's constructive resolution occur when Moore sees that he can share both the brutalization of the dwarf in the boxing match and the divinity of Christ.

The interest in Zora Neale Hurston generated by the coincidental appearance of feminist criticism and Robert E. Hemenway's first-rate biography (1977) should gain stimulation from the appearance of two valuable editions of Hurston's work. *Mules and Men* (Indiana, 1978) originally issued in 1935 was the first book of Afro-American folklore published by a black author with a major publisher. Hemenway introduces the new edition detailing Hurston's process of tale collection during 1927–29 and explaining her use of personae. *I Love Myself When I am Laughing . . . and Then Again When I am Looking Mean and Impressive*, ed. Alice Walker (Feminist Press) offers selections from Hurston's autobiography, folklore collections, five essays, short stories, and excerpts from the novels. The excellence of the introduction by Mary Helen Washington, the editor's afterword, and a superb production job more than justify the book's appearance. Many selections are now unavailable elsewhere.

As for interpretations of Hurston, Lloyd W. Brown concentrates on *Their Eyes Were Watching God* in "Zora Neale Hurston and the Nature of Female Perception" (*Obsidian* 4,iii[1978]:39–45) in order to explicate Hurston's idea that females recreate their thwarted dreams by forgetting what is too painful to remember. In each case of a relationship with a man in the novel Janie seeks to transcend the limitations of her gender-determined role without acknowledging the conventionality of, first, equating marriage with love, and, later, seeking love with Tea Cake, a man as insensitive and possessive as any other man she has known. Less conclusive than Brown is Ellease Southerland in "The Influence of Voodoo on the Fiction of Zora Neale Hurston" (*Sturdy Black Bridges*, pp. 171–83). Nevertheless, the instances of numerology, significant colors, zombie-like characters, tree symbols, and the portrayal of Moses as a voodoo man are suggestive of a way to explore the unique quality of Hurston further.

c. Wright, Motley, Himes. Evelyn Gross Avery's *Rebels and Victims: The Fiction of Richard Wright and Bernard Malamud* (Kennikat) discusses the different modes of response to oppression. Although Avery sees Wright as essentially a Naturalist, she casts his personae as rebels. She describes Wright's protagonists as passive until pro-

402 Black Literature

voked by whites, inarticulate and without strategy for defense, ambivalent about their heritage, and, because of slavery's ravages, living
barren institutional lives. In that debased state they can only be drawn
into purposeless motion leading nowhere. Malamud is paired with
Wright, because in Avery's description his protagonists—the so-called
victims—make a nearly complete contrast. Wright does portray life
bleakly, at least at first glance, but criticism based upon closer examination has uncovered subtleties of style and structure that make it
impossible to class him as a simple Naturalist, or to deny the creative
dimension of his characters. Above all, however, the treatment of
Wright in this book dissatisfies because it is based upon a reductionist method by which the critic extracts details of verisimilitude from
their literary context, as if those details were unmediated social facts.

The year's treatment of *Native Son* includes two comparative
studies. Stephen Corey's "The Avengers in *Light in August* and *Native
Son*" (*CLAJ* 23:200–212) explains that Faulkner and Wright give
social cruelty a human face by pouring the hatred and power of the
white world into Percy Grimm and State Attorney Buckley. "*Native
Son* and *An American Tragedy*: Two Different Interpretations of
Crime and Guilt" (*CentR* 23:208–26) by Yoshinobu Hakutani takes
issue with the commonplace association of the two novels by illustrating structural differences, contrasting modes of rendition, and focus.
Hakutani's is a welcome effort to deter slack use of the term "Naturalism" in criticism of both novels.

Savage Holiday received no reviews when it was originally published in paperback, and very little has been written on it since. This
year J. F. Gounard and Beverley Roberts Gounard study the novel's
psychological conception in "Richard Wright's *Savage Holiday*: Use
or Abuse of Psychoanalysis?" (*CLAJ* 22:334–49) and conclude that
Wright is faithful to Freudianism, perhaps too obviously so. Another
work by Wright that gets little critical attention is *Black Power*, the
book he wrote after visiting Ghana. John M. Reilly argues that the
book deserves consideration, because it marks a turning point. "Richard Wright's Discovery of the Third World" (*MV* 2,ii[1978]:47–53)
points out that Wright first encountered anticolonialism when he was
distressed by Cold War politics and philosophically depressed after
writing *The Outsider*. *Black Power* revived his optimism, since in
writing he could create a drama of his rational, Marxist persona, effectively completing an analysis of historical development of modernism.

Implied in Reilly's article is the need to give new consideration to the exile years of Wright's career. Nina Kressner Cobb does just that in "Richard Wright: Exile and Existentialism" (*Phylon* 40:362–74) where she examines the evidence for French influence on Wright. Wright's awareness of the nexus between freedom and alienation was the source of his existential insight, she concludes, and for that he needed only his experience as an American black. Cobb's essay states the case exceptionally well, and though it is not entirely new in its conclusions, it has value as refutation of the long-lived notion that Wright lost his creative independence when he left America.

Two important contributions to the study of Willard Motley are Robert E. Fleming's literary biography *Willard Motley* (*TUSAS* [1978] 302) and Jerome Klinkowitz' edition of *The Diaries of Willard Motley* (Iowa State). Fleming deals with Motley as both social critic and artist. In the first and best-known role he saw environment deterministically, but in each succeeding work of fiction his artistry became technically more capable of vivifying life lived humanly. The book includes discussion of uncompleted projects, an account of the posthumous revision by the publisher of *Let Noon Be Fair*, and bibliographies of primary and secondary works. Klinkowitz has selectively cut the diaries which fill 28 handwritten volumes in order to highlight the information they give about Motley's early ambitions as a writer in 1926 and his progress toward publication of *Knock on Any Door*, which appeared in 1947, four years after he stopped the diaries. It is also possible, with the editor's help, to trace Motley's method of composition from diary entry to first draft story to completed incident in a novel. Both Fleming and Klinkowitz establish how Motley's decline during the 1950s and 1960s was the fault of his own misplaced Romanticism coupled with a publishing establishment unsympathetic with his attempts to break out of the formula, best-seller mold.

d. **Ellison, Baldwin, Morrison.** There was a time in the years shortly after publication of *Invisible Man* when it was nearly impossible to tell from published comments on the novel that Ralph Ellison had conceived his book out of black experience and imagination. Then it was the vogue to say this novel of identity happened to be written by a Negro who, as chance would have it, used Negro characters. Today critics will talk of the book's universality, but only as it is arrived at through black specificity. Witness these studies of folk-materials. Robert G. O'Meally's "Riffs and Rituals: Folklore in the Work of Ralph Ellison" (*Reconstruction of Instruction*, pp. 153–69) regards Ellison as a leader in the effort to define folklore as a present and dynamic source for literature. On the one hand, Ellison uses narrative like a blues man who copes with predicament after predicament through art, and, on the other hand, creates stories such as "Did You Ever Dream Lucky?" that recreate the folk tale as multidimensional written literature. Susan L. Blake contributes "Ritual and Rationalization: Black Folklore in the Works of Ralph Ellison" (*PMLA* 94:121–36) to the contemporary discussion of blackness. In Blake's interpretation Ellison ritualizes folklore so as to translate the particular into universal myth. For Blake this process is by no means desirable, for it erases black distinctiveness, and in the instance of *Invisible Man* reduces the figure of trickster John to an acquiescent Sambo. Socially derived conflict, embodied in folkloric conceptions of chaos created by whites, becomes ritualized to the extent that it implies that the social chaos is part of a general, inescapable fate. Blake states her case so provocatively that Hortense Spillers has responded in a letter to *PMLA* (95[1980]:107–08) which charges Blake with taking a static view of universalization which, Spillers says, does not remove the experience from history but represents it on a complementary, dialectically related level.

Two articles focusing on image patterns can also be related to the interest in Ellison's folklore. Lynn Veach Sadler, writing about "Ralph Ellison and the Bird-Artist" (*SAB* 44,iv:20–30), relates numbers of occurrences where birds in Ellison's novel and short stories exemplify the idea that everyone can learn to accept life, be an artist, and, as the folk say, fly away to freedom. The multiplicity of Sadler's citations persuades. Emeha Okeke-Ezigbo's "Buzzard/Eagle Symbolism in Ralph Ellison's 'Flying Home'" (*NConL* 9,v:2–3) convinces in shorter space because the image of a buzzard as Jim Crow and the aspiration to fly are so commonly known.

The richness of *Invisible Man* extends to literary reference, too, as Jane Gottschalk shows in "Sophisticated Jokes: The Use of American Authors in *Invisible Man*" (*Renascence* 30[1978]:69–77). Gottschalk spends a good deal of her time on allusions to Booker T. Washington and the leadership issue. These are obvious. But her presentation of references to T. S. Eliot and wasteland images make the article worth reading.

The final article of interest on Ellison is J. T. Hansen's "A Holistic Approach to *Invisible Man*" (*MELUS* 6,i:41–54). Defining holistic as a method that employs a variety of perspectives to emphasize interdisciplinary relationships, Hansen proceeds to describe the novel as a conjunction of picaresque and anthropological elements. The former are accounted for by the narrator in motion, the latter by reference to four black life-styles the narrator encounters and a five-point development of black male identity. The life-style schemes and pattern of male identity are validated by empirical social research, and there can be little doubt they appear in *Invisible Man* too. The article is an attractive version of the reflection theory. On second thought, though, it raises methodological problems. Is literature confirming the findings of science, or is science explaining literature? If either is the case, can we keep an eye on "literariness"?

James Baldwin's career has reached the point where summary articles have begun to appear. Craig Werner in "The Economic Evolution of James Baldwin" (*CLAJ* 23:12–31) believes Baldwin has always been aware of economic issues such as rent exploitation in the ghetto, but since his earliest work he has been de-emphasizing spiritual approaches to social reality and endorsing political action. The transformation is not yet complete, for though Baldwin is increasingly concerned with the class and production system, he phrases resolutions poetically. Despite the latter qualification Werner rides his thesis too hard to allow for the possibility that the poetic language may also contain concepts of chaos and grace that are religious in origin. C. W. E. Bigsby's "The Divided Mind of James Baldwin" (*JAmS* 13:325–42) argues that it is precisely the presence of contradictory conceptions of grace and secular programs, the desire to make history present in white guilt countered by a cry for atonement, and a wish to be free of racial definition but accepted in its terms that makes Baldwin so continually interesting and, indeed, paradigmatic of American culture.

Eleanor Traylor's "I Hear Music in the Air: James Baldwin's *Just Above My Head*" (*First World* 2,iii:40–43), occasioned by the appearance of Baldwin's newest novel, extends into an account of the narrator-witness who has told the tale of suffering and delight through six novels, a short story collection, and two plays. Hortense Spillers also concentrates on one novel—*If Beale Street Could Talk*—in her essay "The Politics of Intimacy: A Discussion" (*Sturdy Black Bridges*,

pp. 87–106) but does so in order to indicate how Baldwin's fiction rehearses the rhetoric of received opinion, particularly in portrayal of
women as tragic heroines. These women experience God-given love
in the symbolic roles they live through men, so despite Baldwin's concern for the power of blacks in history, his female characters are fated
to remain its objects.

Easily the most discussed story of Baldwin's is "Sonny's Blues."
Not surprisingly, then, it receives treatment again in 1979, this time
by Edward Lobb in "James Baldwin's Blues and the Function of
Art" (*IFR* 6:143–48). Lobb accepts some of the previous analyses of
the story, particularly John M. Reilly's, but he means to show that
the blues have a wider significance than Reilly noted. He does this in
two ways: by showing images of light and dark, sound and silence
reconciled in the blue light of the final band scene; and by suggesting
that beyond the narrative lies a level of discourse on the relation of
art and life, art like the blues necessarily including elements it fights
against in life.

Toni Morrison's prominence may be new, but for critics there is
considerable interest in the works she produced before *Song of Solomon* gained her a wide audience. Phyllis R. Klotman's "Dick-And-
Jane and the Shirley Temple Sensibility in *The Bluest Eye*" (*BALF*
13:123–25) describes Morrison's first novel as a female *Bildungsroman*
that marks the character Pecola's movement into madness by the use
of three versions of a school reader that represents the life-style prescribed by school and society. Jacqueline De Weever in "The Inverted
World of Toni Morrison's *The Bluest Eye* and *Sula*" (*CLAJ* 22:402–
14) extends the basic reading Klotman sees to a general pattern of
inverted roles and desires resulting from a struggle to achieve identity
in a world that refuses to acknowledge blacks. Yet another perspective
on struggle against constriction is provided by Barbara Lounsberry
and Grace Ann Hovett in "Principles of Perception in Toni Morrison's
Sula" (*BALF* 13:126–29). Sula, the authors argue, is a character who
refuses to let any one structure or tradition define her life. Still, she
is an ambiguous figure, for despite the ability to see from several
perspectives she dies without realizing any consequent power. Chik-
wenge Okonjo Ogunyemi's "*Sula*: 'A Nigger Joke' " (*BALF* 13:130–33)
points out that Sula is typical of her community, but considered an
evil influence. Such irony seems to couple with the tendency of things
inexplicably to go awry; thus, the grimness of the insider's joke.

e. **Marshall, Major, Reed, A. Walker, McPherson, G. Jones.** "To Be a Black Woman in America: A Reading of Paule Marshall's 'Reena' " by Gloria T. Hull (*Obsidian* 4,iii[1978]:5–15) critically recovers an uncollected short story from 1962, demonstrating how its alternating viewpoints provide both an autobiographical persona and an epitome of the recent history of educated black middle-class women.

Treatments of prose fiction in the special *BALF* issue on Clarence Major include Doug Bolling's "A Reading of Clarence Major's Short Fiction" (13:51–56), which discusses 12 stories in defining Major's aesthetic principles of fluidity, denial of "closure," and verbal freedom; "Major's *Reflex and Bone Structure* and the Anti-Detective Tradition" by Larry McCaffery and Sinda Gregory (13:39–45), a fascinating account of the ways *Reflex* upends the epistemological surety of the detective genre; and Jerome Klinkowitz' "Notes on a Novel-in-Progress: Clarence Major's *Emergency Exit*" (13:46–50) presented in the form of a letter to Major encouraging him in the task of reinventing fiction by sustaining its own inward reality. Klinkowitz properly indicates his letter is a rhetorical device. Major needs no special urging to create "pure writing" that stands apart from any sociological referents.

The techniques of Ishmael Reed provide the subject for four essays. In one, "Politics as an Innovative Aspect of Literary Folklore: A Study of Ishmael Reed" (*Obsidian* 4,i–ii:41–50), Norman Harris contrasts Reed's Neo-HooDoo, an urban folklore that combats the surrounding majority culture, with rural HooDoo devoted to solution of personal problems. Jewell Parker Rhodes testifies to his personal discovery of Reed's significance in "*Mumbo Jumbo* and a Somewhat Private Literary Response" (*AHumor* 6,ii:11–13), and then goes on to a brief justification of parodic plot elements essential to Reed's seriocomic presentation of black soul. The best of the articles, Joe Weixlmann's "Politics, Piracy, and Other Games: Slavery and Liberation in *Flight to Canada*" (*MELUS* 6,iii:41–50) presents Reed as a surrealist fulfilling aesthetic principles anticipated by Ralph Ellison. The continuous assaults on Lincoln and Harriet Beecher Stowe and the parodies of the slave owner's Europeanism constitute a struggle to maintain ethnic culture against arbitrary misinterpretation. In this struggle literature becomes paramount, because the black surrealists, like the folk, know freedom is a state of mind. Marian E. Musgrave's "Sexual Excess and Deviation as Structural Devices in Günter Grass's

Blechtrommel and Ishmael Reed's Free-Lance Pallbearers" (*CLAJ* 22:229–39) establishes both books as works that juxtapose conventionally outrageous behavior against the genuinely evil practices of society.

Alice Walker's affecting domestic fiction gives two critics the chance to explain its dynamics. In "'Cast Out Alone/To Heal/and Re-Create/Ourselves': Family-Based Identity in the Work of Alice Walker" (*CLAJ* 23:71–94) Peter Erickson observes Walker's *oeuvre*, defining a family first by a child's relation to her grandfather and by tension between the elder generations, then by emphasis on a daughter's guilty relationship to her mother. In short fiction and poetry the focus closes in upon a daughter, her search for her mother, and finally her extended mourning. Mary Helen Washington is also comprehensive in "An Essay on Alice Walker" (*Sturdy Black Bridges*, pp. 133–49), but her attention is given wholly to Walker's empathetic treatment of women who are evolving the consciousness necessary to control their own lives. Simply stated, the progression goes from "suspended women" reminiscent of Toomer's female characters thwarted in their creativity, to women who become victims of psychic violence as they follow urgings to enter the mainstream, and finally to a third stage illustrated by women of feminist persuasion of the late 1960s.

The welcome attention to female characters in Afro-American literature naturally encompasses male authors too. For example, Edith Blicksilver's "The Image of Women in Selected Short Stories by James Alan McPherson" (*CLAJ* 22:390–401) discerns great variations resulting from McPherson's carefully managed narrative distance.

Another experimentalist writer gets attention from Claudia C. Tate, who manages in the brief essay "*Corregidora*: Ursa's Blues Medley" (*BALF* 13:139–41) to illuminate the intricate narrative design of Gayl Jones's psychological novel as two interconnecting stories, one of external events, the other of Ursa's recollections which inform all external detail with symbols arising from the core of her memory.

f. **General Criticism of Fiction.** William L. Andrews discusses the context of mulatto fiction in "Miscegenation in the Late Nineteenth-Century American Novel" (*SHR* 13:13–24). "The issue of black rights," Andrews says, "did not come down to a matter of abstract politics but rather of sexual politics in which miscegenation became the ultimate political act of triumph for blacks over the restraints of Southern civilization." Treatment of these politics by white writers such as Thomas Dixon is familiar enough. Less rabid was Rebecca Harding Davis, whose *Waiting for the Verdict* offered white readers the comfort of showing a black doctor who had passed the color bar returning to his people. At least two black writers also tried to re-solve the question of sexual politics in fiction, with results remark-ably similar to those of moderate white authors. Frances Ellen Wat-kins Harper's *Iola Leroy* shows, according to Andrews, that racial assimilation would be a betrayal of blacks. And when Sutton Griggs took up the challenge in *The Hindered Hand* he affirmed a distinct difference between political equality and miscegenation. Because An-drews is not concerned with motive in Griggs's case, the conclusion is starker than it would have been had it included some remarks on nationalism.

"The Utopian Impulse in Early Afro-American Fiction" (*AFs* 1,iii–iv[1978]:59–71) by John M. Reilly addresses the question why Afro-Americans have not used the literary utopia as a genre of social criticism. Only one work, Edward Augustus Johnson's *Light Ahead for the Negro* (1904), can conceivably be defined as utopian fiction, and it limits the vision of a good life to less than comprehensive equality. Considerations of Martin R. Delany's *Blake* and Sutton Griggs's *Imperium in Imperio*, which are motivated by a utopian im-pulse but fail to achieve full generic form, leads to the conclusion that utopia can only be fully expressed when there exists in historical ex-perience some social model adequate to the imagination. For black American writers there has never been such a model. In 1979 Reilly developed his argument about fictional history in "The Reconstruc-tion of Genre as Entry into Conscious History" (*BALF* 13:3–6). This essay begins from Richard Wright's prophecy in *12 Million Black Voices* that the people will become subjects of their own history. The technically notable feature of that prophecy is Wright's use of a collective narrative voice that departs from the convention of em-pirical reportage: thus, it establishes the possibility of historical action taken by overturning the burden of generic convention imposed on writers by the same society that oppresses them as blacks. Wright in *The Outsider*, John A. Williams in *Captain Blackman*, and Ishmael Reed in several works demonstrate the priority of literary imagina-tion over "objective" history.

Chester J. Fontenot does a superior job of black criticism in "Black Fiction: Apollo or Dionysius?" (*TCL* 25:73–84). I say black criticism because the essay uncovers a specific outlook from within fiction that less sensitive observers will overlook. In brief, Fontenot contends that black fiction arises out of conflict between linear history progressively moving to an obscure future that promises to obliterate the conditions of neoslavery and a mythic history that constantly recreates slavery by conditions of segregation and unemployment. In black fiction the protagonist necessarily rejects linear history because of its false promise and tries to move outside of the mythic to create alternate values. This is why for Bigger Thomas, Ellison's invisible man, Zora Neale Hurston's Janie, and Gayl Jones's Ursa Corregidora there is no such thing as a distant past or future, only a radical present. Another fine contribution to the description of black literary characteristics is made by Elizabeth A. Schultz in "The Insistence Upon Community in the Contemporary Afro-American Novel" (*CE* 41: 170–84). Critics of American fiction commonly remark on the isolato: Huck, Natty, Gatsby. And some, taking as their examples Bigger Thomas and the invisible man, say Afro-American writing is equally concerned with an individualistic ethos. With numerous examples from the past 20 years Schultz demonstrates the reverse is the case. Ernest J. Gaines, Margaret Walker, Louise Meriwether, Alex Haley, Al Young, Ron Fair, William Melvin Kelley, Ishmael Reed, and the later works of John A. Williams all have protagonists defining themselves within their community.

Two more items deserve mention in this section because they illustrate the arrival of a feminist consciousness in black criticism. Jerilyn Fisher's "From Under the Yoke of Race and Sex: Black and Chicano Women's Fiction of the Seventies" (*MV* 2,ii[1978]:1–14) notes the increasing number of works in which women characters reevaluate their inherited conditions so that they may assert their integrity as females without losing ties to their community. Alice Walker, Toni Morrison, Toni Cade Bambara, and Gayl Jones provide the examples from Afro-American writing. The politics of scholarship concern Rita B. Dandridge in "Male Critics/Black Women's Novels" (*CLAJ* 23:1–11). Dandridge charges that apathy, chauvinism, and paternalism account for the inadequate criticism of females' writing by prominent male scholars. Afro-Americanists know as well as anyone that unacknowledged politics motivate literary estimates, but Dandridge's article is hard to judge because it combines slight with nearly conclusive evidence for the abuses the author sees while offering unexceptional advice for better criticism.

iii. Poetry

a. **Wheatley, Dunbar.** This year's publications on poets before the Harlem Renaissance period are the work of Mukhtar Ali Isani, who contributes two articles on Phillis Wheatley, and Peter Revell, who provides a book on Dunbar. Isani's " 'Gambia on My Soul': Africa and the African in the Writings of Phillis Wheatley" (*MELUS* 6,i: 64–72) attempts to correct the view that the poet showed little interest in the evils of slavery. Wheatley's deprecating remarks about Africa usually provide the evidence for that interpretation, but Isani claims that the poet's mourning of past life at home reflects pleasure in becoming Christian, rather than lack of sympathy for the enslaved. A poem to the Earl of Dartmouth speaking of the vogue of falsely romanticized Africans, a letter Wheatley wrote in 1774 mentioning the blacks' inherent love of freedom, and a poem to "A Gentleman of the Navy" imagining Gambia as Eden provide Isani his evidence. "Early Versions of Some Works of Phillis Wheatley" (*EAL* 14:149–55), also by Isani, presents a letter describing the nearly impromptu process of composition Wheatley followed in the poem to Dartmouth.

Peter Revell's *Paul Laurence Dunbar* (*TUSAS* 298) presents Dunbar's works according to genre rather than the customary chronological arrangement of some Twayne books; thus, dialect and "literary" poems are separately treated, and so forth. This makes considerable sense for a writer as prolific as Dunbar. Revell opens his study by analyzing the available black audience at the start of Dunbar's career, because the early poems show a desire to write explicitly for that audience. This, however, is neither the explanation nor the source of Dunbar's dialect verse. In that, it seems, he was encouraged by the example of James Whitcomb Riley and the local color movement. The formal literary poetry, in Revell's view, constituted an attempt to enoble themes that involve universal sentiment. An evident purpose of Revell's book is to defend Dunbar against charges of compromise with racist tastes. He accomplishes the task by setting Dun-

bar in the context of his time and against the temper of American
culture. This is successful enough to make a reader realize that Dunbar must be honored for enormous contributions to the development
of black art.

b. **Hughes, McKay, G. D. Johnson.** Melvin Dixon's "Rivers Re-
membering Their Source: Comparative Studies in Black Literary
History—Langston Hughes, Jacques Roumain, and Négritude" (*Reconstruction of Instruction,* pp. 25–43) makes an ambitious, and largely satisfactory, effort to relate Hughes to "the single most resounding
literary achievement of international scale in the twentieth century . . .
the celebration of a black consciousness through literature." By this
broad statement Dixon means that the Renaissance in American Harlem, Négritude in Francophone countries, and Negrissmo in Hispanic
ones constituted a reinvention of the African self through language.
The most important of the movement's several strategies was transformation of folk materials into literature. Hughes participated both
with poems, such as the one alluded to in Dixon's title, and in trans-
lating Roumain, who had already testified to the influence upon him
of Hughes's example. The strength of Dixon's essay inheres in the
view he takes of black writers within Euro-American settings: refusing
the Hobson's choice of impossible isolation or total assimilation, they
combined the best of their oral African heritage with the most useful
European vocabulary to create a bond of language. William H. Hansell's "Black Music in the Poetry of Langston Hughes: Roots, Race,
Release" (*Obsidian* 4,iii:16–38) treats music as a thematic metaphor.
Middle-class blacks and insensitive whites are out of touch with it;
those who accept the pervasive music of black culture find it rejuve-
nating. Patricia A. Johnson and Walter C. Farrell, Jr., in "How Langston Hughes Used the Blues" (*MELUS* 6,i:55–63) explain that between *Fine Clothes to the Jew* (1927) and *Shakespeare in Harlem*
(1942) Hughes abandoned the poetry of jazz and blues, because he
became deeply involved in radical politics. When he once again took
up the patterns of popular black music his verse had become more
narrative, even more organic, because of his developed working-
class perspective.

Future studies of Claude McKay will no doubt take some account
of his newly available book, *The Negroes in America,* ed. Alan L.
McLeod, trans. Robert J. Winter (Kennikat). The poet wrote the book

while attending the Fourth Congress of the Third International in Moscow, 1922–23. It was translated into Russian, but the English manuscript was lost; so until this new rendering into McKay's native language the book had to be neglected by most scholars. For literary study interest probably will center on McKay's expressed opinions that Dunbar's dialect was in tune with black workers' language, that the highest development of protest appears in *Souls of Black Folk*, and that the only literature worth attention is national propaganda. At other periods in his career McKay had different opinions on literature. Similarly the year's scholarship on McKay differs according to the period it considers. William H. Hansell in "Some Themes in the Jamaican Poetry of Claude McKay" (*Phylon* 40:123–39) parallels his work on Hughes by establishing four categories in McKay's two volumes of Jamaican poetry: commonplace things, love, poems of the peasant mind, and racial or social themes. John Hillyer Condit in "An Urge Toward Wholeness: Claude McKay and His Sonnets" (*CLAJ* 22:350–64) gives his attention to the structure of the verse in which McKay broke with dialect, explaining the principle of imbalance within them as a structural representation of feelings McKay hoped to synthesize by the discipline of the sonnet. Condit closely relates the emergence of McKay's poetics to the stage of his life; thus, his article has the value of an abstract for critical biography.

Erlene Stetson has published previously on women writers of the 1920s. Her contribution for 1979 is "Rediscovering the Harlem Renaissance: Georgia Douglas Johnson, 'The New Negro Poet'" (*Obsidian* 5,i–ii:26–34), a model of feminist reevaluation. Since the time of William Stanley Braithwaite critics have either seen Johnson as a simple romantic or relegated her to minor status—a name in a list. One cannot do much about the latter treatment, but in closely analyzing Johnson's three most popular books of verse Stetson shows her deconstructing male fantasies, producing tragic but hopeful verse by placing women in mythic analogy, and rescuing women from the mask of convention.

c. **Tolson, Brooks, Hayden.** For the study of Melvin Tolson the major event of 1979 is publication of *A Gallery of Harlem Portraits*, ed. Robert M. Farnsworth (Missouri). This book-length manuscript, completed around 1935, preceded the publication of the more cerebral and tightly structured *Harlem Gallery: Book I: The Curator* by

30 years. The author spoke of a manuscript of 340 pages; 297 have been recovered for this edition. Thus we have an early adumbration of Tolson's massive lifetime project. Farnsworth includes a discussion of the early poem's development in his introduction, references to related writings, which include Tolson's M.A. thesis on "The Harlem Group of Negro Writers," and biographical notes. Other work on Tolson for the year is limited to Mariann Russell's "Ghetto Laughter: A Note on Tolson's Style" (*Obsidian* 5,i–ii:7–16), which offers instances of wordplay, varied levels of speech, disparate and multiplied images from *Harlem Gallery* to discuss Tolson's ideal of joining sound, sight, and sense—what he called the "S-Trinity of Parnassus"—to control both the visual and linguistic shape of his poetry.

That it is difficult to generalize about the effect of Gwendolyn Brooks's poetry instigates Hortense Spillers' "Gwendolyn the Terrible: Propositions on Eleven Poems" (*Shakespeare's Sisters*, pp. 233–44). Therefore, Spillers examines a range of stunning poems. In "We Real Cool" implicative simplicity attracts; a constellation of temperaments impresses in other works; "The Anniad" marvelously reworks the epic in ironic mode; and in still other poems it is Brooks's intensification of common life by displacing familiar language with the unfamiliar that accounts for Spillers', and our own, joy. In contrast Beverly Guy-Sheftall's "The Women of Bronzeville" (*Sturdy Black Bridges*, pp. 157–70) passes over the technique of the poems to describe the way the characters within them transcend poverty.

Fred M. Fetrow studies Robert Hayden's inversions and irony in "'Middle Passage': Robert Hayden's Anti-Epic" (*CLAJ* 22:304–18). The poem has resisted classification, but Fetrow's notations of the use of slave-ship names as an ironic catalogue, Hayden's transformation of the quest-journey into the middle passage, the short and brutal similes, and the absence of presiding deities seem enough to allow its denomination as a modern anti-epic. Fetrow has written frequently on Hayden in the past, so the fact that he has a second essay in 1979 does not surprise. "Robert Hayden's 'The Rag Man' and the Metaphysics of the Mundane" (*RS* 47:188–90) concerns the strategy of the poet's giving the rag man attributes relatively superior to the speaker of the poem. As we identify with the speaker, we are forced to reconsider our position in the light of the rag man's contrary values. To his essays on Hughes and McKay William H. Hansell adds one on Hayden. "The Spiritual Unity of Robert Hayden's *Angle of Ascent*"

(*BALF* 13:24–31), like Hansell's other pieces, concerns themes, in this case spiritual ones relevant to Hayden's Bahai faith. The article is thorough, highly suggestive, and deserves careful reading, because in asserting that *Angle of Ascent* is Hayden's *Leaves of Grass* Hansell admonishes us to treat the poem not only as an artifact, but as a project in process.

***d.* Baraka, Madhubuti, Emanuel, Major, Harper.**   William J. Harris' "Militant Singers: Baraka, Cultural Nationalism and Madhubuti" (*MV* 2,ii[1978]:29–34) attempts to show the inspirational force of Amiri Baraka's (Leroi Jones) example in essay and poem on Haki R. Madhubuti (Don L. Lee). Baraka was the central theorist of the movement in the 1960s for black cultural nationalism; Madhubuti's position in *Think Black* was already identical, but he took time to find an adequate form, because his sensitivity to language always vies with his politics. Marvin Holdt, writing "James A. Emanuel: Black Man Abroad" (*BALF* 13:79–85), looks back from Emanuel's 1978 Toulouse poems to trace an increasing subtlety and lyricism.

Two essays on Clarence Major's poetry are included in the previously mentioned special issue. The most substantial of these, Nathaniel Mackey's "To Define an Ultimate Dimness: Deconstruction in Clarence Major's Poems" (*BALF* 13:61–68) attributes Major's technical experiments to his stance as the outsider who unmasks the conventional. Necessarily Major must loosen the syntactic and grammatical threads that tie the world view together. He must even question language's access to a consensual reality by undermining its referential function. The consequence is a remarkably dense verse that ultimately threatens to depart from socially shared language altogether. Fanny Howe in "Clarence Major: Poet and Language Man" (*BALF* 13:68–69) devotes her attention to specific experiments in sound, intensity, and visual poetry that create Major's personal linguistic code.

Michael S. Harper's collection from 1977 provides John F. Callahan the occasion to undertake an overview in "The Testifying Voice in Michael Harper's *Images of Kin*" (*BALF* 13:89–92). By 1970 Harper had worked out the problem of voice in his "performance poems," so he became capable of expressing many styles and experiences, while retaining the active voice of consciousness at the center of the poems. Callahan sees profound creativity in Harper's mix of oratorical and intimate language, because the departure from poetic decorum illustrates the combination of love with politics that Callahan is now attempting to document as an American tradition for a book in progress.

e. General Criticism of Poetry. Gloria T. Hull's "Afro-American Women Poets: A Bio-Critical Survey" (*Shakespeare's Sisters*, pp. 165–82) expands an essay originally published in 1975 but not previously noted in *ALS*. Hull announces uniqueness as the framework of her essay: black women poets are not direct heirs to the Anglo-American tradition, and they also stand apart from the dominant Afro-American tradition. Her most provocative statements concern seven women poets of the Renaissance period: Angelina Grimké, Anne Spencer, Georgia Douglas Johnson, Jessie Fauset, Effie Lee Newsome, Gwendolyn Bennett, and Helene Johnson. Why, except for Fauset, are these poets not better known and rarely classified as Renaissance authors? Hull's answer, in keeping with her title, is bio-critical. Most lived away from Harlem, none produced a large body of verse, and all characteristically wrote in ways too easily classified as feminine. Now Hull finds the newer generation of women poets gaining audiences because they do write as females.

Two essays by Andrea Benton Rushing also illustrate the growing interest in women's poetry but arrive at positions that seem to modify Hull's findings about contemporary writers. Rushing's first essay, "Images of Black Women in Afro-American Poetry" in *The Afro-American Woman: Struggles and Images*, ed. Sharon Harley and Rosalyn Terborg-Penn (Kennikat, 1978), pp. 74–84, asserts that poetic images of women rarely reflect their full reality, because they are used mainly to symbolize traits of general racial importance. The second Rushing essay, "Comparative Study of the Idea of Mother in Contemporary African and African American Poetry" (*CLQ* 15:275–88) notes further limitation in the treatment of women in Afro-American verse. Most poems about women concern mothers, not lovers. Moreover, decidedly maternal and female subjects such as pregnancy, childbirth, menstruation, and menopause are absent. In contrast African poetry will employ female imagery as cosmological symbol, but in neither tradition is much made of women's "domination" of the household. To compare fairly the essays by Hull and Rushing it must be noted that the one writes diachronically, the other synchronically.

Moreover, Rushing surveys writing by both sexes. Nevertheless, the feminist perspective of Hull proffers greater insight when it comes down to work that other critics can build on.

Sherley Anne Williams' "The Blues Roots of Contemporary Afro-American Poetry" (*Reconstruction of Instruction*, pp. 72–87) can be read as a companion piece to Melvin Dixon's essay on Hughes and Négritude. Like Dixon, Williams gives her attention to the new forms developed from cultural interfacing. Blues and spirituals are Afro-American examples, and the characteristic blues voice provides a technique readily adaptable to literature.

We have seen that critics as often as poets find great value in the assimilation of popular language to literature, but the matter of dialect has been more problematic. Of course, mock dialect employed by white authors has demeaned the creators of the popular-language, but the careers of Dunbar, James Weldon Johnson, and McKay, who variously sought to enhance literary language with dialect and to show even nobler purpose, were misunderstood. Henry-Louis Gates, Jr., in "Dis and Dat: Dialect and the Descent" (*Reconstruction of Instruction*, pp. 88–119) sees the passage of dialect from written literature as a great loss, despite the "political" problems its presence entailed. Dialect, he says, is the key to a lost tongue. When common, dialect expresses the singular and hermetic world of a distinct people, and when the poet understands its syntactic options he or she fully shares the consciousness of the people. Why, then, did poets let this invaluable means of creating the inner world of Afro-America pass? Because they felt driven to prove a place for the race in the American mainstream.

Robert B. Stepto expresses his interest in the future of black poetry in "After Modernism, After Hibernation: Michael Harper, Robert Hayden, and Jay Wright" (*Chant of Saints*, pp. 470–86). For the purposes of his essay Stepto establishes the conclusion of modernism in the epilogue to *Invisible Man* where the hibernating narrator prepares to act from a newly created consciousness. Each of the poets named in the essay's title writes of self-willed movement into history: Harper through metaphoric creation of the human picture in *Song: I Want a Witness*, Hayden by reembracing his bloodline and kin in "Elegies for Paradise Valley," and Jay Wright by creating an archivist figure from traditional culture to explore *Dimensions of History*.

iv. Drama

a. **Dodson, Hansberry, Baraka, Bullins.** Scholarly attention to Afro-American playwrights in 1979 has been retrospective. Bernard L. Peterson, Jr., in "The Legendary Owen Dodson of Howard University: His Contributions to the American Theatre" (*Crisis* 86:373–78) offers a detailed survey of the author-director-producer who has exerted his influence on black theatre largely through noncommercial channels. The article's listing of works, biographical sketch, and notation of archival collections makes it a necessary starting place for research. Under the title "Who Has Seen the Wind?" Dodson himself has been writing a commentary on the history and development of black theatre. Part 1 appeared in 1977 (*BALF* 11:108–16); part 2 appeared in the same journal this year (13: 20–23). Dodson speaks frankly of his likes and dislikes, but whatever judgment he makes always includes informative statements on stagecraft. A third portion of the survey will appear in 1980.

The special issue of *Freedomways* on Lorraine Hansberry contains mostly appreciative comment by prominent figures in the world of theatre and black culture, but there are also some contributions of practical immediate use. One already noted is the bibliography by Ernest Kaiser and Robert Nemiroff. Others include Jewell Handy Gresham's "Lorraine Hansberry as Prose Stylist" (19:192–204), an urgent call for attention to the linguistic invention and tempo of the nondramatic works; Steven R. Carter's "The John Brown Theatre: Lorraine Hansberry's Cultural Views and Dramatic Goals" (19:186–91), which derives an outline of Hansberry's aesthetic-political principles from the prospectus of an abortive plan for a popular black theatre in Harlem; and Adrienne Rich's "The Problem of Lorraine Hansberry" (19:247–55), given over to raising questions about such possible filters of Hansberry's writing as the inner and outer censors imposed by expectations of audience reception and, more particularly, Nemiroff's editing of *Les Blancs*.

Craig Werner is both ingenious and compelling with his attempt to explain the rhetoric of Amiri Baraka's dramaturgy in "Brer Rabbit Meets the Underground Man: Simplification of Consciousness in Baraka's *Dutchman* and Slave Ship" (*Obsidian* 5,i–ii:35–40). We know that Baraka would reject the underground narrator of *Invisible Man*, but Werner explains that the chief cause lies in Baraka's distrust of portrayal of complex black consciousness which whites can comprehend and destroy with their greater political and economic power. In fact, Baraka's own underground man, the character Clay in *Dutchman*, illustrates the point when his sophisticated awareness disappears with the plunge of Lula's knife into his body. So *Slave Ship* concedes nothing to interior subtlety, but rather conceals it beneath stereotyped black-white relationships.

"Ed Bullins Was Steve Benson (But Who Is He Now?)" by Richard G. Scharine (*BALF* 13:103–09) undertakes a search for the playwright's alter ego in the "Twentieth Century Cycle." If the matter of autobiographical entry into the plays has pertinence, in this case it lies in the contrast between the consciously revolutionary author and the personae of plays set in the 1950s. Scharine believes the character of Benson, who is hardly revolutionary, emblemizes the sources of Bullins' rage. In a reply to Scharine Bullins puts the whole question off by declaring that his characters have multiple identities and a search for an alter ego is not apt in nonrealistic works like his own (*BALF* 13:109).

b. **General Criticism of Drama.** In their special issue on theatre the editors of *BSch* (10,x) compile a selection of essays showing a historical approach to production and performance within the black community. The theoretical dimension of the project appears in Vèvè A. Clark's "The Archaeology of Black Theatre" (pp. 43–55), which explains the value of Michel Foucault's conceptions when aligned with ethnography and oral history. James V. Hatch's "Retrieving Black Theatre History, or Mouth to Mouth Resuscitation" (pp. 58–62) underlines in a practical fashion the value of oral history techniques. The potential and realized results of research are described by Lorraine Brown, who describes materials assembled at George Mason University in "A Story Yet to Be Told: The Federal Theatre Research Project" (pp. 70–78), and by Jeanne-Marie A. Miller's "Successful Federal Theatre Dramas by Black Playwrights" (pp. 79–85), which discusses early productions of *Brother Mose* by Frank Wilson, *The Trial of Dr. Beck* by Hughes Allison, and *Big White Fog* by Theodore Ward. John O'Neal treats more recent theatrical experience in "The Free Southern Theatre: Living in the Danger Zone" (pp. 11–13), while "Finding the People's Ideology: Black Theatre at Brown University" by Rhett Jones (pp. 17–20) carries the account

to the contemporary period. One other notable contribution about research appears in Margaret B. Wilkerson's "Redefining the Black
Theatre" (pp. 32–42), a report of an investigation of community-
based productions that stresses an orientation toward audience interests rather than performers' to create laboratories for collective
response to social issues.

v. Slave Narratives and Autobiography

Despite the evident importance of the life writings by fugitive slaves,
scholarship has been surprisingly limited until recent years. For example, it seems that just three dissertations have been written about
the narratives as literature, and only one of these has made its way
into print—Charles H. Nichols' *Many Thousand Gone* (1963/69).
The historians have done much better by this literature; however,
1979's output may signify the beginning of substantial published literary study. For one thing, Frances Smith Foster has brought us a
volume that ought to become a basic introduction to the form of the
slave narrative, complementing the studies of Sidonie Smith and
Stephen Butterfield on black autobiography and demonstrating the
literary qualities of the materials that have become basic sources for
the investigations of slavery conducted by the historians John W.
Blassingame, Eugene D. Genovese, and Herbert G. Gutman. Foster's
book, *Witnessing Slavery: The Development of Ante-Bellum Slave
Narratives* (Greenwood) opens with a sketch of the evolving cultural context provided for antislavery writing by the development
of the "peculiar institution." The story proper begins with "Adam
Negro's Tryall," the documents surrounding an early 18th-century
slave case, known to students of American literature as the occasion for
Judge Samuel Sewall's *The Selling of Joseph*. Of course, the 19th century, the locus of greatest significance, receives Foster's major discussion of social and literary influences on the narratives and the Judeo-
Christian mythic structure of their plots. In discussing postbellum
influence of the narratives in the concluding section of her book,
Foster makes her most telling points in recounting the myths about
slave family instability enforced by the rhetoric of abolitionism.

   For most of us Frederick Douglass looms as the giant among fugitive slave writers. For some time Philip S. Foner's four-volume *Life
and Writings* (1950–55) has been our most valuable source, but in

1979 the inaugural volume of a definitive edition made its appearance. *The Frederick Douglass Papers, Series One: Speeches, Debates and Interviews,* ed. John W. Blassingame (Yale) covers the first half of Douglass' career as a Garrisonian. Plans are to issue series of volumes containing published writings and letters in addition to the collection of speeches. The editing is superb in the first volume: notes describe each of the sources in newspapers and reports, explanatory footnotes appear as needed, a 48-page introduction discusses rhetorical influences on Douglass, and the volume is fully indexed.

Because Douglass' career so dramatically exemplifies the power of the word, it is no wonder he lends himself so well to literary discussion such as can be found in the three intriguing essays included in *Reconstruction of Instruction.* In the first, "Narration, Authentication, and Authorial Control in Douglass' *Narrative* of 1845" (pp. 178–91), Stepto considers the apparatus of testimonial documents commonly prefacing and appended to slave narratives. Douglass' accomplishment is to integrate all of these into the tale he wishes to tell, so that he assumes complete authorial control over a text that enforces the twin motives of the slaves' struggle for freedom *and* literacy. Robert G. O'Meally's "Frederick Douglass' 1845 *Narrative*: The Text Was Meant to Be Preached" (pp. 192–211) compares the written work to black preachers' sermons in its use of exhortation, parable, and invocation of the Old Testament God's power. In "Binary Oppositions in Chapter One of the *Narrative of the Life of Frederick Douglass, an American Slave, Written by Himself*" (pp. 212–32) Henry-Louis Gates, Jr., uses the work of Roman Jakobson and Morris Halle identifying binary oppositions as a fundamental operation of the mind to examine Douglass' contrasts between nature and culture, the world of the slaves counterposed to the world of the masters. With the aid of irony the oppositions reimagine the form of reality. Jane Matlack's "The Autobiographies of Frederick Douglass" (*Phylon* 40: 15–28) offers a view of the 1845 *Narrative* that differs from these essays. For Matlack the framing documents serve to allay hostile reactions to a slave's story so that its plain style can invoke peaks of intense feeling without irrelevant distractions. Matlack agrees, however, with the view that the work presents an author's self-creation, a theme she finds attenuated in Douglass' next autobiography, *My Bondage and My Freedom,* and subordinated to a version of the rags-to-riches story in his final autobiography, *The Life and Times.*

If antebellum slave narratives have historical value, then so will later ones; and if the earlier narratives are literature, oral statements of former slaves collected as late as the 20th century are at least inherently literary. Since 1971 George P. Rawick has been editing a multivolume collection of narratives titled *The American Slave: A Composite Autobiography*. In 1979 he issued another ten volumes identified as *Supplement Series 2* (Greenwood). Rawick's collections print materials collected by the Federal Writers Project during the 1930s and by researchers from Fisk University. In *Slavery Remembered: A Record of Twentieth Century Slave Narratives* (N.Car.) Paul D. Escott applies statistical and interpretative methods to these collections to judge their documentary value and to summarize their portrayal of life during Reconstruction and after. This is not a literary study, but the ex-slaves' testimony about the bases of black culture must have interest for literary historians.

A clear line of descent appears from slave narratives to modern autobiographies, and among the most prominent works demonstrating the lineage are *Black Boy* and *The Autobiography of Malcolm X*. Charles T. Davis considers the first of these in "From Experience to Eloquence" (*Chant of Saints*, pp. 425–39). The problem with Wright's autobiography for many readers is its denial of the possibility for black humanity in the South. Davis agrees that Wright omitted crucial features of traditional black life, but, he says, their absence results from inspired editing aiming to strengthen the impression of an isolated persona confronting the problems of physical survival and artistic development. We might say one's life always takes the form of a story, but in an autobiography one gets to choose the shape of the story. In "To Be Young, Gifted and Oppressed" (*MELUS* 6,i:73–80) Ellen Schiff also takes account of *Black Boy*'s bleak portrayal of indigenous culture in order to couple it with Chaim Potok's novel *My Name Is Asher Lev* to provide examples of intragroup conditioning by force and fear to control the behavior of the talented young. This universalization of Wright's book has a parallel in H. Porter Abbott's "Organic Form in the Autobiography of a Convert: The Example of Malcolm X" (*CLAJ* 23:125–46). Abbott proposes to use Malcolm X's life writing to test the idea originating with St. Augustine that following religious conversion memory reforms the past life without self-conscious intervention by the will of the autobiographer. Predictably the findings of reformation are positive, but as the example of

Richard Wright has just shown us, deliberate selection is essential to telling one's story.

Now if we want a first-rate example of critical discernment of form organic to the autobiographer's story, we need look no further than Albert Murray's brief examination of *Music Is My Mistress* in "Duke Ellington Vamps 'Til Ready" (*Chant of Saints*, pp. 440–44). Murray reads Ellington's book as the creation of a sequence of routined acts, some jive-riffed, all deeply concerned with the style of black life: dress, cuisine, linguistic exuberance, festivity. For Murray only *Along This Way*, James Weldon Johnson's autobiography, exceeds Ellington's in presenting a full-scale personal record.

vi. Literary History, Criticism

Mukhtar Ali Isani has complete responsibility for this year's treatment, in journals, of the 18th century. In addition to the two articles on Wheatley Isani also published "Far from 'Gambia's Golden Shore': The Black in Late Eighteenth Century American Imaginative Literature" (*WMQ* 36:353–72). Surveying the titles in Charles Evans' *American Bibliography* for the period, he finds images of blacks in varied genres used so exclusively in pleas against slavery that "Black became almost another name for misery itself." Portrayal includes idyllic reminiscences devised by white authors who presented Africans in their homeland as pious, brave, and proud. For coverage of actual as distinct from fancied African heritage, and, what is more crucial, for materials available to black writers we have the research of Mary F. Berry and John W. Blassingame in "Africa, Slavery, and the Roots of Contemporary Black Culture" (*Chant of Saints*, pp. 241–56). Taken from the authors' forthcoming book *Long Memory*, their essay asserts the imperative need to understand the transformative impact of slavery on African culture in the Americas. In the New World, for example, proverbs and folktales came to express plantation experience, and it was in the matrix of slavery that African language and music began its evolution into toasts, boasts, put-downs, and blues.

Robert B. Stepto's remarkable output this year also includes *From Behind the Veil: A Study of Afro-American Narrative* (Illinois). Readers will recognize influences of Northrop Frye, Geoffrey Hartman, and Harold Bloom as indication of Stepto's concern to broaden the theory upon which we base Afro-American literary history. He first presents four types of slave narrative, which are denominated eclectic, integrated, generic, and authenticating and represented by the writings of Henry Bibb, Solomon Northup, Frederick Douglass, and William Wells Brown. The essence of the typology appears also in Stepto's essay on Douglass' 1845 *Narrative* discussed earlier. Booker T. Washington's *Up From Slavery* and W. E. B. DuBois's *Souls of Black Folk* revise and revoice these types. Then he treats *Autobiography of an Ex-Colored Man* as a text echoing DuBois' tale of his immersion in the South, and *Black Boy* as an innovative variation of the slave narrators' ascent to the north and literacy. The study culminates by studying Ralph Ellison's attempt to create out of the dialectic of ascent and immersion a new narrative, organically making art out of art to discover a self beyond imposed definitions. No doubt about it. This is a major book.

The debate between Booker T. Washington and W. E. B. DuBois has fascinated Afro-Americanists because it symbolizes so dramatically the dilemma that faced blacks in the decades on either side of 1900. William Toll's *The Resurgence of Race: Black Social Theory from Reconstruction to the Pan-African Conferences* (Temple) recounts the conflict between the two champions with sufficient complexity to suggest how difficult it was for other black citizens to take sides. The most important feature of the book, however, is Toll's rejection of the usual approach to the debate as a question of tactics and his conception of it as a major event in cultural history turning on questions of the purposes of black life. Danny Champion's "Booker T. Washington Versus W. E. B. DuBois: A Study in Rhetorical Contrasts" in *Oratory in the New South*, ed. Waldo W. Braden (LSU), pp. 174–203, retells the story in its familiar form but provides the flavor of the contest with numerous quotations.

The problems of meeting the expectations of the mainstream audience and dealing with publishers' ideas of what the American public wants to read have always plagued black creative artists; so magazines controlled by and directed to blacks have had unusual literary importance. Abby Arthur Johnson and Ronald Maberry Johnson tell of those magazines in *Propaganda and Aesthetics: The Literary Politics of Afro-American Magazines in the Twentieth Century* (Mass.). They discuss ten major periodicals plus a number of short-lived ones in a chronological arrangement that places the policies of editors and contributors in the context of their perceptions of the appropriate aesthetic responses to black historical needs. Philip Butcher has noted in a review a number of important publications omitted from the account (*AL* 52[1980]:144–45), but the book still is a great service to scholars in its summation of materials existing in special library collections and its discriminating discussion.

The saga of black magazines reached its first literary high point during the Harlem Renaissance when *The Crisis* and *Opportunity* were so instrumental in introducing new writers to the public. David Levering Lewis' excellent article, "Dr. Johnson's Friends: Civil Rights by Copyright during Harlem's Mid-Twenties" (*MR* 20:501–19), recreates the party hosted by Dr. Charles S. Johnson, editor of *Opportunity*, on 21 March 1924 to introduce black creative artists published in his magazine to white sympathizers whom Johnson realized would attend for a variety of motives, including an interest in authenticating their personal ideas about primitive artists. The evening was a success from the standpoint of promoting black writing, for it was then that the idea was conceived for a special issue of *Survey Graphic* that gained a circulation of 42,000 and subsequent republication as *The New Negro*. Since white patronage, for better and for worse, was so important during the 1920s, note must be taken of the publication of *"Keep A-Inchin' Along": Selected Writings of Carl Van Vechten about Black Art and Letters*, ed. Bruce Kellner (Greenwood). The book includes an introduction on Van Vechten's career; explanatory notes; numbers of his photographs of black writers including Walter White, Langston Hughes, Zora Neale Hurston, and Chester Himes; and virtually all the writing about blacks except for the novel *Nigger Heaven*.

The year's general historical treatments of modern writing are few and varied. "Black Literature," by Nathan A. Scott, Jr., in *Harvard Guide*, pp. 287–341, offers a canonical survey repeating many of the views Scott has expressed on other occasions. The *Harvard Guide*, by the way, includes three pages on black writers in Elizabeth Janeway's essay "Women's Literature," and three pages on black playwrights in Gerald Weales's "Drama." Otherwise black writing is absent from the nine additional chapters which include treatments of realism and Naturalism, experimental fiction, and three periods of poetry.

Betty J. Collier and Louis N. Williams in "Black Revolutionary

Literature of the Sixties: The Eurocentric World View Recycled"
(*MV* 2,ii[1978]:57–66) point out, as has James Baldwin in "Everybody's Protest Novel" and Nathan A. Scott, Jr., in the essay named
above, that while protest literature condemns social conditions it may
also support the philosophical base on which the system of oppression
rests. Collier and Williams see the 1960s as a period when the Euro-
American framework was forcefully challenged but with only isolated examples of writers breaking through to an Afrocentric world
view. Kimberly W. Benston writes "Late Coltrane: A Re-Membering
of Orpheus" (*Chant of Saints*, pp. 413–24) to provide the example of
an advanced musician agonistically engaged in unlearning Euro-
American culture in order to reconceive his art. The connection with
literature is more than analogy, since we see time and again black
language leading toward black music and back. It could also be the
case that close focus on folklore will give us more than illustrations
of adaptable subject matter. Robert E. Hemenway's "Are You a Flying Lark or a Sitting Dove?" (*Reconstruction of Instruction*, pp.
122–52) attempts to describe the method for a more functional study.
The premises of the method must include understanding that folklore
consists not in discrete items, but in processes of communication continually being created. In studying the amalgam of folklore and literature, then, one must seek vestiges of oral communication.

As this essay has argued, we are now becoming self-conscious
about the underlying conceptions applied in writing Afro-American
literary history, but the suppositions underlying criticism have long
been a matter of discussion. "Preface to Blackness: Text and Pre-
text" by Henry-Louis Gates, Jr. (*Reconstruction of Instruction*, pp.
44–69) contends that most previous discussion has ignored literature's
primary forms. Since Thomas Jefferson's time black writing has been
put forth by its champions as evidence for inclusion of the race in
humanity; consequently, art and propaganda have been confused. In
recent years, Gates says, the propagandizing has merely become more
subtle. Critics have revised the Marxist conception of base and super-
structure into a scheme where race as a metaphysical concept has become the controlling mechanism of culture and literature. Ultimately,
for Gates, the greatest failing is the disposition to confuse textual
meanings with models of reality outside of literature's linguistic structures. As a rejoinder to Gates, Mari Evans' recent essay "Decoloniza-

tion as Goal, Political Writing as Device (*First World* 2,iii:34–39) may be cited. Evans argues that blacks must see literature politically so long as they live as colonial people. When this necessity is recognized, as it was in the 1960s, literature gains fervor and popular participation because it is steadily demystifying reality.

State University of New York at Albany

20. Themes, Topics, Criticism

Jonathan Morse

When Emerson said, "Our age is retrospective," he wasn't thinking of *ALS*, but the epigram certainly applies to this chapter. The production of criticism these days, for better or worse, is overwhelming, and the only way to think about it is retrospectively, as if American literature had already been written and this really were an age of criticism. Before I start doing that, however, I would like to thank my predecessor, Michael Hoffman, for offering me help and a good example.

i. American Literature

a. **Themes and Topics.** Because seven of the 11 books discussed in this section are treated in two or more chapters elsewhere, I will confine myself to general remarks only about them. *Puritan Influences* contains essays on four Puritan writers who helped form the American mind, and four 19th-century authors whose minds show the Puritan influence. Despite the book's title and Elliott's introductory claims, only one essay is a direct influence study. The early essays on Anne Bradstreet, Edward Taylor, and Jonathan Edwards focus sharply on helping us understand their Puritan texts, and the later ones on Hawthorne, Thoreau, Melville, and Dickinson have little to do with Puritanism directly. In fact, their references to Puritanism tend to be forced. But the quality of the volume is high throughout, and without worrying too much about its title, readers of *ALS* should approach it as they would an unusually good issue of *AL*. *The Stoic Strain* is devoted to analyzing the ways in which stoicism manifests itself, explicitly or implicitly, across a wide range of American writing. The general introductory essay by Peter Buitenhuis is followed by essays discussing stoicism in nine 19th- and 20th-century

This chapter was completed with the aid of a grant from the Office of Research Administration, University of Hawaii—*J.M.*

authors. The common theme keeps the quality of the essays consistent: few surprises, but solid scholarship throughout.

In *Free Will and Determinism*, a full-length study of a related topic, Perry D. Westbrook draws up an account of various philosophical and religious positions regarding free will, then demonstrates where each of two dozen American authors fits into the outline. Thus we learn that Michael Wigglesworth was an orthodox Calvinist, Emily Dickinson was an unorthodox Calvinist, and Oliver Wendell Holmes rejected Calvinism. There is no general conclusion; when the book reaches Hemingway and existentialism, it just stops. The discussions of specific authors are too short and narrow in scope to be of much critical value, and Westbrook's deductive rather than inductive organization hampers the development of his ideas. A more useful study is *Freedom and Fate in American Thought from Edwards to Dewey*, by Paul F. Boller, Jr. (SMU, 1978). This handbook accurately (though with a sunny antideterminist bias) summarizes the attitudes toward freedom and necessity of Edwards, Paine, Emerson, Calhoun, Frederick Douglass, Edward Bellamy, William James, Mark Twain, and John Dewey. It can be recommended for undergraduate use. A related undergraduate-level study is Charles Berryman's *From Wilderness to Wasteland: The Trial of the Puritan God in the American Imagination* (Kennikat). The first four chapters of this book comprise a clear, compact intellectual history of American Puritanism from the early 17th century to the early 19th; the remaining four examine the Puritan mind as it shows itself in the works of Emerson, Hawthorne, Melville, and Eliot. Berryman's own intellectual history seems to date from the 1920s. His Freudian explanation of the Puritans' guilt feelings resembles one of Ludwig Lewisohn's simplifications, and his view of Christianity is pure H. L. Mencken.

"[T]he Puritans . . . [had] an a priori vision of America so strongly conceived through Scripture that it subsumed the physical geography of the new place," writes Cecelia Tichi in *New World*. The subject of Tichi's book is the ideology of that subsumption: the belief that Americans exist in America for the purpose of re-forming chaotic nature. In one way or another, Tichi contends, the Scriptural command to subdue the earth was fundamental to American thinking from the days of John Smith to the early 20th century. Eschewing cheap Sierra Club ironies, Tichi traces the American literary attitude toward this imperative from its Puritan beginnings through Thoreau, Cooper,

George Bancroft, and Joel Barlow to its highest expression in Whitman and its death in *The Waste Land*. Her commitment to reading the topography of the American spirit on its own terms serves Tichi well when she comes to read the books which express that spirit. I especially admire her sensitive treatment of Bancroft's *History of the United States* and Whitman's "Song of the Broad-Axe," and her meditation on Barlow's invention of the characteristically American word "utilize."

I end this section with five unrelated thematic studies. According to Roy R. Male's *Mysterious Stranger*, the subgenre of the cloistral can be defined as a story about the intrusion of a stranger into an isolated setting, followed by an agonistic transaction between the intruder and the characters he intrudes upon, followed by the departure of the intruder. Male's refinement of this definition through the first four chapters of his five-chapter book is full of interesting examples, but one still approaches chapter 5 with the feeling that the taxonomic exercise wasn't really necessary. In chapter 5, however, Male finds a general application by pointing out that Morse Peckham's psychologistic model of fiction—something that invades our "art perceiver's space" bearing a problem and refuses to leave— "specifically fits the basic plot of cloistral fiction. And that plot is one way of indirectly describing the transaction between reader and writer" (p. 84). Male rides this theory very hard, but it works.

John G. Blair's *Confidence Man* is an attractive study of the ways in which the character of the confidence man subverts its embodying text. At the beginning, Blair points out, things were straightforward: Milton's description of the temptation of Eve "clearly identifies the confidence man and the Devil" (p. 31). But from that point on, as we read more complicatedly than Milton's unquestioning audience, the ambiguities of the role grow steadily more prominent. Blair analyzes the evolution of this ambiguity in six novels, two of which are American: Vonnegut's *Cat's Cradle* and Melville's *The Confidence-Man*. He concludes that with few firm moral standards to violate and few unambiguous characters to contrast with, the confidence man is almost out of work in the post-Modern novel, a victim of his own success.

I should briefly mention here Alexander Blackburn's *Myth of the Picaro*. In the course of formalizing an anatomy of the picaresque in its realistic and symbolic forms Blackburn gives us a pair of close readings of *The Confidence-Man* and *Huckleberry Finn* (see chapters 4 and 6).

In *Mark and Knowledge* Marjorie Pryse uses the notion of the "marked" character (Hester Prynne with her letter, Joe Christmas with his blackness, etc.) as the central focus of six extended readings. Her technique owes something to the system of "transcendental meditation" taught by Maharishi Mahesh Yoga, and at times Pryse rides it too hard for the American terrain. But the gauche proselytism dwindles as the book goes along.

If the Laurentian notion of the turbulently anarchic American soul is still current, Sam B. Girgus' *Law of the Heart* will serve as a useful qualifier. On the one hand, as Girgus points out, the American Adam has continued to flee inward to the sheltering solipsism of himself from the days of Cooper through the 1960s; on the other hand, as Girgus demonstrates, other equally American figures have succeeded in reconciling their individualism with an acknowledgment of the external world's claims. Few literary surprises, but a good piece of American Studies workmanship.

b. **Biography: Practice and Theory.** In the last 15 years or so, as the New Criticism has receded into history, the old genre of the literary biography has climbed out of its grave. The revival started some time around 1961 with the publication of Mark Schorer's biography of Sinclair Lewis, and it has been gaining strength ever since. Witness the current Virginia Woolf boom, which can't even be discussed until one has abandoned the old New Critical distinction between the writer and her work.

This new interest in biography has generated a good deal of theoretical work. There is now a journal, *Biography* (Honolulu: Univ. Press of Hawaii, 1978), devoted entirely to the genre, and the one book everybody seemed to be discussing in the Americanist sections of this year's MLA convention was *Madwoman in the Attic* (see chap. 5). I report here on two biographies, two autobiographies, and two books about biography. As is unfortunately usual in these waning days of 20th-century literature, the theory is more interesting than the practice.

Stanley Weintraub's *The London Yankees* is an entertaining study of a dozen or so Americans who pursued their literary careers in England between 1894 and 1914. Some of these men and women, such as Henry James and T. S. Eliot, became thoroughly Europeanized; others, such as Bret Harte, learned to live as Englishmen while continuing to write as Americans; still others, such as Mark Twain and Robert Frost, remained more or less untouched by the English experience. Weintraub makes this point but does little with it; his primary concern is with biography as the higher gossip. Beyond some plot summary, there is little in *The London Yankees* about the writers *as* writers.

Robert E. Humphrey's *Children of Fantasy: The First Rebels of Greenwich Village* (Wiley, 1978) is a psychobiographical study of five of the writers who made the Village's reputation in the years before World War I: Max Eastman, Floyd Dell, John Reed, the liberal journalist Hutchins Hapgood, and George Cram Cook, the hard-drinking Iowan who introduced Eugene O'Neill's plays to the world. Given the undeniable achievements of these Villagers in the days of Elbert Hubbard and Henry Van Dyke, it seems almost ungrateful of Humphrey to claim that the fabled bohemian community of the Ash Can School and *The Masses* was not much more than an unstable group of "individuals whose pursuit of unbridled fantasies precluded a reasonable assessment of their talents and objectives" (p. 253).

Howard Mumford Jones: An Autobiography (Wis.) is a warmly emotional memoir, but, except in the concluding chapters, it is diffident and uninformative about the writing of Jones's books. After reading it, we are left with no accumulated wisdom beyond a few digressions and obiter dicta. Lewis Mumford's *My Works and Days: A Personal Chronicle* (Harcourt), on the other hand, is very much an intellectual autobiography—or rather a large sampling of the raw material of one: 545 pages of letters, uncollected articles, poems, notebook entries, and reminiscences. The wide range accords perfectly with Mumford's self-projected image of himself: an unspecialized culture hero whose intellectual life was inseparable from his life as a man.

Telling Lives is an elegantly printed symposium volume containing contributions by Leon Edel, Justin Kaplan, Alfred Kazin, Doris Kearns, Theodore Rosengarten, Barbara Tuchman, and Geoffrey Wolff, plus a good introductory essay by the editor. The general quality of the book is high—I would especially single out Tuchman's "Biography as a Prism of History"—and three of the essays deal directly with American literature. Edel's "The Figure Under the Car-

Themes, Topics, Criticism

pet" is a plea for the psychological method that Edel has used with such power in his great biography of Henry James. In this essay Edel applies his technique, in passing, to Hemingway, to Thoreau, and to, of all people, Rex Stout. Why would a thin writer named Rex invent a fat character named Nero? asks Edel, and leads us, by way of sketching out an answer, through a tour de force of literary psychology. Kaplan's "The Naked Self and Other Problems" is an extended meditation, rich in circumstantial detail, on the relationship between *Leaves of Grass* and the life Walt Whitman lived. Wolff, a novelist and the biographer of the very minor poet Harry Crosby, makes a case in his essay "Minor Lives" for biography as a purely aesthetic interaction between the biographer and the reader.

   G. Thomas Couser, in contradistinction, grounds *American Autobiography* on a firm sense of biography's "obligation" to empirically determined truth (pp. 6–7). Out of this sense of the genre Couser derives a clear thesis: "A coherent tradition—perhaps the mainstream of American autobiography from the Puritans to the present—is traced through [15] autobiographical works. . . . Generally, these autobiographies are characterized by the conflation of personal and communal history, the conscious creation of exemplary patterns of behavior, and their didactic, even hortatory, impulses. These characteristics derive in turn from the writers' tendency to assume the role of prophet in writing autobiography. While prophetic autobiography is not exclusively American, it is characteristically American, and our tradition of prophetic autobiography seems to be a distinctive achievement of American letters" (p. 1). Couser's method is structural: making the most sparing use of quotation, he holds his primary documents at abstracted arm's length and measures selected narrative incidents against one another. This technique has a drawback: it subordinates to its thesis the crucial experience of *reading* autobiography, an experience which must vary with the texture as well as the ideology of each individual document.

c. **Literary History.** *History as a Tool in Critical Interpretation,* ed. Thomas F. Rugh and Erin R. Silva (Brigham Young, 1978), is a symposium volume devoted primarily to art history, despite the presence on the panel of Monroe Beardsley, E. D. Hirsch, Jr., and René Wellek. The volume ends, however, with a 32-page overview of Edmund Wilson's critical career by Wellek, from which Wilson emerges considerably flattened. A more satisfactory study is *Edmund Wilson: The Man and His Work* (New York Univ. Press, 1978), a collection of essays edited by John Wain. Nothing in this book is as rigorously analytical as Wellek's study, but the spirit is right. For readers of *ALS*, the most useful essay in this volume will be Larzer Ziff's "The Man by the Fire: Edmund Wilson and American Literature."

So far as I know, *The Little Magazine in America: A Documentary History*, ed. Elliott Anderson and Mary Kinzie (Pushcart, 1978), is the first book of its kind since 1946. Given the amazing proliferation of little magazines in the last quarter-century, *The Little Magazine in America* automatically becomes a standard reference book. This two-pound, 770-page volume is not a narrative history; rather, it is a scrapbook of memoirs, reminiscences, interviews, and scholarly articles, concentrating for the most part on what has been achieved since 1950 and followed by an extensively annotated bibliography of 84 influential titles.

Twayne has published a three-volume chronological survey of *American Literary Criticism*. Volume 1, which covers the period from 1800 to 1860, is by John W. Rathbun; volume 2 (1860–1905) is by Rathbun and the late Harry H. Clark; volume 3 (1905–65) is by Arnold Goldsmith. The first two volumes cannot be recommended; they are full of errors, small (Fred Lewis Pattee's first name was not Frederick; Indiana University is not the University of Indiana), medium-sized (Hannah More was not an American), and large (it is technically correct but extremely misleading to assert without qualification that "idealism was the controlling impulse in the thought of both [Poe and Emerson]" [vol. 1, p. 140]). Volume 3, however, covers the major figures in an orderly and reliable fashion.

Goldsmith's choice of 1965 as his history's terminal year was happy, for it was in 1966 that the structuralists landed at Johns Hopkins and started another era in American criticism. One indication of how far we have come since then is Grant Webster's *The Republic of Letters: A History of Postwar American Literary Opinion* (Hopkins). This long book is a historical evaluation of just two critical schools: the New Critics, their predecessors and their succesors from T. S. Eliot to Murray Krieger, and the New York Intellectuals aligned around the Lionel Trilling–Edmund Wilson axis. In his preface (pp. x–xi) Webster promises a continuation which will cover "such critical schools as psychological and myth criticism, Structuralism and hermeneutics, the American Studies movement, and the counterculture of the sixties"—all with the object of "causing a revolution in the history of criticism. I hope," he modestly adds, "that the ideas expressed in this book will cause such a revolution." I will have something to say about Webster's tone in a moment, but let there be no mistake: *The Republic of Letters* nearly brings it off. As a work of criticism it is learned, lively, and toughly argued, and as a work of history it is—if not exactly revolutionary—certainly novel. With its great mass of detail ingeniously organized around a pluralistic model adapted from Thomas Kuhn's *Structure of Scientific Revolutions*, it is a valuable book. But as it now stands it is seriously defective. Here are a few of the defects.

For a book that necessarily deals with personality its psychology is horribly shallow. For instance, Webster's one-sentence analysis of Edmund Wilson's father explains that that complicated man "became a neurotic because he was unable to face the America of the robber-barons" (p. 366). The book's tone is not "hard-hitting," as the blurb proclaims, but just vulgar. For an all-too-typical instance Norman Podhoretz writing about Dwight Macdonald is said to be "the dumb praising the dumb" (p. 228). There are some methodological lapses; the discussion of *Partisan Review* is not much more than an annotated bibliography. Finally, the book was written over too long a period. The chapter on Allen Tate was first published in 1967, and it is perhaps just bad luck that Webster couldn't consult Louis D. Rubin's *The Wary Fugitives* (LSU, 1978)—but what are we to say about the following sentence? "[T]he main reason Eliot is less available to us now than he was is that the revolutionary fervor of the sixties in America, with its renewed interest in the occult, the counterculture, Marxism, rock music, the black revolution, the third world, and the like, seems antithetical to the Puritan restraint and Anglo-European tradition of Eliot" (p. 137). We are to say this: it was first published in 1966; it ought to have been rethought in 1979.

d. Social Criticism. *Images and Ideas in American Culture: The Functions of Criticism: Essays in Memory of Philip Rahv*, ed. Arthur Edelstein (Brandeis), covers the full range of Rahv's concerns. The book begins with two political essays: one more denunciation of the intelligentsia by Noam Chomsky, followed by Stephen J. Whitfield's excellent study of the shifting acceptations of the term "totalitarianism." Then come four literary essays: Robert Alter's "Mimesis and the Motive for Fiction," originally published in *TriQuarterly* 42 (1978): 228–49; a fine exercise in the new literary history, "The Difficulties of Modernism and the Modernism of Difficulty," by Richard Poirier; a study by Robert Brustein of the contemporary playwrights David Rabe, Christopher Durang, and Sam Shepard; and a meditation on children and language by Howard Nemerov. Finally there are two essays about Rahv himself: a study of the criticism by Milton Hindus and a moving personal memoir by the novelist Alan Lelchuk. I place this book in the category of social criticism for a single overriding reason: one finishes reading it with a clear idea that for Rahv literature could never be considered apart from society.

Robert N. Wilson's *The Writer as Social Seer* (N. Car.), is a collection of eight essays in literary sociology, held together by a thesis to the effect that literature can help us understand our societies and ourselves. Readers of *ALS* may take this idea for granted, but Wilson, a sociologist, must be presumed to know how many Gradgrinds there are in his intended audience. At any rate, he sets out his literary claims with a pathetic plea against "the disregard and even pronounced animus shown by social scientists toward art" (p. 4). Given this disregard (Wilson calls it "art blindness"), we should not expect critical sophistication in Wilson's studies of five authors and three single works (Fitzgerald, Hemingway, James Baldwin, Camus, Beckett, *Death of a Salesman, Long Day's Journey Into Night, Doctor Zhivago*). But Wilson wields his blunt instrument with shrewdness and sensitivity, and his book might be used to win arguments with that recalcitrant engineering major in your sophomore American-lit survey.

The remaining books in this section are only indirectly related to the immediate concerns of *ALS*, but they all have things to say about the ways in which literature comes out of language and society. *Language and Responsibility* (Pantheon) is the transcript of a series of conversations between Noam Chomsky and the French linguist Mitsou Ronat, translated into English by John Viertel and revised by Chomsky. In the first four chapters Chomsky discusses linguistics in the broadest sense, as *the* science of human nature, and this leads him naturally into questions of politics, philosophy, and psychology. The remaining five chapters are devoted to an overview

of generative grammar. The book as a whole is a first-rate introduction to the many-sided work of this important thinker; it is of course
authoritative, and Viertel's English is easier to read than Chomsky's
own arrhythmic prose. Ronat knows what questions to ask throughout, and her introductory material is helpful.

At the end of her first interview with Chomsky ("Politics") Ronat
asks, "What can the links be between a theory of ideology and the
concepts of your linguistic theory, generative grammar?" (p. 41).
Chomsky doesn't answer the question, and he later takes some pains
to defend the theoretical purity of linguistics against such practical
applications as sociolinguistics ("very useful on the level of educational practice, in attempting to combat the prejudices of the society
at large . . . but on the linguistic level, this matter is evident
and banal," p. 55) and literary criticism ("Literary criticism . . . has
things to say, but it does not have explanatory principles. . . . [True
research] is concerned to discover explanatory principles of some
depth and fails if it does not do so," pp. 56–57). Given this resolute
defense of the interdisciplinary barriers, we might think that we can
discuss Chomsky's linguistics without regard to Chomsky's slightly
cranky political views. Unfortunately, we would be wrong. At the
heart of Chomsky's rationalist psychology is a political attitude that
is almost paranoid in its abstract elaboration (pp. 89–94), and we
cannot claim an opinion of Chomsky's linguistic work until we have
taken its political dimension into account. In *Liberty and Language*
(Oxford) the English linguist Geoffrey Sampson sets out to do so.

Sampson applies the term "liberal" to himself with a historical
footnote; he is in fact a laissez-faire fundamentalist who in the United
States would be called a Libertarian. His short volume offers, as an
alternative to Chomsky's anarcho-syndicalism and radical rationalism,
an equally radical empiricism and a historically idealized free-market
capitalism. Between Chomsky and Sampson much political logic gets
chopped; as George Orwell said, you can never win an argument with
a Communist or a vegetarian. Sampson does put forward one linguistic thesis, however (chapter 4, especially pp. 117–29). Noting that
Chomsky's theory of innate language rules seems to work for syntax
but not for semantics, Sampson deduces that semantic capacity is not
rule-bound; that is, we human beings have an unlimited capacity to
mean. Meaning implies change, adaptation, innovation—and it follows, according to Sampson, that this fundamental human attribute

should not be trammeled by any restrictions on economic expression. But Chomsky interprets the same semantic data in a more modest, less hypothesis-bound fashion (*Language and Responsibility*, chapter 6, especially pp. 141–43).

The failings of five Philadelphia writers—Charles Brockden Brown, Bayard Taylor, George Boker, the forgotten but once highly respected novelist S. Weir Mitchell, and Owen Wister—form a small part of the body of evidence in E. Digby Baltzell's *Puritan Boston and Quaker Philadelphia: Two Protestant Ethics and the Spirit of Class Authority and Leadership* (Free Press). The purpose of the evidence is to help explain why Philadelphia has contributed so much less than Boston to the intellectual and political leadership of America, and in Baltzell's hands it yields this sociological theory: "[I]t is the proper function of an upper class in any healthy society to wield authority . . . through the respect it commands throughout society for the accomplishments and leadership qualities of its members over several generations. My task in this book is . . . to show how and why Boston Brahmins produced a long tradition of class authority whereas Proper Philadelphians did not. . . . [The reason is that] Bostonians and Philadelphians were and still are motivated by the hierarchical and authoritatrian ethic of Puritanism, on the one hand, and the egalitarian and anti-authoritarian ethic of Quakerism, on the other" (p. x). Baltzell makes no claim to any esthetic interpretation of this thesis; he accepts Philadelphia's deficiencies a priori and claims only to provide a historical explanation with the data he has amassed. But the sheer volume of those data, and their sheer variety—from, e.g., the ideological histories of Harvard and Swarthmore to the comparative political assertiveness of Roman Catholics in Boston and Philadelphia—give *Puritan Boston and Quaker Philadelphia* a literary-historical value that extends far beyond the Main Line. As a study of the persistence and power of colonial attitudes, it has much to tell us about American literature from Anne Bradstreet to Henry James and beyond.

Baltzell is a conservative, with a vision of a class-based ideal world; Frances FitzGerald is a liberal who doesn't like what she sees in the real world. In "Rewriting American History," a three-part *New Yorker* article (26 February, 5 March, 12 March 1979) subsequently published by Little, Brown as *America Revised*, FitzGerald uses literary criticism to help us understand why Americans know so little about the historical nature of that world. Her explanation—that American history has been taught for the last 90 years as a factitious civic ideology bearing little relationship to any real, lived history—is less remarkable than the evidence she supports it with. For FitzGerald has looked at what must have been hundreds of school histories, from Jedidiah Morse's Johnsonian periods and imaginative misinformation ("North America has no remarkably high mountains") to the education-corporation complex's latest efforts to present the Vietnam War in a noncontroversial manner—and what she has found is both fascinating and appalling.

Here, for instance, is an eighth-grade textbook that has gone through several editions between 1931 and 1955. Looking at five of these editions in detail, FitzGerald demonstrates that the book has undergone a complete thematic metamorphosis inside its jacket, shifting as the times dictated from liberal internationalism to Cold War xenophobia. This much we could have guessed, but we may not have realized that in such a book the facts too are subject to ideological control. In 1931, for instance, American eighth-graders were learning from this book that the War of 1812 was a mutual loss. By 1950 they were learning that the War of 1812 was a glorious American moral victory. And if children's ideas of the War of 1812 are to be manipulated this way, think of what the textbook manufacturers are now doing to the history of the civil rights movement.

Unfortunately, FitzGerald leaves us with no usable ideas about all this. Her conclusions are completely negative: textbook A is an ideological Trojan horse, and a boring piece of committee prose to boot; publisher B is pusillanimous; school board C is bigoted; pedagogical expert D is a fool; reformer E is naive; there is none righteous, no, not one. After a while the repeated shocks of FitzGerald's examples are only benumbing. But as an application of literary scholarship to the fundamental notion of what history is, "Rewriting American History" is an elegant piece of work.

I end this section on a depressing note. Paul Copperman's *The Literacy Hoax: The Decline of Reading, Writing, and Learning in the Public Schools and What We Can Do About It* (Morrow, 1978) is a flashback to the post-Sputnik days when James Bryant Conant and Hyman Rickover were stirring up the muddy waters of the American educational system. After presenting us with some statistics and the transcripts of some horrifying interviews with students, teachers, and reading experts, Copperman polishes up the Cold War Purple Hearts once more: the Russian schools and their academic myrmidons (p. 99), the finger of blame leveled at Dr. Spock (p. 161), the call for less democracy and more authority (passim). What is depressing about these pleas and arraignments is not that they are right or wrong but that they are so obviously inadequate to explain what we all know: that students in 1980 don't read or write or think very well. What can anybody do about Copperman's interviewee Steve (pp. 223–29), a 16-year-old functional illiterate, stoned most of the time, whose ambition is to be a drug counselor or, alternatively, "like maybe mak[e] certain types of ice cream"? I don't know, reader, and neither do you. As Richard Mitchell notes in *Less Than Words Can Say*, p. 207, "If we want to do only so simple a thing as ensure that all third-grade teachers will be expert in spelling and punctuation, we will have to change everything that happens at every step of the process by which we now provide ourselves with third-grade teachers." Michel Foucault would argue that in such an *episteme* nobody *can* know what to do.

Less Than Words Can Say (Little, Brown) is an appeal from the depths of a teacher's college for the clarity of thought which can come only from purging our language of jargon and imprecision. As readers of his witty newsletter *The Underground Grammarian* know, Mitchell is a purely private eye who catches the rapists of the language one by one with their pants down, and his most comfortable intellectual size is the pamphlet. *Less Than Words Can Say* is a long pamphlet, and a little diffuse. But it is entertaining from bitter beginning to bitter end.

e. Folk and Ethnic Literature.   Helen Addison Howard's *American Indian Poetry* (Twayne) is a study of eight early 20th-century white writers: three translators of Indian verse and five poets whose original work was influenced by Indian life and song. Whether "translations" or "interpretations" (the distinction is Howard's), most of the poems discussed are burdened with obsolete European poetic diction, and the reader is forced to question the validity of the book's concluding claim to have supplied him with something of "the inherent aesthetic and idealistic values peculiar to [Indian culture]" (p. 157). The eight forgotten authors whom Howard discusses may be worth reconsidering, but anybody who does so should take into account the sophisticated ethnopoetics that has developed in the last decade around the writings of Jerome Rothenberg.

American Indian Literature: An Anthology, edited by Alan R. Ve-lie (Oklahoma), is a much more substantial volume, containing repre-sentative samples of everything from pre-contact myth cycles to a surrealist poem called "For Theodore Roethke." The quality is high, but the ethnicity of the authors is an overriding absolute criterion, and this leads us to some obvious critical problems when we get to Indian material written directly in English. Velie finds it important to inform us, for instance, that William Jay Smith "retains a keen consciousness of his Choctaw heritage" (p. 298). But on the evidence of the three poems that Velie reprints, Smith's few Indian genes have had essentially no effect on his writing, in content or in form. So I wonder why I should care about his genealogy, and on purely theore-tical grounds I question his presence in this company. Still, overinclu-siveness in an anthology is a generous vice. *American Indian Litera-ture* even gives us an Indian science fiction story. The book is attrac-tively illustrated by the Cherokee artist Danny Timmons.

Gordon Brotherston's lavishly and functionally illustrated *Image of the New World: The American Continent Portrayed in Native Texts* (Thames and Hudson) is by far the most intellectually reward-ing of the three Indian books I am reviewing here. Brotherston's range is much wider than Howard's or Velie's; the heavily annotated Native American texts and pictograms which comprise his book come from Alaska and the Amazon, the Great Plains and the Caribbean. And this catholic learning, grouped under nine anthropological head-ings, all comes to bear on a powerful Lévi-Straussian thesis: that pre-contact Native American culture, despite its diversity, was at the fundamental level a unity, a way of looking at the world that was essentially the same throughout the Western Hemisphere. I am not competent to assess Brotherston's anthropological claims as such, but I know that the texts in *Image of the New World* will have great value for structuralists, myth critics, and historians of American litera-ture. The translations, prepared in collaboration with the Black Moun-tain poet Ed Dorn, are also beautiful.

The study of American Indian literature and the history that it represents leads me to a pair of quite different literary histories: Andrew Welsh's *Roots of Lyric: Primitive Poetry and Modern Poetics*

Jonathan Morse 443

(Princeton, 1978; James Russell Lowell Prize, 1979) and William J. Scheick's *The Half-Blood: A Cultural Symbol in 19th-Century American Fiction* (Kentucky).

Welsh's topic is most ambitious: no less than an attempt to define poetic language. He proceeds analytically, first considering language under the aspect of its vocative and evocative powers of image and sound (Pound's "phanopoeia" and "melopoeia") and then examining each of these powers as it manifests itself generically. In order to simplify this enormous task, Welsh proceeds by treating each poetic phenomenon as an effect in search of its theoretical cause. His discussion of phanopoeia, for instance, takes us in just five steps from primitive riddle, which works by mechanically attaching names to things, to Ernest Fenollosa's theory of the ideogram, in which the name is the image is the thing. Welsh takes his five steps to be a progression; his conclusion is that Fenollosa's mimetic theory of language approaches a complete explanation of the phanopoeic phenomenon. Similarly, Welsh tries to demonstrate that the mysterious melopoeic power of poetry to "communicate before it is understood" (the phrase is Eliot's, quoted by Welsh) can be understood with the help of Bronislaw Malinowski's pragmatic theory of language as physical action.

Along the way to this conclusion Welsh devotes two chapters of his book to some of the Indian poems discussed by Howard and Brotherston. In incantation if anywhere, he hypothesizes, we may be able to catch meaning in the act of emerging into consciousness out of the phylogenetic beginnings of speech itself. Welsh's anthropology here is strictly linear and evolutionary; he sees poetry moving from "primitive" to "higher" forms. This programmatic historicism strikes me as the most vulnerable part of his scheme. But considered purely *as* a scheme, a literary device for helping us read poems side by side with other poems, *Roots of Lyric* is admirably provocative. Brotherston, Velie, and Howard give us the Indian poems; Welsh places them in the history of English literature and shows us how good they are.

Scheick's compressed little monograph aims at clarifying the nature of a generic character in 19th-century American fiction. To do this Scheick has mined an enormous collection of books, ranging in quality from *The Confidence-Man* down to dime novels, for the sociological data they could yield. The operation has been, on the whole, a success; in fact, my only real objection to *The Half-Blood* is that it

is too all-inclusive and somewhat unfocused. The fact that a forgotten
novel is "incredibly boring" (p. 42) doesn't save us from a two-page
synopsis of its episodes in miscegenation. Literarily, it matters where
the stereotypic images come from—Mark Twain's Injun Joe is more
worth our attention now than Edward L. Wheeler's *Bob Woolf, the
Border Ruffian*—but Scheick's sociological blender mingles all his
characters into a wholly artificial epistemological homogeneity. This
does not vitiate *The Half-Blood's* value as a source book, however.
Scheick's data are valuable and his conclusions are solid. His concluding comparison of the half-blood with the mulatto has the potential to form the core of a large, radical idea.

Two final notes: Jan Harold Brunvand has supplemented his *Folklore: A Study and Research Guide* (see ALS 1976, p. 417) with a volume of *Readings in American Folklore* (Norton). And Ben Belitt has
collected some of his previously published discussions of the art of
translation in *Adam's Dream: A Preface to Translation* (Grove).

f. **Science Fiction.**   I. F. Clarke's *The Pattern of Expectation, 1644–
2001* (Basic Books) uses the documents of science fiction and utopian-
dystopian speculation to illustrate a history of the idea of the predictable future. But the material he has to work with is repetitious, and
the most interesting part of *The Pattern of Expectation* turns out to
be the unadorned notion that there *is* a pattern of expectation. It is
when this pattern breaks down—after World War I with *Brave New
World* and *Metropolis*, after World War II with Burroughs and
Vonnegut and Orwell and *A Clockwork Orange*—that Clark's analyses work best.

Darko Suvin in *Metamorphoses of Science Fiction: On the Poetics
and History of a Literary Genre* (Yale) sets out to define the genre
and succeeds in erecting a stipulative barrier which excludes the
great majority of the canon. "SF," says Suvin, "is . . . a literary genre
whose necessary and sufficient conditions are the presence and interaction of estrangement and cognition, and whose main formal device is an imaginative framework alternative to the author's empirical
environment" (pp. 7–8). He goes on to explain that "Estrangement
[in the sense of Brecht's *Verfremdungseffekt*] differentiates SF from
the 'realistic' literary mainstream. . . . Cognition differentiates it not
only from myth, but also from the folk (fairy) tale and the fantasy."
By this definition, as Suvin points out, Kafka is a writer of science

fiction but Isaac Asimov isn't. There is a reason for this rigor: Suvin, a Marxist, believes that science fiction has a generic power to help us understand and change our world, but "it is at its worst, its most alienated and alienating, when it honors the parasitism and vampirism of fantasy" (p. 25). This socially oriented poetics controls the critical history of pre–World War II science fiction which follows. *Metamorphoses* is abstract, powerful in argument, and deeply learned: its 22-page bibliography contains items in seven languages. Unfortunately, however, Suvin's English—entirely aside from its heavy load of philosophical terminology—is a tin-eared jargon full of phrases like "a grave disservice and rampantly socio-pathological phenomenon" (p. 9). This is frustrating. *Metamorphoses* is full of exciting temptations to generalize, yet Suvin's own critical instrument isn't sensitive enough to pick up a reading from any genre more aesthetically developed and less overtly ideological than science fiction. But Suvin himself stays within generic limits, and on its own terms his book is a formal construction of great elegance.

Metamorphoses is reviewed in *TLS* (9 May [1980]: 519), along with a book that I haven't been able to obtain: Gary K. Wolfe, *The Known and the Unknown: The Iconography of Science Fiction* (Kent State). Another book that I haven't read is *Voices for the Future: Essays on Major Science Fiction Writers*, vol 2, ed. Thomas D. Clareson (Bowling Green). When he reviewed volume 1 in *ALS 1976*, Michael J. Hoffman noted that it "herald[ed] the long overdue arrival of academic respectability to the study of this area of popular literature." Now that the genre has acceded to the Yale University Press and *TLS*, it appears that science fiction has risen from mere respectability to solid establishmentarianism.

ii. Criticism

a. **Theoretical Criticism: Collections of Essays:** *Critics at Work: Contemporary Literary Theory*, a special number (12, i) of *SLitI*, is a bargain: just three dollars will buy you eight state-of-the-art essays about the most interesting things critics are doing now. Only one of the essays, Joseph Riddel's "H. D.'s Scene of Writing," deals directly with the primary material of American literature, but all eight have important things to say about the ways in which literature is being read in America today. Americanists ought to read two of the essays

in particular: Murray Krieger's "Literature vs. Écriture: Constructions and Deconstructions in Recent Critical Theory" and Vincent B.
Leitch's "The Book of Deconstructive Criticism."

We ought to read these essays for a specifically Americanist reason: they reenact in a different genre the ontological debate about
America that Whitman summed up for our side in "Song of the
Broad-Axe." On this side of the Atlantic, metaphorically speaking,
stands Krieger with an essay claiming that literature has meaning and
therefore partakes of our own treasurable human reality. On the other
side stand Leitch and the deconstructors, with Freud and Nietzsche
and Heidegger behind them, asserting that literature—like talking,
like thinking, like everything—doesn't "mean" anything; the intelligible world around us is nothing but a collection of signifiers, all
randomly recombining in "freeplay" and all to be reduced to mute
uncertainty by the act of reading. The two essays, read together, come
down to the terms of a dialectic about the future shape of our language and our culture, the shapes that will or won't arise. Whitman
worked the dialectic out for his time, but it will have to be done
again in ours. The remaining books in this section offer interesting
samples of the work in progress.

Psychoanalysis and the Text works carefully along the boundary
between the reader and his reading. The result is sometimes dis-
quieting, as when Barbara Johnson reads Jacques Derrida's reading
of Jacques Lacan's reading of "The Purloined Letter" (see chapter
3, section *iii. b.*). But Cary Nelson's useful essay, "The Psychology of
Criticism, or What Can Be Said," discusses in some theoretical detail
the proper place of the self-referential critical ego in criticism, the
attitude we readers should take to a critic's conscious or self-conscious
or unconscious puttings forward of himself. *Psychoanalysis and the
Text* is a solidly good book. And yet it leaves one with a claustrophobic feeling. The main reason is probably cultural; as Hartman
says of Derrida on pages 98–99, in his essay "Psychoanalysis: The
French Connection," "[T]here is little in English letters to compare
with the *involution* of French or German commentary once it has
singled out its exempla. A modern medievalism then takes over. . . .
The allusiveness goes inward rather than abroad. . . ." Derrida himself takes part in the book with a vertiginous deconstruction of Freud's
Beyond the Pleasure Principle.

Deconstruction and Criticism (Seabury; no editor) is a collection of five essays, of which one in particular concerns *ALS*. In this one, "The Breaking of Form," Harold Bloom surveys his system of antithetical criticism, makes a strong point in passing about the weakness of deconstructionism's exclusively synchronic readings, and concludes with a demonstration of his technique on Ashbery's "Self-Portrait in a Convex Mirror." As he goes through the six revisionary ratios once again, Bloom's tone is that of a weary shop instructor explaining the operation of a piece of machinery which, in its current model, operates almost by itself. He assumes that you have read his previous detailed instructions; this exercise is chiefly a refresher course for advanced students. Three of the remaining essays use analyses of English Romantic poems to demonstrate various deconstructionist positions, from Geoffrey Hartman's temperate textuality to the voracious, nothing-means-anything nihilism of Paul de Man and J. Hillis Miller. (Here and in the summer 1980 issue of *CritI* Miller insists that his practice is not nihilistic. But it is, insofar as all his readings tend to resolve their subjects into nil.) I was unable to finish reading Jacques Derrida's contribution, a 102–page attempt to recreate the endless reflexivity of absolute language in a pair of readings of his own readings of his own readings. Depending on its reader's sense of contact with the nonverbal parts of reality, this exercise will be perceived as either a delicately sensitive regression or an act of self-abuse.

Now, for all the self-conscious decadence of their preoccupations and their prose styles, Derrida and the Yale group are scholars of deep learning and deep seriousness. But their method lends itself more easily to irresponsible excess than perhaps any idea since progressive education. A sign of the bad news we may expect on seminar papers in a few years is the 1978 New York Literary Forum volume *Intertextuality: New Perspectives in Criticism*, ed. Jeanine Parisier Plottel and Hanna Cherney. This collection of essays contains, inter alia, five studies of buttons in literature, an essay beginning, "One of the most rewarding aspects of Free Shakespeare (both as adjective and verb) is that it sanctions our own free association" (p. 35), and an essay on Freud's use of the letter "Z." Freud, we learn, employed the Z-heavy Italian word "piazza" in an essay published in 1919, when he was 62 years old; Z is the 26th letter of the alphabet; the number 26 is 62 backwards; this, by way of "castrative privilege" and railroad tracks that look sort of like Z's without their crossbars, tells us something about Freud's repression of the idea of his own death. Of course Freud was actually 63 in 1919, and of course Z is not the 26th letter of the alphabet in either Italian or German, but, well, everybody's got a right to their own opinion, ain't they?

Meanwhile, *Textual Strategies: Perspectives in Post-Structuralist Criticism*, ed. Josué V. Harari (Cornell), offers 16 essays plus a first-rate bibliography. The book's range is broad; it includes Derrida and de Man on the one hand, and, on the other, the more extrinsically oriented Edward W. Said (who asks us to take account of the social "worldliness" of texts and their readers) and Michel Foucault (whose essay "What Is an Author?" raises fundamental questions about the social origins of esthetic response). There is also a brief, lucid essay by Barthes on the idea of a text, and one specifically Americanist contribution. This, unfortunately, almost strangles on its own jargon. On the whole, however, *Textual Strategies* is well worth looking at.

Finally, and more traditionally, vol. 1 of *Comparative Criticism: A Yearbook*, ed. Elinor Shaffer (Cambridge), contains one Americanist contribution: Christopher Heywood's "French and American Sources of Victorian Realism." This essay is an old-fashioned influence study devoted primarily to Zola and Balzac; the only American work discussed in detail is *The Scarlet Letter*.

b. **Theoretical Criticism: Monographs.** When we sit down to read a book, certain conscious or unconscious assumptions—about form, about meaning, about truth and authorial intention and our own situations as readers—sit down beside us. In *Critical Assumptions* (Cambridge), K. K. Ruthven analyzes some of these preconceptions in twelve short, heavily annotated chapters. This modest little handbook lays no particular claim to originality—Ruthven intends it primarily as a graduate-level textbook—but I found it very useful in the way of handbooks: a collection of facts and ideas arranged for maximum heuristic value.

But to go on to current trends: Jacques Derrida's *Spurs: Nietzsche's Styles*, trans. Barbara Harlow, pub. in bi-glot ed. (Chicago), elegantly illustrates the internal logic that drives deconstructionism back to a continuous redeconstruction of its own originating texts. And Paul de Man's *Allegories of Reading: Figural Language in Rousseau, Nietzsche, Rilke, and Proust* (Yale), with less panache but more

discursive readability, attempts a detailed proof of the central deconstructionist paradox that "Literature as well as criticism—the difference between them being delusive—is condemned (or privileged) to
be forever the most rigorous and, consequently, the most unreliable
language in terms of which man names and transforms himself" (p.
19). There is a direct and important connection between this notion
of a panrhetorical universe and Emerson's dictum, "Words are signs
of natural facts," but *ALS* is not the place to go into detail about it.
But for an examination in general terms of the deconstructionist idea
and its implications, I would like to recommend two review-essays:
Dennis Donoghue's "Deconstructing Deconstruction," *NYRB* 12 June
(1980): 37–41, and Gerald Graff's "Deconstruction as Dogma," *GaR*
34 (1980): 404–21. A more detailed and more sympathetic analysis
can be found in Rodolphe Gasché's formidably abstract "Deconstruction as Criticism," *Glyph* 6:177–215.

Meanwhile, three conservative critics have weighed in with their
own arguments against deconstruction. Murray Krieger's *Poetic Presence and Illusion: Essays in Critical History and Theory* (Hopkins)
is a large collection of essays, all but two of them previously published
as long ago as 1967. Their common theme is enunciated in the book's
two-part title essay, which pleads with us to acknowledge the special
reality subsisting in the illusion created around itself by a literary
text. Krieger's argument is subtle, and it erects an almost fideistic barrier to defend the idea of reality against attack from Yale. But inside
the stockade, with a reading of Shakespeare's sonnets in part 1 and a
reading of *Tristram Shandy* in part 2, nothing very hopeful happens.
Krieger's delicately elaborated formalism seems less adapted to practical application than the techniques of the deconstructors.

Like Krieger, Gerald Graff is philosophically a realist. In *Literature Against Itself* Graff takes a stand, on behalf of realism, against
the entire literary sensibility of which deconstructionism is a mani-
festation. "A formidable conglomerate of publicists, theoreticians,
musicians, bards, prophets, therapists, mystagogues, sexualogues, and
ideological dieticians and haberdashers has formed a kind of alienation industry," he concludes on page 224, "supported by the expanding segment of society which predicates its very sense of community
on the type of 'disinherited mind' that was once the monopoly of the
antagonists of bourgeois society." My own sense of the popular cul-

ture, for what it's worth, tells me that this statement of Graff's was truer five or ten years ago than it is today, and in general, *Literature Against Itself* seems to be a not fully successful broadening of the front that Graff opened against New Haven in his dashing essay "Fear and Trembling at Yale" (*ASch* 46 [1977]: 467–78). But an excellent thing about this book is that it reprints and updates Graff's 1974 essay "What Was New Criticism?," a first-rate piece of polemical literary history.

Wayne C. Booth's *Critical Understanding: The Powers and Limits of Pluralism* (Chicago) has had a bad press, and it is easy to understand why. After demonstrating, in three long chapters devoted to R. S. Crane, M. H. Abrams, and Kenneth Burke, that pluralistic approaches to criticism tend to turn into monisms when reduced to method or elevated to first principles (pp. 200, 210), Booth can think of nothing better to throw the foundering pluralist instinct than a leaky psychologistic lifejacket called "understanding," which is defined in italics (p. 262) as *the goal, process, and result whenever one mind succeeds in entering another mind, or, what is the same thing, whenever one mind succeeds in incorporating any part of another mind.*" Even though Booth then succeeds in producing some good miscellaneous readings of James, Goldsmith, and Anatole France, this is clearly unsatisfactory as literary criticism. But Booth admits at the very end of his book that his critical enterprise here arises from a religious impulse, and when one has that fact in hand, understanding does follow. Booth's task—the creation of a truly pluralist critical ethic somewhere between the intolerant monism of the older critics and the anything-goes skepticism of the deconstructors— is a fully necessary one, and one that must finally be based on transcendent values. Read in those terms, the terms of Booth's boldface "Three Inseparable Values: Vitality, Justice, and Understanding" (p. 219), *Critical Understanding* is still not a usable work of literary criticism. But it may form the basis of a future moral criticism.

I end this section with some unrelated studies. Robert L. Caserio's *Plot, Story, and the Novel From Dickens and Poe to the Modern Period* (Princeton) argues that "plot and story make sense of life by reasoning about it with an intellectual and moral narrative reason that is attached to a ground not merely speculative" (p. 91). "Life," of course, is a big word, perhaps too big for efficient use in an activity so circumscribed as literary criticism; at any rate, Caserio's argument didn't carry me very deeply into the books he considers. The American authors discussed are Poe, Melville, James, and Faulkner.

Allegory, says Maureen Quilligan in *The Language of Allegory: Defining the Genre* (Cornell), is a form of writing based on a model of language "felt to have a potency as solidly meaningful as physical fact," out of which "the allegorist's narrative comes, peopled by words moving about an intricately reechoing landscape of language" (p. 156). This medieval way of perceiving language (Quilligan calls it "suprarealism") has been literally unthinkable since the Renaissance, and yet, as Quilligan notes, it bears some interesting affinities to contemporary linguistic philosophy. It therefore follows that allegory can be usefully rethought for our times, and Quilligan sets out to do this. Her chief American examples are *The Scarlet Letter, The Confidence-Man, Pale Fire*, and (at a length greater, I think, than their literary qualities justify) *Gravity's Rainbow* and *The Crying of Lot 49*. Her wide range of reference is illustrated by her unexceptionable conclusion (pp. 221–22) that "anyone armed with the experience of the Lady Meed episode in *Piers Plowman* is not going to find the Confidence Man's requests for money quite as perplexing, or miss the ambivalent ambiguity of the Confidence Man's title."

Saul's Fall: A Critical Fiction (Hopkins) is a combination of *Pale Fire* and *The Pooh Perplex*: a play surrounded by an elaborate biographical fiction and followed by several critical studies in the very latest styles. All of this is the work of Herbert Lindenberger— "who," the jacket copy tells us in a moment of faintheartedness, "really does exist." Some of Lindenberger's parodies are pointless but others rival the works of Myron Masterson and Simon Lacerous, and this intertextual artifact is full of high spirits.

Another venturesome study of intertextuality from Johns Hopkins must receive brief mention. Susan Stewart's *Nonsense: Aspects of Intertextuality in Folklore and Literature* is a study of the ways in which nonsense—"a radical shift towards the metaphoric pole [of Jakobson's metaphoric/metonymic model of language] accompanied by a decontextualization of the utterance" (p. 35)—short-circuits utterance, separates form from content, and insures that every society will bear within the codes of its structure an anticode of anarchy and terror.

Stewart analyzes a corpus of examples ranging all the way from jump-rope rhymes to *Finnegans Wake*, and her readings are sharp-eyed and stimulating.

The farthest-reaching and most powerful study in this section is Frank Kermode's *The Genesis of Secrecy: On the Interpretation of Narrative* (Harvard). Though this hermeneutic study of the Gospel of Mark has almost nothing directly to do with American literature, I want to mention it here, however briefly, because it is full of extraordinarily suggestive ideas about the nature of narrative reading.

c. Linguistics and Semiotics.   In addition to Noam Chomsky's *Language and Responsibility*, which I discuss in another section, several linguistic studies bear on the concerns of *ALS*. Oswald Ducrot's and Tzvetan Todorov's *Encyclopedic Dictionary of the Sciences of Language*, trans. from the 1973 French edition by Catherine Porter (Hopkins), is divided into a historical section ("Schools"), a section arranged by disciplines ("Fields"), and two sections devoted to concepts: "Methodological Concepts," which deals with such general linguistic ideas as the *langue/parole* distinction, and "Descriptive Concepts," which deals with such empirical matters as the phoneme. This analytical arrangement allows the book to be read through for many uninterrupted pages at a time: an improvement over the conventional alphabetical arrangement. The book's linguistic ideology is of course completely post-Saussurean; an appendix, "Toward a Critique of the Sign," summarizes the radical linguistic metaphysics of Lacan, Derrida, and Kristeva.

George L. Dillon's *Language Processing and the Reading of Literature: Toward a Model of Comprehension* (Indiana, 1978) is Empson formalized: a sensitive linguistic study of the ways in which we fill in the ellipses, sort out the relative pronouns, wait for the suspended verbs, and do all the other things that make up the action of literary reading. The book is full of practical examples; Americanists will especially appreciate Dillon's demonstration of how the difficult beauties work in James, Faulkner, and Stevens.

A complementary volume is Michael Riffaterre's *Semiotics of Poetry* (Indiana, 1978), which shifts the critical focus from the reader to the intertextual sign systems of poetic discourse. This discourse, in Riffaterre's view, is a "semiotic circularity" which forces its readers to engage in "a continual recommencing, an indecisiveness resolved one moment and lost the next with each relieving of revealed significance. . . ." (p. 166). That is, the poem is a self-enclosing verbal structure, defined by its unique semiotic norms and therefore not mimetic. In fact, what a poem does is to transcend mimesis through language's power of overdetermination, which is why the poem's "Significance . . . [can] be more than or something other than the total meaning deducible from a comparison between variants of the given" (p. 12). Riffaterre's demonstrations of this far-reaching idea are all based on French examples, but their power makes them generally applicable to the entire structure of Western literary language. *Semiotics of Poetry* can be read profitably alongside Justus George Lawler's *Celestial Pantomime: Poetic Structures of Transcendence* (Yale), an amazing scrapbook of tiny, acute readings of such microstructural devices as parentheses and refrains, loosely held together by an airy phenomenological thesis and one of the most narcissistic prose styles in New Haven. The examples are the thing here, and as a collection of examples Lawler's book complements Riffaterre's very well.

Another, more theoretical, complement to Riffaterre is Barbara Herrnstein Smith's *On the Margins of Discourse: The Relation of Literature to Language* (Chicago), a collection of essays based on J. L. Austin's speech-act theory of language. *ALS* is not the place to go into detail about the philosophy of language, but I would like to call attention to two of the essays. One, "The Ethics of Interpretation," is an attack on the notion that authorial intention, or any other historically determinate datum, can serve as a valid critical criterion. The other, the book's title piece, is an extended definition of poetry in terms of the interpretive consequences that the utterance of poetry invites. I found the first essay a concise, rigorous statement of the antihistoricist position, and the second a stimulating complement to the poetics of Welsh (see section *i.e.*) and Riffaterre.

A more extensively developed monograph is Wolfgang Iser's *The Act of Reading: A Theory of Aesthetic Response* (Hopkins), which aims to produce a comprehensive theory of "the reader's role [as] prestructured by three basic components: the different perspectives represented in the text, the vantage point from which he joins them together, and the meeting place where they converge" (p. 36). This is a project of the most fundamentally interesting kind, and I think Iser may well have succeeded. Certainly *The Act of Reading* will

have to be read by anyone concerned with the philosophy of literature, if only because other models of reading are incorporated into
Iser's step-by-step exposition. Again, *ALS* is not the place to go into
detail about this important analysis of the meaning of reader response,
but I would like to encourage readers by noting that Iser's style is
necessarily dense and abstract but quite graceful.

d. **Feminism and Related Studies.**   Three major works of specific
concern to *ALS* were published this year: *The Madwoman in the
Attic, Shakespeare's Sisters,* and *The Homosexual Tradition in American Poetry.* These are reviewed elsewhere in this volume, but I
would like here to call attention to two good general studies not directly related to American literature, Laurence Lerner's *Love and
Marriage: Literature and Its Social Context* (St. Martin's) and Tony
Tanner's *Adultery in the Novel: Contract and Transgression* (Hopkins). Lerner's attractively written study examines our society's idea
of love, as it has been expressed in literature from the Minnesingers
to Doris Lessing, and attempts to show how this idea gave rise to
the literary convention that love and marriage coexist in a state of
conflict. This is an ambitious topic for a relatively short book, and
Lerner's self-imposed restriction to English and German literature
automatically excludes some monuments of documentation, such as
Madame Bovary and *Anna Karenina.* And his exclusion of American
authors has forced him to omit Henry James and, most regrettably,
William Carlos Williams, the poet of married love. Such omissions,
along with a concentration on breadth rather than depth and a certain
excessive reasonableness in discussing passion and its social outcomes,
limit the power of *Love and Marriage.* But Lerner's eye for detail is
very sharp. Witness his analysis of the reader's feelings when Esther
Summerson, the preternaturally pure heroine of Dickens' *Bleak
House,* receives a proposal of marriage from the silly but not evil
Mr. Guppy: "Mr. Guppy's offence is that he did not stay in his part
of the book. He belongs among the Dickensian humours. . . . Esther
is the heroine . . . and a proposal like this threatens to draw her into
the comedy, where respect gives way to gusto" (p. 94). *Love and Marriage* is full of small, acute insights like this.
     Adultery in the Novel is a structuralist study of Rousseau's *La
Nouvelle Héloïse,* Goethe's *Die Wahlverwandtschaften,* and Flaubert's *Madame Bovary,* prefaced by a sprawling 110-page introduction

which lays out the topography of a strikingly interesting map of reading. "[T]he connections or relationships between a specific kind of
sexual act, a specific kind of society, and a specific kind of narrative
seem to me to be worth exploring," Tanner says (p. 12), because (p.
15) "marriage is *the* central subject for the bourgeois novel . . . marriage in all its social and domestic ramifications in a demythologized
society. . . . It is the structure that maintains the Structure. . . . As
bourgeois marriage loses its absoluteness, its unquestioned finality,
its 'essentiality,' so does the bourgeois novel. On another level we
may say that as the cont[r]act between man and wife loses its sense
of necessity and binding power, so does the contract between novelist
and reader." The test of such an extreme hypothesis, of course, is its
ability to help us read, and here Tanner performs with great daring.
Pushing his idea to its limits, laying himself fully open to the charge
of being thesis-bound, he consistently comes up with wonderful readings. I wish—to take one example at random—that I had the space to
quote Tanner's analysis (pp. 254–58) of the functioning of Monsieur
Homais' hundreds of unused napkin rings in the narrative economy
of *Madame Bovary*. In the absence of that luxury, I will second Edward W. Said's jacket endorsement, "one of the two or three really
important books on the novel," deplore the book's terrible proof-
reading (as in "contact" for "contract" above), and note with anticipation that Tanner promises (p. 12, n.) to consider some American
novels in a subsequent volume.

e. **Miscellaneous.** Oxford has published collections by two of
HudR's ace reviewers, Marvin Mudrick and Roger Sale. *Books Are
Not Life But Then What Is?* gives us Mudrick in his best form as the
learned Groucho Marx of American criticism. "His unfailing impolite-
ness gets to be very funny": this is Mudrick on Nabokov's quarrel
with Edmund Wilson (p. 76, n. 10), but it is also Mudrick's literary
ideal. Certainly he hits some barn doors with a wonderful bang: D. H.
Lawrence in his prophetic mood ("Delphic snottiness," p. 135),
Jacques Derrida's metaphysical style ("When the French get heavy,
they make the Germans look like ballerinas," p. 215). When things
get subtle, though, Grouchism isn't enough. Franz Kafka was not
just "Portnoy's bachelor uncle" (p. 118), Roland Barthes was not a
"jerk" (p. 225), and "contemptible" (p. 189) is really not the right
word for *Troilus and Cressida*. But *ALS* readers should make a point

of looking at "Issues and Answers," Mudrick's judicious dismantling of Edmund Wilson.

Books Are Not Life ends with four previously uncollected essays, oddly old-fashioned "appreciations" which tend to confirm Sale's judgment that Mudrick is "temperamentally . . . completely a reviewer." Sale thus reviews Mudrick in *On Not Being Good Enough: Writings of a Working Critic* (p. 169), a collection of reviews dating back to 1966. The essay on Mudrick is a good one; Sale's temperament is different enough from Mudrick's to allow for the proper degree of perspective. Mudrick uses his epigrams to dismiss, Sale uses his to introduce. For example, Sale begins a discussion of Lionel Trilling's *Sincerity and Authenticity* by cutely noting that "reading Trilling in bulk does bear certain affinities with eating a meal consisting entirely of Thousand Island dressing" (p. 150). But he doesn't stop there; four pages later his contemplation of Trilling's orotundity has led him to a critical insight much larger and more useful than Mudrick's average: "Trilling treats himself as an institution. . . . [h]e unfailingly does think that he can recover enough [of the past] to make it relevant for any question that happens to be pressing; all you do is make patterns, continuities, trends, emphases." This is good, but the whole essay is just nine pages long. Not good enough, as Sale says. The format of the book review cramps his style.

Robert Scholes has published a retrospective collection of his critical pieces, *Fabulation and Metafiction* (Illinois). Most of these are short and many are superannuated (discussions of the obsolete novelists Terry Southern and Jerome Charyn; a wildly over-enthusiastic explication of *Giles Goat-Boy* with no reference to Barth's later work). *Fabulation and Metafication* is a revised and expanded edition of *The Fabulators* (1967). The years have not been kind.

Giles Gunn's *The Interpretation of Otherness: Literature, Religion, and the American Imagination* (Oxford), a series of five essays on the relationships between literature and religion, is addressed primarily to theologians; that is, to a group of learned, sensitive men and women who stand outside literature and ask what it is ultimately for. Gunn's critical perspective, therefore, is different from most of ours. This difference was most valuable for me in the long, subtle essay "The American Writer and the Formation of an American Mind: Literature, Culture, and Their Relation to Ultimate Values," in which Gunn establishes a reciprocal relationship between our discipline's insights into the nature of expression and theology's insights into the nature of mind. Of the remaining four essays, one is a brief historical introduction to the religious study of literature and two are apologias for the religious value of literary criticism. In the last, "American Literature and the Imagination of Otherness," Gunn uses specific examples to demonstrate how American literature defines us American human beings in relation to what lies beyond us. Gunn's literary criticism has less freshness than its theological applications; the deer in Frost's "The Most of It" reminds Gunn, infelicitously, of "the beaching of an enormous landing craft or outer space machine" (p. 197), and I take it as conclusively established that no one can say anything new about *The Great Gatsby.* But as an extended religious meditation on the nature of mind in America, *The Imagination of Otherness* is worth considering.

Van Wyck Brooks: The Critic and His Critics, ed. William Wasserstrom (Kennikat), is a well-rounded collection of essays written about Brooks between 1924 and 1973, plus a bibliography.

Northwest Perspectives contains two essays in folklore, three essays in history, and eight discussions of the literature of the region. A collection like this one is always susceptible to regionalist hyperbole, and Bingham and Love have occasionally succumbed when they should have been blue-penciling. Every region has its local colorists whose only claim to glory is getting the place names right, none of their productions is as interesting as Franz Kafka's geographically impossible novel *Amerika,* and it is banal to deck out such merely commemorative art in the regalia of literary scholarship. But there are broadly useful things in *Northwest Perspectives.* I especially liked Barbara Meldrum's feminist reading of Vardis Fisher and Kermit Vanderbilt's strained but sensible case for Roethke as a regional poet.

Another regionalist study, Anne E. Rowe's *The Enchanted Country: Northern Writers in the South, 1865–1910* (LSU, 1978), examines the southern image portrayed in the postbellum works of Harriet Beecher Stowe, John W. DeForest, Albion Tourgée, Constance Fenimore Woolson, Lafcadio Hearn, Owen Wister, and Henry James. The book's thesis, supported in detail, is that even the most antisouthern writers, such as the Reconstructionist Judge Tourgée, had favorable things to say about southerners and the South. Few surprises here, but a useful study of the growth of the magnolia-blossom novel after the Civil War.

Themes, Topics, Criticism

Finally, I would like to call attention to James Monaco's *American Film Now* (Oxford), a detailed, up-to-the-minute critical survey written from the triple points of view of aesthetics, economics, and sociology. As his excellent textbook *How to Read a Film* (Oxford, 1977) shows, Monaco possesses a sophisticated critical sense, an insider's knowledge of the film industry, and an admirably lucid way of explaining complicated things. *American Film Now*, however, is a project big enough to spread even Monaco's talents thin. By necessity, Monaco has had to abandon the semiotic style of *How to Read a Film* in favor of a flexible Veblenian economic anthropology that verges on impressionism, and I, at least, miss the formal power of the older book. But it is a good sign when one wishes that a long book were longer still. *American Film Now*, as it stands, is a literate, informed, intelligent overview.

f. **Conclusion.** This was a slow year for traditional Americanist studies of the kind usually published in *AL*. On the one hand, there were a great many books—so many that I had to pass over a number of good articles. On the other hand, many of the best books were only indirectly related to American literature. This seems to me to indicate that Americanist scholars as a group have some theoretical homework to do. *Glyph* and *Diacritics* may be too esoteric for our immediate concerns, but now is probably the time for more of us to start reading *NLH* and *CritI*.

But reading this year's big pile of books has been a rewarding experience for me. My favorites, Baltzell's *Puritan Boston and Quaker Philadelphia*, Riffaterre's *Semiotics of Poetry*, Tanner's *Adultery in the Novel*, and Welsh's *Roots of Lyric*, cover a very wide intellectual range, and I take this to be a good sign. It indicates that American literary scholarship is powerful enough to venture across its own disciplinary frontiers.

University of Hawaii

21. Foreign Scholarship

i. East European Contributions[1]

F. Lyra

I regret that the indispensable selectivity of the two-year material below is to a large extent due not so much to acts of discretion as to limited access to the pertinent publications. It is simply beyond one man's capacity to provide a comprehensive survey of scholarship on American literature in Eastern Europe without some kind of co-operation on the part of Americanists from the particular countries. Sad to say, solicitations for cooperation have so far remained unheeded in Roumania and Bulgaria, and there has been little reaction from Yugoslavia.

In the Soviet Union scholarship on American literature in 1978 and 1979 was with very few exceptions concerned with the 20th century. Among the books the most representative in this respect is *Literatura SSHA XX veka. Opyt tipologicheskogo isledovaniya. (Avtorskaya pozytsiya konflikt, geroi)* [Literature of the USA of the 20th Century. An Attempt at a Typological Analysis. The Position of the Writer, Conflict, Hero] (Moskva Nauka, 1978) which was published in 1978 and not in 1977 as reported in *ALS 1977*. Edited by Yasen N. Zasurski, who also wrote the Introduction (pp. 3–11), the volume contains nine studies by seven scholars. "The Spiritual Crisis of Society and the Moral Position of the Individual" by Maya Koreneva (pp. 12–68) is the most literary in that Koreneva explores at length a number of works of 20th-century representatives of American literature with an eye on the types of solution of the conflict between the individual and society. In "Crisis of Bourgeois Democratic Ideals and Roads Toward Socialist Ideals" (pp. 69–108) A. P. Sarukhanyan traces the evolution of socialist ideology among such American writers as Randolph Bourne, Jack London, John Reed,

---

1. This essay covers Eastern European scholarship for both 1978 and 1979. To save space I have omitted the Russian titles of individual contributions published in books.—F. L.

Albert Maltz, Lars Lawrence, Philip Bonosky, Walter Lowenfels, and a few others. Sarukhanyan discusses in greater detail the ideological meanderings of Upton Sinclair and John Dos Passos.

N. A. Anastas'ev's "Mass Consciousness and the American Writer" (pp. 109–33) deals with another type of conflict illustrated by brief discussions of the works of O'Hara, Vidal, and Shirley Ann Grau. Anastas'ev expresses the conviction that "the latest books of Vonnegut, Baldwin, and Heller confirm that in America there is a rebirth of the tradition of truly socialist art." A. M. Zverev's essay "The American Dream and the American Tragedy" (pp. 134–208) explores well-known concepts without saying anything new. Koreneva's second article on "Literature and War" (pp. 209–38) covers familiar ground starting with novels about the First World War. Koreneva stresses Faulkner's opposition to the southern idealization of war, but chooses not to discuss A Fable. She criticizes all the writers for not understanding the social, political, and economic causes of the First World War. The ambiguities of the Second World War novels reflect the double role the United States played in that war. The novelists have failed to separate false from true heroism and to grasp the significance of heroic acts. The only meaning the novels convey is the senselessness of war. G. V. Anikin's essay "The Literature of the USA and the Struggle Against Fascism" (pp. 239–84) is surveyish and topical. S. A. Chakovski deserves praise for his unconventional treatment of black literature in his "Race Conflict and 20th Century American Literature" (pp. 285–312). Not neglecting the ideological implications to be found in black authors' works, Chakovski concentrates on their aesthetic values, especially Wright's Native Son, Ellison's The Invisible Man, and Baldwin's Another Country.

In his second contribution to the volume "Industrialism and American Literature" (pp. 313–88) Zverev attempts to contrive a poetics of American literary works exploring the problem of industrialism. In his view the "synthesis of documentalism and fiction" constitutes the "artistic model" of which Sinclair's The Jungle is an exemplary prototype. Zverev discusses the book perspicaciously, but he does not examine other works with comparative proficiency. Two hundred pages of the collection (pp. 359–560) are devoted to T. L. Morozova's "A Typology of the Hero." This scholar distinguishes eight types of heroes in 20th-century American literature. Except for the black protagonist whom Morozova considers to be the only uniquely American hero having no counterparts among other types, Morozova connects all types with models in European literature, mostly French and Russian. The American heroes of the Sorel type, for example, Martin Eden, Gatsby, Clyde Griffiths, are "tragic conquerors." The model for the "triumphant conqueror" is Rastignac. This type is represented by Horatio Alger, Newman, Cowperwood, Sutpen. Other types are the alienated hero of the lost generation and the wrecked generation, the average American, the intellectual, the antihero. The eighth type includes characters who "struggle for a new world." Their lives are emblematic of "active humanism." Unfortunately, Morozova's perceptive discussion of representatives of this type— among them Dreiser's Ernita, Hemingway's Robert Jordan, Faulkner's Linda Snopes—does not extend to characters of leftist authors who are only mentioned: Philip Bonosky, Lars Lawrence, Albert Maltz, Lillian Hellman, Alvah C. Bessie. Fast is absent.

While retaining in various degrees the traditionally social and ideological perspective on American literature, many Soviet contributions reveal a strong emphasis on its humanistic values. This approach is typified in A. M. Zverev's introductory essay to the impressive edition (*tirage*: 50,000 copies) of Vonnegut's four novels in one volume, containing *Slaughterhouse-Five, Cat's Cradle, Breakfast of Champions, God Bless You, Mr. Rosewater* (Moskva: Khudozhestvennaya Literatura, 1978), and in his article "Faulkner—Short Story Writer," one of two pieces concluding the superbly edited first complete Russian translation of Faulkner's *Collected Stories* (Moskva: Nauka [1978], pp. 369–97). The other one is on "Yoknapatawpha and its People" (pp. 598–606). Zverev's comments exemplify the general empathy with which Soviet literateurs and scholars regard those American writers whose works have been translated into Russian. This empathy is rooted in the widespread opinion that the American writer is ill treated at home by the critics.

"The critic is not an ally of literature, but its adversary," declares Zverev in "SSHA: Itogi goda—'moralnoe porazhenie'?" [USA. Results of the Year—Moral Defeat?] (*Inostrannaya Literatura* 5:209–14). He disagrees with John Gardner's pessimistic judgment of American literature. Inasmuch as Zverev censures Barthelme, Walker Percy, Joan Didion, and Pynchon for "the banal stereotypes of modern thinking," he commends "the ethical consciousness of John Cheever's collected stories, Ernest Gaines's *In My Father's House*, the latest

work of Vidal, Mary Gordon, and John Irving, and undertakes a qualified defense of Mario Puzo's *Fools Die* and James Michener's *Ches-
apeake*.

The period was dominated by interest in Modernism, as if Soviet scholars and critics were vying for the best answer to D. V.
Zatonskii's question, "What Is Modernism?," which is the title of his
piece in his collection of essays *V nashe vremya* [In Our Times]
(Moskva: Sovetskii Pisatel', pp. 31–61). Soviet scholars are unani-
mous in viewing Modernism as a cultural phenomenon indicative
of the decline of bourgeois society and humanistic values, but they
differ in approach to and evaluation of Modernist literature and
criticism. One of the two books on Modernism, *Literatura i dvizhenie
vremeni* [Literature and the Movement of Time] by Dimitri N. Urnov
and Mikhail V. Urnov (Moskva: Khudozhestvennaya Literatura,
1978), is meant as a polemics with Modernist thought in the West
in general and American criticism in particular, although the authors' underlying intention is grounded in concern with the question
of literary tradition. Appreciating with different degrees of qualification the artistic achievements of such Modernists as Henry James,
Virginia Woolf, James Joyce, T. S. Eliot, Ernest Hemingway, and
others, the Urnovs point out the deficiencies of their art and especially
the discrepancies between their work and theory. They adjudge one
or the other, defending rather than disparaging them either as
theorists or writers. They do, however, ostracize those who happened also to be critics. Eliot, for instance, comes in for severe judgment for creating criticism with a capital "c," for transforming criticism into its own object, for his and James's justification of "dullness"
and artistic decrepitude under the guise of consciousness and complexity. In addition Eliot is blamed for creating the cult of "failure."
The Urnovs charge that Anglo-American criticism has lost its basic
function, which is to provide guidance to both the reader and the
writer. They mete out harsh words to "the critical industry," which
has the power to make or destroy the reputation and worth of an
author, as was the case with Faulkner, whose reputation, they claim
—not without some justification as Faulkner experts know—was made
entirely by the critics.

The Urnovs' book, and particularly the authors' high-handed
opinion of Faulkner's work as being too difficult for the reader and
thus detached from the tradition of the classical novel, provoked N. A.

Anastas'ev to publish a long article, "Preodolenie ili razvitie (Folkner v svete klassicheskogo opyta)" [Defeat or Development: Faulkner in the Light of Classical Experience] (*Voprosy Literatury* 9:86–125), in which he accuses the Urnovs of arbitrary opinions about the Modernists. Anastas'ev states that "twentieth-century literature was and is a field of the relentless struggle between realism and modernism," adding that "the writers' realism is sometimes complicated by elements of modernist aesthetics." If I understand him correctly, he wants to rescue the Modernists from Modernism. Anastas'ev substantiates his defense with a detailed analysis and evaluation of *Absalom, Absalom!*. In all fairness, his attack on the Urnovs is not always justified. His charge that they have made of Conrad a chief representative of Modernism simply is not true. As a matter of fact, the Urnovs do not even consider Joyce a full-blooded Modernist.

D. Urnov amplifies one of the themes of the book, pertaining to the close reading of literary works in "Parodosky pristalnogo chteniya" [Paradoxes of Close Reading] (*Voprosy Literatury* 3[1978]:110–36). The article is a devastating criticism of F. R. Leavis and his followers, who practice the principle of intensive reading. The paradox of their method, says Urnov, is that "they wanted to learn to read, but in reality they unlearned reading."

In contrast to the Urnovs' book, which is topical, Zverev's *Modernism v literature SSHA* [Modernism in American Literature] (Moskva: Nauka) is comprehensive, systematic, and historical in approach. Like no other Soviet scholar Zverev demonstrates a sensitive understanding of the complexity of Modernism. He recognizes both the antithetical and evolutionary nature of particular movements and authors, stating that postwar American Modernism is discontinuous with earlier modernism in some respects and continuous in others. For a brief characterization of latest Modernist tendencies in American literature, Zverev, following Ihab Hassan, applies the term "post-Modernism" but refrains from discussing any works which he considers post-Modern. Unlike Hassan, however, he views post-Modernism as the final stage of decline of literary art intrinsic in Modernism. The work of such Modernists as Gertrude Stein, Ezra Pound, T. S. Eliot, Wallace Stevens, William Carlos Williams, and even E. E. Cummings appears to him as genuine achievements in comparison with that of the existentialists, the Beatniks, the black humorists, the New Left, and the practitioners of pop art. In deploring the decline of Modernist literature, Zverev departs from the earlier Marxist negative attitude toward prewar Modernism. He separates what he considers valuable in Modernist literature from avant-gardism to characterize the postwar varieties of Modernism. A measure of Zverev's unconventional approach (within the tradition of Soviet scholarship, of course) is his treatment of Richard Wright as a precursor of American existentialism, and the conspicuous absence of Faulkner, whose name he does not even mention.

Several studies deal with the literature of the 1960s and 1970s. In "V poiskakh utrachennogo puti: Literaturovedenie Anglii i SSHA poslednikh let" [In Search of a Lost Course: Literary Scholarship in England and the USA of Recent Years] (*Voprosy Literatury* 12:312–40) D. Urnov shows little reason to commend present-day American criticism and scholarship which lack a coherent "platform" of past schools, for instance, New Criticism. Urnov advocates Geoffrey Hartman's demand for the democratization of criticism and demystification of the muses. After all, American and English literary theorists and critics have a long tradition and rich experience to draw from to improve their views on literature. Such practical criticism of recent American literature is demonstrated by Aleksandr S. Mulyarchik in several articles published in *SSHA-Ekonomika, Politika, Ideologiya* ii and x; *Neva* iii; *Sovetskava Literatura* viii. Denouncing Modernist works, Mulyarchik directs attention to realistic novels critical of American society.

There were two books on genre, one on the short story and another on the drama. Valentina I. Oleneva's *Sotsialnye motivy v amerikanskoi novelistike* [Social Motives in the American Short Story] (Kiev: Naukova Dumka, 1978) is marred by a disproportion between the literary and the sociological in favor of the latter. Extensive portions of the book are actually devoted to the denunciation of various aspects of American society, culture, and ideology. Except for detailed exploration of some works of a few black writers—Hughes, Wright, Baldwin—Oleneva forbears analyzing particular authors' works. This leads her occasionally to sweeping generalizations: "In the short story of the '60s and '70s, the tradition of realism and social psychologism of Sh. Anderson, E. Hemingway, J. Steinbeck, W. Faulkner is continued by J. D. Salinger, J. Updike, J. Cheever, B. Malamud, J. Baldwin, Joyce C. Oates, and many others." Predictably, she disapproves of Modernists like Barth, Friedman, and Barthelme, for "their stories subvert and degrade man," but she commends those of Barthelme's which reflect a realistic mode.

Justifying her book *Amerikanskaya dramaturgiya pervoi poloviny XX veka* [American Dramaturgy of the First Half of the 20th Century] (Leningrad: Iskusstvo, 1978) Anna S. Romm acknowledges that notwithstanding the contributions of Koreneva, A. A. Aniks, G. Zlobin, and a few others, American drama has been rather neglected by Soviet scholars, and the public remains ignorant of a great many prominent American playwrights. With these exigencies in mind, Romm wrote a book that is halfway between hard-core academic scholarship and popular criticism. Almost three-fourths of the book is taken by seven essays, each dealing with one playwright: O'Neill, Rice, Lawson, Odets, Hellman, Anderson, and Wilder. Romm's criticism of their work is discerning. So is her treatment of a host of other playwrights discussed in three topical chapters preceding the monograph essays.

Realism continues to be the only touchstone of artistic value of a literary work in the Soviet Union. The concept, however, has been widened enough to include such authors as Vonnegut as well as Cheever. The latter is the subject of an article by P. B. Balditsin, "Osobennosti realisticheskoi prozy SSHA 60. godov i tvorchestvo Dzhona Chivera" [The Characteristics of American Realistic Prose in the '60s and the Work of John Cheever] (*Filologicheskie Nauki* [1978] 2:37–46). Contrary to widespread opinion (certainly to Jerome Klinkowitz'), Balditsin sees in the '60s "a new growth of realism in American literature" as an extension of the realistic tradition of the 1920s and 1930s. Cheever is one of its chief upholders, although his realism is tinged with Modernist satire.

Whether Cheever's work will eventually contribute to the improvement of American realism in the measure that E. E. Cummings "contributed to the improvement of realism" during an earlier period remains to be seen. Precisely such credit is given to the author of *The Enormous Room* by Zverev in "Kammings i chistaya poetika" [Cummings and Pure Poetics] (*Inostrannaya Literatura* [1978] 7: 200–209). The article can be read as a vindication—in the context of past Soviet criticism—of Cummings. Zverev accomplishes his purpose by admitting the pluralistic nature of 20th-century art.

Cummings is also the subject of a long contribution by the Yugoslav scholar Mladen Jovanović: "e. e. kamings i pesnicka sloboda"

[E. E. Cummings and poetic license] (*Zbornik Radovo Filozofskogo Fakulteta u Nisu* 5). Following an elaborate discussion of poetic license based on linguistic and semantic criteria Jovanović subjects "anyone lived in a pretty how town" to microscopic analysis, concluding that poetic license is but a deviation from linguistic norm.

As in the past, monograph studies of American authors published during 1978–79 are of unequal quality. S. Baturin's *Portrety amerikanskikh pisatelei* [Portraits of American Writers] (Moskva: Khudozhestvennaya Literatura), which includes literary biographies of L. Steffens (pp. 3–57), Jack London (pp. 59–117), and Theodore Dreiser (pp. 119–420) is addressed to the general reader and contains little that might be of value to the literary scholar.

This is not the case with Aleksandra K. Savurenok's *Romany U. Folknera 1920–1930kh godov* [William Faulkner's Novels of the '20s and '30s] (Leningrad: Izdatel' stvo Leningradskogo Universiteta). This scholar's proclaimed aim is to demonstrate that *Light in August, Absalom, Absalom!*, and *The Hamlet* are Faulkner's greatest achievements because of his superior presentation of social problems under the impact of "the Red decade." Though approaching Faulkner's work in terms of social realism tenets, Savurenok devotes considerable attention to formal questions of his art, discussing, for instance, the structural analogy between *The Hamlet* and *The Wild Palms*, or arguing the superiority of *Flags in the Dust* over *Sartoris*. She succeeds in correcting some earlier perceptions of Faulkner in the Soviet Union in three respects: (1) she concentrates on Faulkner's earlier work (much of Soviet scholarship and criticism dealt with his later novels, especially the Snopes trilogy); (2) by tracing the "internal logic of his creative evolution" she departs from the dichotomous fallacy which differentiates between Faulkner the Modernist and Faulkner the realist; (3) she skillfully interrelates exegesis, interpretation, social criticism, and philosophy, confirming or expanding what other scholars have already ascertained from different points of view. Savurenok is almost exceptional in stressing the importance of *Mosquitoes* in Faulkner's literary development. Incidentally, she insists plausibly that his intuitivism was not shaped by Bergson directly, but through William James's *A Pluralistic Universe*. The omission of *As I Lay Dying* from the study, however, stains her achievement.

Among shorter monograph studies the most interesting is perhaps D. V. Zatonskii's on "Faulkner—Short Story Writer" included in his above-mentioned collection of essays *In Our Times* (pp. 283–303), in which he demonstrates that—like Dostoyevski—Faulkner was mainly concerned with "the soul of man."

Other contributions on single American authors deserve at least passing notice. A. Mulyarchik's "Voyna i mir Dzhemsa Dzhonsa" [James Jones's War and Peace] (*Inostrannaya Literatura* 9[1978]: 205–13) commemorates eloquently Jones's death. Mulyarchik has also published a good article on Norman Mailer, "V pogone za begushchim vremenem" [In Pursuit of Flying Time] (*Voprosy Literatury* 10[1978]:128–65). Lyudmila Gvishchiani has brought to light new material about Albert R. Williams, author of numerous publications about the Soviet Union (*Inostrannaya Literatura* 8[1978]:189–99). M. Landor in "Otkrytyi espilog 30-kh godov (O romane Tomasa Vulfa Domoi vozvratata net)" [A Discovered epilog of the '30s; on Thomas Wolfe's novel *You Can't Go Home Again*] (*Inostrannaya Literatura* 9[1979]:191–200) traces Wolfe's evolution as a democrat in life and writing, and notes the revival of interest in his work in the 1960s. A similar revival in Richard Wright is perceptively discussed by B. Gilenson in " 'Vtoroe rozhdenie' Richarda Raita" ['The Second Birth' of Richard Wright] (*Voprosy Literatury* 6[1979]: 278–90).

Soviet scholarship on pre-20th-century American literature is represented by Yu. Kovalev's "Problemy periodizatsi amerikanskogo romantizma" [The Problems of Periodization of American Romanticism], (*Vestnik Leningradskogo Universiteta* [1978] 2:80–90), and *Amerikanskaya literatura: Problemy romantizma i realizma* [American Literature: Problems of Romanticism and Realism] (Krasnodar: Kubanskii Gosudarstvennyi Universitet). Taking issue with R. N. Nikolyukin's periodization presented in *Amerikanskii romantizm i sovremennost* [American Romanticism and Contemporaneity] (Moskva [1977]: Iskusstvo), in which Nikolyukin fixes the beginnings of American Romanticism in the 1770s, Kovalev relegates its inception to half a century later. He attributes great importance to the problem of periodization in anticipation of a future Soviet history of American literature based on "principles of dialectics and historical materialism, and on the best traditions of Soviet literary scholarship." Whether and when his call will become reality, remains to be seen. (In the meantime Soviet scholars have concluded the translation of the *LHUS* in three volumes.)

The Kuban State University publication is only partly devoted to pre-20th-century literature. Its title claims more than the work delivers. It is a collection of ten articles of unequal quality by as many scholars writing on a variety of mostly familiar topics connected with the work of 11 authors ranging from Poe to Heller. Only two of the contributions deal with American Romantics: E. K. Apenko writes about Poe's aesthetic theory, and L. P. Bashmakova traces thematic links between Melville and Hemingway. Of the other contributions, three deserve notice. L. I. Tur-Pikina presents a survey of Russian criticism of Walt Whitman during the pre–October Revolution period without even mentioning V. A. Libman's *Bibliography* (*ALS 1978*, pp. 463–64). A. I. Lozovskii writes solidly on the theme of art in Dreiser's *Twelve Men*. N. I. Samokhvalov claims predictably that Faulkner's use of folklore material—if nothing else—qualifies him as a realistic writer. There is also P. B. Balditsin with another piece on Cheever, in which he offers a survey of the critical reception of the author in America, stating that "the social content of his works is mostly ignored or distorted there." Balditsyn is wrong when he maintains that "there has not appeared a monograph on Cheever's work." The other writers discussed in the papers are W. D. Howells, Hemingway, Thomas Wolfe, Heller, and Lorraine Hansberry.

Outside the Soviet Union the most serious work on American literature has been accomplished in Hungary.[2] Nowhere in Eastern Europe is scholarship on American literature more vigorous and diversified than there. Earlier books, such as Zsolt Virágos's *A Néger-ség és az Amerikai Irodalom* [Blacks and American Literature] (Budapest: Akadémiai Kiadó, 1975) or Miklósné Kretzoi's *Az Amerikai Irodalom Kezdetei 1607–1750* [The Beginnings of American Literature 1607–1750] (Budapest: Akadémiai Kiadó, 1976) are impressive contributions in the field. In 1978–79 there were two books and one major dissertation. The first of these, *T. S. Eliot a költöi nyelvhasz-nálatáról* [T. S. Eliot's Poetic Use of Language] (Budapest: Akadémiai Kiado, 1978) by Ferenc Takács is an attempt at defining Eliot's views on poetic language and the concept of dissociation of sensibility in historical, sociological, philosophical, linguistic, and stylistic perspectives. The major fault with the work is its excessive versatility

2. The material with English summaries of studies in Hungarian was procured for this report through the generous cooperation of Zoltan Abádi-Nagy of the English Department of Kossuth University, Debrecen.

of problems and ideas which the author fails to support with analyses of Eliot's poems. The dissociation of sensibility is also the topic of Takács's article "Some Themes of Unification in T. S. Eliot's Criticism" (*ALitASH* 20[1978]:164–72). Bálini Rozsnyai's "Reflections of T. S. Eliot's Imagery in the Novels of W. Golding" in the same journal, pp. 172–75, reveals five instances of lexical parallels between the two writers.

The other book, *Henry James világa* [The World of Henry James] (Budapest: Europa) is by Aladár Sarbu. Written for a popular series, the book reviews the life and work of James, making ample use of autobiographical material as well as the findings of recent scholarship. Because of the attention it gives to James's experiments and to his penetrating social criticism in the major phase, it also can be of interest to the scholar. Contrary to what is commonly believed, the author sees in the last novels a deepening of James's understanding of British society. Sarbu contributed another piece on James, "Illusion and Reality in *The Ambassadors*," in *Annales Universitatis Scientiarum Budapestiensis de Rolando Eötvös nominatae, Sectio Philologica Moderna* (Budapest [1978], pp. 19–31). He discerns in the novel three levels of meaning.

The dissertation is Zoltan Abádi-Nagy's "Válságérzet és komikum osszefuggései a hatvanas évek amerikai regényében" [Crisis and Comedy in the American Novel of the Sixties]. This bulky study (350 pages) deals with the interrelationship between entropic and comic elements. Abádi-Nagy isolates entropic themes and weighs their significance against the satiric mode, and then turns to the American novelists' use of ironic messianism. He offers a new approach to satire and black humor in the American novel of the 1960s. Some of the themes are dealt with in several of his articles: "The Entropic Rhythm of Thomas Pynchon's Comedy in *The Crying of Lot 49*" (*HSE* 11:117–30); "Ironic Messianism in Recent American Fiction" (*SEA* 4[1978]: 63–84); "Ironic Treatment of Conformism in Recent American Fiction" (*ALitASH* 20 [1978]:146–55). In the last he examines 20 novels published between 1952 and 1974. The second of these articles was part of a conference held in Budapest in 1977, seven papers from which appeared in *SEA* 4 (see *MLA International Bibliography*).

The diversity of Hungarian scholarship in the field is also reflected in the joined numbers i–ii of *ALitASH* 20, which contain a

large number of articles on American literature ranging from new
prosodies in 20th-century verse to Melville's use of mythology (see
also listings in the MLA bibliography). Other articles by Hungarian
scholars in 1979 include Zoltán Szilassy's "Az istenek halnak, az em-
ber él . . ." /Gods Die, Man Lives . . ./ (*Nagyvilág* 12:1898–99), an
essay on Barris Stavis' historical drama-tetralogy: *Lamp at Midnight,
Harpers Ferry, Coat of Many Colors,* and *The Man Who Never Died.*
Szilassy expresses his opinion that Stavis is one of those very few
dramatists since World War II who—somewhat in the spirit of Arthur
Miller's *The Crucible*—still believe in the possibility of "humanistic
alternative." And there is Z. Virágos' "Myth: The Dilemma of the
American Novelist" (*HSE* 12:107–19), which rounds up fitfully
recent Hungarian contributions to American literary scholarship.
Virágo vigorously condemns the fallacy of the intrinsic value of myth
as used by contemporary fiction writers. He blames the critical industry for making myth "the supreme vehicle of creative imagination" and "an automatic measure of value" sanctified by the critics'
and scholars' invocation of Eliot and Jung. Virágos points out their
ambiguous and contradictory conceptions of myth and archetype as
material and method. Unfortunately, he does not support his compelling criticism with an analysis of fictional works.

An analysis of such a work was presented by the Czech scholar
Eva Stehlíková in "The Function of Classical Myths in John Updike's
The Centaur (*Listy Filologické* 1[1978]:1–12). Stehlíková traces the
ways Updike introduces mythological motifs; she perceives their ambivalent character and demonstrates their shaping the structure of
the novel. The lack of the latter in a work of the imagination is what
Virágos most disapproves of.

In Poland scholarship on American literature has been rather
meager. The only book-length publication is a slender dissertation by
Irena Przemecka, *The Work of Robert Penn Warren and the Main
Trends in American Literature* (Kraków: Uniwersytet Jagielloński,
1978). Useful and informative, the study is too kaleidoscopic to offer
deep insight into any aspects of Warren's versatile work. The scholar
simply compresses too much material into 104 pages. Arranged thematically, the volume contains—in that order—chapters on Warren's
view of history; man, nature, and idea; the tragic; links with Kentucky tradition; the Negro; the question of identity. These themes are

in turn compared with those in the works of other southern writers. Finally, there is a chapter on Warren and his critics. Traditionally, of all American writers, Hemingway, Faulkner, and T. S. Eliot have been drawing the greatest attention. This time Eliot's work is the subject of scholarly scrutiny in only one article, "The Problem of Time in T. S. Eliot's 'The Rock' and 'Murder in the Cathedral'" by Jadwiga Dudkiewicz (*Acta Universitatis Lodziensis Seria I* 46[1978]:29–51). Dudkiewicz explores lucidly the thematic and structural function of time in the plays "which are constructed so that the deeper levels of meaning of these dramas intensify the surface meanings and make them universal." The same issue of the periodical contains two other pieces on American literature: Agnieszka Salska's fine essay on an old theme, "Hester and Dimmesdale: The Pattern of Moral Development" (pp. 55–62), and Katarzyna Skoniecka's "Przedstawienie życia miejskiego w *Manhattan Transfer*" [The Presentation of Urban Life in *Manhattan Transfer*] (pp. 65–75), which is little more than a first-rate summary of the novel.

Hawthorne's *The Blithedale Romance* is the subject of analysis by Grażyna Branny, "Hawthorne's 'Cold Arcadia': The Collapse of the American Dream in *The Blithedale Romance*" (*KN* 26:477–87). Drawing parallels between history and fiction, Branny regards the novel as an illustration of the archetypal American dream, not just the failure of a utopian community. Another American myth is examined by Teresa Kieniewicz in "The Concept of Success in Late Nineteenth Century American Prose" (*KN* 26:215–33). Other scholars have dealt with the topic in greater depth.

While there was nothing significant on Faulkner, Hemingway received his best Polish biography so far in the form of a 116-page introduction, by Leszek Elektorowicz, to a new and excellent edition of *For Whom the Bell Tolls* (Wroclaw: Ossolineum, 1978).

Superior among modest contributions from Poland is Maciej Hołota's "'Zródło' Katarzyny Anny Porter przykładem 'noweli postaci'" [K. A. Porter's "The Source" as Example of the "Story of Character"] (*KN* 26:489–97). Hołota's incisive analysis extracts the most pertinent aesthetic features of the all-too-rarely discussed important piece which introduces the Miranda stories.

American criticism and scholarship commands great interest here, but Poles, like most other East Europeans, find it difficult to keep up with current publications systematically. Under these circumstances Zbigniew Lewicki's thoughtful review-article "Opracowania krytyczne współczesnej prozy amerykańskiej" [Critical Studies of Contemporary American Prose] (*Przeglad Humanistyczny* 9[1978]: 61–67) provides useful service to the Polish literary community. Regretfully, Lewicki limits his survey to works published between 1970 and 1975. Not surprisingly, he considers Tony Tanner's *City of Words* the most important of them all.

There is no better indication of the state of Polish scholarship in American letters than the *Poznań Proceedings*. Of the 19 contributions only one is by a Polish scholar, Andrzej Kopcewicz, "The Rocket and the Whale: Thomas Pynchon's *Gravity's Rainbow* and *Moby Dick*" (pp. 145–50). Inspired by Edward Mendelson's "Encyclopedic Narrative: From Dante to Pynchon" (*MLN* 6:[1976]1267–75), Kopcewicz comments chiefly on the symbolic value of the whale and the rocket. The paper is more important for its suggestions than its analysis. Kopcewicz' general statements about both works invite substantiation. The reason Pynchon is linked to Melville's art and technique "in the aesthetics of Postmodernism" is not given. By way of extenuation I might add that the symposium, from which these papers resulted, was held in 1977. The contributions published since then and here reported suggest a gradual increase of participation by Polish scholars in American literary studies.

University of Warsaw

ii. French Contributions

Maurice Couturier

Never in the past have so many books been published in France on American literature in a single year. Until this year my essays in *American Literary Scholarship* were mostly concerned with articles published by my colleagues in French or American periodicals. We still find the same amount of periodical literature this year, but it is surpassed, both in quantity and quality, by the book-length studies. This welcome change is partly due to the fact that French scholars are increasingly specialized in contemporary literature and consequently find it easier to get their dissertations and essays published.

a. Bibliography. Two outstanding specialists in Afro-American literature, Geneviève and Michel Fabre, have put together, with the help of Amritjit Singh and William P. French, a very important bibliography, *Afro-American Poetry and Drama, 1760–1795: A Guide to Information Sources* (Gale). (See chapter 19, section *i.*).

***b.* 18th- and 19th-Century Literature.** Most of the recent research on the literature of the late 18th and early 19th centuries has been done by Jean Beranger's group at the University of Bordeaux III and published in *Annales du Centre de Recherches sur l'Amérique Anglophone*. In volume 4 of this review we find first Jean-Marie Bonnet's article "Critique littéraire et système" (pp. 11–17), which provides an epistemological reflection on literary criticism in general, with emphasis on American literary criticism in the early 19th century. In "Comique et rhétorique dans *The Patriots* de Robert Munford" (pp. 19–28) Rolande Diot offers an excellent structural analysis of this sentimental comedy. Jean Béranger, who has abundantly worked on Crèvecoeur, publishes an article on "Conscience ethnique et frontière chez Crèvecoeur" (pp. 65–80), in which he draws attention to the portraits of the various ethnic groups sketched in *Letters from an American Farmer*. In another article, "Charles Brockden Brown's *Wieland*: A Psychoanalytical Approach," included in *Poznań Proceedings*, pp. 7–19, Béranger applies the critical grid invented by Charles Mauron to Brown's novel, insisting particularly on doubling, incest, repetitions, and revenge. These proceedings also contain an article on "Jones Very's Conception of Mystic Rebirth" (pp. 43–58) by Colette Gerbaud, who tries to prove here, through her study of the "Epistle on Prayer" and the mystic poems, that Very is not an outmoded thinker but a very modern one. Colette Gerbaud has also an article on Very's contemporary Thoreau in *EA* (32:303–11), entitled "Thoreau et la nourriture dans le journal," in which she spells out the various attributes and virtues of food according to Thoreau.

This year Roger Asselineau has edited three tales of Washington Irving, "Rip Van Winkle," "The German Student," and "The Adalantado of the 7 Cities," which are published both in English and in French (in Henri Parisot's translation), in a book called *Washington Irving* (Paris: Aubier). In his introduction Asselineau tries to assess the importance of Irving in American literature and to outline a portrait of the writer, and he suggests an interpretation of each tale, inveighing against those who, like Philip Young and Jean Béranger, take the tales too seriously and decipher them scientifically without realizing that they are mere entertainment. The book also provides a convenient chronology and a useful bibliography.

Two doctoral dissertations also have been published on this period. First, Claude Pérotin's *Les écrivains anti-esclavagistes aux Etats-Unis de 1808 à 1861* (Paris: Presses Universitaires de France), which is a comprehensive study of the abolitionist campaign through American literature before the Civil War. The first part deals with the prophets of abolitionism, Garrison, Channing, Phillips, Parker, who were pugnacious militants rather than *littérateurs*, and the second with the great poets and novelists of the period (Whitman, Whittier, Lowell, Harriet Beecher Stowe, Melville, Emerson, and Thoreau). The book is above all an analysis of the views of individual writers as they appear in their works, taken therefore as documents. Claude Pérotin helps us acquire a better understanding of that tormented period.

The second dissertation is Claude Richard's epoch-making *Edgar Allan Poe: Journaliste et critique* (Paris:Klinksieck, 1978), a very thick (962 pp.) and dense volume, which, far from repeating what Robert D. Jacobs wrote in *Poe: Journalist and Critic* (LSU, 1969), considerably adds to Poe studies. Baudelaire had almost entirely avoided this subject; Marie Bonaparte in her psychoanalytical study had been concerned with the unconscious of the writer but not with his conscious project. Claude Richard has here filled an important gap: by perusing scattered, and often unexploited, documents he has managed to define the self-acknowledged principles which governed Poe's working habits and literary activities. The book is divided into four long chapters: in the first one Richard scrutinizes the main stages in Poe's journalistic career; in the second one he draws attention to the temptations facing an American journalist at the time (erudition, polemics, poetesses!). With the third chapter he continues to describe and analyze Poe's literary tastes in various fields, which brings him, in chapter 4, to define Poe's poetics. This brilliant work is supplemented with a 100-page bibliography of Poe's works, the best we have in France at the present time, and a seven-part appendix which completes the bibliography and deals with such varied subjects as Poe's relation to Schlegel and Prescott, the origins of *Marginalia*, or Baudelaire's criticism of Poe. A must for Poe scholars.

c. 20th Century. *c-1.* Poetry. Though a good number of French Americanists have been working on poetry for some time, they have published comparatively little until now, with the exception of Roger Asselineau, the Whitman specialist. This year may signal a new beginning, judging from the quality of what I am about to review. In the October issue of *RFEA* F. J. Cebulski published an article on "The Satiric Attitude of Ezra Pound" (8:135–55), which shows that Pound's special use of metaphors and ideograms "forces the reader to form a hierarchy of values by the evaluation of subjects presented from many different points of view." In a special issue of *Delta* entitled "Ezra Pound et l'Imagisme" Nancy Blake has gathered the main documents and exemplary poems of the movement whose story she briefly summarizes in two articles, "Ezra Pound et l'Imagisme" and "De part et d'autre de l'Atlantique" (pp. 1–14). This issue also contains two interesting articles, Gérard-Georges Lemaire's "La rupture imagiste" (pp. 15–21), which tries to assess the importance of the movement in the Modernist revolution, and Kenneth White's "L'Orient des Imagistes" (pp. 23–34), which takes stock of the Oriental influences on imagist prosody in particular. This collection will be a useful document in the classroom.

There are also some articles on contemporary poetry scattered in the proceedings of two conferences. First, Jean Guiget's "A propos de l'obscurité de Hart Crane: Communication et poésie," in *Rhétorique et Communication* (Paris: Didier), pp. 268–75, which reassesses the concept of obscurity as "suspended meaning" in Hart Crane's poetry. Then "A Neglected Transcendentalist Poet of the 20th Century: Walter Lowenfels," in *Poznań Proceedings*, pp. 31–42, by Roger Asselineau, which provides a short presentation of the poet and a study of his main themes, with emphasis on socialism and Transcendentalism. Finally, in the same book, Marc Chénetier has an article on "Lindsay and Imagism" (pp. 161–74), in which he explains Lindsay's attitude toward the "ivory-towered, intellectual poets of the East" and shows that the beggar poet behaved largely as a painter.

Marc Chénetier, the leading French specialist on Lindsay, has also edited *The Letters of Vachel Lindsay* (Burt Franklin). This volume, which is extremely well presented, illustrates the various aspects of Lindsay's taste and personality, and bears witness to the modernity of his poetic practice. See also chapter 16, section *v.*).

The publication of a dissertation on an American poet is a rare and welcome event. This year we have Jacqueline Saunier-Ollier's scholarly as well as fervent dissertation on *William Carlos Williams: L'homme et l'oeuvre poétique* (Nice: Les Belles Lettres), which is probably one of the most important books to date on this poet. The first part (pp. 13–267) is a well-documented biography, based on letters and manuscripts, which covers the various facets of Williams' life. The second part is a thematic and prosodic study of his poetry, under the following titles: Things, The Others, The Tapestry, A Very Simple Language, A Form for the Future, A New Prosody for a New Verse, A True Contemporary (his influence). This very useful intelligent book ends with a 20-page bibliography.

c-2. Theatre and fiction. Except for a few surveys, the French Americanists have published comparatively little on the American theater until now. Pierre Nordon, in "Le jeu des stéréotypes dans *Un tramway nommé désir*" (EA 32:154–61), tries to isolate the cultural (North vs. South) archetypes in *A Streetcar Named Desire* and to assess its ideological impact. Liliane Kerjean's dissertation, *Le théâtre d'Edward Albee* (Paris: Klincksieck, 1978), is one of the first important studies published in France on an American playwright. The first part provides a biography and a portrait of Albee and offers a selection of articles and letters he wrote about his practice, his public, and society. In the second part, "Signs and Myths," Kerjean examines the physical and philosophical dimension of Albee's plays as well as the topics he writes about. Finally, in the third part, she touches three unrelated subjects: Albee's other forms of writing, the financial appraisal of the Seascape Co., and the American theatre in the 1970s. This book stresses one theme, the loss of innocence and the corruption of the American Dream.

The bulk of French criticism in American literature deals with 20th-century fiction. Michel Terrier's *Le roman américain 1914–1945* (Paris: Presses Universitaires de France) has no other claim but to present to a comparatively large public the American novel between the two World Wars. Each author is briefly introduced, and one of his works is studied at some length. Nathanael West deserved more than three pages, however. In "Dos Passos et la guerre d'Espagne" (*ACRAA* 4:93–106) Pierre Dussange questions Dos Passos' communism and the significance of his trip to Spain in 1937. André Muraire's "Upton Sinclair: *The Brass Check*. L'organisation rhétorique d'une révolte" *ACRAA* 4:107–19) deals with Sinclair's rebellion against the servility of a gagged press and the main periodicals in particular and studies the ideological dimension of *The Brass Check*. Muraire has another excellent article on Sinclair in *Rhétorique et Communication* (previously cited, pp. 285–97), "Communication et propagande: Upton Sinclair ou l'art engagé," which starts with two letters Sinclair and William Carlos Williams exchanged in 1951 and goes on to demonstrate that all art is propaganda for Sinclair.

One of the most important contributions of the French Americanists this year is no doubt André Le Vot's *Scott Fitzgerald* (Paris: Julliard), a thick and beautifully presented volume which retraces the romantic life of the novelist. This is not a novelistic biography, a florid rehash of Mizener or Turnbull, but a scholarly work in its own right. André Le Vot marvellously applies his critical mind to a study of the letters and novels and gives a new shape and a new life to all these materials as the New Historians have done in other fields in recent decades. No one had so accurately portrayed the imagination of this great figure. American scholars will be pleased to hear that this exciting book will soon be available in translation in the United States. Along with this new book André Le Vot has reissued an earlier (1967) study, *The Great Gatsby* (Paris: Colin). This little book is not only an excellent student's guide to the novel but a scholarly inquiry into its sources and a thematic and rhetorical study of its structure, which cleverly makes use of the concepts evolved by the French New Criticism.

André Bleikasten, a specialist in Faulkner, studies the father-son relationship in *Sartoris, The Sound and the Fury*, and *Absalom, Absalom!*, in "Les Maîtres Fantômes: Paternité et filiation dans les romans de Faulkner" (*RFEA* 8:157–81). Michel Fabre has prefaced the first French translation of Erskine Caldwell's *The Bastard, Le Bâtard* (Paris: Editions des Autres). He is aware that this early novel lacks the vitality of the following ones, but he thinks that he can sense in it the qualities which made Caldwell famous later on. The book also includes a translation of Caldwell's letters to Duhamel, earlier published in *Afternoons in Mid-America*. In "The Rhetoric of Saul Bellow's Novels" (*Rhétorique et Communication*, pp. 277–

84), Edmond Schraepen shows how Bellow has moved away from
rhetoric in his latest novels toward a more direct form of presentation.
This year *Delta* again presents an important and unjustly neglected
author to the French public, William Goyen. This special issue,
edited by Patrice Repusseau, begins with an interview given by
Goyen to Rolande Ballorain in 1974 (9:3–45) in which Goyen em-
phatically repeats: "I'm extremely involved in trying to find the
spiritual way in life." There follow two sets of letters written by
Goyen to Zoë Léger and Maurice-Edgar Coindreau (one of his
French translators), and two unpublished pieces, "Come Back to the
Show" (pp. 105–12), which is an excerpt from a novel in progress,
and "The Seadown's Bible" (pp. 113–19), a short fiction Goyen wrote
in his sophomore year at college and clearly announced the novel
The House of Breath. The novel is studied at some length in three
articles. "La première oeuvre d'un jeune Américain" (pp. 123–31)
is the translation of a preface written originally in German by Ernst
Robert Curtius, which stresses the poignant nostalgia of the novel.
Hélène Rozenberg's "Le roman du puits de la rose dans *La maison
d'haleine*" (pp. 133–40) is a poetic comment. Simone Vauthier's
article "The Teller-Listener Situation: Notes on *The House of Breath*"
(pp. 141–69) offers an excellent analysis of Goyen's rhetorical devices,
with emphasis on the problem of the "narratee" (the built-in desti-
nator). It is followed by two articles about the short stories, Robert
Phillips' "*Ghost and Flesh*: William Goyen's Patterns of the Invisible
and of the Visible" (pp. 173–85) and Gabriel Merle's "Les liens du
sang et les liens du temps dans *The Faces of Blood Kindred*" (pp.
187–94). Patrice Repusseau probes Goyen's "mystical eroticism of re-
pletion" in "The Concentrated Writing of William Goyen: Reflections on *Come, the Restorer*." This excellent issue ends with a useful
bibliography compiled by Clyde L. Grimm and Patrice Repusseau.
    The French public has long been acquainted with the novels of
William C. Burroughs, but it has so far received little help from the
critics to understand them better. Serge Grunberg's marvellous book,
*A la recherche d'un corps: Langage et silence dans l'oeuvre de William
S. Burroughs* (Paris: Seuil), will largely contribute to fill this gap.
This is a Freudian, Lacanian, and Marxist study of Burroughs' work
which tries to make sense of the author's obsession with sex, drugs,
and the body in general. The psychoanalytic jargon is used sparingly;
Grunberg provides a global interpretation of Burroughs' writing,

which, as he says, "is literally a 'science of dreams'" (p. 192), an initiator of silence in the midst of chaos.

For a number of reasons, some of them political, the French public never has had the same reverence for another writer, however, who is much closer to its cultural traditions, Vladimir Nabokov. Now Maurice Couturier has published the first book-length study in French on this very important writer: *Nabokov* (Lausanne: L'Age d'Homme). Couturier deals mostly with the referential problem, the narrative voices, and the magic of language in Nabokov's Russian and English novels. He takes the work as a whole and assesses its revolutionary dimension. As he shows, Nabokov has succeeded in abolishing the separation between signifier and signified, which fiction has traditionally taken for granted, and created a new genre. The book also contains a chronology and a translation of "Details of a Sunset." Couturier also has an article on Nabokov, "The Subject on Trial in Nabokov's Novels," *Poznań Proceedings,* pp. 121–36, in which he outlines the three stages in Nabokov's development as represented by *The Defense, Pale Fire,* and *Look at the Harlequins!.*

The members of the CRLAC (Research Center on Contemporary American Literature of the University of Paris III, headed by André Le Vot), who specialize in so-called post-Modern fiction, again have published a number of articles. Régis Durand's "Donald Barthelme and the Art of Displacement" (*Poznań Proceedings,* pp. 137–44) offers a Freudian approach to Barthelme's fiction, "a fiction which involves a weak sense of identity in the central self." "Barthelme's Uppity Bubble: 'The Balloon'" (*RFEA* 8:183–201) by Maurice Couturier is a textual analysis of the famous fiction, in terms of semiotics and speech acts, which concludes that Barthelme is here trying to blur the distinction between subject and object.

The members of the CRLAC also have put together a special issue of *Delta* on four of the major post-Modern fiction writers, Gass, Barthelme, Pynchon, and Coover. Almost half of the articles are about Gass. There is first a short piece by Gass, taken from *The Tunnel,* a novel in progress, and then an interview by Durand (8:7–19) in which Gass discusses this same work and his special sense of language and metaphor. Durand's "La métaphore comme texte" (8:87–104) demonstrates that the metaphor is "a place of exchange between body and language" in the works of Gass. In *"Omensetter's Luck,* roman post-freudien" (8:21–36) Michèle Poli says that Gass gives in his masterpiece a sample of aborted and successful analyses. Jeanne Blandin's "Pike ou l'enfantement rhétorique" (8:37–45) underlines the importance of Pike as a "dead witness" in the Furber chapter of *Omensetter's Luck*. Pierre Gault's "Les désordres du récit dans 'The Pedersen Kid'" (8:47–63) is a good rhetorical study of that fiction both as a discourse and a story. Finally Olga Scherer examines the linguistic, mythical, and narrative stylization of *In the Heart of the Heart of the Country* and *Omensetter's Luck* in "William Gass: instances de la stylisation" (8:65–85).

There are two articles in the chapter on Barthelme. First, Maurice Couturier's "Barthelme ou la contamination" (8:107–26), which considers the complex relationship betwen the text and the drawings from the point of view of the reader. Secondly, "Post-Modern Paternity: Donald Barthelme's *The Dead Father*" (pp. 127–40), in which Robert C. Davis (Univ. of Oklahoma) states that "the postmodern novel . . . must deal with the residue of the father images."

The Pynchon chapter contains two articles about *The Crying of Lot 49*, Marion Brugière's "Les avatars de la quête dans *The Crying of Lot 49*" (8:143–54), which views the novel as a new genesis and a quest for a metaphorical alternative, and Marie-Claude Profit's "La rhétorique de la mort dans *The Crying of Lot 49*" (8:155–74), where the novel is shown to work like "a machine generating uncertainty" and a sense of doom.

The first article in the Coover chapter, Pierre Vitoux's " 'The Magic Poker': récit et narration" (8:177–87), deals with the absence of a separation between the story and the narrative act in Coover's fiction. In "Les jeux de l'énonciation dans 'Panel Game'" (8:189–203) Monique Armand tries to distinguish the voices and the various "narratees," and emphasizes the absence of preexisting codes to read this type of fiction. The last article, "Coover et l'histoire, ou Clio Doesn't Live Here Any More" (8:205–40) by Marc Chénetier, is an excellent essay on Coover's sense of history as it transpires through his fiction; it concludes that Coover sets off "on a quest to discover a world so far canceled by a preexisting order."

The French Americanists are still exploiting, with considerable success, the concepts developed by the structuralists, but, more and more, they are concerned again with the ideological or historical dimension of literature, as the last commented article testifies. They seem to be becoming aware of the dangers inherent in a certain type of criticism which would completely overlook the fact that the critic is willy-nilly socially involved. Jean-Paul is dead. Long live Sartre! Let us hope, however, that Roland Barthes will remain with us for a long time.

Université de Nice

iii. German Contributions
Hans Galinsky

The year 1979 saw a telling shift of interests. Literary history and multiperiod studies, the post-1945 years, and literary didactics were the winners, while the 20th century up to 1945 suffered a setback. The number of book-length publications increased considerably, that of articles fell off slightly. As usual, many of the latter were contributed to collections of essays. The total number of scholarly contributions, excluding those to broadly cultural periodicals, rose to almost 130. A new quarterly, *Englisch-Amerikanische Studien* (Cologne: Phal-Rugenstein) was launched. Its subtitle, 'Journal for Teaching, Scholarship and Politics,'[3] defines its scope. Also a new bibliographical tool, *New Contents: English Language and Literature, A Bimonthly List of Contents of Current Periodicals*, comp. Barbara Krettek and Werner Tannhof (Göttingen: Niedersächsische Staats- und Universitätsbibliothek) was begun. "English Literature" is to be understood as literature written in English.

a. **Literary History—General.** A rare single-handed effort covers if not the whole of American literature yet several of its periods along lines of motif research. Horst Kruse's *Schlüsselmotive der amerikanischen Literatur* (Düsseldorf: Bagel) selects for 'key motifs' (1) "I Can Swim Like a Top," with examples from Franklin's *Autobiography* through John J. McNamara's *The Money Maker*, (2) "Dr. Materialismus," with illustrative materials ranking from Irving's "Dolph Heyliger" through W. Francis' "The Professor's Jealousy: The Honor of a Great Discovery," (3) "The Haunted House," with paradigms extending from Irving's Heyliger story to Wilder's *Theophilus North*, (4) "Dynamite," a technological motif linking Twain's "The

3. Material set off by single quotation marks is translated from German.

Story of the Good Little Boy" and many other tales to Bellow's *Henderson the Rain King* and John Masters' *Trial at Monomoy*. As a motif-oriented inquiry this book is also of considerable methodological interest. Other multiperiod presentations are the joint product of several authors. One that comes close to a complete historical survey of American literature is *Einführung in die Amerikanische Literaturgeschichte*, ed. Jakob J. Köllhofer (Heidelberg: Deutsch-Amerikanisches Institut). It largely preserves its original shape of lectures for high-school seniors and university undergraduates. Colonial writing ("Amerikanische Literatur: Die Kolonialzeit," pp. 1–33) is discussed by Astrid Schmitt- v.Mühlenfels, whose task is most difficult in view of readers' little knowledge and few sympathies. Schmitt-v. Mühlenfels tackles it by providing ample background information about discovery, exploration, and settlement, and by focusing on the 17th-century literature of New England, predominantly Massachusetts. Information given about the southern and middle colonies' writing is marginal. However, the picture of the age is not unduly unified because controversies within New England Puritanism are not glossed over. Unfortunately, Teut A. Riese's lecture on the Age of Enlightenment and the War of Independence could not be reproduced from tape and was not replaced. Martin Christadler's "Neu-Englands Romantik und Transzendentialismus: Eine intellektuelle Protestbewegung" (pp. 34–76) looks upon the New England Renaissance as an "intellectual protest movement." The implied analogy to the 1960s is persuasively handled so as to illuminate the past and the present. The Transcendentalist 'theory of the autonomous individual' unfolds as a 'criticism of scientific discourse and concept of nature,' as 'the mythology of the Self' and as social theory. Theory is compared to practice, with slavery and the Civil War putting the theory to the test. The chief interest is in the untraditional role of the intellectual in a society changing from an agricultural to an industrial one; it is not in the works of the imagination. Emerson and Thoreau are at the center. Hawthorne, Melville, and Whitman are introduced to confirm the picture drawn of the economic conditions of American Renaissance intellectuals. Shortest of all contributions, yet consummate because of a firm sense of proportion is Hans-Joachim Lang's "Vom Bürgerkrieg zur Jahrhundertwende" (pp. 77–103). The situation of the nation considered as a 'field of tension' and literature 'living' in this field furnish the principles of organization. The literature part is structured by authors' age-group as well as by genre and tone of works. The novel as chief genre is described with reference to major writers; 'tasks,' both ethnic and socioeconomic, of presentation; and the revolutionary possibilities unfulfilled owing to early deaths (Norris, Crane) or publishers' censorship (Dreiser). The drama, the short story, and nonimaginative prose are dealt with in lesser detail.

Explicitly aware of his principles of severely limited selection, Klaus Lubbers in "Die 'Lost Generation' " (pp. 104–38) *starts* from the origin of the term "Lost Generation" as reported in Hemingway's *A Moveable Feast* and defines its literary scope but limits it to the 1920s. The four stages of the generation's development as delineated in Malcolm Cowley's *Exile's Return* are, with critical reservations, applied to its major literary members. Interpretations, geared to plot, tone, and ideas, are given of Hemingway's *The Sun Also Rises* and Fitzgerald's *The Great Gatsby*. Consistently drama and poetry are excluded. What is lost in expansiveness is gained in depth of interpretation. Like Lubbers, attentive to a single decade, i.e., the 1930s, and like Christadler, attracted to the functions of the intellectual in American society, Olaf Hansen in " 'Red Decade'? Das Jahrzehnt als Palimpsest!" (pp. 139–77) comments upon conditions, possibilities, preferred forms, and reality experiences of politically engaged artists, mostly literary ones. Hansen complements Lubbers' picture of the 1920s by tracing the 'Red' theory of literature and culture to its forerunners in that decade. Waldo Frank, J. T. Farrell, and Calverton in his later years serve to illustrate the tendency to accentuate the mediating function of the symbol, with Michael Gold and Joseph Freeman stressing the immediacy of literary subject matter. The 'fatal absence of dialectic reasoning' is rightly noted. With Susanne Vietta's "Die 'Beat Generation' " (pp. 178–210) inquiry proceeds to post-1945 literature and culture. Central figures such as Ginsberg for poetry and Kerouac for the novel are represented by interpretation of several samples. Gary Snyder, however, is not given a hearing as a poet. The effects of the Beat Generation on the "generations of the 1960s and 1970s" are found in the subculture, ecology, and poetics.

The last two contributions abandon the temporal principle of century, decade, or generation, and shift to groupings by ethnicity and sex. Berndt Ostendorf's "Marginal Men: Jüdische und schwarze Autoren in Amerika" (pp. 211–45) develops a comparative typology of Jewish and black American writing, mainly of the 20th century. The

typology applies to Jewish literature the three-generation model of
immigrant assimilation drawn up by Marcus Lee Hansen. Ostendorf's
corresponding thesis that 'the grandchildren reconstruct as literary
subjects their ancestors' experience of being mere objects of history'
is exemplified by Isaac Rosenfeld, Irving Howe, Clement Greenberg,
Saul Bellow, and Bernard Malamud. Ostendorf does not deny that
Abraham Cahan's *Yekl*, which he soundly interprets, was published
as early as 1896, but refers to its rediscovery and screen adaptation
as phenomena of recent date. Similarities and differences in the evolution of black writing are explained in terms of incongruity between the Jewish and the black experience of their marginality in
American society. The process of acculturation involving black imitation, white parody, and black travesty is seen as bilateral, resulting
in a "blackening of America" (Ellison) and a "Judification of America" (L. Fiedler). Bettina Friedl's "Frauen in der Literatur: Amerikanische Autorinnen des 20. Jahrhunderts" (pp. 246–78) justly takes
issue with the disproportion of women authors over against their male
colleagues in the preceding offerings. Friedl builds her complementary but necessarily highly selective presentation around the lack
of a "room of one's own," a phrase, both in its literal and figural
senses, borrowed from Virginia Woolf, and around the gradual conquest of that "room" by American women. After a brief retrospect
on pre-20th-century women writers, she confines herself to Edith
Wharton, Willa Cather, Ellen Glasgow, Carson McCullers, K. A.
Porter, and Lillian Hellman, only the last of whom is not a fiction
writer, none of whom is a poet, and none a nonwhite. Selectivity has
its price. True to its title, this teamwork of three women and five men
Americanists has produced an introduction to American literary history, and even to literary theory and criticism.

Internationality of contributors is the distinguishing mark of *Vistas
of a Continent: Concepts of Nature in America*, ed. Teut Andreas
Riese on behalf of the European Association for American Studies,
Anglistische Forschungen 136 (Heidelberg: Winter). It assembles
essays by American, British, French, German, Italian, and Norwegian
authors. Among the German ones are Frieder Busch, Riese, and Ursula Brumm. In his Introduction the editor aptly sets off "the attitude
of the newcomer to a new world" from "the changes and recurrences
in the development of ideas and literary structures from the eighteenth to the twentieth century as they appear in American fiction."

The former is predominantly voiced in Busch's "Nature in the New World: Its Impact on European Observers and Settlers in the Colonial Period"(pp. 19–34), and in Riese's "Man's Rebirth in the Wilderness: The Immigrant Writer's View" (pp. 51–60). Busch paints a representative picture of early reactions to American nature. Spanish, French, and English, they range from Ribault to William Bartram or in terms of period from the Late Renaissance to Early Romanticism. American literature's precedence as to "sublimity" of nature and as to a feeling unifying "Nature, Natural Man, and God" is solidly documented. Riese recognizes the topic of man's rebirth in Cooper's *The Crater*, Melville's *Typee*, and Sealsfield's "Die Prairie am Jacinto," the first story in *Das Cajütenbuch*. A comparative glance is given Adalbert Stifter's novella *Der Waldsteig*. It is on Sealsfield's Texan story that Riese concentrates the exploration of his overall theme and of its ramifications in Sealsfield's whole work. Brumm's essay turns to the native-born writer's image of nature in a specific genre. The thesis that "landscape as seen in fiction is very often a flirtation with the visual arts" is propounded with reference to Cooper's *The Pioneers*. This scenic role is traced back to travel literature as its playground proper and followed up to Howells' *The Landlord at Lion's Head*. A different trend is seen to lead to the encounter of nature as wilderness, "the place and the occasion of [man's] confusion, a symbol of 'the world as maze.'" Fittingly, Charles Brockden Brown's *Edgar Huntly* commands the central part of this well-reasoned essay. Affinities with this view of nature as the testing ground and as "an agent in the formation of the American self" are suggested to exist in Hawthorne's "Young Goodman Brown" and "Roger Malvin's Burial" as well as in Norris' *McTeague* and Faulkner's "The Bear" (in *Go Down, Moses*).

More than a century of American literature is also covered by a volume including essays on Afro-American writing, *Black Literature*. Only the editor's preface and his Introduction, "Einleitung: Zum Rahmen einer afrikanischen und afroamerikanischen Literatur" (pp. 12–58) deal with black writing in the United States inclusively. Only one of the three contributions which treat of it exclusively, Heiner Bus's "Afroamerikanische Autobiographie von Frederick Douglass bis Elridge Cleaver" (pp. 255–94) cuts across more than one period. In his preface Breitinger maintains that 'the unifying factors outweigh the factors of regional differentiation so much that a synopsis of these amphi-Atlantic literatures is not only legitimate but imperative." In the 'Introduction' this thesis is supported by the common West African, West Indian, and Black American experience of 'colonialism' and its linguistic consequences, but also by the continuity of a 'Pan-african cultural tradition' basically oral. Four short surveys, 'Beginnings,' which include Jupiter Hammon, Phillis Wheatley, and Olaudah Equiano, 'The West Indies,' 'Africa' and 'America,' provide historical and contemporary illustrations of "black literature" in the amphi-Atlantic sense. The contention as such is not new. It might be nearer the truth to say that every transplanted ethnic literature (or its oral equivalent) can be studied adequately only with dual reference to its functioning in its post-transplantation social environment, and to its original country and its poetry, past and present. Bus's essay, subtitled "Dokumente der Suche nach persönlicher, sozialer und literarischer Identität," succeeds in establishing a pattern of continuity and change in the development of Afro-American autobiography since 1945. Douglass' *Narrative*; W. E. B. DuBois' *Darkwater, Dusk of Dawn*, and *The Autobiography*; James Baldwin's *Notes of a Native Son, Nobody Knows My Name, The Fire Next Time*, and *The Autobiography of Malcolm X.*, and Elridge Cleaver's *Soul on Ice* are analyzed along the lines indicated in the subtitle. An ambitious aim has been achieved within a limited compass.

Even more ambitious is Bernd Peyer's attempt in the adjacent field of native American literature. His essay, "Reconsidering Native American Fiction" (*Amst* 24:264–74), is one of the two investigations which traverse several periods in the narrow scope of a periodical article. Short as it is, it paints the first German picture of native American fiction that does not lack a background of early 17th- and 18th-century Indian writing in English. Of recent works Hyemeyohsts Storm's *Seven Arrows* receives the most penetrating interpretation. Moving on more familiar ground is Herwig Friedl's "Problemgeschichtliche Überlegungen zum Stellenwert der Kunst in amerikanischen Künstlererzählungen" (*Anglia* 97:153–67). The article links analysis of American artist tales of different periods to comparative aesthetic theory, German, English, American, of these periods. Therefore it will be reviewed in section *b*.

a-1. **Colonial, Revolutionary, and 19th Century.** With one exception, to be dealt with later in the context of Comparative Studies,

Ursula Brumm's "Passions and Depressions in Early American Puritanism" (*La Passion dans le Monde Anglo-Américain aux XVIIe et XVIIIe Siècles, Actes du Colloque tenu à Paris les 27 et 28 Octobre 1978* [Bordeaux Université III]), pp. 85–96, is the only representative of colonial studies. Skillfully Brumm contrasts "passion," the prevailing story content, and a frequently used word in Hawthorne's *The Scarlet Letter*, with what "seems to be very little talk about human passions in early New England." Brumm's question of "When, where, and how were (the historical Puritans) concerned with passions?" is answered with quotations from Nathaniel Ward's *The Simple Cobler of Aggawam*, Thomas Shepard's *Journal*, Cotton Mather's *Diary* and *Magnalia* as well as Samuel Willard's *Compleat Body of Divinity*. A pre-Emigration source, Thomas Wright's *The Passions of the Mind* (1601), highlights differences of an Englishman's and a New England Puritan's way of handling the knotty problem of the passions. Repression of passion is studied with special reference to Cotton Mather's portrait of, and funeral elegy on, William Thompson. Brumm's is a truly seminal study bound to promote further inquiry.

Revolutionary literature goes entirely unnoticed. The late 18th century, however, comes up for attention. Alfred Weber, a Brown scholar of long standing, has edited *Charles Brockden Brown: Somnambulism, and Other Stories, with an introduction and notes*, Studien und Texte zur Amerikanistik, Texte 4(Lang).

Studies in the 19th century or parts of it were geared to two general topics which furnish the titles to such collective enterprises as *Mythos und Mythologie in der Literatur des 19. Jahrhunderts*, ed. Helmut Koopmann (Frankfurt: Klostermann) and *Romantic Reassessment*, ed. James Hogg, the latter being the title of SaSEL 87. Lothar Hönnighausen's "Zum literaturwissenschaftlichen Problem einer amerikanischen Mythologie im 19. Jahrhundert" (*Mythos und Mythologie*, pp. 213–33) pursues a line of research seldom followed by Germans before. The subject as such lends itself to comparative treatment and for this reason will recur in this report at one of the intersections of literary criticism and comparative studies. Katrina Bachinger's "A Fit Horror: Edgar Allan Poe's "The Raven" (*Romantic Reassessment*, pp. 48–60) returns to the aspect of horror in the interpretation of a much-analyzed poem. Not flinching from an equally much-discussed short story, the same scholar's essay "The Poetic Distance of the House of Usher" (pp. 61–74) adds the pictorial angle

of distance to previous debate. A gratifying echo of a 1971 essay by
Gerhard Hoffman, "Raum und Symbol in den Kurzgeschichten Edgar
Allan Poes," cited in *ALS 1973*, p. 61, is its reprint in *PoeS* 12:1–14.
Translated as "Space and Symbol in the Tales of Edgar Allan Poe,"
it opens an announced series of articles representative of contemporary Germany's critical responses to Poe. Ulrich Broich's expert
knowledge of the detective genre once more manifests itself in a
concise 'Afterword' he has written for *Edgar Allan Poe, Detektiv-
geschichten*, trans. Hans Wollschläger (Munich: Deutscher Tas-
chenbuch Verlag), pp. 195–207.

Aside from Poe traditional scholarly interest attaches to Emerson,
Melville, and Dickinson. Reincreasing curiosity about the interrelations of literature and language reflects itself in Roland Hagenbüchle's
"Sign and Process: The Concept of Language in Emerson and Dickinson" (*ESQ* 25:137–55). (See also chapters *1.ii-b. and 5.ii.*) Manfred
Siebald's *Auflehnung im Romanwerk Herman Melvilles*, MSzA 13
(Frankfurt:Lang) applies the well-founded and useful distinction of
rebellion as a 'pot motif' and as a 'theme of reflection' (of the narrator
and other figures), while following both motif varieties from *Typee*
to *Billy Budd*. A characteristic feature of Melville's moral, cosmological, and religious universe has received a detailed and competent
treatment. Franz H. Link's *Zwei amerikanische Dichterinnen: Emily
Dickinson und Hilda Doolittle*, Schriften zur Literaturwissenschaft
2 (Berlin: Duncker & Humbolt), combines two essays already reviewed separately in *ALS 1979*, pp. 449 and 451. In a newly added
preface, which follows historical and comparative lines, Link stresses
both women poets' function in establishing a transition from the 19th
to the 20th century. According to Link, these women explored and
expressed new realms of inner reality instead of, like men, critically
reflecting on their poetry.

The antebellum drama, a subject usually neglected by German
19th-century researchers, is examined in Jürgen Wolter's "Die Hel-
den der Nation: Yankee, Pionier und Indianer als nationale Stereotyp-
en im amerikanischen Drama vor dem Bürgerkrieg" (*Amst* 24:246–
63). The stereotype of the stage Yankee is traced from Royall Tyler's
The Contrast through H. J. Conway's *Our Jemimy; Or, Connecticut
Courtship*, that of the frontiersman from Robert Rogers' *Ponteach*
through George Aiken's stage adaptation of Mrs. Stowe's *Uncle Tom's
Cabin*, and that of the Indian from James Nelson Barker's *The Indian*

Princess through John Brougham's parody *Pocahontas; Or, The Gentle Savage.* Functioning both as auto- and hetero-stereotypes, they are interpreted as theatrical embodiments of the quest for nationality. Their transformations, and their changing popularity with dramatists and theatergoers are linked to social and political history, especially to Jeffersonianism, Jacksonianism, the Westward Movement, and the Civil War.

A large segment of post–Civil War literature is surveyed in Heinz Ickstadt's "The Novel and the People: Aspects of Democratic Fiction in Late 19th Century Literature," *Poznań Proceedings*, pp. 89–106. As with Wolter, literature is approached and appraised in terms of political and social function. Response to individual fiction writers such as Twain and Stephen Crane has remained steady. An instructive comparison between Twain's Hannibal as described in *Old Times on the Mississippi* and Eseldorf as delineated in version D of *The Mysterious Stranger* is drawn by Horst Kruse in "Realismus und Idylle: Zu einem Stil-problem Mark Twains," *Mertner Festschrift*, pp. 189–201. Kruse singles out characteristics of the idyllic genre in both descriptions. He examines the strategies by which Twain has fitted them into a thoroughly realistic context. Among such characteristic traits is the restriction of the idyllic to figurative narration, to contrastive function, and to the consciousness of a narrator recalling his childhood. The continuity of the idyllic in works decades apart is explained as an inner need of Twain's creative personality and as complementary to the drive toward the 'real.' Jürgen Wolter's "Drinking, Gambling, Fighting, Paying: Structure and Determinism in 'The Blue Hotel' " (*ALR* 12:295–97) discovers that the four activities mentioned in the title of his short article form a "thematic chain" which "occurs three times and subdivides the first eight sections [of this short story] into three parts." This is a brief but useful contribution to the discussion of the broad subject of "structure as embodiment of world view."

A new trail through late 19th-century literary history is blazed by Heinz Ickstadt's and Hartmut Keil's "A Forgotten Piece of Working-Class Literature: Gustav Lyser's Satire on the Hewitt Hearings of 1877" (*Labor History* 20:127–40). The article saves from oblivion a German immigrant journalist of Milwaukee and Chicago and reprints this Social Democrat's satire. This essay is linked by its socio-economic and ethnic elements to the comprehensive, if local, topic of

German immigrant working-class culture in late 19th-century Chicago. With their companion article "Elemente einer deutschen Arbeiterkultur in Chicago zwischen 1880 und 1890" (*Geschichte und Gesellschaft* 5:103–21) the same authors may justly claim to be the first to have investigated the pertinent sources inclusive of literary ones. They are available in America's German-language press and general publishing of the period. Themes, forms, functions, and representatives of this kind of literature are vividly described. The article does not conceal tensions between an ethnic subculture, rooted in the German Enlightenment, Classicism and pre-1848 revolutionary poetry, on the one hand, and, on the other, American working-class solidarity cutting across ethnicity. Traces of assimilation to American working-class culture and its literature are not overlooked. It is not only Dreiser research that will benefit from this joint pioneering effort.

a-2. **20th-Century Poetry, Drama, and Fiction to 1945.** The impulse to link American literature to the country's industrial society persists in 20th-century studies. Dietmar Haack's "Turm, Rad und Brücke: Motive amerikanischer Maschinenbegeisterung in den 20er Jahren," *Literatur und Industriegesellschaft*, Schriften der Gesellschaft der Freunde der Niederrheinischen Universität Duisburg 10 (Duisburg: Universität) pp. 32–55, explores symbolic leitmotifs of American enthusiasm for the machine in the decade following World War I. The author enters a discussion that has never calmed down since Frederick J. Hoffman's *The Twenties* (1955) resumed "the problem of the machine as poetic subject" (p. 255).

As for individual pre-1945 poets only Stevens and Pound have books or articles devoted to them. Stevens is not a regular guest in German scholarly circles. The more gratifying is the appearance of Klaus Martens' *Negation, Negativität und Utopie im Werk von Wallace Stevens*, Neue Studien zur Anglistik und Amerikanistik 17 (Lang). The theme chosen results from Martens' hypothesis that 'Stevens' concept of a "supreme fiction" springs from a polarity that structures his work. On the one hand there exists "a poverty of imagination in the real world"; on the other hand there lives an intuited possibility of an existence grasped imaginatively as a new reality.' Martens wants to demonstrate that Stevens' "supreme fiction" in *Notes Toward a Supreme Fiction* and in his whole literary theory contains traces of the utopian, the term being understood in Ernst

Bloch's extended sense. Whether this 'lyrical utopia' can be realized in part by language is the final problem taken up by the author. 'Comparable phenomena in the works of Emily Dickinson, T. S. Eliot, and Paul Valéry' are adduced for precision and enlargement of results arising from the analysis of Stevens' selected texts. An ambitious project has been realized. Readers of Stevens' "Prologues to What Is Possible," "The World as Meditation," "The Sail of Ulysses," and "Presence of an External Master of Knowledge" will be particularly grateful for Martens' explications. Just as helpful is Franz H. Link's detailed study "Mythos und Image in der frühen Dichtung Ezra Pounds" (*LJGG* 20:209–60). It conceives of Pound's early poetry as a communication of knowledge. As accesses to it the study distinguishes "metamorphosis," "persona," "poet," "woman and beloved," "epiphany," and "Image." Link stresses Pound's relatively constant notion of image and myth in the early poems. "A Girl," one of the metamorphosis poems, recurs in Link's brief note "Pound's 'A Girl' and Ovid's *Metamorphoses*, I, 547–555" (*Paideuma* 7:409–10). Also a source study, but of quite another kind, is Max Nänny's "The Oral Roots of Ezra Pound's Methods of Quotation and Abbreviation" (*Paideuma* 8:381–87) (see chapter *8.i-b.*).

As for pre-1945 prose, researchers have been attracted to Dreiser, Stein, Faulkner, Hemingway, and Chandler. Interest in Dreiser has never ceased. Latest proof comes from Christa Drescher-Schröder's *Das Bild Chicagos in der Cowperwood-Trilogie Theodore Dreisers mit besonderer Berücksichtigung von "The Titan"* (Frankfurt: R. G. Fischer). The spirit of place is distilled through a systematic study of selected sample passages whose function in the context is carefully described and assessed. Drescher-Schröder's interpretive, work-centered method returns but serves purposes of sophisticated theoretic reflection in Jürgen Schlaeger's *Grenzen der Moderne: Gertrude Steins Prosa*, ed. Gerherd Hess, Konstanzer Universitätsreden 103 (Konstanz: Universitätsverlag [1978]). Regrettably overlooked last year, it is among the few German monographs on Stein that make use of the author's achievement not only to highlight the nature and success of Modernism in literature but also to define its limits. It combines the interpretation of the works, especially *The Making of Americans*, with the investigation of the literary-theoretical essays. Schlaeger seeks to account for the dynamism characteristic of 20th-century literary history by literature and literary history "driving each

492 Foreign Scholarship

other to extremes." Gertrude Stein is chosen for her 'extreme modernity' to prove this assertion. It is acutely observed that with her 'the
text becomes the attempted aesthetic realization of a theoretical
process,' i.e., of acts of increasing abstraction. The retreat from concrete meanings is found to correspond with the increasing frequency
of the term 'emotion' in Stein's essays, and with a turning to religious
themes.

Faulkner and Hemingway are reapproached from various directions of interest. Ernst Ulrik Lettau's *Faulkner's "Intruder in the
Dust": Argumente für eine kritische Würdigung*, Trierer Studien zur
Literatur 2 (Lang) selects for critical appreciation a novel which so
far has met with scanty scholarly attention in Germany. Lettau holds
that *Intruder in the Dust* has been misinterpreted as merely a detective novel or initiation story, and wrongly assessed as an artistically
inadequate, polemical articulation of Faulkner's attitude toward the
race problem. In the course of attempted clarification Lettau investigates such 'constituent elements' of the novel as narrative devices,
setting, treatment of time, weight of the characters if considered
as individuals and as members of group constellations of characters.
'Individual themes' are elaborated last. Chapter 5, which includes
an inquiry into Chick Mallison's relations to his mother and his uncle,
will not meet with universal approval for assigning to Chick the role
of 'skeptical judge,' but the analysis in chapter 6 of 'contrary conceptions of right and wrong as examples of the novel's bipolar structure'
is convincing. When read against the background of this study, as a
rule text-explicating yet heavily theory-freighted at places, Heinrich
Straumann's succinct essay "Black and White in Faulkner's Fiction"
(*ES* 60:462–70) makes particularly instructive reading.

As problem oriented as Straumann's but not work-centered like
Lettau's Faulkner studies are Peter Nicolaisen's and Rudolf Haas's
inquiries into Hemingway's works. Nicolaisen's *Ernest Hemingway:
Studien zum Bild der erzählten Welt* (Neumünster: Wachholtz) is
most responsive to such early pieces as *The Sun Also Rises, A Farewell to Arms*, and the short stories later collected in *The First Forty-
Nine Stories. Death in the Afternoon* and *Green Hills of Africa* are
included, though, while *The Torrents of Spring* is not. The later
novels figure in the context of a brief but rewarding comparison.
Nicolaisen aims to discover 'essential traits characteristic of Hemingway's narrated world.' The world of things, the world of processes,

and the image of man as presented by the novelist thematically and technically fill the first three chapters. The study of the recurrence of thematic and formal characteristics in Hemingway's works is paralleled by a comparative scrutiny of the contemporaneous novels of Dos Passos, Fitzgerald, and Faulkner. The results are often not new but more detailed, and sensibly systematized. What for Nicolaisen was a matter of literary ontology and anthropology in Haas's "Hemingway und die Wahrheit," *Mertner Festschrift*, pp. 203–14, becomes a threefold problem pinpointed in Kant's classic questions of 'What can I know?,' 'What ought I to do?,' and 'What may I hope for?' With a great deal of the same terrain to traverse, the two explorers often agree and sometimes disagree, especially as to continuity and change in Hemingway's experience and expression of 'reality' and 'truth.' Haas's criticism is axiological and therefore more incisive than Nicolaisen's.

With Renate Giudice's *Darstellung und Funktion des Raumes im Romanwerk von Raymond Chandler*, MSzA 14 (Lang) we are on less familiar ground. Sharing Drescher-Schröder's attraction to the aesthetics of literary setting but covering all of her author's novels and taking in even Chandler's unfinished "The Poodle Springs Story," Giudice completely analyzes the great variety of places within a limited California southland area. She clearly and systematically defines constant and variable functions and styles of setting in each of the works. Still less familiar to German researchers is the achievement of Jean Toomer. Udo O. H. Jung's "Die Dichtung Jean Toomers und die Negerrenaissance" (*Black Literature*, pp. 295–316) is among the few German attempts to assess Toomer's place in pre-1945 black and generally American writing. Jung brings to his essay the knowledge and empathy acquired while writing his doctoral dissertation on Toomer. As *Cane* intermingles narrative prose, poetry, and drama, Jung's outline of Toomer's life and literary career up to the Harlem Renaissance includes concise interpretations of such poems as "Portrait in Georgia," "Conversion," "Reapers," and, combining verse and prose, "Calling Jesus." The socioeconomic conditions on which the literary rise of black America occurs are rendered by thumbnail sketches of Booker T. Washington, Marcus Garvey, W. E. B. DuBois, Alain Locke, and Langston Hughes. White American sponsors are not disregarded. Toomer's self-distancing from this movement and its consequences are explained. Jung agrees, though in a qualified manner, with Arna Bontemps' optimistic statement on American, West

Foreign Scholarship

Indian, and African Negro writing continually reflecting the "mood" and often [the] "method" of Toomer's achievement, and of its "influenc[ing] the writing about Negroes by others." It is symptomatic that Toomer's name occurs only in an annotation appended to Maria Diedrich's more than 400-page monograph *Kommunismus im afroamerikanischen Roman: Das Verhältnis afroamerikanischer Schriftsteller zur Kommunistischen Partei der USA zwischen den Weltkriegen, Amst* Eine Schriftenreihe 53 (Stuttgart: Metzler). Well-informed and aware of the difficult problems of distinguishing between authorial mouthpiece figures and fully realized objective ones in a political novel, this comprehensive study deserves special mention. It is the first German exploration of interrelations of political party, i.e., Communist party history, and ethnic literary history during a crucial period. Exceeding the scope indicated in the title, its sections encompass not only the years from the end of World War I to the Great Depression, and from it to the end of World War II, but also the time from 1945 through 1957, the 'nadir' of the party. Themes characteristic of each of these period sections are represented by selected novels. They comprise Walter White's *The Fire in the Flint*, Langston Hughes's *Not Without Laughter*, and Claude McKay's *Home to Harlem: A Story Without a Plot* and *Banana Bottom* as spokesmen for "the Golden Twenties," William Attaway's *Let Me Breathe Thunder* and *Blood on the Forge*, George S. Schuyler's *Black No More*, and Arna Bontemps' *Black Thunder* as examples of "the Red Decade," with Richard Wright's novels linking the late 1930s to the two following decades. The 1950s have Ralph Ellison's *Invisible Man* as an additional representative. The restriction of the study's topic to the genre of the novel bids fair to generate complementary inquiries into black American poetry and drama.

The complete lack of scholarly attention paid pre-1945 drama, Afro-American or other, dramatically underscores that change of interest which has manifested itself much less in the decrease of publications on the poetry and fiction of the period. On the whole the most curiosity has been reserved for the immediate present, preferably for its fiction.

a-3. **General and Fiction since 1945.** Richard Wright, linking as he did in Maria Diedrich's monograph the pre-1945 period to its sequel, turns up again in the last essay of *Black Literature*. In "Der Protest-roman Richard Wrights" (pp. 317–44) Kurt Otten judiciously examines this novelist's work. Otten points up Wright's acquaintance with Nietzsche and Unamuno. Both are seen to affirm Wright's view of the tragedy involved in the cultural integration of an ethnic minority. Ethnicity-centered as *Black Literature* is but without its bicontinental African and American dimension and its multiperiod vista, *Der moderne Roman des amerikanischen Negers: Richard Wright, Ralph Ellison, James Baldwin*, ed. Rolf Franzbecker, assisted by Peter Bruck and Willi Real, Erträge der Forschung 108 (Darmstadt: Wissenschaftliche Buchgesellschaft) presents a useful account of the state of international research on the modern black novel. Real is in charge of the Wright section, while Bruck is responsible for the Baldwin part. Most demanding in view of the intensity of international critical discussion, the Ellison section has been left to Franzbecker. The account is selective in many respects: it disregards shorter and very short articles because of the mostly highly specialized partial aspects treated in them; it limits the time span covered from 1940, the year Wright's *Native Son* was published, to the spring of 1977; it leaves out the critiques of 'around 180 to 200 black novelists of the last 35 years,' concentrating instead on three novelists thought to be known to the European and German readers, too, and, presumably, having effected the integration of black American literature into the mainstream of the country's present-day literature; it focuses on 'the general critical tendencies and their most significant representatives'; the principle of organization is systematic. Within these clearly stated limits the report is useful, not the least for its comments in chapter 4 on the 'bibliographical situation' in the field of criticism of the black American novel. In spite of its international scope, the account does not venture into tracing foreign national characteristics, if any, in extra-American modes of critical reception. For this reason the book has been reviewed here, and not within the comparative studies section.

A third collective enterprise, jointly Austrian and American, is *American Imagination*. The volume is prefaced by Arno Heller, one of the four editors, who confines himself to pointing out connections within each of the two parts of the volume. The first deals with literary and cultural criticism, the second with authors and works since 1945. Among the individual contributors Walter Hölbling proceeds along a thematic, problem-oriented line when examining 'war, the individual, and society' in "Kreig, Individuum und Gessellschaft: Überlegungen zum amerikanischen Kriegsroman seit 1945" (pp. 67–84). Six other contributors in the area of fiction choose one another each, occasionally concentrating on only one of his works. The gallery of literary portraits embraces Saul Bellow as delineated in Brigitte Scheer-Schäzler's "Epistemology as Narrative Device in the Works of Saul Bellow" (pp. 99–110). As this substantial piece was pre-published in a Brussels symposium volume, it was cited in *ALS 1978*, p. 457. A portrait of John Hawkes emerges from Elisabeth Kraus's "A Tasteful Executioner: John Hawkes' Travesties" (pp. 121–32). One of the first English-language publications of Polish-American author Jerzy Kosinski, his novel *Steps*, furnishes the topic for Sepp L. Tiefenthaler's "Jerzy Kosinski's dichterische Imagination: Bemerkungen zu seinem Roman *Steps*" (pp. 13–46). The critic has produced a very useful introduction to a post-Modernist. Quite a different kind of narrative imagination at work is encountered in Michael Friedbichler's contribution, "Toward a Redeemed Imagination: The Role of Paranoia in the novels of Thomas Pynchon" (pp. 147–56). This is a welcome sign for many, indicative of the increasing response in German-speaking countries to a complex author. Myth criticism and reception aesthetics take over in Sonja Bahn's "The Existential Monster: The Use of Mythic Patterns in John Gardner's *Grendel*" (pp. 157–64) and in Arno Heller's " 'Experienced meaning': Wirkungsästhetische Betrachtungen zur Kurzprosa Flannery O'Connors" (pp. 163–80). Displaying a whole spectrum of methods of interpretation, these six essays are a notable achievement of Austrian scholarship in the field of American letters. Leo Truchlar and Arno Heller add to them two articles of a more general interst. Truchlar's "Imaginativer Text und politischer Kontext: Von der Funktionsweise amerikanischer Gegenwartsliteratur" (pp. 49–56) and Heller's "Literarischer Wandel und kritsche Reaktion: Bermerkungen zur Rezeption des zeitgenössischen amerikanischen Romans" (pp. 57–66) center on such basic concepts as 'imagination,' 'function,' and 'reception.' The 'implied reader' would seem to be the common target of post-Modernist fiction and its interpreters. These two essays anticipate problems to be discussed in the "Literary Criticism and Theory" part of section *b.*

A much rarer activity than the editing of collected essays on post-1945 literature is the editing of translated texts. The latter has yielded only one volume, which, moreover, is not of strictly literary significance throughout. It does throw light, however, on American writers' involvement in politics, particularly in the late 1940s and the 1950s. *Sind oder waren Sie Mitglied?*, ed. Hartmut Keil, das neue buch 131 (Reinbek: Rowohlt) makes the translated minutes of the Un-American Activities Committee hearings of 1947–56 accessible to German readers.

Regarding monographs devoted to more than one author and more than one decade of the post-1945 period, hence in both respects rivaling the aforementioned collective volumes, a courageous effort by Kurt Dittmar regrettably went unnoticed last year: *Assimilation und Dissimilation: Erscheinungsformen der Marginalitätsthematik bei jüdisch-amerikanischen Erzählern 1900–1970* (Frankfurt: Lang). As the title indicates, Dittmar's book is not only concerned with the post-1945 years but is of chief interest to students of this period. It basically agrees, in subject matter and theoretical reflection, with Ostendorf's contribution to *Einführung in die Amerikanische Literaturgeschichte* (see section *a*). Ostendorf's argumentation in part relies on it but modifies it in extending it to black literature.

Among individual novelists attracting periodical articles or, predominantly, book-length monographs, an older group comprising Ellison, Malamud, and Salinger holds its own against younger, chiefly post-Modernist writers and against native Americans. Karl Wilhelm Dietz's *Ralph Ellisons Roman "Invisible Man": Rezeptionsgeschichte und Interpretation*, MSzA 13 (Lang) renders a most extensive account of this novel's reception by international critics. Besides, it tests the validity of the criticism by a fresh interpretation of the work itself. The examination emphasizes its space and time structure as well as the character drawing. In number 9 of the same series Karl Ortseifen's *Kritische Rezeption und stilistische Interpretation von J. D. Salingers Erzählprosa* adopts the same method of testing, by fresh interpretation of the text, the results of previous international criticism. But the focus is on the style of the early short stories and its continuity in the later work. The study closely follows the evolution of Salinger's style from "The Young Folks" to "Franny." Tobias Hergt's *Das Motiv der Hochschule im Romanwerk von Bernard Malamud und John Barth*, MSzA 11 (Lang), by way of a common motif, links an older to a younger post-1945 novelist. Leading to what at first sight looks like a strange grouping indeed, this motif-oriented approach permits instructive comparisons. It confirms the value of a method already encountered in Horst Kruse's monograph (see section *a*).

Barth returns in the company of an older and a younger fellow-novelist, William Burroughs and Thomas Pynchon, in Klaus Poenicke's essay, "Jenseits von Puer und Senex: der Pikaro und die Figurenphänomenologie der Postmoderne" (*Amst* 24:221–45). Poenicke relates the changes of the figure of the picaro from the late Renaissance to the present, predominantly the present of the post-1945 American novel, to the *senex-puer* dichotomy, formerly known as a topos, introduced into depth psychology as archetypal polarity by C. G. Jung, and reinterpreted by post-Jungian James Hillman. Poenicke demonstrates that Hillman's description of this archetypal (and mythological) pair can illuminate figures and situations in Ellison's *Invisible Man* and Bellow's *Augie March*, with *puer* as protagonist but *senex* consciousness influencing the act of writing. Interpretation with the aid of Hillman's concepts grows more detailed as Poenicke turns to William Burroughs' *The Naked Lunch* and *The Ticket That Exploded*, Barth's *The Sot-Weed Factor*, and particularly Pynchon's *V*, and *Gravity's Rainbow*. Implied in this application of consciousness concepts is its limitation to a profounder understanding of central figures and situations in post-1945 picaresque novels. But the observation of the growing ambiguity of the ego helps the observant critic grasp the shift from first- to third-person narration and abrupt changes between the two within one and the same novel. The equation of the *senex-puer* with the father-son contrast, eliminating the customary grandfather-father-son model and its reconciliatory potential, will meet with objection. Even so, the critical energy at work is undeniable. This is also true for Manfred Pütz's *The Story of Identity: American Fiction of the Sixties*, *Amst*, Eine Schriftenreihe 54 (Stuttgart: Metzler). This book incorporates "material or parts" of five articles whose topics range from Nabokov to Pynchon (see *ALS 1974*, p. 443, *1976*, p. 440; *1977*, p. 486). The articles have been enlarged and entirely new chapters added. The ones on "Luke Rhinehart: The Hero as Theoretician and the Self-Negation of Fictional Autobiography" (pp. 158–75), and on "Ronald Sukenick: Connections Proliferate" (pp. 176–93) explore areas rather new to German research.

So does Bernd Peyer's *Hyemeyohsts Storm*, "*Seven Arrows*": *Fiktion und Ethnologie in der Native American Novel*, Arbeiten aus dem Seminar für Völkerkunde der Johann Wolfgang Goethe-Universität

Frankfurt am Main 9 (Wiesbaden: Steiner). Peyer undertakes an even more detailed examination of a novel he had also concentrated on in his historical survey of native American fiction (see section *a*). Increasing German attention to this new field shows again in Thekla Zachrau's article, "N. Scott Momaday: Towards an Indian Identity," *DQR* 9:52–70. Momaday's works are found to "reflect a sociological development" apparently indicating "a reversal of roles," *i.e.* the Indian way of life "as an example to be followed by the white man."

a-4. **Drama and Poetry since 1945.**   Only Arthur Miller and black drama continue exciting interest whereas curiosity aroused by Chicano drama is entirely new. In "*The Creation of the World and Other Business:* Arthur Millers Spekulationen über die Urspünge des Bösen" (*LWU* 12:37–48) Rolf Högel examines this play partly in the context of Miller's previous works, partly with reference to its Biblical, both canonic and apocryphal, as well as to its non-Biblical sources. As for the latter, Milton's Lucifer and Goethe's Mephistopheles are credited with probable influence on Miller's Lucifer. Evil is seen to originate from God's presumed 'intellectual and moral inadequacies,' Lucifer's feeling of personal insufficiency, and Eve's sensuality. Otto Heigl, Dieter Herms, Wolfgang Schneider, and Bianca Witzel are the joint authors of *Von James Baldwin zum Free Southern Theater: Positionen schwarzamerikanischer Dramatik im soziokulturellen Kontext der USA.* Bremer Afrika-Archiv 7 (Bremen: Übersee-Museum). The volume encompasses constant and changing features in the development of black drama and theatre organization since Baldwin's dramatic work. Chief attention is paid the 'positions' taken up in close relation to continuing and changing trends in American culture and society. In this respect the volume is complementary to the drift of Herms's single-handed effort to depict another ethnic area of recent American drama. "Zwischen Mythos, Anpassung und Rebellion: El Teatro Campesino 1978," *Iberoamericana* 3,ii:14–32, with the exception of an article to be reviewed in the Comparative Studies section *b*, Herms's report is the only one to open up to the Iber-American, especially Chicano, contribution to American literature and its Indian heritage. Based on observations on the spot, and on an interview given him by Los Angeles dramatist and theater manager Luis Valdez in December 1978, the article analyzes the four-play "cycle of San Juan Bautista," "Fin del Mundo" (still unpublished), *La Carpa de los Ras-*

quachis, shown also in Europe, and *Zoot-Suit*, produced at Los Ange-les' Mark Taper Forum and taken to Broadway. The literary-historical tradition as well as the ethnic and socioeconomic message of the plays are investigated.

Mentioned by Herms as playing a subordinate role in Chicano drama, poetry as a dominant or exclusive topic of research is confined to a single, Austrian, contribution. With a wide vista on four post-1945 poets, hence along comparative lines, Waltraut Mitgutsch's "Ichverlust als Weltgewinn in den Deep Imagists," *American Imagi-nation*, pp. 181–201, studies the correlation of 'loss of self' and 'gain of external reality' in the poetry of James Dickey, Robert Bly, James Wright, and Galway Kinnell. With an exquisite sensitivity, controlled empathy, and a trained talent for drawing subtle distinctions, this contribution ranks among the best of the year.

b. **Literary Criticism and Theory, Comparative and Didactic Studies.** In 1979 American literary criticism and theory have be-come a major field of German study. In part this is due to the appear-ance of volume 2 of *Englische und amerikanische Literaturtheorie: Studien zu ihrer historischen Entwicklung*, ed. Rüdiger Ahrens and Erwin Wolff (Heidelberg: Winter) and to the share accorded in it to American literary critics and theorists. Since in this volume of 612 pages subjects are arranged chronologically, the commentary on their individual treatments will obey the same order. General themes discussed systematically, and multiperiod topics dealt with outside this collective enterprise will be reviewed first.

Dieter Meindl's "Die fiktionsgemässe Lektüre und ihre gattungs-theoretischen Implikate, besonders für das Erzählen," *GRM* 60:261–81, takes up a very general problem. Meindl exemplifies, however, the extent to and the purpose for which American literary theory, in addi-tion to French and German, and individual American literary works have come to be used by young German Americanists when oc-cupying themselves with themes of general literary theory. This subtly reasoned article on fiction-adjusted reading and its implications for genre theory, especially narrative genre, draws, though not exclusive-ly, on E. D. Hirsch's *Validity in Interpretation* (1967), John Ellis' *Theory of Literature* (1974), and essays by Barbara Herrnstein Smith, Henryk Markiewicz, and John R. Searle. Meindl puts their ideas to good use when studying fictionality as a mode of reception. External and internal signals for bringing about a fiction-adjusted reception of the dramatic, narrative, and lyrical genres are pointed out. Of American texts and art forms Franklin's *Autobiography*, Melville's *Moby-Dick*, and the "happening" provide examples. Involving questions of general literary theory and history, yet keeping their American aspects in the foreground, Gustav Blanke's "Das Problem eines nationalamerikanischen Stiles" (*Mertner Festschrift*, pp. 215–32) and Herbert Foltinek's "Wie amerikanisch ist der amerikanische Roman?" (*American Imagination*, pp. 11–24) approach the problem of Americanness from a stylistic and a generic angle. According to Blanke, a national style, defined in functional terms, is 'the highest service American English renders for the everyday interaction of the members of American society and for the symbolic interpretation of each of its members.' Blanke names five categories of American "cultural style" elaborated by cultural anthropologist Florence Kluckhohn, collecting from nonliterary and literary discourse prosodic, lexical, semantic, and syntactic features assignable to "activism," "moralist connotation," "pragmatism," "optimism," and "democracy." Selected literary texts ranging from Brackenridge's *Modern Chivalry* to works by Hemingway and Dashiell Hammett are used for theoretical statements made in them and as stylistic examples. Foltinek proceeds along comparative lines with especially the English novel in full view. But both methods, the applied cultural-anthropological and the comparative-literary one, will keep up that time-honored debate on national characteristics in literature, any literature for that matter.

As to individual critics and theorists or groups of them as spokesmen of particular periods of American literature, *Englische und amerikanische Literaturtheorie*, vol. 2, presents American 19th- and 20th-century developments sometimes in separate chapters, sometimes together with British literary theory. It strikes the reader that neither Poe nor Whitman receives separate treatment. Both are included, though only for comparison's sake, in Franz H. Link's "Ralph Waldo Emerson: Der Dichter als Repräsentant" (pp. 106–26). Minor figures such as Bryant and Fuller are not included by anyone. Link rightly stresses the close connections of Emerson's poetics and view of reality. Disentangling the connecting threads, he first follows the conceptual one of 'representativeness.' A political sense of the term is differentiated from a broadly human one. Beauty, the organic form, the function of nature in poetics, the place within it of the ugly and the obscene, inspiration, fancy and imagination, and finally, the effect of poetry furnish special topics of a clear and coherent exposition. Similarities with, and differences from, Poe and Whitman are explained. For post-Whitman trends of American literary theory the reader has to turn to Bernd Lüking's "Von Matthew Arnold zu T. S. Eliot: Versuch einer kommunikativen Literaturtheorie" (pp. 143–212). The value of this comprehensive essay lies in (1) the systematic comparison of three complexes of literary theory and criticism from the angles of 'notion of criticism,' 'concept of literature,' each theorist's and critic's 'understanding of history and the self,' 'intention of each theoretical model,' (2) in the evaluation of these critics as predecessors of a present-day 'communicative literary theory.' Based on Lüking's earlier study of the New Humanism (see *ALS 1973*, p. 448), the comments on this group of critics are especially well-founded. More specific as to author and genre is Ulrich Halfmann's " 'A Faithful Representation of Our Experience of Life': Zur Romantheorie von William Dean Howells" (pp. 240–65). Halfmann investigates Howells' 'revolt against the "romanticistic" novel,' basic traits of the author's doctrine of the realistic novel as well as the 'ideological premises and aims' underlying the doctrine. Its sources, relation to his practice, and critical reception are elucidated with great care.

Of early 20th-century theorists and critics Pound is served exceptionally well by a monograph, Miriam Hansen's *Ezra Pounds frühe Poetik und Kulturkritik zwischen Aufklärung und Avantgarde*, SAVL 16 (Stuttgart: Metzler). This is an in-depth study. Limited to the years 1910–15, it digests and links some 200 British and American periodical contributions by Pound to a network of literary, artistic, economic, social, and political trends of the time and to many of their historical precedents. The polarity posited in the title interprets Pound's poetics and cultural criticism of those years as an 'attempt to rescue an Enlightenment poetics' in and for the 20th century, an effort followed by Pound's turning to English Vorticism as an insular (modified) equivalent to Continental, French, Italian, German, Russian, avant-gardes. The author's account for both positions taken is of great literary-sociological interest. This is the most penetrating inquiry into English Vorticism and Pound's role in it that so far has come out of Germany. The minutely traced impact of Worringer and Kandinsky and its transformation are of special significance to American-British-German relations in the field of aesthetics. Pound and

Eliot are included in Wolfgang Riedel's *Die Arbeit der Dichter: Vergleichende Studien zur dichterischen Subjektivität in der englischen Romantik und Moderne*, Sprache und Literatur, Regensburger Arbeiten zur Anglistik und Amerikanistik 14 (Lang). The broad philosophical context of this monograph reaches back to Bacon and Descartes, with special reference to the function both assign to subjectivity. Not in terms of creative process but as establishment of the relationship between the subject (the poet) and the object (the 'world'), "Arbeit" is studied in Eliot's "The Death of Saint Narcissus" and "The Love Song of J. Alfred Prufrock." Theory and practice of the image, in Pound's terms, is discussed with regard to two classics, Pound's "In a Station of the Metro" and Hilda Doolittle's "Oread." Riedel's general conclusion that 'the modern age represents the contradiction immanent in the Romantic subjectivity to the, preferably social, reality' meets with a less philosophy- than literature-oriented complementation supplied by Hans-Werner Ludwig's "Tradition und Innovation in der Literaturtheorie des Modernismus: Pound, Eliot und die Imagisten" (*Englische und amerikanische Literaturtheorie*, vol. 2, pp. 312–41). Previous research results are tested by reexamining Pound's and Eliot's theoretical and critical writings during the "critical," i.e., the second, decade of the 20th century. The process of their redefining, by selection for their own practical uses, a 'living tradition' truly comes to life. The growing awareness, on the part of English critics of the 1960s and 1970s, of 'modernism' as an American 'intermezzo' in a 'genuinely English tradition' has not escaped Ludwig's observation.

The post-1919 phase of American literary theory and criticism is viewed from two perspectives, one predominantly historical, another prevailingly conceptual. In "Amerikanische Literaturtheorie im 20. Jahrhundert: Entwicklungsphasen und besondere Aspekte" (pp. 362–85) Gustav H. Blanke unfolds a panorama not only of literary theory and criticism but also of literary history from the New Humanism to the New Historicism. The achievement of the New Criticism is assessed with fairness. So are, on a larger scale, the importation of European tendencies and their Americanization. On the whole it is less the individual representatives than the general trends that interest Blanke. The one which aims at the social function of literature and its criticism is thought to be most characteristically American. With Armin Paul Frank's "Literarische Strukturbegriffe in der amerikanischen Literaturtheorie" (pp. 386–419) we turn from the history of trends to the history of a single concept, 'structure,' and of its synonyms in 20th-century literary terminology. While an earlier version of this essay (1972) ranged from Edwin B. Burgum to Kenneth Burke, this later one extends to Norman N. Holland's depth-psychological, R. H. Pearce's neo-historicist, Murray Krieger's co-textualist and Americanized French-structuralist uses of "structure" and "system." It stops at "design" and "pattern" in Leo Marx's *The Machine in the Garden*, at Northrop Fry's terminology and at the one employed in Claudio Guillen's *Literature as System*. Frank's is a well-planned and informative survey.

Not an author-critic but a scholar-critic receives the honor of the most detailed portrait drawn in this collective volume. Lothar Fietz's "René Welleks Literaturtheorie und der Prager Strukturalismus" (pp. 501–23) rightly assigns to him the role of idiosyncratic mediator, shared with Roman Jakobson, in the triangular contact of American literary criticism, Russian Formalism, and Prague structuralism. Austin Warren ought to have been given his due, too. Not a single critic but a single trend is at the center of Bernhard Ostendorf's "Der amerikanische *Myth Criticism*: Überlegungen zu den Grenzen und Möglichkeiten einer literarischen Anthropologie" (pp. 524–56). Ostendorf aims to systematize 'interests and background assumptions of myth criticism.' He stresses four of them: (1) 'the desire for an autonomous literary scholarship with a "central hypothesis,"' (2) 'the critique of the inadequacy of history-oriented models for ordering and explaining [reality],' (3) 'the postulate of an ahistorical deep structure of culture,' (4) 'the substitution of a mythological-literary evaluation, if often only implied, for an historical-literary one.' Aside from Canadian Northrop Fry, whose central position is acknowledged, a great many American myth critics are mentioned peripherally. The applicability of myth criticism, via literary anthropology, to literary historiography is discussed with critical reservations. Essays on Henry James and Allen Tate as critics and on the New Historicism have been supplied by American contributors. Even so the total neglect of Charles Olson and the but fleeting attention paid Gertrude Stein, W. C. Williams, Randall Jarrell, and psychoanalytical critics up to recent American disciples of French post-Freudian Jacques Lacan are hard to explain.

A minor facet of 20th-century literary theory, implied in the self-understanding and self-justification of practitioners of nonmimetic poetry, is investigated in Klaus Weiss's "Theorie und Ästhetik konkreter Poesie: Zum Verständnis einer nicht-mimetischen Dichtung" (*LJGG* 20:261–76). Weiss approaches his international subject adequately, i.e., as comparatist. Aided by photos of this combinatory, pictorial-cum-lingual type of poetic communication, he sketches the history of concrete poetry, links it to prior concrete art, and includes such American practitioners as Emmett Williams, Mary Ellen Solt, Ronald Johnson, and Jonathan Williams. Mrs. Solt's "Moonshot Sonnet" is singled out for analysis. Weiss's appraisal of the significance of this trend of poetry is level-headed. Concrete poetry and its poetics do not turn up in the subject index of *Englische und amerikanische Literaturtheorien*. Nor does ethnopoetics, the topic of Reinhold Schiffer's "Ethopoetics: Some Aspects of American Avant-Garde Primitivism" (*DQR* 9:39–51). Schiffer aims "to place ethnopoetics against the larger background of contemporary American artistic and social concerns, to introduce the main figures and their poetics and to comment on the ethnopoetic quality of their poetry." The first aim is achieved with the help of Jerome Rothenberg, the second and third with Rothenberg, Gary Snyder, David Antin, and Jackson MacLow.

Interest in American literary aesthetics broadens into response to perception aesthetics in Horst Oppel's "Zur Problematik des bildkünstlerischen und des literarischen Interpretationsmodells der amerikanisch-englischen Perzeptionsästhetik" (*Anglia* 97:398–419). Accompanied by several reproductions, this essay asks 'whether methodological experiences made by perception esthetics in its dealings with pictorial art may enrich the interpretation of literature.' The question is raised and answered with a delightful sense of humor quickened by the ambiguity of the "Wittgenstein-Gombrich figure" of 'rabbit or duck' reproduced from Gombrich's classic *Art and Illusion*. The answer emerges in a brilliant discussion of critics, artists, poets, and novelists. America is represented by Wayne C. Booth, Harold Bloom, and M. H. Abrams for the critics, Dickinson and post-Modernists like Barthelme and Pynchon, makers of collaged prints like Claes Oldenburg and 'analytical conceptualists' like Emmett Williams. The possibility of the illumination of literary by pictorial art is demonstrated. Its limits are defined by Williams' "13 Variations on 6 Words by Gertrude Stein."

The point at which literary and broadly aesthetic theory intersects with comparative studies marks the place of Herwig Friedl's "Problemgeschichtliche Überlegungen zum Stellenwert der Kunst in amerikanischen Künstlererzählungen." As a literary analysis of tales about artists written in different periods of American literature this essay was already mentioned in section *a*. Kant's *Kritik der Urteilskraft*, Schiller's *Über die ästhetische Erziehung des Menschen*, Shelley's *Defence of Poetry*, Emerson's "Art" and Henry James's *The Tragic Muse* provide the trinational frame. In it Poe, Hawthorne, James, and Wharton are consulted as to their expository and imaginative presentation of art vs. socioeconomic 'reality' and 'life.' Poe's "The Poetic Principle," James's *The Art of Fiction*, and Wharton's *The Writing of Fiction*, on the one hand, Poe's "The Oval Portrait" and "The Domain of Arnheim," Hawthorne's "The Prophetic Pictures," "Drowne's Wooden Image" and "The Artist of the Beautiful," James's "The Lesson of the Master" and "The Figure in the Carpet," and Wharton's "The Potboiler" and "The Daunt Diana" exemplify 'conflicts' reflecting 'historic changes of the place of art' in society. Implicitly comparative, too, is a pair of instructive state-of-research accounts. In Roland Hagenbüchle's "New Developments in Dickinson Criticism" (*Anglia* 97:452–74) and in Wolfgang Riehle's *T. S. Eliot*, Erträge der Forschung 106 (Darmstadt: Wissenschaftliche Buchgesellschaft), one major author each is refracted in the prism of American and foreign critiques, which in their turn reflect trends of 20th-century literary criticism. Problems requiring further exploration are indicated.

Explicitly comparative studies keep flourishing. They cover such varied fields as general, period-oriented, reception- and adaptation-centered investigations, imagology, and comparison of works of literature with works of the other arts. The role, often central, which American literary works and the image of the country play in this most international branch of literary scholarship is seldom realized by specialists in American literature. A seemingly familiar subject of literary concept studies assumes new aspects in Walter Pache's "Symbolism vs. Allegory: Whiteness in Poe's *Narrative of Arthur Gordon Pym*, Melville's *Moby-Dick* and Thomas Mann's *Der Zauberberg*," *Proceedings of the International Comparative Literature Association 1973*, ed. Milan V. Dimić and Eva Kushner (Stuttgart: Bieber), vol. 1, pp. 493–99. With Pache, who compares three "variations of an archetypal theme: whiteness as the color of the confrontation with the absolute," the subject serves to "exemplify tendencies of modern symbolism." *Der Zauberberg* is seen to "follow the initiation pattern with an even higher awareness of the problems of symbol and allegory than we found in *Pym* and *Moby-Dick*. The 'Schnee' chapter achieves a subtle balance of realism and symbolic stylization which Mann's 'predecessors' lack." Much less familiar is the treatment of a whole epoch of American literature, the colonial age, in a comparative context. This approach is tried out in Hans Galinsky's " 'Colonial Baroque': A Concept Illustrating Dependence, Germinal Independence and New World Interdependence of Early American Literatures" (pp. 43–51). On the basis of selected passages from colonial writings in Spanish, Portuguese, French, English, and German, their themes, forms, social functions, and the origin of their authors are compared as to similarities and dissimilarities over against their equivalents in the literatures of the European mother countries, and in each of these Colonial literatures. The results are evaluated in terms of literary dependence, independence, and interdependence. The inter-American literary applicability of the term 'Colonial Baroqe' borrowed from art history is recommended with qualifications.

Not transplantation from Europe but reception in Europe is the concern of Friedel H. Bastein's "A Note on the Contemporary German Reception of Stephen Crane's *The Red Badge of Courage*" (*ALR* 12:151–54). Bastein has located what so far is "the only German magazine" reflex of this work, which was in *Die Neueren Sprachen* (1897): 290. Jürgen Wolter's "Recent German Criticism of American Drama and Theatre: 1970–1977" (*LWU* 12:135–50) takes us from the reception of a single author's fiction in the 1890s to the reception of a whole genre, American drama, in the 1970s. Wolter asserts that "no other period of seven years has seen so many German publications on American drama and theatre as that from 1970–1977." True as this may be for academic criticism, it will need proof with reference to criticism in general, especially magazine and newspaper criticism. The appended checklist is indispensable. Limited to only one post-1945 dramatist but blending critical reception at home with reception abroad is the procedure of Martin Brunkhorst's "Albees Frühwerk im Kontext des absurden Theaters: Etappen der Deutungsgeschichte" (*LWU* 12:304–18). American, British, and German critical

responses to the earlier plays are evaluated as attempts at interpretation. The influence of the French and British 'theatre of the absurd'
is appraised and Albee's own view of his production stated. The bibliographical information extending to Albee's *Seascape* (German tr.:
Seeskapade) is valuable.

Investigation of the image of a country in the literature of another
('imagology') has three America-centered ones to its account. Manfred Durzak's *Das Amerika-Bild in der deutschen Gegenwartsliteratur: Historische Voraussetzungen und aktuelle Beispiele*, Sprache und
Literatur 105 (Stuttgart: Kohlhammer) presents three varieties of
content and genre of America's image in 19th-century German literature, and five in its 20th-century development. Attraction and re-
pulsion, often intermingling, are diagnosed from Ernst Willkomm's
Die Europamüden (1838) and Ferdinand Kürnberger's counterblast
Der Amerika-Müde (1855) up to the most recent contemporary
novel. The travel report and the American short story and its German
acculturation, besides American drama and its impact, e.g., that of
Wilder's *The Skin of Our Teeth* on Swiss playwright Max Frisch, are
adduced as vehicles for images of America. Hence Durzak combines
image study with reception and influence research. His is a thoughtful and well-written monograph on major aspects of American-Ger-
man literary relations. With Martin Schulze's "Das England- und
Amerikabild im Englischunterricht der DDR dargestellt am Lehr-
werk *English for you*," *Zur Analyse fremdsprachlicher Lehrwerke*, ed.
Gerhard Neuner (Lang), pp. 118–66, we are on the way not only
from the exclusive literary image of America to its inclusive, bina-
tional treatment but also from comparative to didactic studies. Likewise to both areas one may assign Hartmut Lutz's exclusively Amer-
ica-oriented image study " 'North American Indians' in Kinder- und
Jugendliteratur: Ein Bericht über *American Studies* in der Schule"
(*Amst* 24:122–51). This is an amply documented pioneer study in
the image of the Indian conveyed by German children's books, juve-
nile fiction, and teaching materials. 'Historical, cultural and geographical authenticity,' ideological indoctrination and typologies of
the fiction and the classroom materials are discussed. Some of the
arguments have to be taken with a grain of salt.

Before briefly commenting on exclusively didactic studies, a
glimpse of another area of comparative studies in American literature,

i.e., research on its interrelations with the other arts, is rewarding. Interest in American popular culture, often viewed anthropologically, leads to art forms in which language, dance, and music coalesce. This interest permeates Berndt Ostendorf's compact but soundly structured essay "Minstrelsy & Early Jazz" (*MR* 20:574–602). From the various stages of minstrelsy Ostendorf concludes that in it "popular culture opened itself to the massive influence and influx of black American culture, however travestied the first items may have been." Interest in the American song as language wedded to music reveals itself in Peter Urban's *Rollende Worte—die Poesie des Rock: Von der Strassenballade zu Pop. Eine wissenschaftliche Analyse der Pop-Song-Texte* (Frankfurt: Fischer). Chapter 6 (pp. 204–45) is relevant for its investigation of themes and forms of 'Anglo-American popular music texts.'

Blendings of the lingual and visual art forms are profitably examined in Christine Noll-Brinckmann's "Fiktion und Geschichtsmythos in *Young Mr. Lincoln*," an essay contributed to *Young Mr. Lincoln: Der Text der "Cahiers du Cinéma" und der Film von John Ford*, ed. Winfried Fluck, Materialien 10 (Berlin: John F. Kennedy Institut). The literary medium as functioning in the more than merely architectural context of urban, nay capital, planning is of less than central but more than peripheral significance in one of the essays making up *Haupstadt: Entstehung, Struktur und Funktion*, ed. Alfred Wendehorst and Jürgen Schneider, Schriftenreihe des Zentralinstituts für Fränkische Landeskunde und Allgemeine Regionalforschung an der Universität Erlangen-Nürnberg 18 (Neustadt an der Aisch: Degener). In "Bundeshauptstadt Washington: Entwurf und Realität" (pp. 113–22) Hans-Joachim Lang and Friedrich Horlacher have produced a portrait of a 'planned' capital in which neither its visiting men of letters nor its literary image, mostly of American and British provenience, is forgotten. Thomas Moore, Frances and Anthony Trollope, Henry Adams, Henry James, and Thomas Nelson Page pronouncing on Washington, D.C., are introduced, mostly tongue-in-cheek. This is an urbane study on an urban subject.

The comparative studies, numerous as they are, are outnumbered by exclusively didactic studies in American literature. The veritable flood of these, mostly authored or edited by professional Americanists, evidence a general awakening to the fact that university studies of American writing cannot retain their vigor and attraction without cooperative English teachers and their well-trained high-school students. Essays such as Peter Bischoff's "The Genesis of the Modern Short Story: Sherwood Anderson's 'I Want to Know Why,'" *Literatur im Englischunterricht der Sekundarstufe II*, ed. Peter Freese and Peter Noçon (Münster: Regensberg), pp. 26–48, and Arno Heller's "Zu den Erscheinungsformen der Gewalt: Amerikanische *stories of violence* von Stephen Crane bis Flannery O'Connor," *Die Short Story im Englischunterricht der Sekundarstufe II: Theorie und Praxis*, ed. Peter Freese, Horst Groene, and Liesel Hermes (Paderborn: Schöningh), pp. 256–94, stand out as excellent examples of scholarly work for classroom use. The latter collection of essays also contains Freese's "Amerikanische *stories of initiation* von Nathaniel Hawthorne bis Joyce Carol Oates" (pp. 206–55). Thus the historic vista is by no means missing in these didactic studies. Nor are post-Modernist fiction and its theory. In the same author's essay "Donald Barthelmes 'The Educational Experience' (1973)," *Anglistik: Beiträge zur Fachwissenschaft und Fachdidaktik*, ed. Freese et al. (Münster: Regensberg), pp. 65–83, a single work is interpreted, while in his " 'Things Don't Appear to Happen According to Aristotle Any More'" (*Literatur im Englischunterricht*, pp. 150–81) the same work helps illustrate themes and methods of post-Modernist narration.

Studies in American literature as an educational subject do not overlook its occasional role in political didactics. An example of this awareness is offered by *Die zarte Pflanze Demokratie: Amerekanische Re-education in Deutschland im Spiegel ausgewählter politischer und literarischer Zeitschriften (1945–1949)*, ed. Hans Borchers and Klaus Vowe (Tübingen: Narr). The book conveys a detailed picture of American literature used for didactic purposes in the postwar task of reestablishing democracy in Germany. An informative introduction, assisted by reproductions of source material, precedes an anthology of passages extracted from articles published in five American-sponsored, and three American-licensed German magazines of the period. The image of American literature and of its German reception, which results from the collected extracts, is limited but basic to many facets of the present-day image in German critical and didactic studies.

Undoubtedly, this selective survey, ranging from literary history in general to specifics of didactic uses of American literature, testifies to the still increasing vitality and variety, both thematic and methodological, of German contributions in 1979.

Johannes Gutenberg Universität, Mainz

iv. Italian Contributions

Rolando Anzilotti

The patterns that emerge in the work done on American literature by Italian scholars in 1979 are fundamentally the same as those of the last few years. There is still diversification of subjects, periods, and genres; more attention is given to prose than poetry (though less conspicuously this year); and translations of contemporary poets are attempted and successfully carried out. The number of books far exceeds that of articles and essays, however. Whether this is a real trend or just the result of circumstances it is too early to say.

Three books are composed of essays. *Robert Lowell: A Tribute*, ed. Rolando Anzilotti (Pisa: Nistri-Lischi) originates from a commemoration of the late poet held at Pisa University in 1978, but it goes far beyond such a eulogistic occasion. It opens with an unpublished Lowell essay on "Epics," which has since appeared in America (*NYRB* 20 Feb. [1980]:3–6). This first part includes a few pieces (in Italian with English translation) by some prominent Italian poets who had known Lowell and admired him; though mainly biographical, they offer interesting clues for understanding and appreciating Lowell's poetry. In the second part Italian and American scholars discuss some aspects and phases of the poet's work. Agostino Lombardo deals with the early poetry and finds Lowell's historical vision linked with his religious one, both springing from an "active and dynamic internal experience." Gaetano Prampolini thoughtfully and painstakingly investigates the presence of Dante in Lowell's whole work, completing a chart of borrowings and adaptations and finally concluding that Dante remained for Lowell the exemplary figure of the Poet. M. L. Rosenthal in "Our Neurotic Angel: Robert Lowell (1917–1977)," an overall appraisal of Lowell's poetical achievement, stresses the importance of *Life Studies*, both as a "demonstration of what the confessional mode can do" and as a successful form of poetic sequence. Helen Vendler, writing about Lowell's last poems and last days, brilliantly argues in favor of the poetry of the "poor passing facts" of *Day by Day*. Other articles on Lowell's imitations of modern Italian poetry (by Alfredo Rizzardi), on the problems of word interpretation posed by his poetry to his translator (by Rolando Anzilotti), on his "literary fortune" in Italy help to give a full view of Lowell's relationship with our country.

The second volume (for vol. 1 see *ALS 1978*, pp. 466–67) of *L'esotismo nella letteratura angloamericana* (Roma: Lucarini) comprises six essays which deal with as many episodes of what editor Elémire Zolla, in his brief introduction, calls "a peculiarly American inclination": the desire for cultural syncretism that manifests itself throughout the 19th century, characterizes Ezra Pound's literary program and practice, and is so deeply felt in contemporary literature. As for articulateness and depth there is a certain unevenness in the way the six essays illustrate the common theme. The best two are Cristina Giorcelli's on E. A. Poe's "Israfel" and Marina Camboni's on Allen Ginsberg's "Wichita Vortex Sutra." The former is a punctilious (though at times overingenious) recognition of how subtly Poe combines elements from Greek mythology and Islamic theology, showing how both appropriate and inventive is the poet's exoticism in shaping one of his earliest poetical quests for cosmic oneness; the latter carefully and assiduously (if not always lucidly) demonstrates how oriental philosophy, especially the *mantra yoga* method of illumination, works at all levels in Ginsberg's poem, mingling with and indeed leavening the poet's earlier Whitmanism. Both studies are also very valuable as close readings that can increase our understanding of these particular poems. As for the other contributions, Andrea Mariani diligently examines the letters written by Henry Adams during his 1890 journey around the world and gives the reasons for the writer's peevish disillusionment with South Seas cultures; Caterina Ricciardi illustrates Pound's syncretistic method of composition by concentrating on the "Light" theme in the *Cantos*; Alessandra Contenti in her rather hastily written essay points out Gary Snyder's shamanistic idea and practice of poetry writing and traces the Japanese influences of his verse; Fedora Giordano clearly delineates the history and meaning of Voodoo from G. W. Cable to Ishmael Reed, giving a more descriptive than critical appraisal of the latter's work.

Thirteen essays are included in *Saggi sulla cultura afro-americana*, ed. Alessandro Portelli (Roma: Bulzoni), and are devoted to various aspects of black American culture. Mostly written in a spirit of personal involvement and sympathetic enthusiasm during or immediately after the "black rage" years, these essays are the outcome of a series of seminars held at the Faculty of Letters of the University of Rome. As Agostino Lombardo quite rightly remarks in his "Foreword," there is indeed something "dogmatic and even schematic and biased" in the analyses and judgments contained in the book; in fact the reader is often disturbed to find lack of scholarly detachment, second-hand and uncritically accepted views on black American history and culture, an all but exclusive concern with the contents of the works under scrutiny, indulgence in the rhetorics of political passion and moral zeal, hastiness and redundancy in writing. Nonetheless some of the essays do not conform to this description; and, in spite of prolixities, repetitions, and overlappings, the range is certainly wide. In my opinion four contributions rank higher than the others: the two companion pieces on black drama—Gabriella Ferruggia's clear overview of the black theatre movement in the 1960s and Valentina Guerra's lengthy report on the 1975–76 activities of the Black Theatre Alliance and other New York black theatre avant-garde groups; Ugo Rubeo's able discussion of Etherige Knight's prison poems; and editor Portelli's essay on *Invisible Man*. For originality of insight (but not for methodological correctness) this last one deserves more than a simple mention. After convincingly showing how the riot in the last chapter of Ellison's novel is shaped on the same pattern and performs the same function of mere ritualistic liberation that religious feasts have in traditional societies, Portelli argues that this episode is homologous with others in the novel in evidencing Ellison's distrust of revolutionary action—which is something Portelli feels bound to reprove the writer for. The remaining contributions deal with black American folk culture, with authors like W. E. B. DuBois, Ishmael Reed, and Nikki Giovanni, with the relationships between black American and African writers, with black women's verse. Stefania Piccinato, who furnishes a diligent account of the poetics of the Harlem Renaissance writers, is also the author of the accurate and comprehensive bibliography of the Italian contributions to black American literary studies that completes the volume.

A few thematic works by individual scholars deal with interesting subjects, and though failing in general to provide a distinctly original approach, they are accurately informed or stimulating, or clearly useful. Rosella Mamoli Zorzi's *Utopia e letteratura nell'Ottocento americano* (Brescia: Paideia) is a well-written survey of utopian fiction in 19th-century America, from C. B. Brown's *Alcuin* to E. Bellamy's *Looking Backward*, including nonprofessional, minor writers like George Tucker, Mary Griffith, Sylvester Judd, and others. The author stresses the practical bent or bias of American utopias as opposed to the merely theoretical quality of European utopian fiction. The accuracy and range of information that are displayed in this compact book constitute its principal merit.

The purpose of Lina Unali in her *Descrizione di sé: Studio sulla scrittura autobiografica del '700* (Roma: Lucarini) is to examine the autobiographical writings of 18th-century authors (William Penn, Cotton Mather, Madam Knight, Ethan Allen, the Holyoke Diaries, Jonathan Edwards, Benjamin Franklin, John Woolman, Sally Wister) in order to verify the "theatrical" projection of their idealized selves into the written page. Assuming that the "written text is more in the power of the one who observes than the one who lives it," Unali singles out the common traits of the different writings and arrives at a description of the autobiographical model that is more precise than the descriptions commonly provided. The analysis of each author's personality as it emerges from zero to full evidence in the various texts is conducted with the help of a structuralist framework which does not blend with the more traditional method of close reading skilfully employed by Unali. This is perhaps the main fault in a book that appears well constructed and clearly written.

Angela Giannitrapani's *Pantheon dell'Ottocento americano* (Napoli: Istituto Universitario Orientale) is as weak in construction as it is rich in scholarship. The "Pantheon" of the title alludes to the "tribe" of New England men of letters of the 19th century (chiefly, E. P. Whipple, J. R. Lowell, Emerson, Rufus Choate) who composed a revered and venerated group. Giannitrapani surveys the memorialistic production of these men, seeing in it their capacity to reflect and write about themselves as a definite body of intellectuals; their collectivistic attitude, which differs from the individualistic quest for identity of the European Romantics, is taken to derive from their Puritan outlook. This guiding idea, however, does not seem to be carried throughout the book. One cannot understand how the chapter on Francis Grierson's *The Valley of Shadows* fits into it. Certainly there is lack of direction and coherence in the general plan, even if each page of the volume may have its own validity. Haste in assembling the essays must be responsible for the lack of unity; nonetheless ample reading and intellectual curiosity are revealed—and also, at times, thoughtful criticism.

Henry James's international theme is the subject of Sergio Perosa's *L'Euro-America di Henry James* (Vicenza: Neri Pozza). Meant to be a sort of illustration of some important aspects and problems that were considered peripheral to the author's lengthier study *Henry James and the Experimental Novel* (Virginia, 1978), this highly readable book traces the development of the novelist's ambivalent attitude toward Europe and America through his letters and prose writings. Competence, discrimination, and accurate writing make it successful within its self-imposed limits, and it will be undoubtedly useful to all who are interested in James in Italy.

Two complete studies on single authors deserve particular attention. Alessandro Portelli's *Il re nascosto: Saggio su Washington Irving* (Roma: Bulzoni) is a reexamination of the Romantic author conducted with intellectual earnestness and founded on both an intensive reading of the Irving canon and an extensive knowledge of Irving scholarship. It is a pity therefore that the reader's grasp of the subject should be made more difficult than necessary by digressions, opportunistic eclecticism of method, and the arrangement of the argument itself. It happens in fact that the critic inclines to deviate from the principal line of his demonstration; that his method, based on Marxian and Freudian ideas, uses critical tools derived from the sociology of literature, semiotics, rhetoric, and stylistics; above all, that so much of the subject matter that is propounded in the first half of the book becomes clear only when the patient reader reaches the second half. However, the ruling ideas of Portelli's interpretation can be outlined as follows: Irving's works reflect the author's keen awareness of the contradictions ingrained in American history, especially of the changes and conflicts that characterized the formative years of the United States, but at the same time they also reflect the author's conscious and/or unconscious tendency to deemphasize those contradictions, to ignore those changes, to reconcile those conflicts. Evidence of this is in Irving's style—the painstakingly sought-for product of rhetorical devices intended to keep troubling realities out of the written page. A nostalgic dreamer of a more humane past, aristocratically adverse to "rabble power" and "money getters," Irving later turned into an admirer of Jacksonian democracy and a celebrator of "free enterprise" and "progress": a true counterpart to this evolution is to be found in Irving's changing attitude toward the Indian, as can be traced from *History of New York* to the works on the frontier written in the 1830s. Although the letter of the author's texts is often forced to comply with the spirit of the critic's interpretation, Portelli's book provides a number of stimulating suggestions, and while verifying Irving's importance as a fountain-head of American literature, it is also a useful reminder of his continuing relevance.

In her *Testo e contesto della poesia di Langston Hughes* (Roma: Bulzoni) Stefania Piccinato, after describing the black poet's historical and intellectual background and his contribution to the formation of a "black aesthetics," analyzes a fair number of his lyrics from a structuralist viewpoint. Piccinato follows a thematic division in her analysis, first examining the African theme (from Africa as a golden-age myth to modern Africa as a "mirror and test"), then shifting to the beloved and hated South of roots and violence, to Harlem's jazz and its rhythmic and emotional effects, to the American Dream that gradually comes to evolve, in Hughes's later years, into a substantial identification with the revolutionary ideals of the 1960s. The author's attention is always successfully turned to that network of symbols and images (light/shadow, color, music and dance, dreams) that recur and combine, together with "the poetic I, the interpreter of the collective I" linked with the oral tradition, to give Hughes's poetry a peculiar strength, flavor, and coherence over the years. Written with intelligence, sound scholarship, and precision of style, this study's principal merit is its detailed examination of the linguistic and stylistic elements that make up Hughes's poetic system. The main faults I find in the book are two. First, there is the stiff, almost mechanical application of two different approaches: historical in the early part, and structuralist in the later—each part standing as a separate entity. Second, the structural analysis applied to all the poems leaves the reader with no criterion to help him distinguish the authentic poetry from the rhetorical or the merely commonplace.

A third monograph of much less importance is *Howard Phillips Lovecraft* (Firenze: La Nuova Italia) by Gianfranco de Turris and Sebastiano Fusco, two admirers of "the solitary gentleman from Providence." Written for a current series on contemporary writers, it is more an informative than a critical work; it testifies to the popularity of the novelist in Italy, and includes a complete bibliography of Italian translations and articles on the subject.

Interest in contemporary poetry was also reflected in translations that appeared either in book format or in a section of a volume. To confine myself to those that seem fine, or at least competent, and at the same time useful to the student and general reader, I would first mention Liana Borghi's *Esplorando il relitto* (Roma: Savelli), a faithful and able rendering of Adrienne Rich's *Diving into the Wreck*. In her sound introductory essay, after placing Rich's work in the context of feminist poetry, Borghi briefly examines the themes of all the poems and provides a key to their interpretation. Eleven representative poems by Anne Sexton were translated by Laura Coltelli for the annual *Almanacco dello Specchio* (8:181–209). Coltelli's versions deserve praise for their faithfulness to the meaning and tone of these poems, and her brief introduction appears exemplary in its objective evaluation of the poet's achievement. A new anthology of 20th-century American poetry (texts and translations), ed. Sergio Perosa, is *Da Frost a Lowell: Poesia americana del '900* (Milano: Nuova Accademia). Each of the 46 poets, from E. A. Robinson to Richard Howard is represented by a few poems, a total of 165 in all, judiciously selected and, on the whole, faultlessly rendered into Italian. Rosella Mamoli Zorzi and Giovanni Zanmarchi, together with Perosa himself, are responsible for most of the work, including the detailed introductory note to each poet. Perosa also contributes an interesting introduction to the volume, outlining the historical development and contemporary trends of modern American poetry, which he sees as being conditioned by the models of Emily Dickinson's lyrical fragments and Walt Whitman's epic-dramatic poem.

Among the few articles that were published this year, Giovanni Cianci's "Futurismo e avanguardia inglese: il primo Pound tra Imagismo e vorticismo" (*Quaderno 9, Futurismo/Vorticismo* [Instituto di Lingue e Letterature Straniere, Facoltà di Lettere, Università di Palermo]) represents an important contribution to Ezra Pound studies. It is a lengthy essay, carefully written and well documented, which throws light on the relationship between Italian Futurism and British Vorticism. Pound's rejection of Marinetti's theories—until now uncritically accepted in literary circles—is seen in a closer and more discriminating perspective: Futurism was actually indispensable (both as a vital stimulus and as a set of principles to react to) in the genesis of Vorticist aesthetics and style. The extent of Pound's debt to Futurism is aptly and soundly established through constant reference to critical *dicta* and literary texts. Two other articles deal directly or indirectly with two other poets. In his " 'The Dolphin' di Robert Lowell" (*Spicilegio moderno* 10:17–25) Rolando Anzilotti argues, against the general opinion of American critics who discount it as too private and fragmentary, that *The Dolphin* is a "poem" which takes its form from the felt rhythm of life playing deliberately on a multiplicity of moods and voices. Anzilotti finds that the unique tone of Lowell's verse is the unifying element in this collection of sonnets, which are sustained by an almost flawless taste for language. "Wilder e Masters fra ordine e caos" (*Studi e richerche* 1:151–75 [Facoltà di Magistero, Università di Bari]) by Salvatore Simone is a reasoned and readable essay in which *Our Town* is contrasted with *Spoon River Anthology*. Simone points out that Wilder's concern with universal values and positive virtues deprives his play of historical specificity, whereas Masters' realism places his characters firmly and vividly in their own individual time and space.

Last mention, but not the least, must go to an interesting structural essay, " 'Bartleby': il sistema semantico della doppia negazione" (*Calibano* 3:121–33), coauthored by Paola Cabibbo and Paola Ludovici. The two critics find the distinctive sign of the structure of "Bartleby" in the negative and double negative; their purpose is "to verify this presence at various levels . . . and to analyse its semantic function." The discoveries and observations they make are, on the whole, pertinent and convincing when they explore the level of grammar and syntax as well as those of plot (the couple of opposing characters, Turkey/Nippers and Bartleby/Narrator) and drama (Bartleby's refusal which sparks off the action of the story). As to the semantic function, which may be called the "ideology" behind the narration, too little is said, and only in relationship to the Melvillean criticism of society. An exploration of the Melvillean theme of "otherness" and "unspeakableness" would have given more substance to the conclusive part of the essay, showing how the writer surprisingly anticipated some modern theorizations.

University of Pisa

v. Japanese Contributions

Keiko Beppu

The year 1979 recorded significant achievements in reconstructing our perspectives, both looking after and before, on American literature. A symposium was held in October 1979, where some 350 books published between the year 1930 and 1979 were presented for careful examination and assessment in search of new guidelines for future studies on American literature in this country. (See Kenzaburo Ohashi's report of the symposium, "Japanese Scholarship on American Literature: Its Problems and Its Future" [*EigoS* 125:434–36]). This retrospective and prospective scholarly investigation may well be reflected in the recent compilation of bibliographies of Japanese scholarship (and translations) on American authors. New England Puritan writers (1977); Melville (1978); Faulkner (1979); and similar projects are now under way on Dickinson and Fitzgerald. Important works produced in 1979 are grouped for the present survey as follows: general studies and literary criticism; 19th-century American literature; 20th-century American fiction; contemporary American literature; American poetry; and American studies. As usual, with a few exceptions articles are restricted to those published in our major scholarly journals: *SELit*, *SALit*, and *EigoS*; also the Japanese titles for the articles are omitted.

Significant in the first group are Tetsuji Akasofu's *Gendai Hihyobungaku Ron: Hoho to Jissen* [*Literary Criticism Today: Method and Practice*] (Tokyo: Chukyoshuppan) and Koji Oi's *America no Shinwa to Genjitsu: Parrington Saiko* [*Myth and Reality in America: Parrington Reconsidered*] (Tokyo: Kenkyusha). *Literary Criticism Today: Method and Practice* is an anthology of Akasofu's essays, most of which have previously appeared in various journals. Like his book on Faulkner (1977), Akasofu's work under review is no easy reading; it is an ambitious attempt at a new philosophy of literature. As his constant reference to Raymond Federman's essay in *Partisan Review* (40,iii) indicates, the critic's concern is still with the art of fiction, and *Literary Criticism Today: Method and Practice* is not a treatise on radical structuralism nor a new symbology of criticism. The irony in the literal translation of the Japanese title of the book—literature of criticism—is indeed the burden of Akasofu's work that literary criticism need not have a philosophical thesis nor does fiction need to depend on its conventional form.

Oi's *Myth and Reality in America: Parrington Reconsidered* combines both our recent interest in the 1930s and our efforts to locate (or relocate) that decade in the literary history of the United States. Oi's approach to his subject, as in his study on Hawthorne (1974), is clear-cut and classic, that is, to see America as the New Eden and American writers as critics of that age-old vision. The most revealing chapter and the paean of the book is the discussion of James and Fitzgerald entitled "The Two Daisies" (pp. 122–44). The analyses of the works in question show the critic at his best, in style and in ingeniousness of applying Parrington's paradigm to the writers who did not fare well with the literary historian. Oi contends that *The Great Gatsby* is a denial of Parrington's historical vision and *Daisy Miller* an illustration of that thesis, both of which points Parrington misses. Well supported by Judith Fryer's *The Faces of Eve* (1976), the juxtaposition of the two Daisies is a happy one. By no means an enthusiast of James, Oi exploits James's "cultural heroine" well to serve his purpose. Another interesting discussion is his comparison again of *The Great Gatsby* with Nathanael West's *A Cool Million* (pp. 146–67). Thus, Oi clarifies the near-sightedness of the literary historian he sets out to reevaluate; his reassessment is double-edged, and it is indeed a shrewd reconsideration of the renewed interest in Parrington's *Main Currents in American Thought* and the 1930s.

The year 1979 was low in academic explorations of 19th-century American writers, even though a reference has been made above to Oi's interesting discussion of James's "Daisy Miller" in his *Myth and Reality in America*. Worth mentioning here is Keiko Beppu's *The Educated Sensibility in Henry James and Walter Pater* published in English (Tokyo: Shohakusha), a study of the dichotomies between aesthetics and morality registered in the fiction of James and Pater (see also chapter 7, section *ii*). Among the articles on 19th-century authors, the following deserve our attention: Shizuo Asai's "*The House of the Seven Gables*: A Story of Time" (*SALit* 16:28–49), another essay on Hawthorne—Noriaki Nakai's discussion of a "would-be" artist in 19th-century America, "Coverdale's Narrative: A Portrait of the Artist as a 19th-century American in *The Blithedale Romance*" (*The American Review* [Doshisha University] 14:144–62); two essays on 19th-century cultural milieu and mores are Keiko Beppu's "Huck's 'Conscience' and Strether's 'Consciousness': An American Ethos in the 19th Century" (*Kansai America Bungaku* [Kansai Chapter of The American Literature Society of Japan] 16:18–30), Kaeko Mochizuki's "Before *The Awakening*: Kate Chopin's Short Stories before 1899" (*SALit* 16:50–76). Mochizuki presents Kate Chopin as an antithesis to the then-dominant, as she phrases it, "WASP literature and secularized Puritanism," and her essay makes an interesting contrast with Beppu's article on James.[3] Also Toru Mori's "Lafcadio Hearn: His Later Essays and Meditations" (*EigoS* 125:290–91) deserves comment, since this expatriate American writer receives little critical attention in the United States. In his article Mori establishes a continuity of Emerson's transcendental ideas in the meditations of this 19th-century American-Japanese writer. Besides the works mentioned above, it seems only appropriate to refer to the chapters dealing with such 19th-century American authors as Thoreau and Hawthorne in Shunsuke Kamei's *Bus, bus, bus . . . Bus in America*, which will be surveyed later in this review.

Unflagging interest in major 20th-century American writers continues among our scholars. Significant book-length studies on the subject for 1979 are: Tateo Imamura's *Hemingway: Shoshitsu Kara Henkyo o Motomete* [*Ernest Hemingway: From Disillusionment to the Terra Incognita*] (Tokyo: Tohjusha), a new addition to the Tohjusha Series of British and American Authors, Shoichi Saeki's *Kaita, Koishita, Ikita: Hemingway Den* [*I Wrote, Loved, and Lived: Hemingway Biography*] (Tokyo: Kenkyusha), and Kenzaburo Ohashi's *Faulkner Kenkyu II* [*Faulkner Studies II*] (Tokyo: Nan'undo).

In his *Ernest Hemingway: From Disillusionment to the Terra Incognita* Imamura sees the ambience of Hemingway's works in the novelist's national identity, that is, a perennial urge to discover the

3. Prof. Beppu's juxtaposing of Huck and Strether as "birds of a feather of the Puritan ethos" is a neat *aperçue* linking two writers who wouldn't have given each other the time of day—Ed.

terra incognita; he regards Nick as Hemingway's projection, and his early experience more crucial to the ambience of his writings than his experience of the wars in Europe. Therefore throughout the book a great emphasis is given to the Nick Adams stories and to the protagonist. In a loosely chronological order Imamura discusses Hemingway's major writings: the first two chapters are devoted to *The Sun Also Rises* and *A Farewell to Arms*; the next three chapters to the Nick Adams stories; then follow the chapters on African stories and nonfiction, on *For Whom the Bell Tolls*, and on *The Old Man and the Sea*; the concluding chapter examines Hemingway's style. On the whole the book is a good standard study of Hemingway, but partly due to the critic's great concern with the Nick Adams stories the discussion meanders between biographical accounts and analyses of the stories and novels treated in the book. A redeeming feature is Imamura's excellent analysis of Margot Macomber and his discussion of "The Short Happy Life of Francis Macomber" (pp. 133–45). Also, the bibliography of Hemingway scholarship at the end of the book is well prepared, and with succinct comments on the works cited it is valuable for scholars as well as for students.

Shoichi Saeki's *Ernest Hemingway* is this renowned scholar-critic's second biography of the novelist. Saeki makes full use of relevant scholarship, former biographies—*not* excepting Carlos Baker's definitive biography (1968) and including his own (1966)—and what Saeki calls the "facts of Hemingway's life"—personal memoirs, letters, and witnesses of the novelist's friends and relatives. He begins his biography with the hypothesis that Hemingway's romantic vulnerability has always been the source of his creativity, the observation he takes over from the novelist's own son Gregory. Saeki discovers that Gregory's insight is valid and is useful to explain Hemingway's contradictory character traits; he succeeds in giving relief to both the artist and the daring virile man, without any attempt at synthesis, a pitfall for a Freudian critic, of the conflicting forces within the man. It cannot be denied that the biographer is slightly complacent with the image he creates of the man who "wrote, loved, and above all lived"—the trinity in Stendhal's epigraph which Saeki uses in the subtitle of his book—but this biography is an excellent and very readable portrait by one of the aficionados of the novelist.

Kenzaburo Ohashi's *Faulkner Studies II* is the second volume of this three-volume study on Faulkner. It must also be added that

Ohashi is the chief editor of the Faulkner journal in Japan—*Faulkner Studies: Bibliography, Research, Criticism*. The present volume deals in chronological order with the following novels by Faulkner: *Sanctuary, Light in August, Pylon, Absalom, Absalom!, The Unvanquished, Wild Palms*, and *The Hamlet*. Ohashi's *Faulkner Studies II* is an example of solid scholarship and the fruit of cumulative research, and when completed, *Faulkner Studies* will be a landmark in our scholarship on American literature, as Faulkner received serious critical attention in this country before he was acclaimed by many of his own scholars and countrymen. Three articles on the novelist are worth mentioning here, Ryo Haraguchi's "From Poet to Novelist: On the Transitional Aspects of William Faulkner's *Soldier's Pay*" (*SALit* 16:117–36), Takako Tanaka's reflections on "The World of *As I Lay Dying*: In the Midst of Chaos" (ibid., pp. 137–50) and Takeaki Fukuda's "Bessie Smith and the American Writers" (*EigoS* 125:447–48). Haraguchi's essay is a careful analysis of *Soldier's Pay*, which sheds light on Faulkner's apprenticeship as a literary artist. The last-mentioned also needs a few remarks. Fukuda's article begins with a reference to Albee's play, *The Death of Bessie Smith*, but its real subject is Faulkner's short story, "That Evening Sun." Fukuda traces the influence of jazz and blues on the language and tone of Faulkner's short stories, but especially "That Evening Sun," Faulkner's "St. Louis Blues," as Fukuda says. Using the words and nuances of that famous blues, he offers an interesting reading of the story's end that Nancy's former husband is *not* coming back to kill her, as she fears he is, but that Nancy imagines this because she would rather choose death by the hand of her lover than indifference and neglect by him.

F. Scott Fitzgerald is another much discussed 20th-century writer among Japanese scholars; reference has been made earlier to the discussions of the novelist in Koji Oi's *Myth and Reality in America*. It has also been mentioned at the beginning of this review that a Fitzgerald bibliography is in preparation. Curiously enough, the following articles are the by-products, as it were, discoveries made in compiling some 200 publications on the novelist by Japanese scholars: Shigenobu Sadoya's "F. Scott Fitzgerald's 'On Your Own' " (*EigoS* 125:32) and Sadao Nagaoka's "On the First Japanese Translation of Fitzgerald's Stories" (pp. 68–69). The first mentioned is a marginal note on "On Your Own," a phantom piece, which is now collected in

The Price Was High: Last Uncollected Stories of F. Scott Fitzgerald
(1979). The writer of the other essay is the editor of the aforementioned bibliography; Nagaoka identifies the first Fitzgerald story
translated into Japanese in 1930 as "The Bridal Party." He also discovers that the first translation of "At Your Age" was collected with
the original story in *An Anthology of Contemporary American Short
Stories* (Tokyo: Shunyodo, 1933). Other American writers included
in the *Anthology* Nagaoka mentions are: Sherwood Anderson, Theodore Dreiser, Ernest Hemingway, Ben Hecht, and Michael Gold. He
finds some careless and silly mistakes in the translations of Fitzgerald's
stories, and judges the introductory remarks about the novelist and
the stories naive and meagre, but such a discovery, Nagaoka realizes,
gives us an inkling into our early reception of American literature and
is therefore valuable for our future scholarship.

The year 1979 saw no significant work on individual contemporary writers except Masao Takahashi's book on some postwar novelists: *America Sengo Shosetsu no Shoso* [*Aspects of Post-War Novel in
America*] (Tokyo: Toyamashobo). This is the fourth and the last
volume in the series on the 20th-century American novel, and gives
us a quick glance at our own contemporary literary scene. The writers selected for discussion in Takahashi's book are: Robert Penn Warren, Saul Bellow, Norman Mailer, J. D. Salinger, William Styron, and
John Updike. The list is neither startling nor original, but it is a
fairly good indicator of our reception of contemporary American
novelists. Two essays of some interest on this subject are Hiroshi
Narasaki's "John Hawkes's Trilogy: Design and Debris in Contemporary Literature" (*SALit* 16:77–92) and Shigeo Hamano's "On
Reading Malamud's *Dubin's Lives*" (*EigoS* 125:166–68). The first
mentioned is a judicious evaluation of a novelist who has yet received
little criticism here, and credits should be given to Narasaki's essay.
Avid reader and energetic critic of contemporary American authors,
Hamano contends in his article that *Dubin's Lives* is a breakthrough
from Malamud's earlier novels, which are characterized by his Jewish heritage, and that Malamud's Jewishness is more bookish than
natural. His point is well taken, even though some reservations should
be made for an inference based on the novelist's single work.

The retrospective stance in our scholarship for 1979 referred to
earlier is also recognized in the following articles on American poetry.
Kunizo Kishi, an elderly poet, recalls his first translations of *his*

contemporary American poets (1930)—Carl Sandburg and Sara Teasdale—and acknowledges Edgar Lee Masters' influence on his early poems in his article, "*An Anthology of Contemporary American Poetry*" (*EigoS* 125:211). A more extensive and thorough account of influences and confluences among American and Japanese poets of the time is given in Kichinosuke Ohashi's "*The Anthology of American Proletarian Poetry* and Sherwood Anderson," which appeared in installments in *EigoS* (125:28–29, 73–74, 110–12, 158–59, 209–10, 252–53, 313–14, 351–52, 406–07). Ohashi's study of Sherwood Anderson and his contemporaries is a valuable scholarly exploration into the social issues shared by both American and Japanese poets—Kunizo Kishi, especially Shimpei Kusano, and Juzaburo Ono.

Greater contribution was made in 1979 to our studies of contemporary American poetry than to that of fiction. Two noteworthy additions are: Noriko Mizuta's *Junan no Joseishijin* [*Sylvia Plath: The Martyred Poetess*] (Tokyo: Bokushinsha), and Shozo Tokunaga's *Kotoba no Soyogi: Gendai America Shi* [*The Frisson Nouveau: Contemporary American Poetry*] (Tokyo: Chukyoshuppan). In her *Sylvia Plath: The Martyred Poetess* Mizuta attempts to place Plath in the tradition of Poe, Hawthorne, and Dickinson, but not wholly successfully. Yet, considering the fact that it is the first book-length study on Plath in this country, due credit should be given to Mizuta's scholarly efforts.

Shozo Tokunaga's *The Frisson Nouveau: Contemporary American Poetry* is a collection of the author's essays which have appeared previously in various scholarly journals; in the present book these essays are arranged into five chapters: (1) a general survey of modern American poetry; (2) discussions of Hart Crane, John Berryman, and in particular Robert Lowell—their contributions to American poetry; (3) Sylvia Plath and Ann Sexton as representatives of confessional poetry in America; (4) Elizabeth Bishop and A. R. Ammons; (5) miscellaneous essays, which include one entitled "American Poets and Japan." Like Mizuta's in her book on Plath, Tokunaga's purpose in *Contemporary American Poetry* is to evaluate leading contemporary poets against the literary tradition of the United States; this is accomplished by careful explications *and* translations of individual poems cited as illustrations. Often Tokunaga is hesitant about his assessments of the poets, but in the context of his book his argument stands firm, substantiated by the examples he selects for the demonstration of his thesis. Of special interest is the section on A. R. Ammons in chapter 4 (pp. 265–318), which was originally published in English; Tokunaga rates Ammons highly as a new Romantic who combines the poetic traditions of the 19th and 20th centuries—Emerson and Whitman on one hand, and Frost and Williams on the other. This is the first extensive study on Ammons in this country and a valuable contribution to our scholarship on American poetry.

In recent years it has become a favorite critical strategy among our scholars to include some comparative remarks on American and Japanese writers or poets and to claim a certain influence of our culture on American literature. Tokunaga's discussion in "American Poets and Japan" (chapter 5, pp. 321–34) is an illustration of such practice. Tokunaga enumerates some American poets whose acquaintance with Japanese culture have enriched their poetic imagination: Robert Bly, Gary Snyder, and Stephen Sandy. No further comment on the first two is necessary here; but the observations Tokunaga makes about Stephen Sandy, onetime Fulbright professor at Tokyo University, are worth our attention. Tokunaga argues that when the poet is a "transparent" receptacle, an exposure to a foreign culture becomes a vital nourishment for the poet's creative imagination. He quotes Sandy's long poem, "This Jammed Intersection of the Present Japan," as the quintessence of a felicitous combination of his deep-rooted Anglo-Saxon poetic heritage and his immersion into Japanese culture, which has provided the poet not only exotic subject matters but also a new poetic vision. Tokunaga even declares that Sandy's poems collected in *Roofs* (1971), his second book of poems, are American "Songs of Experience." While this may be an overestimation of this obscure poet, the critic does make his point; and a final judgment rests with American scholars rather than with us.

The following four books published in the area of American studies for 1979 reflect the increasing amount of interdisciplinary research done by Japanese scholars of American literature: Hiroko Yoshikawa's *American Wooman* [*The American Woman*] (Tokyo: Kohdansha), Shimpei Tokiwa's *America no Mieru Mado* [*The Window Opening to America*] (Tokyo: Tohjusha), Shunsuke Kamei's *Basu no America* [*Bus, bus, bus . . . Bus in America*] (Tokyo: Tohjusha), and the same scholar's *Jiyu no Seichi: Nipponjin no America* [*The Sacred Land of Liberty: The Japanese Image of America*] (Tokyo: Kenkyusha). These works all deal with American culture and literature, but simultaneously they are cross-cultural studies of the two countries on both sides of the Pacific.

Yoshikawa's *The American Woman* is a lively and adept account of the women's movement in America and its varied impact on the American woman; her keen observations give us an insight into motherhood and the family system in our country as well. With the kind of resources Yoshikawa has at her command, it is hoped that she will engage in a similar work on the Japanese woman, which might enlighten her American counterpart.

Shimpei Tokiwa's *The Window Opening to America* is a collection of the author's sketches and articles which were serialized in *The Signature* (1977–78); it is a showcase of such popular magazines as *The New Yorker, Esquire,* and *Playboy* and *Penthouse,* which gives us illuminating side-glances at contemporary American culture *and* literature. Professional translator of American authors, Tokiwa includes chapters on Saroyan, Singer, and Doctorow; a few of his translated works are *The New Yorker Stories,* Gay Talese's *Honor Thy Father,* Irwin Shaw's *Voices of a Summer Day,* and Woodward's and Bernstein's *All the President's Men.* But *The Window Opening to America* is, in essence, a unique study of *The New Yorker,* the "window" through which Tokiwa looks at America and its culture.

Like Tokiwa's book, Shunsuke Kamei's *Bus, bus, bus . . . Bus in America* is a collection of his travel sketches and essays published in our major newspapers and literary magazines. Vigorous and fluent in style, Kamei's book is a talk-show in print about American culture and literature. His perceptive (and sometimes lop-sided) observations and commentaries make his book a subtle and sly critique of the workaday American life and ours, which are strikingly similar. The intellectual flexibility and interdisciplinary approach of this scholar also characterize his discussions of such 18th- and 19th-century American writers as Franklin, Thoreau, and Hawthorne in the chapter, "Studies of Foreign Literature" (pp. 221–32). *Bus, bus, bus, . . . Bus in America* is an interesting cross-cultural study of the two countries, which is Kamei's proper field of study and the subject of his other book, *The Sacred Land of Liberty: The Japanese Image of America.*

The latter is the fruit of solid scholarship and long painstaking research. It is a historical survey of cultural interchanges between the two countries since Japan's first acquaintance with the United

States in 1853—the date Kamei regards as the very beginning of American studies in this country. *The Sacred Land of Liberty* records the shock and veneration America caused among political and religious leaders, educators, and literary men in 19th-century Japan. It traces the changing attitudes of the Japanese through the years toward this "sacred land of liberty"—the model for democratic society, the sanctuary of Christianity, and the labor market. Kamei's arrangement of valuable archives, historical documents, and literary works, with succinct and judicious commentaries, is such that these materials speak for themselves. Of special interest to the readers of this *Annual* are Kamei's discussions of some leading modern Japanese writers who were exposed to American literature—Kafu Nagai and Takeo Arishima in particular—and those of 18th- and 19th-century American writers whose ideas and literary works had a great impact on our political and religious leaders and literary men during the Meiji Era: Franklin, Jefferson, Thoreau, Emerson, and Whitman. Kamei's remarks about these American writers, together with his discussions of Thoreau and Hawthorne in *Bus, bus, bus, . . . Bus in America,* should also be claimed as part of our scholarly achievements in 19th-century American literature for the year 1979.

Kobe College

vi. Scandinavian Contributions

Rolf Lundén

Certain American writers—such as Poe, Twain, Henry James, Eliot, Faulkner, and O'Neill—are more regularly subjected to the interest of Scandinavian scholars than others. In that respect 1979 was no exception. But there is a growing appreciation of the more recent and less well-known authors, which can be seen in some of this year's contributions dealing with, for instance, William Burroughs, James Wright, Joyce Carol Oates, and John Hawkes. This year there was furthermore a new emphasis on the American short story, a field of study which has earlier been neglected.

One of the short stories to be examined is Edgar Allan Poe's "The Fall of the House of Usher." Frederick S. Frank focuses in "Poe's House of the Seven Gothics: The Fall of the Narrator in 'The Fall of the House of Usher'" (*OL* 34:331–51) not on the Ushers but on the "trespassing materialist who invades the House of Usher." According to Frank, the narrator is a threat to the invisible order and higher beautiful form of Roderick's "kingdom of inorganization." Through his skepticism the narrator sets in motion a series of "falls" which culminates in the destruction of the domicile of art itself. He becomes the tale's unconscious villain, an agent of disorder in a world of imagination. The House of Usher falls "because the alien intruder fails to rise to a new consciousness of aesthetic responsibility." The external fall of the mansion symbolizes the internal collapse of the narrator's analytic faculty. The article is well argued, but, like the House of Usher, it seems built on sand and threatens to sink into the deep and dank tarn. Frank is unwilling, or incapable, of supporting his argument from the text. He speculates, for instance, that Usher has summoned his friend in the hope that he will "be able to envision the artistic problem in form and will then ascend to Usher's stewardship of the mansion as new keeper of order in the kingdom of inorganization," a suggestion which is a mere figment of the critic's mind (see also chapter 3, section *iii-a*).

Two other articles devoted to 19th-century literature are Øyvind Gulliksen's "Mark Twain og Folkemålet" (Mark Twain and Vernacular Language?) (*Språklig Samling* 20:15–22) and Per Winther's "On Editing Emily Dickinson" *AmerSS* (11:25–40). After a discussion on how the protagonists of *Huck Finn* are characterized by their speech, Gulliksen scrutinizes three Norwegian translations of Twain's novel, revealing how the translators distort the characters, and thereby the meaning of the book, by using literary, even genteel, language. Per Winther is concerned with the lack of a good reader's edition of Dickinson's poems. He investigates numerous editorial problems and reaches what he calls a "purist" stance. The future editor of a reader's edition should reproduce as carefully as possible the typically Dickinsonian features, the capitals and the punctuation, and should organize the poems into a chronological, rather than thematic, arrangement (see also chapter 5. *ii-a*).

In a repetitive discourse called "Nineteenth-Century American Theory of the Short Story: The Dual Tradition" (*OL* 34:314–30) Walter Evans outlines the history of a neglected aspect of short-story criticism. There are two modes of American short stories, the traditional plot-story and the "formless," "lyrical" story. Evans argues that his orians and theorists have failed to see that 19th-century critics were aware of this dual tradition, and gives examples, more or less convincing, from Washington Irving, Longfellow, Poe, Henry Tuckerman, Brander Matthews, and Henry James.

Henry James is also the object of analysis in Ralf Norrman's lengthy article, "Referential Ambiguity in Pronouns as a Literary Device in Henry James's *The Golden Bowl*" (*SN* 51:31–71). In his thorough study Norrman presents a close reading of James's novel with special focus on referential ambiguity in pronouns. He points to the fact that the four main characters form a sort of *ménage à quatre*, and that the entanglements in the relationships are effectively exploited by the use of referential ambiguity. Employing many quotations from the text, Norrman disentangles and clarifies blurred passages. He further shows in detail how James uses this device for various purposes: to keep the reader alert, to foreshadow coming events, and to dramatize the combinations of characters and thereby create intensity (see also chapter 7, section *iv.*).

One of the few book-length studies this year is Barbro Ekman's *The End of a Legend: Ellen Glasgow's History of Southern Women* (Uppsala: Almqvist & Wiksell International). This monograph examines Ellen Glasgow as a historian of southern women from before the Civil War up to World War II. Ekman sees three main groups of women: The Victorian Woman, The Liberated Woman, and the "New Woman." The largest section is devoted to the first group, which includes many subcategories of women; what they have in common is that they all have been victimized by the genteel tradition in which they have been raised. Ekman's investigation renders a painstaking picture of southern women and their sufferings as Glasgow saw them. Ekman comes to the conclusion that Glasgow, because of her aristocratic background, gives a faithful account of the Victorian woman, whereas she knew little of the more liberated types of women appearing after the Great War.

Gayle Greene attempts to explain the presence of the references to Shakespeare's *The Tempest* in Eliot's *The Waste Land*. The larger part of "Shakespeare's *Tempest* and Eliot's *The Waste Land*: 'What the Thunder Said'" (*OL* 34:287–300) is devoted to Shakespeare's conception of art's redemptive powers and how these are expressed primarily through Prospero. A secondary interest to Greene is how these ideas in *The Tempest* are used by Eliot to suggest the need for rebirth and redemption. According to Greene, what the thunder demands in Eliot's poem is, in the deepest sense, what Shakespeare says: art has redemptive powers, restores us to ourselves and "a clear life ensuing" because it teaches us to "give, sympathize, and control."

In "The Trapped Female Breaking Loose: William Faulkner's 'Elly' (1934)" (*AmerSS* 11:15–24) Hans H. Skei analyzes one of the short stories from Faulkner's *Doctor Martino and Other Stories*, but points also to parallels in many other early Faulkner stories. Skei is convinced that Faulkner's females do not represent, as has often been argued, some kind of inborn female quality for evil, but that they have been molded by the social order in which they are living. Even though narcissism, hedonism, and self-gratification are motivational forces behind some of the female characters' attempts to break loose from their bondage, "Faulkner more often than not gives sufficient motivation in the social environment to explain their behavior."

Emphasis on society also characterizes a collection of articles, *America in the Fifties*, ed. Anne R. Clauss (Copenhagen: University of Copenhagen). The volume is of an introductory nature and does not pretend to be conclusive. In "Fiction of the Fifties: Alienation and Beyond" Paul Levine selects *Catcher in the Rye*, *The Naked and the Dead*, and *Invisible Man* for an analysis of the sense of alienation that characterized the decade. However, another choice of novels may have resulted in a different picture of the era. Henrik Rosenmeier's "The Sense of Public Responsibility and American History in Some Poetry of the Fifties" examines the growing political awareness in such poets as Lowell, Duncan, Adrienne Rich, and James Wright. Rosenmeier states that in the poetry of the 1950s there is a "determination to reassert a genuine national identity and to record what went wrong on the historical journey toward a respectable outcome." In a somewhat rambling article, "Hip–Bop–Beat," Bruce Clunies Ross concentrates on Kerouac, Ginsberg, and Burroughs and their intentions and sources of inspiration. A special emphasis is put on the role that jazz played for these writers. The volume is concluded with a survey of "Postwar American Drama" by Anne R. Clauss.

Pirjo Ahokas compares two recent short stories in "Two Immigrations: Singer's 'The Joke' and Malamud's 'The German Refugee'" (*AmerSS* 11:49–60). The basis for the comparison is that both writers are Jewish and that both stories deal with a German refugee trying to adapt to American life. However, the writers and the stories are so widely different that little is said about the art of the respective authors. Ahokas prefers Malamud's story because of its greater depth and tighter structure. Another contemporary short story is probed in Michael Böss's "Our Universal Fears: An Essay on a Story by John Hawkes" (*AmerSS* 11:61–66). Böss uses "The Universal Fears" as the focal point for a discussion of Hawkes's presentation of fear and the sense of morality that pervades his fiction.

The moral stance of a writer is also central to Monica Loeb's *Vonnegut's Duty-Dance with Death: Theme and Structure in Slaughterhouse-Five* (Umeå: Univ. of Umeå). The thesis of this monograph is that by means of stylistic devices Vonnegut consciously tries to persuade the reader to accept his view of life; Loeb even calls Vonnegut "didactic." The structural elements studied are point of view, treatment of time, characterization, use of other sources, and imagery. The result of the investigation is unfortunately unsatisfactory. The book is not well researched and many important aspects, such as Vonnegut's ambiguity, are left out.

One of the best-known introducers of Modern foreign literature to Swedes is Artur Lundkvist. In his new book, *Fantasi med Realism* [Realistic Imagination] (Stockholm: Liber Förlag), Lundkvist presents such American writers as Joyce Carol Oates, John Gardner, Pynchon, Barthelme, and Nabokov. The essays on the first two are the longest and the best. The author underlines specifically Oates's remarkably broad scope; it is as if Oates has the collected experience of several lives. In Gardner's production Lundkvist admires the author's ability to portray the tension existing in many Americans: they live on two noninterrelated levels, the poor level of reality and the sensational level of imagination. Lundkvist fears, however, that both Oates and Gardner are heading for destruction, Oates because of her growing emotional involvement and Gardner because of his growing lust for exhibitions of stylistic brilliance.

University of Uppsala

22. General Reference Works

James Woodress

Not only is this an age of criticism, but also it is an age of reference works. American scholars and publishers currently are producing an unending stream of bibliographies, biographical dictionaries, collections of criticism, anthologies of this or that, surveys of the state of things, and reference works too miscellaneous to categorize. All this activity gives us bigger and better research tools, but the utility and quality vary considerably, and the prices outstrip inflation. Few libraries can afford all the books, reviewed here, as the total cost of the 34 volumes I describe comes to more than $1,000. There are only a few titles that individuals can afford.

One such, however, is that indispensable *vade mecum* now in its fourth avatar, *A Handbook to Literature* (Bobbs-Merrill). C. Hugh Holman, who revised the original version of 1936 by William Thrall and Addison Hibbard for the second and third editions in 1960 and 1972, now has revised once again. This compilation is too well known to need description, as most students and teachers keep it within reach, but the fourth edition is better than ever. It contains 200 new entries and reflects the changes in the profession, especially the greater interest today in criticism over history. New terms such as "structuralism," "semiotics," and "phenomenology" have been added, but also old terms previously overlooked, such as "parataxis" and "pasquinade," have been included. Its dictionary-type organization runs from Abby Theatre to Zoom Shot and contains besides an outline of Pulitzer and Nobel prize winners.

Another reference work that calls itself a handbook, though it will come to three volumes and probably cost $75 when completed, is the *Handbook of Popular Culture*. The book, as Thomas Inge's preface states, "is the first organized effort to assemble in one place the basic bibliographic data needed to begin the study of several of the major areas of popular culture." This work reflects the growth of the Popular Culture Society and the maturing of popular culture as an academic discipline. Various chapters, each written by a specialist, provide chronological surveys of the subject, guides to bibliographies, reference works, and other sources. There are too many typographical errors affecting names and dates, but this handbook will be a valuable reference source.

No less than five biographical dictionaries appeared in 1979. Perhaps the most ambitious is the *DLB* (Gale), a projected multivolume series, of which the third volume, *Antebellum Writers in New York and the South*, ed. Joel Myerson, came out this year. (Volumes one and two were reviewed here by Professor Robbins last year.) This handsome, well-edited, and lavishly illustrated volume treats 67 authors, 15 of whom are sufficiently major to receive extended coverage. These larger essays range from 20 pages to G. R. Thompson's excellent 48-page treatment of Poe. All the essays are equipped with lists of works and bibliography, and all are written by reputable scholars: Hennig Cohen on Melville, Myerson on Whitman, Joseph Ridgely on J. P. Kennedy, Rayburn Moore on Hayne, and so forth. Unfortunately this volume costs $42.

Gale also has produced another volume in its Contemporary Authors Series, issued as volumes 85–88, which also contains an index for the entire series. These volumes, professionally edited and updated every five years, constitute an *omnium gatherum* of biographical data. Everyone who ever wrote a book, play, movie scenario, television drama, or work of nonfiction of any description seems to be included. At $48 per volume these compilations are strictly for libraries, but for wide coverage they are indispensable. The same cannot be said for *American Women Writers: A Critical Reference Guide from Colonial Times to the Present*, ed. Lina Mainiero (Ungar). In 1979 the first volume, from A through E, appeared, greatly overpriced at $45 for about 350 very brief biographies ranging from Edith Abbot (the first woman dean of an American graduate school) to Sarah Ann Evans (author in 1825 of a single novel called *Resignation*). The feminist rationale for this work is that Americans have until now been deprived of adequate biographical information on women. This may well be true, but it is hard to know who will need a page and a half of information on Sarah Bolton, who wrote *Paddle Your Own Canoe and Other Poems* in 1897.

Although no male was asked to contribute to this work, many established woman scholars wrote for it: Josephine Piercy, Winifred Frazer, Ann Stanford, and others. Yet the quality control seems faulty. I read carefully the sketches of two authors I know well: Cather and Dickinson. The Cather essay contains seven factual errors, two misspellings of proper names, one misquotation, and seven critical judgments that Cather scholars, male or female, would find very odd. The Dickinson essay contains four factual errors and information outdated by Sewall's biography, but the critical analysis is good. The essay on Didion begins: "D was graduated from the University of Berkeley at California." The coverage of living authors is highly arbitrary, and one wonders why Marian Anderson, who has written only an autobiography, was included at the expense of other women writers who are found in abundance along with the men in Gale's *Contemporary Authors*.

Another contribution to biographical reference books in 1979 is one that will have considerable usefulness. Issued in a paperbound edition at $7.95, it is within the reach of individuals who want a ready source of information on its subject: *Southern Writers: A Biographical Dictionary*, ed. Robert Bain, Joseph Flora, and Louis D. Rubin, Jr. (LSU). Gracefully dedicated to Lewis Leary, whose sketch appears in the front matter, it gathers 379 biographical articles ranging from one to three pages. The definition of southern writer is too elastic, for it includes authors who merely happened to be born in the South or who spent a few years there but whose careers have little southern association. The sketches, which are written by scholars, are reliable, but it is hard to see much value in a two-page account of Jefferson or three pages on Faulkner, but having brief sketches of Madison Cawein, Jay Hubbell, or George Sandys, etc. should be very handy.

The final entry in the biographical derby is an ambitious three-volume set: *Great Writers of the English Language*, ed. James Vinson (St. Martin's). Separate volumes are devoted to novelists and prose writers, poets, and dramatists, and the coverage is from the Middle Ages to the present. The critical commentaries written by a large group of scholars are accurate, but occasional errors appear in the summaries of biographical facts and lists of works, both of which were prepared by in-house staff. Since both English and American writers are included, some 1200 in all, this is an economical way for small libraries to acquire an up-to-date biographical work covering two literatures, but at $45 per volume it is out of the reach of individuals. The critical commentaries range from 500 words to 1500, and one is pleased to see excellent scholars signed to the articles: George Bennett on Howells, John Gerber on Twain, Donald Stanford on Taylor, Keneth Kinnamon on Ellison, and so forth.

The most numerous general reference works in any year are the bibliographies. This year among the 15 such volumes I have for review from seven different publishers, perhaps the most important for scholars in American literature is the long-needed third volume in the series that Lewis Leary began in 1954: *Articles on American Literature*. Professor Leary has added eight years to the coverage of the previous volumes so that all three gatherings span 75 years of periodical scholarship. The new volume also makes additions and corrections in the previous compilations. These three volumes offer dramatic proof of the increased interest in American literature and the explosion of knowledge over the years. The 1954 compilation, covering the years from 1900 to 1950, came to 17,000 items; the 1970 volume, spanning the years 1951 through 1967, ran to 20,000 items, the latest gathering totals over 27,000 items.

Also having a high degree of utility is the sixth edition of *Selective Bibliography for the Study of English and American Literature*, comp. Richard D. Altick and Andrew Wright (Macmillan). As an inexpensive paperback, this bibliography can be required for majors and graduate students and supplies an up-to-date winnowing of the many reference works in the field. The sixth edition has more than ten percent new items among its 636 numbered entries. More than ten percent also have been altered to take account of the new editions or supplemental volumes.

Vito J. Brenni's *The Bibliographic Control of American Literature: 1920–1975* (Scarecrow), even though priced at $10, is a book of little utility. With a cut-off date of 1975 it was already obsolete when it appeared, as a skimming through *ALS* for 1976–78 quickly makes clear. But its 218 pages simply don't begin to list all the items of bibliographic control or give complete information: for example, Walter Blair's *Native American Humor* is listed but not Constance Rourke's *American Humor*; Willis Buckingham's bibliography of Emily Dickinson is listed but not Sheila Clendenning's; The Gibson-Arms Howells bibliography is listed as having appeared serially in *BNYPL* but not issued separately nor later reprinted. It is strange to discover that author bibliographies are alphabetized by compiler, not subject, and the general index does not include the sources from which this volume itself was compiled. Finally the omissions are glaring. To list a few: general bibliographies by Donald Bond and Altick and Wright; *Sixteen Modern American Authors, Fifteen American Authors before 1900, Eight American Authors,* and the crowning omission, *ALS* itself appears nowhere in the book.

Among the other bibliographies two attest to the current strong interest in women's studies: *Poetry by American Women, 1900–1975: A Bibliography,* comp. Joan Reardon and Kristine A. Thorsen (Scarecrow) and *More Women in Literature: Criticism of the Seventies* by Carol Fairbanks (Scarecrow). The former volume lists the more than 9,500 volumes of poetry published in the first three-quarters of the century by more than 5,500 American Women and is equipped with a title index. The latter volume is an expansion of a similar work published by Scarecrow in 1976. Its concern is only partly with American literature, for the organizing principles were to gather articles and books examining women characters in various contexts, to list essays in feminist criticism, to collect biographical studies of women writers, interviews with women writers, and some book reviews. The entries are drawn from various literatures and from classic Greek to the present. Dissertations also are included.

Four more bibliographies that concern themselves only partly with American literature are devoted to science fiction, fantasy literature, utopian literature, and Gothic novels. The most impressive is *Science Fiction and Fantasy Literature,* comp. R. Reginald, 2 vols. (Gale), which provides both a checklist of science fiction, fantasy literature, and supernatural literature in book form and 1,443 biographical sketches of modern science fiction writers living and dead. This is a very extensive work, listing 15,884 books and pamphlets brought out between 1700 and 1974. Besides the author entries, there is both a title and a series index so that one can find, for example, all 38 of the Tom Swift books listed neatly together. These two big volumes at $62 the set seem appropriately priced. *The Literature of Fantasy: A Comprehensive, Annotated Bibliography of Modern Fantasy Fiction,* comp. Roger C. Schlobin (Garland), despite its title, is far less comprehensive and is mostly subsumed in the Gale compilation. Its beginning date is the middle of the 19th century, and its total listings come to 1,249 items. It does have plot summaries of novels, which the other work does not have, and it contains author and title indexes. *British and American Utopian Literature, 1516–1975* by Lyman T. Sargent (Hall) is a very thorough, well-organized list. Beginning with More's work, which gave the genre its name, it is arranged chronologically, gives library locations (many of these utopias are hard to come by), and includes an extensive bibliography of secondary works on utopian literature. It is remarkable how many people have been moved to write utopias in the past four and one-half centuries, my rough estimate being more than 4,000, of which half have appeared in the last 60 years, the majority by Americans. Sargent prefaces his compilation with a careful essay of definition. *Gothic Novels of the Twentieth Century: An Annotated Bibliography* by Elsa J. Radcliffe (Scarecrow) seems a work of limited usefulness for scholars, though not for readers with a taste for the modern Gothic. Radcliffe has read hundreds of these novels and of the 1,973 items she lists many are graded from A to F according to her appraisal of their quality. Her introduction attempts to define this genre, but it is a tricky business.

The final trio of bibliographies all are useful compilations but fall into no particular category. The first is a 168-page bibliography of Irish-American fiction, both primary and secondary sources, which accompanies *Irish-American Fiction*. Fifty-two writers are included from William Alfred to Jim Tully. Better and more extensive listings are available, of course, for Fitzgerald, Flannery O'Connor, and such, but no doubt brief bibliographies of writers like Peter Finley Dunne, or FitzJames O'Brien will be useful. Another general volume in Gale's Information Guide Series has appeared with *Author Newsletters and Journals*, comp. Margaret C. Patterson. The coverage is international, listing 1,087 titles devoted to 420 authors and published in 28 countries. The number of journals dedicated to single authors seems to increase every year, and it is fairly astonishing to find listed here 70 American authors to whose work 130 journals are now or have been devoted. Many are inconsequential and short-lived publications, often merely a newsletter for *aficionados*, but many are substantial and have lasted for years, such as *ESQ, PoeS, WWR*, etc. The final bibliography for review is *Index to Reviews of Bibliographical Publications*, vol. 2 for 1977, comp. Terry Oggel and Rosalie Hewitt (Hall). This is the second volume in an annual series and lists reviews of all books that have any bibliographical interest, not just bibliographies but letter collections, indexes, editions, catalogues, papers, and so forth. Among the volumes of reprinted material appearing in 1979 I want to notice two continuing series from Gale: *Contemporary Literary Criticism,* comp. Dedria Bryfonski, vols. 10 and 11, and *Twentieth Century Literary Criticism,* by Bryfonski and Sharon K. Hall, vol. 2. These two series complement each other, the first reprinting excerpts from criticism of the works of authors now living or deceased since 1960, the second collecting excerpts about the work of writers who died between 1900 and 1960. Although both volumes treat authors of all nationalities, the first devotes nearly half of its space to Americans, the second less than one-third. These are useful volumes for libraries with limited resources, as the excerpts are often generous, though scholars with access to even moderately well-equipped libraries will not need the sections of these volumes devoted to the likes of Hemingway, Henry James, and Ezra Pound. If one wants critical comment, however, on Peter Devries, James Jones, or wants to know what Gore Vidal thinks of Edgar Rice Burroughs, these collections have a place.

Three important catalogues/indexes appeared in 1979. In *American Periodicals, 1741–1900: An Index to the Microfilm Collections,* ed. Jean Hoornstra and Trudy Heath (Univ. Microfilm) we have at last a one-volume index for the microfilm project originally begun by the William L. Clements Library in 1941. All three series, the 18th century, 1800–1850, and 1850–1900, have been conflated in this single volume providing easy access to more than 1,100 periodicals on microfilm. There is a title index, giving full bibliographical data and location by reel number, also subject and editor indexes. Each title entry also carries a brief history of the magazine. *Guide to Literary Manuscripts in the Huntington Library* (Huntington Library), the second of four guides to Huntington holdings, has a great deal for Americanists in its catalogue of about 125,000 pieces by more than 1,000 authors and is indispensable for scholars planning a visit. In fact, no one should attempt the study of any American author without consulting this catalogue, as the Huntington's collection of American literary manuscripts, letters, and documents is extensive. Although the information contained here is briefly summarized in *American Literary Manuscripts* (see *ALS 1977,* p. 511), the *Guide* describes literary manuscripts instead of merely counting them. The increasing importance of oral history is reflected in the fourth edition of *The Oral*

History Collection of Columbia University (New York: Columbia Univ. Oral History Research Office). This research tool contains half again as much information as the 1973 edition. Although the emphasis is on history, government, and the arts in general, there is a moderate amount here for scholars in American literature. Only a few authors have recorded their memoirs, but a good many are talked about in the material catalogued. There are entries for "Authors," "Books and Book Publishing," "Poets on Their Poetry," etc., enough so that anyone writing on a contemporary writer should check this source. Willa Cather, for example, is discussed in the 325 pages recorded by Alfred Knopf.

For humanists who have resisted learning about computers and their humanistic capabilities and possibilities because the subject seemed too arcane, Robert Oakman's *Computer Methods for Literary Research* (S. Car.) comes in the nick of time. Oakman is both professor of English and computer scientist and able to explain in clear nontechnical English how computers work and what they can do for the literary scholar. He focuses both on computer fundamentals and literary applications: concordances, automated bibliography, lexicography, textual collation, disputed authorship, and content and stylistic analysis. Examples are chosen with literary possibilities in mind, and the entire enterprise gives the nonscientist reader a clear idea of how the machine can be made to do respectable literary projects.

Although many of the essays have been discussed in other parts of this book, *The Harvard Guide* contains two essays not yet mentioned: Alan Trachtenberg's opening chapter, "Intellectual Background" and A. Walton Litz' "Literary Criticism." The former is a competent summary of intellectual/social/cultural developments since World War II by a professor of American studies. While it contains no surprises for those of us who have lived through this period, it provides a springboard for younger readers into the rest of the volume. The latter essay also is an able roundup of its subject, though, as Litz says, his task was "like writing a brief guidebook to a continent." Beginning with the "New Criticism," he takes the reader through literary study as "theology" (Frye et al.) to the theoretical speculations of Hartman, J. Hillis Miller, and Bloom.

Collectible Books: Some New Paths, ed. Jean Peters (Bowker), is a remarkably good collection of essays for would-be book collectors in times of inflation and the increasing scarcity of rare books. As a follow-up volume to *Book Collecting: A Modern Guide*, also edited by Peters (Bowker, 1977), which explains what book collecting is all about and how to do it, *Collectible Books* is full of ideas for collecting other books than rare and expensive first editions. G. Thomas Tanselle suggests buying nonfirst editions, and Charles Gullans and John Espey urge the collecting of American trade bindings and the work of specific designers. William Todd advocates hunting for books in series and discusses his search for Tauchnitz editions, and Peters proposes collecting publishers' imprints and describes her pursuit of Hogarth Press titles. These chapters and others can make collectors out of bibliophiles without bankrupting them.

A final item of significant interest comes from a journal, the work of a scholar from the University of Groningen: J. G. Riewald, "The Translational Reception of American Literature in Europe, 1800–1900: A Review of Research" (*ES* 60:562–602). Riewald has surveyed the translations of Irving, Cooper, Poe, Longfellow, Emerson, Hawthorne, Stowe, Melville, Whitman, Dickinson, Thoreau, Twain, and James. The purpose of this survey is to give a reasonably complete picture of the state of scholarship relating to the translations of the authors considered. Riewald's findings are summary in nature, and there is plenty of work left to be done on this subject.

Author Index

Subject Index